SAS® Enterprise Guide®: ANOVA, Regression, and Logistic Regression

Course Notes

SAS® Enterprise Guide®: ANOVA, Regression, and Logistic Regression Course Notes was developed by Melinda Thielbar and Catherine Truxillo. Additional contributions were made by Peggy Cavalieri, Paul Marovich, Mike Patetta, Jill Tao, and Susan Walsh. Editing and production support was provided by the Curriculum Development and Support Department.

SAS® Enterprise Guide®: ANOVA, Regression, and Logistic Regression Course Notes

Book code 60416, course code EGBS, prepared date 08Feb05.

Table of Contents

Course Description

This three-day course covers a range of statistical topics and uses SAS Enterprise Guide to carry out statistical analyses. Topics include statistical inference, analysis of variance, multiple regression, categorical data analysis, and logistic regression. You learn to construct graphs to explore and summarize data, construct confidence intervals for means, test hypotheses, apply multiple comparison techniques in ANOVA, assess and correct collinearity in multiple regression, use diagnostic statistics to identify potential outliers in multiple regression, use chi-square statistics to detect associations among categorical variables, and fit a multiple logistic regression model.

To learn more…

SAS Education

A full curriculum of general and statistical instructor-based training is available at any of the Institute's training facilities. Institute instructors can also provide on-site training.

For information on other courses in the curriculum, contact the SAS Education Division at 1-919-531-7321, or send e-mail to training@sas.com. You can also find this information on the Web at support.sas.com/training/ as well as in the Training Course Catalog.

SAS Publishing

For a list of other SAS books that relate to the topics covered in this Course Notes, USA customers can contact our SAS Publishing Department at 1-800-727-3228 or send e-mail to sasbook@sas.com. Customers outside the USA, please contact your local SAS office.

Also, see the Publications Catalog on the Web at www.sas.com/pubs for a complete list of books and a convenient order form.

Prerequisites

Before attending this course, you should

- have completed an undergraduate course in statistics covering *p*-values, hypothesis testing, analysis of variance, and regression.
- be able to perform analyses and create SAS data sets with SAS Enterprise Guide software. You can gain this experience by completing the *Querying and Reporting Using SAS® Enterprise Guide®* course.

General Conventions

This section explains the various conventions used in presenting text, SAS language syntax, and examples in this book.

Typographical Conventions

You will see several type styles in this book. This list explains the meaning of each style:

UPPERCASE ROMAN	is used for SAS statements and other SAS language elements when they appear in the text.
italic	identifies terms or concepts that are defined in text. Italic is also used for book titles when they are referenced in text, as well as for various syntax and mathematical elements.
bold	is used for emphasis within text.
`monospace`	is used for examples of SAS programming statements and for SAS character strings. Monospace is also used to refer to variable and data set names, field names in windows, information in fields, and user-supplied information.
select	indicates selectable items in windows and menus. This book also uses icons to represent selectable items.

Syntax Conventions

The general forms of SAS statements and commands shown in this book include only that part of the syntax actually taught in the course. For complete syntax, see the appropriate SAS reference guide.

PROC CHART DATA = *SAS-data-set*;
    HBAR | VBAR *chart-variables </ options>*;
RUN;

This is an example of how SAS syntax is shown in text:

- **PROC** and **CHART** are in uppercase bold because they are SAS keywords.
- DATA= is in uppercase to indicate that it must be spelled as shown.
- *SAS-data-set* is in italic because it represents a value that you supply. In this case, the value must be the name of a SAS data set.
- **HBAR** and **VBAR** are in uppercase bold because they are SAS keywords. They are separated by a vertical bar to indicate they are mutually exclusive; you can choose one or the other.
- *chart-variables* is in italic because it represents a value or values that you supply.
- *</ options>* represents optional syntax specific to the HBAR and VBAR statements. The angle brackets enclose the slash as well as *options* because if no options are specified you do not include the slash.
- **RUN** is in uppercase bold because it is a SAS keyword.

Chapter 1 Introduction to Statistics

1.1 Fundamental Statistical Concepts

Objectives

- Decide what tasks to complete before you analyze your data.
- Distinguish between populations and samples.

3

Two Broad Categories of Statistics

Inferential

Descriptive

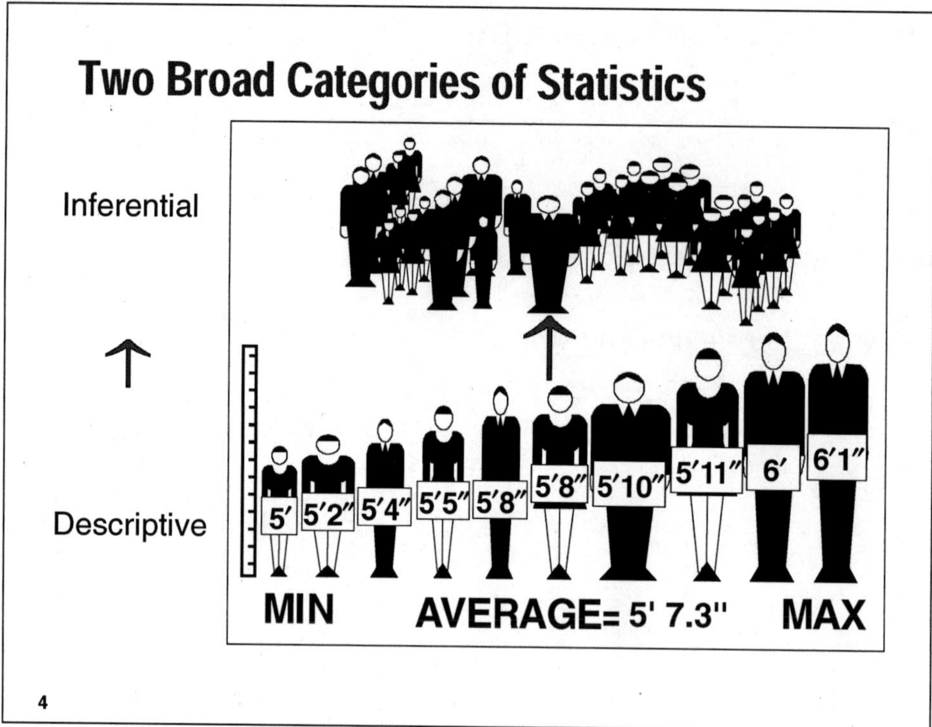

4

Descriptive statistics are used to organize, summarize, and focus on the main characteristics of your data, which make the data more usable.

Inferential statistics make generalizations or inferences from your data to a larger set of data, based on probability theory.

Defining the Problem

Before you begin any analysis, you should complete certain tasks.

1. Outline the purpose of the study.
2. Document the study questions.
3. Define the population of interest.
4. Determine the need for sampling.
5. Define the data collection protocol.

5

Cereal Example

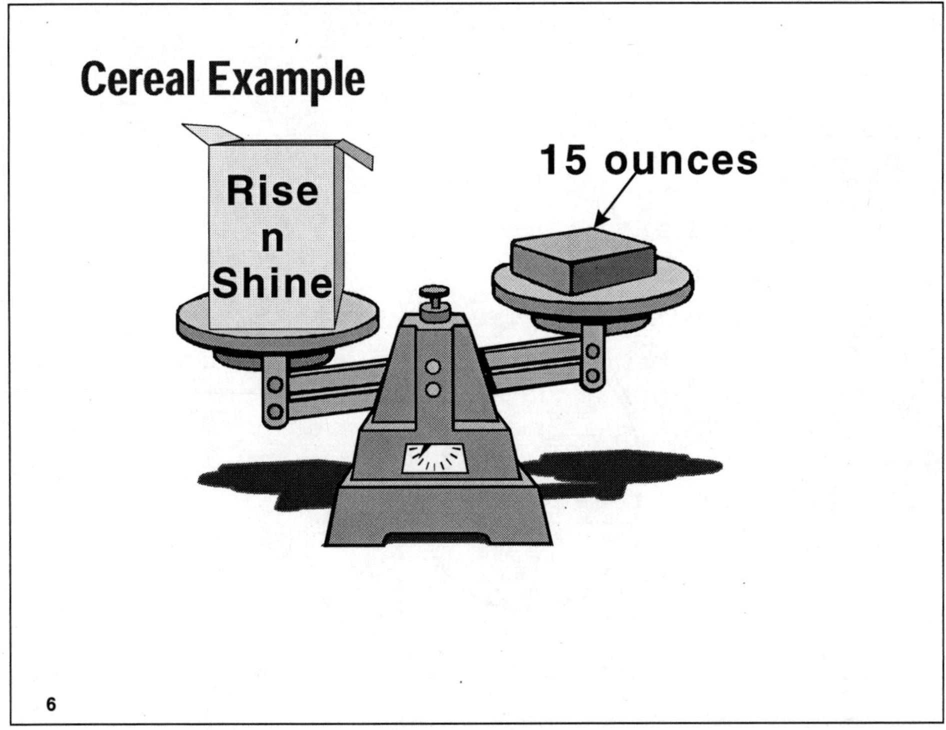

6

Example: The manufacturer of Rise n Shine cereal wants to test if the company is producing the specified amount of cereal. Each box is supposed to contain 15 ounces. There are approximately one million boxes of Rise n Shine cereal available to customers.

Defining the Problem

The purpose of the study is to determine whether Rise n Shine cereal boxes contain 15 ounces of cereal.

The study question is whether the average amount of cereal in Rise n Shine boxes is equal to 15 ounces.

7

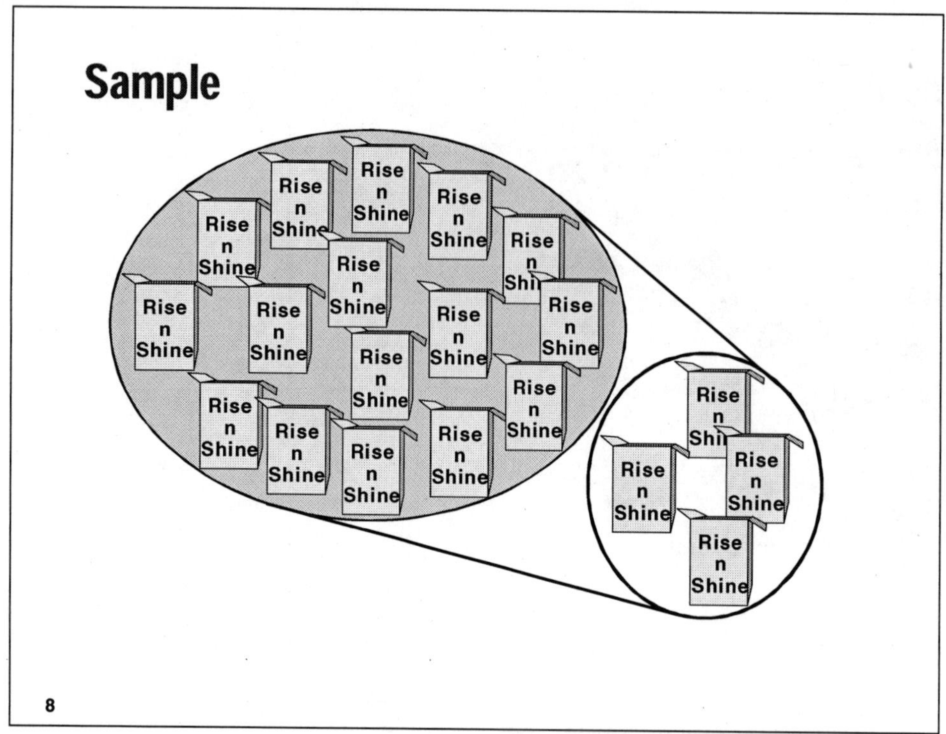

A *population* is the set of all measurement values of interest.

In the cereal example, the population is the number of ounces of cereal in each Rise n Shine cereal box, not the actual cereal boxes.

Populations can be categorized as either concrete or theoretical:

- A population is referred to as *concrete* if you can identify every subject in the population. For example, at any one point in time (that is, as of June 30, 2004), you can identify each person on the company payroll. These people constitute a concrete population.
- A population is referred to as *theoretical* if the population is constantly changing. For example, because Rise n Shine cereal continues to be produced and packaged, the population changes almost continuously.

Because there are approximately one million cereal boxes in the grocery stores, you would need to record approximately one million measurements to examine the entire population.

Is it feasible to examine the entire population?

No, the population consists of approximately one million measurements. This would require too much time and too many resources to conduct the study and analyze the results.

A *sample* is a subset of the population. The sample should be random to help ensure that it is representative of the population.

A representative sample has characteristics that are similar to the population's characteristics.

For the cereal example, that means the average weight of cereal in a representative sample of Rise n Shine boxes should be close to the average weight of all Rise n Shine boxes.

Parameters and Statistics

Statistics are used to approximate population parameters.

	Population Parameters	Sample Statistics
Mean	μ	$\bar{x}$
Variance	σ^2	s^2
Standard Deviation	σ	s

9

Parameters are characteristics of populations. Because populations usually cannot be measured in their entirety, parameter values are generally unknown. *Statistics* are quantities calculated from the values in the sample.

Suppose you have $x_1, x_2, \ldots, x_n$, a sample from some population.

- $\bar{x} = \frac{1}{n}\sum x_i$ the mean is an average, a typical value in the distribution.
- $s^2 = \frac{1}{n-1}\sum (x_i - \bar{x})^2$ the variance measures the sample variability.
- $s = \sqrt{\frac{1}{n-1}\sum (x_i - \bar{x})^2}$ the standard deviation measures variability. It is reported in the same units as the mean.

Describing Your Data

The goals when you are describing data are to

- screen for unusual data values
- inspect the spread and shape of continuous variables
- characterize the central tendency
- draw preliminary conclusions about your data.

10

After you select a random sample of the data, you can start describing the data. Although you want to draw conclusions about your population, you first want to explore and describe your data before you use inferential statistics.

Why?

- Data must be as error-free as possible.
- Unique aspects, such as data values that cluster or show some unusual shape, may be missed.
- An extreme value of a variable could be missed and cause gross errors in the interpretation of the statistics.

Some scientists have suggested that all great scientific discoveries have been due to outliers. The outlying observation indicates an event that is unexpected and does not follow existing theories. In resolving the anomaly, new theories are born.

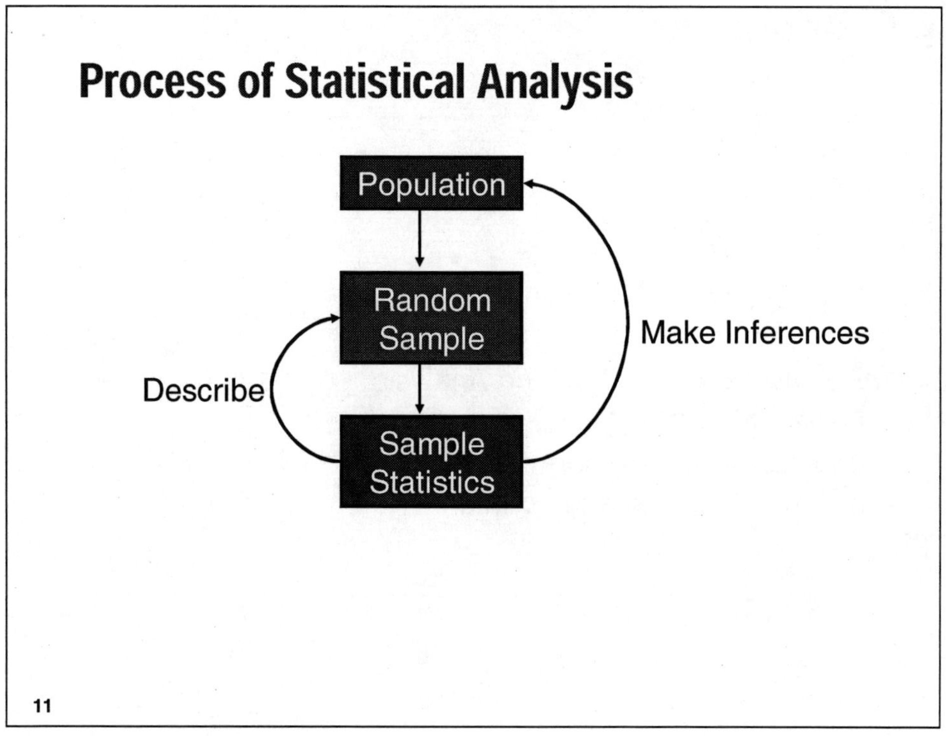

These processes are involved in a statistical analysis:

1. Identify the population of interest.
2. Draw a random sample.
3. Compute sample statistics to describe the sample.
4. Use sample information to make inferences about the population.

1.2 Examining Distributions

Objectives

- Examine distributions of data.
- Explain and interpret measures of location, dispersion, and shape.
- Use the Summary Statistics and Distribution Analysis tasks to produce descriptive statistics.
- Use the Distribution Analysis task to generate histograms, box-and-whisker plots, and normal probability plots.

13

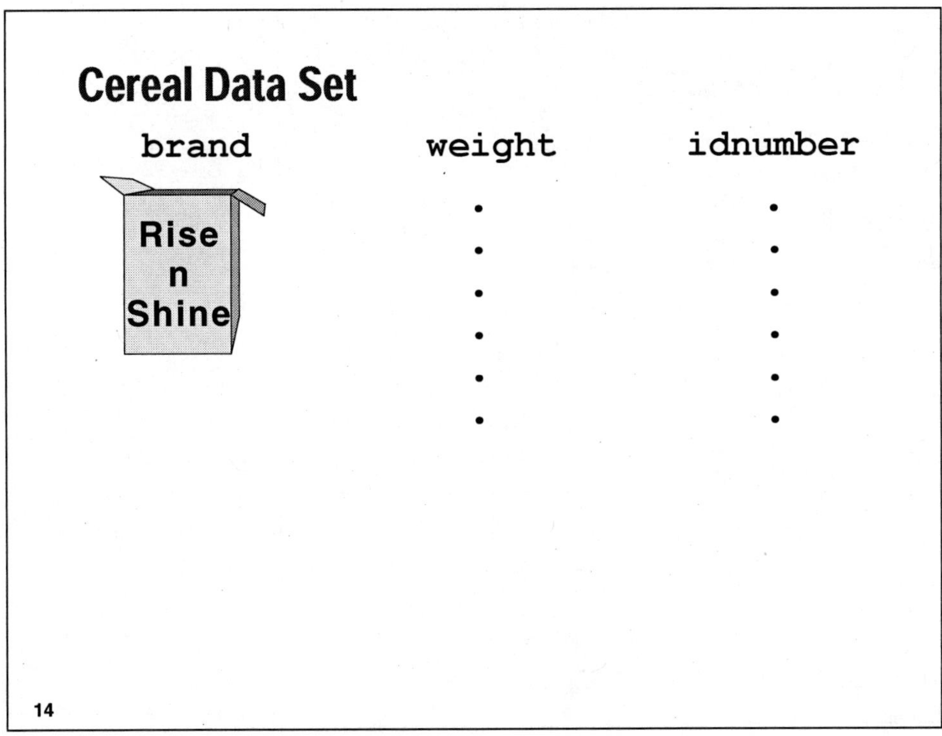

Example: A consumer advocacy group wants to determine whether Rise n Shine cereal boxes contain 15 ounces of cereal. A random sample of forty boxes was selected. The identification number of each box (**`idnumber`**) and the amount of cereal in ounces (**`weight`**) were recorded. The data is stored in the **`RISECEREAL`** data set.

Assumption for this Course

- The sample drawn is *representative* of the entire population.
  - In other words, the sample characteristics should reflect the characteristics of the population as a whole.

15

One sampling method that helps ensure a representative sample is *simple random sampling.*

In a simple random sample, every member of the population has an equal chance of being included.

In the cereal example, the number of ounces of cereal in each box has an equal chance of being selected from the population.

See the Appendix entitled Random Samples for information on how to generate random samples without replacement and with replacement.

Why not select cereal boxes from one grocery store near your home?

When you select values in a population that are easily available to you, you are using *convenience sampling*.

A *biased* sample is one that is not representative of the population from which it is drawn. Convenience sampling may lead to biased samples.

In the cereal example, the average weight of a biased sample may not be close to the true average of the population. This may cause the consumer advocacy group to draw erroneous conclusions about the cereal Rise n Shine.

Distributions

When you examine the distribution of values for the variable **`weight`**, you can find out

- the range of possible data values
- the frequency of data values
- whether the data values accumulate in the middle of the distribution or at one end.

16

A *distribution* is a collection of data values arranged in order, along with the relative frequency. For any kind of problem, it is important that you describe the location, spread, and shape of your distribution using graphical techniques and descriptive statistics.

For the cereal example, these questions can be addressed using graphical techniques.

- Are the values of **`weight`** symmetrically distributed?
- Are any values of **`weight`** unusual?

You can answer these questions using descriptive statistics.

- What is the best estimate of the average **`weight`** for the population?
- What is the best estimate of the average spread or dispersion of the values of **`weight`** for the population?

"Typical Values" in a Distribution

- Mean: The sum of all the values in the data set divided by the number of values

$$\frac{\sum_{i=1}^{n} x_i}{n}$$

- Median: The middle value (also known as the 50th percentile)

- Mode: The most common or frequent data value

17

Descriptive statistics that locate the center of your data are called *measures of central tendency*. The most common measure of central tendency is the sample mean.

A property of the sample mean is that the sum of the differences of each data value from the mean is always 0. That is, $\sum(x_i - \bar{x})=0$.

The mean is the physical balancing point of your data.

Percentiles

98	
95	
92	75th Percentile=91
90	
85	
81	50th Percentile=80
79	
70	
63	25th Percentile=59
55	
47	
42	

The quartiles break your data up into quarters.

You can use percentiles as typical values or measures of dispersion.

18

Percentiles locate a position in your data larger than a given proportion of data values.

Commonly reported percentile values are

- the 25th percentile, also called the first quartile
- the 50th percentile, also called the median
- the 75th percentile, also called the third quartile.

The Spread of a Distribution: Dispersion

Measure	Definition
range	the difference between the maximum and minimum data values
interquartile range	the difference between the 25th and 75th percentiles
variance	a measure of dispersion of the data around the mean
standard deviation	a measure of dispersion expressed in the same units of measurement as your data (the square root of the variance)

19

Measures of dispersion enable you to characterize the dispersion, or spread, of the data.

Formula for sample variance: $s^2 = \frac{1}{n-1}\sum(x_i - \bar{x})^2$

Another measure of variation is the coefficient of variation (C.V.), which is the standard deviation as a percentage of the mean. It is defined as $\frac{s}{\bar{x}} \times 100$.

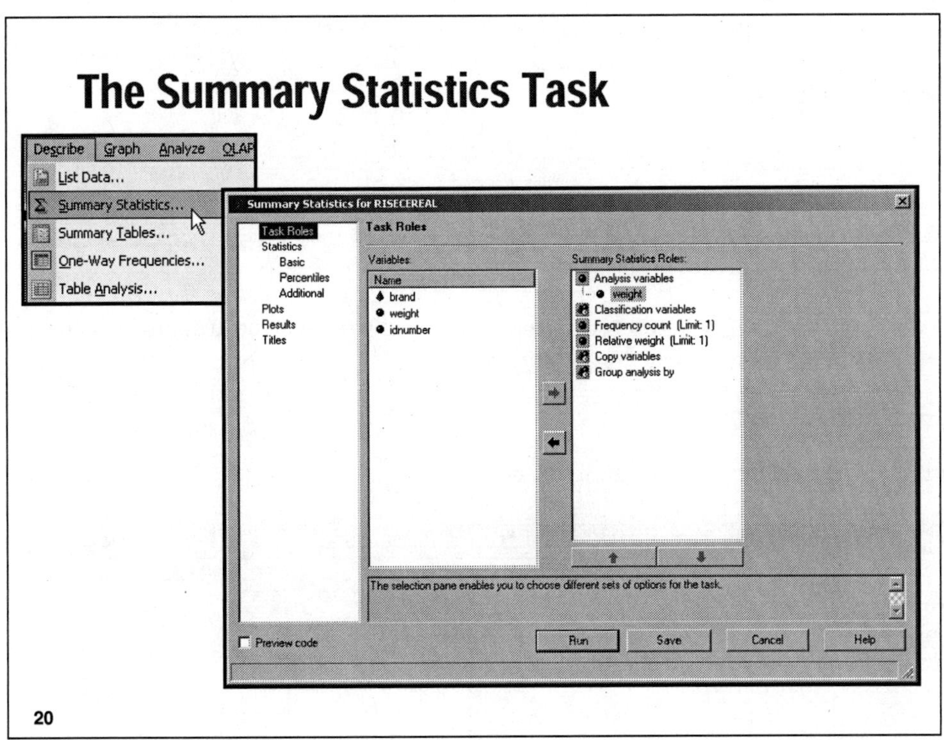
The Summary Statistics Task
Describe
Graph
Analyze
OLAP
List Data...
Summary Statistics...
Summary Tables...
One-Way Frequencies...
Table Analysis...
Summary Statistics for RISECEREAL
Task Roles
Statistics
Basic
Percentiles
Additional
Plots
Results
Titles
Task Roles
Variables:
Name
brand
weight
idnumber
Summary Statistics Roles:
Analysis variables
weight
Classification variables
Frequency count (Limit: 1)
Relative weight (Limit: 1)
Copy variables
Group analysis by
The selection pane enables you to choose different sets of options for the task.
Preview code
Run
Save
Cancel
Help
20

Descriptive Statistics

Example: Create the data sets for the course by running the SAS program in the class project. Then use the Summary Statistics task to create descriptive statistics.

1. When you open SAS Enterprise Guide 3.0, you see a dialog that asks whether you want to create a new project or open an existing project. Select **New Project**.
2. Select **File** ⇨ **Open** ⇨ **From My Computer**.
3. Navigate to the location of the `EGBS.sas` program.

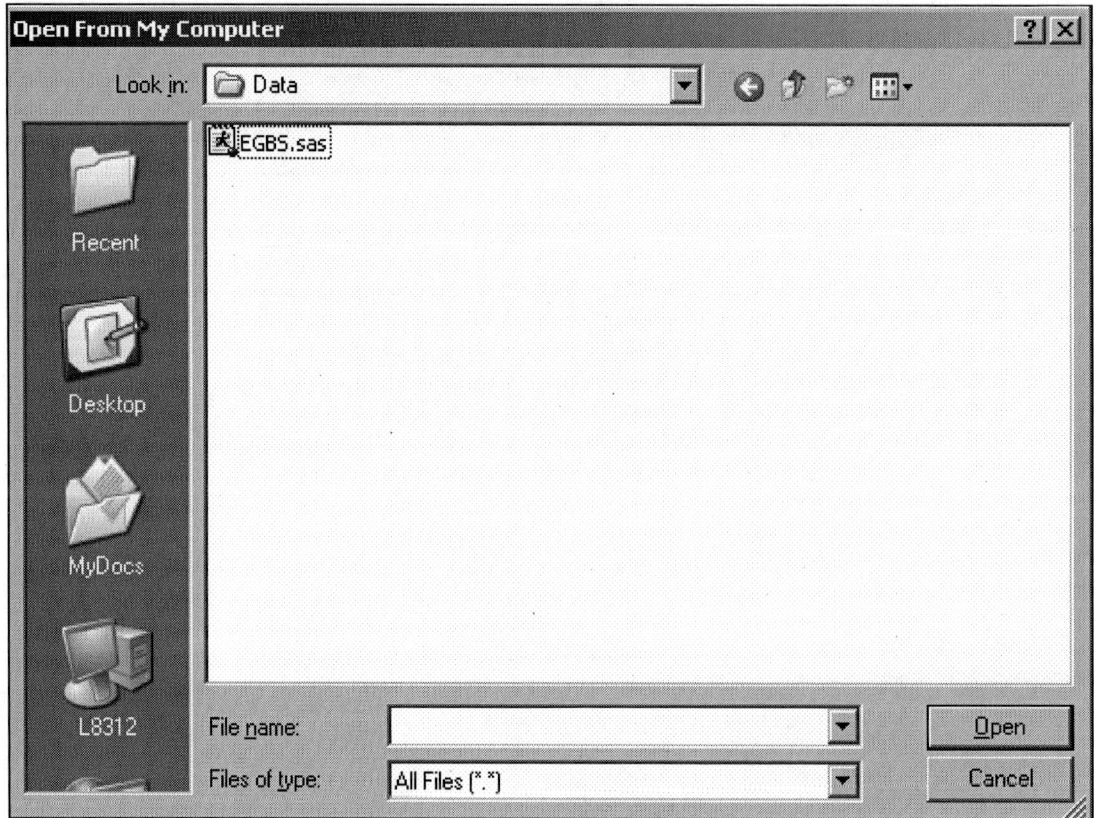

Your instructor will show you where to find the program. You may write the path below:

____

4. Select **EGBS.sas**. This SAS program generates all the data sets used in demonstrations and exercises for this course.

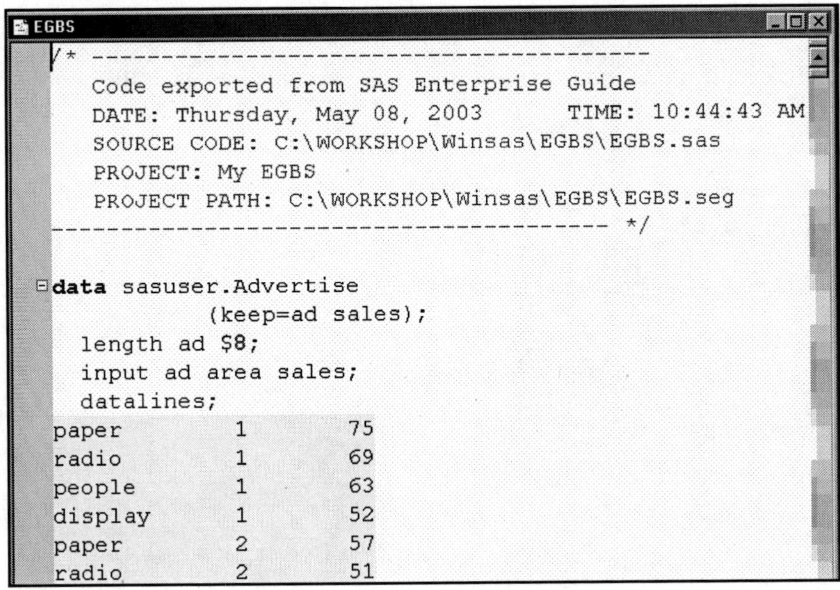

5. Right-click on the program and select **Run on Local**.

   A series of SAS data sets will appear in the project process flow. The **VEHICLESAFETY** data set is opened at the bottom of the SAS Enterprise Guide work area because it was the last data set created.

6. Close **VEHICLESAFETY** by selecting X in the upper-right corner of the pane.

7. Close **EGBS.sas** in the same manner.

   ✎ You can also close all the open windows at the same time by selecting **Window** ⇨ **Close All.**

8. Save the project by selecting **File** ⇨ **Save Project**. Save it in the location specified by your instructor and give it the name **EGBSProject.egp**.

Example: Now you are ready to begin your analyses. Locate the data set **RISECEREAL** in the project tree and examine its contents. Use the Summary Statistics task to generate descriptive statistics for **weight**.

1. To view a data set, double-click on its node in the project tree. The data table opens at the bottom of the screen.

   Partial Listing

   SASUSER.RISECEREAL (read-only)

	brand	weight	idnumber
1	Rise n Shine	15.0136	33081197
2	Rise n Shine	14.9982	37070397
3	Rise n Shine	14.993	60714297
4	Rise n Shine	15.0812	9589297
5	Rise n Shine	15.0418	85859397
6	Rise n Shine	15.0639	99108497
7	Rise n Shine	15.0613	70847197
8	Rise n Shine	15.0255	53750297
9	Rise n Shine	15.0176	3873197

   There are three variables in the **RISECEREAL** data set. One variable, **brand**, is a character variable that contains the brand name of the cereal. The other two variables, **weight** and **idnumber**, are numeric variables that contain the weight of each box in ounces and an identifying code for each box of cereal.

   Create a summary statistics report for the **RISECEREAL** data set.

2. Select **Describe** ⇨ **Summary Statistics...** from the menus.

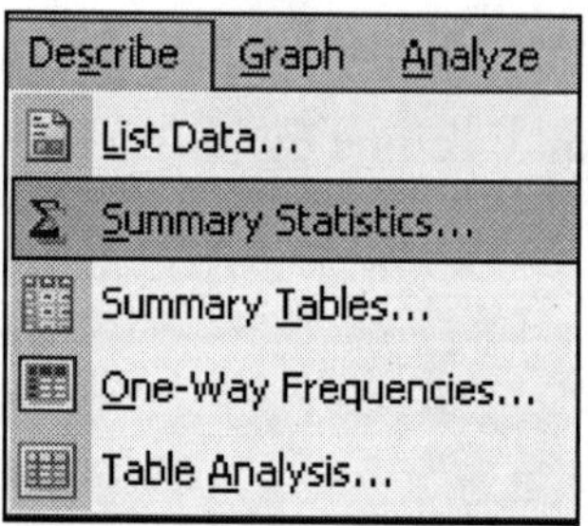

3. With Task Roles selected on the left, drag the variable `weight` from the **Variables** pane to the Analysis variables role in the **Summary Statistics Roles** pane, as shown below:

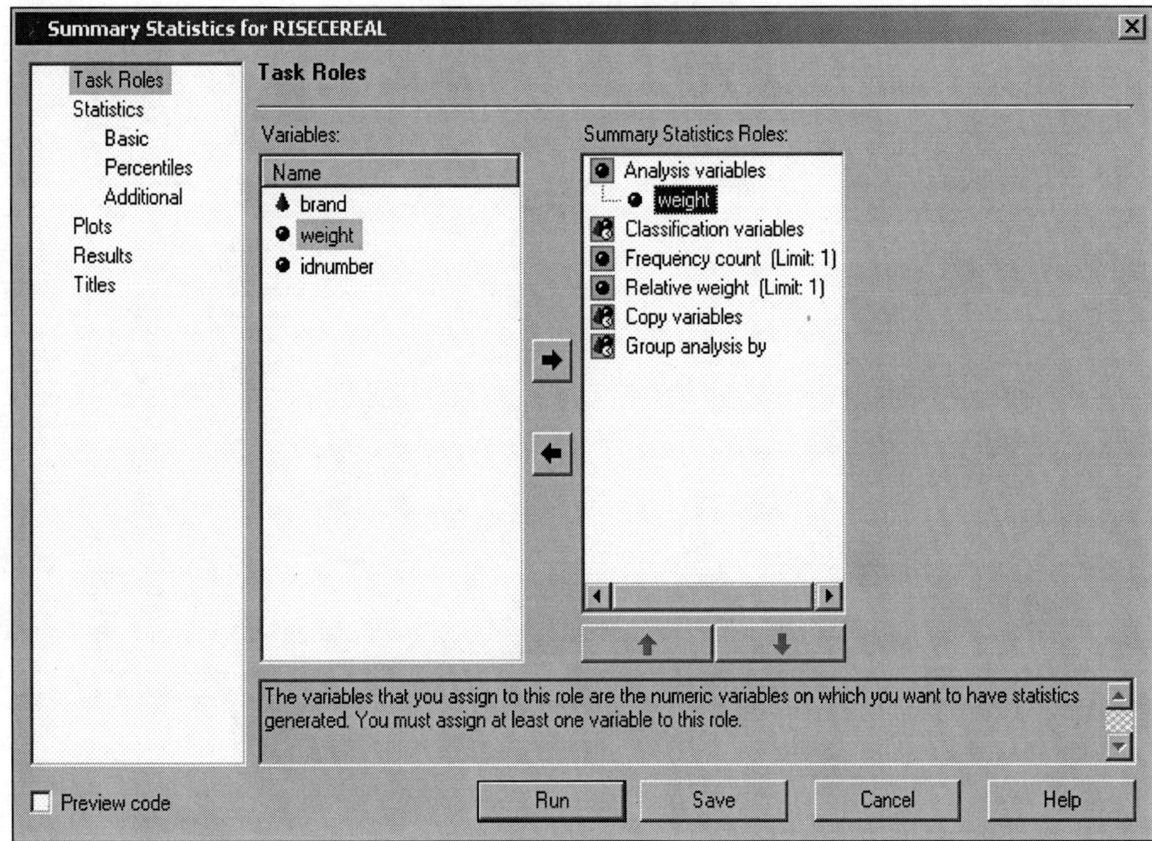

4. Select **Basic** under Statistics on the left. Leave the default basic statistics. Change the Maximum decimal places from Best fit to 4.

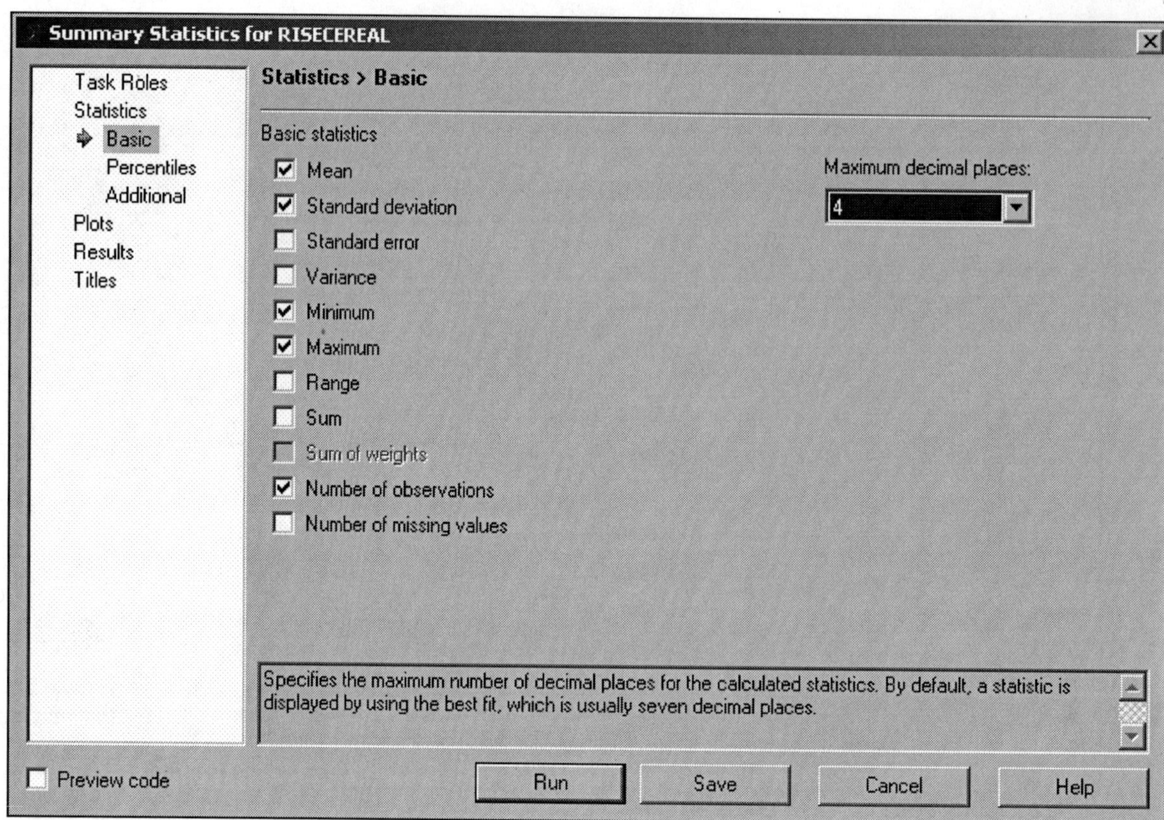

5. Select **Percentiles** on the left. Check the boxes next to **Median**, **Lower quartile**, and **Upper quartile**.

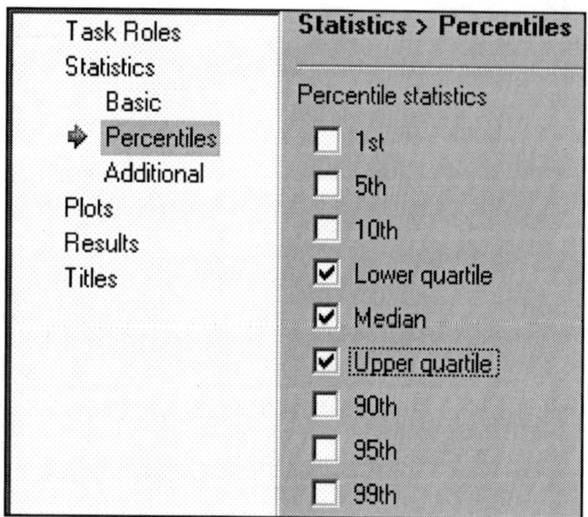

6. Select **Titles** on the left. Select **Analysis** and uncheck **Use default text**. Select the default text in the box and type `Descriptive Statistics for RISECEREAL`. Leave the default footnote text.

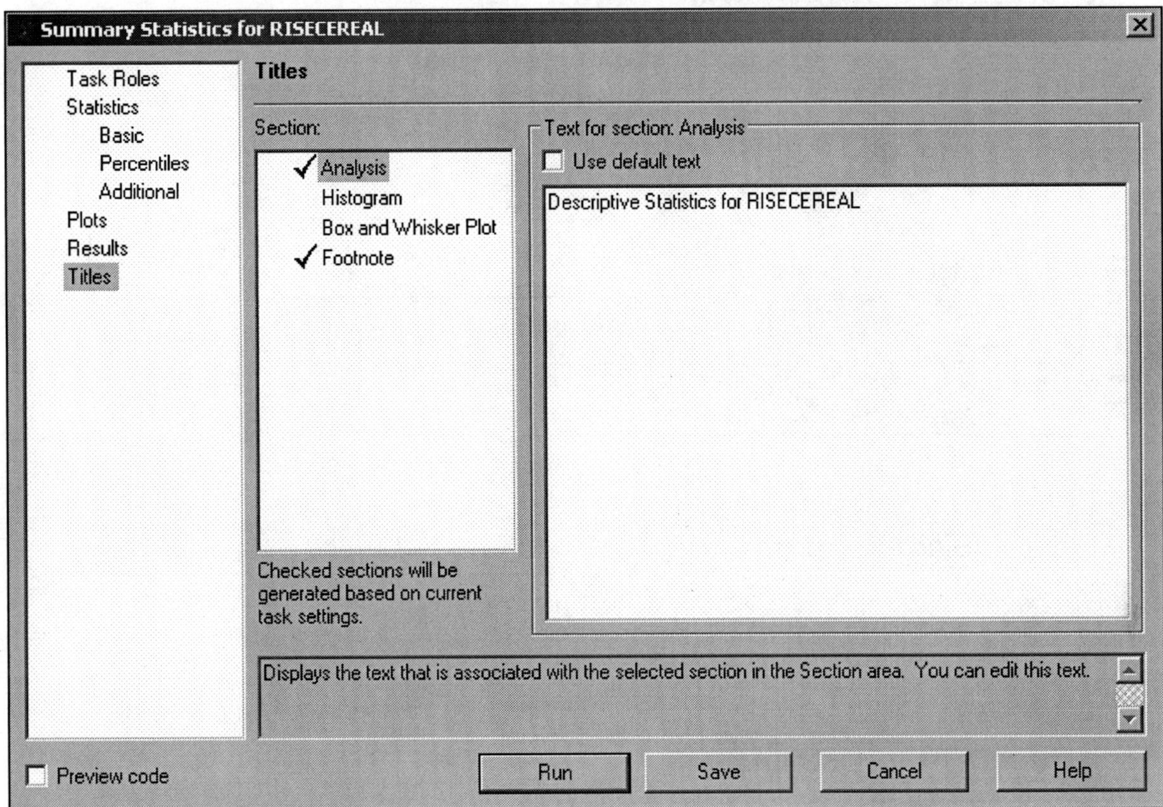

7. Select **Run** to run the analysis.

The report is shown below:

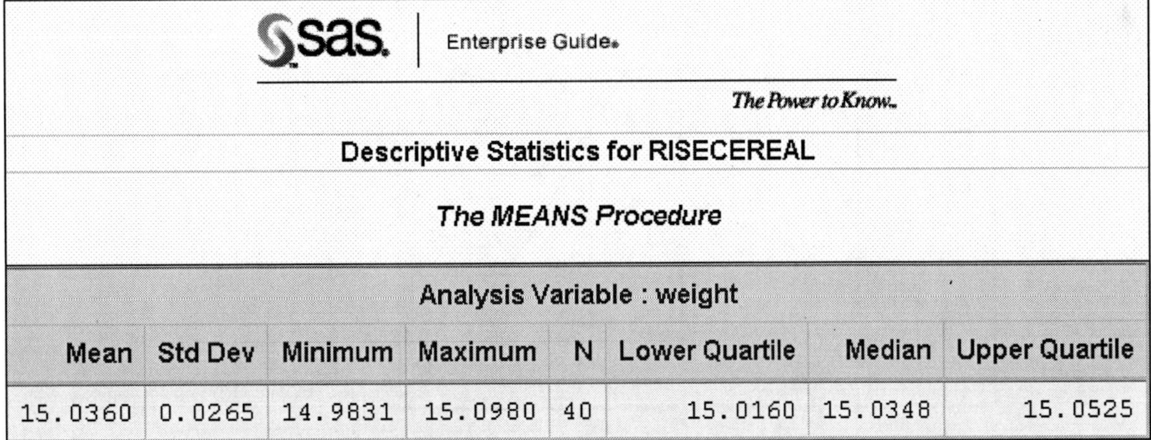

Descriptive Statistics for RISECEREAL

The MEANS Procedure

Analysis Variable : weight

Mean	Std Dev	Minimum	Maximum	N	Lower Quartile	Median	Upper Quartile
15.0360	0.0265	14.9831	15.0980	40	15.0160	15.0348	15.0525

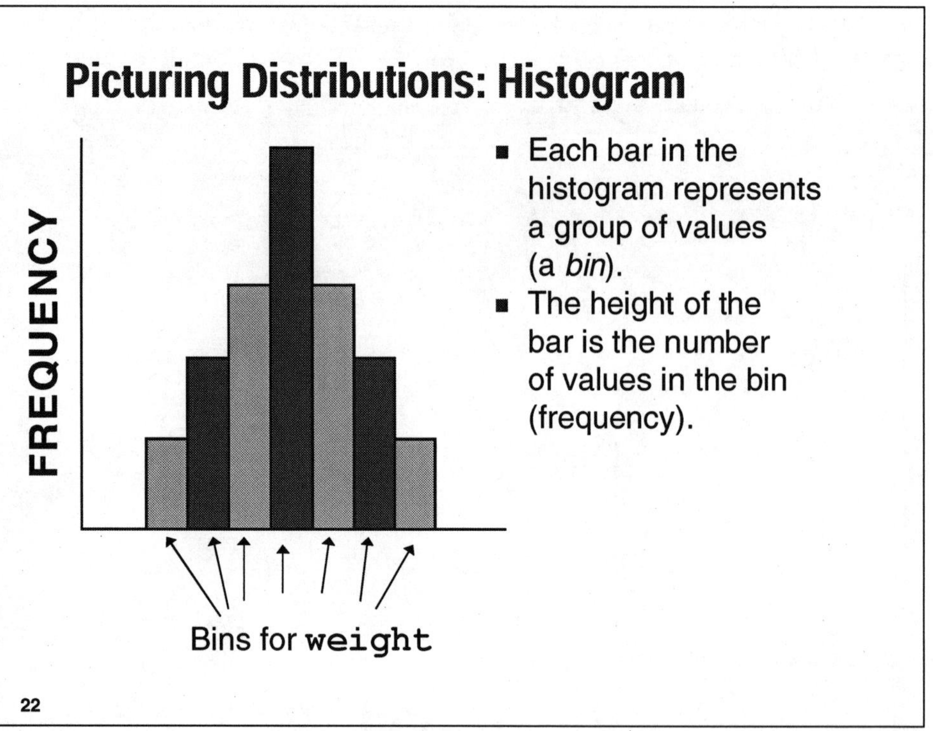

Picturing Distributions: Histogram
FREQUENCY
Each bar in the histogram represents a group of values (a *bin*).
The height of the bar is the number of values in the bin (frequency).
Bins for weight
22

The Normal Distribution

The normal distribution is a common distribution, characterized by its bell-curved shape.

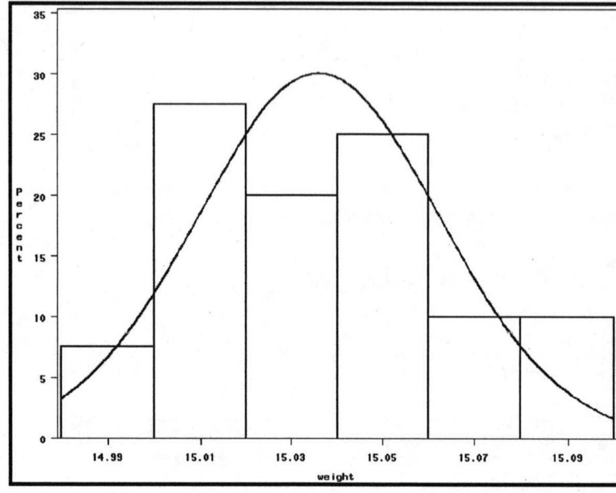

23

Normal Distribution

The normal distribution

- is a symmetric distribution. If you draw a line down the center, you get the same shape on either side.
- is fully characterized by the mean and standard deviation. If you know those two parameters, you know all there is to know about the distribution.
- is bell-shaped.
- has mean≈median≈mode.

The blue line on each of the following graphs represents the shape of the normal distribution.

24

Distribution Shapes: Normal

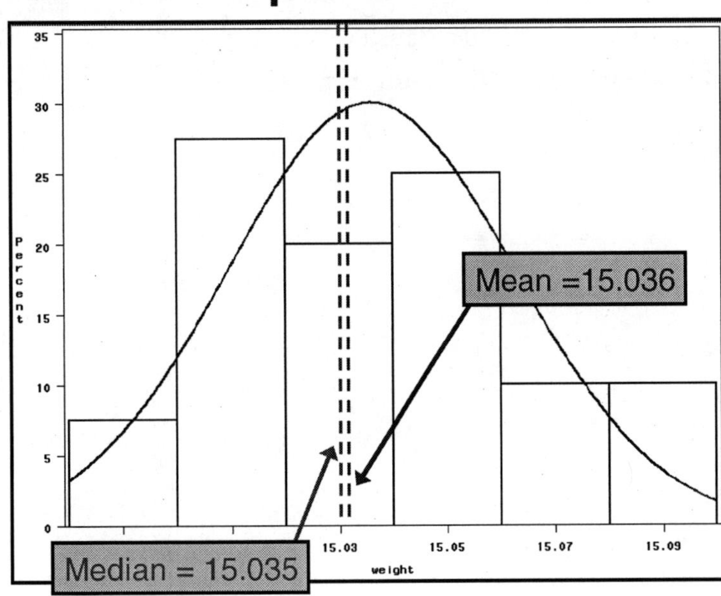

25

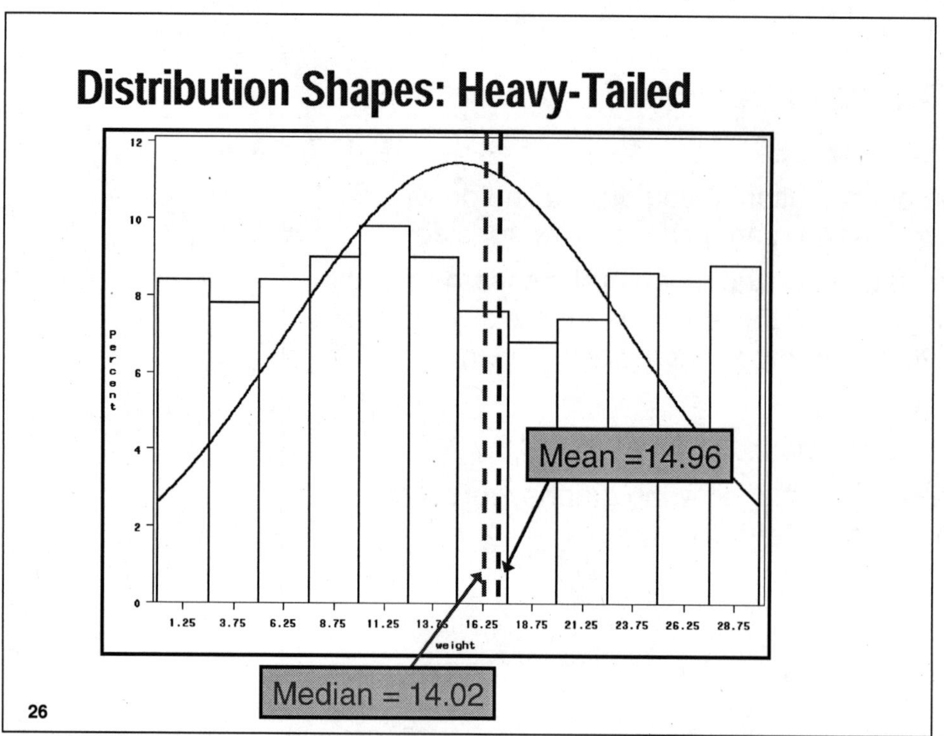

The *kurtosis* statistic measures the tendency of your data to be distributed toward the tails, or ends, of the distribution. A distribution that is approximately normal has a kurtosis statistic close to 0.

If your distribution has

- heavy tails compared to the normal distribution, then the statistic is positive
- light tails compared to the normal distribution, then the statistic is negative.

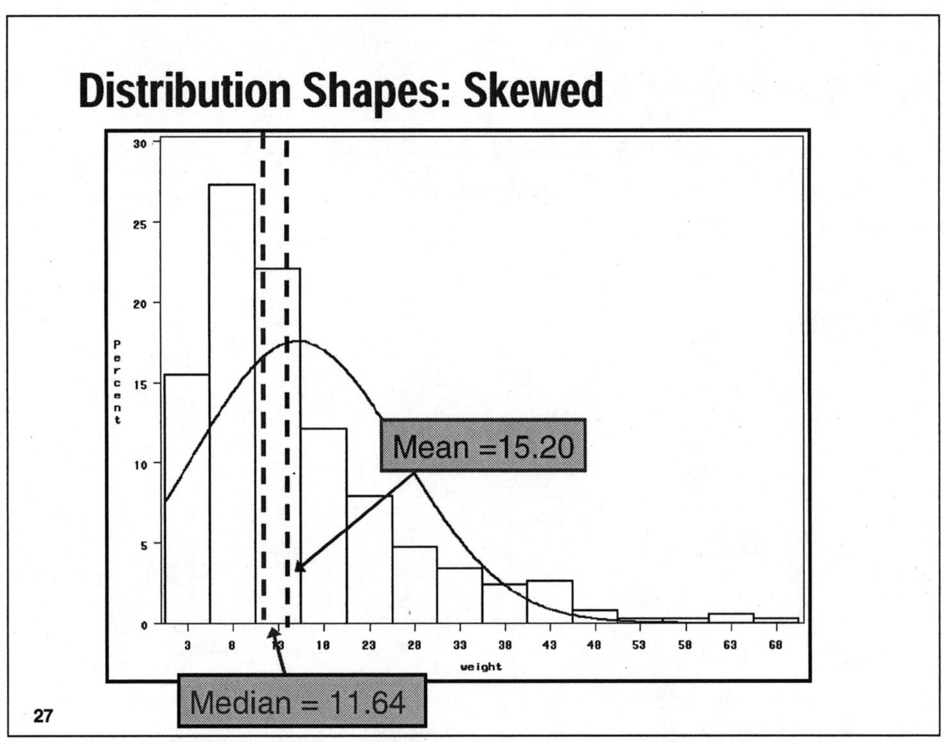

The *skewness* statistic measures the tendency of your distribution to be more spread out on one side than the other. A distribution that is approximately symmetric has a skewness statistic close to 0.

If your distribution is more spread out on the

- left side, then the statistic is negative, and the mean is less than the median.
- right side, then the statistic is positive, and the mean is greater than the median.

Graphical Displays of Distributions

The Distribution Analysis task produces several kinds of plots for examining the distribution of your data values:

- normal probability plots
- histograms
- box-and-whisker plots.

28

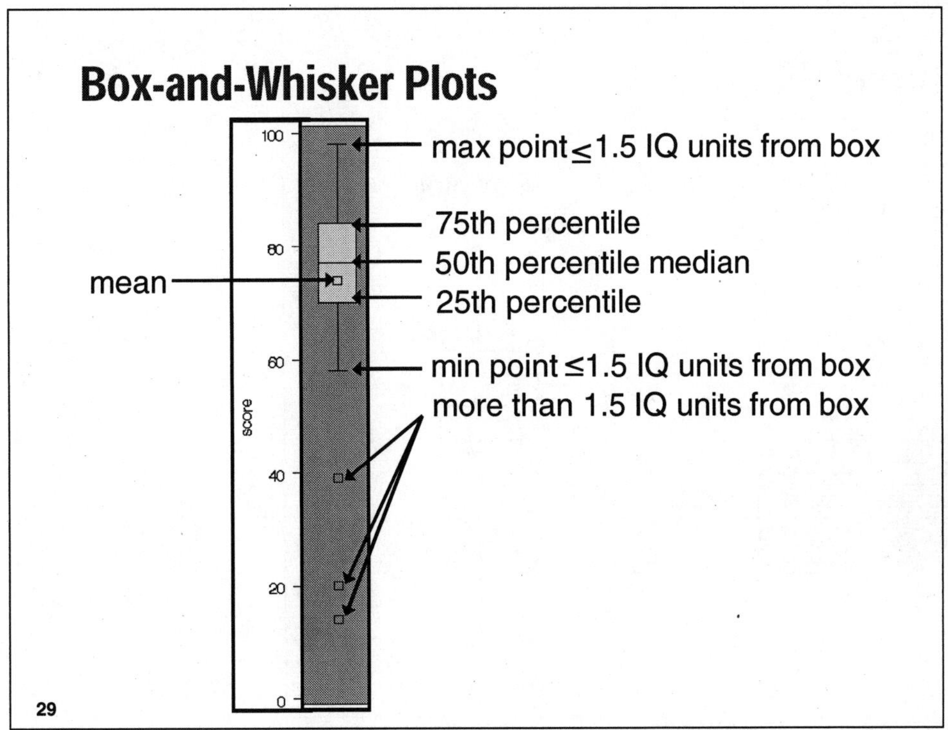

Box-and-whisker plots provide information about the variability of data and the extreme data values. The box represents the middle of your data, and you get a rough impression of the symmetry of your distribution by comparing the mean and median. The whiskers extend from the box as far as the data extend, to a distance of, at most, 1.5 interquartile units. An interquartile unit is the 75th percentile minus the 25th percentile. The square symbols denote points that are 1.5 or more interquartile units from the box, respectively.

The above plot is of the test scores from a statistics exam. The plot shows the data is skewed and has a few extreme values.

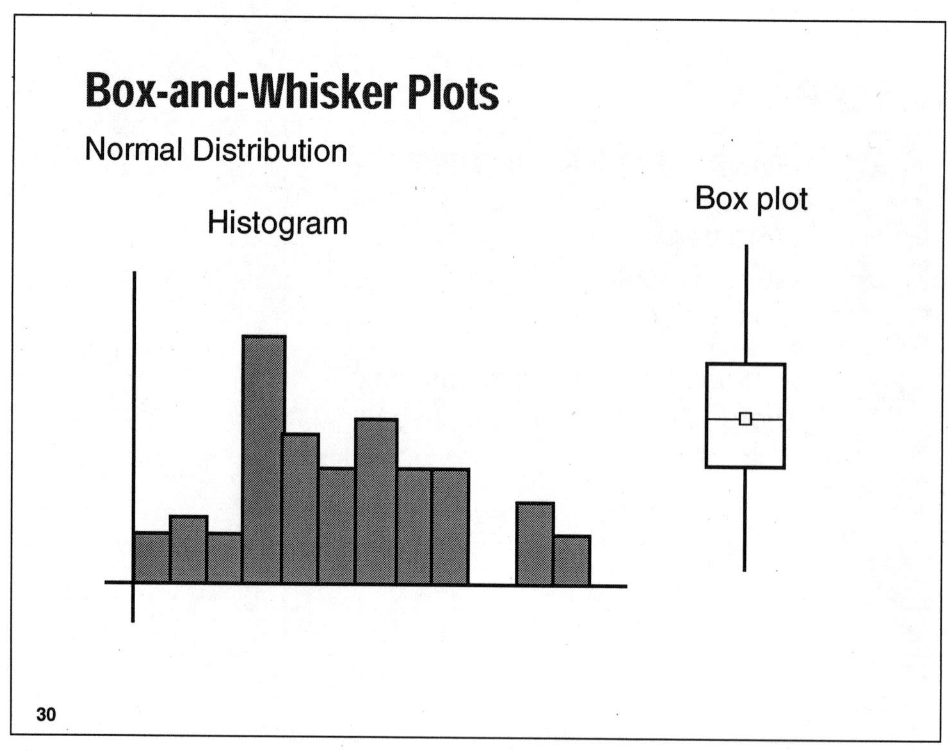
Box-and-Whisker Plots
Normal Distribution
Histogram
Box plot
30

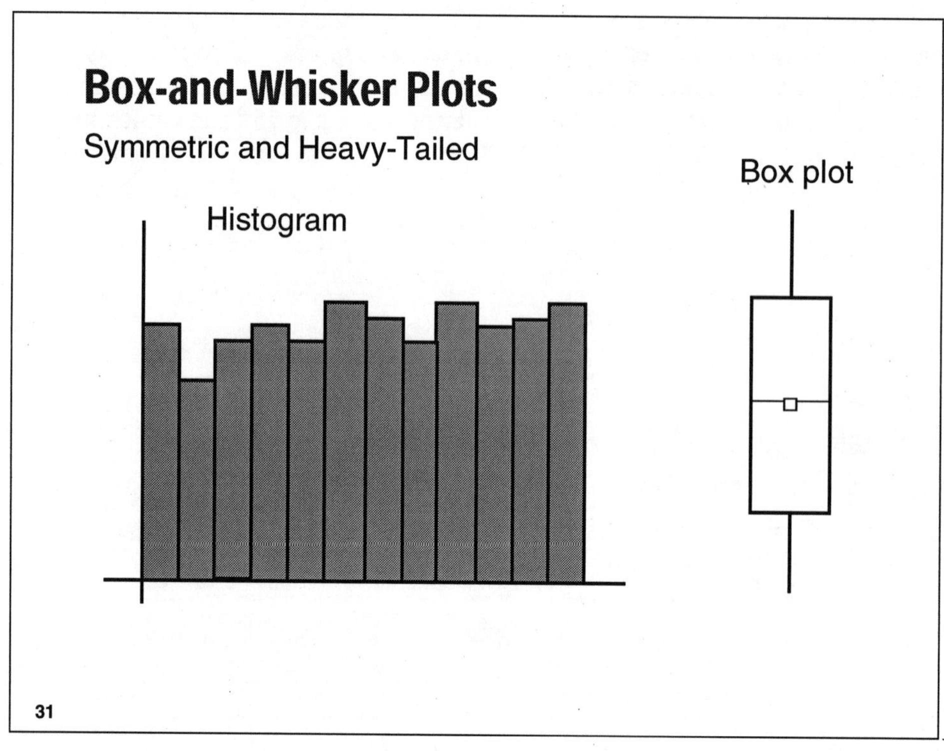
Box-and-Whisker Plots
Symmetric and Heavy-Tailed
Histogram
Box plot
31

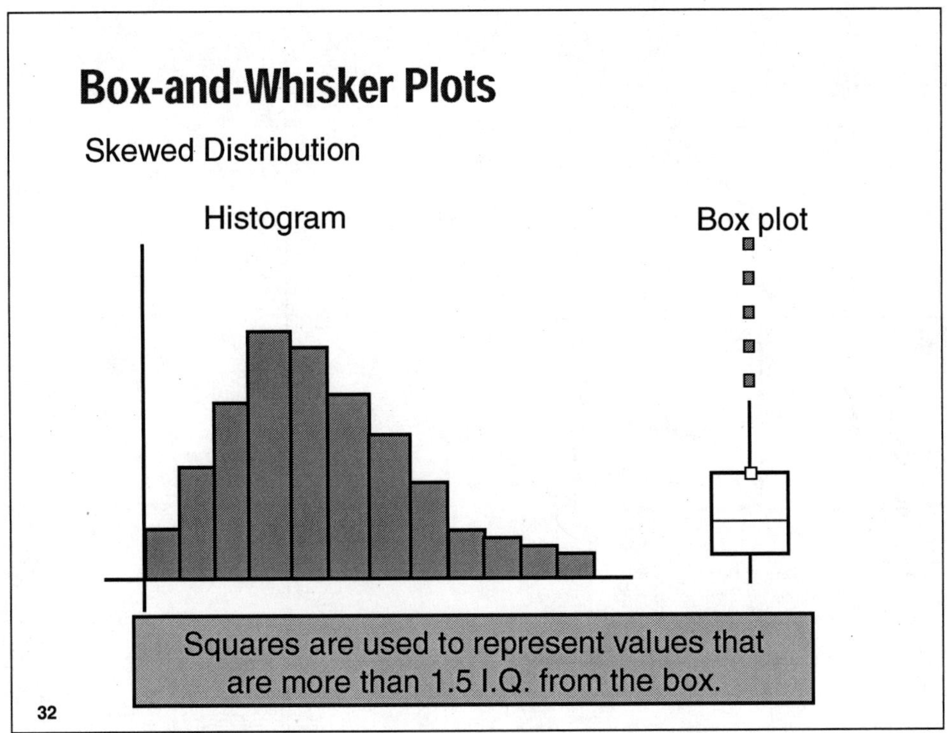
Box-and-Whisker Plots
Skewed Distribution
Histogram
Box plot
Squares are used to represent values that are more than 1.5 I.Q. from the box.
32

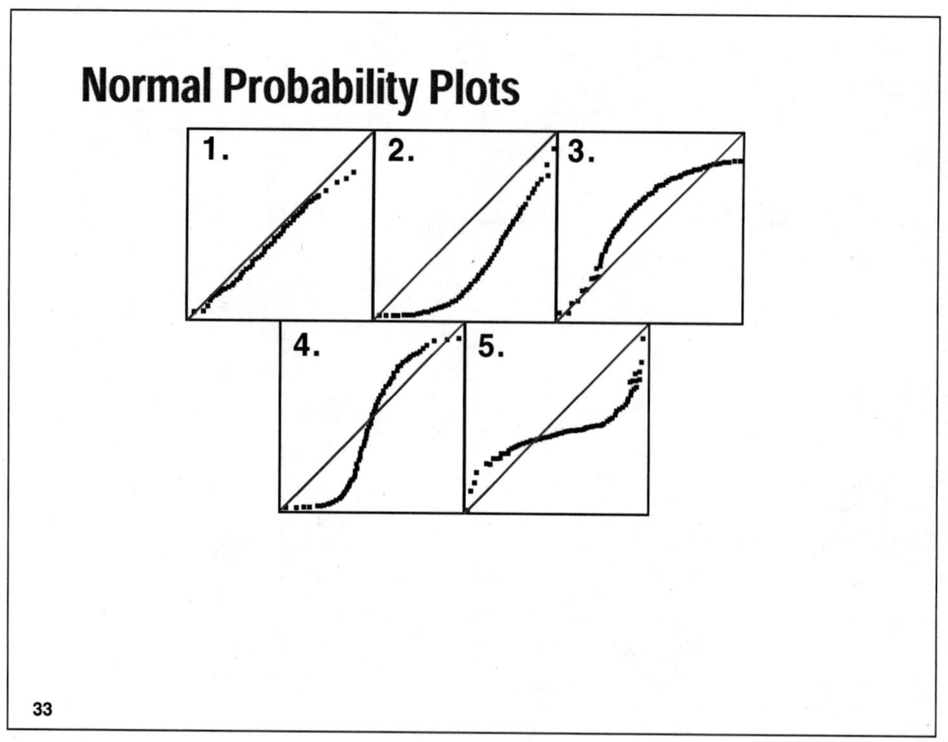

A *normal probability plot* is a visual method for determining whether or not your data comes from a distribution that is approximately normal. The vertical axis represents the actual data values while the horizontal axis displays the expected percentiles from a standard normal distribution. In other words, the plot is an overlay plot of your observed data versus your expected data if your data came from a normal distribution.

The above diagrams illustrate some possible normal probability plots for data from a

1. normal distribution (the observed data follow the reference line)
2. skewed-to-the-right distribution
3. skewed-to-the-left distribution
4. light-tailed distribution
5. heavy-tailed distribution.

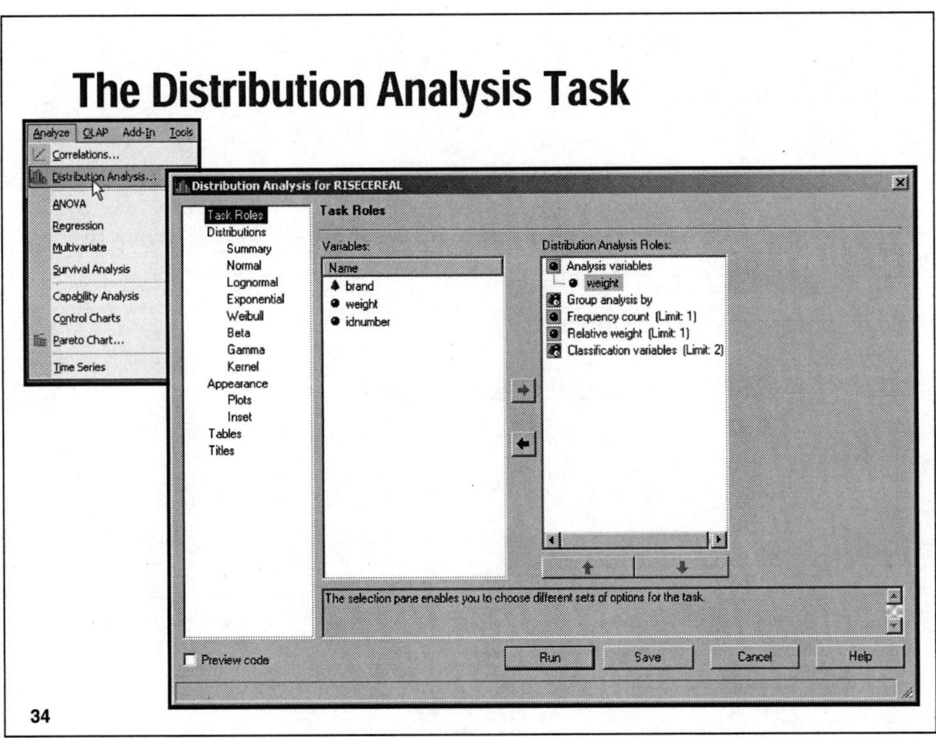
The Distribution Analysis Task
Analyze
OLAP
Add-In
Tools
Correlations...
Distribution Analysis...
ANOVA
Regression
Multivariate
Survival Analysis
Capability Analysis
Control Charts
Pareto Chart...
Time Series
Distribution Analysis for RISECEREAL
Task Roles
Distributions
Summary
Normal
Lognormal
Exponential
Weibull
Beta
Gamma
Kernel
Appearance
Plots
Inset
Tables
Titles
Task Roles
Variables:
Name
brand
weight
idnumber
Distribution Analysis Roles:
Analysis variables
weight
Group analysis by
Frequency count (Limit: 1)
Relative weight (Limit: 1)
Classification variables (Limit: 2)
The selection pane enables you to choose different sets of options for the task.
Preview code
Run
Save
Cancel
Help
34

Examining Distributions

Examine the shape of the distribution of weights in the **SASUSER.RISECEREAL** data set using the Distribution Analysis task.

1. Select the **RISECEREAL** data set in the process flow.

2. From the pull-down menus, select **Analyze** ⇨ **Distribution Analysis…**.

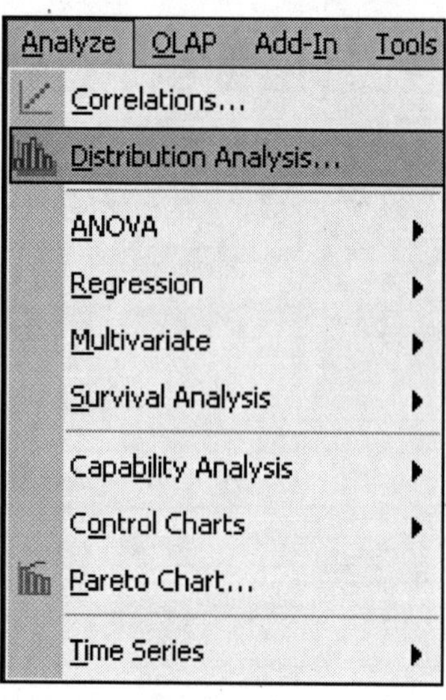

3. With **Task Roles** selected on the left, drag and drop `weight` to Analysis Variables.

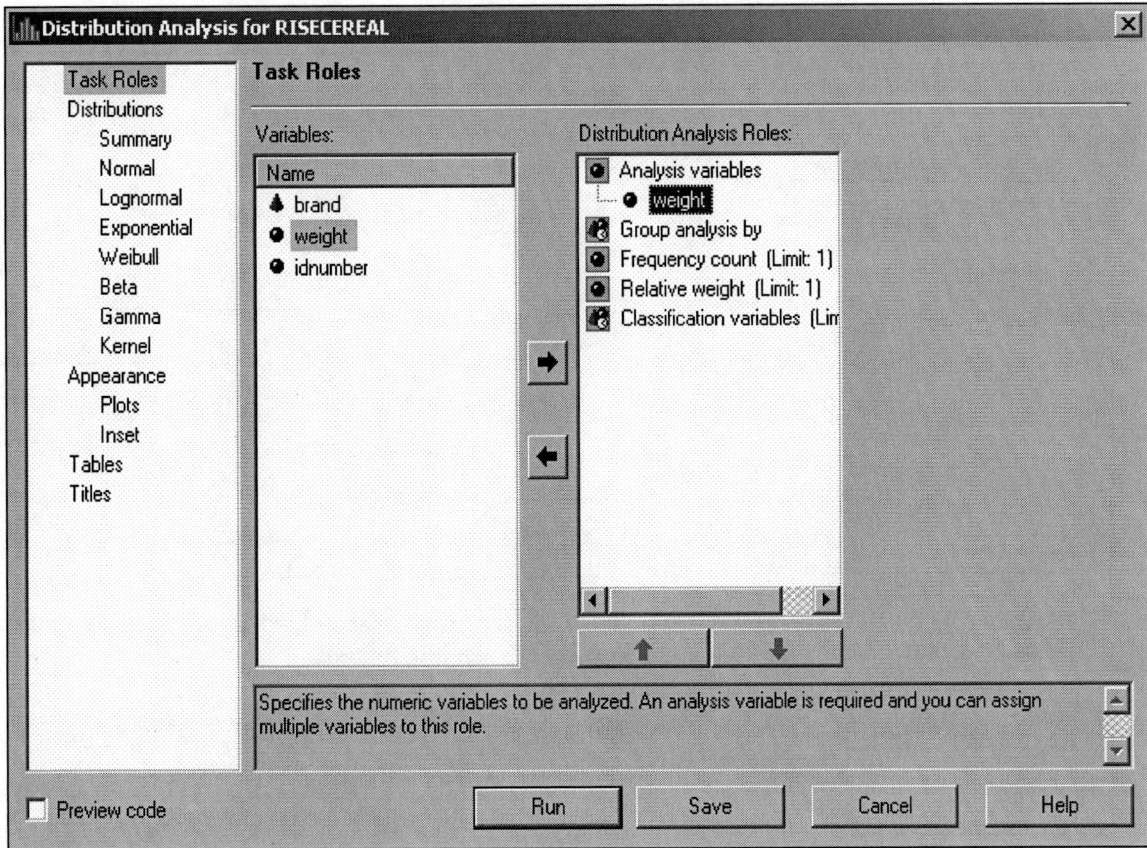

4. Select **Normal** under Distributions on the left. Select the check box next to **Normal** and give the reference line a width of 2.

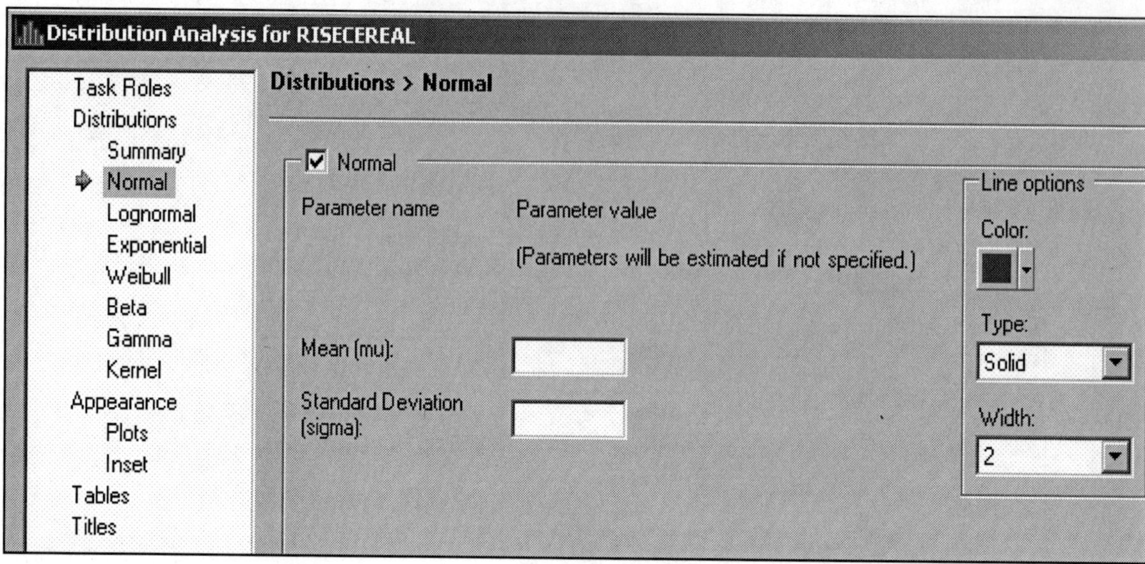

5. Select **Plots** under Appearance on the left, and check the boxes next to **Histogram Plot**, **Probability Plot**, and **Box plot**. Change the background color for each plot to white.

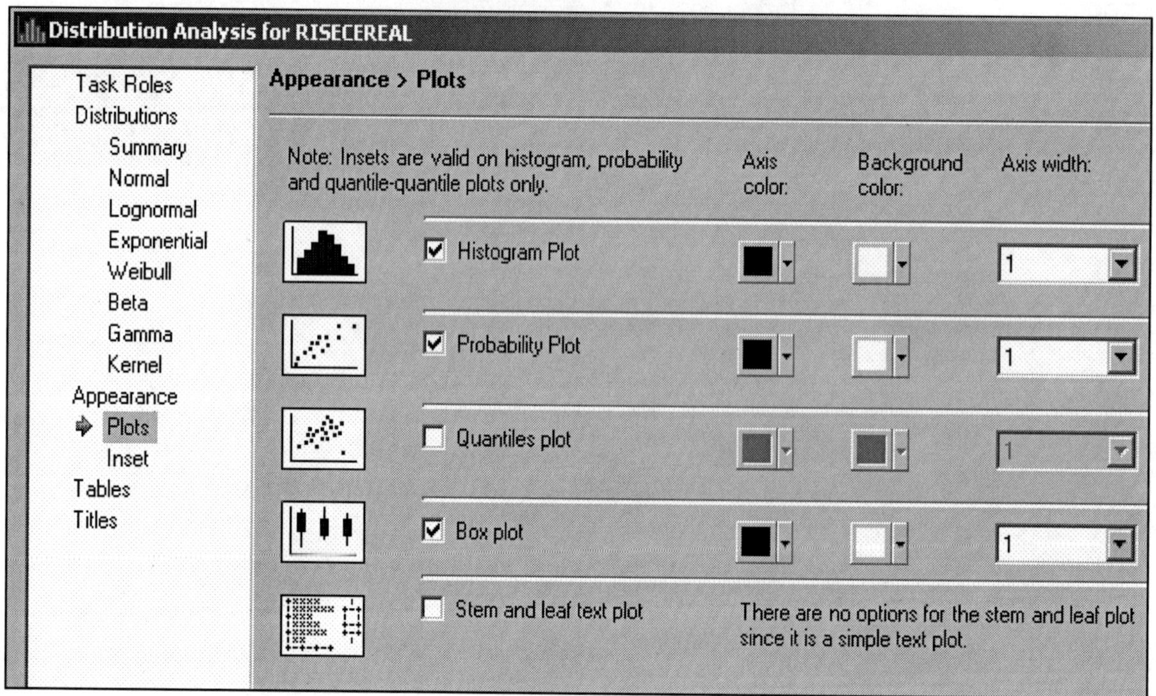

6. Select **Tables** on the left. Uncheck the boxes next to **Basic confidence intervals** and **Tests for location**. Check the boxes next to **Moments** and **Extreme values**.

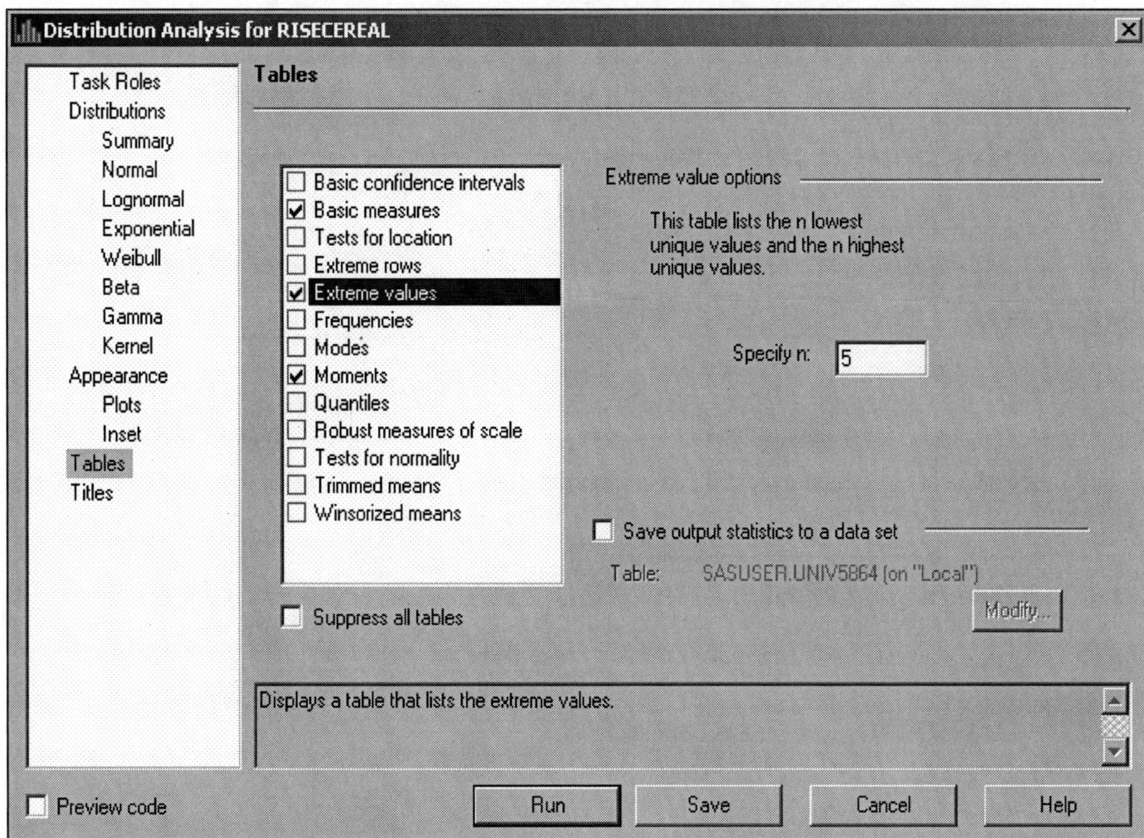

7. Select **Run** to submit the analysis.

Moments			
N	40	Sum Weights	40
Mean	15.03596	Sum Observations	601.4384
Std Deviation	0.02654963	Variance	0.00070488
Skewness	0.39889232	Kurtosis	-0.1975717
Uncorrected SS	9043.23122	Corrected SS	0.02749044
Coeff Variation	0.17657424	Std Error Mean	0.00419787

The Moments table shows many of the statistics from the Summary Statistics task, plus some measures of shape.

Basic Statistical Measures			
Location		Variability	
Mean	15.03596	Std Deviation	0.02655
Median	15.03480	Variance	0.0007049
Mode	15.01220	Range	0.11490
		Interquartile Range	0.03650

Note: The mode displayed is the smallest of 2 modes with a count of 2.

The Basic Measures table shows some standard statistics on location and variability. The output also notes that there are two modes and shows which of the two choices is displayed.

Extreme Observations			
Lowest		Highest	
Value	Obs	Value	Obs
14.9831	37	15.0639	6
14.9930	3	15.0812	4
14.9982	2	15.0858	21
15.0093	14	15.0868	27
15.0096	40	15.0980	35

The Extreme Observations table shows the five lowest and five highest values in the data set. This is a good opportunity to search for outliers.

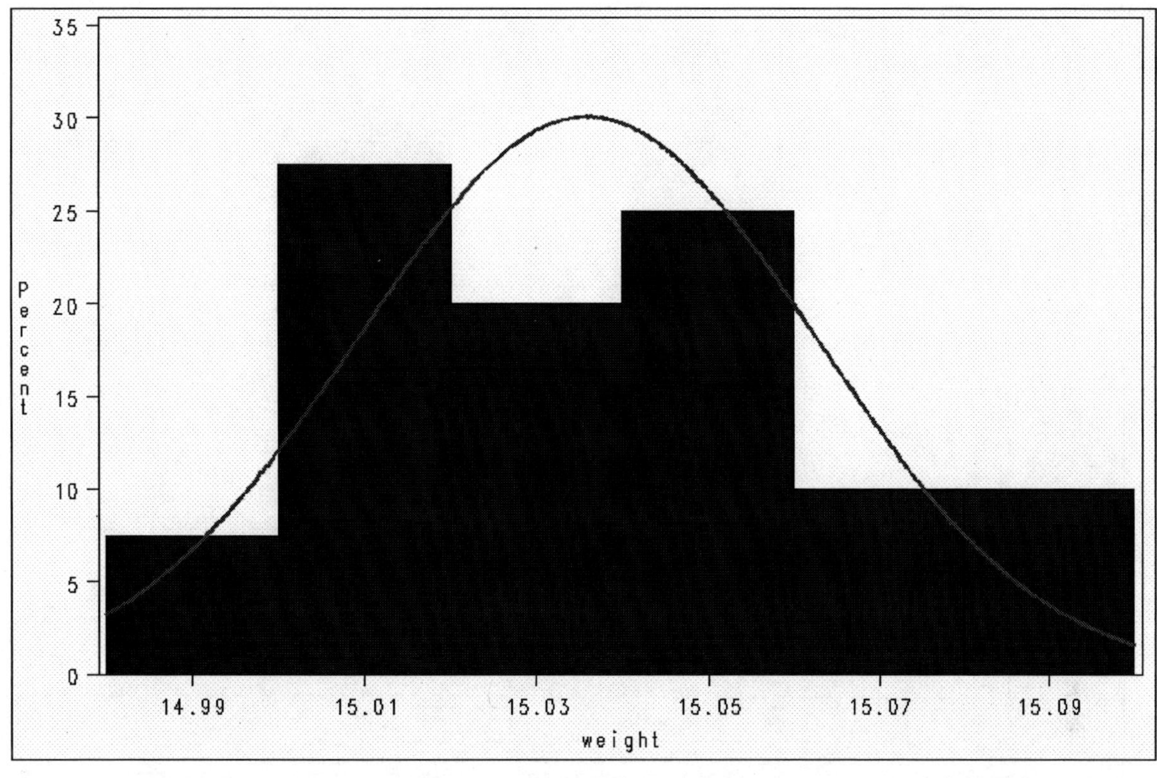

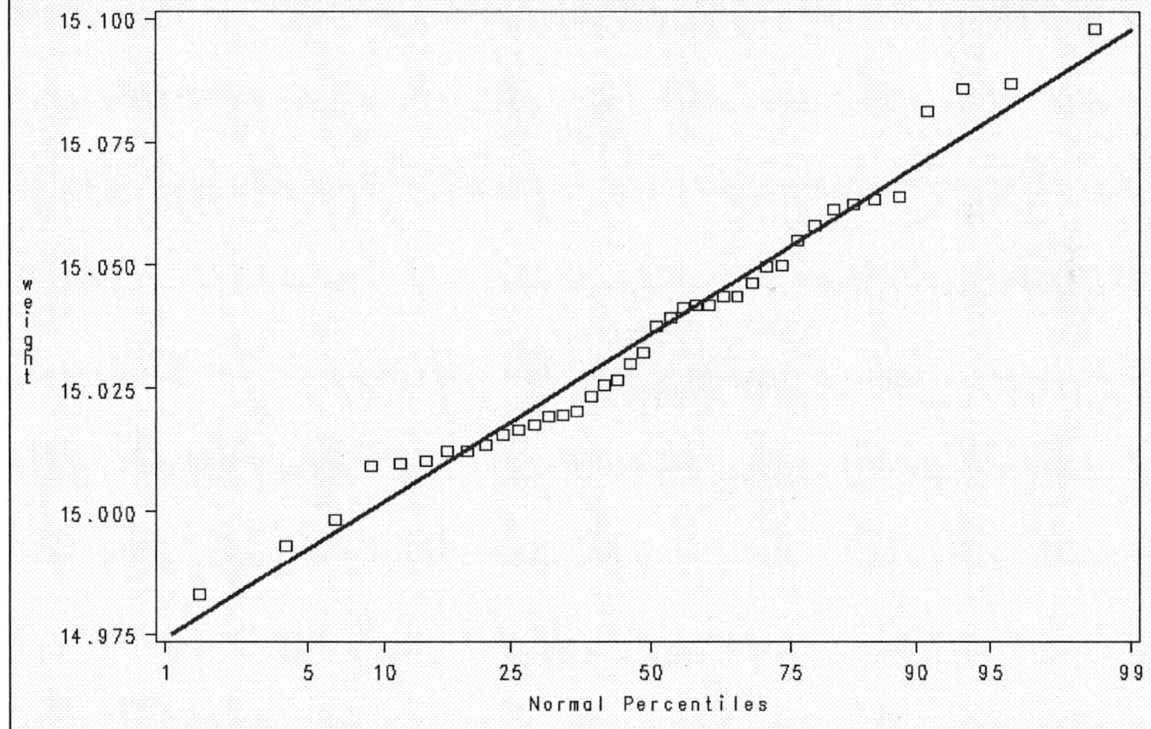

The normal probability plot and histogram show that the data follows a normal distribution.

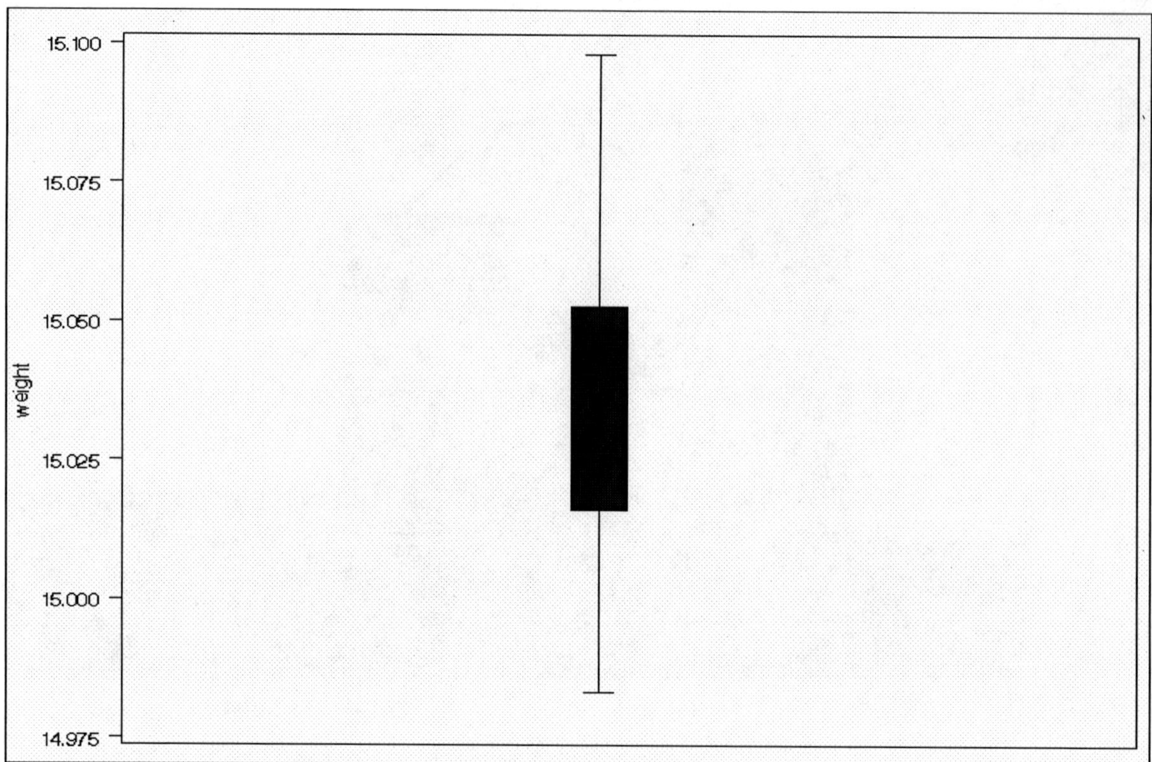

The high-resolution box plot gives further evidence that the data is normal.

1.3 Confidence Intervals for the Mean

Objectives

- Explain and interpret the confidence intervals for the mean.
- Explain the central limit theorem.
- Calculate confidence intervals using the Summary Statistics task.

37

Point Estimates

$\overline{X}$ estimates μ

S estimates σ

38

A *point estimate* is a sample statistic used to estimate a population parameter.

- An estimate of the average `weight` is 15.036, and an estimate of the standard deviation is 0.027.
- Because you only have an estimate of the unknown population mean, you need to know the variability of your estimate.
- A point estimate does not take into account the accuracy of the calculated statistic.

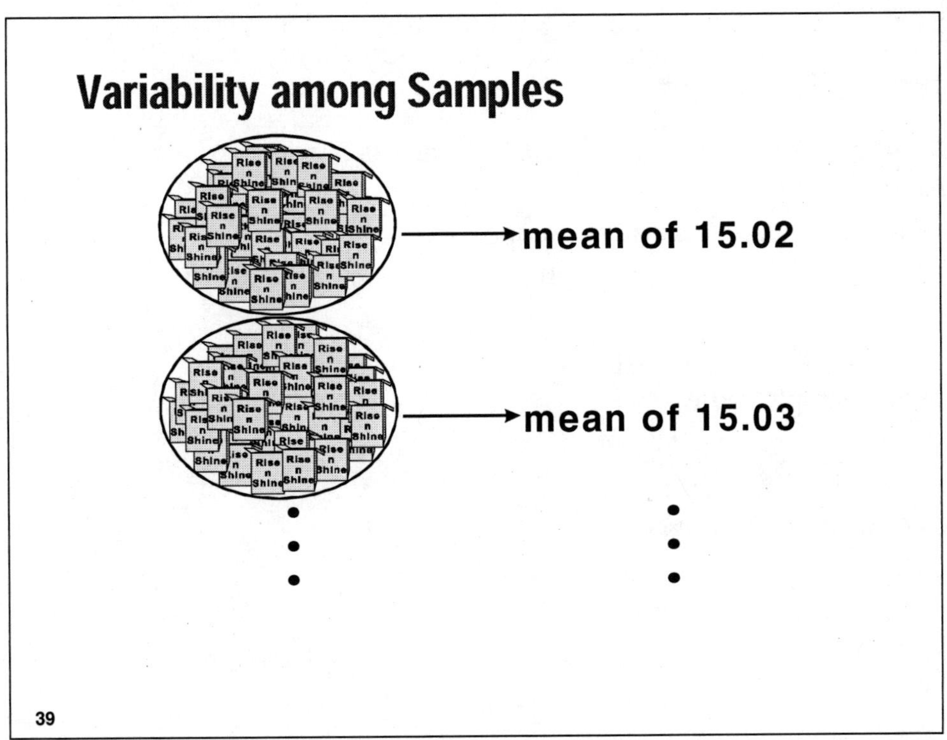

Why are you not absolutely certain that the mean weight for Rise n Shine cereals is 15.036?

The answer is because the sample mean is only an estimate of the population mean. If you collected another sample of cereal boxes, you would have another estimate of the mean.

Therefore, different samples yield different estimates of the mean for the same population. How close these sample means are to one another determines the variability of the estimate of the population mean.

Standard Error of the Mean

A statistic that measures the variability of your estimate is the *standard error of the mean.*

It differs from the sample standard deviation because

- the sample standard deviation deals with the variability of your data
- the standard error of the mean deals with the variability of your sample mean.

$$\text{Standard error of the mean} = \frac{s}{\sqrt{n}}$$

40

The standard error of the mean is estimated as

$$s_{\bar{x}} = \frac{s}{\sqrt{n}}$$

where

s	is the sample standard deviation
n	is the sample size.

The standard error of the mean for the variable `weight` is 0.02654963 / 6.324555, or approximately 0.004. This is a measure of how much error you can expect when you use the sample mean to predict the population mean. Therefore, the smaller the standard error is, the more accurate your sample estimate is.

Confidence Intervals

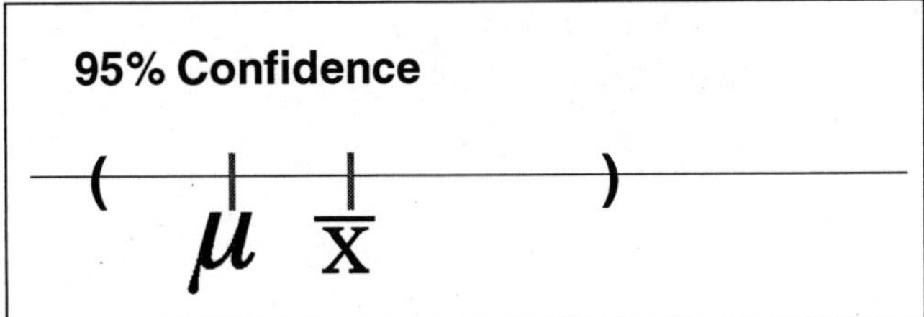

- A 95% confidence interval states that you are 95% certain that the true population mean lies between two calculated values.
  - In other words, if 100 different samples were drawn from the same population and 100 intervals were calculated, approximately 95 of them would contain the population mean.

41

A *confidence interval*

- is a range of values that you believe to contain the population parameter of interest
- places an upper and lower bound around a sample statistic.

To construct a confidence interval, a significance level must be chosen.

A 95% confidence interval is commonly used to assess the variability of the sample mean. In the cereal example, you interpret a 95% confidence interval by stating you are 95% confident that the interval contains the mean number of ounces of cereal for your population.

Do you want to be as confident as possible?

- Yes, but if you increase the confidence level, the width of your interval increases.
- As the width of the interval increases, it becomes less useful.

Assumption about Confidence Intervals

The types of confidence intervals in this course make the assumption that the sample means are normally distributed.

42

Confidence Intervals for the Mean

$$\bar{x} \pm t \cdot s_{\bar{x}} \quad \text{or} \quad (\bar{x} - t \cdot s_{\bar{x}},\ \bar{x} + t \cdot s_{\bar{x}})$$

where

$\bar{x}$ is the sample mean.

t is the *t* value corresponding to the confidence level and *n*-1 degrees of freedom where *n* is the sample size.

$s_{\bar{x}}$ is the standard error of the mean.

$$s_{\bar{x}} = \frac{s}{\sqrt{n}}$$

43

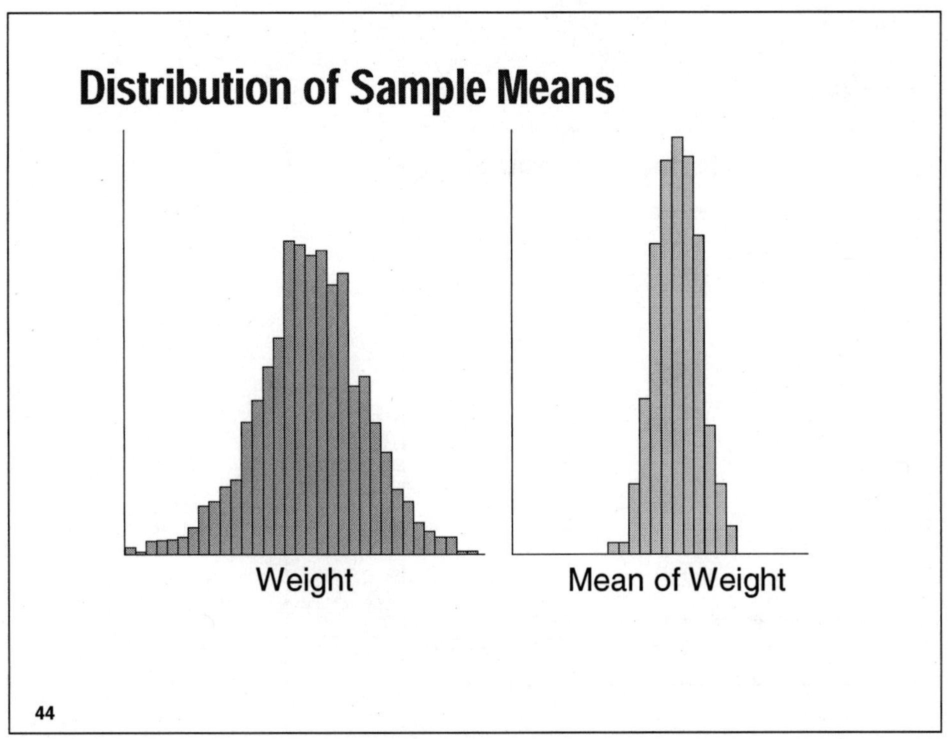

What is a distribution of sample means?

In the cereal example, it is the distribution of all possible sample means of ounces of cereal.

If you collect another sample of weights of cereal boxes, you would have another sample mean. In fact, if you collect 100 more samples, you could have 100 different sample means.

To illustrate the distinction between the distribution of the data values and the distribution of the sample means, suppose 500 samples of cereal weights were collected.

- The first chart may represent all 5000 observations in the data.
- The second chart may be a plot of the means from each of 500 samples of size 10.
- The distribution of sample means is not as wide. In other words, the distribution of sample means has a smaller variance.

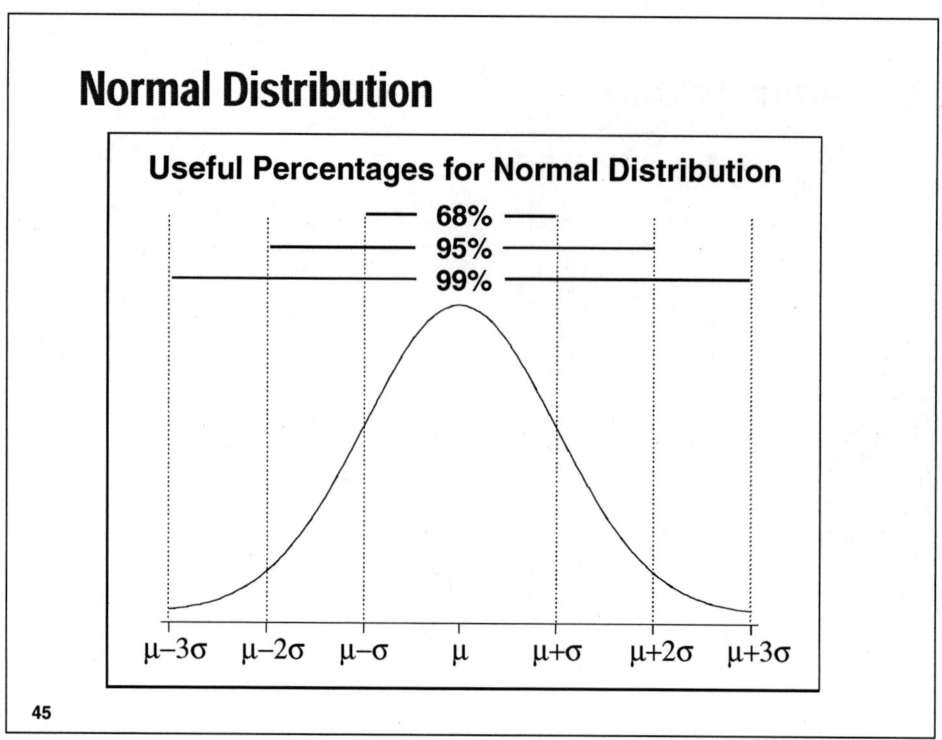

Why does the distribution of sample means have to be normally distributed?

The normal distribution describes probabilities. For example, approximately

- 68% of the data fall within one standard deviation of the mean
- 95% of the data fall within two standard deviations of the mean
- 99% of the data fall within three standard deviations of the mean.

If the distribution of sample means is normal, you can use the probabilities described by the normal distribution when constructing a confidence interval. The probability corresponds to the confidence level.

Therefore, if you construct a 95% confidence interval, you have a 95% probability of constructing a confidence interval that contains the population mean.

If the distribution of sample means is not normal, you have no idea what probability corresponds to a 95% confidence interval (unless the distribution of sample means is a known distribution).

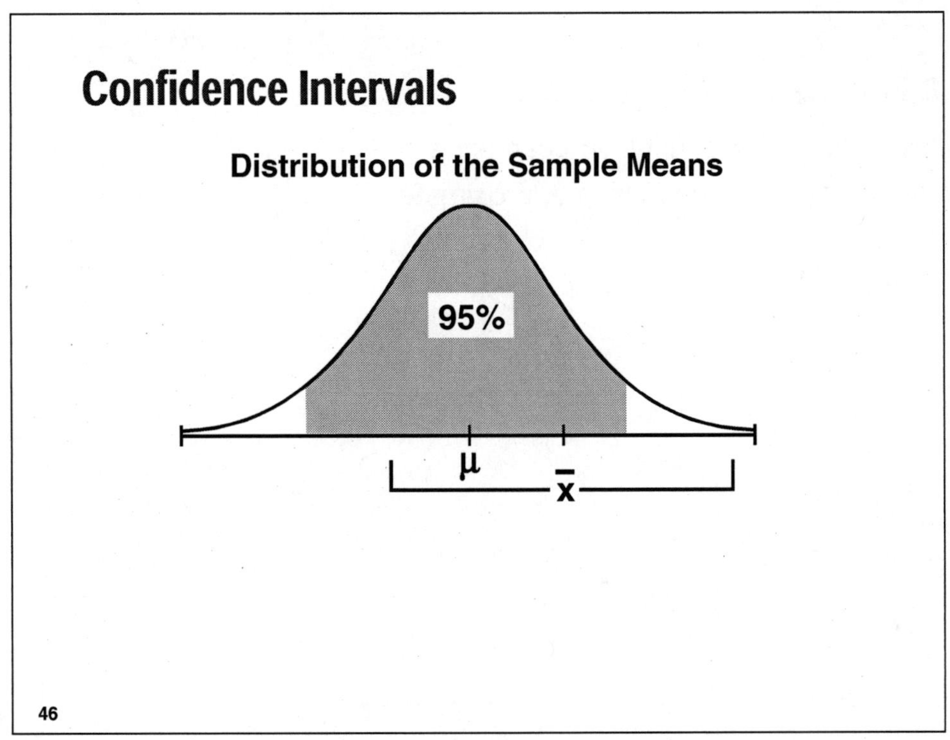

The graph above is the distribution of sample means. The shaded region represents 95% of the area in the distribution.

When constructing a 95% confidence interval, the length of the interval

- covers 95% of the area under the distribution of sample means when it is centered over μ, the population mean
- corresponds to a 95% probability of capturing the population mean when the interval is constructed.

Therefore, if the sample mean falls in the shaded region in the distribution of sample means, the interval constructed will contain the population mean.

Notice that μ is captured in this interval.

Verifying the Normality Assumption

To satisfy the assumption of normality, you can either

- verify that the population distribution is approximately normal, or
- apply the central limit theorem.

47

To verify that the population distribution is approximately normal, you can determine whether the data values in your sample are normally distributed.

Central Limit Theorem

The central limit theorem states that the distribution of sample means is approximately normal, regardless of the distribution's shape, if the sample size is large enough.

"Large enough" is usually about 30 observations: more if the data is heavily skewed, fewer if the data is symmetric.

48

To apply the central limit theorem, your sample size should be at least 30. The central limit theorem holds even if you have no reason to believe the population distribution is not normal.

Because the sample size for the cereal example is 40, you can apply the central limit theorem and satisfy the assumption of normality for the confidence intervals.

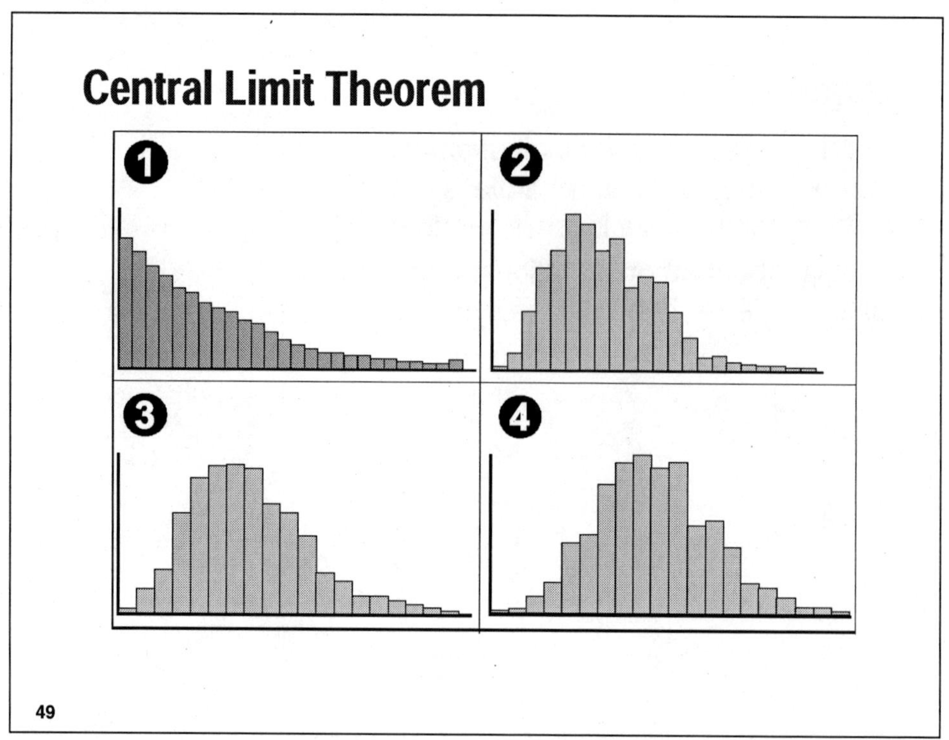

The graphs illustrate the tendency of a distribution of sample means to approach normality as the sample size increases.

The first chart is a histogram of data values drawn from an exponential distribution. The remaining charts are histograms of the sample means for samples of differing sizes drawn from the same exponential distribution.

1. Data from exponential distribution
2. 1000 samples of size 5
3. 1000 samples of size 10
4. 1000 samples of size 30

For the sample size of 30, the distribution is approximately bell-shaped and symmetric, even though the sample data is highly skewed.

Confidence Intervals

Example: Use the Summary Statistics task to generate a confidence interval for the mean of `weight` in the `RISECEREAL` data set.

1. Open the Summary Statistics dialog you created earlier by double-clicking on it in the project tree.

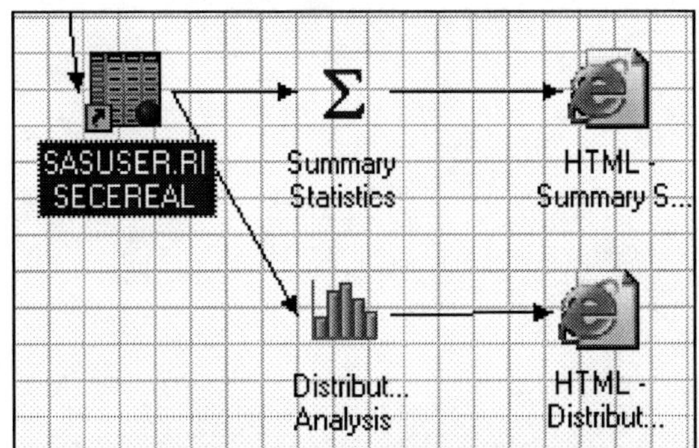

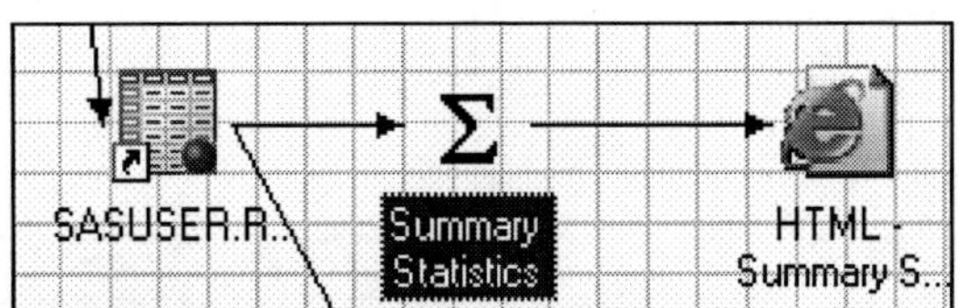

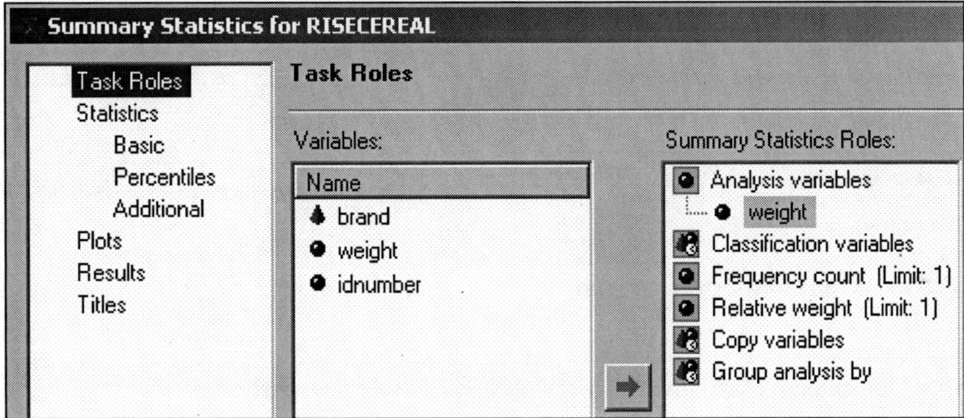

2. On the left, select **Percentiles**. Uncheck the boxes next to **Lower quartile**, **Median**, and **Upper quartile**.

3. On the left, select **Additional**. On the right, check the box next to **Confidence limits of the mean**.

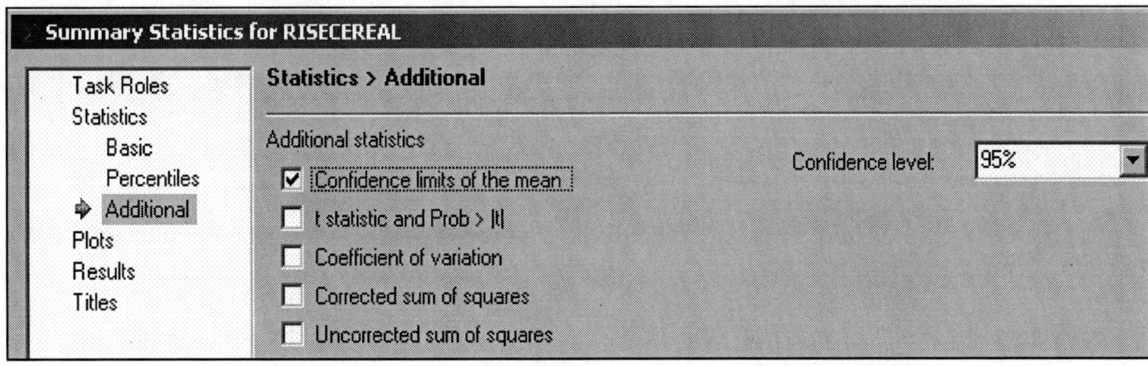

You can change the confidence level by selecting from the pull-down at the upper right.

4. On the left, select **Titles**. Change the title to `Confidence Limits for the Mean of weight`.

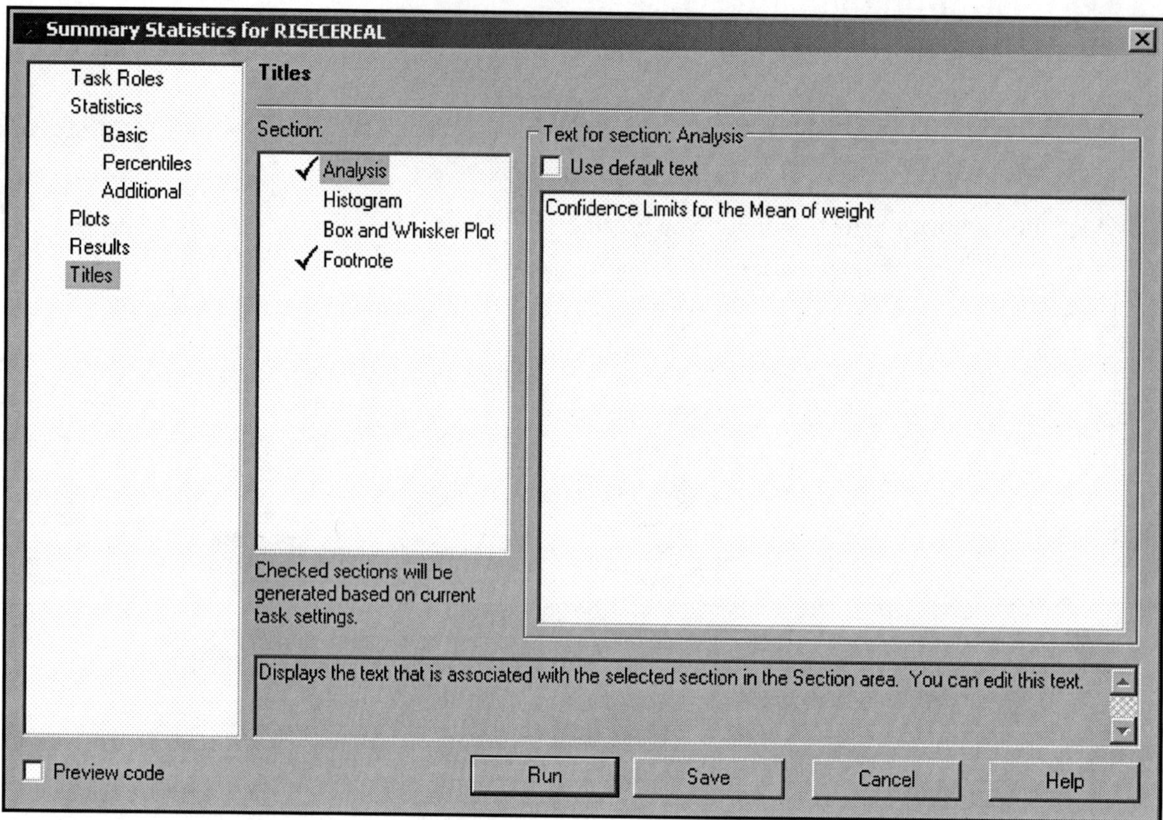

5. Select **Run** to run the task.

6. Select **No** to keep the results of the previous run. A second Summary Statistics task appears in the process flow.

Confidence Limits for the Mean of weight

The MEANS Procedure

Analysis Variable : weight						
Mean	Std Dev	Minimum	Maximum	N	Lower 95% CL for Mean	Upper 95% CL for Mean
15.0360	0.0265	14.9831	15.0980	40	15.0275	15.0445

The reported confidence interval says you are 95% confident that the true population mean is between 15.0275 and 15.0445.

1.4 Hypothesis Testing

Objectives

- Define some common terminology related to hypothesis testing.
- Perform hypothesis testing using the Distribution Analysis task.

52

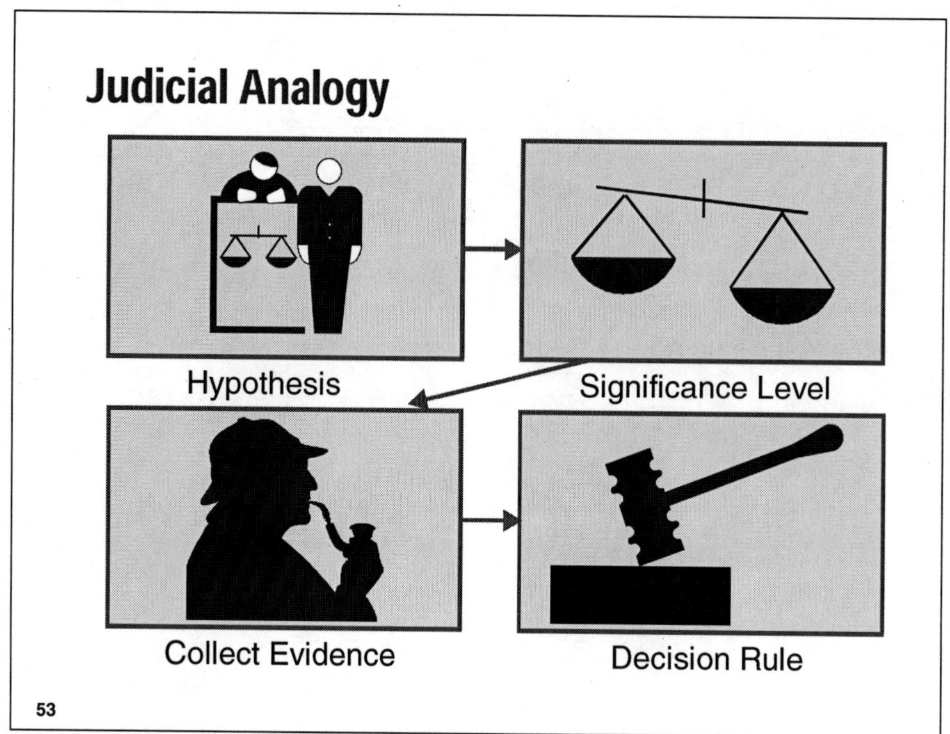

In a criminal court, you put defendants on trial because you suspect they are guilty of a crime. But how does the trial proceed?

Determine the null and alternative hypotheses. The *alternative* hypothesis is your initial research hypothesis (the defendant is guilty). The *null* is the logical opposite of the alternative hypothesis (the defendant is not guilty).

Select a *significance level* as the amount of evidence needed to convict. In a court of law, the evidence must prove guilt "beyond a reasonable doubt."

Collect evidence.

Use a *decision rule* to make a judgment. If the evidence is

- sufficiently strong, reject the null hypothesis.
- not strong enough, fail to reject the null hypothesis. Note that failing to prove guilt does not prove that the defendant is innocent.

Statistical hypothesis testing follows this same basic path.

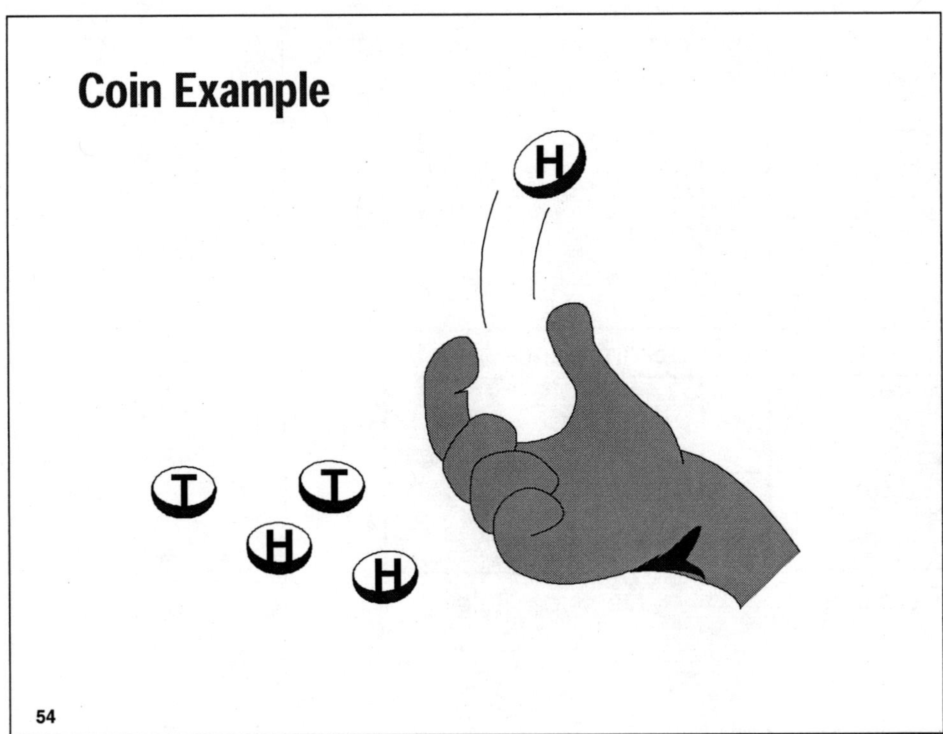

Suppose you want to know whether a coin is fair. You cannot flip it forever, so you decide to take a sample. Flip it five times and count the number of heads and tails.

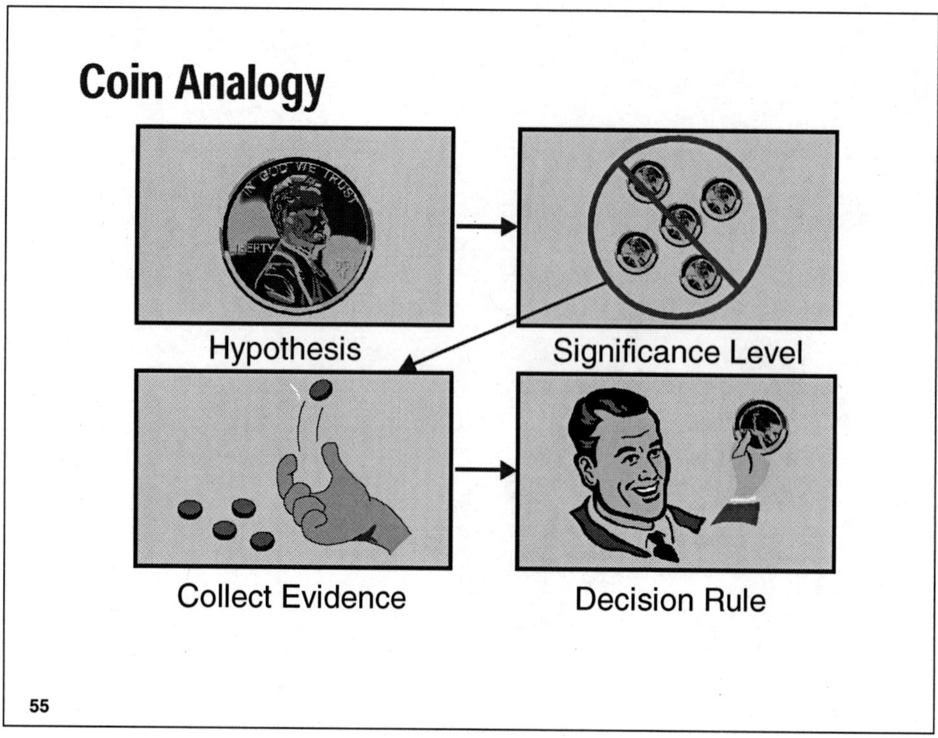

Test whether a coin is fair.

1. You suspect that the coin is **not** fair but recall the legal example and begin by assuming the coin is fair.

2. You select a significance level. If you observe five heads in a row or five tails in a row, you conclude the coin is not fair; otherwise, you decide there is not enough evidence to show the coin is not fair.

3. You flip the coin five times and count the number of heads and tails.

4. You evaluate the data using your decision rule and make a decision that there is
   - enough evidence to reject the assumption that the coin is fair
   - not enough evidence to reject the assumption that the coin is fair.

Types of Errors

You used a decision rule to make a decision, but was the decision correct?

	ACTUAL	
DECISION	H_0 Is True	H_0 Is False
Fail to Reject Null	Correct	Type II Error
Reject Null	Type I Error	Correct

56

Recall that you start by assuming that the coin is fair.

The probability of a Type I error, often denoted α, is the probability you reject the null hypothesis when it is true. It is also called the significance level of a test. In the

- legal example, it is the probability that you conclude the person is guilty when he or she is innocent
- coin example, it is the probability that you conclude the coin is not fair when it is fair.

The probability of a Type II error, often denoted β, is the probability that you fail to reject the null hypothesis when it is false. In the

- legal example, it is the probability that you fail to find the person guilty when he or she is guilty
- coin example, it is the probability that you fail to find the coin is not fair when it is not fair.

The power of a statistical test is equal to $1-\beta$, where β is the Type II error rate. This is the probability that you correctly reject the null hypothesis.

Modified Coin Experiment

Flip a fair coin 100 times and decide whether it is fair.

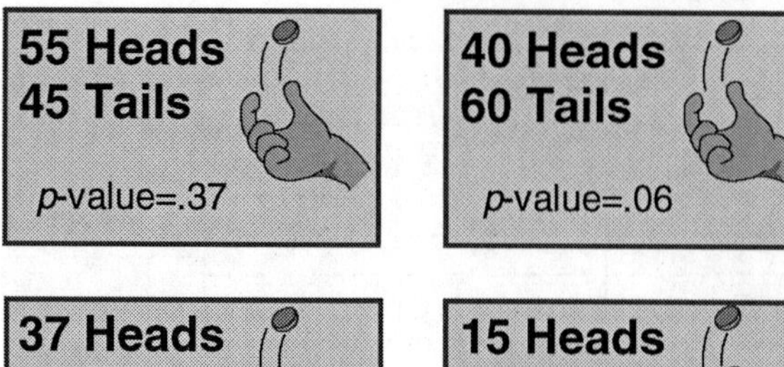

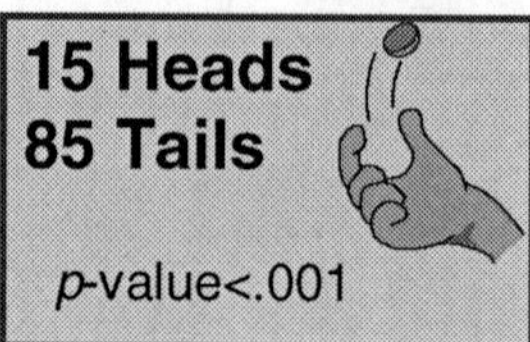

57

If you flip a coin 100 times and count the number of heads, you do not doubt that the coin is fair if you observe exactly 50 heads. However, you may be

- somewhat skeptical that the coin is fair if you observe 40 or 60 heads
- even more skeptical that the coin is fair if you observe 37 or 63 heads
- highly skeptical that the coin is fair if you observe 15 or 85 heads.

In this situation, the greater the difference between the number of heads and tails, the more evidence you have that the coin is not fair.

A *p-value* measures the probability of observing a value as extreme or more extreme than the one observed. For example, if your null hypothesis is the coin is fair and you observe 40 heads (60 tails), the *p*-value is the probability of observing a difference in the number of heads and tails of 20 or more from a fair coin tossed 100 times.

If the *p*-value is large, you often see a difference this large in experiments with a fair coin. If the *p*-value is small, however, you rarely see differences this large from a fair coin. In the latter situation, you have evidence that the coin is not fair.

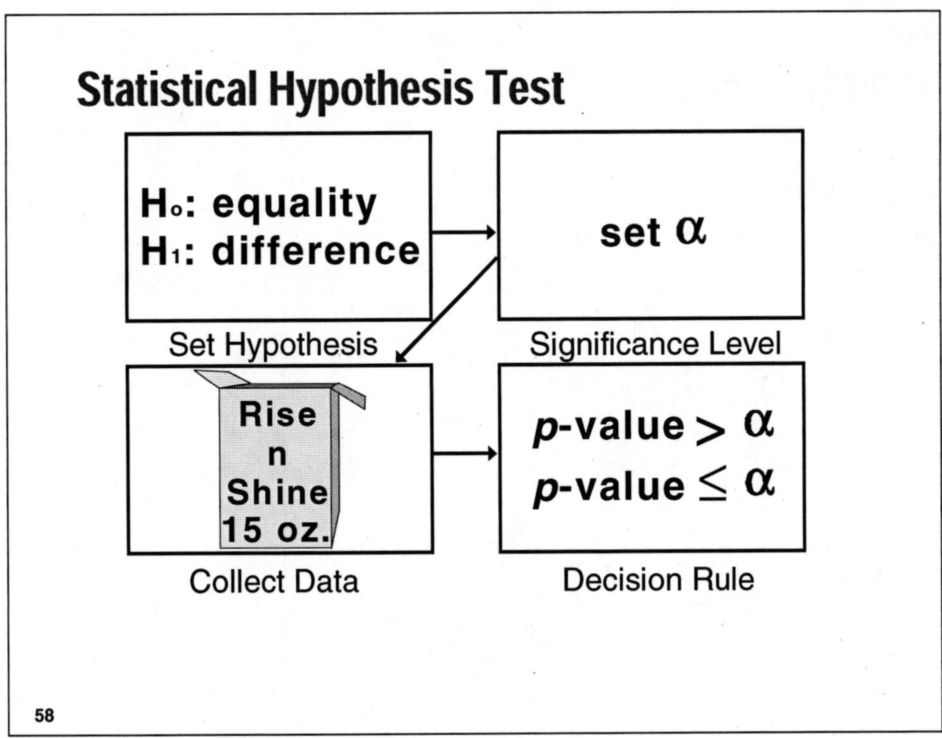

In statistics,

1. the null hypothesis, denoted H_0, is your initial assumption and is usually one of equality or no relationship. For the cereal example, H_0 is that the mean population weight for Rise n Shine cereal is 15 ounces.

2. the significance level is usually denoted by α, the Type I error rate.

3. the strength of the evidence is measured by a *p*-value.

4. the decision rule is
   - fail to reject the null hypothesis if the *p*-value is greater than or equal to α
   - reject the null hypothesis if the *p*-value is less than α.

You never conclude that two things are the same or have no relationship; you can only fail to show a difference or a relationship.

Comparing α and the *p*-value

In general, you

- reject the null hypothesis if p-value $\leq \alpha$
- fail to reject the null hypothesis if p-value $> \alpha$.

59

It is important to clarify that

- α, the probability of Type I error, is specified by the experimenter before collecting data
- the *p*-value is calculated from the collected data.

In most statistical hypothesis tests, you compare α and the associated *p*-value to make a decision.

Remember, α is set ahead of time based on the circumstances of the experiment. The level of α is chosen based on what it costs to make a mistake. It is also a function of your knowledge of the data and theoretical considerations.

For the cereal example, α was set to 0.05, based on the consequences of making a Type I error (if you conclude that the mean cereal weight is not 15 ounces when it really is 15 ounces). For example, if making a Type I error causes serious problems, you may want to lower your significance level.

Performing a Hypothesis Test

To test the null hypothesis H_0: $\mu = \mu_0$, the t statistic is calculated as

$$t = \frac{(\bar{x} - \mu_0)}{s_{\bar{x}}}$$

60

For the cereal example, μ_0 is the hypothesized value of 15 ounces, $\bar{x}$ is the sample mean weight of the cereal, and $s_{\bar{x}}$ is the standard error of the mean.

- This statistic measures how far $\bar{x}$ is from the hypothesized mean.
- To reject a test with this statistic, the t statistic should be much higher or lower than 0 and have a small corresponding p-value.
- The results of this test are valid if the distribution of sample means is normally distributed.

Performing a Hypothesis Test

The null hypothesis is rejected when the actual value of interest is either less than or greater than the hypothesized value.

H_0: $\mu = 15.00$

H_1: $\mu \neq 15.00$

$$t = \frac{(\bar{x} - 15)}{s_{\bar{x}}}$$

61

For the cereal example, if discrepancies in either direction (above 15 ounces or below 15 ounces) are of interest, then the cereal manufacturer would conduct a two-sided test of the hypothesis.

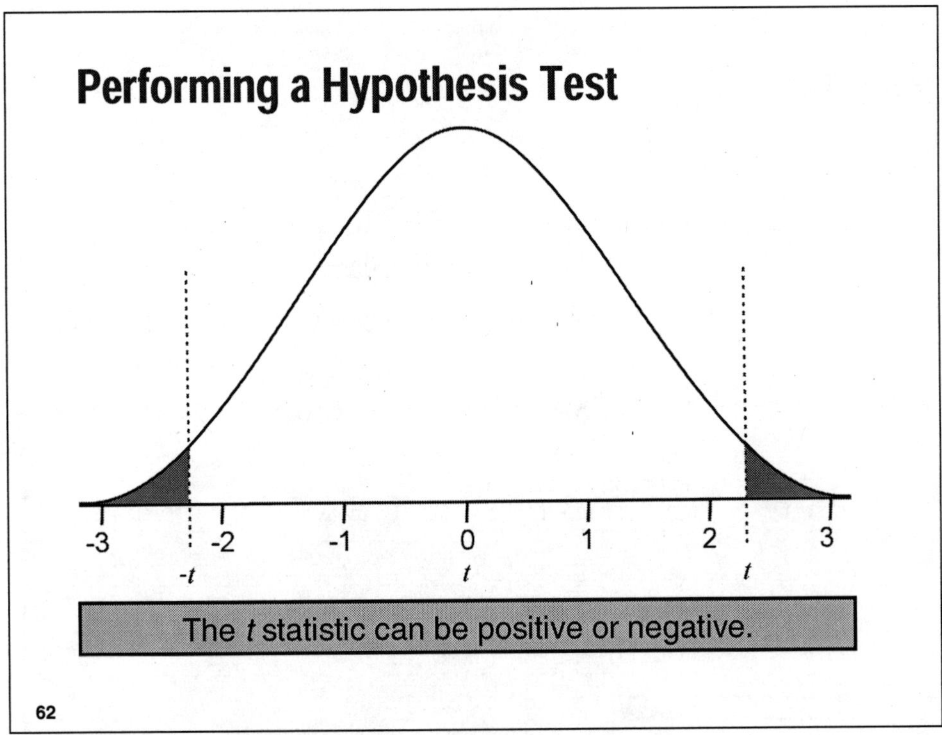

For a two-sided test of hypothesis, the rejection region is contained in both tails of the distribution of *t* statistics. If the *t* statistic falls in the rejection region, then you reject the null hypothesis. Otherwise, you fail to reject the null hypothesis.

The area in each of the tails corresponds to $\frac{\alpha}{2}$ or 2.5%.

It is also possible to have a one-sided test of hypothesis where the question is whether the mean of the population is greater than or less then a certain amount. For example, a consumer advocacy group may suspect that Rise n Shine is not giving consumers enough cereal. Their hypothesis would therefore be

H_o: $\mu \geq 15$

H_1: $\mu < 15$

The *p*-value for a one-sided test of hypothesis is half the *p*-value for a two-sided test of hypothesis. Therefore, in order to perform a one-sided test, you must do the following:

1. Check to see if the *t* statistic is the right sign (negative if H_1 is <, positive if H_1 is >).
2. If the sign of the *t* statistic is correct, then divide the reported *p*-value by 2.
3. Compare the new *p*-value to alpha.

Hypothesis Testing

Example: Modify the Tests for Location table options in the Distribution Analysis task to test the null hypothesis that the mean of the cereal example is equal to 15 ounces.

1. Navigate to **RISECEREAL** and open the Distribution Analysis dialog you created earlier by right-clicking and selecting **Open**.

2. Select **Tables** on the right, check the box next to **Tests for location**, and change the H_0: Mu= value to 15.

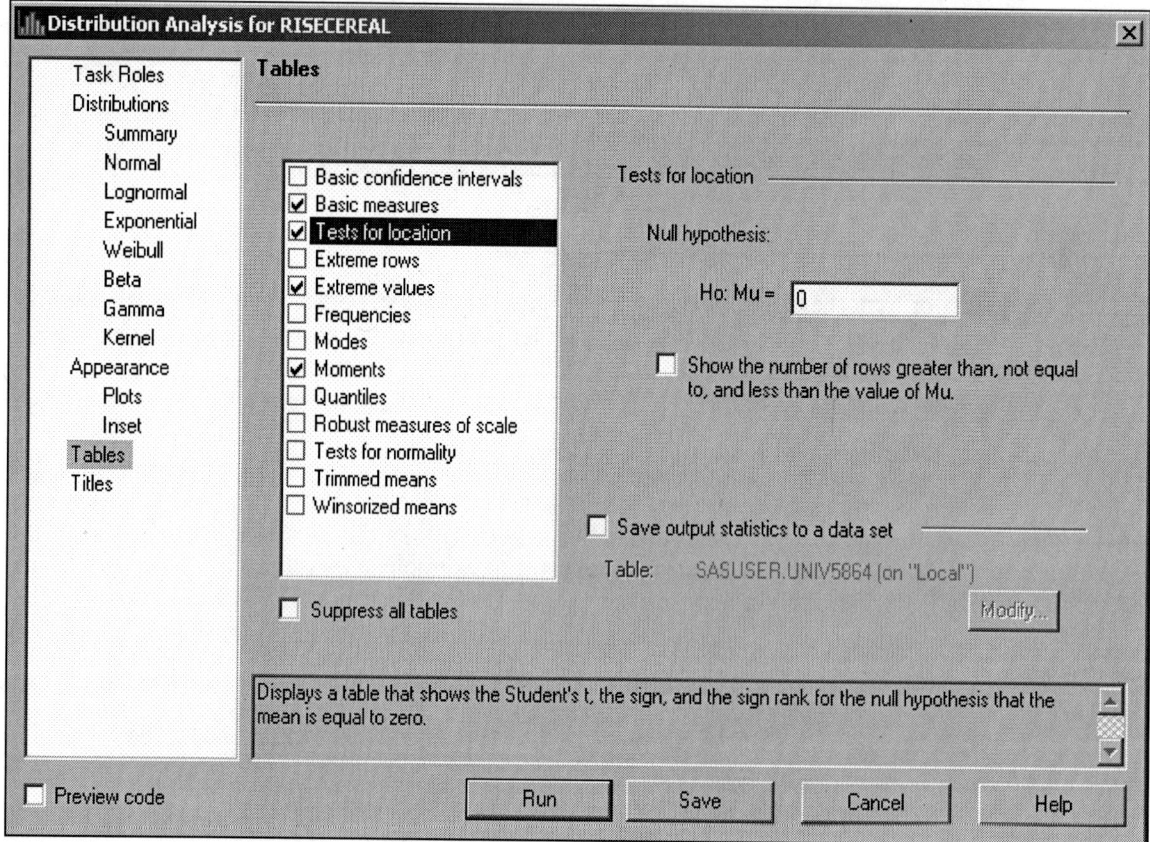

3. Select **Run** to run the task.

4. Select **Yes** to replace the results of the previous run.

5. The report appears in the work area at the bottom of the screen.

<table>
<tr><th colspan="5">Tests for Location: Mu0=0</th></tr>
<tr><th>Test</th><th colspan="2">Statistic</th><th colspan="2">p Value</th></tr>
<tr><td>Student's t</td><td>t</td><td>3581.811</td><td>Pr > |t|</td><td><.0001</td></tr>
<tr><td>Sign</td><td>M</td><td>20</td><td>Pr >= |M|</td><td><.0001</td></tr>
<tr><td>Signed Rank</td><td>S</td><td>410</td><td>Pr >= |S|</td><td><.0001</td></tr>
</table>

The *t*-test is called the Student's t. The Pr >|t| is the *p*-value for a two-sided *t*-test (the probability that a *t* this large or larger in terms of absolute value would appear if the null hypothesis were true.)

With alpha=0.05, you reject the null hypothesis and accept the conclusion that the amount of cereal in Rise n Shine cereal boxes is not equal to 15. This may suggest a need for additional quality control on the part of the plant manager.

1.5 Exercises

1. Producing Descriptive Statistics

A random sample of 50 observations pertaining to 50 male runners in the 1997 Boston Marathon was obtained. The data is in the data set **BOSTONMARATHON**. The data pertaining to the top 87 males who were in the top 100 (men and women) is in the data set **BOSTONTOP100**. Both data sets have these variables:

age runner's age in years

tottime total time in seconds it took the runner to complete the course

halftime time it took in seconds to complete the first half of the distance.

a. Complete the following table of descriptive statistics for each of the variables in the data set **BOSTONMARATHON**. Do the variables appear to be normally distributed?

	age	tottime	halftime
Mean			
Standard Deviation			
Skewness			
Kurtosis			
Median			
Minimum			
Maximum			
Is distribution normal?	Yes/No	Yes/No	Yes/No

b. Complete the following table of descriptive statistics for each of the variables in the data set `BOSTONTOP100`. Do the variables appear normally distributed?

	`age`	`tottime`	`halftime`
Mean			
Standard Deviation			
Skewness			
Kurtosis			
Median			
Minimum			
Maximum			
Is distribution normal?	Yes/No	Yes/No	Yes/No

2. Producing Confidence Intervals

a. Generate the 95% confidence interval for the total time it takes for participants in the data set `BOSTONMARATHON` to complete the marathon.

1) Is it appropriate to obtain a confidence interval for this data?

2) What is the confidence interval?

3) How do you interpret this interval?

3. Performing a One-Sample *t*-Test

a. Do a one-sample *t*-test to determine whether the mean of the random sample of participants in the data set `BOSTONMARATHON` is significantly different from the average time it took for the top 87 male participants, 8891.37 seconds.

1) What is the value of the *t* statistic and the corresponding *p*-value?

2) Do you reject or fail to reject the null hypothesis at the .05 level that the average time for the participants is 8891.37 seconds?

3) Are the assumptions of the one-sample *t*-test validated in this example?

1.6 Chapter Summary

Statistics provide information about your data so that you can answer questions and make informed decisions. The two major branches are descriptive and inferential statistics. When you analyze data, it is imperative to state the purpose(s) of the analysis, identify specific questions to be answered, identify the population of interest, determine the need for sampling, and, finally, evaluate the data collection process.

Descriptive statistics describe the characteristics of the data. They include measures of location, dispersion, and shape. Some measures of location are the mean, median, and percentiles. Measures of dispersion describe the variability in a set of values and include the range, interquartile range, variance, standard deviation, and coefficient of variation. Skewness and kurtosis are measures of shape and enable you to compare your data's distribution to symmetric and normal distributions respectively.

The initial stage of data analysis includes an examination of the distribution of the data. A distribution is a collection of data values arranged in order, along with the relative frequency. In a symmetric distribution, the right side of the distribution is a mirror image of the left side, and the mean is equal to the median. In a skewed distribution, many data values accumulate at one end of the distribution.

Box-and-whisker plots and normal probability plots, when used in conjunction with the mean, median, skewness, and kurtosis statistics, can help determine if the data is normally distributed.

A population is the set of all measurement values of interest. Most of the time, you cannot collect information for the entire population, so you select a sample. A sample is a subset of the population. If the sample is a random sample, it helps ensure that it is representative of the population as a whole. Descriptive statistics describe the sample's characteristics, and inferential statistics draw conclusions about the population.

A point estimate is a sample statistic used to estimate a population parameter. A point estimate does not take into account the variability of the calculated statistic. Therefore, rather than relying on point estimates, you use confidence intervals to estimate population parameters. A confidence interval is a range of values that you believe to contain the population parameter of interest.

Confidence intervals for the mean make the assumption that the sample means are normally distributed. This normality can be verified by assessing the normality of the data or by invoking the central limit theorem. The central limit theorem states that as the sample size becomes sufficiently large for independent random samples from almost any population, the distribution of the sample means becomes normally distributed.

There are four basic steps when you conduct a test of hypothesis:

1. Determine the alternative and null hypotheses. The alternative hypothesis, H_1, is your initial research hypothesis. The null hypothesis, H_0, is the logical opposite of H_1 and is usually one of equality or no relationship. You assume the null hypothesis is true.

2. Select a significance level, the amount of evidence needed to reject the null hypothesis. The significance level is usually denoted by α and is the Type I error rate. This is the probability that you incorrectly reject the null hypothesis.

3. Collect evidence. The strength of the evidence is measured by a *p*-value.

4. Use a decision rule to make a judgment. You fail to reject the null hypothesis if the *p*-value is greater than or equal to α. You reject the null hypothesis if the *p*-value is less than α.

The one-sample *t*-test for the mean is based on the assumption that the sample means are normally distributed. SAS automatically generates a two-tailed *t*-test, so care must be taken when using a one-sided test. Only the researcher/analyst knows whether a one-sided test is appropriate.

When you conduct a test of hypothesis, there are two types of errors you can make. A Type I error is when you incorrectly reject the null hypothesis. The probability of making a Type I error is denoted by α. A Type II error is when you fail to reject the null hypothesis and the null hypothesis is false. The probability of making a Type II error is denoted by β. The power of a statistical test is equal to $1-\beta$ and is the probability that you correctly reject the null.

The following tasks were introduced in this chapter:

- Summary Statistics
- Distribution

The Summary Statistics task uses the MEANS procedure, a Base SAS procedure for generating descriptive statistics and confidence intervals. To locate the Summary Statistics task, select **Describe** ⇨ **Summary Statistics**.

The Distribution Analysis task performs distribution analysis, descriptive statistics, histograms, box-and-whisker plots, and normality probability plots, and tests that a mean is equal to a specific value. It invokes the UNIVARIATE procedure in Base SAS. You can invoke the Distribution Analysis task by selecting **Analyze** ⇨ **Distribution Analysis…**.

1.7 Solutions Exercises

1. Producing Descriptive Statistics

a. Use the Distribution Analysis task to produce descriptive statistics.

1) Select the `BOSTONMARATHON` data set and open the Distribution Analysis task by selecting **Analyze** ⇨ **Distribution Analysis…**.

2) With **Task Roles** selected on the left, drag and drop `age`, `tottime`, and `halftime` to the Analysis variables role.

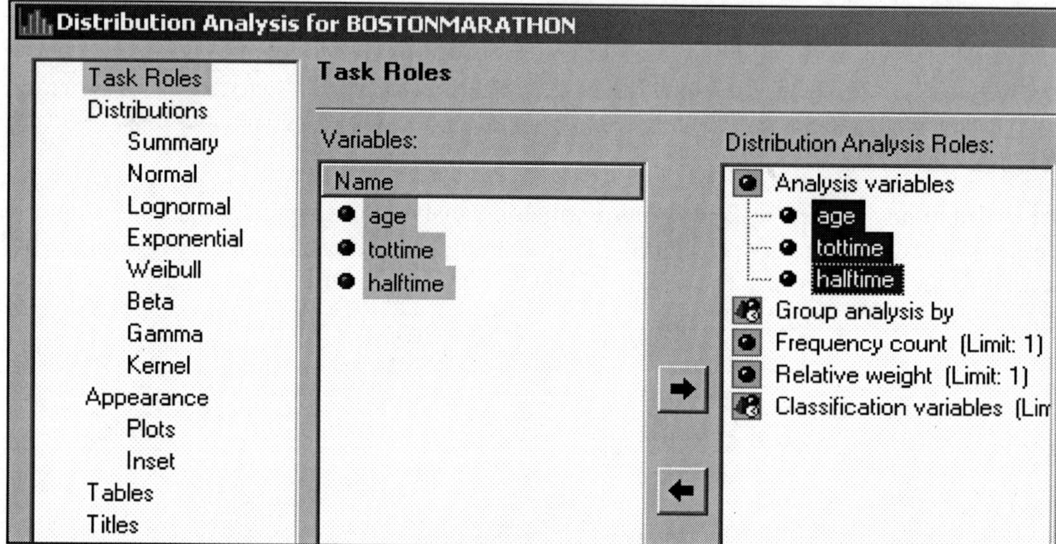

3) On the left, under Distributions, select **Normal** and check the box next to **Normal**. Make any desired changes to the line color or width.

4) On the left, select **<u>Tables</u>**. Check the boxes next to **Moments** and **Extreme values**. Uncheck the boxes next to **Basic confidence intervals** and **Tests for location.**

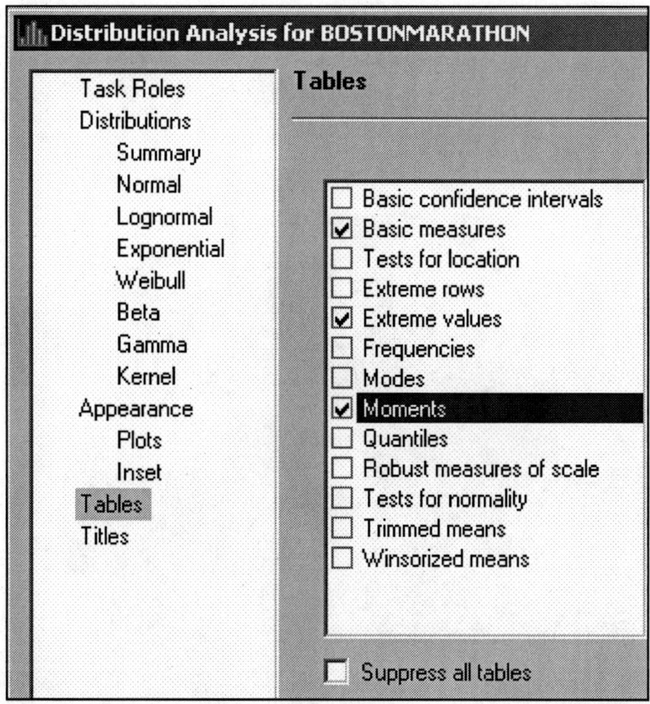

5) Select Plots on the left, and check the boxes next to **Histogram**, **Probability Plot**, and **Box plot**. Make any desired changes to the plot colors.

6) Select **<u>Run</u>** to run the task.

A summary of the output is below:

	age	tottime	halftime
Mean	38.92	13018.98	6187.00
Standard Deviation	7.97	2143.90	1006.07
Skewness	0.09	0.27	0.28
Kurtosis	-0.49	-0.31	-0.70
Median	39.00	12506.00	5980.00
Minimum	25.00	7834.00	3976.00
Maximum	55.00	17340.00	8146.00
Is distribution normal?	Yes	Yes	Yes

An examination of normal probability plots, combined with an interpretation of the skewness and kurtosis statistics, leads to the conclusion that all three variables are normally distributed.

The histograms, normal probability plots and box plots for each variable have been included below in the following order: **age**, **tottime**, and **halftime**.

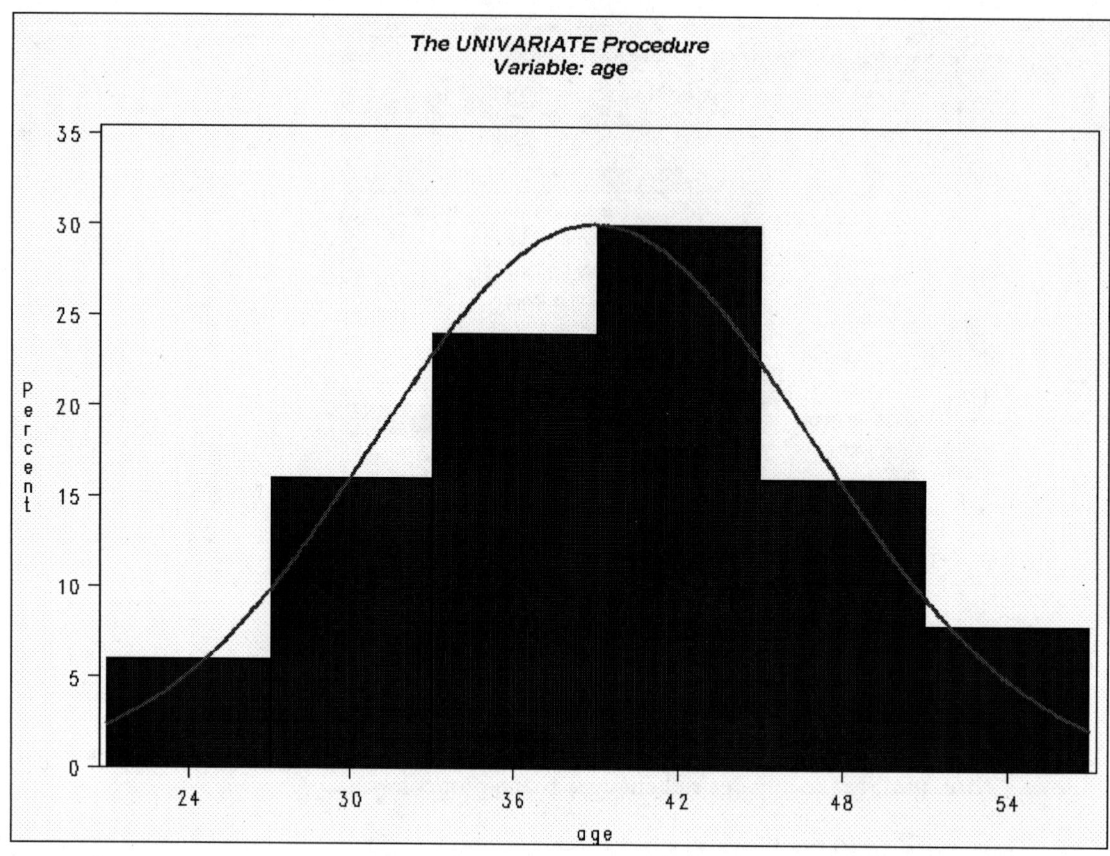

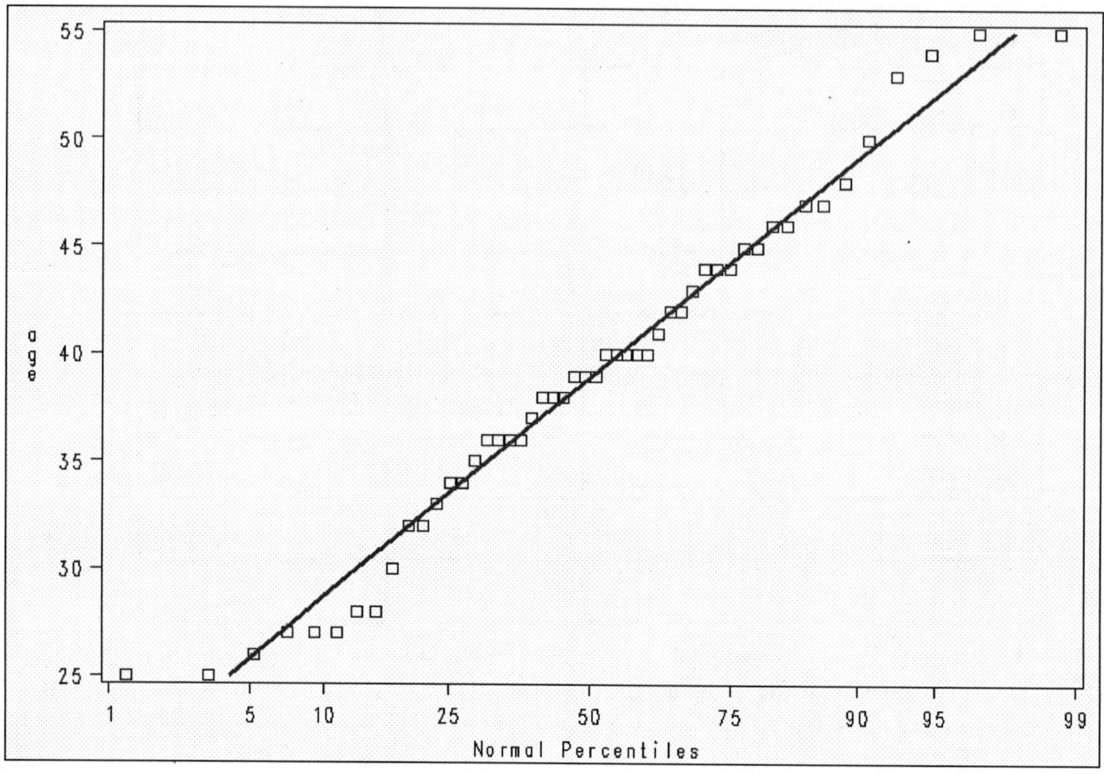

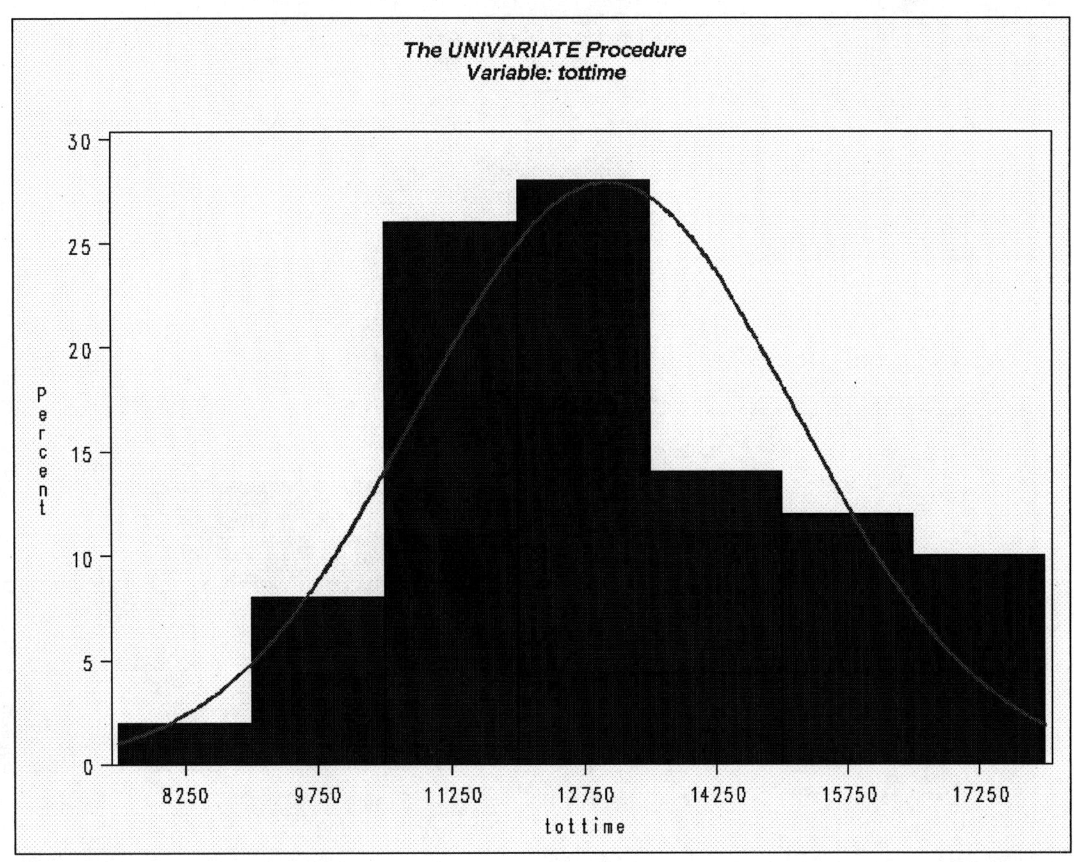
The UNIVARIATE Procedure
Variable: tottime
Percent
30
25
20
15
10
5
0
8250
9750
11250
12750
14250
15750
17250
tottime

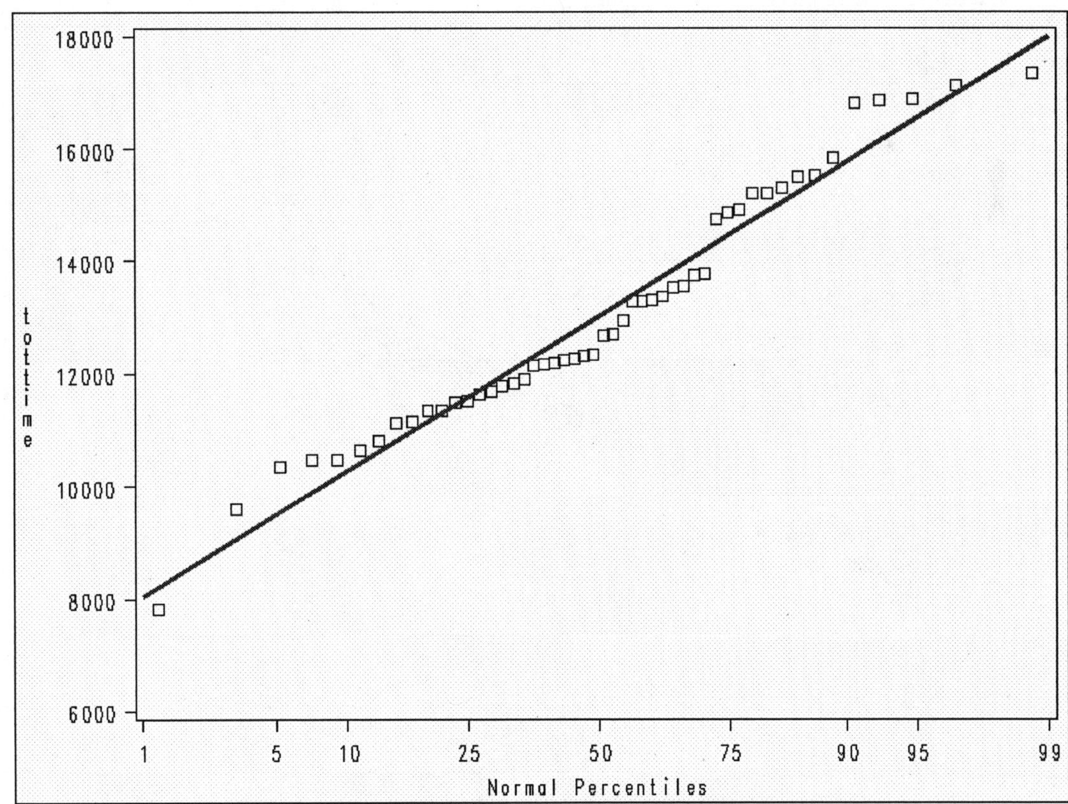
tottime
18000
16000
14000
12000
10000
8000
6000
1
5
10
25
50
75
90
95
99
Normal Percentiles

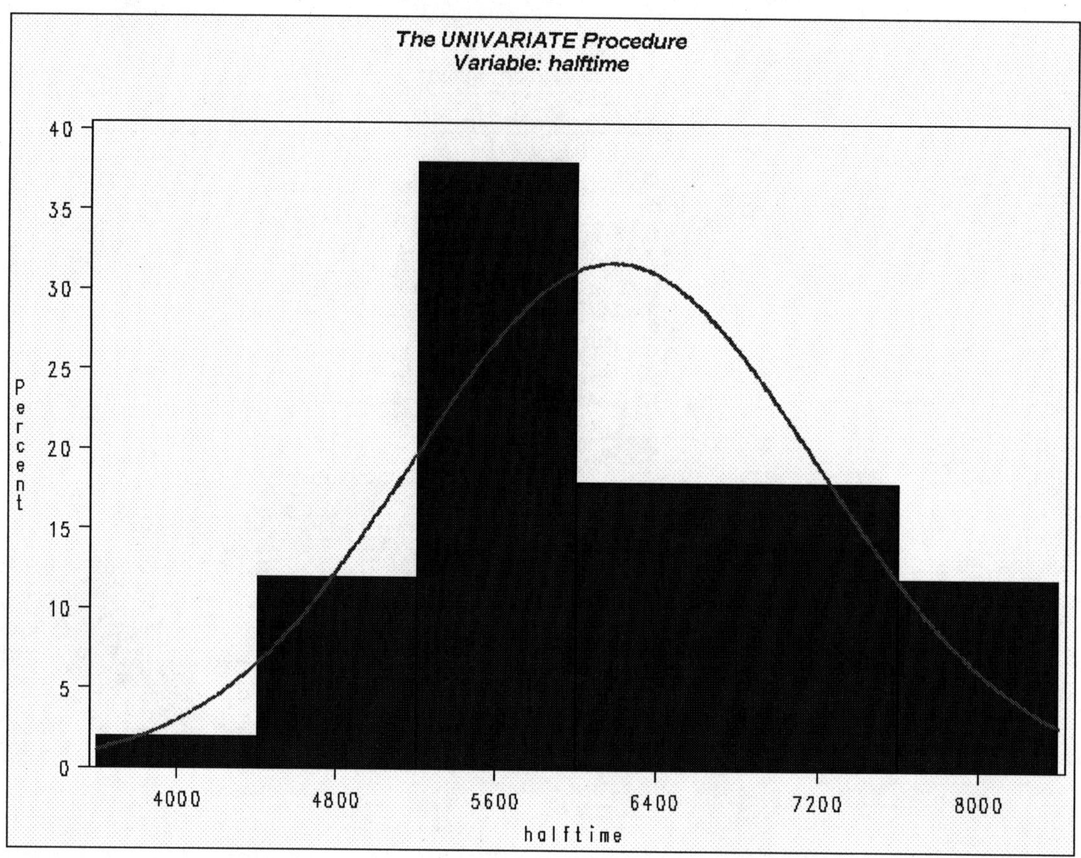
The UNIVARIATE Procedure
Variable: halftime
Percent
0
5
10
15
20
25
30
35
40
4000
4800
5600
6400
7200
8000
halftime

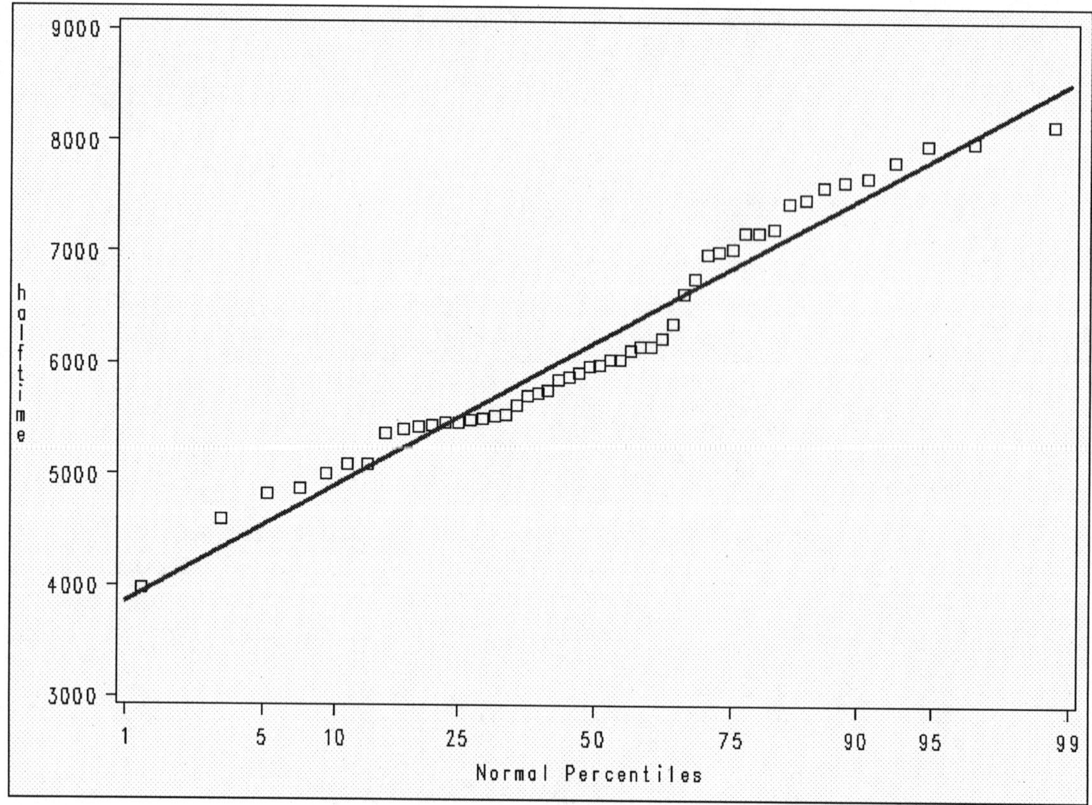
halftime
3000
4000
5000
6000
7000
8000
9000
1
5
10
25
50
75
90
95
99
Normal Percentiles

b. Use the Distribution Analysis task to produce descriptive statistics for the **BOSTONTOP100** data set.

1) Select the **BOSTONTOP100** table and follow the steps outlined above. A summary of the output is shown below.

	age	tottime	halftime
Mean	33.01	8891.38	4276.95
Standard Deviation	6.03	550.14	253.16
Skewness	0.44	-0.55	0.11
Kurtosis	-0.38	-1.09	-1.45
Median	32.00	9027.00	4279
Minimum	22.00	7834.00	3971.00
Maximum	47.00	9539.00	4723.00
Is distribution normal?	Yes	No	No

A close examination of the high-resolution normal probability plots and an interpretation of the skewness and kurtosis statistics leads to the conclusion that **age** appears normally distributed but **tottime** and **halftime** are skewed.

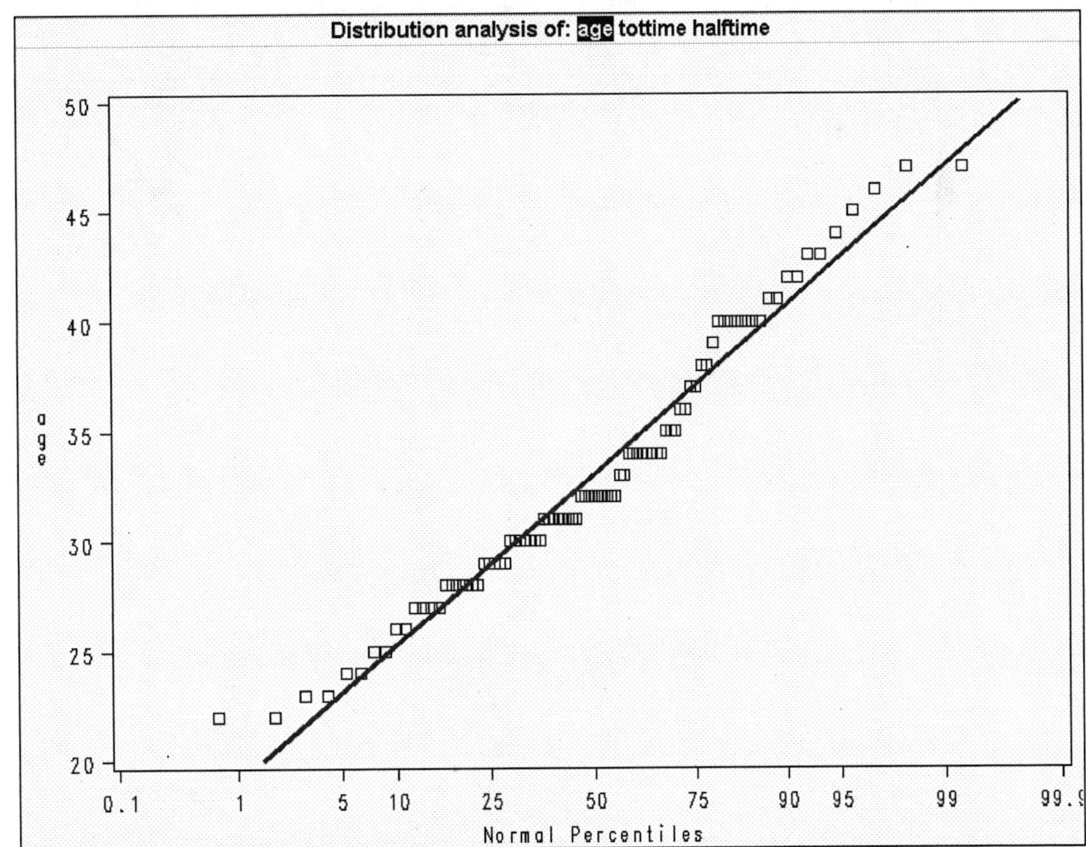

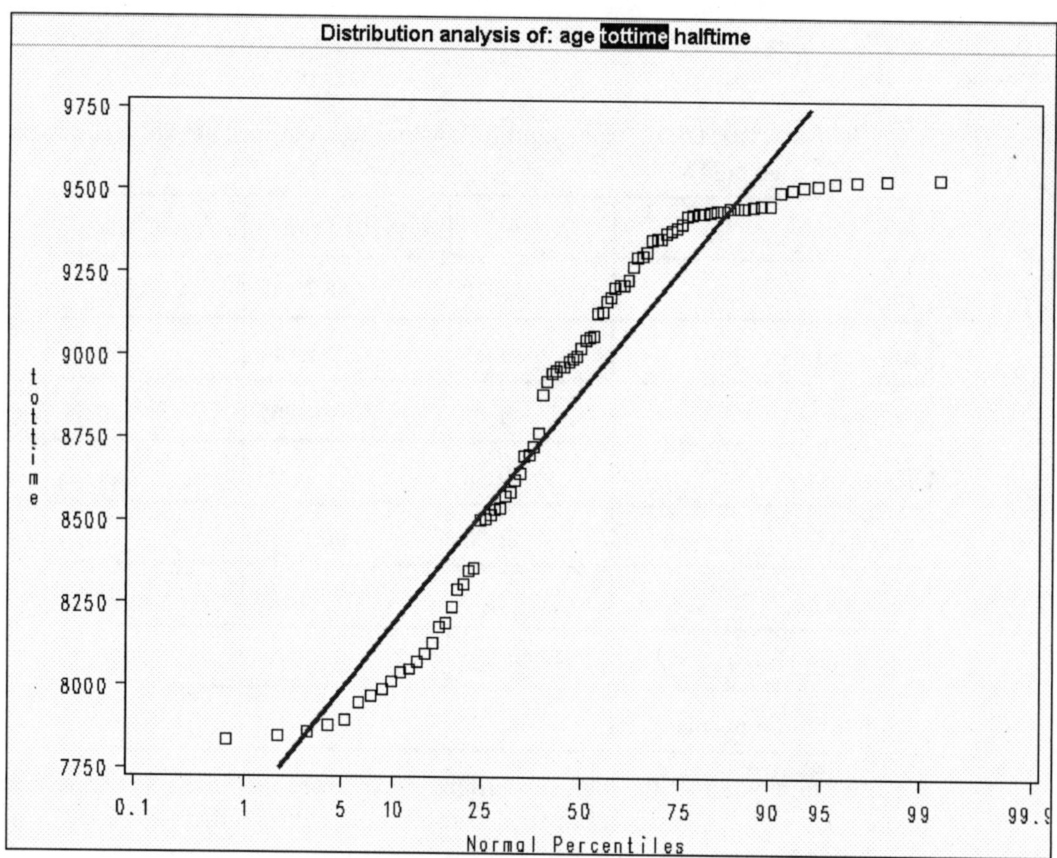
Distribution analysis of: age tottime halftime
9750
9500
9250
9000
8750
8500
8250
8000
7750
tottime
0.1
1
5
10
25
50
75
90
95
99
99.9
Normal Percentiles

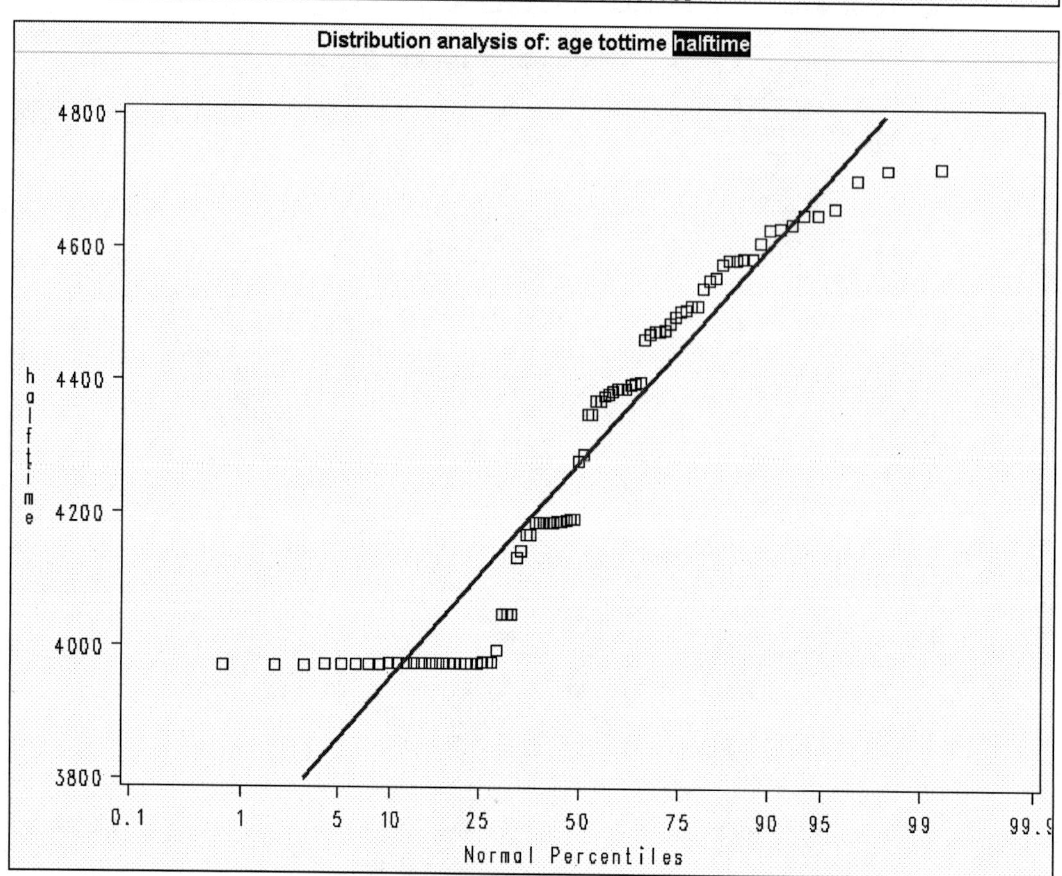
Distribution analysis of: age tottime halftime
4800
4600
4400
4200
4000
3800
halftime
0.1
1
5
10
25
50
75
90
95
99
99.9
Normal Percentiles

2. Producing Confidence Intervals

a. Use the Summary Statistics task to produce confidence intervals.

Select the `BOSTONMARATHON` data set. Select **Describe** ⇨ **Summary Statistics.**

With **Task Roles** selected on the left, drag and drop `tottime` to Analysis Variables.

Select **Additional** on the left, and check the box next to **Confidence limits of the mean**.

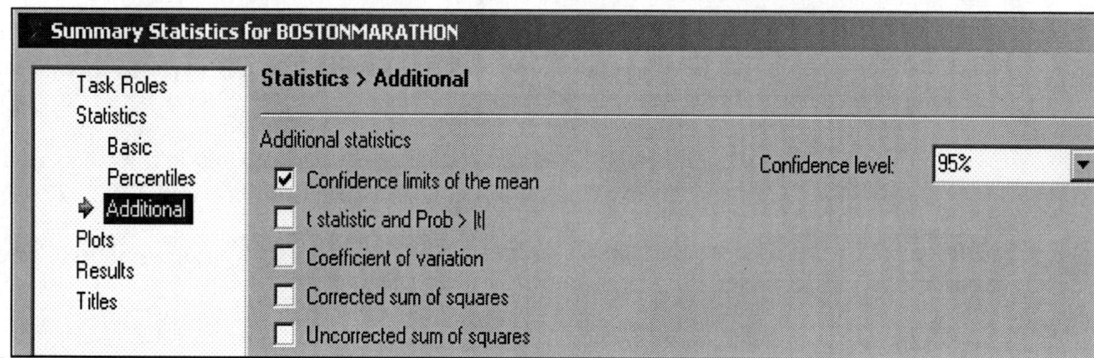

Make any desired changes to titles, footnotes, or additional statistics.

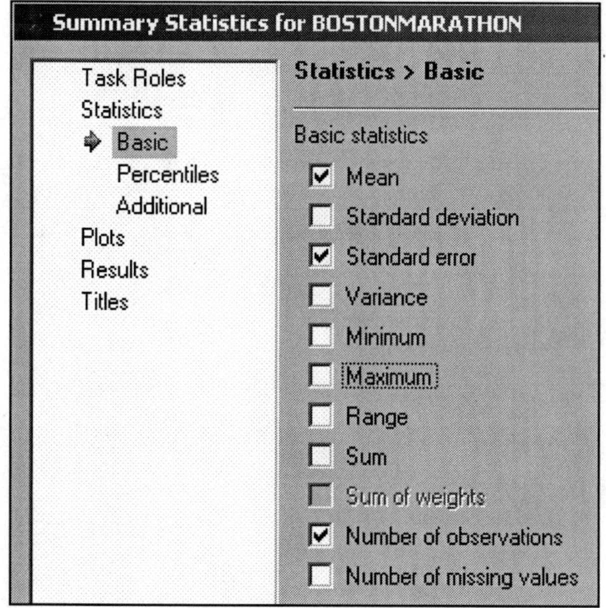

Click **Run** to run the task.

A summary of the output is shown below.

Analysis Variable : tottime				
Mean	Std Error	N	Lower 95% CL for Mean	Upper 95% CL for Mean
13018.98	303.1929748	50	12409.69	13628.27

1) Because the sample size is large enough, the central limit theorem is invoked to validate the assumption of normality of the sample mean.

2) The 95% confidence interval for the total time it takes for participants in the data set **BOSTONMARATHON** to complete the marathon is between 12409.69 and 13628.27 seconds.

3) You have 95% confidence that the above interval includes the true mean total time it takes for participants to complete the marathon.

3. **Performing a One-Sample *t*-Test**

   a. Use the Distribution Analysis task to perform a one-sample *t*-test.

   Select the **BOSTONMARATHON** data set. Select **Analyze** ⇨ **Distribution Analysis...**.

   With **Task Roles** selected on the left, drag and drop **tottime** to the Analysis variables role.

   Select **Tables** on the left, and check the box next to **Tests for location**. Change the H_0: Mu= value to 8891.37.

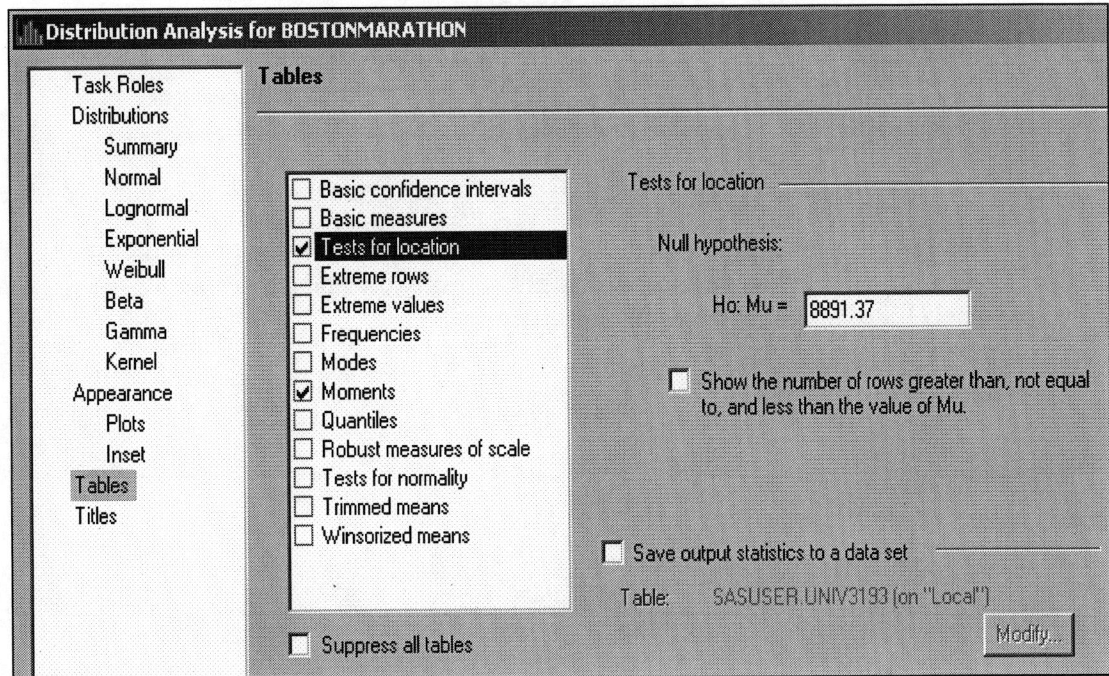

   Make any desired changes to titles and footnotes.

   Select **Run** to run the task. Part of the output is shown below.

Partial Output

Tests for Location: Mu0=8891.4				
Test	**Statistic**		**p Value**	
Student's t	t	13.6138	Pr > |t|	<.0001
Sign	M	24	Pr >= |M|	<.0001
Signed Rank	S	635.5	Pr >= |S|	<.0001

1) The *t* statistic is 13.61 and the corresponding *p*-value is less than 0.0001.

2) You reject the null hypothesis that the average time for the participants is 8897.13 seconds.

3) Because the values of **`tottime`** are normally distributed, the assumptions of the one sample *t*-test are validated. If **`tottime`** were not normally distributed, the sample is large enough to apply the central limit theorem.

Chapter 2 Analysis of Variance (ANOVA)

2.1 One-Way ANOVA: Two Populations

Objectives

- Analyze differences between population means using the Linear Models task.
- Verify the assumptions of analysis of variance.

3

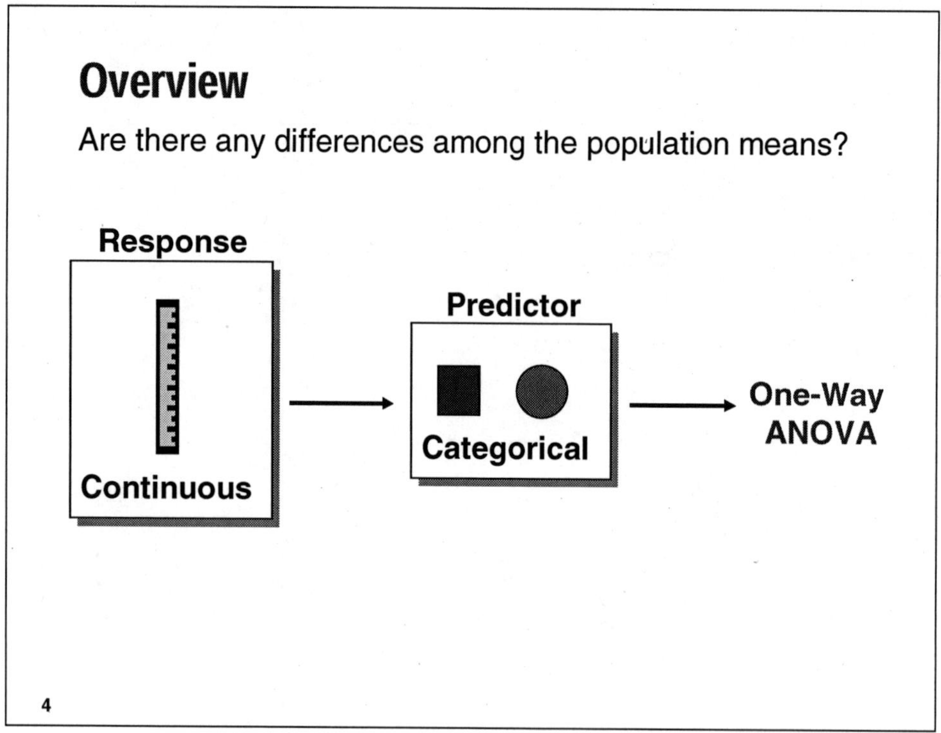

Analysis of variance (ANOVA) is a statistical technique used to compare the means of two or more groups of observations or treatments. In this section, you apply analysis of variance to examine problems where there are two treatments. For this type of problem, you have a

- continuous dependent variable, or *response* variable
- discrete independent variable also called a *predictor* or *explanatory* variable.

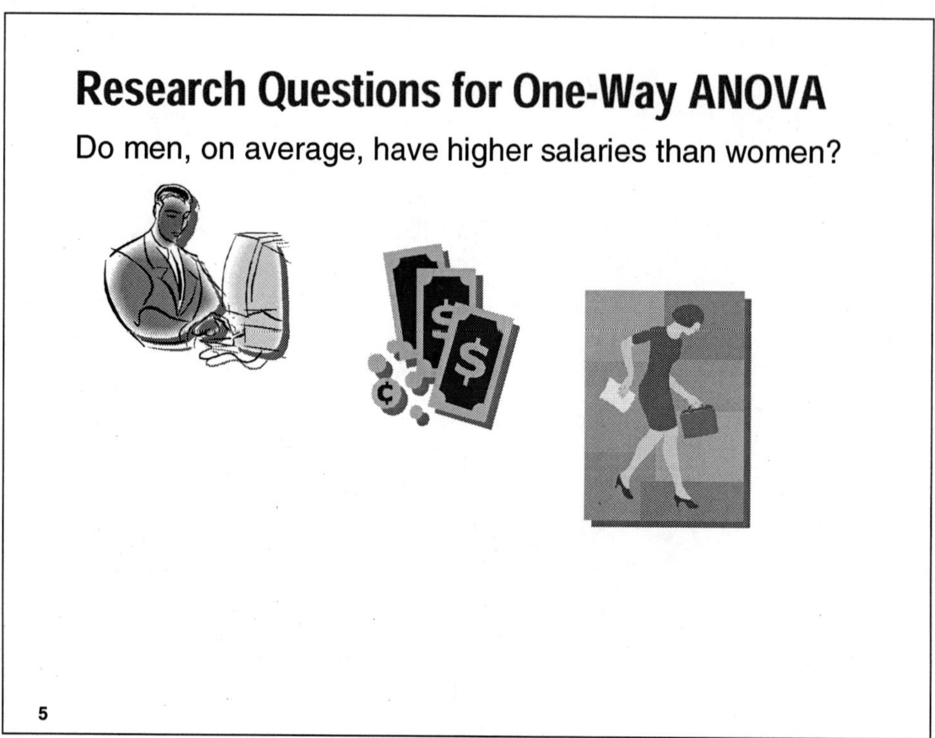

Research Questions for One-Way ANOVA

Do people in the treatment group have a higher average T cell count than people in the control group?

Placebo

Treatment

6

Research Questions for One-Way ANOVA

Do two different factory lines produce juice boxes with the same average amount of juice?

7

Research Questions for One-Way ANOVA

Do the brands Morning and Rise n Shine have the same average amount of cereal per box?

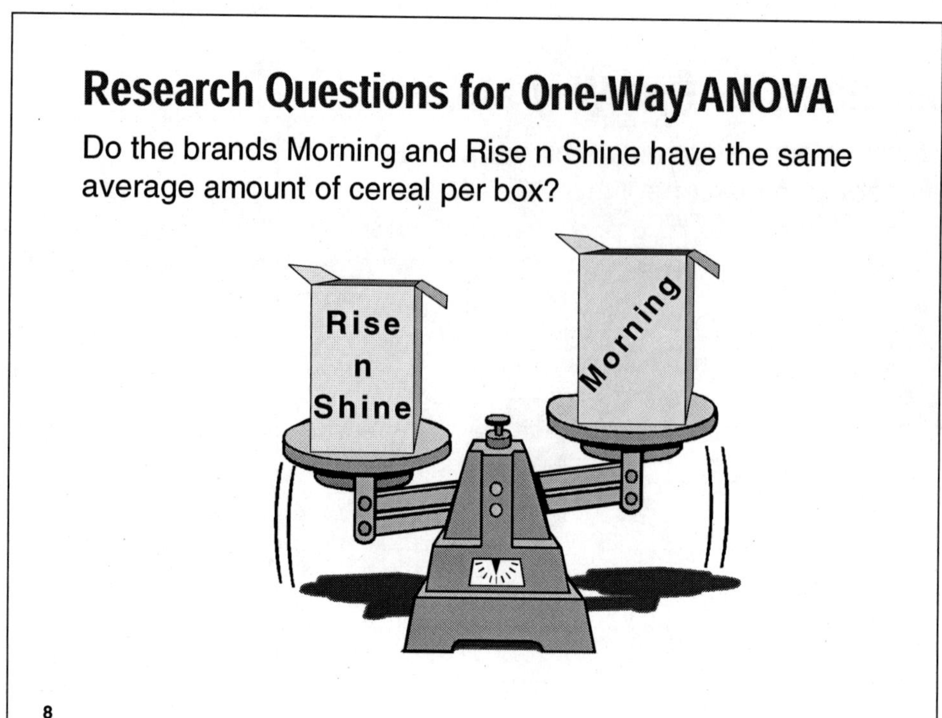

8

Example: The same manufacturer makes Rise n Shine and Morning cereal. They want to make sure their two different processes are putting the same amount of cereal in each box. Both brands should have 15 ounces of cereal per box. A random sample of both brands is selected and the number of ounces of cereal is recorded. The data is stored in a data set called **`CEREALS`**.

The variables in the data set are

`brand` two groups, `Rise n Shine` and `Morning`, corresponding to the two brands

`weight` weight of the cereal in ounces

`idnumber` the identification number for each cereal box.

Descriptive Statistics for Multiple Populations

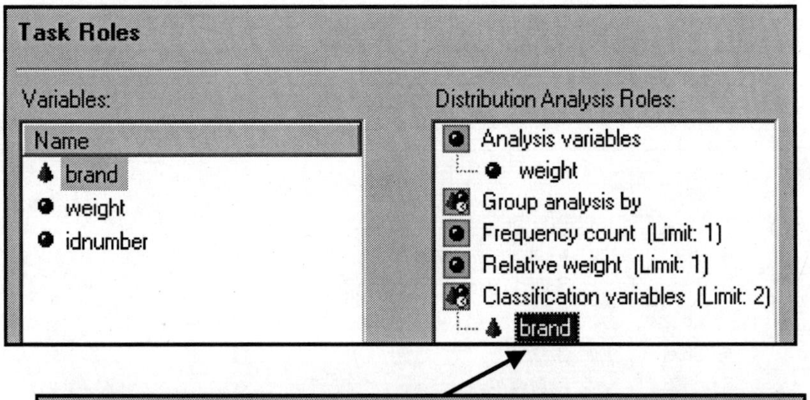

Adding a Classification variable produces a separate analysis for each value of the class variable.

9

Descriptive Statistics Across Groups

Examine the **CEREALS** data set and use the Distribution Analysis task to produce summary statistics.

1. Open the **CEREALS** data set by double-clicking it in the process flow.

SASUSER.CEREALS (read-only)

	brand	weight	idnumber
1	Morning	14.9982	61469897
2	Rise n Shine	15.0136	33081197
3	Morning	15.01	68137597
4	Rise n Shine	14.9982	37070397
5	Morning	15.0052	64608797
6	Rise n Shine	14.993	60714297
7	Morning	14.9733	16907997
8	Rise n Shine	15.0812	9589297
9	Morning	15.0037	93891897
10	Rise n Shine	15.0418	85859397

2. Close the data set by selecting the X at the upper left corner, and go to **Analyze** ⇨ **Distribution Analysis…**. The Distribution Analysis task opens.

3. With **Task Roles** selected on the left, drag and drop **brand** to the Classification variable role and drag and drop **weight** to the Analysis variables role.

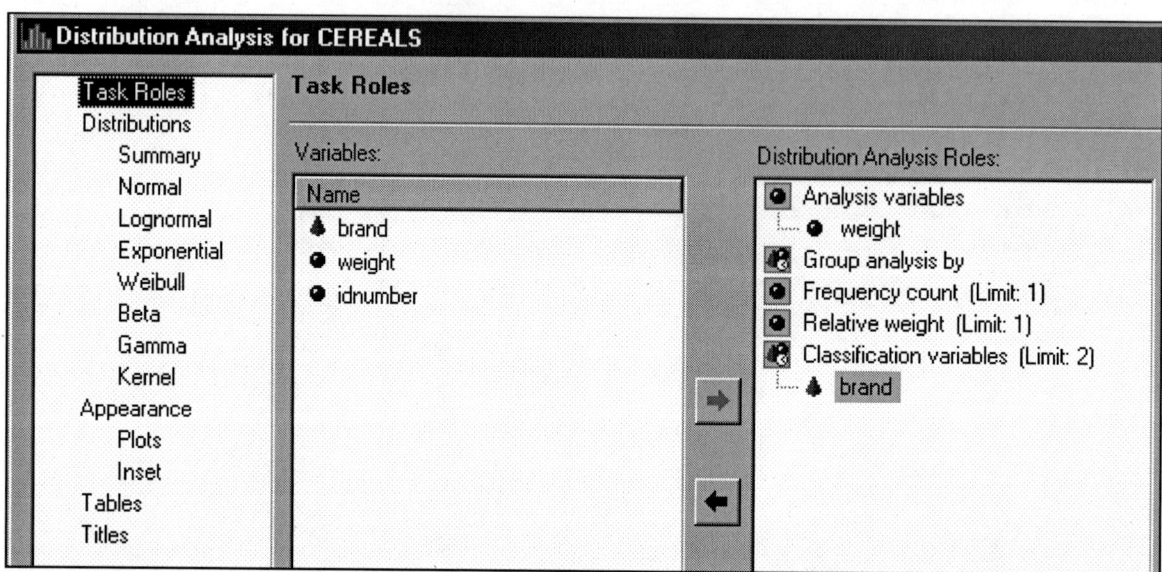

4. Select **Normal** under Distributions on the left and check the box next to **Normal**. Change the line color to red.

5. Select **Plots** on the left and check the boxes next to **Histogram**, **Probability**, and **Box plot**. Change the plot background colors to white.

6. Select **Tables** on the left and check the box next to **Moments**.

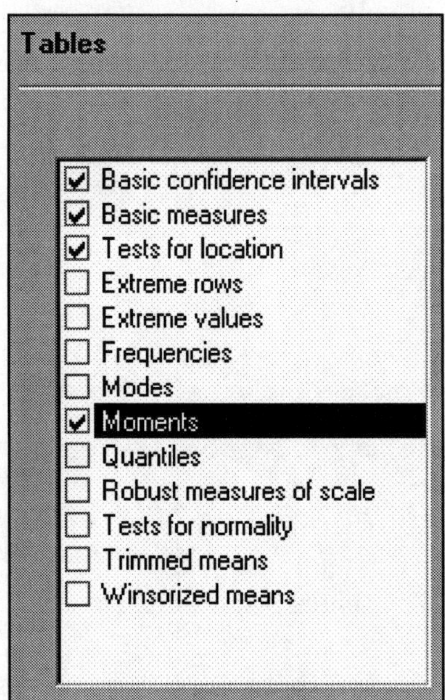

7. Select **Run** to run the task.

A summary of the output is shown below. Assigning **brand** as a classification (also called a *class* variable) produces separate statistics for each level of brand.

The UNIVARIATE Procedure
Variable: weight
brand = Morning

Moments			
N	40	Sum Weights	40
Mean	14.9970125	Sum Observations	599.8805
Std Deviation	0.02201048	Variance	0.00048446
Skewness	0.87481049	Kurtosis	2.07993397
Uncorrected SS	8996.43425	Corrected SS	0.01889398
Coeff Variation	0.14676575	Std Error Mean	0.00348016

The UNIVARIATE Procedure
Variable: weight
brand = Rise n Shine

Moments			
N	40	Sum Weights	40
Mean	15.03596	Sum Observations	601.4384
Std Deviation	0.02654963	Variance	0.00070488
Skewness	0.39889232	Kurtosis	-0.1975717
Uncorrected SS	9043.23122	Corrected SS	0.02749044
Coeff Variation	0.17657424	Std Error Mean	0.00419787

In the output, the two different sets of statistics are stacked vertically.

Assigning **brand** as a Classification variable also produces side-by-side histograms, normal probability plots, and box plots.

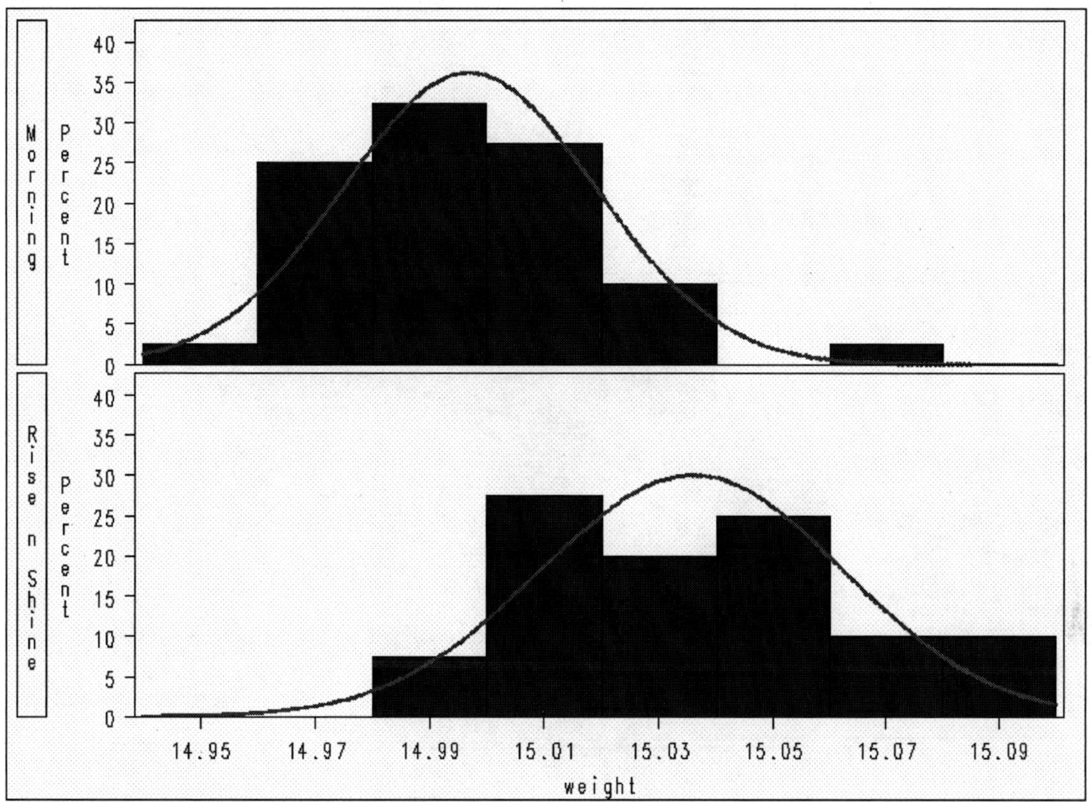

For a full-sized graph for each value of **brand**, assign **brand** as a Group analysis by variable instead of a class variable.

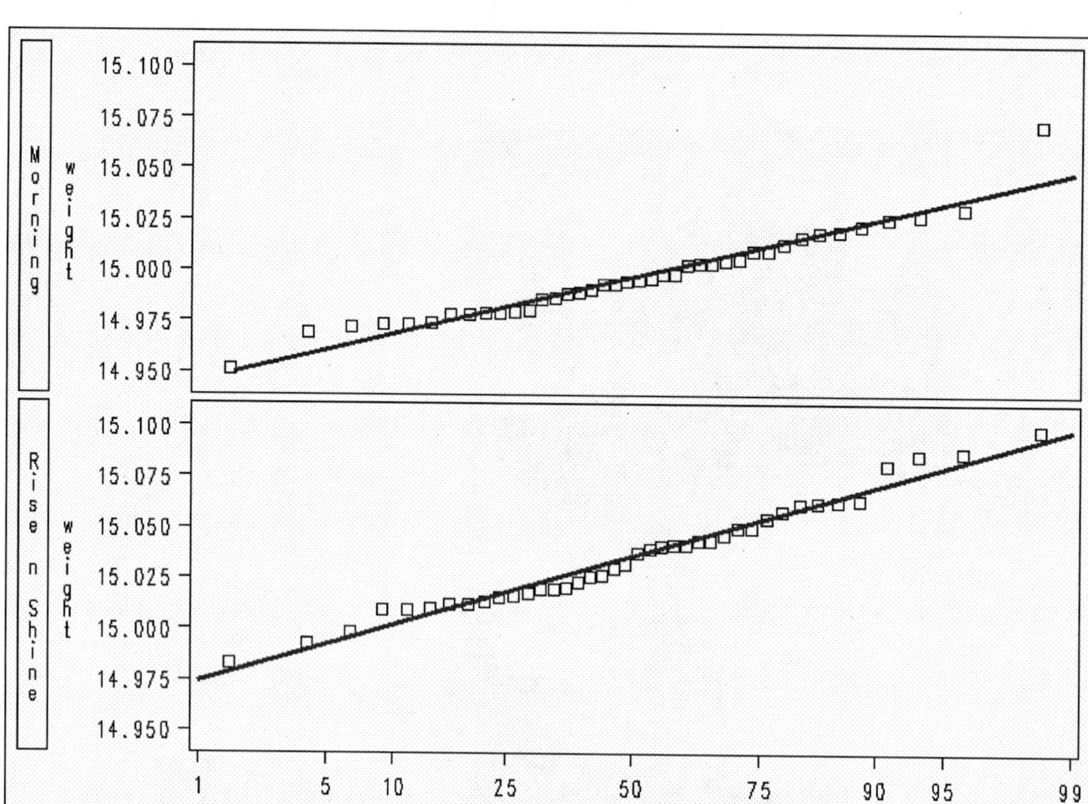

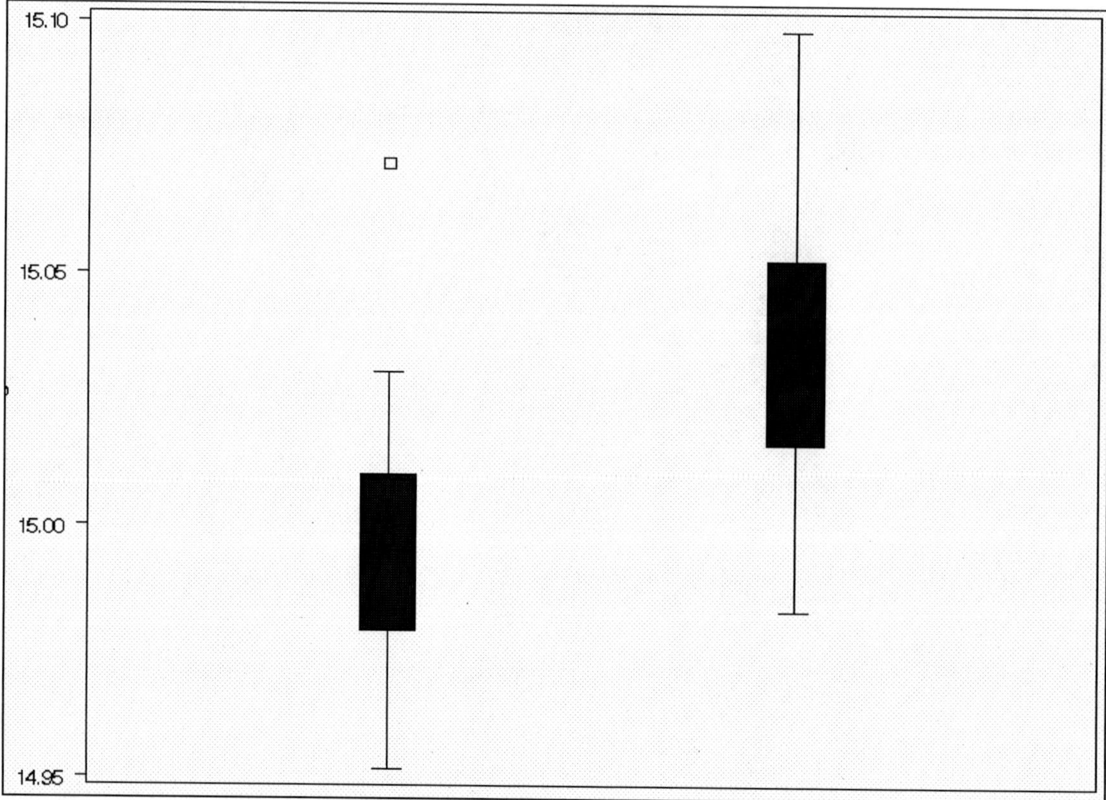

The side-by-side box-and-whisker plots seem to indicate that there is a difference between the Morning and Rise n Shine cereals, but is this difference statistically significant?

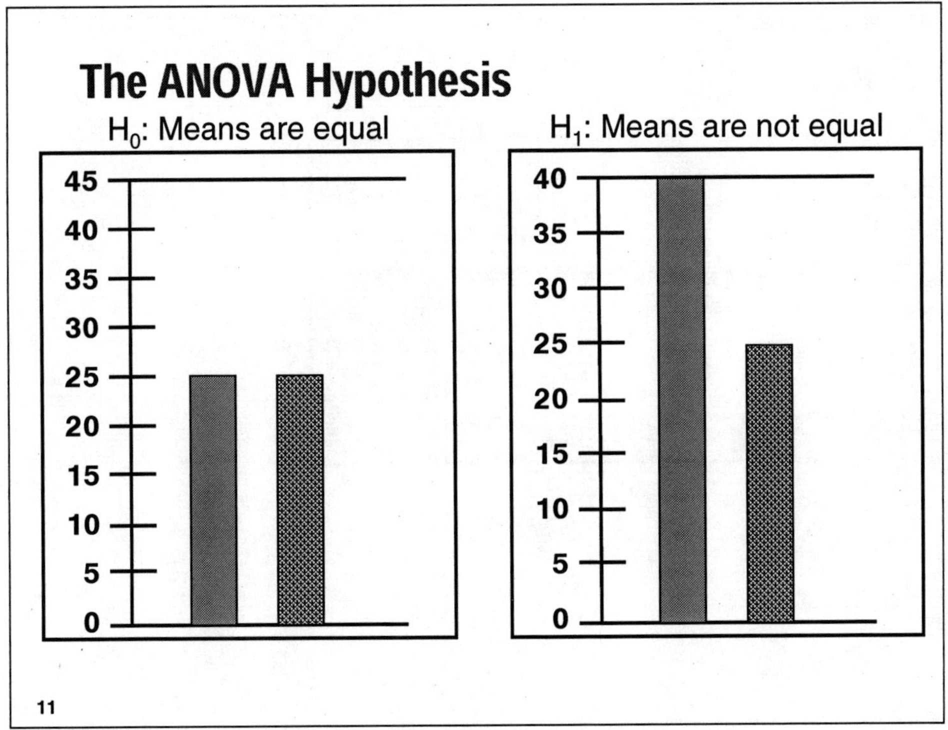

Small differences between sample means are usually present. The objective is to determine whether these differences are significant. In other words, is the difference more than what might be expected to occur by chance?

The assumptions for ANOVA are

- independent observations
- normally distributed error terms for each treatment
- approximately equal error variances for each treatment.

The ANOVA Model

Weight = Base Level + Brand + Unaccounted for Variation

$$Y_{ik} = \mu + \tau_i + \varepsilon_{ik}$$

12

Y_{ik} the kth value of the response variable for the ith treatment.

μ the overall population mean of the response, for instance cereal weight.

τ_i the difference between the population mean of the ith treatment and the overall mean, μ. This is referred to as the effect of treatment i.

ε_{ik} the difference between the observed value of the kth observation in the ith group and the mean of the ith group. This is called the error term.

Because you are only interested in these two specific brands, `cereal` is considered fixed. In some references this would be considered a fixed effect.

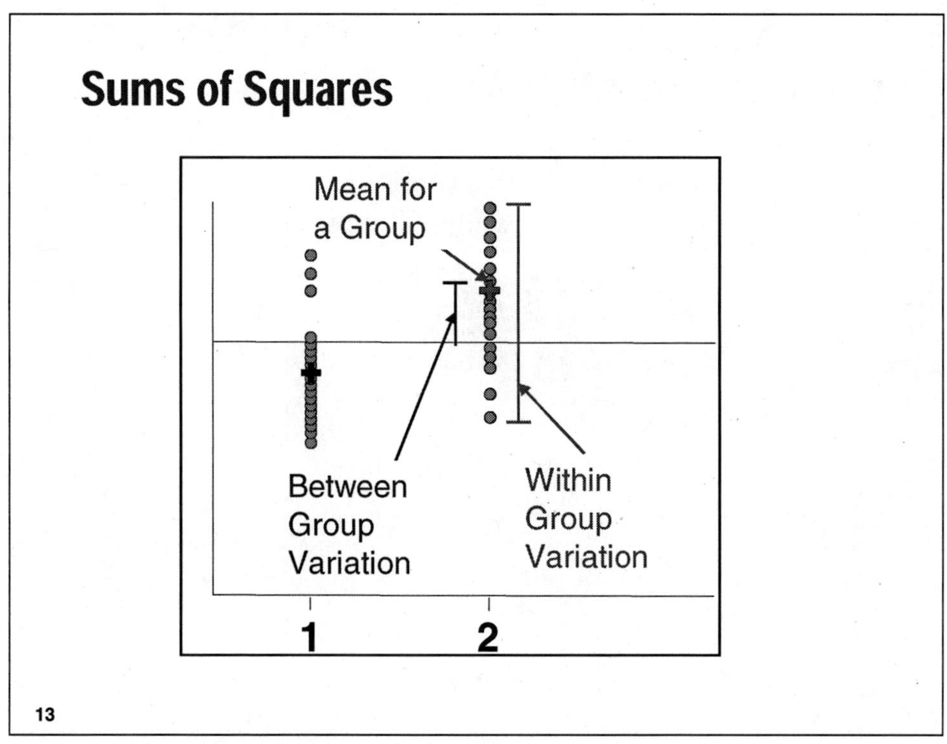

As its name implies, analysis of variance analyzes the variances of the data to determine whether there is a difference between the group means.

Between Group Variation — the sum of the squared differences between the mean for each group and the overall mean, $\Sigma n_i(\tau_i)^2$.

Within Group Variation — the sum of the squared differences between each observed value and the mean for its group, $\Sigma\Sigma(Y_{ij}-(\mu+\tau_i))^2$.

Total Variation — the sum of the squared differences between each observed value and the overall mean, $\Sigma\Sigma(Y_{ij}-\mu)^2$.

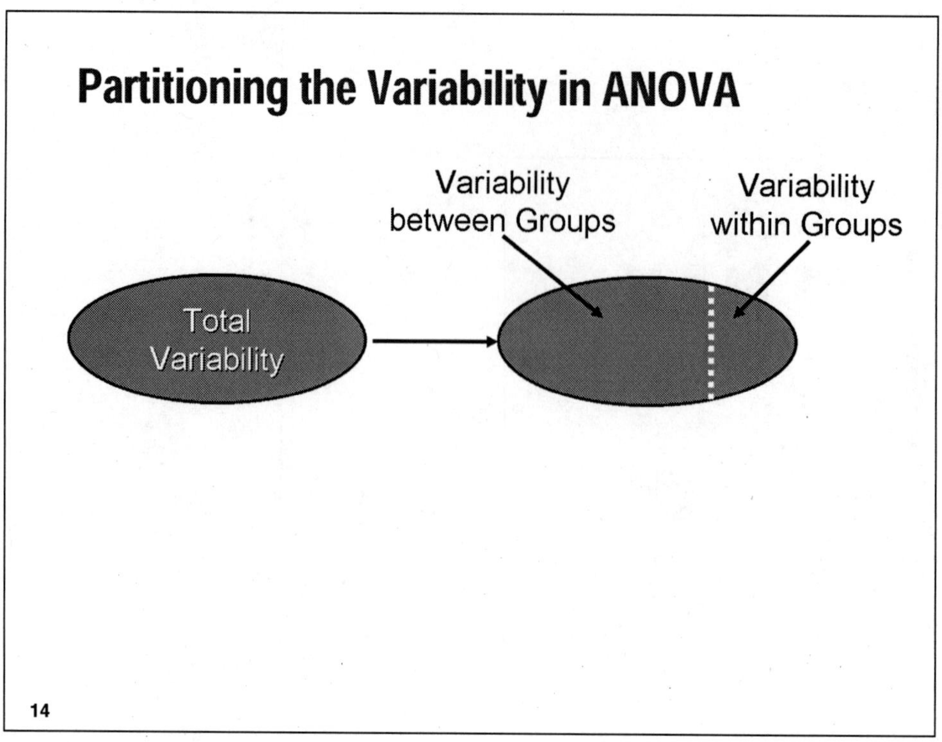

In ANOVA, the corrected total sum of squares is partitioned into two parts, the Model Sum of Squares and the Error Sum of Squares.

Model Sum of Squares (SSM)	the variability explained by the independent variable and therefore represented by the **between** treatment sums of squares.
Error Sum of Squares (SSE)	the variability not explained by the independent variable. Also referred to as **within** treatment variability, or residual sum of squares.
Total Sum of Squares (SST)	the **overall** variability in the response variable. SST=SSM + SSE.

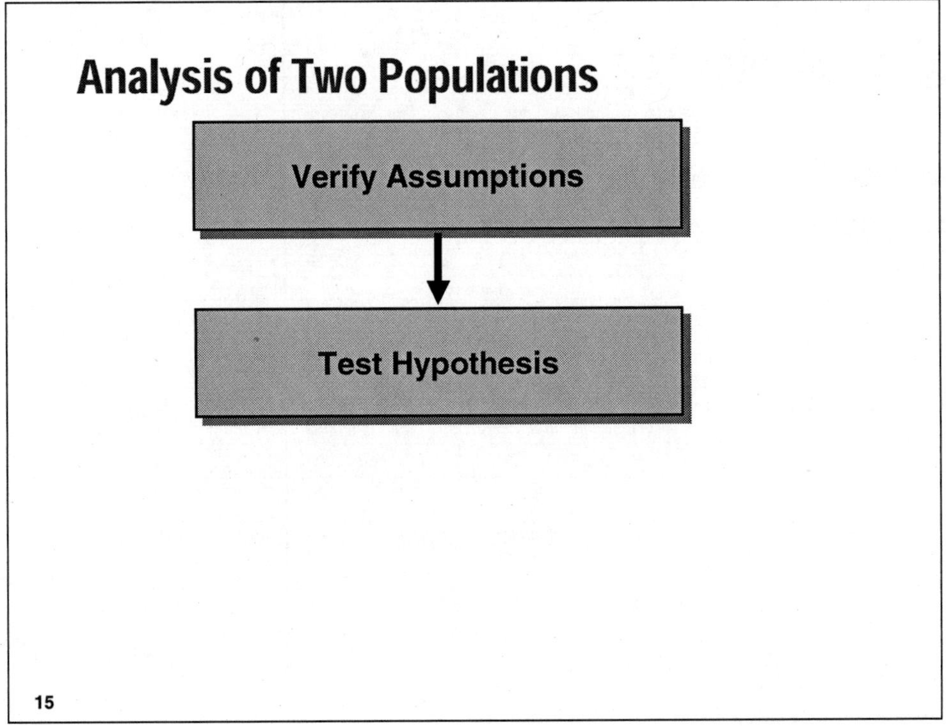
Analysis of Two Populations
Verify Assumptions
Test Hypothesis
15

Assumptions for ANOVA

- Observations are independent.
- Pooled errors are approximately normal.
- All groups have approximately equal response variances.

16

Pooled error terms refer to the error terms for all groups, that is, each individual group does not have to be normally distributed as long as the errors as a whole are normally distributed.

One assumption of ANOVA is approximately equal error variances for each treatment. Although you can get an idea about the equality of variances by looking at the descriptive statistics and plots of the data, you should also consider a formal test for homogeneity of variances. The Linear Models task has a homogeneity of variance test option.

The observations being independent implies that ε_{ij}s in the theoretical model are independent. The independence assumption should be verified with good data collection. In some cases, the residuals can be used to verify this assumption.

Predicted and Residual Values

The predicted value in ANOVA is the group mean.

A residual is the difference between the observed value of the response and the predicted value of the response variable.

Cereal Residuals

Brand	Weight	Pred	Resid
M	15.00	15.00	0.00
RS	15.01	15.04	-0.03
M	15.02	15.00	0.02
RS	15.07	15.04	0.03
M	14.98	15.00	-0.02

17

The residuals from the ANOVA are calculated as (the actual value – the predicted value). These residuals can be examined with the Distribution task to determine normality. With a reasonable-sized sample, only severe departures from normality are considered a problem.

In ANOVA with more than two predictor variables, the test for homogeneity of variances is unavailable. In those circumstances, you can plot the residuals against their predicted values to verify that the variances are equal. The result will be a set of vertical lines equal to the number of groups. If the lines are approximately the same height, the variances are approximately equal. Descriptive statistics can also be used to determine if the variances are equal.

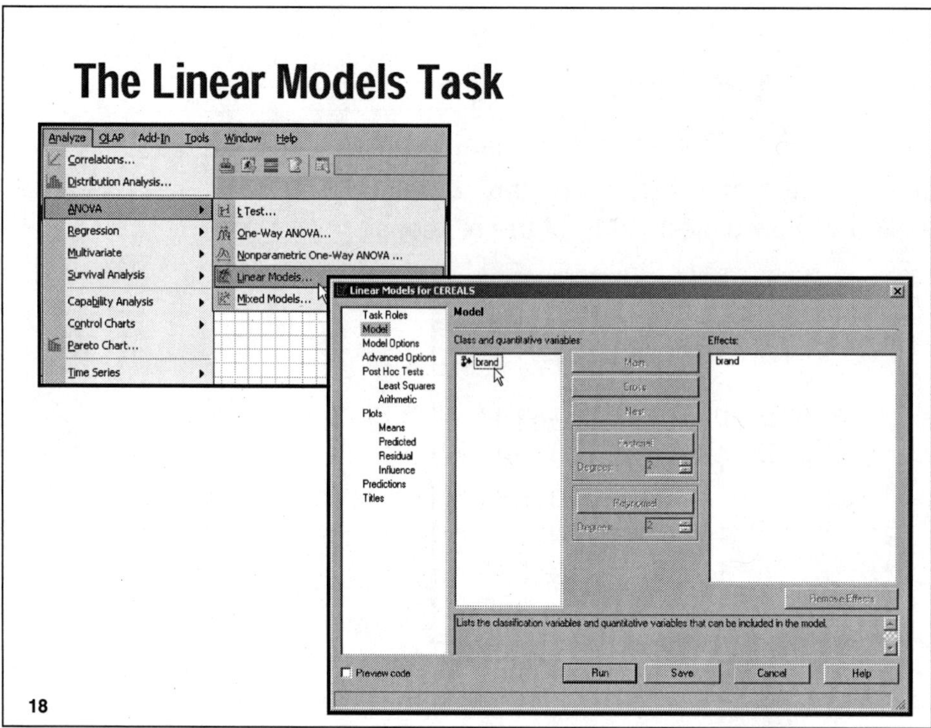

The Linear Models task allows the user to fit general linear models, including ANOVA and regression models.

Assessing ANOVA Assumptions

- Good data collection methods help ensure the independence assumption.
- The Distribution task can be used on data output from the Linear Models task to test the assumption that pooled residuals are approximately normal.
- The Linear Models task produces a hypothesis test. Null for this hypothesis test is that the variances are approximately equal for all populations.

19

One-Way ANOVA with the Linear Models Task

Example: Determine if the difference between the Morning and Rise n Shine cereal brands is statistically significant using the Linear Models task.

1. Make sure `CEREALS` is the active data set. Select **Analyze** ⇨ **ANOVA** ⇨ **Linear Models**. The Linear Models task opens.

2. With **Task Roles** selected on the left, drag and drop `weight` to the Dependent variables role and `brand` to the Classification variables role.

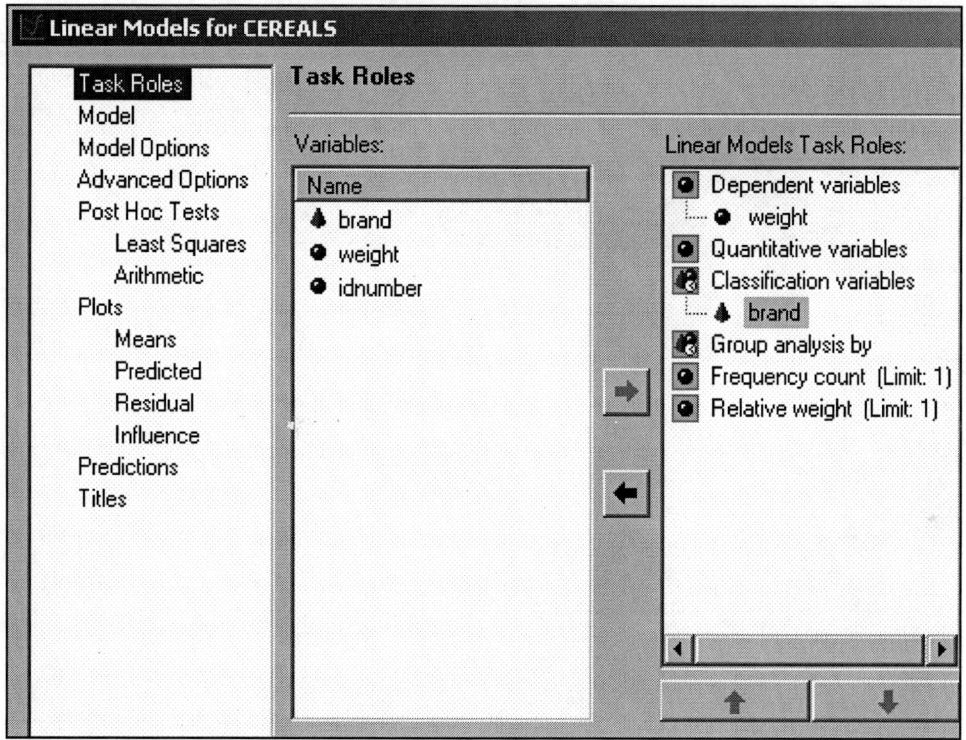

3. Select **Model** on the left. Select **brand** and click **Main** to set `brand` as a main effect. A main effect is any model term that is not involved with any other term. In other words, a main effect is the effect of a single variable only.

4. Select **Model Options** on the left. Uncheck the box next to **Show parameter estimates**.

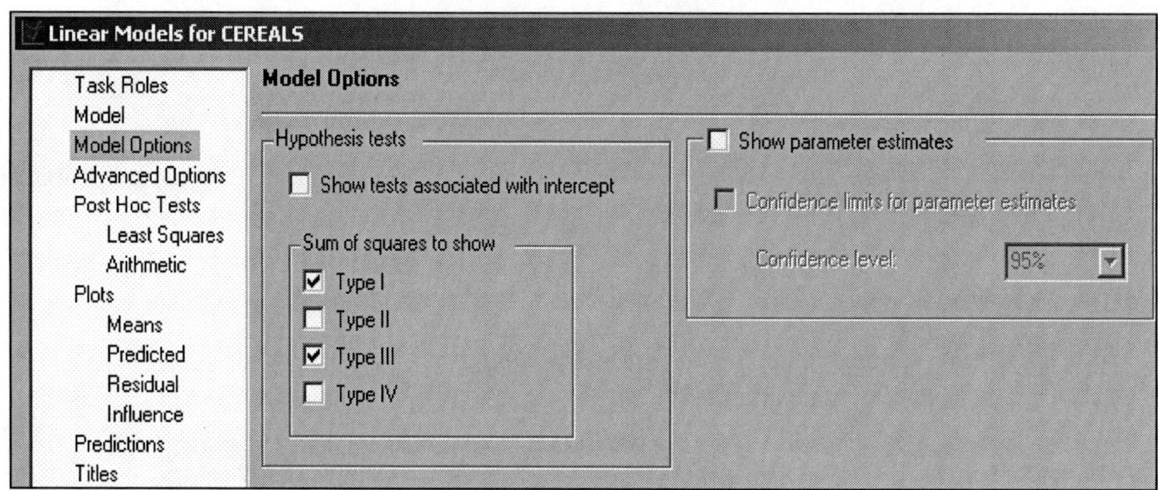

5. On the left, under Post Hoc Tests, select **Arithmetic**.

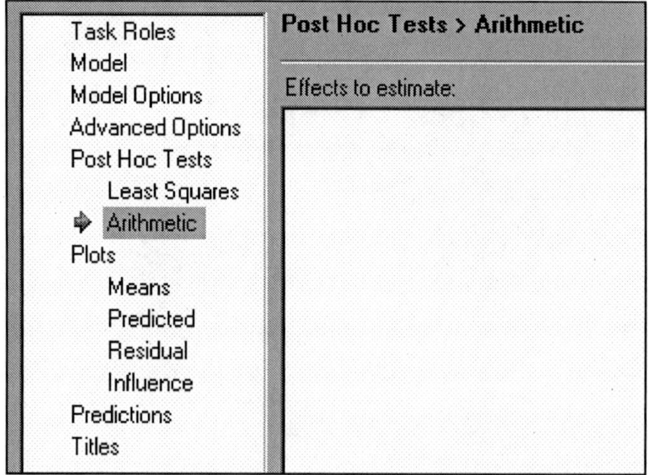

6. Click **Add** at the bottom of the **Effects to estimate** box. The right-hand side populates with a group of choices.

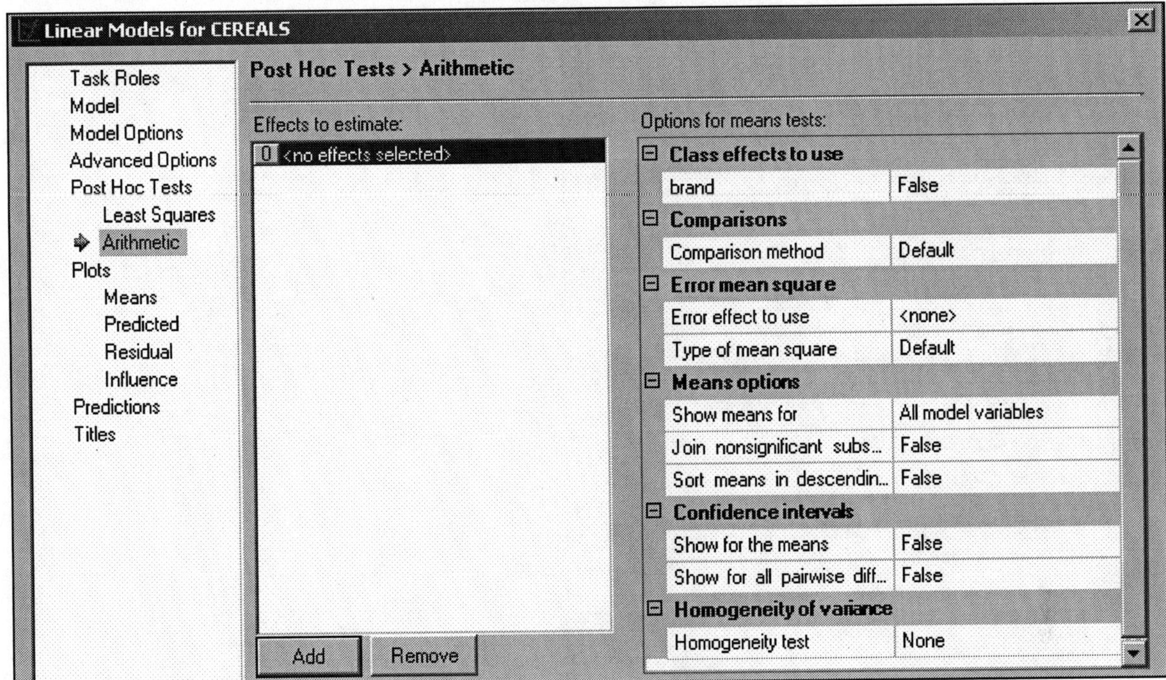

7. Under **Class effects to use**, change the selection for `brand` to `True`.

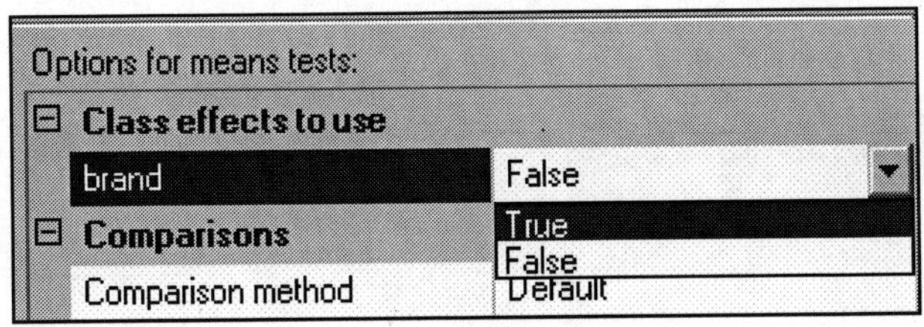

8. To request homogeneity of variance tests, change the **Homogeneity of variance** option from `None` to `Levene (square residuals)`. This option enables you to test the equal variances assumption.

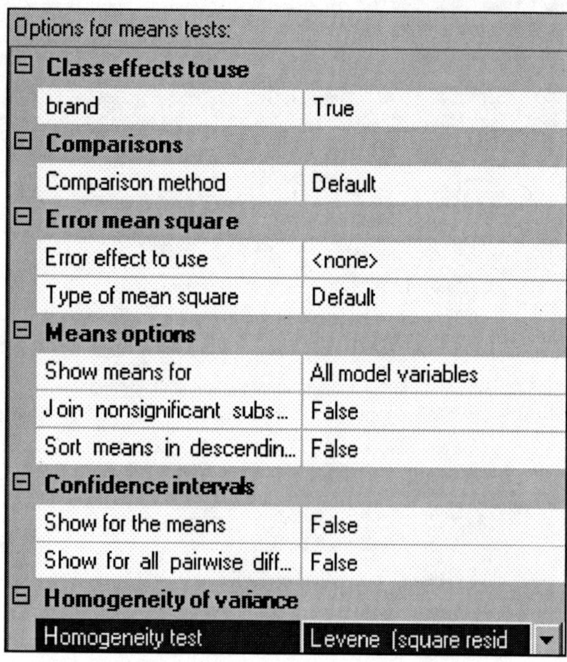

9. On the left, select **Means** under the Plots group. Check the box next to **Dependent means for main effects**. This will create a plot of the means of Morning and Rise n Shine cereal, which will aid in interpretation.

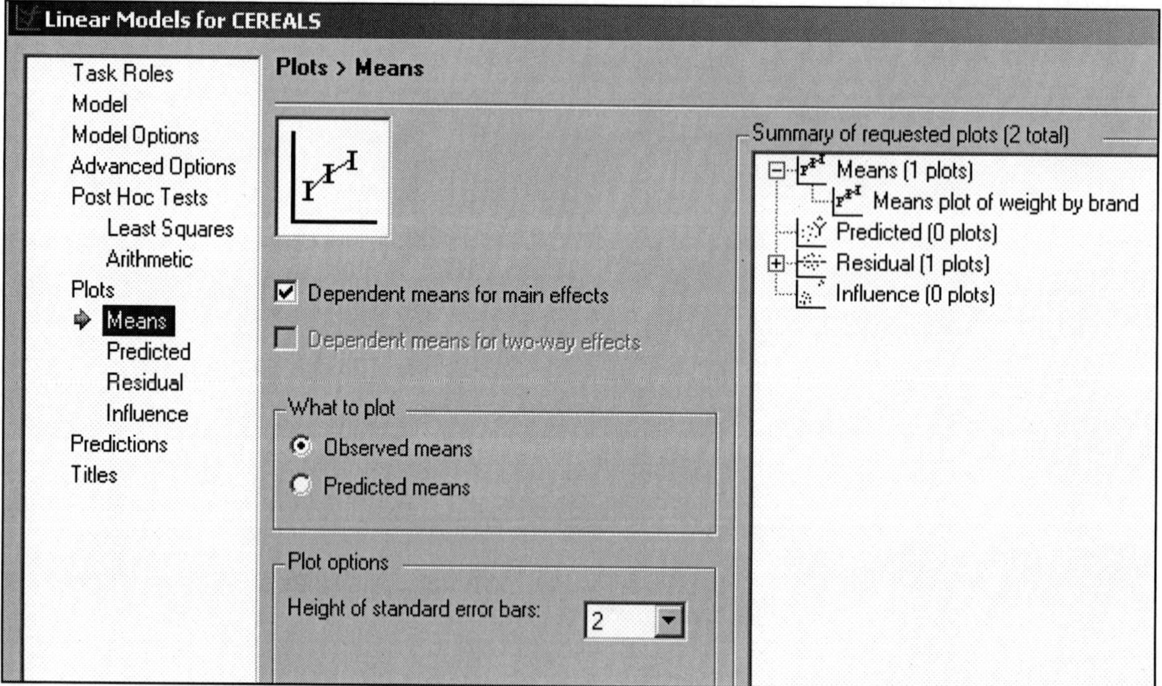

10. To get plots of the residuals versus the predicted values, select **Residual** under Plots. Check the box next to **Ordinary vs Predicted Y**. This will help in validating the assumptions of ANOVA.

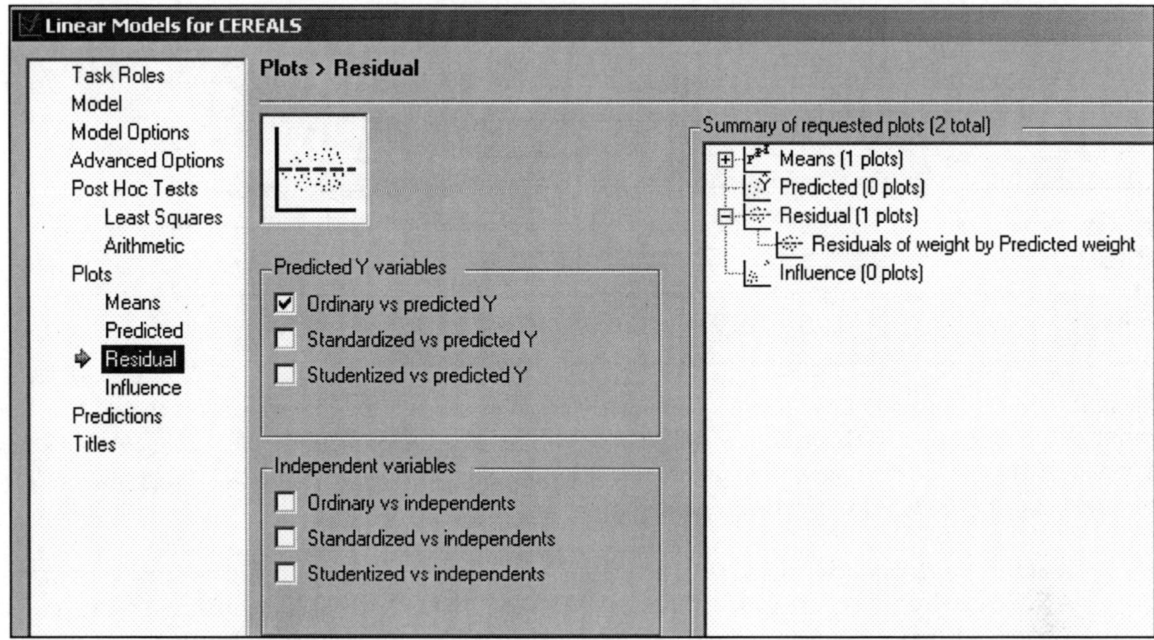

11. In order to test whether the residuals are approximately normal, you have to request that SAS create a data set with the residuals. To do this, select **Predictions** on the left. Under **Data to predict**, check the box next to **Original sample**, and check the lower-left box marked **Residuals** to request that the residuals be added to the output data set.

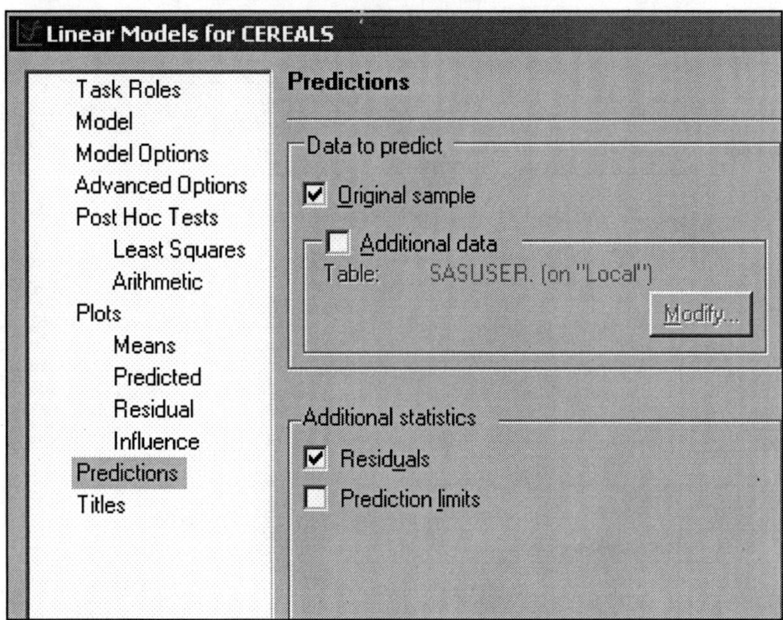

12. Select **Run**.

The output presented below is presented in the order in which it should be viewed: Assumption verification is first, followed by analysis. The actual order in the output shows the assumption verification last.

Levene's Test for Homogeneity of weight Variance ANOVA of Squared Deviations from Group Means					
Source	**DF**	**Sum of Squares**	**Mean Square**	**F Value**	**Pr > F**
brand	1	9.237E-7	9.237E-7	1.12	0.2942
Error	78	0.000065	8.283E-7		

The null hypothesis for the Levene's test is that the variances are equal. Failing to reject the null hypothesis verifies the equal variance assumption. The Pr > F is the probability of getting an *F* as large as the one reported or larger if the null hypothesis is true (in other words, the *p*-value). The *p*-value is less than 0.05, so you fail to reject the assumption that the variances are equal.

If at this point you determined that the variances were not equal, you could use the One-Way ANOVA task and request Welch Variance-Weighted ANOVA on the **Tests** panel. This requests Welch's (1951) variance-weighted one-way ANOVA. This alternative to the usual ANOVA is robust to the assumption of equal variances.

Residual of weight

0.080
0.045
0.010
-0.025
-0.060

14.990 15.003 15.015 15.028 15.040

Predicted weight

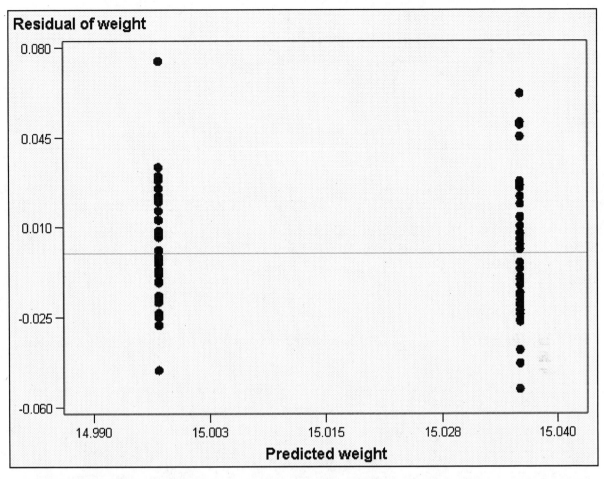

The graph above is a plot of the residuals versus the fitted values from the ANOVA model. Essentially, you are looking for a random scatter about the zero reference line for each of the fitted values. Any patterns or trends in this plot can indicate model assumption violations.

The Predictions selection creates a new data set that is linked to the Linear Models task in the process flow.

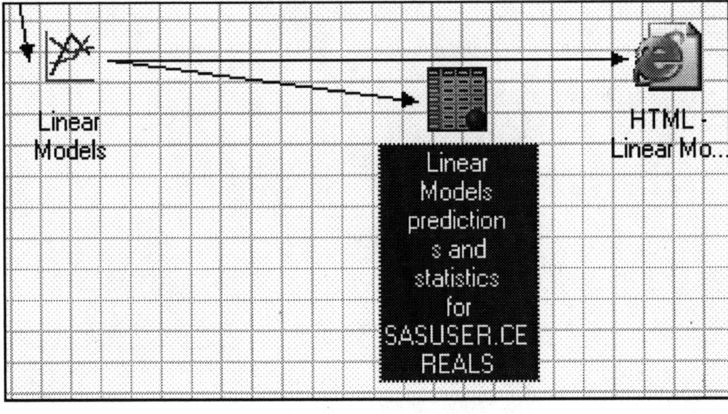

Double-click the data set to view it.

HTML - Linear Models | Linear Models predictions and statistics for SASUSER.CEREALS (read-only)

	brand	weight	idnumber	predicted_weight	residual_weight	student_weight	rstudent_weight
1	Morning	14.9982	61469897	14.9970125	0.0011875	0.0493165341	0.0490001467
2	Rise n Shine	15.0136	33081197	15.03596	-0.02236	-0.928604382	-0.927775213
3	Morning	15.01	68137597	14.9970125	0.0129875	0.5393671471	0.5369006878
4	Rise n Shine	14.9982	37070397	15.03596	-0.03776	-1.568161961	-1.583234672
5	Morning	15.0052	64608797	14.9970125	0.0081875	0.3400245249	0.3380885106
6	Rise n Shine	14.993	60714297	15.03596	-0.04296	-1.784116469	-1.809958543
7	Morning	14.9733	16907997	14.9970125	-0.0237125	-0.984773319	-0.98458012
8	Rise n Shine	15.0812	9589297	15.03596	0.04524	1.8788042144	1.9104511405
9	Morning	15.0037	93891897	14.9970125	0.0066875	0.2777299554	0.2760804334
10	Rise n Shine	15.0418	85859397	15.03596	0.00584	0.2425335237	0.2410647212

The variable `residual_weight` is the actual value of each variable minus the value predicted by the model (in this case, the brand's group mean). To verify that this distribution is approximately normal, use the Distribution Analysis task.

1. Make sure the output data set from Linear Models is selected and select **Analyze** ⇨ **Distribution Analysis…**.

2. With **Task Roles** selected on the left, drag and drop `residual_weight` to the Analysis variables role.

3. Select **Normal** on the left and check the box next to **Normal** in the resulting pane. Change the line color to green and the line width to 2.

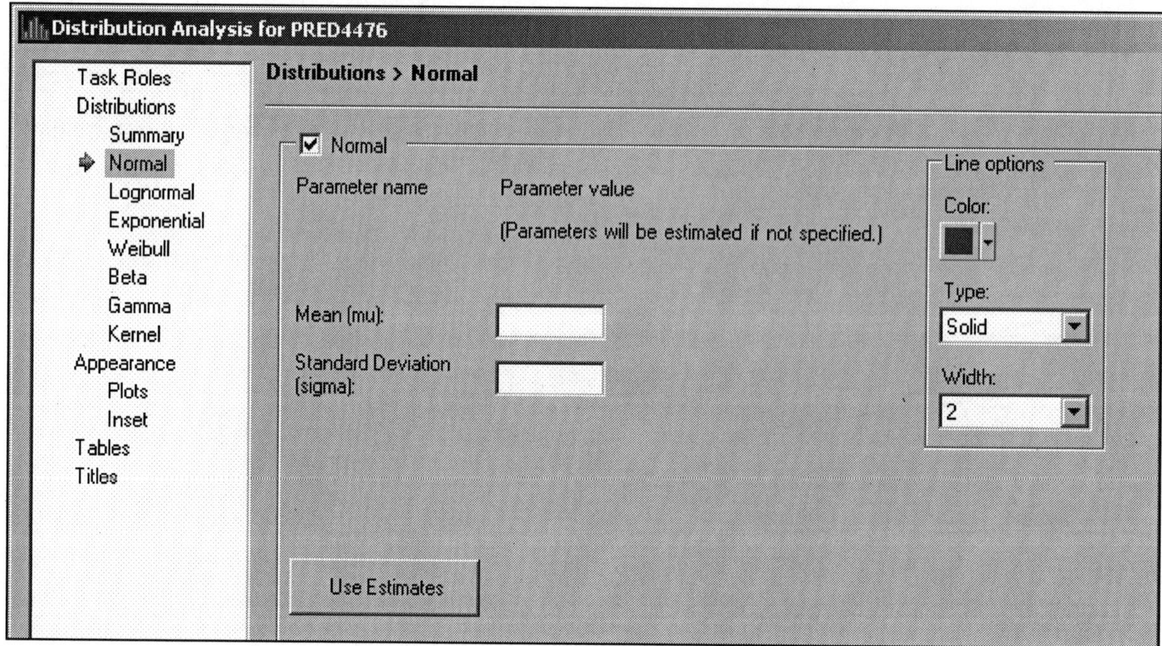

4. Select **Plots** on the left and check the box next to **Histogram**, **Probability**, and **Box plot**.

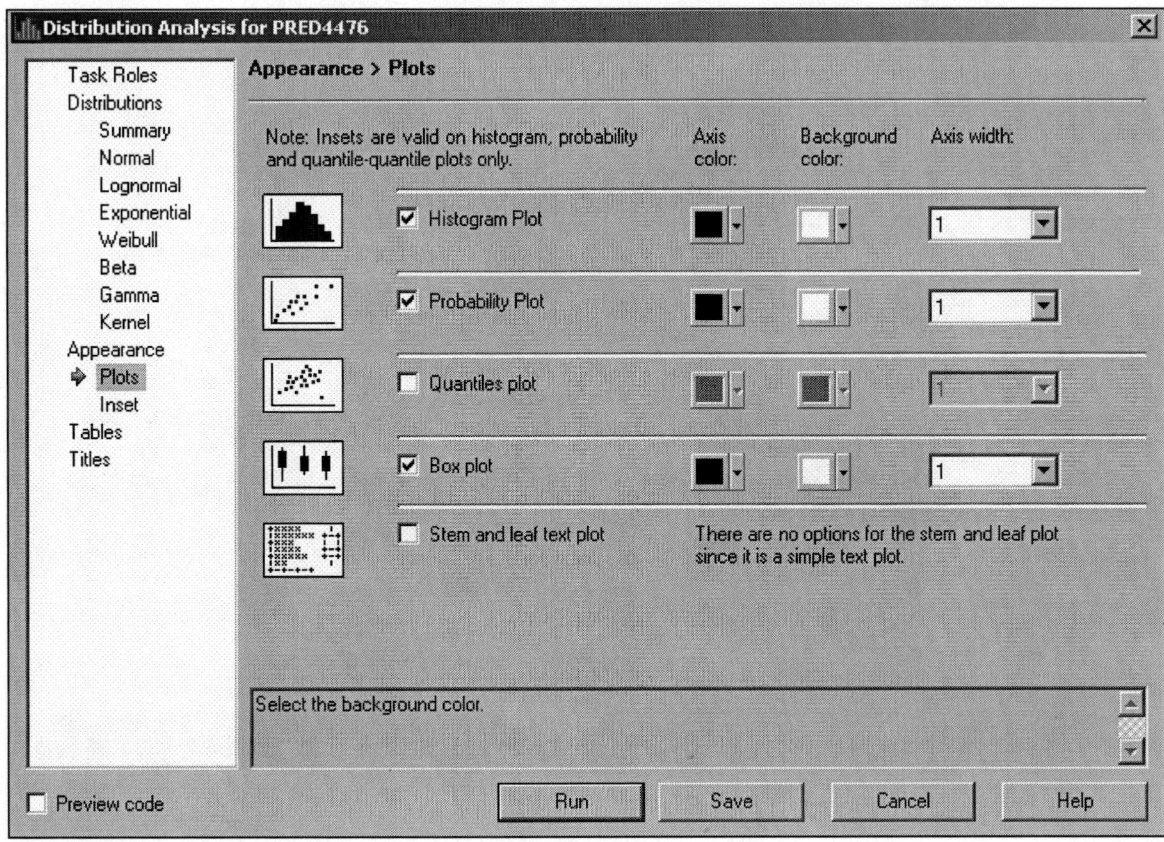

5. Select **Run**.

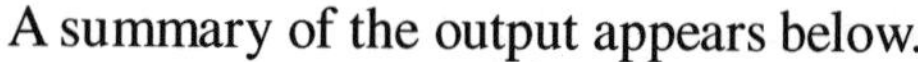

A summary of the output appears below.

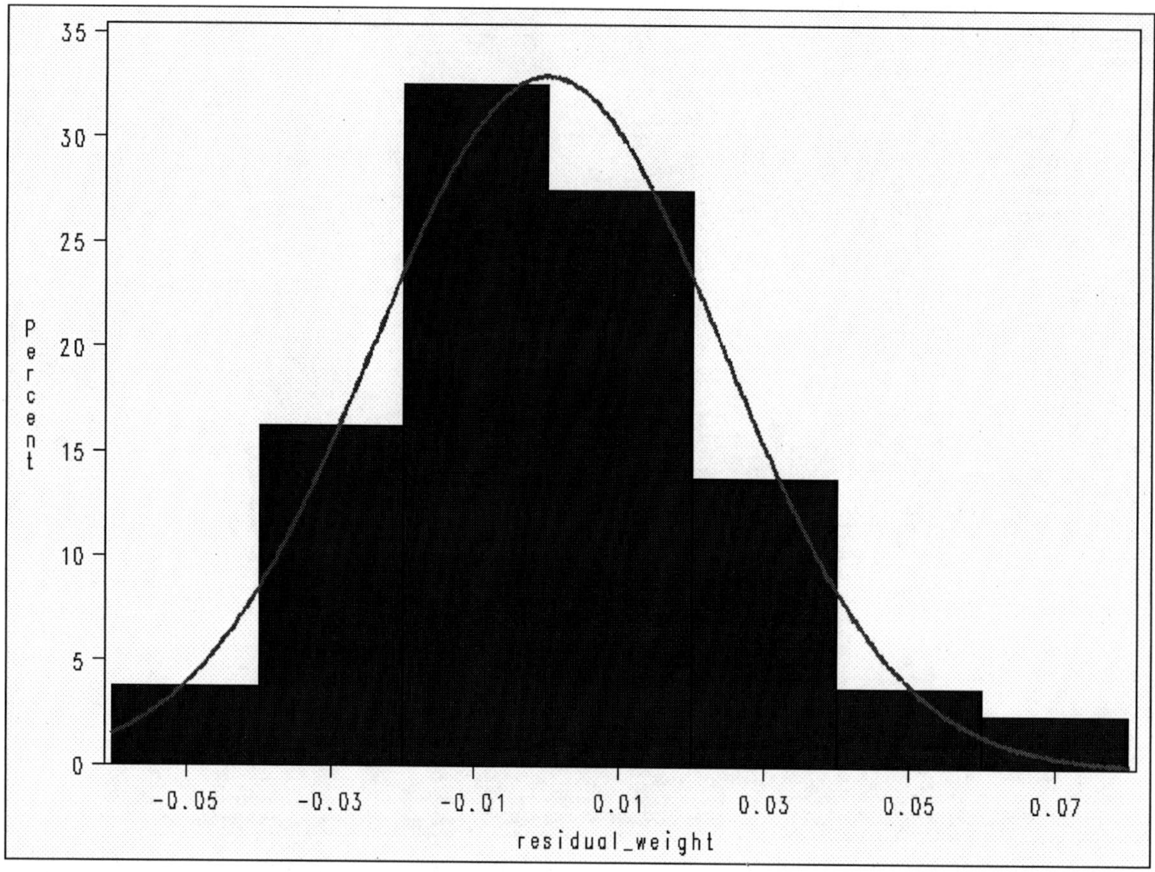

The histogram indicates that the residuals are normal.

Selecting the **Normal** box also creates hypothesis tests for whether the distribution is normal.

Goodness-of-Fit Tests for Normal Distribution				
Test	**Statistic**		**p Value**	
Kolmogorov-Smirnov	D	0.07711238	Pr > D	>0.150
Cramer-von Mises	W-Sq	0.08755262	Pr > W-Sq	0.167
Anderson-Darling	A-Sq	0.61754096	Pr > A-Sq	0.105

The null assumption for the Goodness-of-Fit tests is that the distribution of the data is normal. Failing to reject the null hypothesis indicates that the residuals are normally distributed. Be careful when interpreting these tests, as they depend upon and reflect the sample size. Large samples tend to produce small *p*-values even for slight departures from normality. Small samples tend to produce large *p*-values even for badly skewed or heavy tailed data. The plots shown earlier should always be used in conjunction with these tests.

The *p*-values for all of the Goodness-of-Fit tests are greater than alpha. You fail to reject the null hypothesis that the residuals for the analysis are normal.

After the ANOVA assumptions have been verified, you interpret the output from the analysis.

To locate the previous results, right-click on the Linear Models task. Select **Results** ⇨ **0 HTML - Linear Models**.

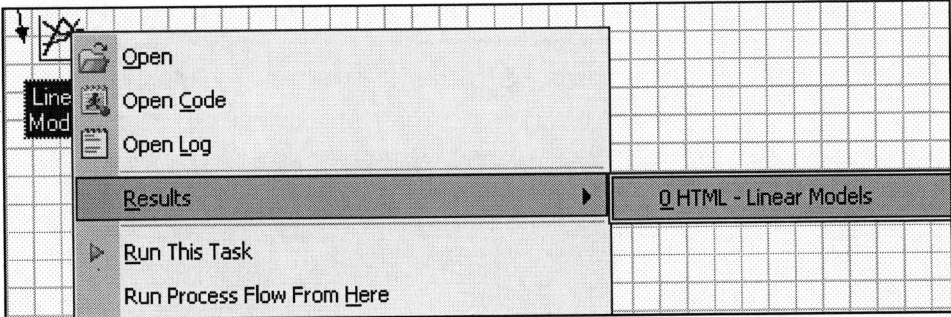

Turn your attention to the first page of the PROC GLM output, which specifies the number of levels, the values of the class variable, and the number of observations read versus the number of observations used. If any row has missing data for a predictor or response variable, that row is dropped from the analysis.

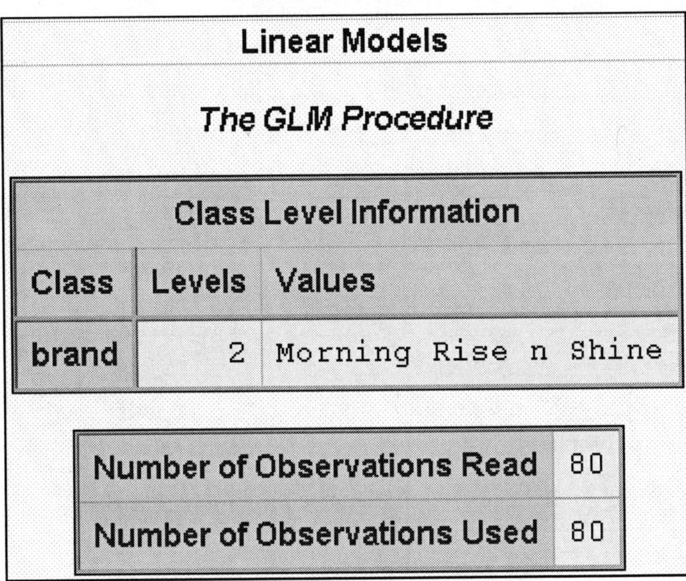

Linear Models

The GLM Procedure

Class Level Information		
Class	Levels	Values
brand	2	Morning Rise n Shine

Number of Observations Read	80
Number of Observations Used	80

The next table is the Analysis of Variance table, which contains information about the overall model, including the explained and unexplained variation.

Dependent Variable: weight

Source	DF	Sum of Squares	Mean Square	F Value	Pr > F
Model	1	0.03033816	0.03033816	51.02	<.0001
Error	78	0.04638442	0.00059467		
Corrected Total	79	0.07672257			

In general, *degrees of freedom* (DF) can be thought of as the number of independent pieces of information.

- Model DF is the number of treatments minus one.
- Corrected total DF is the sample size minus one.

Mean squares are calculated by taking sums of squares and dividing by the corresponding degrees of freedom.

- Mean square for error (MSE) is an estimate of σ^2, the constant variance assumed for all treatments.
- If $\mu_1 = \mu_2$, the mean square for the model (MSM) is also an estimate of σ^2.
- If $\mu_1 \neq \mu_2$, MSM estimates σ^2 plus a positive constant.
- $F = \dfrac{MSM}{MSE}$.

Based on the above, if the *F* statistic is significantly larger than one, it supports rejecting the null hypothesis, concluding that the treatment means are not equal.

The *F* statistic and corresponding *p*-value are reported in the analysis of variance table. Because the reported *p*-value is less than 0.0001, you conclude that there is a statistical difference between the means.

The next statistics are often used to compare different models.

R-Square	Coeff Var	Root MSE	weight Mean
0.395427	0.162394	0.024386	15.01649

The *coefficient of determination*, R^2, denoted in this table as R-Square, is a measure of the proportion of variability explained by the independent variables in the analysis. This statistic is calculated as

$$R^2 = \frac{SSM}{SST}.$$

The value of R^2 is between 0 and 1. The value is

- close to 0 if the independent variables do not explain much variability in the data
- close to 1 if the independent variables explain a relatively large proportion of variability in the data.

Although values of R^2 closer to 1 are preferred, judging the magnitude of R^2 depends on the context of the problem.

The coefficient of variation (denoted Coeff Var) expresses the root MSE (the estimate of the standard deviation for all treatments) as a percent of the mean. It is a unitless measure that is useful in comparing the variability of two sets of data with different units of measure.

The `weight` Mean is the mean of all of the data values in the variable `weight` without regard to `brand`.

The last two tables, Type I and Type III Sums of Squares, allow you to gauge the relative importance of different predictor variables.

Source	DF	Type I SS	Mean Square	F Value	Pr > F
brand	1	0.03033816	0.03033816	51.02	<.0001

Source	DF	Type III SS	Mean Square	F Value	Pr > F
brand	1	0.03033816	0.03033816	51.02	<.0001

If there is only one predictor (as is the case here) both tables repeat the information in the top line of the ANOVA table.

2.2 ANOVA With More Than Two Populations

Objectives

- Recognize the difference between a completely randomized design and a randomized block design.
- Differentiate between observed data and designed experiments.
- Analyze data from the different types of designs using the Linear Models task.

22

Defining the Objectives

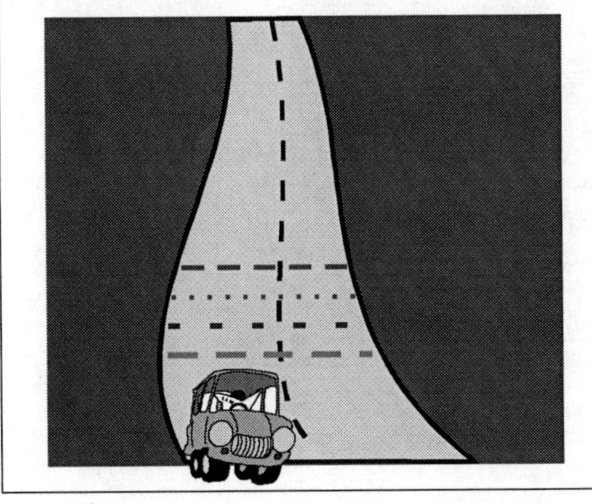

23

Question: Which paint formula is the brightest on the town roads?

Population: The seven busiest roads in town

In this case, you have a designed experiment. Treatments are assigned, and observed values of the response are recorded. It is also possible to have observed data, where treatments are not assigned, but instead observed from the individuals in the sample.

The question is specific, indicating that you are interested only in the effect paint formula has on brightness. The target population is also specific, indicating that inferences are only to be drawn on the seven busiest roads in the town.

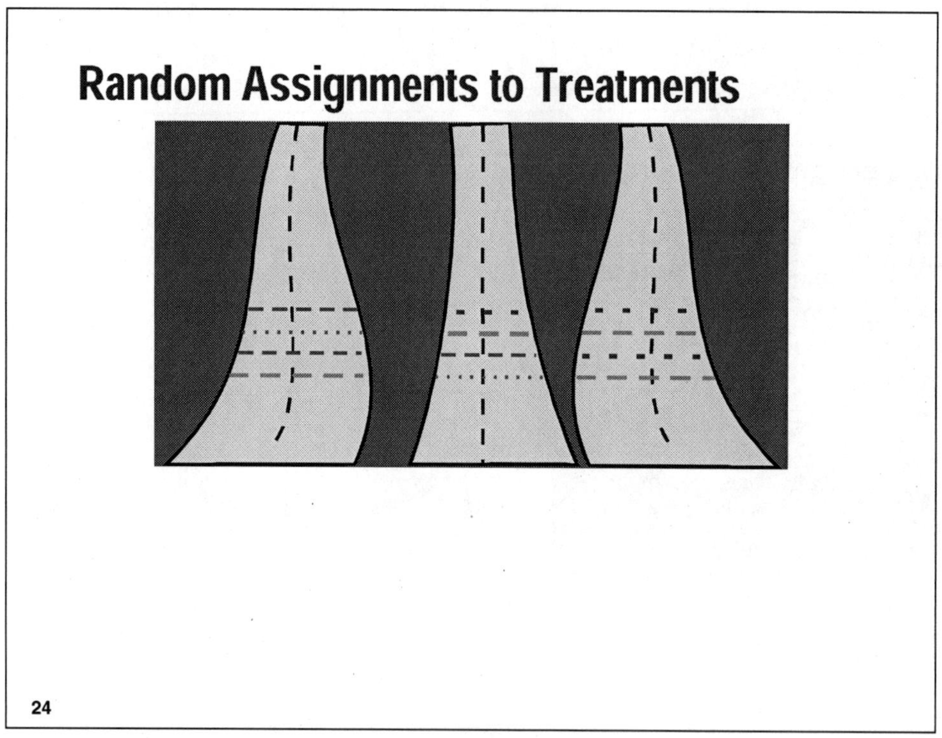

Example: You have identified the seven roads to paint and the four paint formulas to test. You plan to paint four stripes of paint on each road, a total of 28 stripes. One paint formula is randomly assigned to each of the 28 stripes.

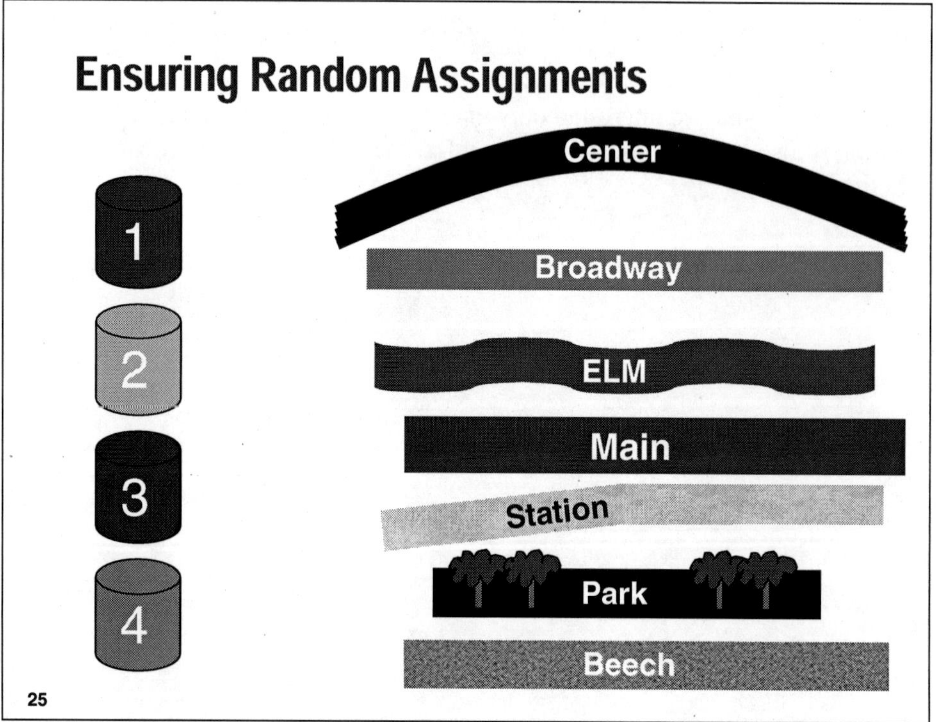

Careful planning is required to ensure that the paints are randomly assigned to each of the 28 stripes. The Appendix entitled Randomization Technique contains a possible program to accomplish this task.

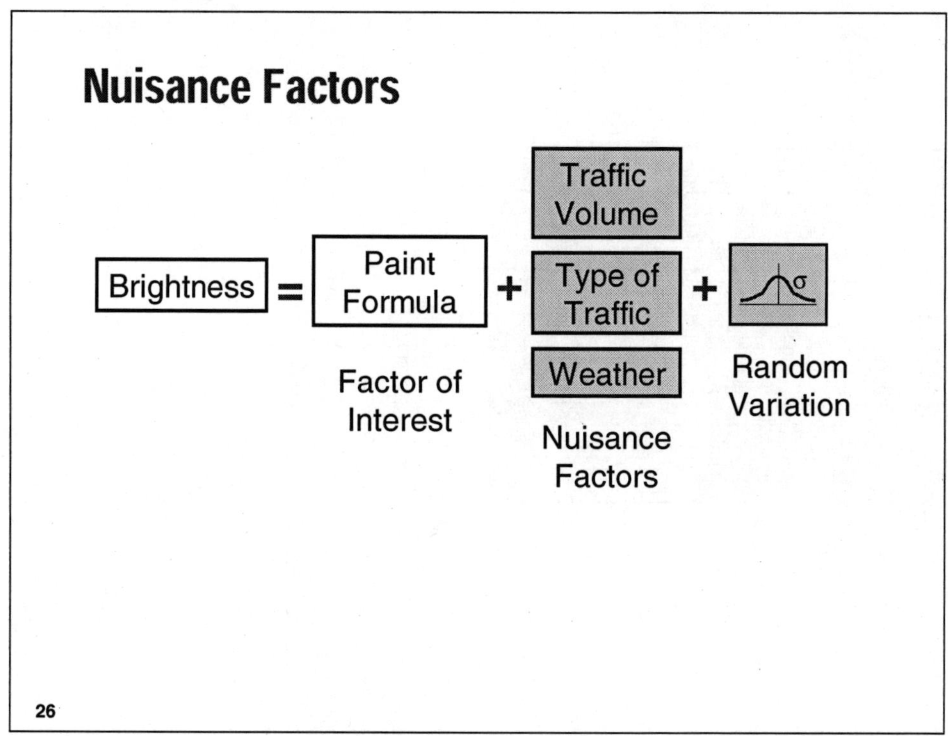

Factors that can affect the outcome but are not of interest in the experiment are called *nuisance factors*. The variation due to nuisance factors becomes part of the random variation.

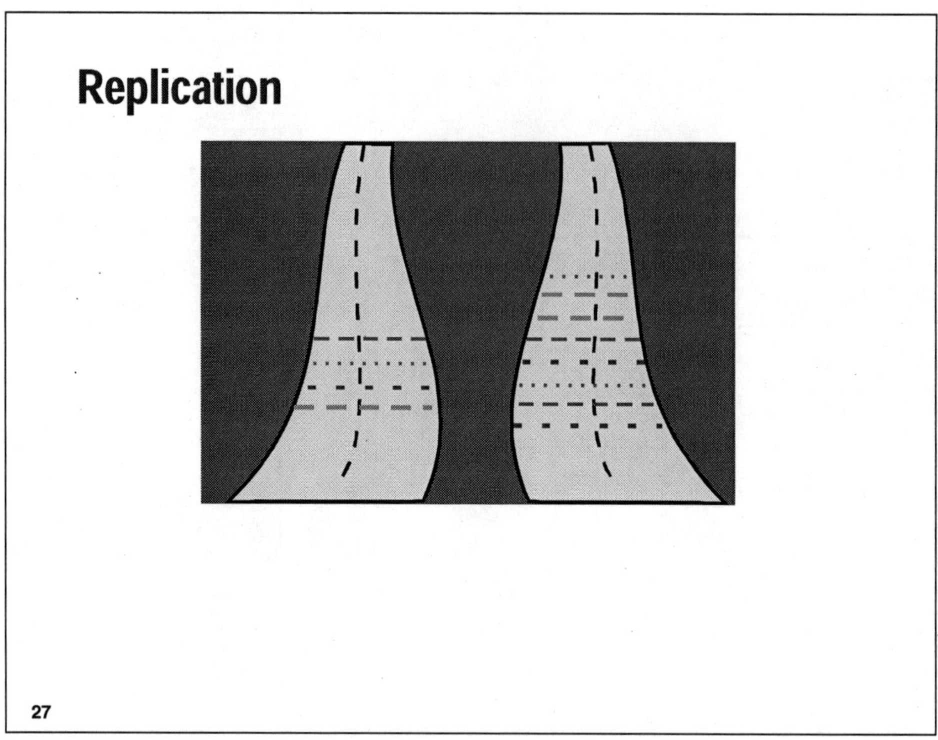

A *replication* occurs when you assign each treatment to more than one experimental unit.

In the picture, there is one stripe of each paint formula applied to the road on the left. If you are concerned that a sample size of one for each treatment is insufficient, then you might consider dividing each stripe into two pieces and measuring the brightness of each piece. You reason that this gives you two observations, or replicates, for each treatment. What is wrong with this approach?

You cannot apply different treatments (paint formulas) to part of a stripe of paint, but only to each stripe. By dividing the stripes and using each piece as an experimental unit, you have done pseudo-replication but not true replication. To have true replication you would have to paint more stripes as shown in the picture on the road on the right.

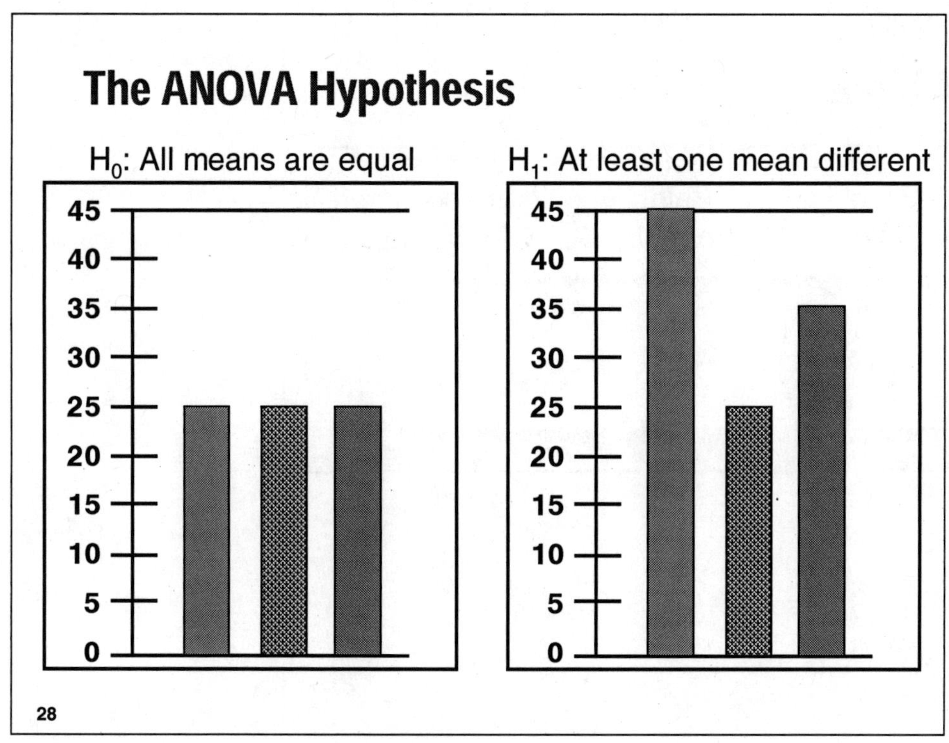

The basic concepts are the same when analyzing more than two populations as when analyzing two populations. The model and its assumptions are identical.

Consider the experiment to determine the best paint formula for roads with a completely randomized design. You want to determine whether the brightness of the paint is significantly different for the various paint formulas. There are seven roads, and four paint formulas are randomly assigned to each road.

Recall that the objective is to determine whether there are differences between population means. Now, with more than two populations, you are testing the hypothesis

- H_0: all means are equal
- H_1: at least one mean is different from one of the other means.

The ANOVA Model

Brightness = Base Level + Paint Formula + Unaccounted for Variation

$$Y_{ik} = \mu + \tau_i + \varepsilon_{ik}$$

29

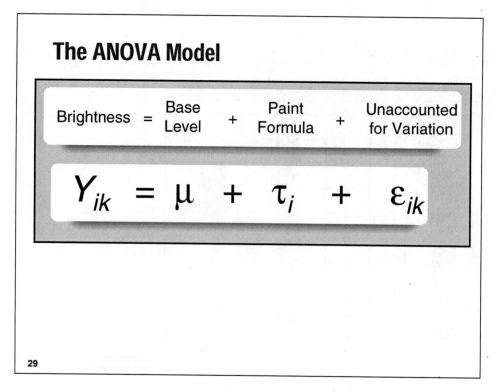

The model is the same as ANOVA for two treatments.

Analysis of More Than Two Populations

Use descriptive statistics to examine the differences between the four types of paint. Use the Linear Models task to verify the assumptions of ANOVA and determine if there is a statistically significant difference due to paint formula.

1. With the **`PAINTS`** table highlighted, select **Analyze** ⇨ **Distribution Analysis…**.
2. Drag and drop **`bright`** to the Analysis variables role and **`paint`** to the Classification variables role.
3. On the left, select **Plots** under Appearance. Check the box next to **Box plot**. Change the box plot background color to white.
4. Select **Run** to submit the task.

Investigation of the output reveals that the means do seem to be different. There are no unusual values that require investigation.

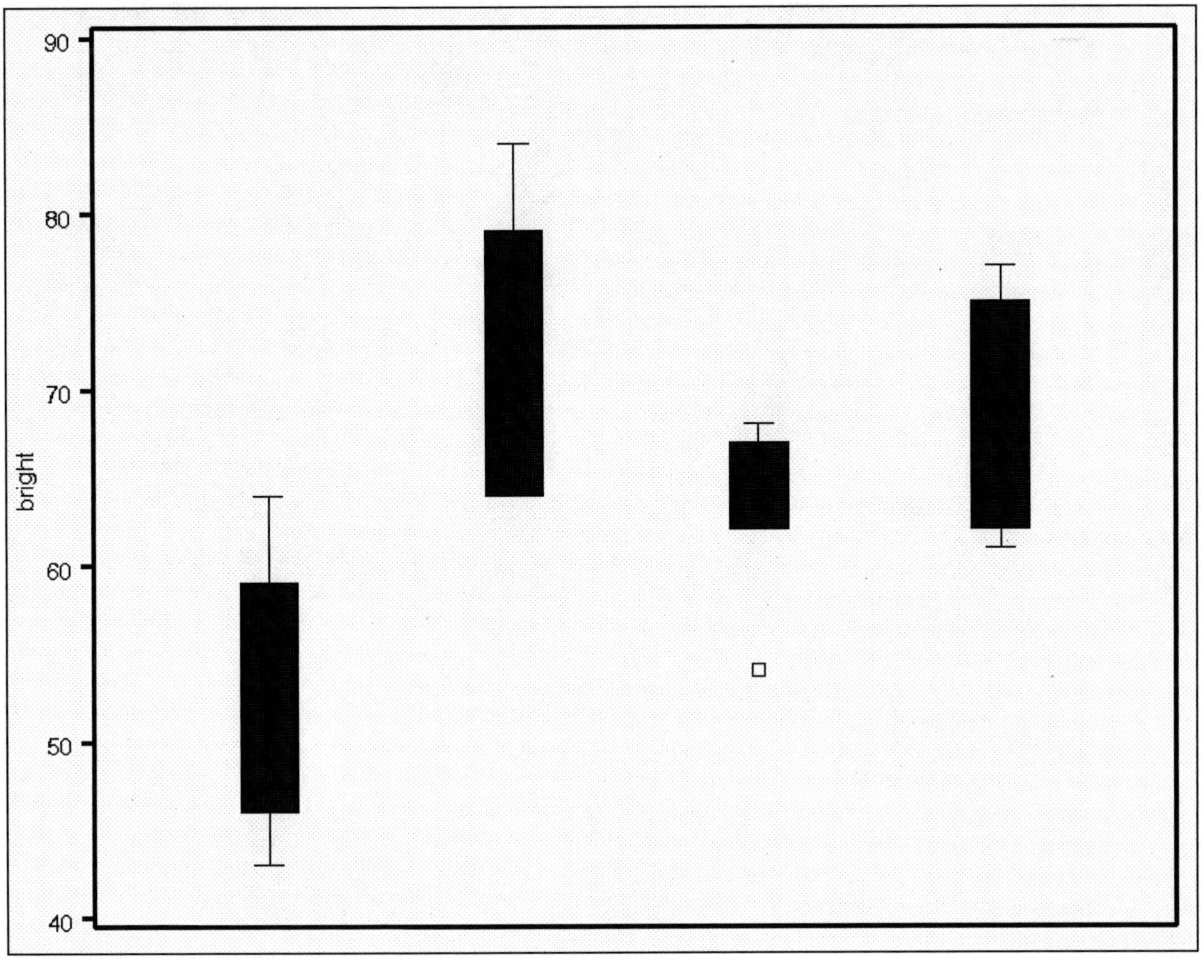

To investigate whether the means are statistically significantly different, use the Linear Models task.

1. With the **PAINTS** table highlighted, select **Analyze** ⇨ **ANOVA** ⇨ **Linear Models**.
2. With **Task Roles** selected on the left, drag and drop **bright** to the Dependent variable role and **paint** to the Classification variables role.
3. Select **Model** on the left. Select **paint** under **Class and quantitative variables** and select **Main** to move it to the **Effects** panel.

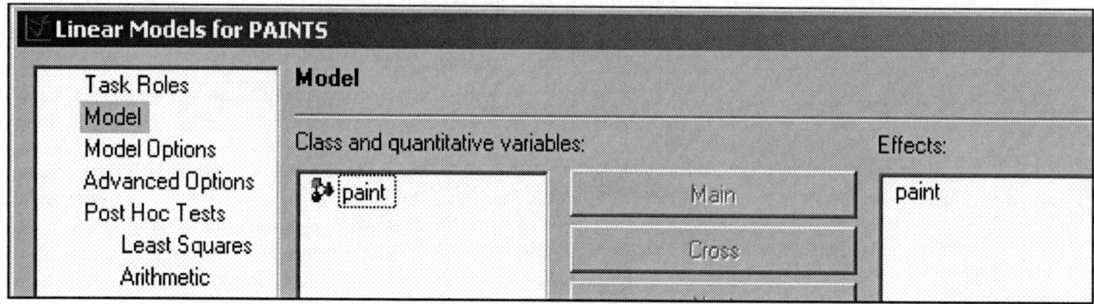

4. Select **Model Options** on the left. Uncheck the box next to **Show parameter estimates**.

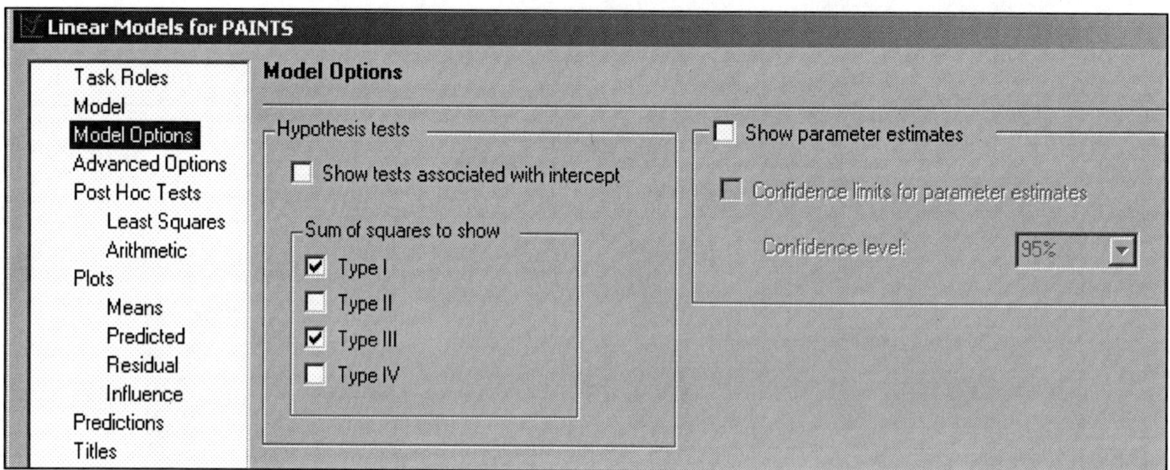

5. On the left, select **Arithmetic** under Post Hoc Tests.

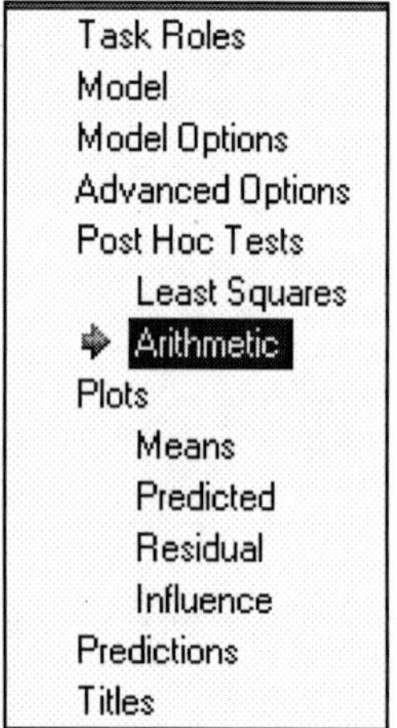

6. Select **Add** at the bottom. The right-hand panel automatically populates with a set of choices.

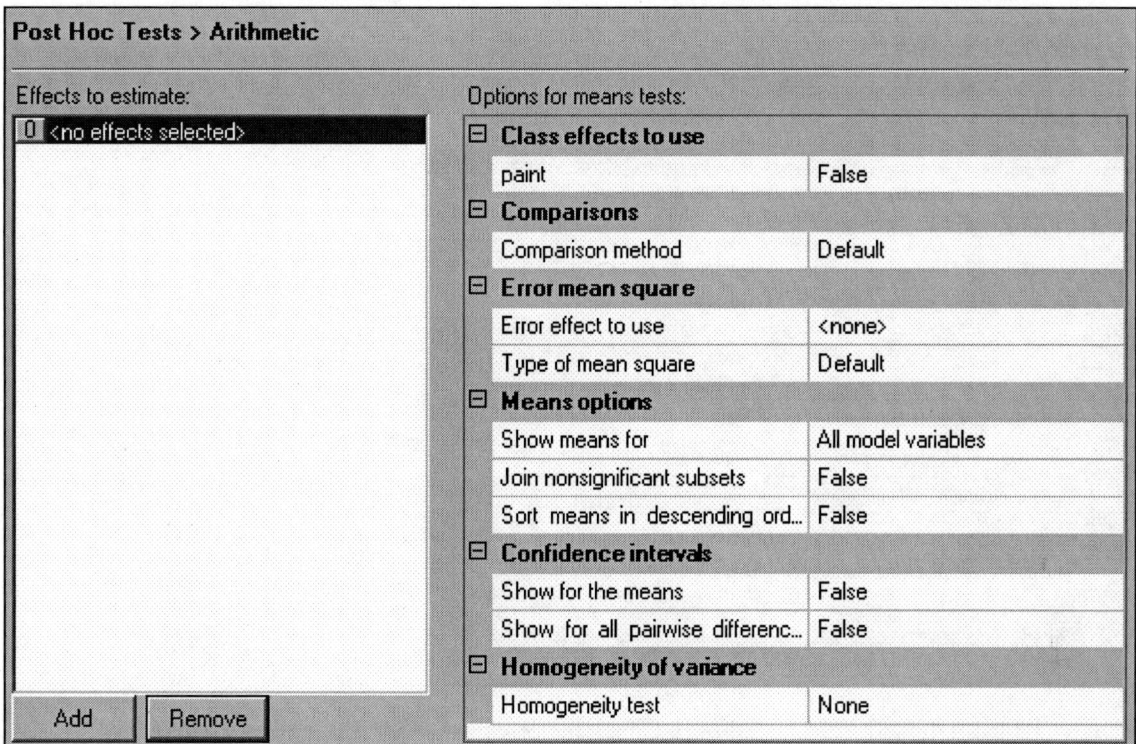

7. Change the **Options for means tests** selection for `paint` to `True` (instead of False).

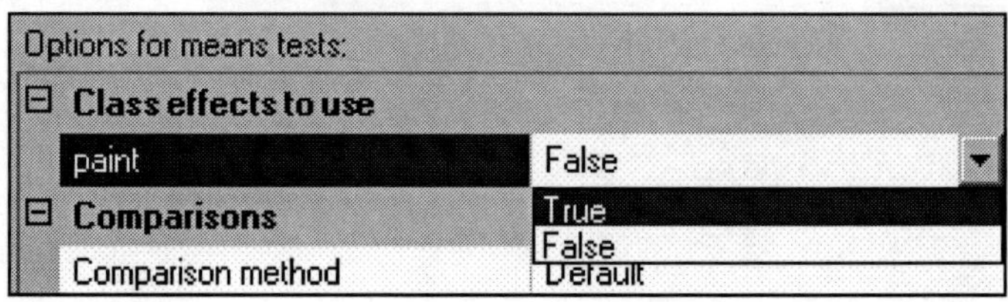

8. Change the Homogeneity of variance test to **`Levene (square residuals)`**.

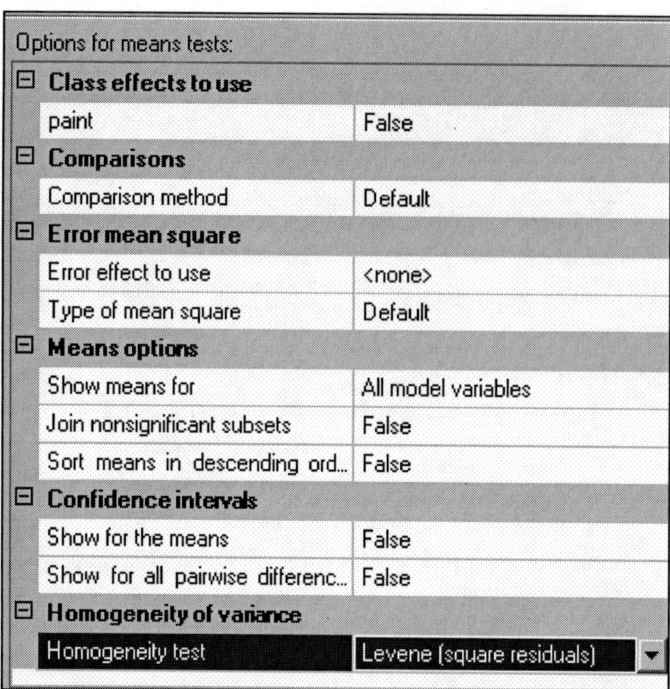

9. Under Plots on the left, select **<u>Residual</u>**. Check the box next to **Ordinary vs Predicted Y**.

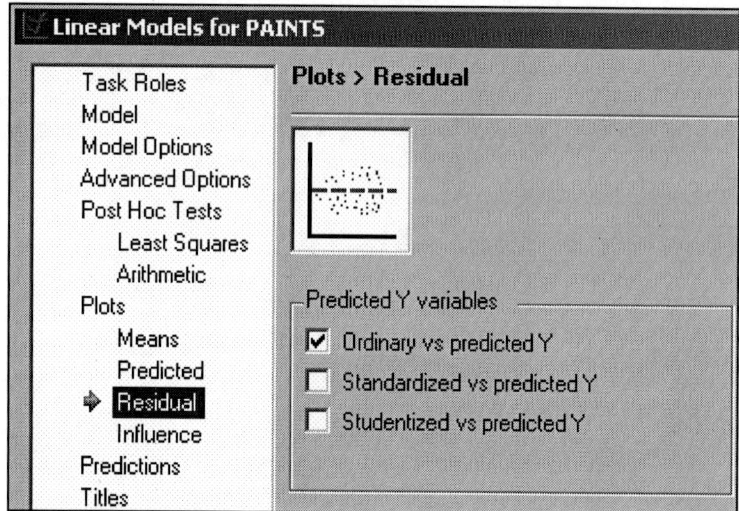

10. Select **<u>Predictions</u>** on the left. Check the boxes next to **Original Sample** and **Residuals**.

11. Select **<u>Run</u>**.

Before checking the results of the analysis, check to make sure the model assumptions are verified.

Levene's Test for Homogeneity of bright Variance ANOVA of Squared Deviations from Group Means					
Source	DF	Sum of Squares	Mean Square	F Value	Pr > F
paint	3	4505.0	1501.7	0.97	0.4224
Error	24	37090.8	1545.5		

Using the Levene's test you fail to reject the null hypothesis that the variances are equal. Therefore, the equal variance assumption is met.

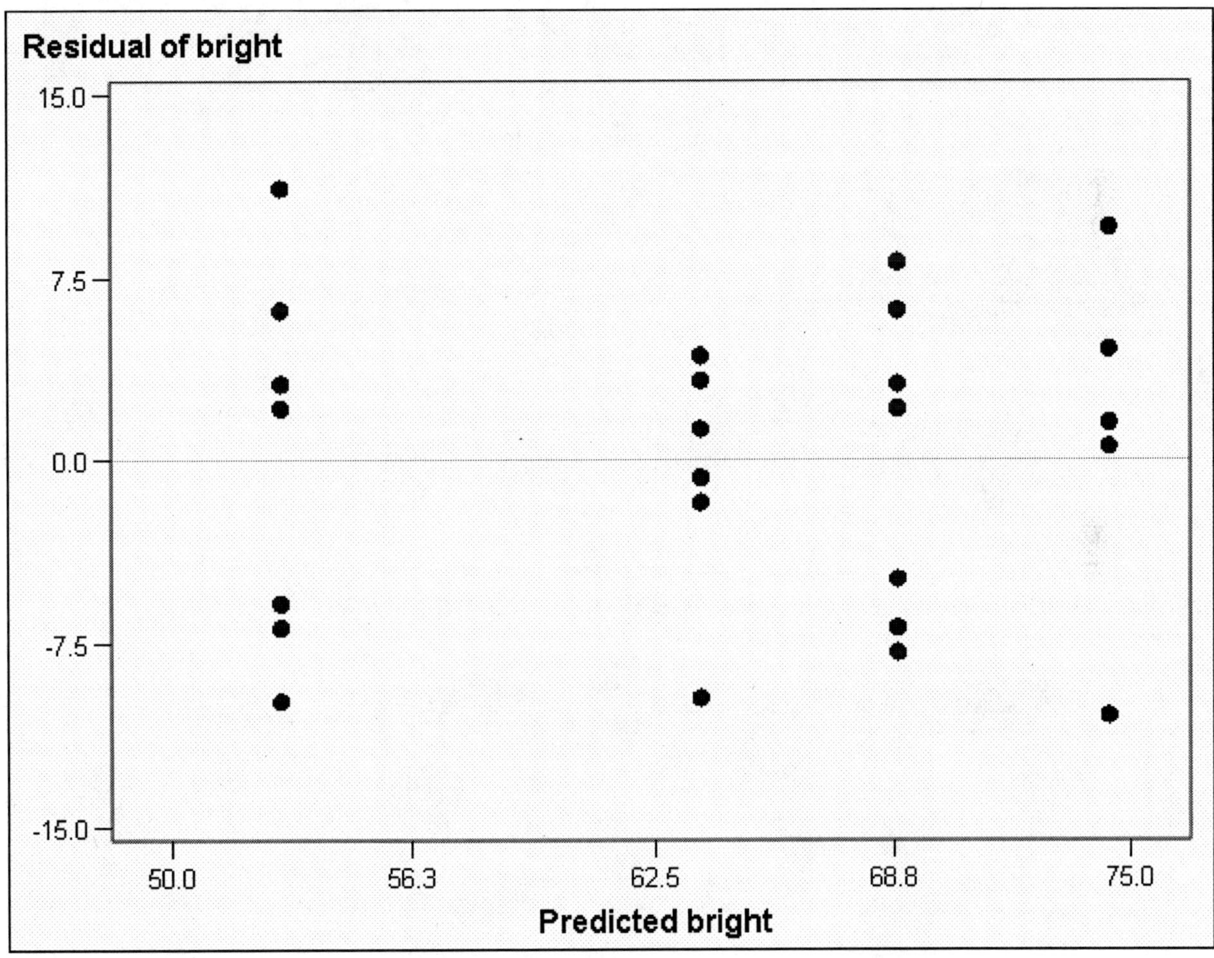

There are no patterns in the scatter plot of the residuals against the predicted values.

In order to test whether the residuals are normally distributed, examine the residuals from the output data set.

1. Choose the result data set in the process flow and select **Analyze** ⇨ **Distribution Analysis…**.

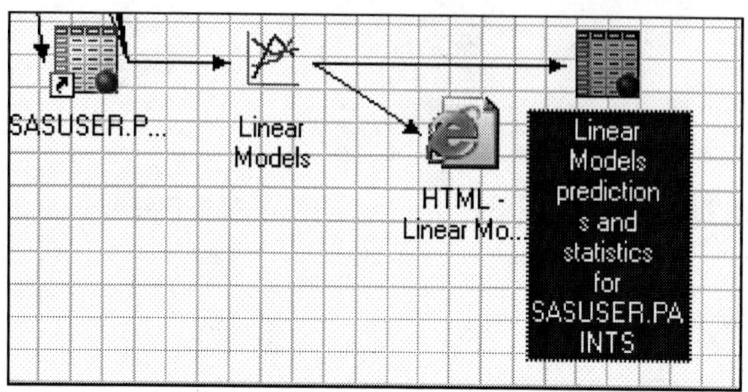

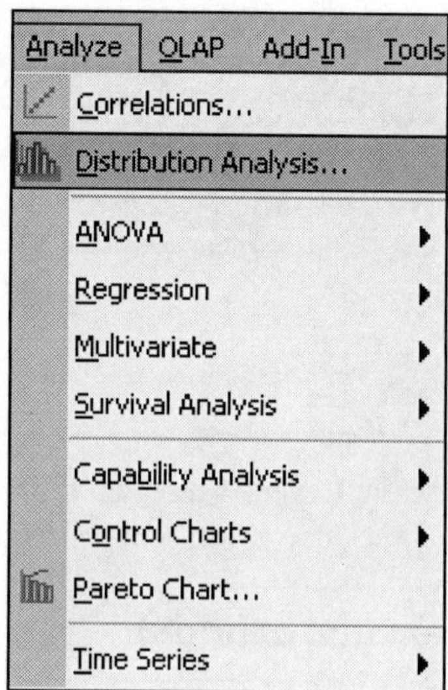

2. Drag and drop `residual_bright` to the Analysis Variables role.

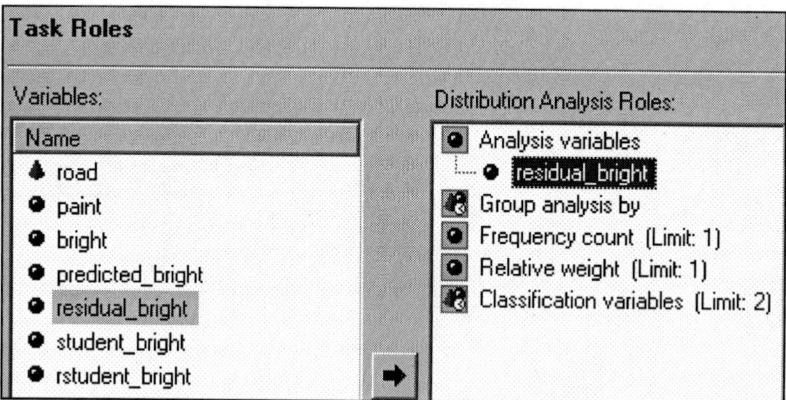

3. Under Distributions, select **Normal** and check the box next to **Normal** in the resulting pane. Change the color to green and the width to 2.

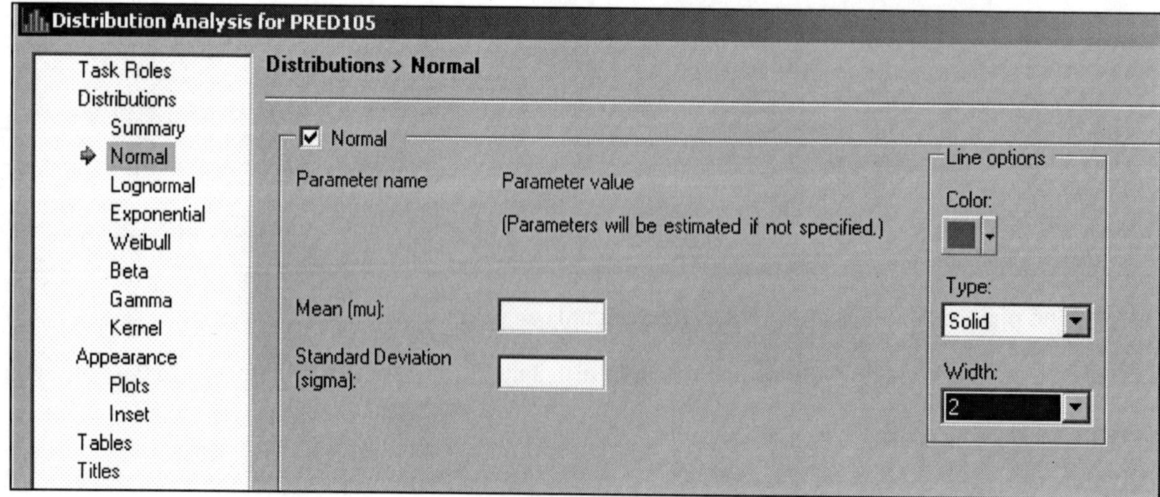

4. Under Appearance, select **Plots** and check the boxes next to **Histogram**, **Probability**, and **Box plot**. Change the background colors to white.

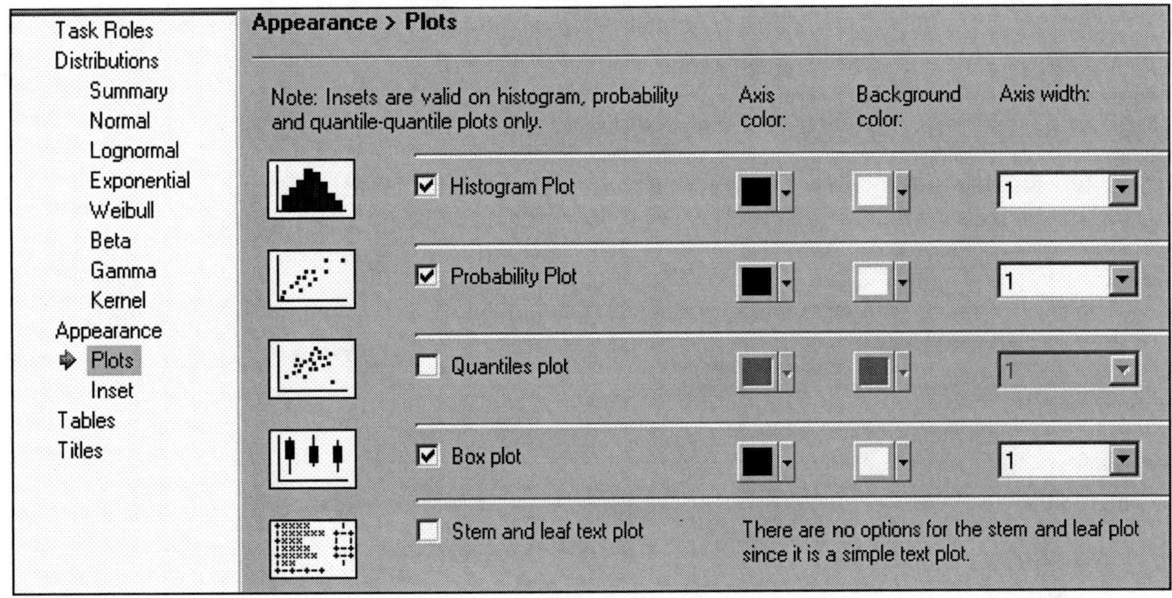

5. Select **Run** to submit the analysis.

None of the resulting plots show severe departures from normality.

Partial Output

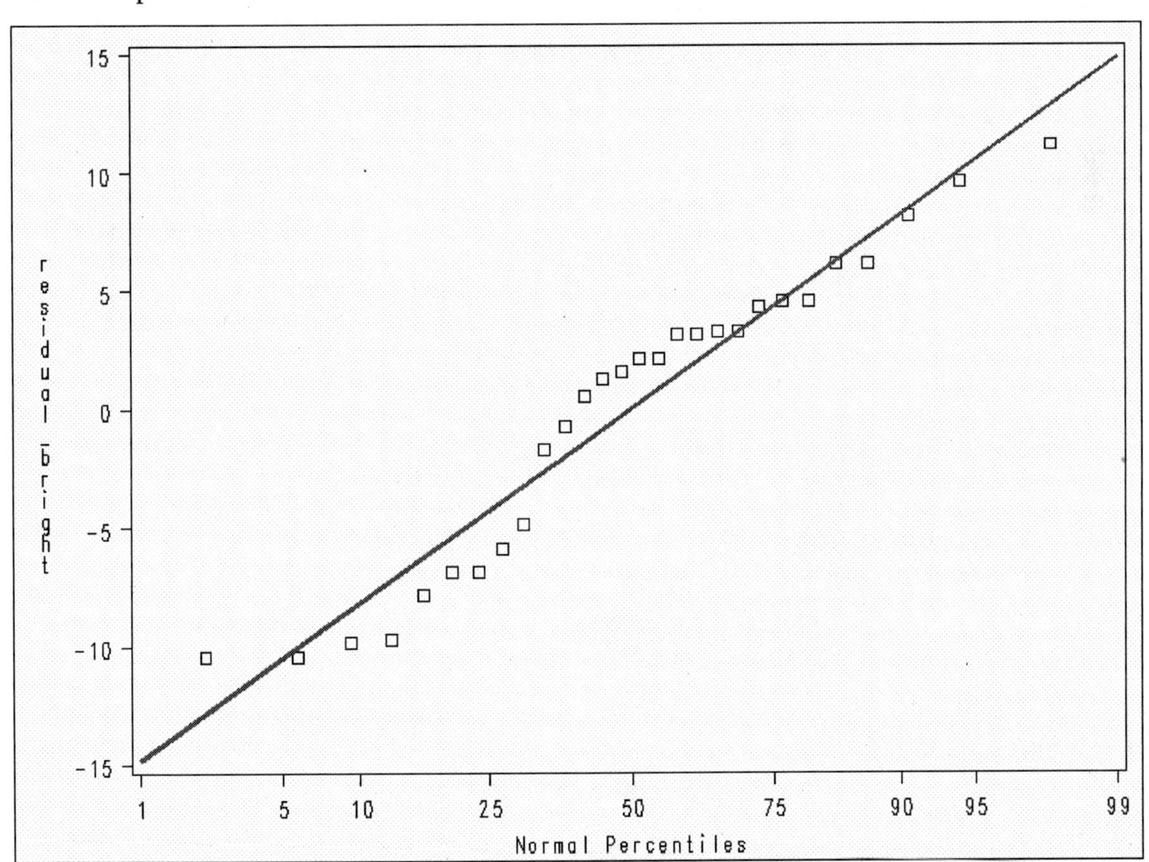

Now that you have verified the assumptions, go back to the output from Linear Models and view the results.

If you did not close the Linear Models output earlier, you can click its tab in the work area to display the results.

If you did close the Linear Models output, you can double-click the HTML file in the process flow or right-click the Linear Models task attached to the `PAINTS` data set and select **Results** ⇨ **0 HTML Linear Models.**

The first page of the output, shown below, specifies the number of levels and the values of the class variable, as well as the number of observations read from the data and used in the analysis.

Class Level Information		
Class	Levels	Values
paint	4	1 2 3 4

Number of Observations Read	28
Number of Observations Used	28

Dependent Variable: bright

Source	DF	Sum of Squares	Mean Square	F Value	Pr > F
Model	3	1770.107143	590.035714	12.89	<.0001
Error	24	1098.857143	45.785714		
Corrected Total	27	2868.964286			

R-Square	Coeff Var	Root MSE	bright Mean
0.616985	10.41574	6.766514	64.96429

The ANOVA table shows a *p*-value of <.0001 for the overall *F* test, leading you to reject the null hypothesis that all the means are equal to each other.

Because `bright` is the only predictor variable, the Type I and Type III Sums of Squares tables have the same information as the ANOVA table.

Rejecting the null hypothesis for the overall *F* test leads to the conclusion that not all the treatment means are the same, but which ones are different?

Level of paint	N	bright	
		Mean	Std Dev
1	7	52.8571429	7.69043933
2	7	74.4285714	7.67804539
3	7	63.7142857	4.82059076
4	7	68.8571429	6.46602844

The table of mean values gives some indication. It can reasonably be concluded that paint 1 is different from paint 2 (because paint 1 is the smallest mean and paint 2 is the largest), but what about the others?

Further testing is needed.

Multiple Comparison Methods

Comparisonwise Error Rate	Number of Comparisons	Experimentwise Error Rate
.05	1	.05
.05	3	.14
.05	6	.26
.05	10	.40

EER $\leq 1 - (1 - \alpha)^{nc}$ where *nc*=number of comparisons

31

When you control the comparisonwise error rate (CER), you fix the level of alpha for a single comparison without taking into consideration all the pairwise comparisons you are making.

The experimentwise error rate (EER) uses an alpha that takes into consideration all the pairwise comparisons you are making. Presuming that no differences exist, the chance you falsely conclude at least one difference exists is much higher when you consider all ten comparisons.

If you want to make sure the error rate is 0.05 for the entire set of comparisons, use a method that controls the experimentwise error rate at 0.05.

There is some disagreement among statisticians about the need to control the experimentwise error rate.

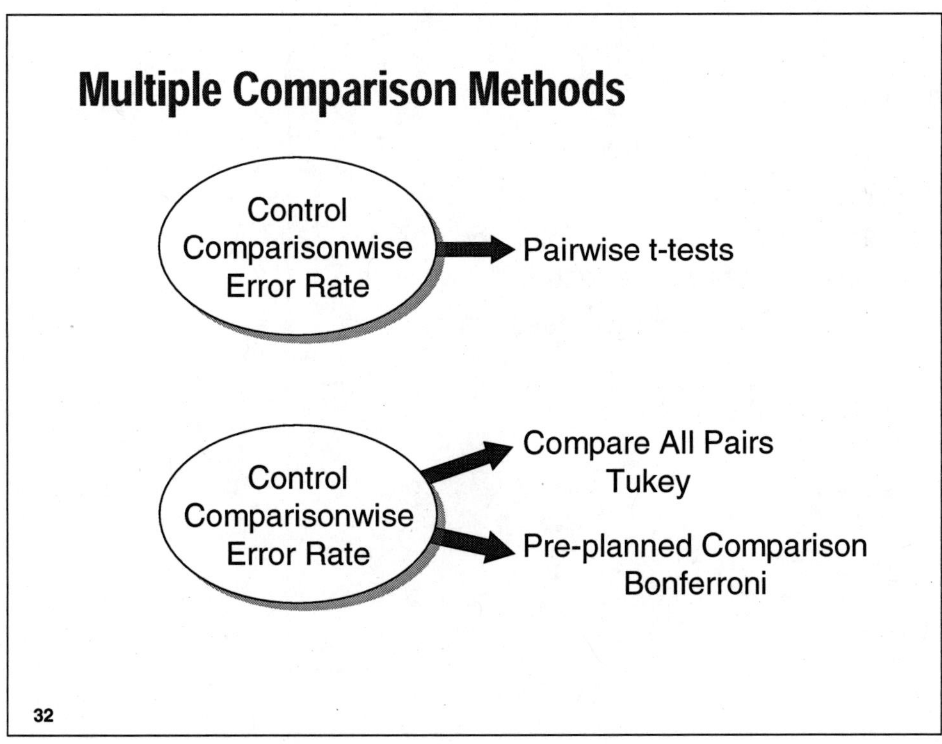

All of these multiple comparison methods are requested in the **Least Squares** panel under Post Hoc Tests in the Linear Models task.

This course addresses these options:

Comparisonwise Control	Using the default adjustment.
Experimentwise Control	Using the Tukey and Bonferroni adjustment.

There are many other options available that control the experimentwise error rate. For information about these options see the SAS online documentation.

Bonferroni's Method

Bonferroni's multiple comparison method

- is used only for preplanned comparisons
- adjusts for multiple comparisons by dividing the alpha level by the number of comparisons made
- ensures an experimentwise error rate less than or equal to alpha
- is the most conservative method.

33

Bonferroni's method is not generally considered appropriate for comparisons made after looking at the data, because the adjustment is made based on the number of comparisons you intend to do. If you look at the data to determine how many and what comparisons to make, you are using the data to determine the adjustment.

A conservative method tends to find fewer significant differences than might otherwise be found.

While Bonferroni's method can be used for all pairwise comparisons, Tukey's method is generally less conservative and more appropriate.

Tukey's Multiple Comparison Method

This method is appropriate when considering pairwise comparisons only.

The experimentwise error rate is

- equal to alpha when **all** pairwise comparisons are considered
- less than alpha when **fewer** than all pairwise comparisons are considered.

34

A pairwise comparison examines the difference between two treatment means. All pairwise comparisons are all possible combinations of two treatment means.

Tukey's multiple comparison adjustment is based on conducting all pairwise comparisons and guarantees the Type I experimentwise error rate is equal to alpha for this situation. If you choose to do fewer than all pairwise comparisons, then this method is more conservative.

Multiple Comparison Methods

Modify the earlier Linear Models task to perform multiple comparisons.

1. Open the pervious Linear Models task by double-clicking it in the process flow or by right-clicking and selecting **Open**.

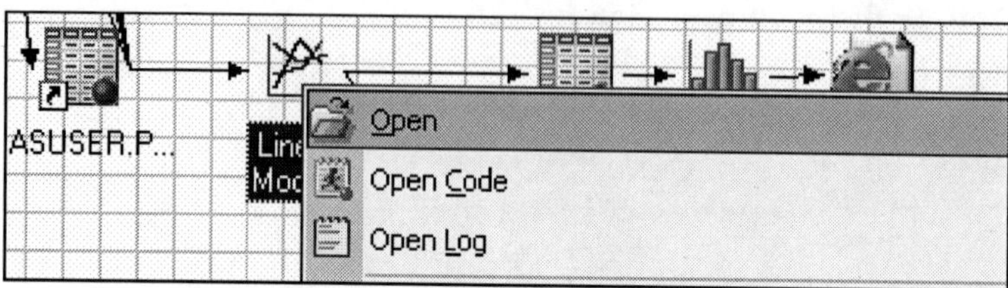

2. Select **Least Squares** under Post Hoc Tests.

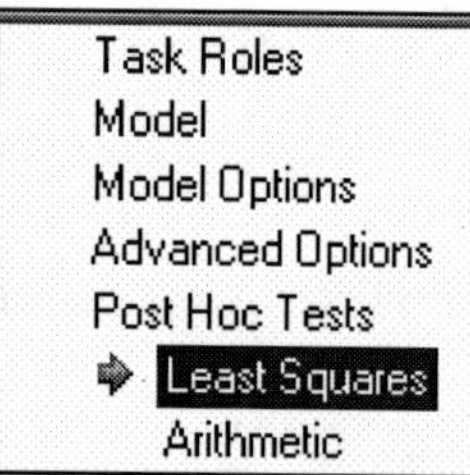

3. At the bottom left, select **Add**. The right-hand pane populates with options.

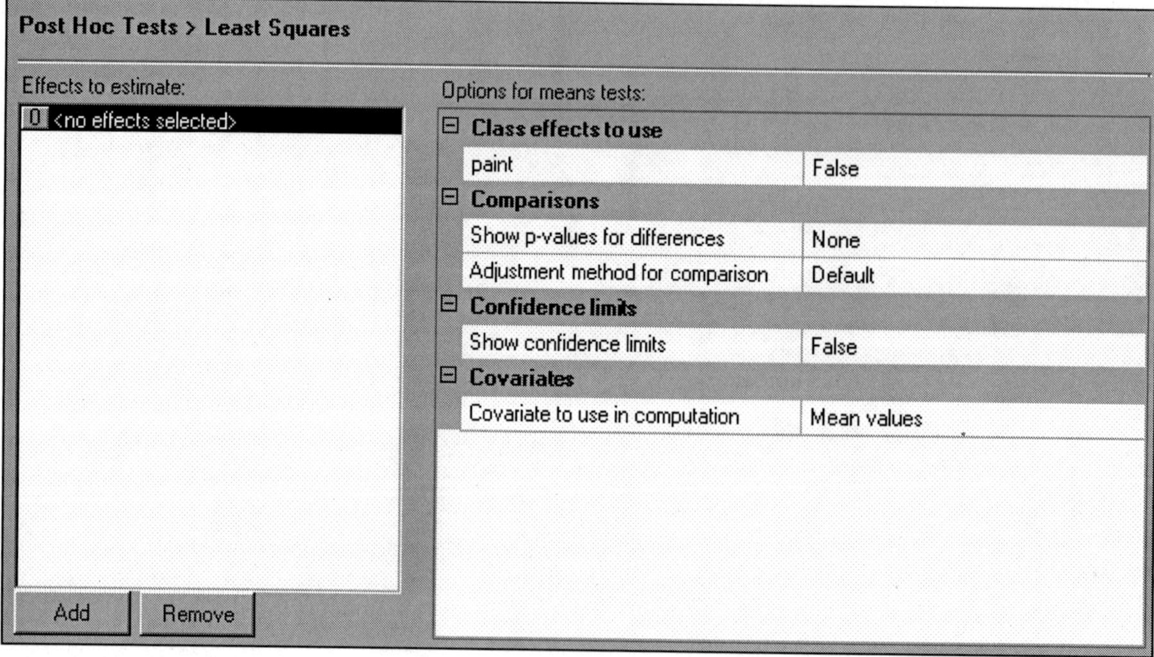

4. Change the selection for `paint` from `False` to `True`.

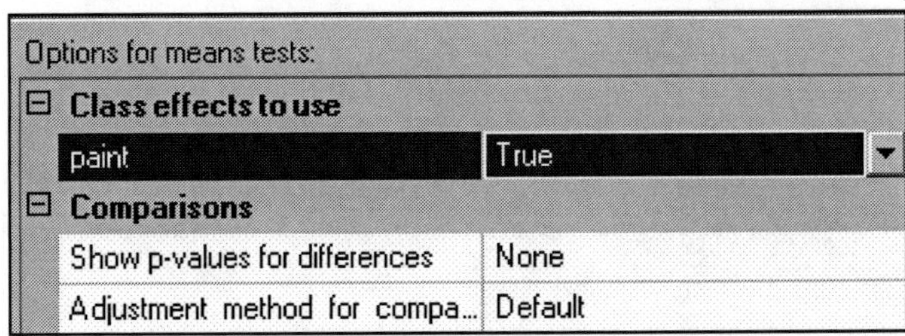

5. Change **Show p-values for differences** from `None` to `All pairwise differences`.

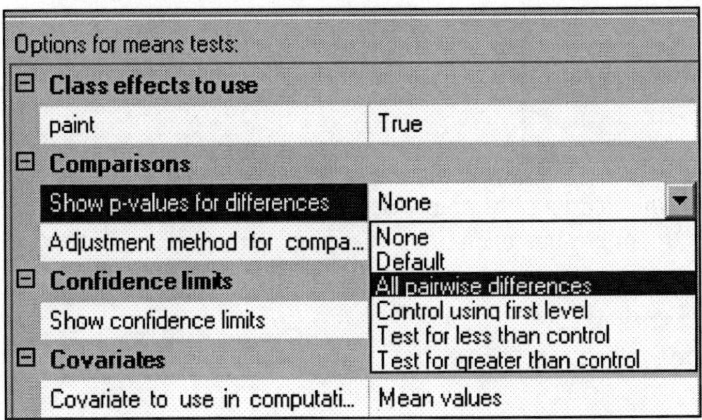

6. Change the **Adjustment method for compa...** from `Default` to `No adjustment`.

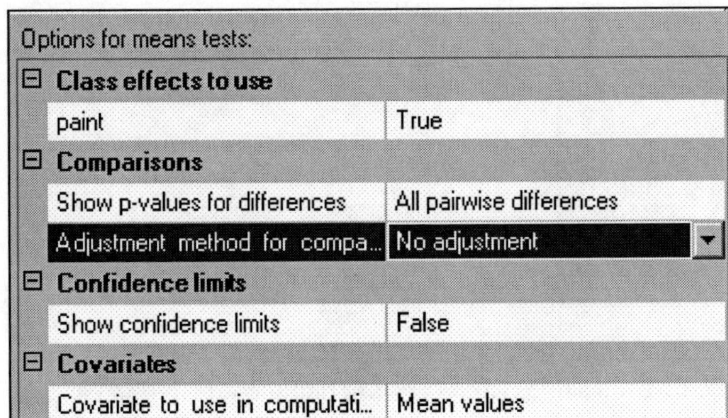

7. Select **Run** to submit the task.

8. Select **Yes** to replace the results of the previous run.

The resulting output is the same with the addition of two tables.

The GLM Procedure
Least Squares Means

paint	bright LSMEAN	LSMEAN Number
1	52.8571429	1
2	74.4285714	2
3	63.7142857	3
4	68.8571429	4

The first table shows a set of adjusted means for each level of paint. Because there is only one predictor variable, the adjusted means are the same as the non-adjusted.

Least Squares Means for effect paint
Pr > |t| for H0: LSMean(i)=LSMean(j)
Dependent Variable: bright

i/j	1	2	3	4
1		<.0001	0.0062	0.0002
2	<.0001		0.0068	0.1365
3	0.0062	0.0068		0.1679
4	0.0002	0.1365	0.1679	

The next table shows a set of *p*-values for pairwise comparisons of means. Notice that row 2--column 4, has the same *p*-value as row 4--column 2, because the same two means are being compared in each case. Both are displayed as a convenience to the user. Notice also that row 1--column 1, row 2--column 2, and so forth, are left blank, because it does not make any sense to compare a mean to itself.

The table shows that there is a statistically significant difference between paints 2 and 4, between paints 2 and 3, and between paint 1 and all other levels of paint with alpha=0.05.

Note: To ensure overall protection level, only probabilities associated with pre-planned comparisons should be used.

The note below the table warns you that you are not controlling for the number of comparisons you are making.

Because you are considering all the pairs, a more valid test would be to use the Tukey adjustment method.

9. Reopen the Linear Models task and change the Adjustment method from **`No adjustment`** to **`Tukey`**.

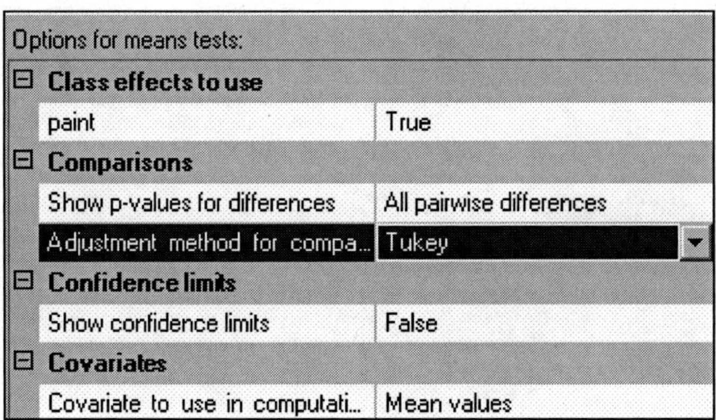

10. Select **Run** to rerun the task. Select **Yes** to replace the results of the previous run.

The GLM Procedure
Least Squares Means
Adjustment for Multiple Comparisons: Tukey

paint	bright LSMEAN	LSMEAN Number
1	52.8571429	1
2	74.4285714	2
3	63.7142857	3
4	68.8571429	4

Least Squares Means for effect paint
Pr > |t| for H0: LSMean(i)=LSMean(j)
Dependent Variable: bright

i/j	1	2	3	4
1		<.0001	0.0294	0.0010
2	<.0001		0.0321	0.4302
3	0.0294	0.0321		0.4985
4	0.0010	0.4302	0.4985	

The output indicates that paint formula 1 is different from all other formulas and that paint formulas 2 and 3 are different from each other at the .05 level. There are fewer differences than were found without controlling the experimentwise error rate. Also notice that the *p*-values are larger when the experimentwise error rate is controlled.

If you had used Bonferroni, an even more conservative test, the *p*-values would have been even larger, but in this case, the conclusions are the same.

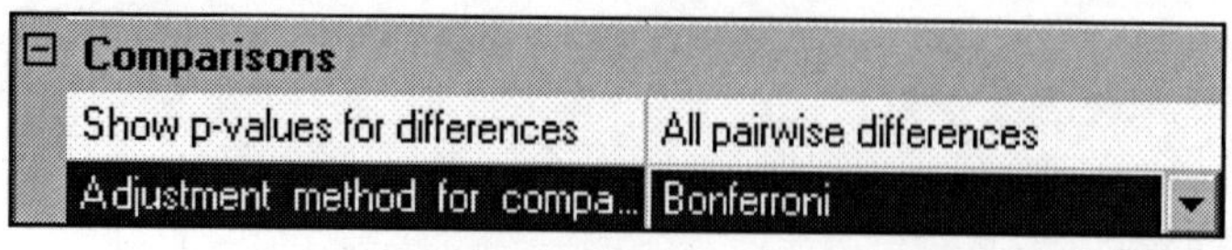

The GLM Procedure
Least Squares Means
Adjustment for Multiple Comparisons: Bonferroni

paint	bright LSMEAN	LSMEAN Number
1	52.8571429	1
2	74.4285714	2
3	63.7142857	3
4	68.8571429	4

Least Squares Means for effect paint
Pr > |t| for H0: LSMean(i)=LSMean(j)
Dependent Variable: bright

i/j	1	2	3	4
1		<.0001	0.0371	0.0011
2	<.0001		0.0407	0.8193
3	0.0371	0.0407		1.0000
4	0.0011	0.8193	1.0000	

Assigning Treatments within Blocks

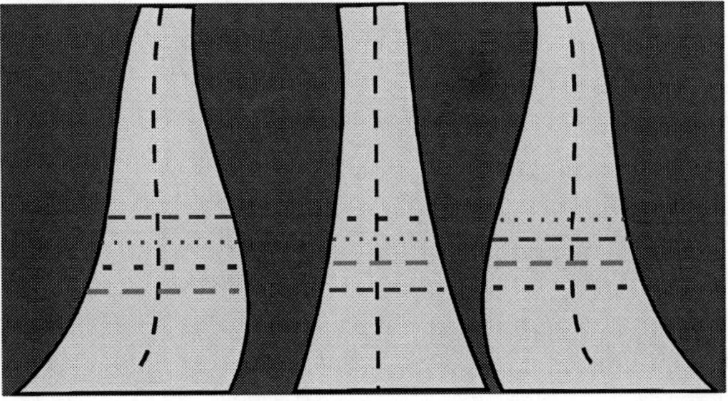

36

An experienced road paint expert might anticipate that there would be so much variability in brightness caused by the nuisance factors that the statistical test would not detect differences caused by paint formulas alone. By including road in the model, you could account for some nuisance factors.

In order to estimate the model properly, you would need at least one stripe for each paint/road combination.

An experimental design like this is often referred to as a *randomized block design*, where `road` is the blocking factor. The variable road is included in the model, but you are not interested in the effect of `road`, only in controlling the variation it represents. By including `road` in the model, you could account for a nuisance factor.

Blocking is a restriction on randomization.

Including a Blocking Factor in the Model

Brightness = Base Level + Road + Paint Formula + Unaccounted for Variation

$$Y_{ijk} = \mu + \alpha_i + \tau_j + \varepsilon_{ijk}$$

37

Nuisance Factors

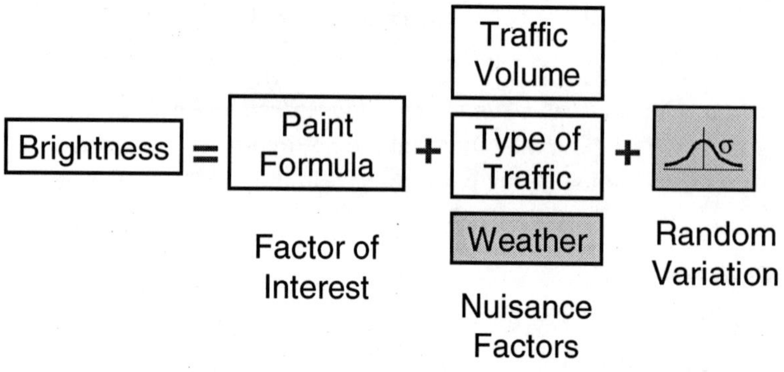

Brightness = Paint Formula + Traffic Volume / Type of Traffic / Weather + σ

Factor of Interest

Nuisance Factors

Random Variation

38

Weather is just one of many possible nuisance factors.

Including a Blocking Factor in the Model

Additional assumptions are

- treatments are randomly assigned within each block
- the effects of the blocking factor are additive.

In the paint example, the design is balanced, which means that there is the same number of paint stripes for every paint/road combination.

39

If the effects of the blocking factor are not additive, then this condition is called *interaction*. You can still analyze the data, but be sure to collect enough data to include the blocking factor in the model. Interactions are discussed in the next section.

In most randomized block designs, the blocking factor is treated as a *random effect*. Treating an effect as random changes how standard errors are calculated and can give different answers from treating it as a fixed effect (as in the example).

In this example, you have the same number of paint stripes for every paint/road combination. This is a balanced design. When treatment groups are going to be compared to each other (in other words, not to 0 or some other specified value), the results from treating the block as a fixed or random effect are exactly the same.

A model that includes both random and fixed effects is called a *mixed model* and can be analyzed with the Mixed Models task or the MIXED procedure. The SAS class *Mixed Models Analyses Using the SAS System* focuses on analyzing mixed models. *Statistics II: ANOVA and Regression* has more detail about how to analyze nonbalanced designs and data that does not meet the ANOVA assumptions, and it is a prerequisite for *Mixed Model Analysis Using the SAS System.*

For more information on mixed models in SAS, you can also consult the SAS online documentation or the SAS Book By User *SAS System for Mixed Models*, which also goes into detail about the statistical assumptions for mixed models. You can learn more about different types of experimental designs by taking the SAS class *Designing Experiments Using the ADX Interface.*

Two-Way ANOVA

Use the **PAINTSBLOCKEDROAD** data set to analyze the difference between paint formulas using **road** as a blocking factor.

To view the new data set, double-click **PAINTSBLOCKEDROAD** in the process flow.

SASUSER.PAINTSBLOCKEDROAD (read-only)

	road	paint	bright
1	Broadway	1	48
2	Main St.	1	49
3	Center St.	1	49
4	Center St.	3	56
5	Elm St.	1	57
6	Main St.	3	57
7	Station Rd.	1	58
8	Broadway	3	59
9	Beech St.	1	60
10	Park Dr.	1	61

Notice there is one row for every paint/road combination.

1. With the **PAINTSBLOCKEDROAD** table highlighted, select **Analyze** ⇨ **ANOVA** ⇨ **Linear Models**.

2. With **Task Roles** selected on the left, drag and drop **bright** to the Dependent variable role and **paint** and **road** to the Classification variables role.

3. Select **Model** on the left. Select **paint** and **road** under **Class and quantitative variables** and click **Main** to move them to the **Effects** panel.

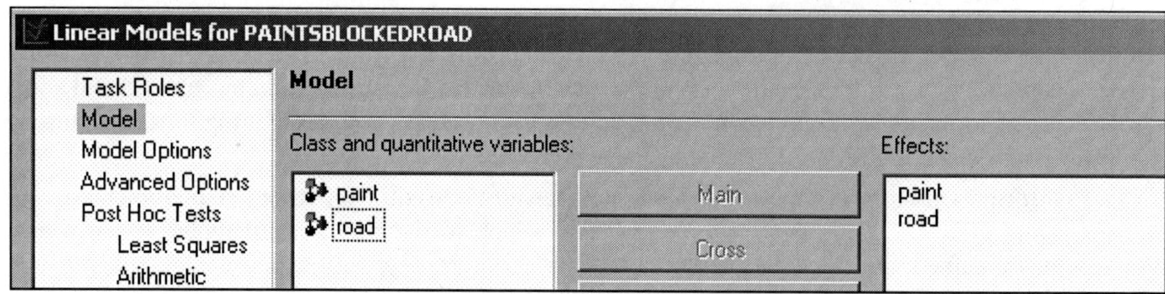

4. Select **Model Options** on the left. Uncheck the box next to **Show parameter estimates**.

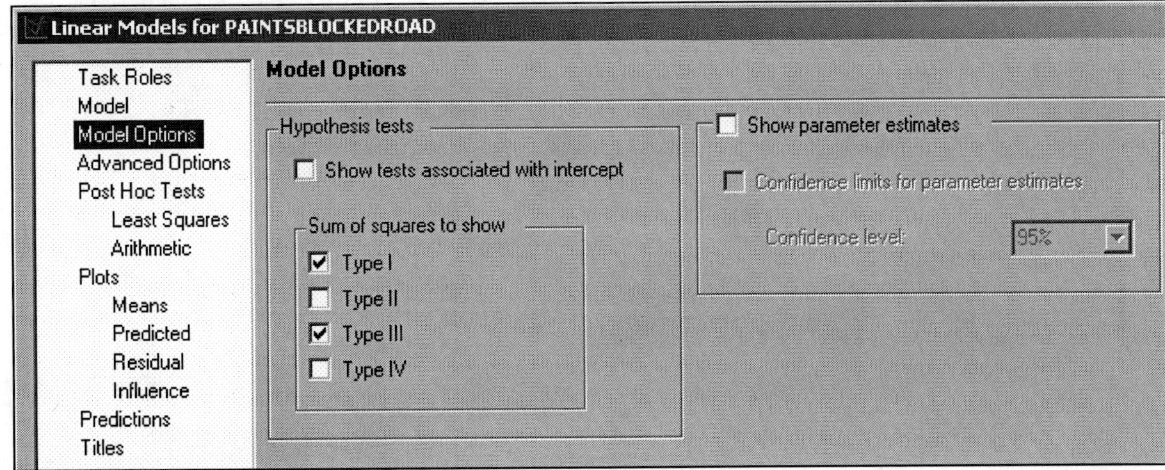

5. On the left, select **Least Squares** under Post Hoc Tests.

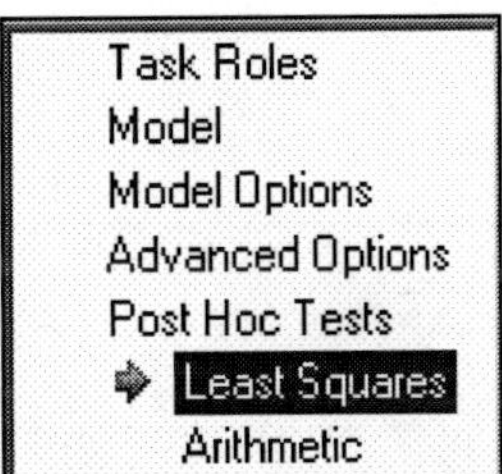

6. Select **Add** at the bottom. The right-hand panel automatically populates with a set of choices.

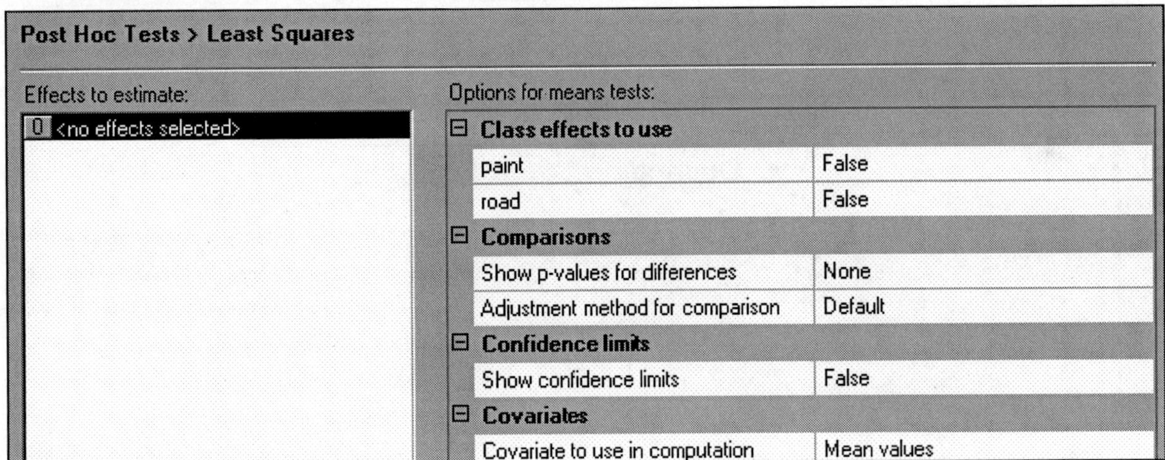

7. Change the Effects to use selection for `paint` to **True** (instead of `False`). Change the **Show p-values for differences** selection to `All pairwise differences`. Change the **Adjustment method** to `Tukey`.

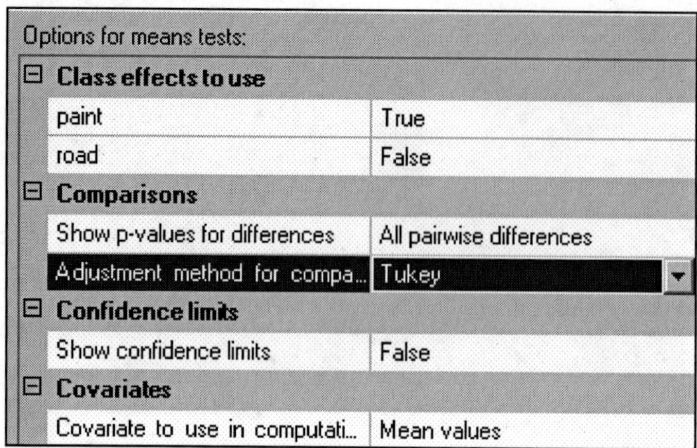

8. Select **Run** to submit the analysis.

The GLM Procedure

Class Level Information

Class	Levels	Values
road	7	Beech St. Broadway Center St. Elm St. Main St. Park Dr. Station Rd.
paint	4	1 2 3 4

Number of Observations Read	28
Number of Observations Used	28

Dependent Variable: bright

Source	DF	Sum of Squares	Mean Square	F Value	Pr > F
Model	9	1804.857143	200.539683	60.16	<.0001
Error	18	60.000000	3.333333		
Corrected Total	27	1864.857143			

R-Square	Coeff Var	Root MSE	bright Mean
0.967826	2.833746	1.825742	64.42857

As expected, the overall *F* test indicates there are significant differences between the means. However, because there are two predictor variables, the differences could be due to **road**, **paint**, or both.

What have you gained by including **road** in the model? The estimate of the experimental error variance or mean square estimate (MSE) has decreased compared to the model that included **paint** only (3.33333 versus 45.78571). Depending on the magnitude of the decrease, this may affect the comparisons between the treatment means by finding more significant differences than the **paint** only model.

Source	DF	Type I SS	Mean Square	F Value	Pr > F
paint	3	1100.000000	366.666667	110.00	<.0001
road	6	704.857143	117.476190	35.24	<.0001

Source	DF	Type III SS	Mean Square	F Value	Pr > F
paint	3	1100.000000	366.666667	110.00	<.0001
road	6	704.857143	117.476190	35.24	<.0001

In determining the usefulness of having **road** included in the model you can consider the *F* value for the block. Some statisticians suggest that if this ratio is greater than 1, then the new variable is useful. But if the ratio is less than 1, then adding the variable is detrimental to the analysis. If you find that including the **road** effect is detrimental to the analysis, then you can exclude it from future studies, but it must be included in ANOVA models calculated with the sample you have already collected.

In this case, the Type I and Type III SS are the same because the design is *balanced* (there is an equal number of observations for each paint/road combination). Unbalanced designs will produce Type I and Type III SS that are different.

The GLM Procedure
Least Squares Means
Adjustment for Multiple Comparisons: Tukey

paint	bright LSMEAN	LSMEAN Number
1	54.5714286	1
2	69.7142857	2
3	63.4285714	3
4	70.0000000	4

Least Squares Means for effect paint
Pr > |t| for H0: LSMean(i)=LSMean(j)
Dependent Variable: bright

i/j	1	2	3	4
1		<.0001	<.0001	<.0001
2	<.0001		<.0001	0.9910
3	<.0001	<.0001		<.0001
4	<.0001	0.9910	<.0001	

In this case, with the blocking factor in the model, paint formulas 2 and 4 are the only ones found not to be significantly different. Also note that all of the *p*-values have decreased as compared to the `paint` only model.

2.3 Two-Way ANOVA with Interactions

Objectives

- Fit a two-way ANOVA model.
- Detect interactions between factors.
- Analyze the treatments when there is a significant interaction.

42

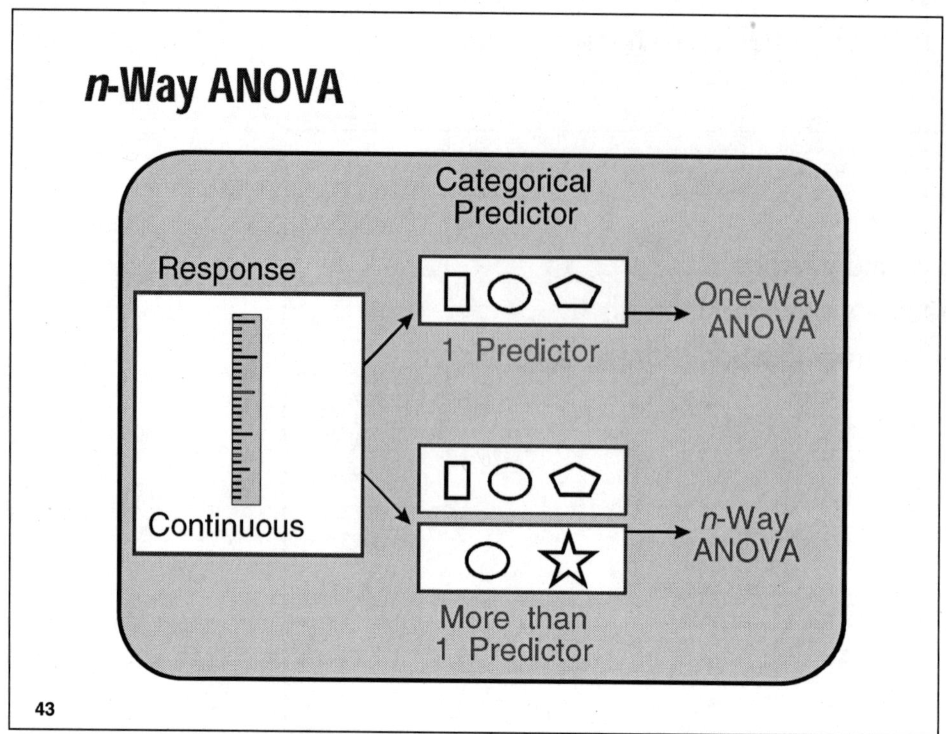

In the previous section, you considered the case where you had one categorical predictor and a blocking variable. In this section, consider a case with two categorical predictors. In general, any time you have more than one categorical predictor variable and a continuous response variable, it is called *n*-way ANOVA. The *n* can be replaced with the number of categorical predictor variables.

The analysis for a randomized complete block design is actually a special type of *n*-way ANOVA.

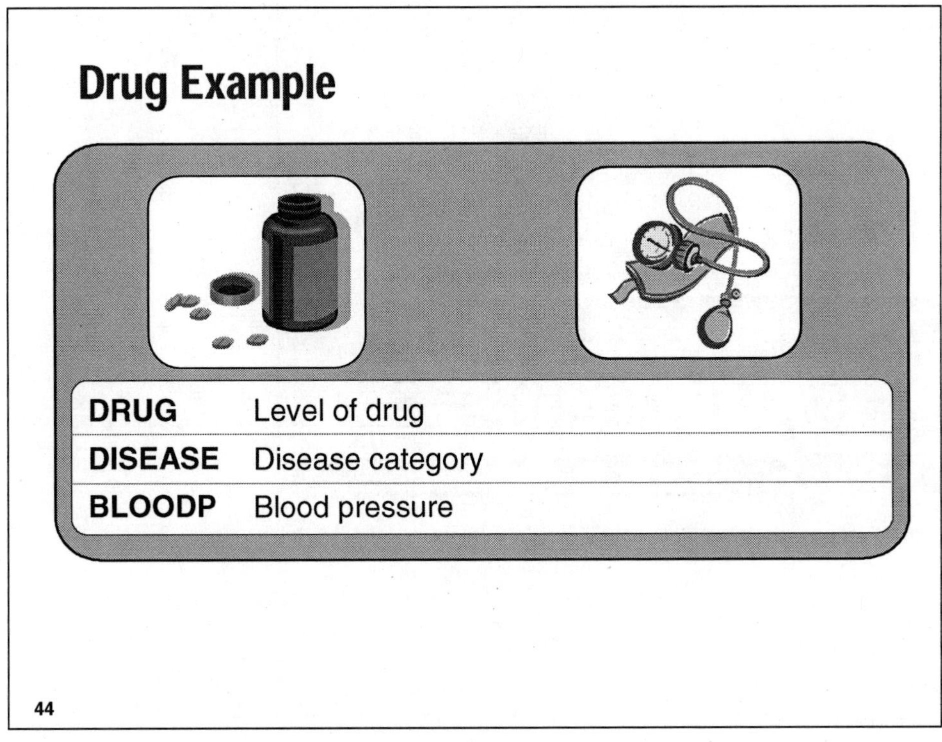

Drug Example
DRUG Level of drug
DISEASE Disease category
BLOODP Blood pressure
44

Data was collected in an effort to determine whether different levels of a given drug have an effect on blood pressure for people with a given disease.

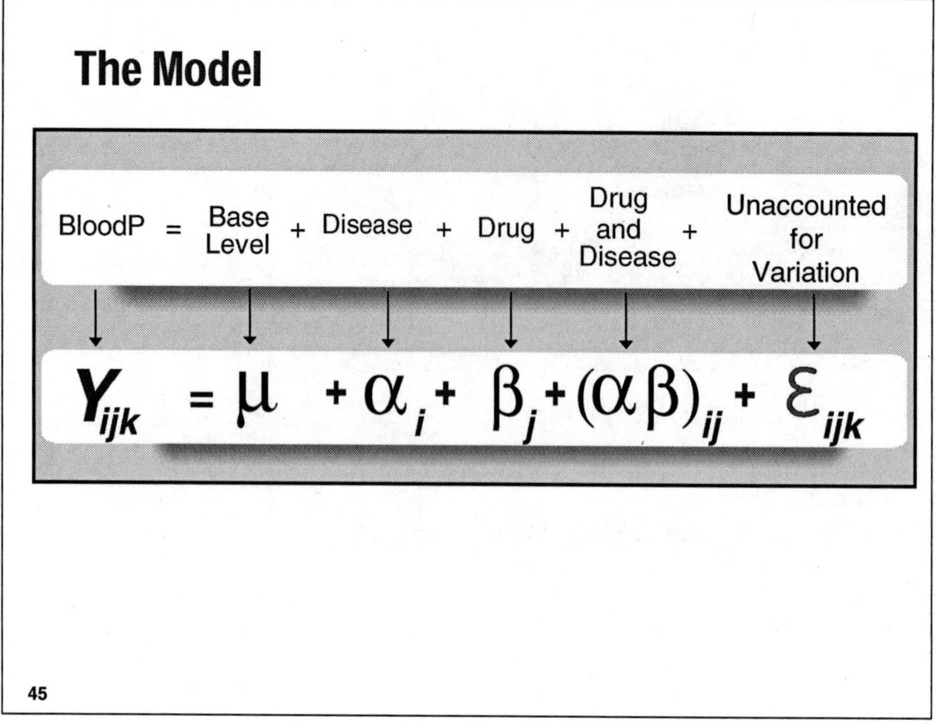

The Model
BloodP = Base Level + Disease + Drug + Drug and Disease + Unaccounted for Variation
$Y_{ijk} = \mu + \alpha_i + \beta_j + (\alpha\beta)_{ij} + \varepsilon_{ijk}$
45

Y_{ijk} the observed **BloodP** for each subject

μ the overall population mean of the response, **BloodP**

α_i the effect of the *i*th **Disease**

β_j the effect of the *j*th **Drug**

$(\alpha\beta)_{ij}$ the effect of the interaction between the *i*th **Disease** and the *j*th **Drug**

ε_{ijk} error term, or residual

In the model it is assumed that the

- observations are independent
- data is normal for each treatment
- variances are approximately equal for each treatment.

Verifying ANOVA assumptions with more than two variables is covered in *Statistics II: ANOVA and Regression.*

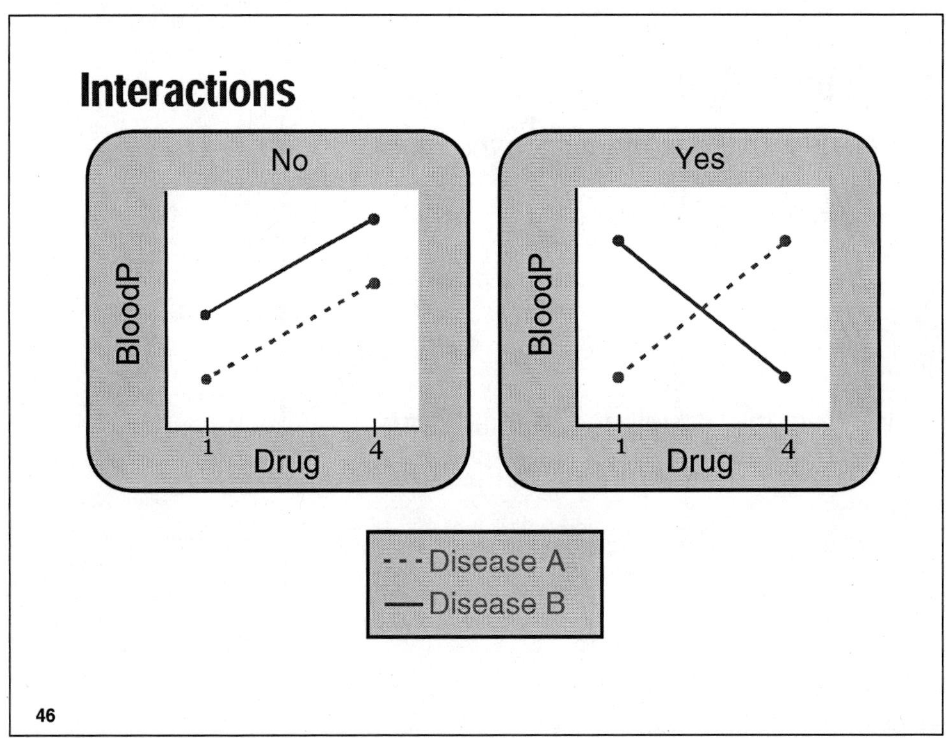

An interaction occurs when changing the level of one factor results in changing the difference between levels of the other factor.

The plots displayed above are called means plots. The average blood pressure over different levels of the drug were plotted and then connected for disease A and B.

In the left plot above, different types of disease show the same change across different levels of drug.

However, in the right plot, the average blood pressure increases for disease A and decreases for disease B. This indicates an interaction between `Drug` and `Disease`.

When you analyze an *n*-way ANOVA, the first consideration must be to determine whether or not there is interaction between the factors. This is done by looking at the test for interaction on the ANOVA table.

If there is no interaction between the factors, then the tests for the individual factor effects can be considered in the table to determine the significance/nonsignificance of these factors.

If there is an interaction between the factors, the tests for the individual factor effects might be misleading due to masking of these effects by the interaction.

In the previous section, you used a block variable and a categorical predictor as effects in the model. It is generally assumed that blocks do not interact with factors.

Nonsignificant Interaction

Analyze the main effects with the interaction in the model.

$$Y_{ijk} = \mu + \alpha_i + \beta_j + (\alpha\beta)_{ij} + \varepsilon_{ijk}$$

...or...

$$Y_{ijk} = \mu + \alpha_i + \beta_j + \varepsilon_{ijk}$$

Delete the interaction from the model, and then analyze the main effects.

47

When the interaction is not statistically significant, the main effects can be analyzed with the model as originally written. This is generally the method used when analyzing designed experiments.

However, even when analyzing designed experiments, some statisticians suggest that if the interaction is nonsignificant, then the interaction effect can be deleted from the model and then the main effects are analyzed. This increases the power of the main effects tests. A suggested guideline for deleting the interaction from the model is when

- there are fewer than 5 degrees of freedom for the error, **and**
- the mean square for the interaction divided by the error mean square is less than 2.

Neter, J., Kutner, M.H., Wasserman, W., and Nachtsheim, C.J. (1996), *Applied Linear Statistical Models*, Fourth Edition, New York: WCB McGraw Hill.

When you analyze data from an observational study, it is more common to delete the nonsignificant interaction from the model and then analyze the main effects.

Two-Way ANOVA with Interactions

To view the **DRUG** data set, double-click it in the project tree.

SASUSER.DRUG (read-only)

	Drug	Disease	Bloodp
1	1	A	119.70095982
2	1	A	121.36188924
3	1	A	119.69180851
4	1	A	119.60217745
5	1	A	120.96573695
6	1	A	119.18963686
7	1	A	120.04126616
8	1	A	120.6485107
9	1	A	121.39677755
10	1	A	121.2941861

You can produce descriptive statistics for **BloodP** by **Drug** and **Disease** using the Summary Statistics task.

1. With the **DRUG** data set highlighted, select **Describe** ⇨ **Summary Statistics**.
2. Drag and drop **BloodP** to the Analysis variables role. Drag and drop **Disease** and **Drug** to the Classification variables role, as shown below.

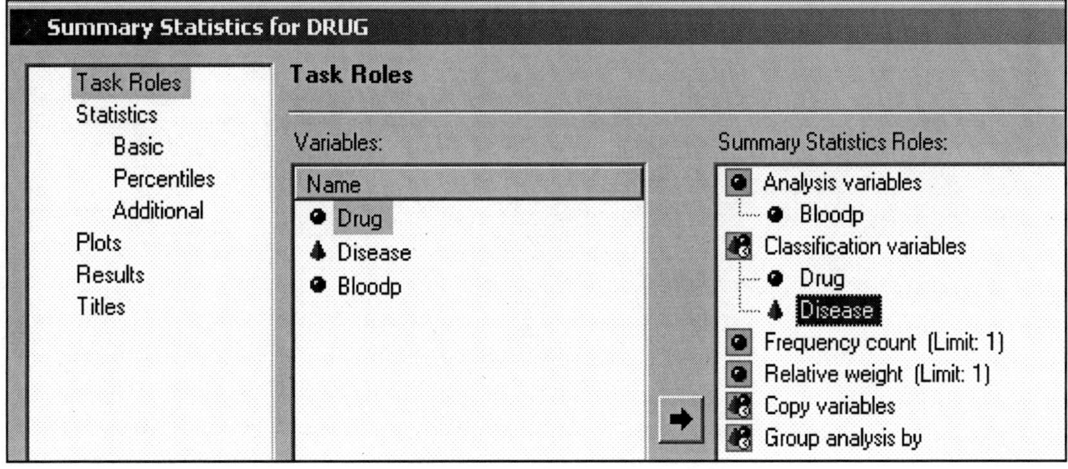

3. Select **Run** to submit the task.

Analysis Variable : Bloodp							
Drug	Disease	N Obs	Mean	Std Dev	Minimum	Maximum	N
1	A	10	120.3892949	0.8379484	119.1896369	121.3967776	10
	B	10	159.8746313	1.4696801	157.8492618	162.4582518	10
	C	10	124.8205390	1.1230988	122.9747579	126.2390290	10
2	A	10	135.3892949	0.8379484	134.1896369	136.3967776	10
	B	10	149.7218911	0.8476733	148.4310401	151.6754030	10
	C	10	124.8345403	1.0161806	123.2942123	126.5964724	10
3	A	10	139.7062141	0.6271086	139.1767099	141.1651971	10
	B	10	140.0273514	0.5443927	139.3493057	140.8466318	10
	C	10	124.6400672	0.7675940	123.7285012	126.0078360	10
4	A	10	149.9168917	1.0654820	148.4562866	151.2275231	10
	B	10	130.1873041	0.7652515	129.0574219	131.6361968	10
	C	10	125.1261637	0.8759408	123.2269428	126.4101276	10

A graph might also be useful in picturing the relationship between `Disease` and `Drug` and `BloodP`.

1. With the `DRUG` data set highlighted, select **Graph** ⇨ **Line Plot**.

2. In the **Line Plot** pane, select **Multiple line plots by group column**.

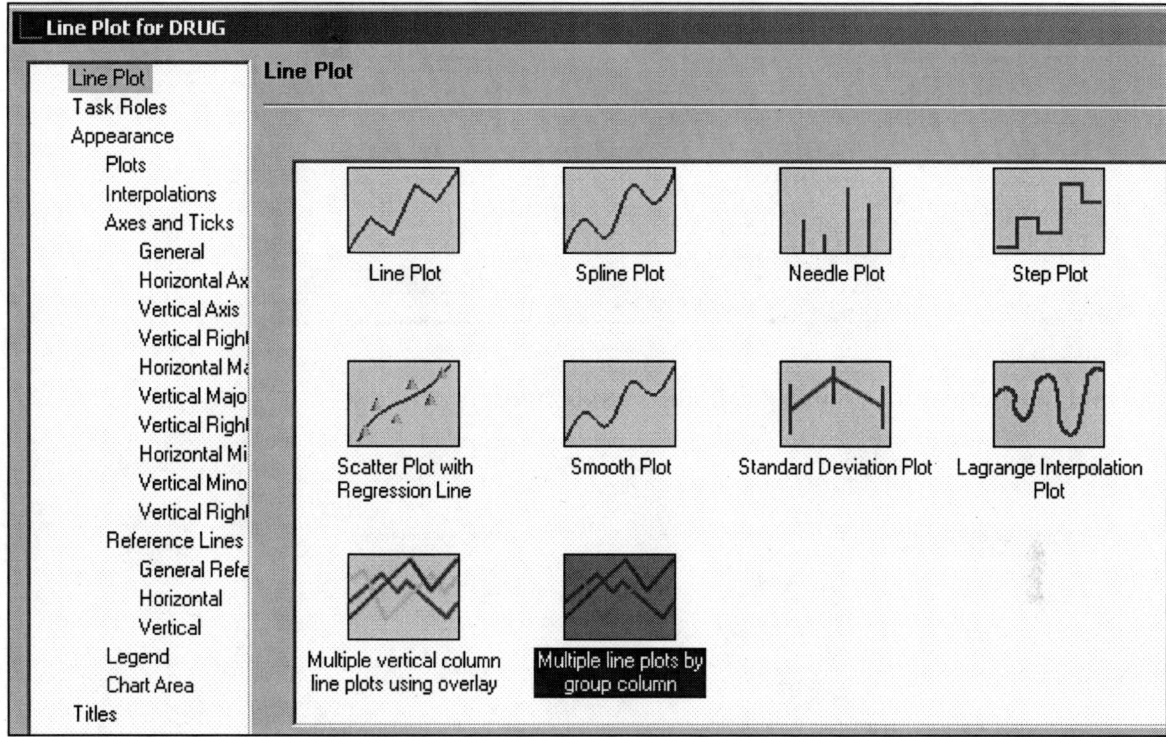

3. Select **Task Roles** on the left. Drag and drop `Drug` to the Horizontal role, `BloodP` to the Vertical role, and `Disease` to the Group role.

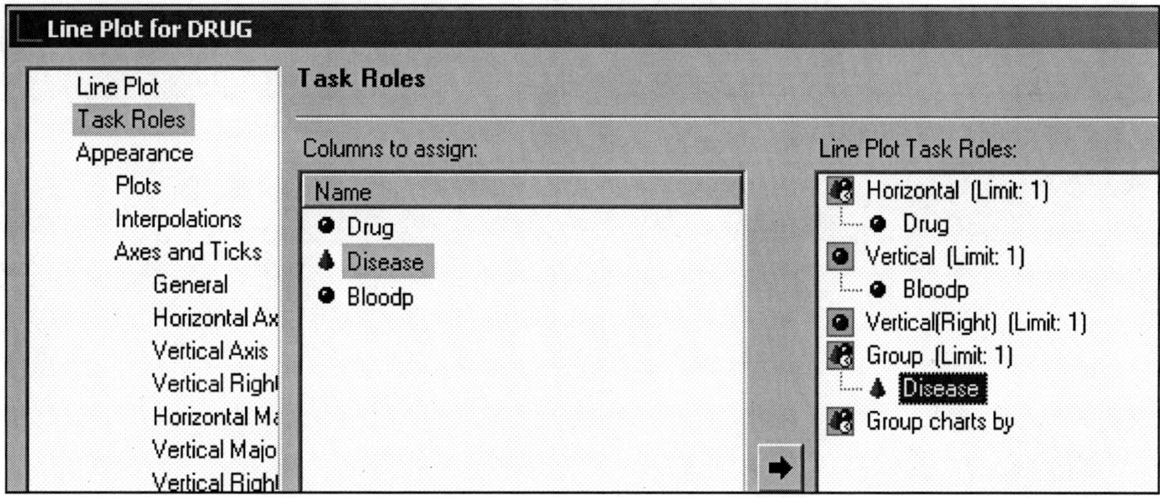

4. Select **Interpolations** on the left under Appearance.

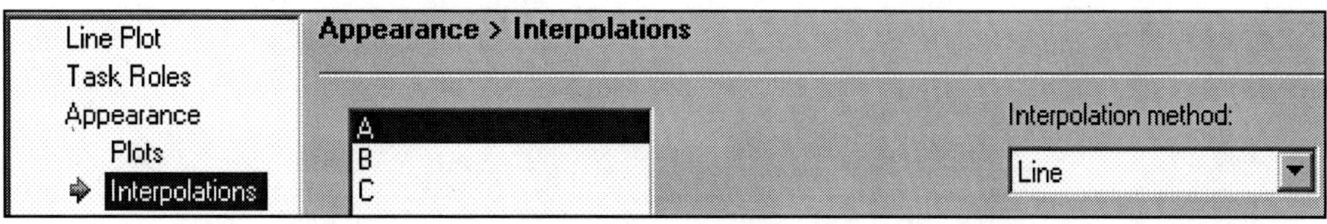

5. For each value of `Disease`, change the interpolation method from `Line` to `STD`.

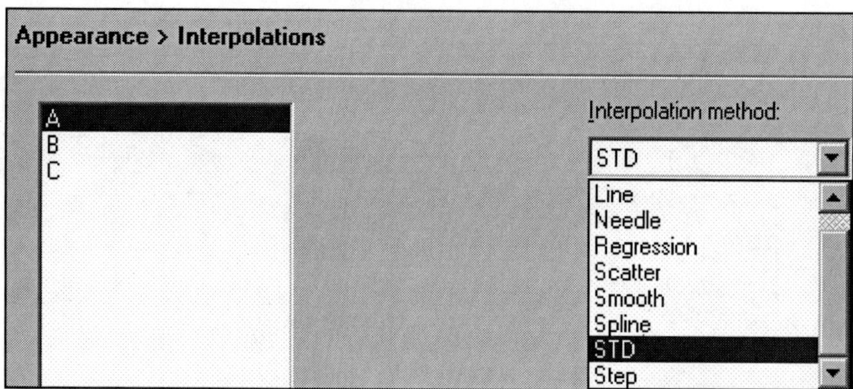

6. For each value of disease, check the boxes next to **Join the means with a line** and **Add tops and bottoms to each line**.

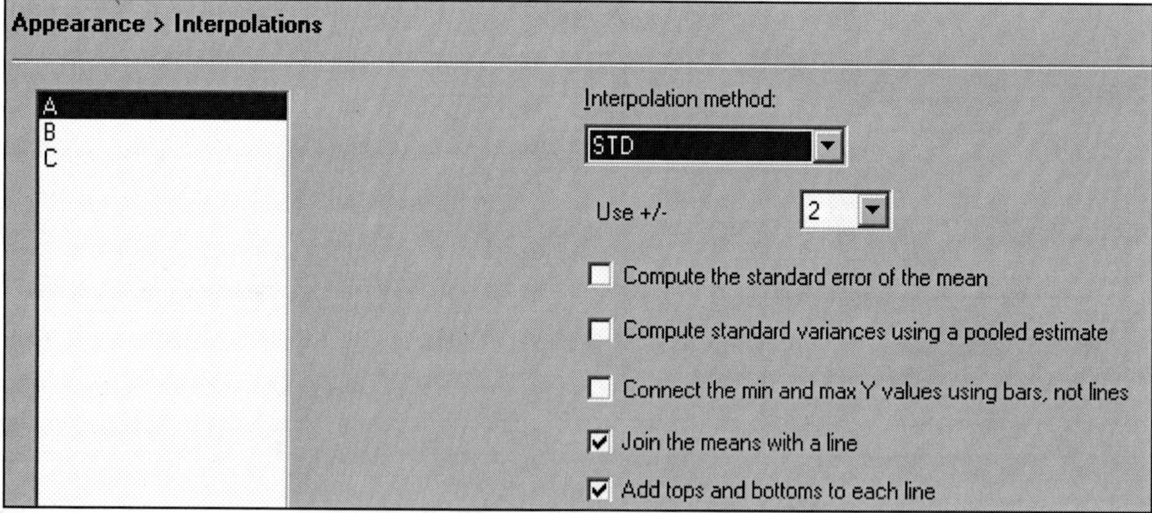

7. Select **Run** to submit the task.

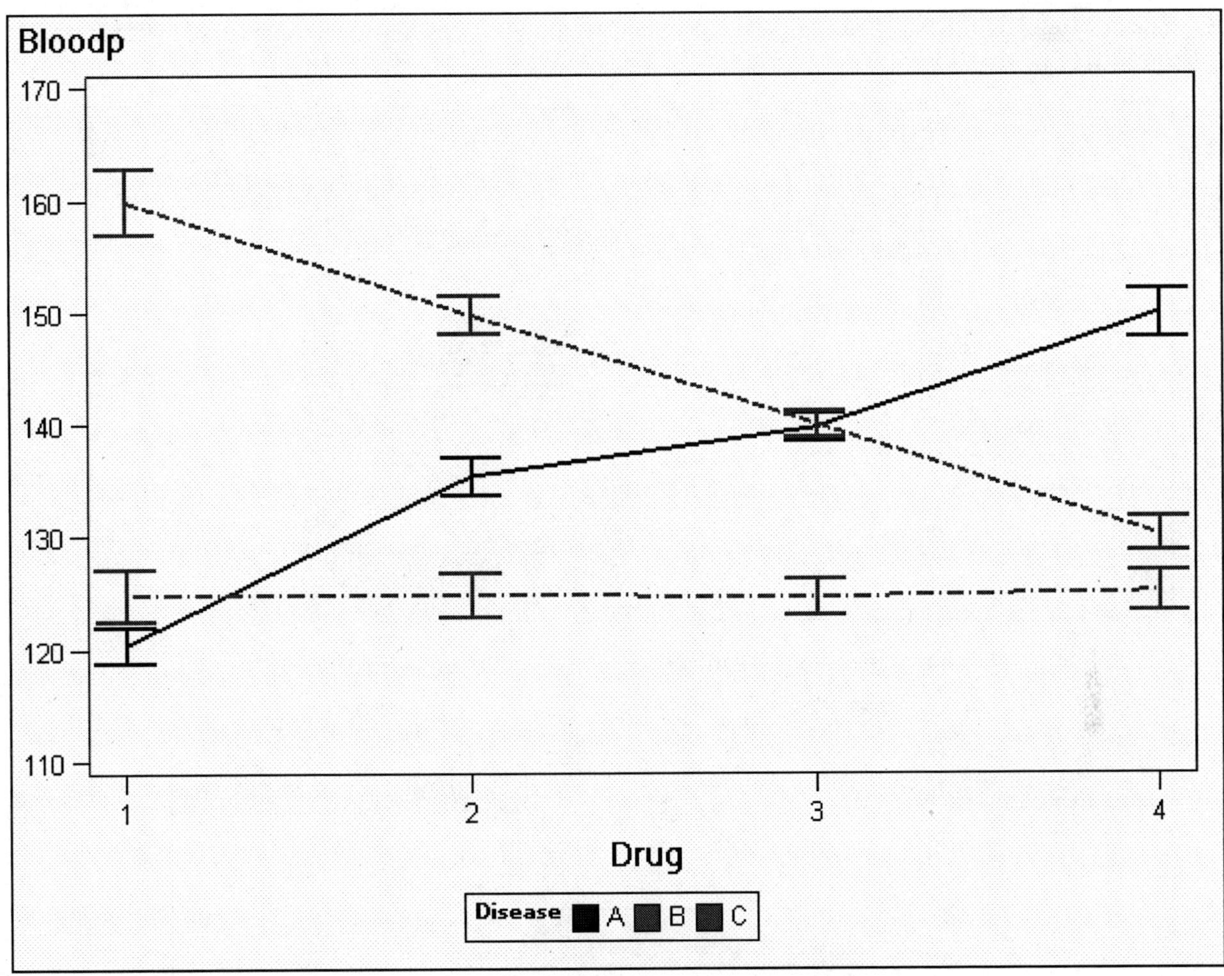

The dotted and dashed lines shown in the book were created for printing purposes. You can change the line style on the **Plots** panel under Appearance.

The graph shows the same relationship that was seen in the Summary Statistics output. For people with disease A (solid line), the blood pressure value seems to rise for increased levels of drug. For disease B (dashed line), the blood pressure value seems to fall for increased values of drug, and for disease C (dashed and dotted line), the blood pressure value seems to stays the same no matter what the value for drug.

To see if this interaction and these differences by `Drug` are statistically significant, use the Linear Models task.

1. With the `DRUG` table highlighted, select **Analyze** ⇨ **ANOVA** ⇨ **Linear Models**.

2. With **Task Roles** selected on the left, drag and drop `BloodP` to the Dependent variable role and `Disease` and `Drug` to the Classification variables role. Be sure `Disease` is first, followed by `Drug`.

3. Select **Model** on the left. Select **Disease**. Hold down the Shift key and select **Drug** under **Class and quantitative variables**.

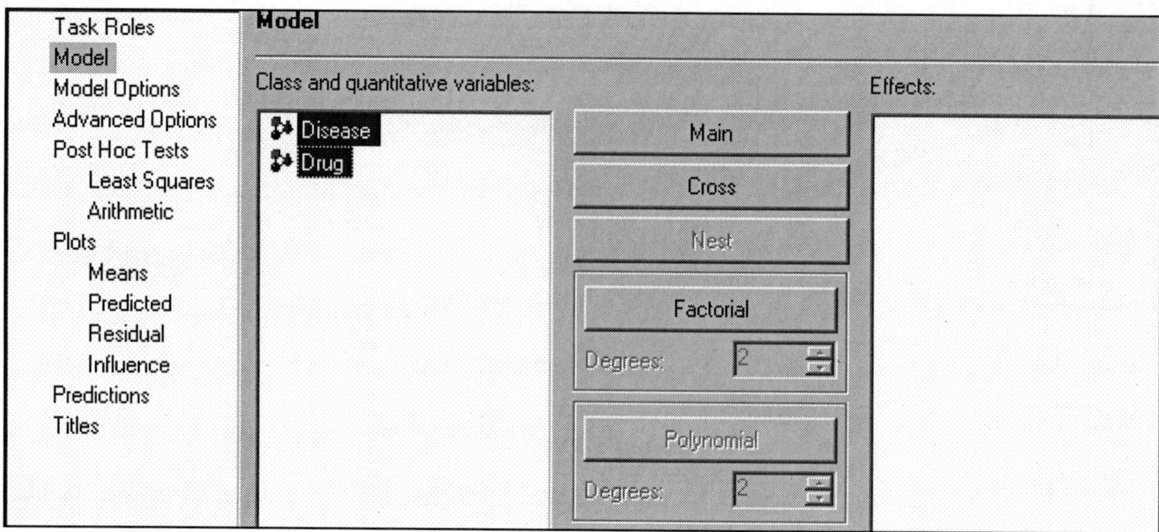

4. Click **Factorial** to move them to the **Effects** panel and create an interaction.

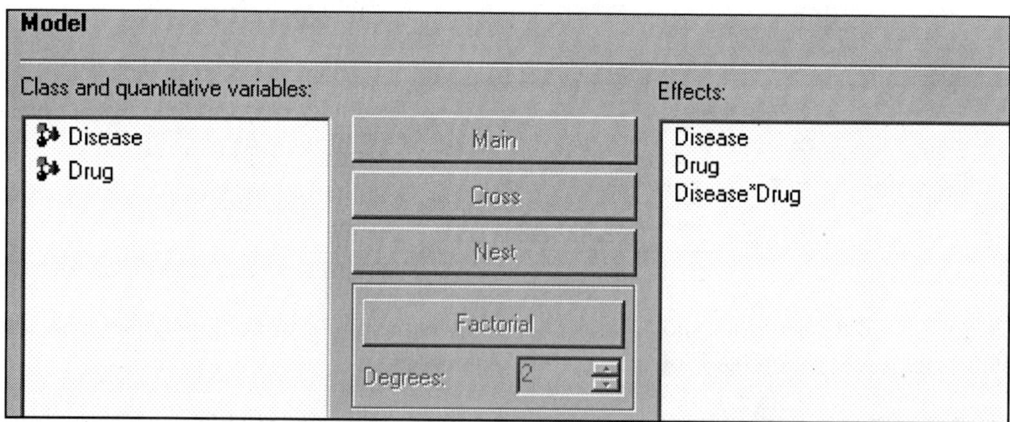

5. Select **Model Options** on the left. Uncheck the box next to **Show parameter estimates**.

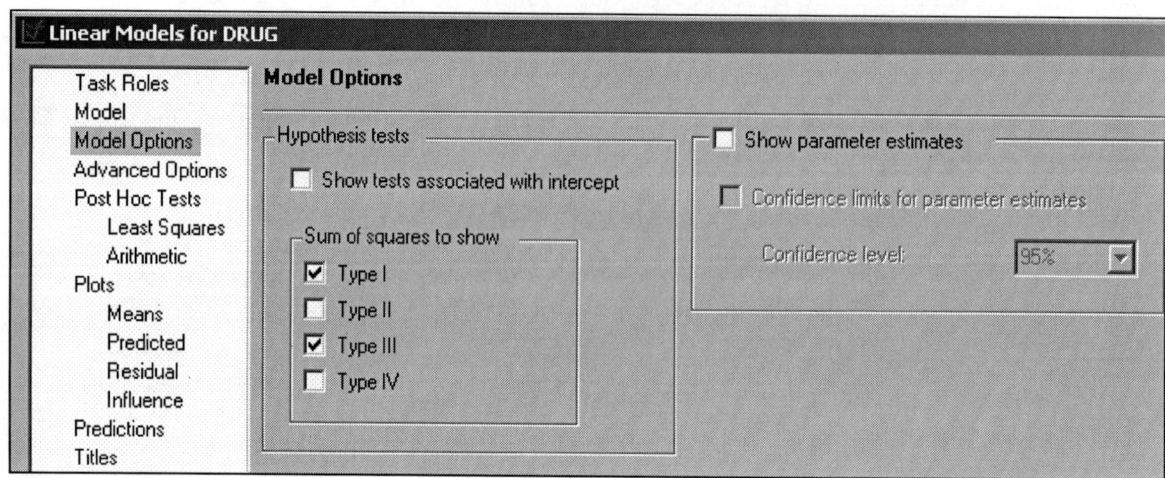

6. Select **Run** to run the analysis.

The first page of the output specifies the number of levels and the values of the class variables in the model, as well as the number of observations. You can verify that your variables were specified correctly here.

Linear Models

The GLM Procedure

Class Level Information		
Class	Levels	Values
Disease	3	A B C
Drug	4	1 2 3 4

Number of Observations Read	120
Number of Observations Used	120

The next part of the output, below, shows the source table with the *F* test for the overall model. This tests the null hypothesis that none of the effects in the model are statistically different, in other words, that there is no difference between the group means.

Dependent Variable: Bloodp

Source	DF	Sum of Squares	Mean Square	F Value	Pr > F
Model	11	17521.93235	1592.90294	1847.96	<.0001
Error	108	93.09386	0.86198		
Corrected Total	119	17615.02621			

R-Square	Coeff Var	Root MSE	Bloodp Mean
0.994715	0.685763	0.928429	135.3862

The descriptive statistics indicate that the average blood pressure for all observations is 135.3862. The R^2 for this model is approximately 0.994715.

The *p*-value given is <0.0001. Presuming an alpha equal to 0.05, you reject the null hypothesis and conclude that at least one treatment mean is different from one other treatment mean. Which factor(s) cause this difference?

The next part of the output shows tests of the main effects and the interaction.

Source	DF	Type I SS	Mean Square	F Value	Pr > F
Disease	2	8133.949263	4066.974632	4718.18	<.0001
Drug	3	65.146099	21.715366	25.19	<.0001
Disease*Drug	6	9322.836989	1553.806165	1802.60	<.0001

Source	DF	Type III SS	Mean Square	F Value	Pr > F
Disease	2	8133.949263	4066.974632	4718.18	<.0001
Drug	3	65.146099	21.715366	25.19	<.0001
Disease*Drug	6	9322.836989	1553.806165	1802.60	<.0001

The sums of squares are used to test the null hypothesis that the effect of the individual terms in the model is not significant. You should consider the test for the interaction first. The *p*-value is <0.0001. Presuming an alpha of 0.05, you reject the null hypothesis. You have sufficient evidence to conclude that there is an interaction between the two factors. As shown in the graph, the effect of the level of drug changes for different disease types.

Because of the interaction, you do not want to test the factors separately for differences between the means. Instead, specify that differences across treatment groups are supposed to be tested for both factors simultaneously.

1. Reopen the Linear Models task by double-clicking or right-clicking and selecting **Open**.

2. On the left, select **Least Squares** under **Post Hoc Tests**. Select **Add** at the bottom. The right-hand panel automatically populates with a set of choices.

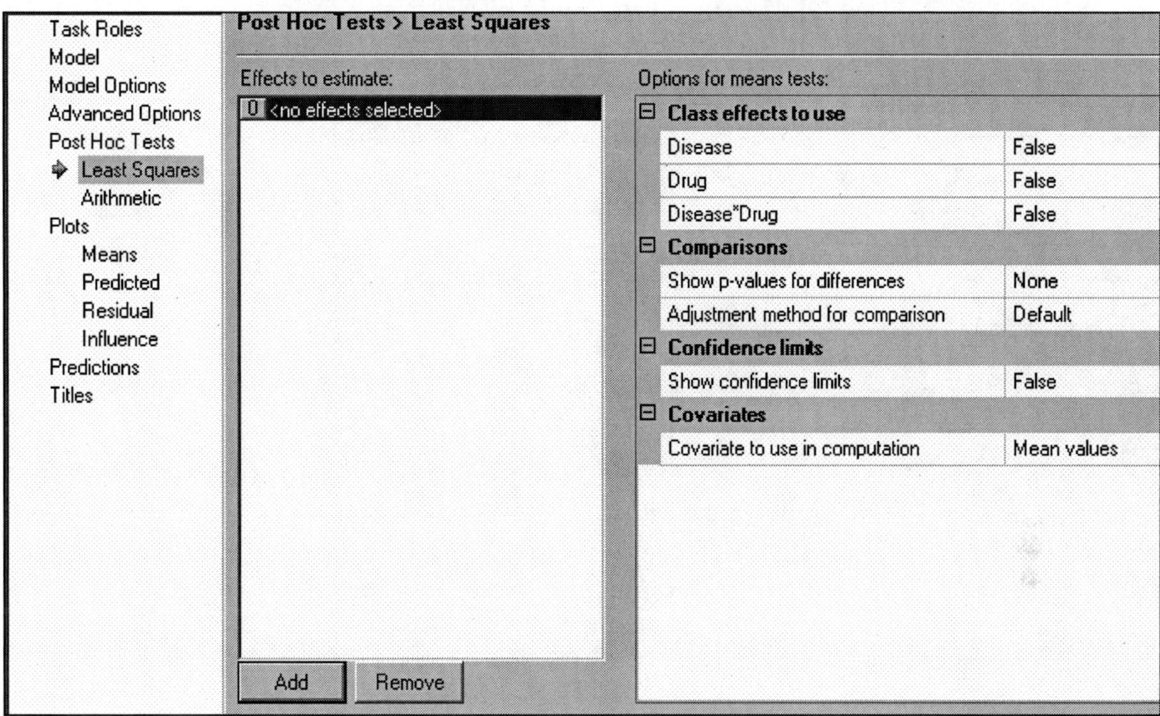

3. Change the **Class effects to use** option for `Disease*Drug` to `True` (instead of `False`). Change the **Show p-values for differences** selection to `All pairwise differences`. Change the **Adjustment method** to `Tukey`.

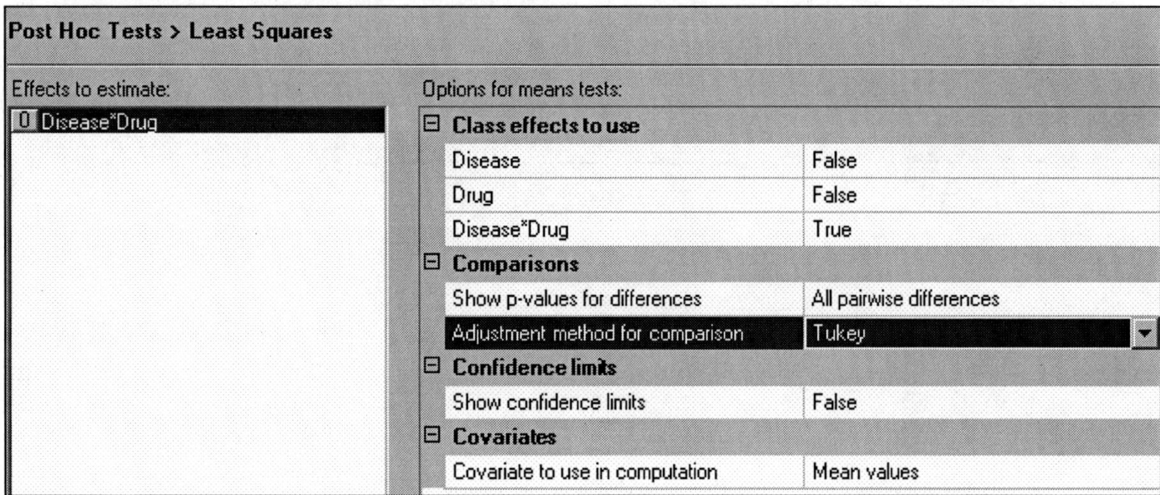

4. Select **Run** to submit the analysis. Select **Yes** to replace the results from the previous run.

The results are the same with the addition of two tables. The first shows each possible grouping of `Disease` and `Drug`, assigns it a number, and reports the mean for the group.

The GLM Procedure
Least Squares Means
Adjustment for Multiple Comparisons: Tukey

Disease	Drug	Bloodp LSMEAN	LSMEAN Number
A	1	120.389295	1
A	2	135.389295	2
A	3	139.706214	3
A	4	149.916892	4
B	1	159.874631	5
B	2	149.721891	6
B	3	140.027351	7
B	4	130.187304	8
C	1	124.820539	9
C	2	124.834540	10
C	3	124.640067	11
C	4	125.126164	12

Least Squares Means for effect Disease*Drug Pr > |t| for H0: LSMean(i)=LSMean(j) Dependent Variable: Bloodp												
i/j	1	2	3	4	5	6	7	8	9	10	11	12
1		<.0001	<.0001	<.0001	<.0001	<.0001	<.0001	<.0001	<.0001	<.0001	<.0001	<.0001
2	<.0001		<.0001	<.0001	<.0001	<.0001	<.0001	<.0001	<.0001	<.0001	<.0001	<.0001
3	<.0001	<.0001		<.0001	<.0001	<.0001	0.9998	<.0001	<.0001	<.0001	<.0001	<.0001
4	<.0001	<.0001	<.0001		<.0001	1.0000	<.0001	<.0001	<.0001	<.0001	<.0001	<.0001
5	<.0001	<.0001	<.0001	<.0001		<.0001	<.0001	<.0001	<.0001	<.0001	<.0001	<.0001
6	<.0001	<.0001	<.0001	1.0000	<.0001		<.0001	<.0001	<.0001	<.0001	<.0001	<.0001
7	<.0001	<.0001	0.9998	<.0001	<.0001	<.0001		<.0001	<.0001	<.0001	<.0001	<.0001
8	<.0001	<.0001	<.0001	<.0001	<.0001	<.0001	<.0001		<.0001	<.0001	<.0001	<.0001
9	<.0001	<.0001	<.0001	<.0001	<.0001	<.0001	<.0001	<.0001		1.0000	1.0000	0.9999
10	<.0001	<.0001	<.0001	<.0001	<.0001	<.0001	<.0001	<.0001	1.0000		1.0000	0.9999
11	<.0001	<.0001	<.0001	<.0001	<.0001	<.0001	<.0001	<.0001	1.0000	1.0000		0.9901
12	<.0001	<.0001	<.0001	<.0001	<.0001	<.0001	<.0001	<.0001	0.9999	0.9999	0.9901	

How do you interpret this table of *p*-values? Presuming an alpha equal to 0.05, the following interpretation and conclusions can be drawn:

- Row 10 in each of the two tables represents disease A, drug 4.
- The *p*-values compare people with disease A and drug dosage level 4 to all other combinations of factors. Because they are all less than the alpha value, you can assume there is a statistically significant difference between that combination and all other combinations of factors.
- Row 9 compares disease C with the other drug/disease group means. Notice that with disease C, drug dosages 1, 2, 3, and 4 are not statistically significantly different from each other, which is consistent with what is seen in the graph.

2.4 Exercises

1. Analyzing Data in a Completely Randomized Design

a. Consider an experiment to study four types of advertising: local newspaper ads, local radio ads, in-store salespeople, and in-store displays. The country is divided into 144 locations, and 36 locations are randomly assigned to each type of advertising. The level of sales is measured for each region in thousands of dollars. You want to see whether the average sales are significantly different for various types of advertising. The data set **ADVERTISE** contains data for these variables:

`ad`	type of advertising
`sales`	level of sales in thousands of dollars.

1) Examine the data using the Distribution Analysis task. What information can you obtain from looking at the data?

2) Test the hypothesis that the means are equal. Be sure to check that the assumptions of the analysis method you choose are met. What conclusions can you reach at this point in your analysis?

3) Conduct pairwise comparisons with a comparisonwise error rate of α=0.05. Which types of advertising are significantly different? Conduct pairwise comparisons with an experimentwise error rate of α=0.05. Which types of advertising are significantly different?

2. Analyzing Data in a Randomized Block Design

a. Suppose that when you design the advertising experiment in the first question you are concerned that there is variability caused by area of the country. You are not particularly interested in what differences are caused by the area, but you are interested in isolating the variability due to this factor. The data set **ADVERTISEBLOCKED** contains data for these variables:

`ad`	type of advertising
`area`	area of the country
`sales`	level of sales in thousands of dollars.

1) Test the hypothesis that the means are equal. Include all of the variables in your model. What can you conclude from your analysis? Was adding the blocking variable **area** into the model detrimental to the analysis?

2) Conduct pairwise comparisons with an experimentwise error rate of α=0.05. Which types of advertising are significantly different?

3. Two-Way ANOVA

a. Consider an experiment to test three different brands of cement and whether an additive makes the cement stronger. Thirty test plots are poured and the following features are recorded in the data set `sasuser.cement`:

`Strength`	the measured strength of a cement test plot
`Additive`	whether an additive was used in the test plot
`Brand`	the brand of cement being tested.

1) Examine the data using the Distribution Analysis task. What information can you obtain from looking at the data?

2) Test the hypothesis that the means are equal. Be sure to verify assumptions and check for interactions. What conclusions can you reach at this point in your analysis?

3) Do the appropriate multiple comparisons test for statistically significant effects.

2.5 Chapter Summary

An analysis of variance (ANOVA) is used to determine whether the means of a continuous measurement for two or more groups are equal. The response variable, or dependent variable, is of primary interest and is a continuous variable. The predictor variable, or independent variable, is a discrete variable. A one-way ANOVA has one independent, or grouping, variable.

Three analyses were discussed: completely randomized, randomized block, and two-way ANOVA.

If the result of an analysis of variance is to reject the null hypothesis and conclude that there are differences between the population means of groups, then multiple comparison tests are used to determine which pairs of means are different. The least significant difference test controls only the comparisonwise error rate. There are many multiple comparison techniques that control the experimentwise error rate.

The assumptions of an analysis of variance are

- observations are independent
- pooled residuals are approximately normal
- all groups have approximately equal response variances.

These assumptions can be verified using a combination of statements and options from the Distribution Analysis and Linear Models tasks:

- Examine the residual versus predicted value plot; you look for an equal number of observations above and below the zero reference line.
- Examine the distribution of the residuals using the Distribution results; look for values for skewness and kurtosis close to zero, a symmetric box-and-whisker plot, nonsignificant measures for the normality statistics, and a normal-appearing normal probability plot and histogram.
- Locate and examine the Levene's F test from the linear models results to determine if the groups have equal variance. Compare the p-value with alpha; the null hypothesis for this test is that the variances are approximately equal. If you reject the null hypothesis, then you have sufficient evidence to conclude that the variances are not equal.

If these assumptions are not met, the probability of drawing incorrect conclusions from the analysis may be increased. Some alternative analysis techniques are to transform the response variable and to generate a Welch ANOVA.

When you analyze an n-way ANOVA, the first consideration must be to determine whether or not there is interaction between the factors. This is done by looking at the test for interaction on the ANOVA table. If there is no interaction between the factors, then the tests for the individual factor effects can be considered in the table to determine the significance/nonsignificance of these factors. If there is interaction between the factors, then the tests for the individual factor effects might be misleading due to masking of these effects by the interaction. In the case of a significant interaction, the Linear Models task can be used to perform multiple comparison tests to compare treatment means.

The Linear Models task was introduced in this chapter. It uses the GLM procedure from SAS/STAT to conduct the appropriate statistical tests for One-Way ANOVA. To validate two of the assumptions, residuals were generated using the Linear Models task.

Two-way ANOVA, which is a subset of n-way ANOVA, also uses the Linear Models task.

2.6 Solutions Exercises

1. Analyzing Data in a Completely Randomized Design

a. Analyze the data in the **ADVERTISE** data set.

1) The Distribution Analysis task will allow you to create descriptive statistics separately for each value of **ad**. Follow the steps in the first demonstration, selecting **ADVERTISE** as the data set to use and setting **sales** as the Analysis variable and **ad** as the Classification variable. Check the box next to **Box plot** in the **Plots** pane to create the side-by-side box plot you see below. Check the box next to **Histogram Plot** to create histograms for each level of **sales** and choose **Normal** under Distributions to superimpose a normal curve for each level.

The box plot gives a visual summary of the four different kinds of ads. It appears that there are a few outliers, that most of the data is approximately normal, and that the mean for display is definitely different from the other kinds of advertising.

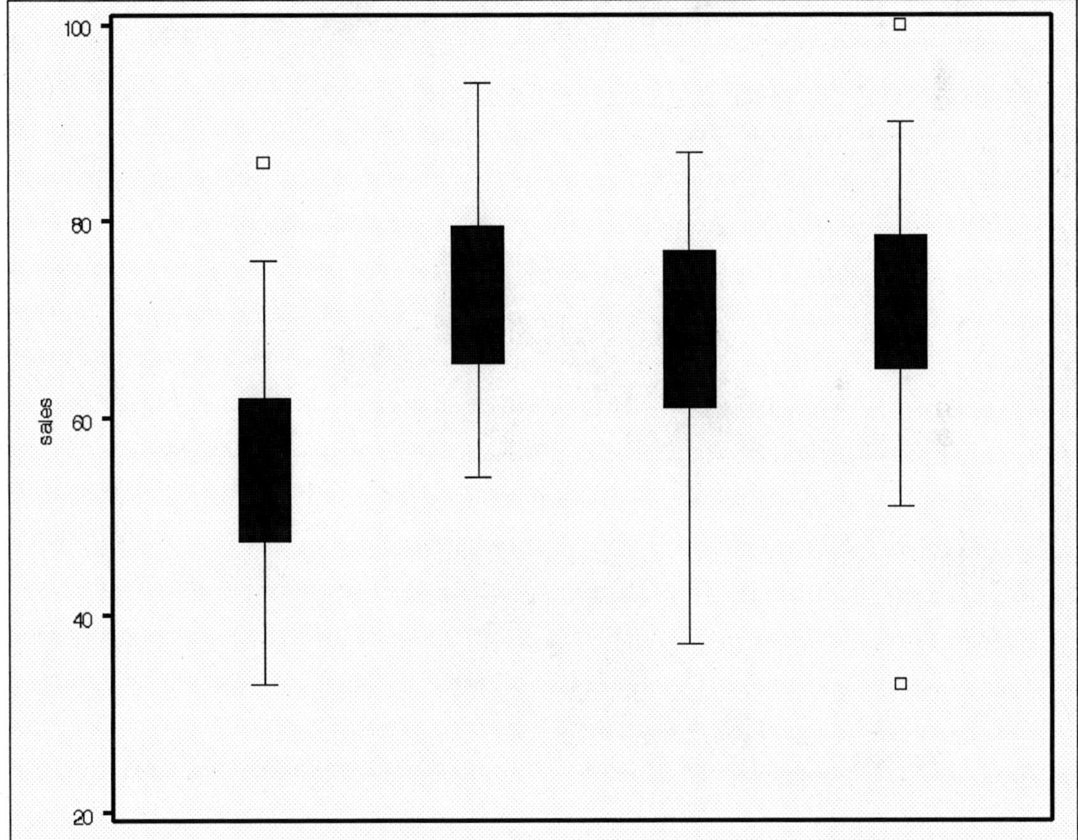

The univariate statistics for each type of advertising give you point estimates, or the means, standard deviations, and ranges. The standard deviations appear to be fairly close to one another. There are a few outliers (one in display and two in radio), but there do not appear to be any extremely unusual data values. The group means lead you to believe that the in-store display method of advertising results in lower sales than the other advertising methods. The remaining methods appear to be fairly close to one another.

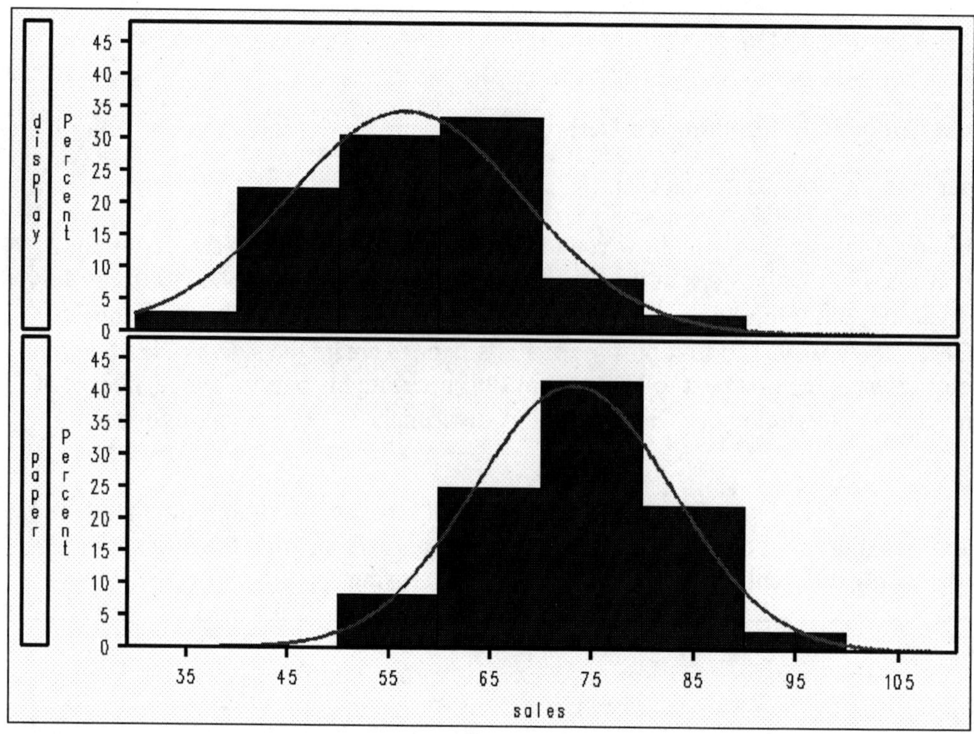
display
paper
Percent
0
5
10
15
20
25
30
35
40
45
35
45
55
65
75
85
95
105
sales

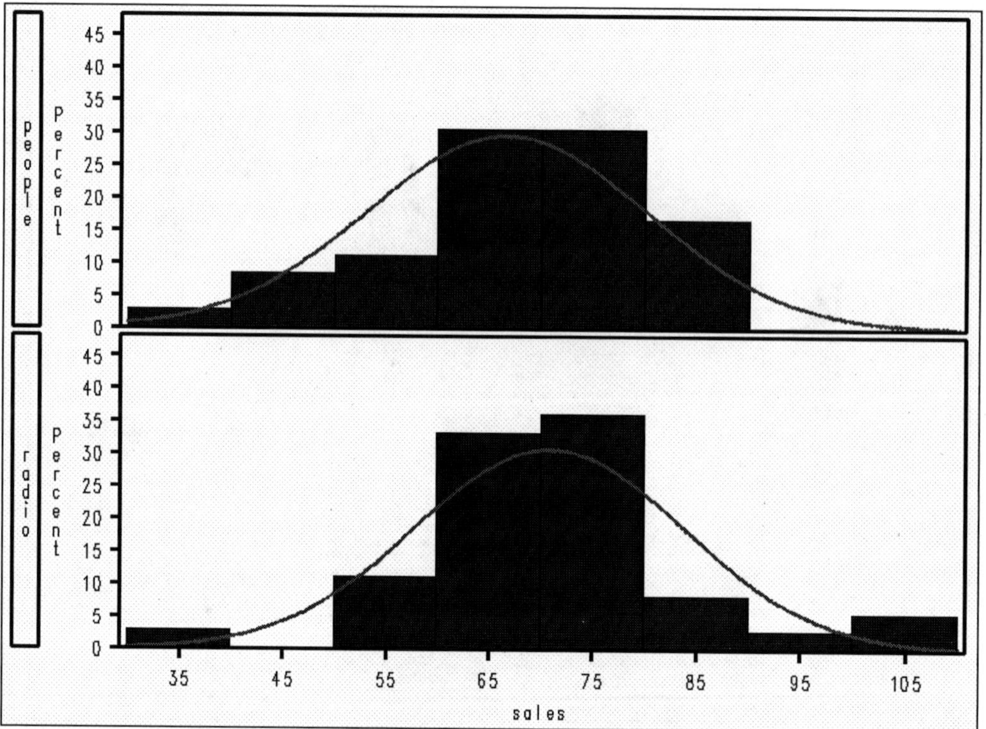
people
radio
Percent
0
5
10
15
20
25
30
35
40
45
35
45
55
65
75
85
95
105
sales

2) Use the Linear Models task to check the equal variances assumption and plot the residuals for the model. Then use the Distribution Analysis task to perform distribution analysis on the saved residuals.

   a) With **Task Roles** selected on the left, drag and drop **sales** to the Dependent variable role and **ad** to the Classification variables role.

   b) Select **Model** on the left. Select **ad** and click **Main** to set **ad** as a main effect (a main effect is any model term that is not an interaction or a higher-order term such as a square).

   c) Select **Model Options** on the left. Uncheck the box next to **Show parameter estimates**.

   d) On the left, under Post Hoc Tests, select **Arithmetic**. Click **Add** at the bottom of the **Effects to estimate** box. The right-hand side populates with a group of choices.

   e) Under **Class effects to use**, change the selection for **ad** to **True**.

   f) To request homogeneity of variance tests, change the **Homogeneity of variance** option from **None** to **Levene (square residuals)**. This option will test the equal variances assumption.

   g) On the left, select **Means** under the Plots group. Check the box next to **Dependent means for main effects**. This will create a plot of the means of the different types of advertising, which will aid in interpretation.

   h) To get plots of the residuals versus the predicted values, select **Residual** under Plots. Check the box next to **Ordinary vs Predicted Y**. This will help in validating the assumptions of ANOVA.

   i) In order to test whether the residuals are approximately normal, you have to request that SAS create a data set with the residuals. To do this, select **Predictions** on the left. Under **Data to predict**, check the box next to **Original sample**, and check the lower left box marked **Residuals** to request the residuals be added to the output data set.

   j) Select **Run** to run the task.

   k) Using the steps outlined in the demonstration, run a Distribution Analysis task on the resulting data set to determine if the residuals are normally distributed.

When you check the model assumptions, you find

- Levene's test for equality of variance has a p-value of 0.3532. Therefore, you do not reject the null hypothesis that the variances are equal.
- The plot of the residuals versus the predicted values does not indicate any problems with the model assumptions.
- The normal probability plot indicates that there is no severe departure from the assumption that the residuals have a normal distribution.

Levene's Test for Homogeneity of sales Variance
ANOVA of Squared Deviations from Group Means

Source	DF	Sum of Squares	Mean Square	F Value	Pr > F
ad	3	154637	51545.6	1.10	0.3532
Error	140	6586668	47047.6		

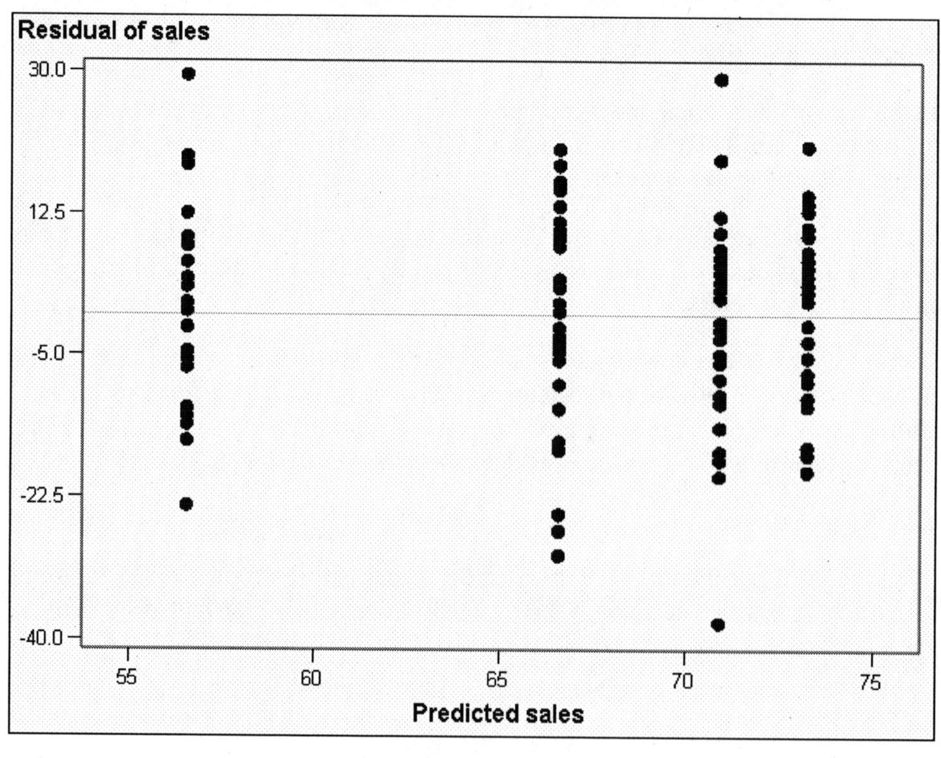

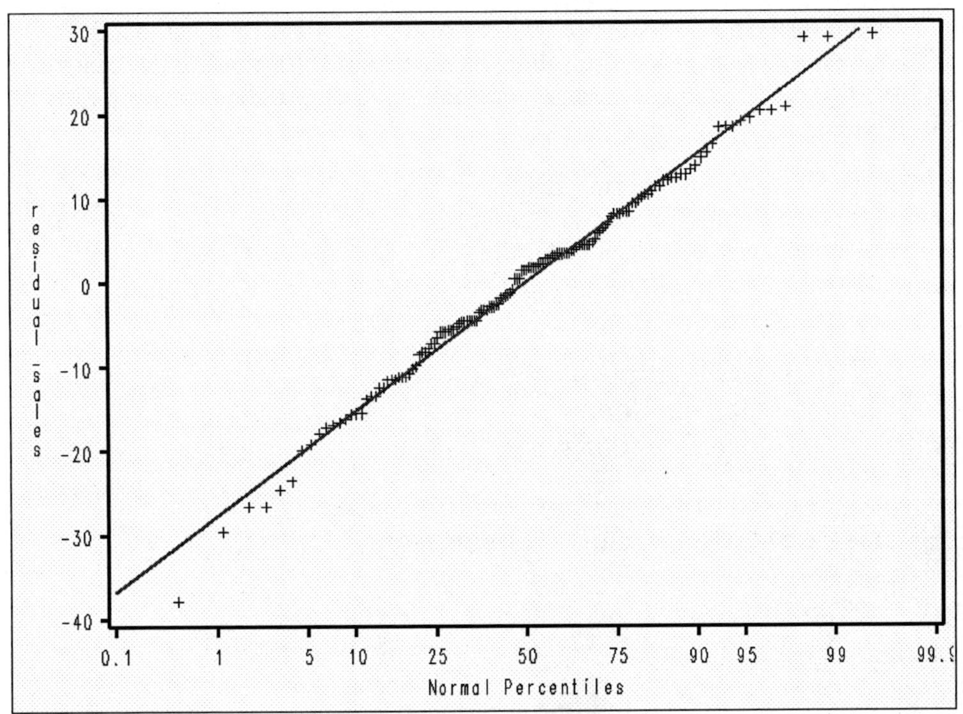

Dependent Variable: sales

Source	DF	Sum of Squares	Mean Square	F Value	Pr > F
Model	3	5866.08333	1955.36111	13.48	<.0001
Error	140	20303.22222	145.02302		
Corrected Total	143	26169.30556			

R-Square	Coeff Var	Root MSE	sales Mean
0.224159	18.02252	12.04255	66.81944

Source	DF	Type I SS	Mean Square	F Value	Pr > F
ad	3	5866.083333	1955.361111	13.48	<.0001

Source	DF	Type III SS	Mean Square	F Value	Pr > F
ad	3	5866.083333	1955.361111	13.48	<.0001

The overall *F* test from the analysis of variance table has a *p*-value less than or equal to .0001. Presuming that all assumptions of the model are valid, you know that at least one of the treatment means is different from one other treatment mean. At this point, you do not know which means are significantly different.

3) Reopen the Linear Models task and perform pairwise comparisons controlling for comparisonwise error rate. Do this by selecting **Least Squares** under Post Hoc Tests on the left side. Click **Add** at the lower left. Change **Ad** from `False` to `True`. Under **Comparisons**, select **All pairwise differences** and **Tukey** for the adjustment method.

The GLM Procedure
Least Squares Means
Adjustment for Multiple Comparisons: Tukey

ad	sales LSMEAN	LSMEAN Number
display	56.5555556	1
paper	73.2222222	2
people	66.6111111	3
radio	70.8888889	4

Least Squares Means for effect ad
Pr > |t| for H0: LSMean(i)=LSMean(j)
Dependent Variable: sales

i/j	1	2	3	4
1		<.0001	0.0030	<.0001
2	<.0001		0.0964	0.8440
3	0.0030	0.0964		0.4360
4	<.0001	0.8440	0.4360	

Based on Tukey's multiple comparison method, using in-store displays is significantly different from all other types of advertising. None of the other types are statistically significantly different.

2. Analyzing Data in a Randomized Block Design

a. Follow the steps outlined in Exercise **1**, part 2) to create a linear model. Use the **ADVERTISEBLOCKED** data set with **sales** as the Dependent variable and **ad** and **area** as classification variables. Do not forget to use the **Model** pane to set **ad** and **area** as main effects.

Assumption verification for ANOVA with more than two variables is not discussed in this class. Those topics are covered in *Statistics II: ANOVA and Regression*.

Partial Output

Class Level Information

Class	Levels	Values
area	18	1 2 3 4 5 6 7 8 9 10 11 12 13 14 15 16 17 18
ad	4	display paper people radio

Number of Observations Read	144
Number of Observations Used	144

Partial Output (continued)

Dependent Variable: sales

Source	DF	Sum of Squares	Mean Square	F Value	Pr > F
Model	20	15131.38889	756.56944	8.43	<.0001
Error	123	11037.91667	89.73916		
Corrected Total	143	26169.30556			

R-Square	Coeff Var	Root MSE	sales Mean
0.578211	14.17712	9.473076	66.81944

Source	DF	Type I SS	Mean Square	F Value	Pr > F
ad	3	5866.083333	1955.361111	21.79	<.0001
area	17	9265.305556	545.017974	6.07	<.0001

Source	DF	Type III SS	Mean Square	F Value	Pr > F
ad	3	5866.083333	1955.361111	21.79	<.0001
area	17	9265.305556	545.017974	6.07	<.0001

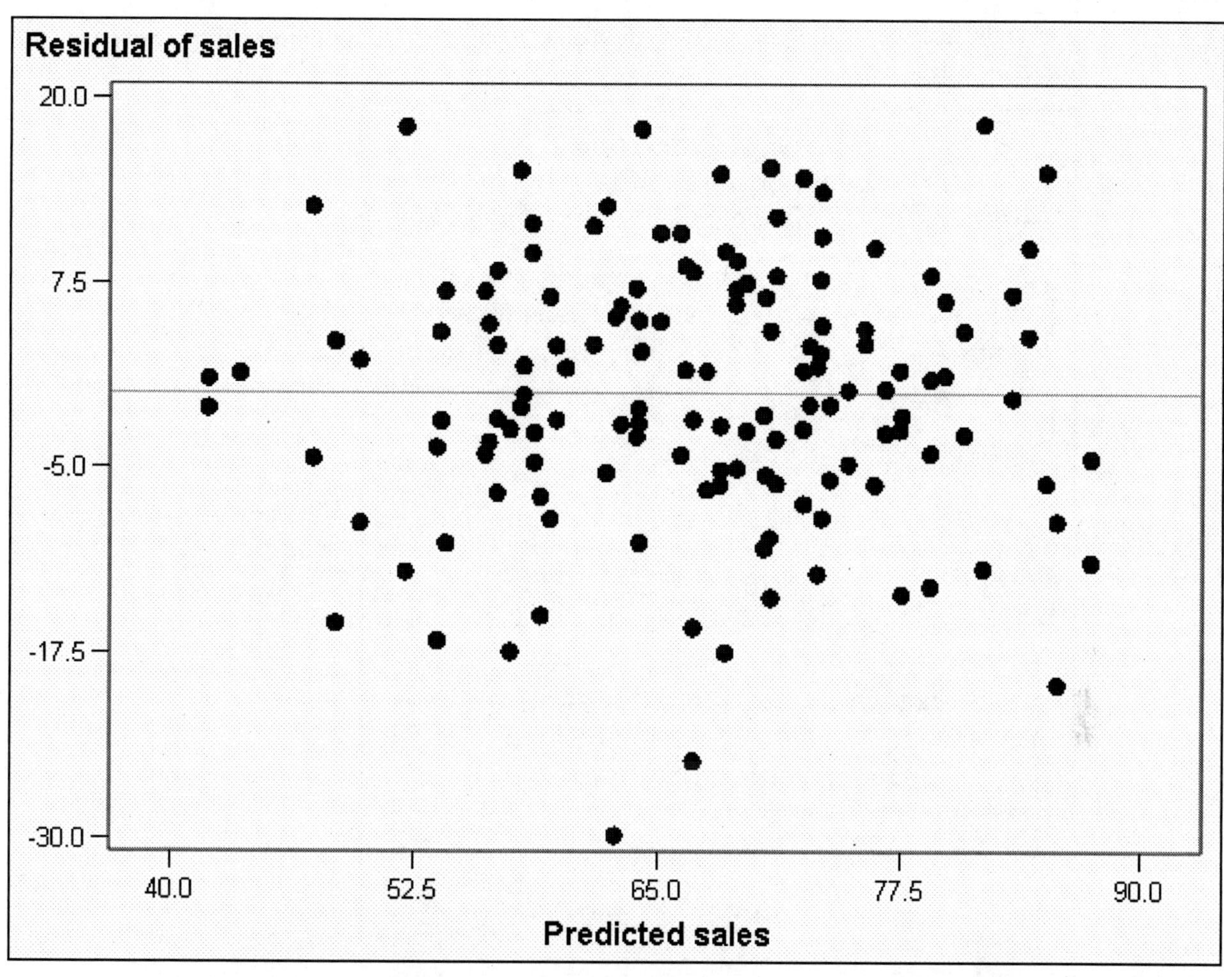

1) The overall *F* test with a *p*-value of less than or equal to 0.0001 means that you reject the null hypothesis that all treatment means are equal and conclude that at least one treatment mean is significantly different from one other treatment mean. Note that the mean square error is much smaller than the model that does not include the blocking factor. Also note the increase in the R^2. This indicates that the addition of the blocking factor was not detrimental to the analysis. The plots of the residuals and the test for normality do not indicate any serious departures from the model assumptions.

2) Rerun the analysis adding the Tukey pairwise comparisons from the **Least Squares** pane under Post Hoc Tests.

The GLM Procedure
Least Squares Means
Adjustment for Multiple Comparisons: Tukey

ad	sales LSMEAN	LSMEAN Number
display	56.5555556	1
paper	73.2222222	2
people	66.6111111	3
radio	70.8888889	4

Least Squares Means for effect ad
Pr > |t| for H0: LSMean(i)=LSMean(j)
Dependent Variable: sales

i/j	1	2	3	4
1		<.0001	<.0001	<.0001
2	<.0001		0.0190	0.7233
3	<.0001	0.0190		0.2268
4	<.0001	0.7233	0.2268	

There are more differences found when blocking on `area`.

3. Two-Way ANOVA

a.

1) Follow the steps outlined earlier to create a distribution analysis on **Strength** by **Brand** and by **Additive**

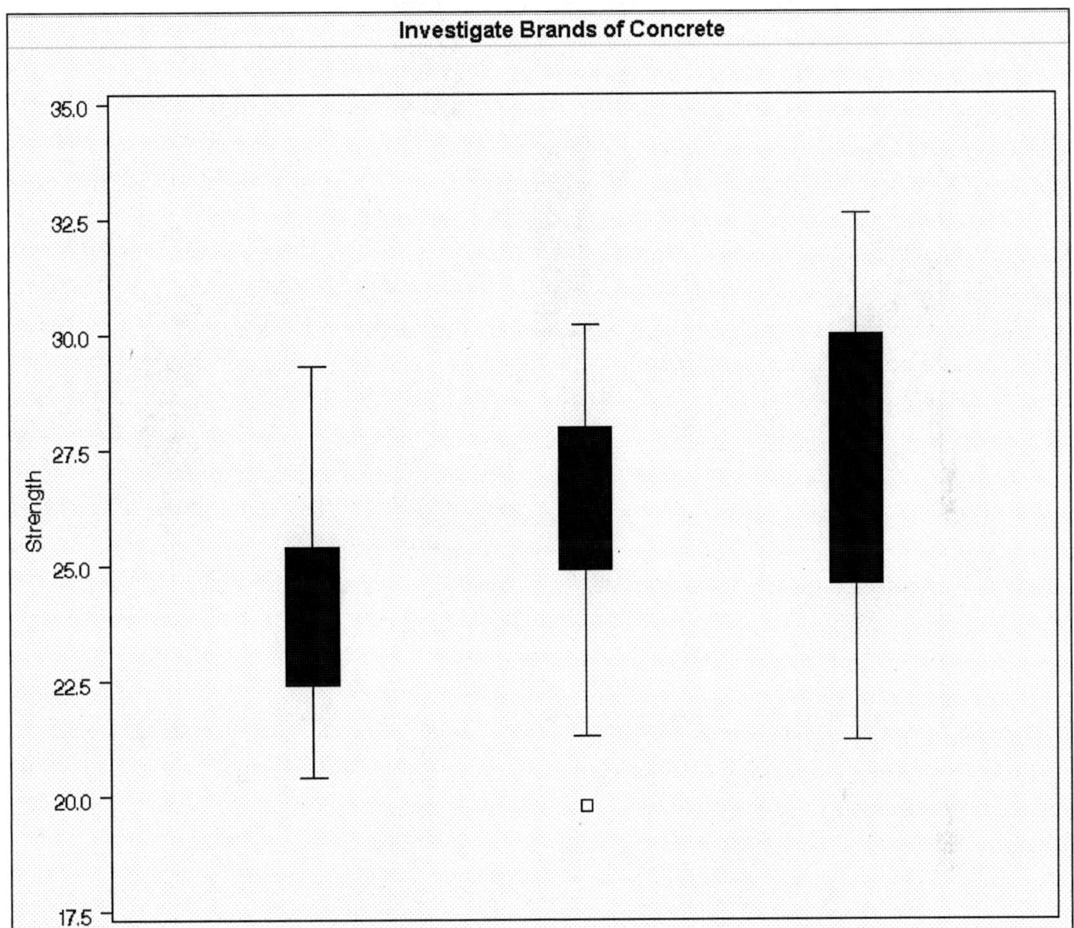

The box plots show that the **Brand** means are slightly different.

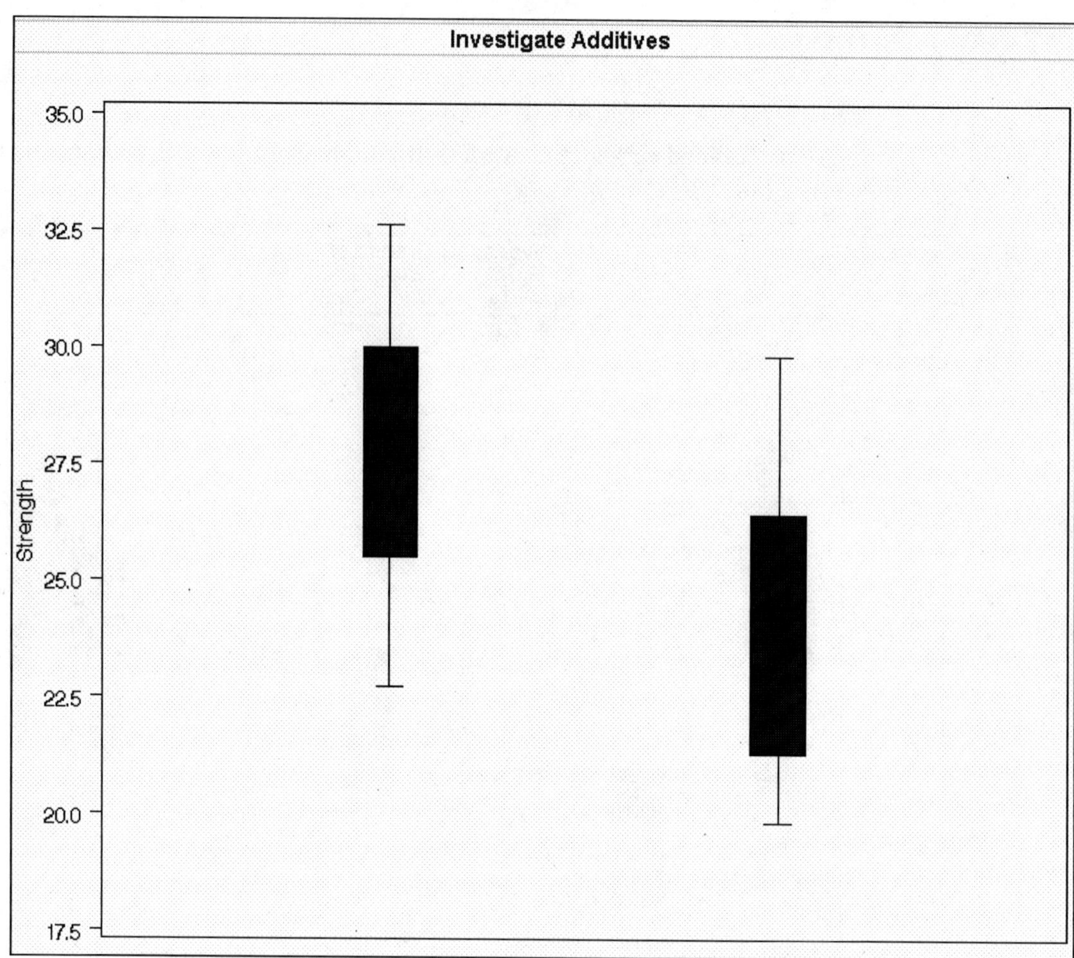

The box plots show that the **Additive** means are different

2) Follow the steps outlined in Exercise **1**, part 2) to create a linear model. Use the **`CEMENT`** data set with **`Strength`** as the Dependent variable and **`Brand`** and **`Additive`** as Classification variables. Use the **Model** pane to set **`Brand`** and **`Additive`** as main effects and to specify an interaction using the Factorial button.

Source	DF	Sum of Squares	Mean Square	F Value	Pr > F
Model	5	189.9080000	37.9816000	6.04	0.0009
Error	24	150.9520000	6.2896667		
Corrected Total	29	340.8600000			

R-Square	Coeff Var	Root MSE	Strength Mean
0.557144	9.645849	2.507921	26.00000

Source	DF	Type I SS	Mean Square	F Value	Pr > F
Additive	1	109.0613333	109.0613333	17.34	0.0003
Brand	2	71.4980000	35.7490000	5.68	0.0095
Brand*Additive	2	9.3486667	4.6743333	0.74	0.4862

The overall *F* test with a p-value of 0.0009 means that you reject the null hypothesis that **`Strength`** is not affected by **`Brand`** or **`Additive`**. The Type I and Type III sums of squares, which test each effect separately, show that both **`Brand`** and **`Additive`** are statistically significant. The table indicates that the interaction is not statistically significant. You can remove the interaction from the model before testing the differences between the means.

3) Follow the steps below to create post-hoc tests on **`Brand`**. Because there are only two levels of **`Additive`**, paired t-tests are not necessary.

   a) Reopen the Linear Models task by double-clicking.

   b) Go to the Model tab. Select **Additive*Brand** in the **Effects** area and select **Remove Effects** at the bottom right.

   ✎ Assumption verification for ANOVA with more than two variables is not discussed in this class. Those topics are covered in *Statistics II: ANOVA and Regression*.

c) Select **Least Squares** under Post Hoc Tests on the left and select **Add** at the bottom of the pane. Change the selection for `Additive` to `True` and `Brand` to `True`. Change the selection for **Show p-values for differences** to `All pairwise differences`. Change the **Adjustment method** to `Tukey`. Be sure to make these changes for both `Additive` and `Brand`.

Additive	Strength LSMEAN	H0:LSMean1=LSMean2 Pr > |t|
reinforced	27.9039944	0.0003
standard	24.0912339	

The additives are significantly different.

The GLM Procedure
Least Squares Means
Adjustment for Multiple Comparisons: Tukey

Brand	Strength LSMEAN	LSMEAN Number
Consolidated	24.2000000	1
EZ Mix	25.8300000	2
Graystone	27.9700000	3

Least Squares Means for effect Brand
Pr > |t| for H0: LSMean(i)=LSMean(j)
Dependent Variable: Strength

i/j	1	2	3
1		0.3224	0.0061
2	0.3224		0.1512
3	0.0061	0.1512	

It appears that Consolidated and Graystone are statistically significantly different from each other.

The tests show that there is a significant difference between the Consolidated and Graystone brands. There also seems to be a significant difference due to `Additive` (reinforced cement is stronger than standard). Pairwise comparisons are not necessary for `Additive` because it only has two levels, but they are easy to produce in the Linear Models task.

Chapter 3 Regression

3.1 Exploratory Data Analysis

Objectives

- Examine the relationship between two continuous variables using a scatter plot.
- Quantify the degree of linearity between two continuous variables using correlation statistics.
- Understand potential misuses of the correlation coefficient.
- Obtain Pearson correlation coefficients using the Correlations task.

3

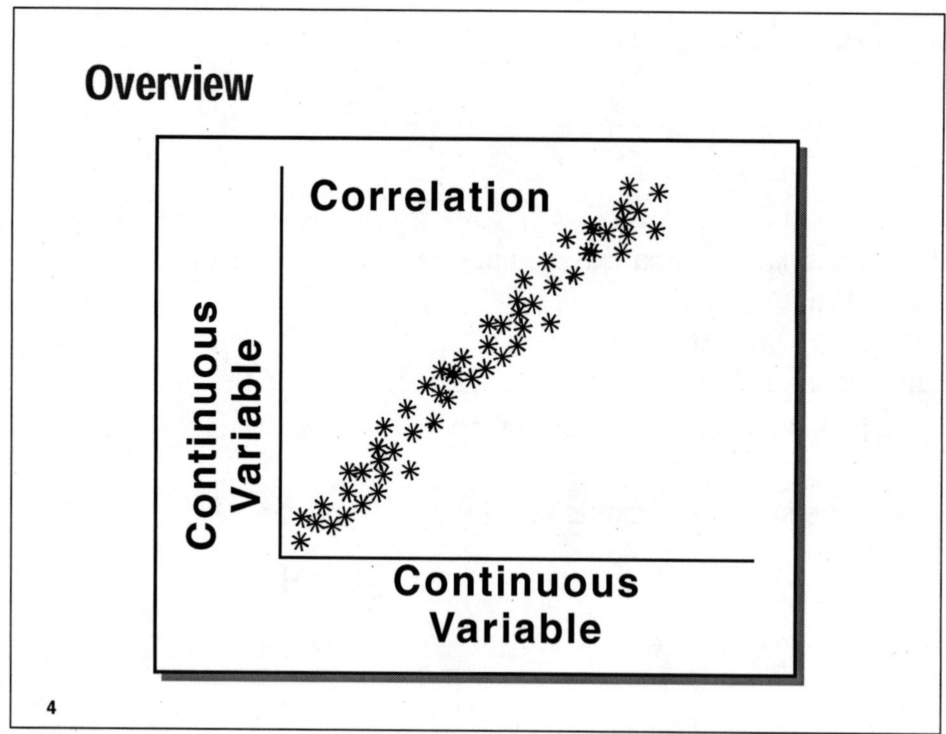

In the previous chapter, you learned that when you have a discrete predictor variable and a continuous outcome variable, you use ANOVA to analyze your data. In this section, you have two continuous variables.

You use correlation analysis to examine and describe the relationship between two continuous variables. However, before you use correlation analysis, it is important to view the relationship between two continuous variables by using a scatter plot.

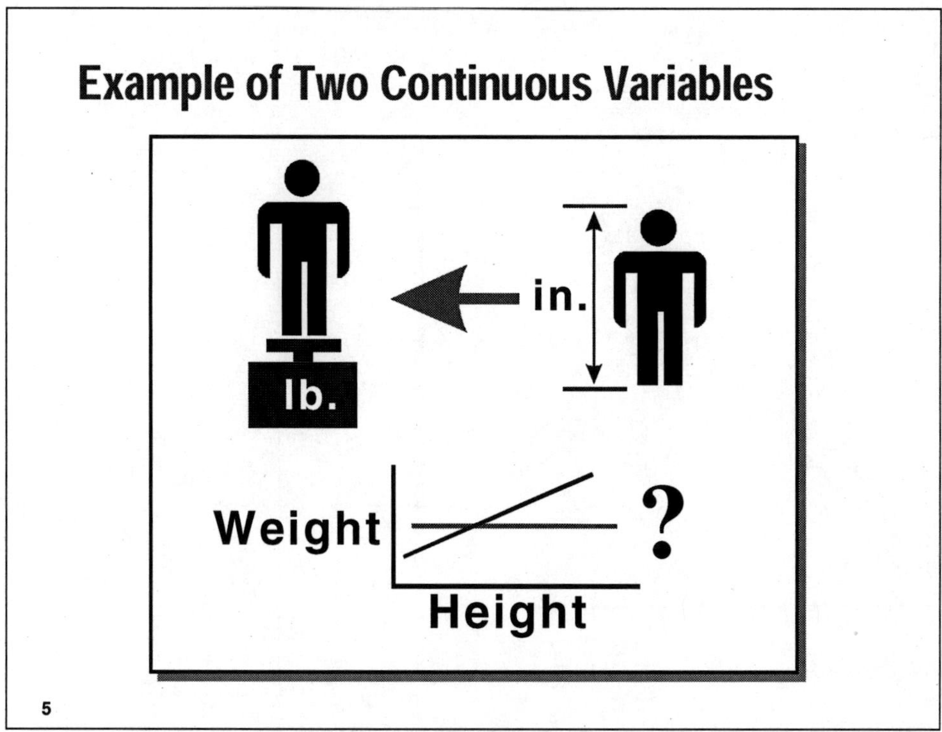

Example: A random sample of high school students is selected to determine the relationship between a person's height and weight. Height and weight are measured on a numeric scale. They have a large, potentially infinite number of possible values, rather than a few categories such as short, medium, and tall. Therefore, these variables are considered to be continuous.

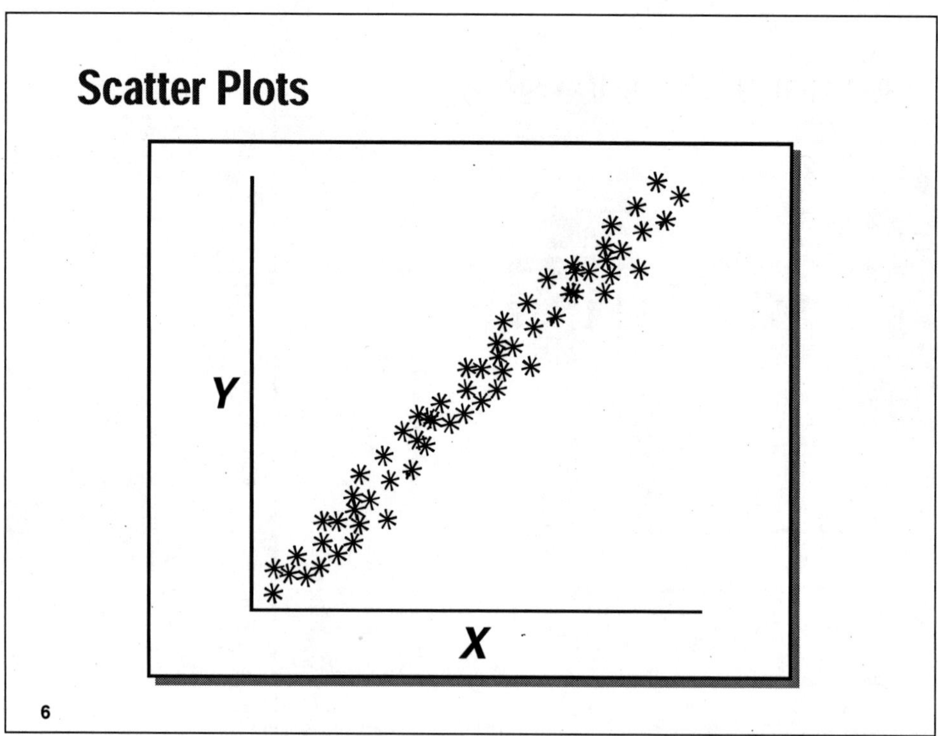

Scatter plots are two-dimensional graphs produced by plotting one variable against another within a set of coordinate axes. The coordinates of each point correspond to the values of the two variables.

Scatter plots are useful to

- explore the relationships between two variables
- locate outlying or unusual values
- identify possible trends
- communicate data analysis results.

Relationships between Continuous Variables

1. 2.

3. 4.

7

Describing the relationship between two continuous variables is an important first step in any statistical analysis. The scatter plot is the most important tool you have in describing these relationships. The diagrams above illustrate some possible relationships.

1. A straight line describes the relationship.
2. Curvature is present in the relationship.
3. There might be a cyclical pattern in the relationship. (You might see this when the predictor is time.)
4. There is no clear relationship between the variables.

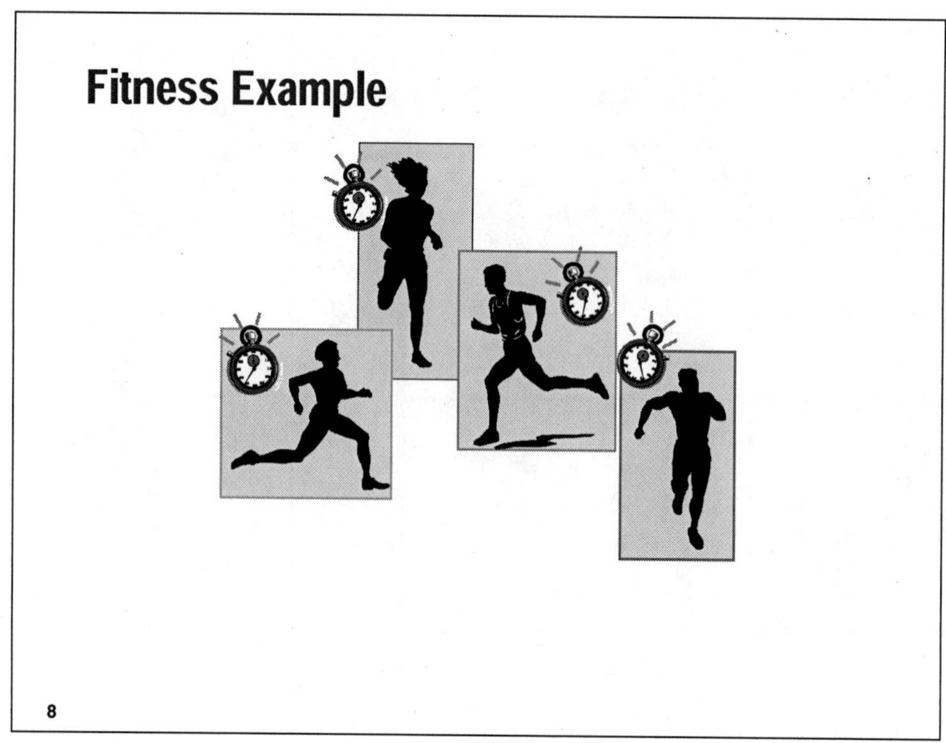

In exercise physiology, an object measure of aerobic fitness is how fast the body can absorb and use oxygen (oxygen consumption). Subjects participated in a predetermined exercise run of 1.5 miles. Measurements of oxygen consumption as well as several other continuous measurements, such as age, pulse, and weight were recorded. The researchers are interested in determining whether any of these other variables can help predict oxygen consumption. Certain values of **Maximum_Pulse** and **Run_Pulse** were changed for illustration. **Name**, **Gender**, and **Performance** were contrived for illustration.

The data set **FITNESS** contains the following variables:

Name	name of the member
Gender	gender of the member
Runtime	time to run 1.5 miles (in minutes)
Age	age of the member (in years)
Weight	weight of the member (in kilograms)
Oxygen_Consumption	a measure of the ability to use oxygen in the blood stream
Run_Pulse	pulse rate at the end of the run
Rest_Pulse	resting pulse rate
Maximum_Pulse	maximum pulse rate during the run
Performance	a measure of overall fitness.

Rawlings, J. O. (1988) Applied Regression Analysis: A Research Tool, Pacific Grove, CA: Wadsworth & Brooks.

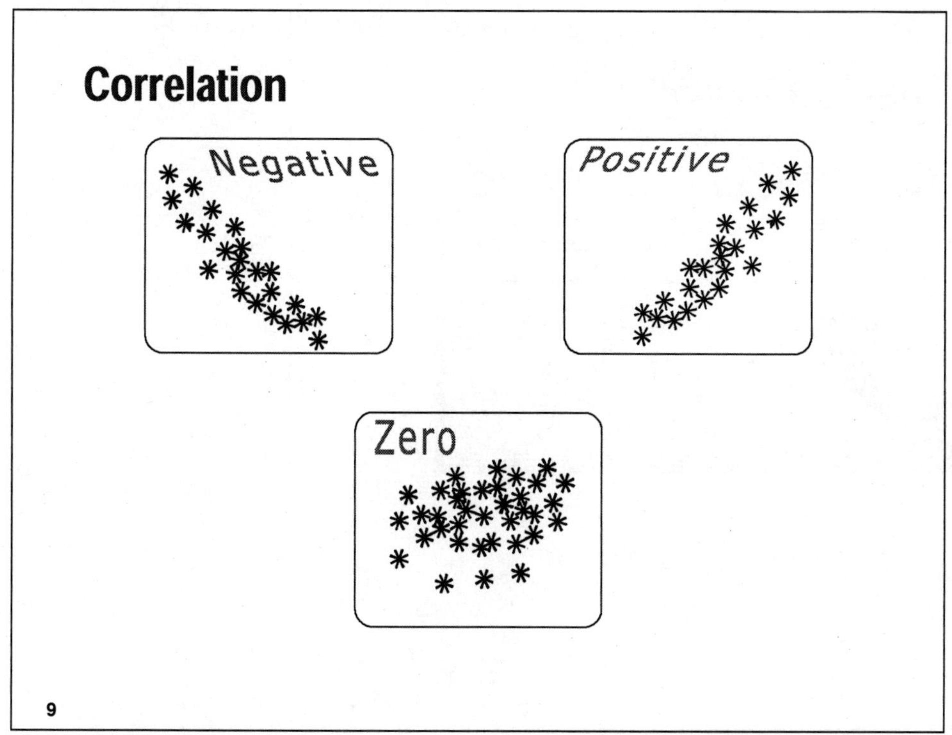

After you examine the scatter plot, you can quantify the relationship between two variables with correlation statistics. Two variables are correlated if there is a **linear** relationship between them. If not, the variables are uncorrelated.

You can classify correlated variables according to the type of correlation:

positive	one variable tends to increase in value as the other variable increases in value
negative	one variable tends to decrease in value as the other variable increases in value
zero	no linear relationship exists between the two variables (uncorrelated).

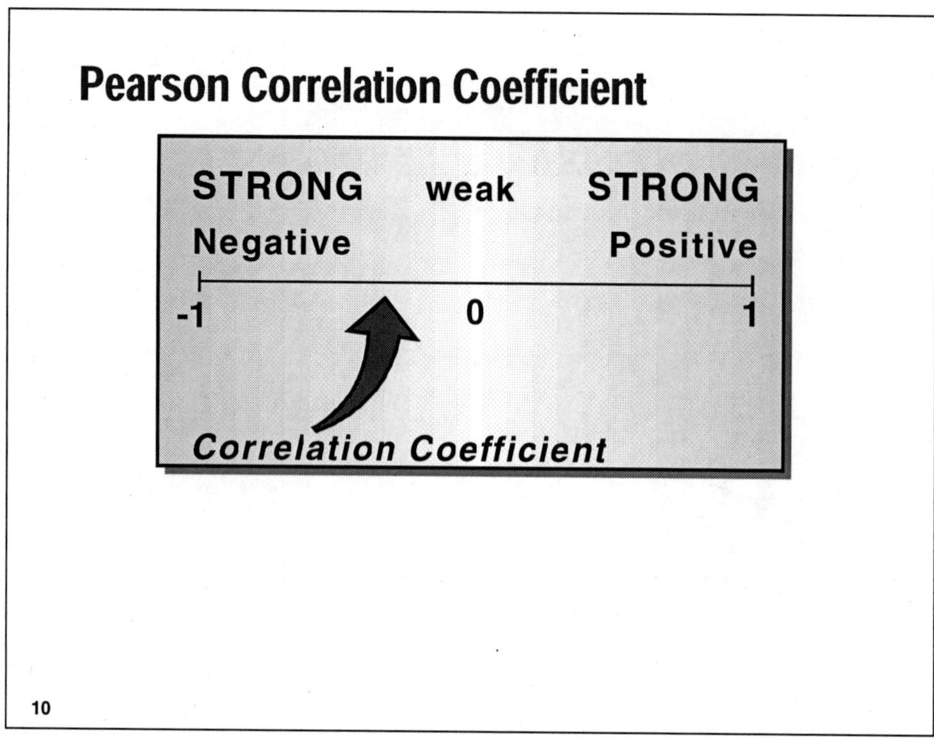

Correlation statistics measure the degree of linear relationship between two variables. A common correlation statistic used for continuous variables is the Pearson correlation coefficient. Values of correlation statistics are

- between –1 and 1
- closer to either extreme if there is a high degree of linear relationship between the two variables
- close to 0 if there is no linear relationship between the two variables
- close to 1 if there is a positive linear relationship
- close to –1 if there is a negative linear relationship.

Misuses of the Correlation Coefficient

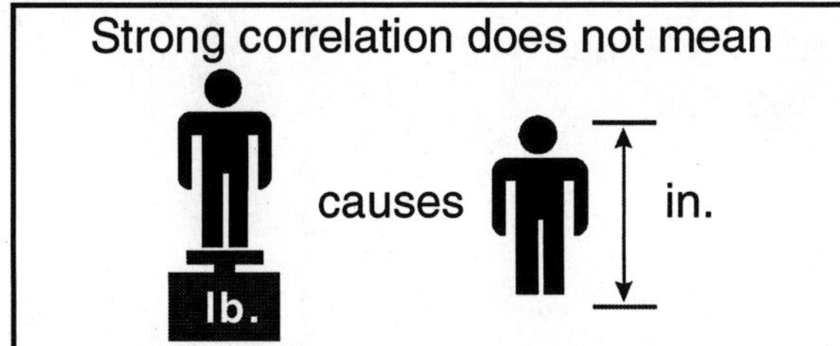

11

Common errors can be made when interpreting the correlation between variables. One example of this is using correlation coefficients to conclude a cause-and-effect relationship.

- A strong correlation between two variables does not mean change in one variable causes the other variable to change, or vice versa.
- Sample correlation coefficients can be large because of chance or because both variables are affected by other variables.

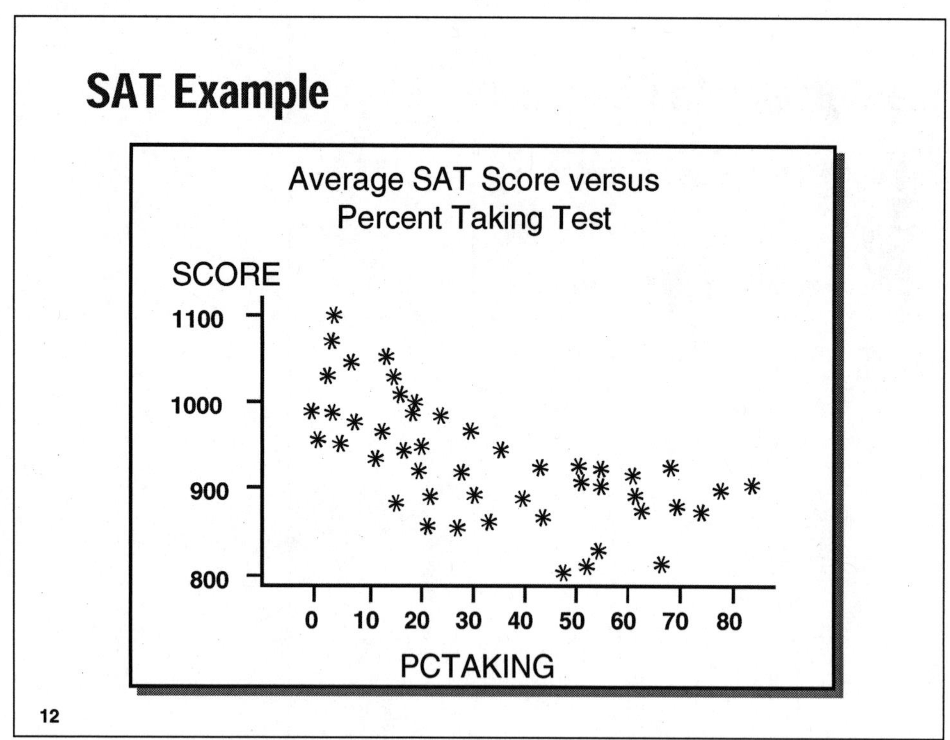

An example of improperly concluding a cause-and-effect relationship is illustrated using data from the Scholastic Aptitude Test (SAT) from 1989. The scatter plot shown above plots each state's average total SAT score (`SCORE`) versus the percent of eligible students in the state who took the SAT (`PCTAKING`). The correlation between `SCORE` and `PCTAKING` is –0.86867. Looking at the plot and at this statistic, an eligible student for the next year can conclude, "If I am the only student in my state to take the SAT, I am guaranteed a good score."

Clearly this type of thinking is faulty. Can you think of possible explanations for this relationship?

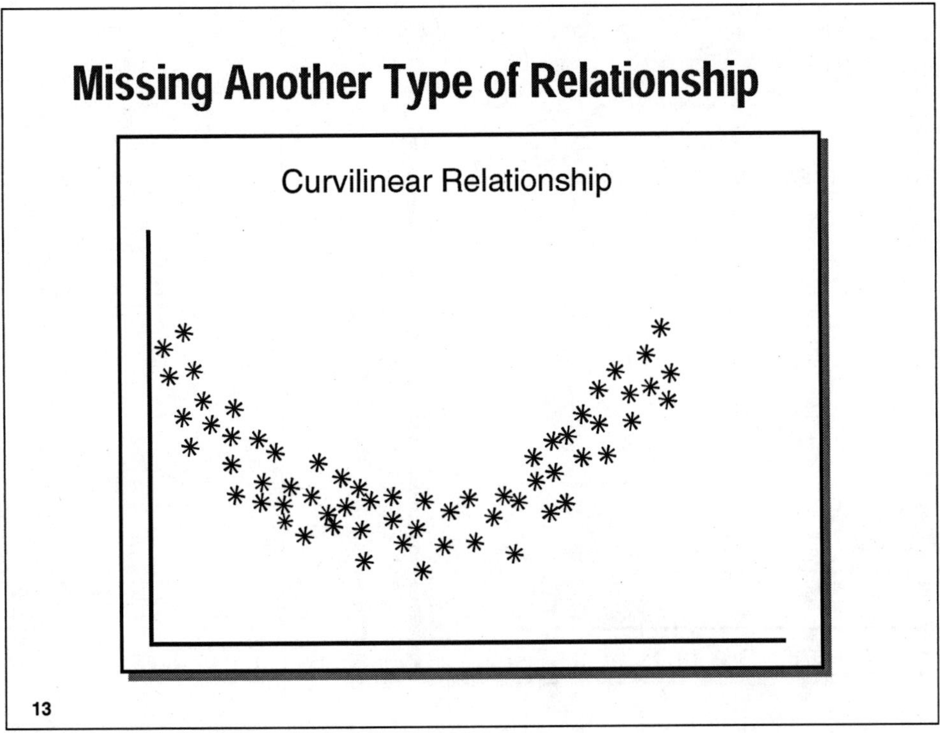

In the scatter plot above, the variables have a fairly low Pearson correlation coefficient. Why?

- Correlation coefficients measure linear relationships.
- A correlation coefficient close to 0 indicates that there is not a strong linear relationship between two variables.
- A correlation coefficient close to 0 does **not** mean that there is any relationship of any kind between the two variables.

In this example, there is a curvilinear relationship between the two variables.

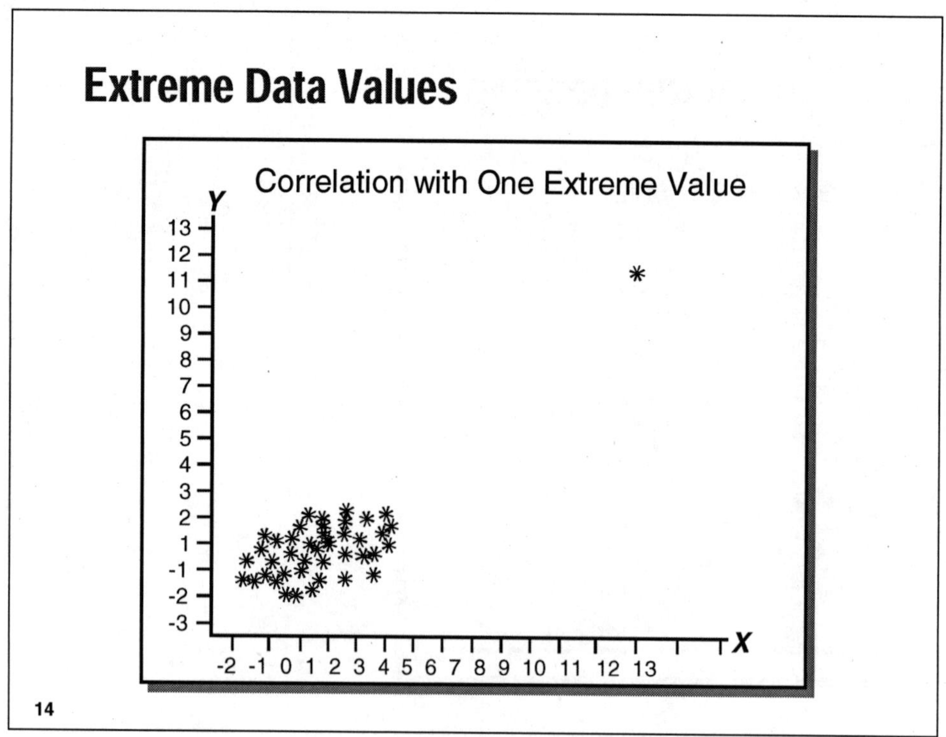

Correlation coefficients are highly affected by a few extreme values of either variable. The scatter plot above shows that the degree of linear relationship is mainly determined by one point. If you delete the unusual point from the data, the correlation is close to 0.

In this situation, follow these steps:

1. Investigate the unusual data point to make sure it is valid.
2. If the data point is valid, collect more data between the unusual data point and the group of data points to see whether a linear relationship unfolds.
3. Try to replicate the unusual data point by collecting data at a fixed value of x (in this case, x=11). This determines whether the data point is unusual.
4. Compute two correlation coefficients, one with the unusual data point and one without it. This shows how influential the unusual data point is in the analysis.

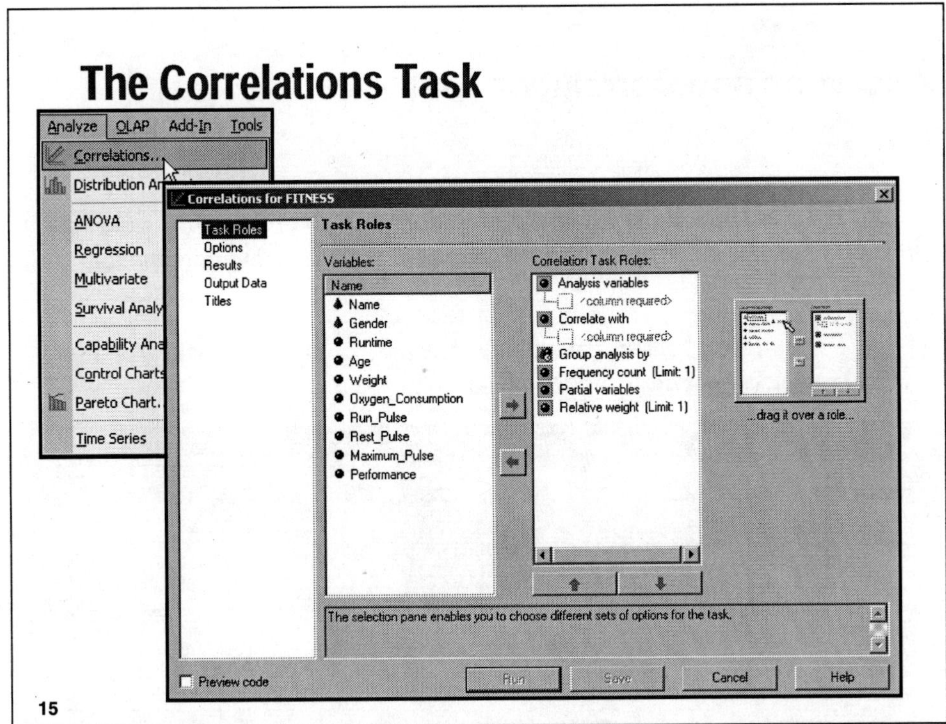

You can use the Correlations task to create bivariate scatter plots of variables and produce correlation statistics for your data. By default, the Correlations task produces Pearson correlation statistics and corresponding *p*-values.

Data Exploration and Correlation Statistics

Explore the properties of the **FITNESS** data set and use the Correlations task to produce bivariate scatter plots and Pearson correlation coefficients for **Oxygen_Consumption** with the other continuous variables.

1. First, explore the data table. Select the **FITNESS** data table in the project tree. Right-click on the table in the process flow and select **Properties** from the menu that appears.

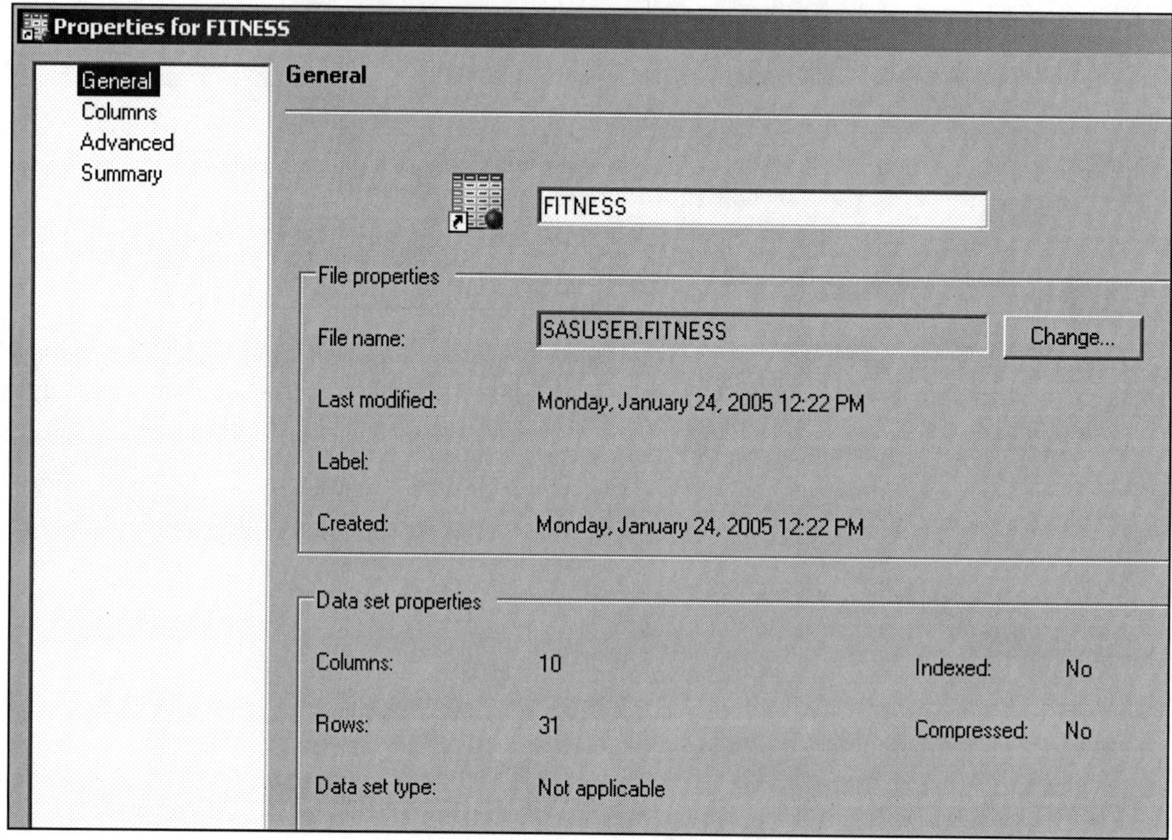

On the **General** pane, you see that the data table is in the SASUSER library and contains 10 columns and 31 rows.

2. Select the **Columns** pane from the left.

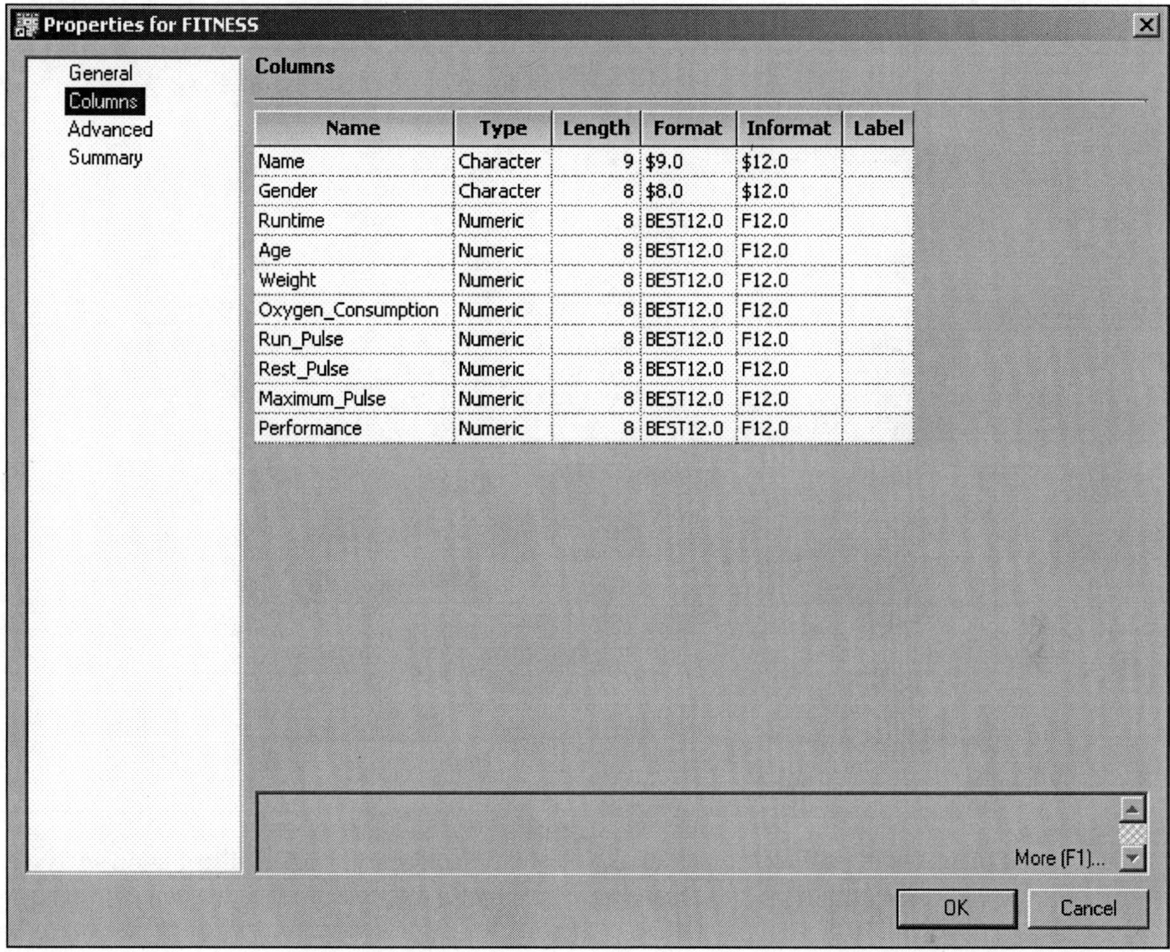

It contains the name, type, length, format, informat, and label (where applicable) for each variable in the data. Numeric variables are typically saved as length 8 variables (using 8-byte floating-point storage), even though they may display with more than 8 characters in your table preview.

3. Select **Cancel** to close the window.

4. Double-click on the table name to preview it. The columns of the table were reduced in order to view all column values.

FITNESS (read-only)

	Name	Gender	Runtime	Age	Weight	Oxygen_Consumption	Run_Pulse	Rest_Pulse	Maximum_Pulse	Performance
1	Donna	F	8.17	42	68.15	59.57	166	40	172	14
2	Gracie	F	8.63	38	81.87	60.06	170	48	186	13
3	Luanne	F	8.65	43	85.84	54.3	156	45	168	13
4	Mimi	F	8.92	50	70.87	54.63	146	48	155	11
5	Chris	M	8.95	49	81.42	49.16	180	44	185	11
6	Allen	M	9.22	38	89.02	49.87	178	55	180	12
7	Nancy	F	9.4	49	76.32	48.67	186	56	188	10
8	Patty	F	9.63	52	76.32	45.44	164	48	166	10
9	Suzanne	F	9.93	57	59.08	50.55	148	49	155	9
10	Teresa	F	10	51	77.91	46.67	162	48	168	9
11	Bob	M	10.07	40	75.07	45.31	185	62	185	9
12	Harriett	F	10.08	49	73.37	50.39	168	67	168	9
13	Jane	F	10.13	44	73.03	50.54	168	45	168	9
14	Harold	M	10.25	48	91.63	46.77	162	48	164	9
15	Sammy	M	10.33	54	83.12	51.85	166	50	170	8
16	Buffy	F	10.47	52	73.71	45.79	186	59	188	8
17	Trent	M	10.5	52	82.78	47.47	170	53	172	8
18	Jackie	F	10.6	47	79.15	47.27	162	47	164	8
19	Ralph	M	10.85	43	81.19	49.09	162	64	170	7
20	Jack	M	10.95	51	69.63	40.84	168	57	172	7
21	Annie	F	11.08	51	67.25	45.12	172	48	172	7
22	Kate	F	11.12	45	66.45	44.75	176	51	176	7
23	Carl	M	11.17	54	79.38	46.08	156	62	165	7
24	Don	M	11.37	44	89.47	44.61	178	62	182	6
25	Effie	F	11.5	48	61.24	47.92	170	52	176	6
26	George	M	11.63	47	77.45	44.81	176	58	176	6
27	Iris	F	11.95	40	75.98	45.68	176	70	180	5
28	Mark	M	12.63	57	73.37	39.41	174	58	176	4
29	Steve	M	12.88	54	91.63	39.2	168	44	172	4
30	Vaughn	M	13.08	44	81.42	39.44	174	63	176	2
31	William	M	14.03	45	87.66	37.39	186	56	192	0

At this point in your data exploration, you should perform univariate distribution analysis on each variable of interest to find out the descriptive statistics as well as the general shape of the distribution for each variable. It is a good idea to look over histograms of the data as well as other plots that you prefer.

Use the Correlations task to generate scatter plots and Pearson's correlation coefficients for all the numeric variables with `Oxygen_Consumption`.

5. Select **Analyze** ⇨ **Correlations…**.

6. Assign `Runtime`, `Age`, `Weight`, `Run_Pulse`, `Rest_Pulse`, `Maximum_Pulse`, and `Performance` to the Analysis variables role.

7. Assign `Oxygen_Consumption` to Correlate with.

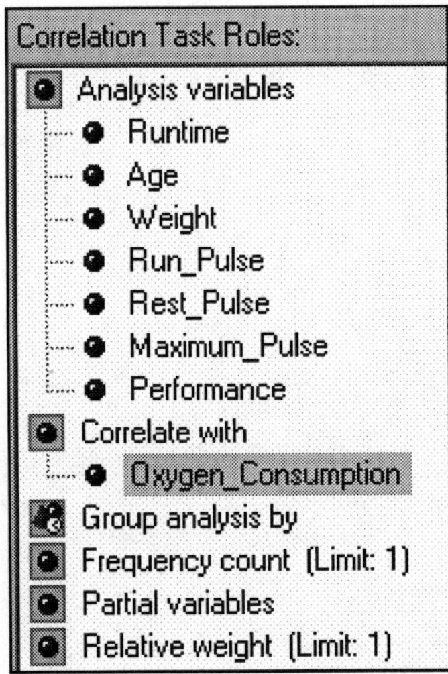

If you only specify variables in the Analysis variables role, SAS produces pairwise correlations for all combinations of variables in the list. The **Correlate with** role enables you to subset these results to pairs of variables that include the **Correlate with** variable.

8. Select the **Options** pane.

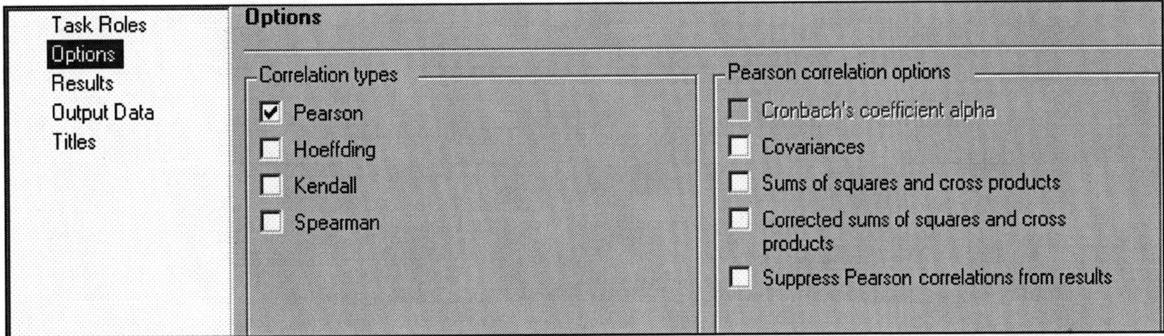

The Pearson correlation is selected by default. Three other (nonparametric) statistics can also be selected:

Spearman	produces Spearman's rho statistic, which is a measure of the monotonic association used for ordinal scale data. Spearman's rho is similar to Pearson's r, but the data values are ranked before computing the statistic.
Kendall	produces Kendall's tau b correlation, which is a measure of association for ordinal data. It may be preferable to Spearman's rho because of its handling of tied values.
Hoeffding	produces Hoeffding's D statistic, which is a more general measure of independence that detects nonmonotonic association among pairs of variables. The range of possible values of Hoeffding is different than Pearson's r. The values range from -.5 to 1 for Without ties. The values can exceed -.5 and 1 for With ties.

9. Leave the default options selected in the **Options** pane.

10. Select **Results** from the left.

11. In addition to the default selections, select **Create a scatter plot for each correlation pair** and **Show correlations in decreasing order of magnitude**.

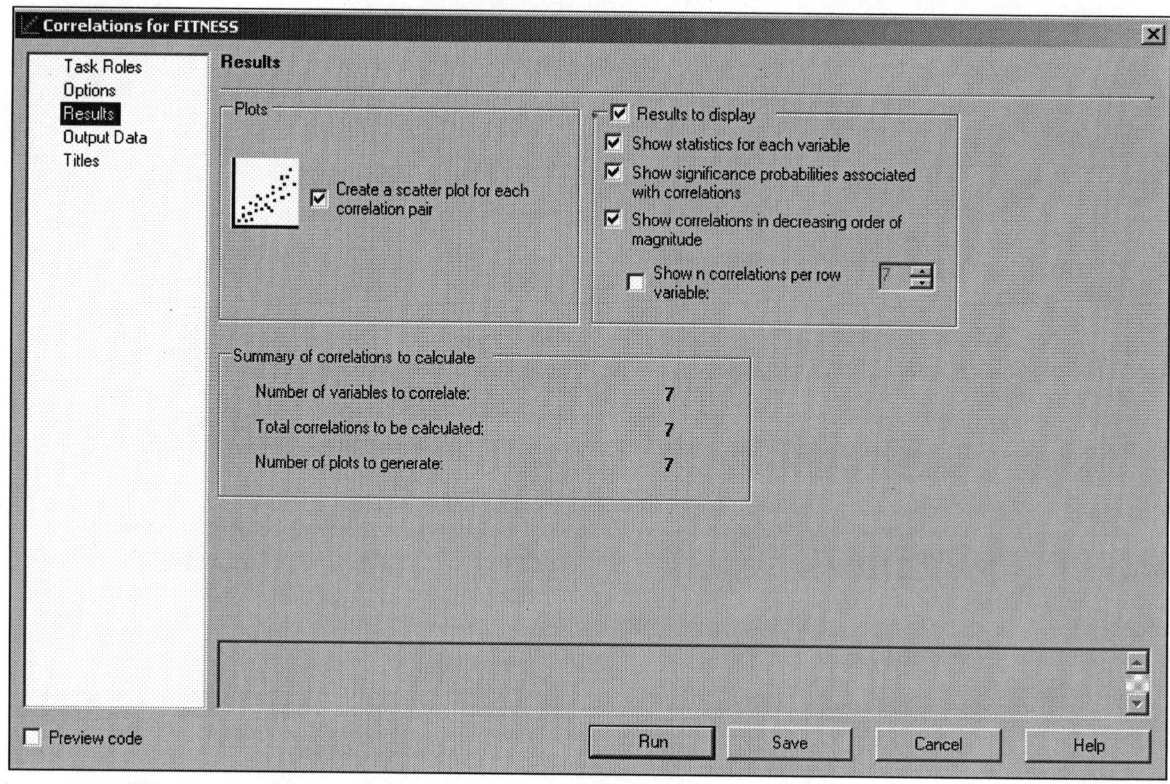

The **Summary of correlations to calculate** pane shows that seven correlations will be calculated from the data.

The Show correlations in decreasing order of magnitude option displays the correlations in order by the absolute value of the coefficient, so the strongest pairwise relationships (positive or negative) are displayed first, followed by weaker relationships.

12. Select **Run**.

By default, the analysis generates univariate statistics for the analysis variables and a correlation statistic. Before looking at these, scroll through the results to view the bivariate scatter plots first.

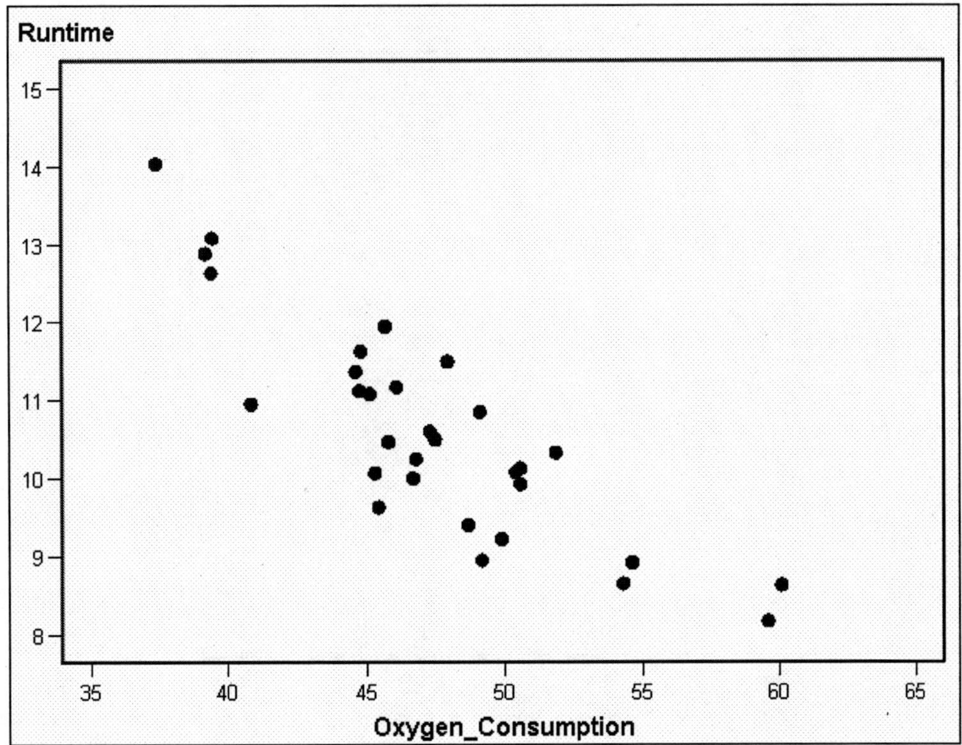

This plot suggests that the longer an individual takes to run 1.5 miles, the lower the oxygen consumption measurement is.

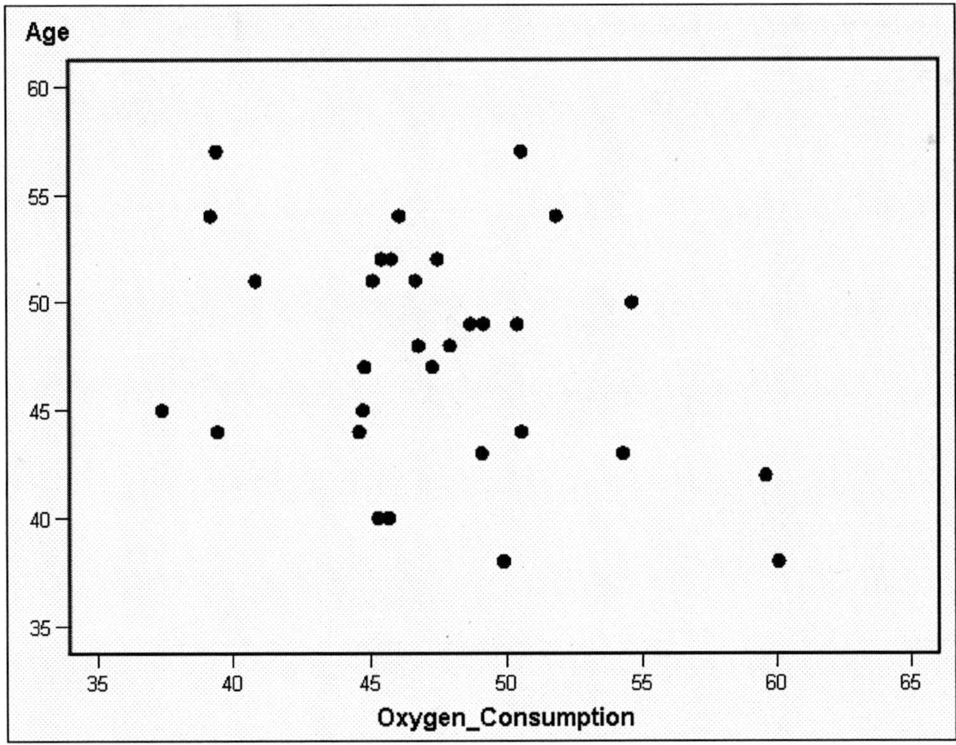

There appears to be a weak linear relationship between `Oxygen_Consumption` and `Age`.

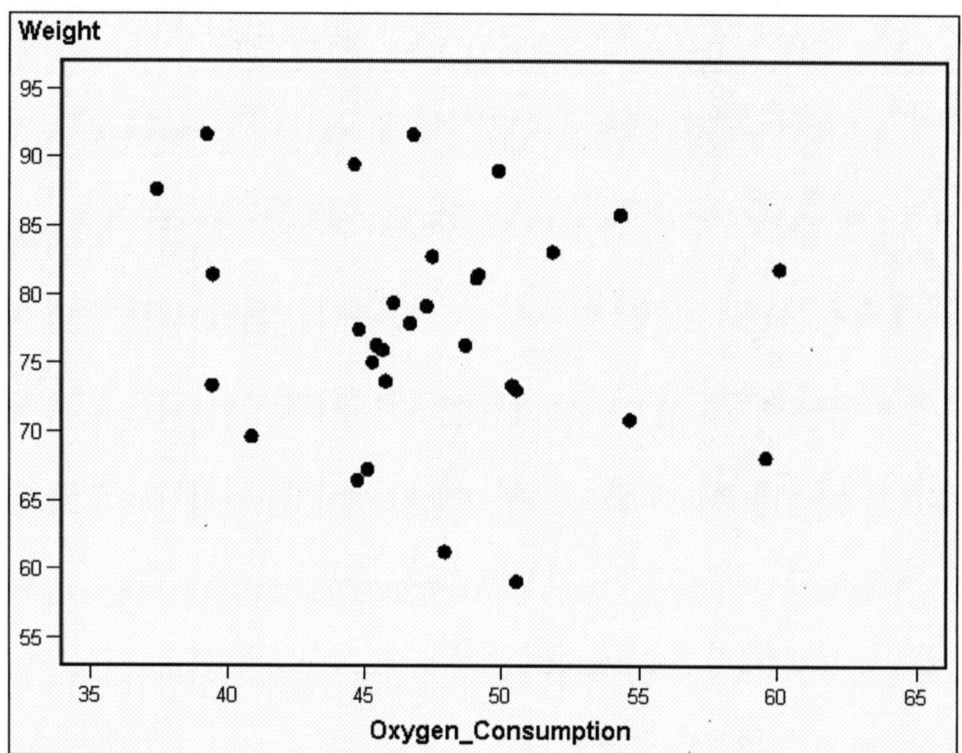

There does not appear to be a relationship between **Oxygen_Consumption** and **Weight**.

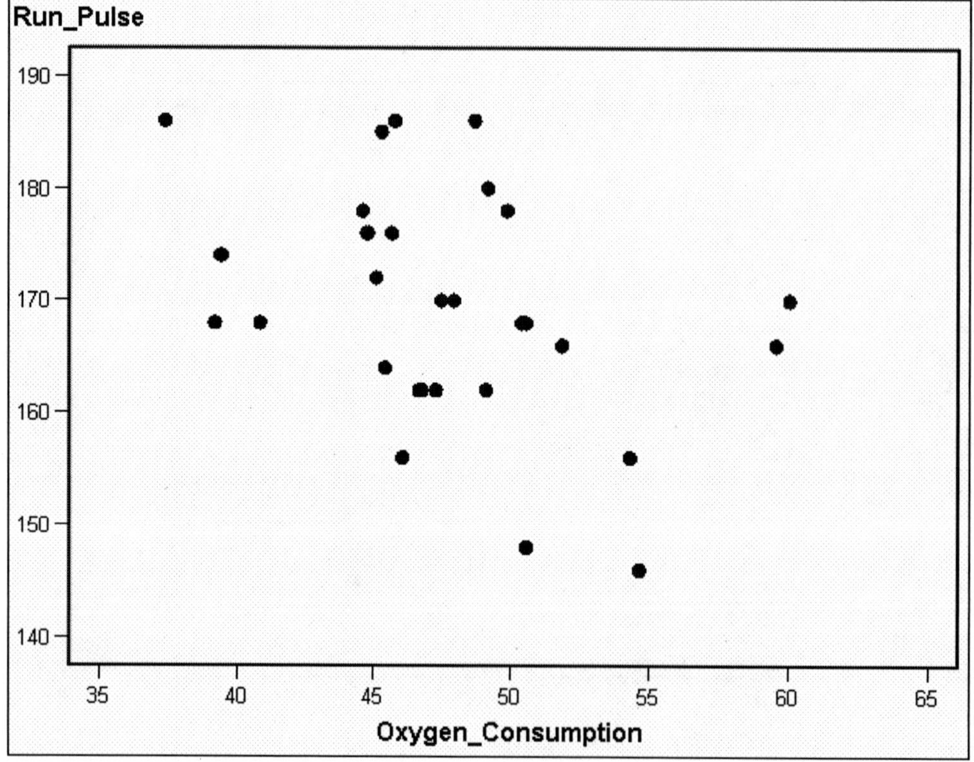

Oxygen_Consumption and **Run_Pulse** show a potential weak association.

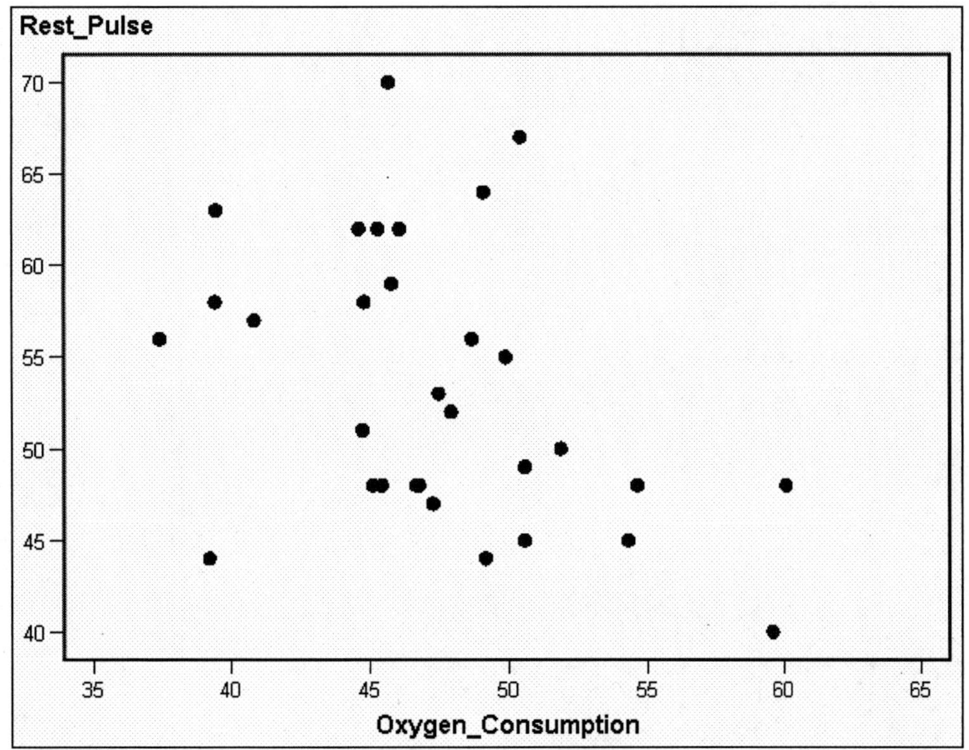

A weak linear association may exist between `Oxygen_Consumption` and `Rest_Pulse`.

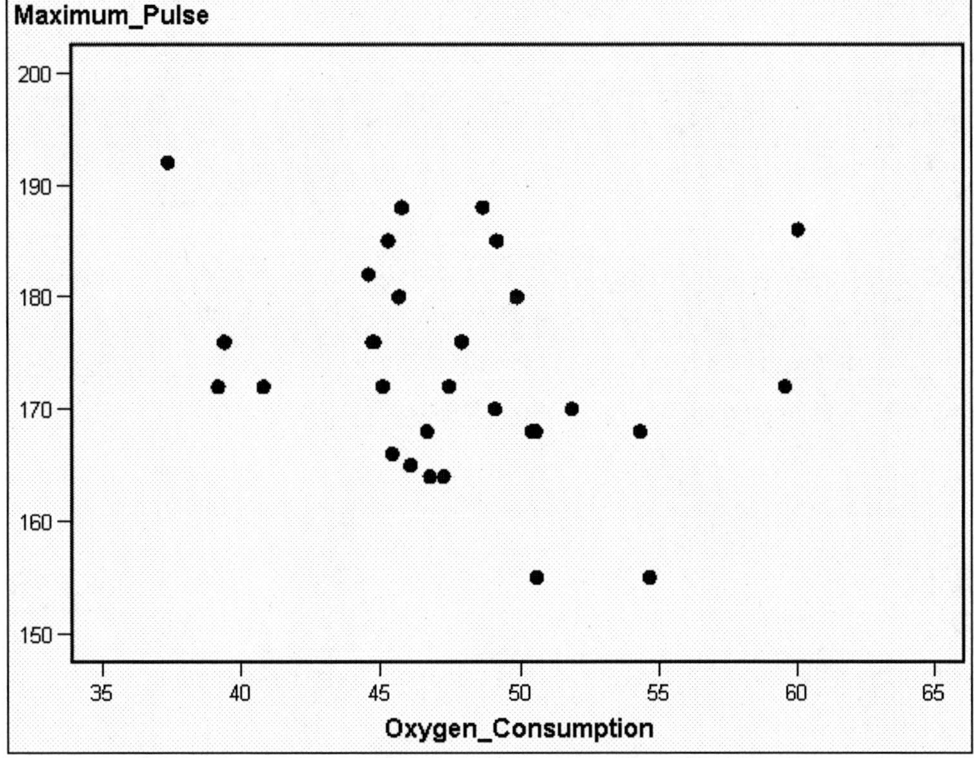

There appears to be no relationship between `Oxygen_Consumption` and `Maximum_Pulse`.

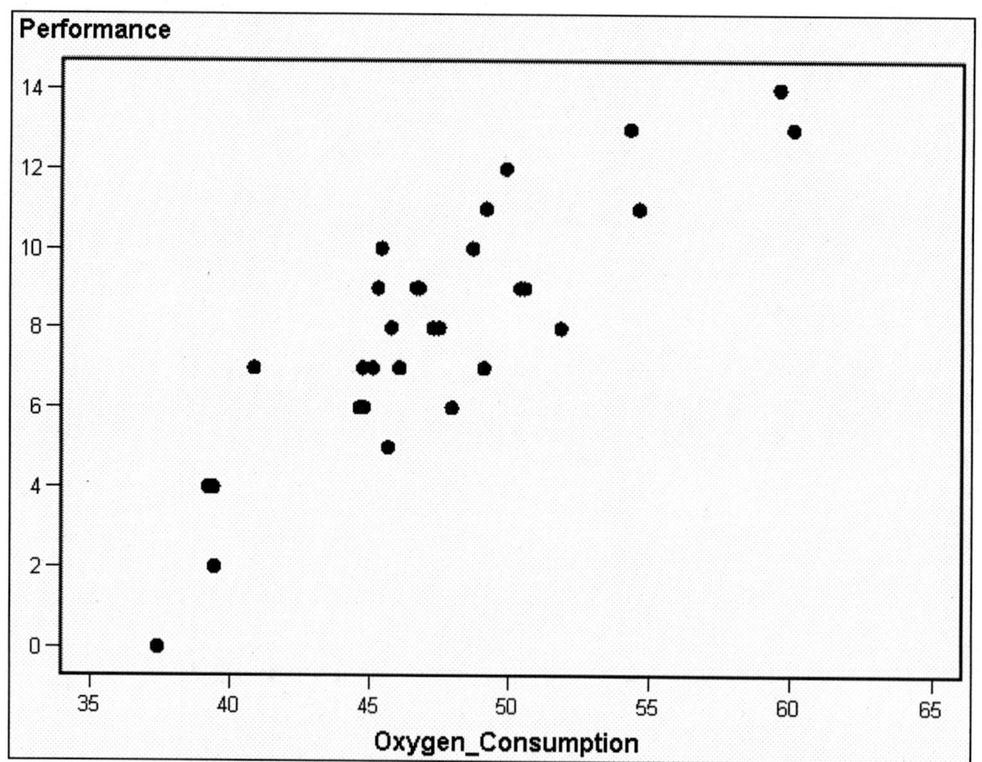

As **Performance** increases, **Oxygen_Consumption** appears to increase as well.

Return to the top of the Correlations task results. A table of simple statistics is included for all variables.

1 With Variables:	Oxygen_Consumption
7 Variables:	Runtime Age Weight Run_Pulse Rest_Pulse Maximum_Pulse Performance

Simple Statistics

Variable	N	Mean	Std Dev	Sum	Minimum	Maximum
Oxygen_Consumption	31	47.37581	5.32777	1469	37.39000	60.06000
Runtime	31	10.58613	1.38741	328.17000	8.17000	14.03000
Age	31	47.67742	5.26236	1478	38.00000	57.00000
Weight	31	77.44452	8.32857	2401	59.08000	91.63000
Run_Pulse	31	169.64516	10.25199	5259	146.00000	186.00000
Rest_Pulse	31	53.45161	7.61944	1657	40.00000	70.00000
Maximum_Pulse	31	173.77419	9.16410	5387	155.00000	192.00000
Performance	31	8.00000	3.11983	248.00000	0	14.00000

Pearson Correlation Coefficients, N = 31 Prob > |r| under H0: Rho=0							
Oxygen_Consumption	Performance 0.86377 <.0001	Runtime -0.86219 <.0001	Rest_Pulse -0.39935 0.0260	Run_Pulse -0.39808 0.0266	Age -0.31162 0.0879	Maximum_Pulse -0.23677 0.1997	Weight -0.16289 0.3813

If your results become too wide to see quickly in HTML format, you can select the RTF or PDF output style from **Tools** ⇨ **Options** ⇨ **Results** to see results with printer-style line breaks.

The correlation coefficient between **Oxygen_Consumption** and **Performance** is 0.86377. The *p*-value is small, which indicates that the population correlation coefficient (Rho) is significantly different from 0. The second largest correlation coefficient, in absolute value, between **Oxygen_Consumption** and **Runtime** is -0.86219.

The correlation analysis indicates that several variables might be good predictors for **Oxygen_Consumption**.

When you prepare to conduct a regression analysis, it is always good practice to examine the correlations between the potential predictor variables. The Correlations task can be used to generate a matrix of correlation coefficients for the predictor variables.

1. Double-click on the Correlations task under **FITNESS** in the process flow.
2. Select the **Task Roles** pane.
3. Select **Oxygen_Consumption**, Using the left-pointing arrow, move it back to the **Variables to assign** list.

   The **Correlate with** field should now be empty.

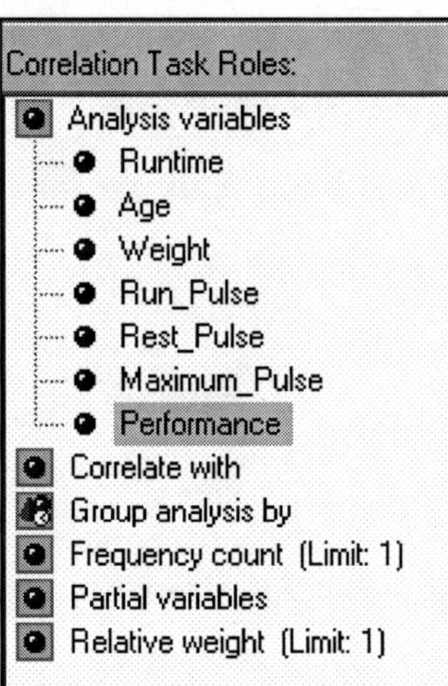

4. Select the **Results** pane.

5. Deselect the options **Create a scatter plot for each correlation pair**, **Show statistics for each variable**, and **Show correlations in decreasing order of magnitude**.

   The Simple Statistics table might be redundant if you have already performed a distribution analysis. This eliminates the table of default descriptive statistics for each variable.

   Notice that the **Summary** pane shows that 21 correlations will be calculated from the 7 variables. Because no **Correlation with** variable was specified, all possible pairwise correlations are generated.

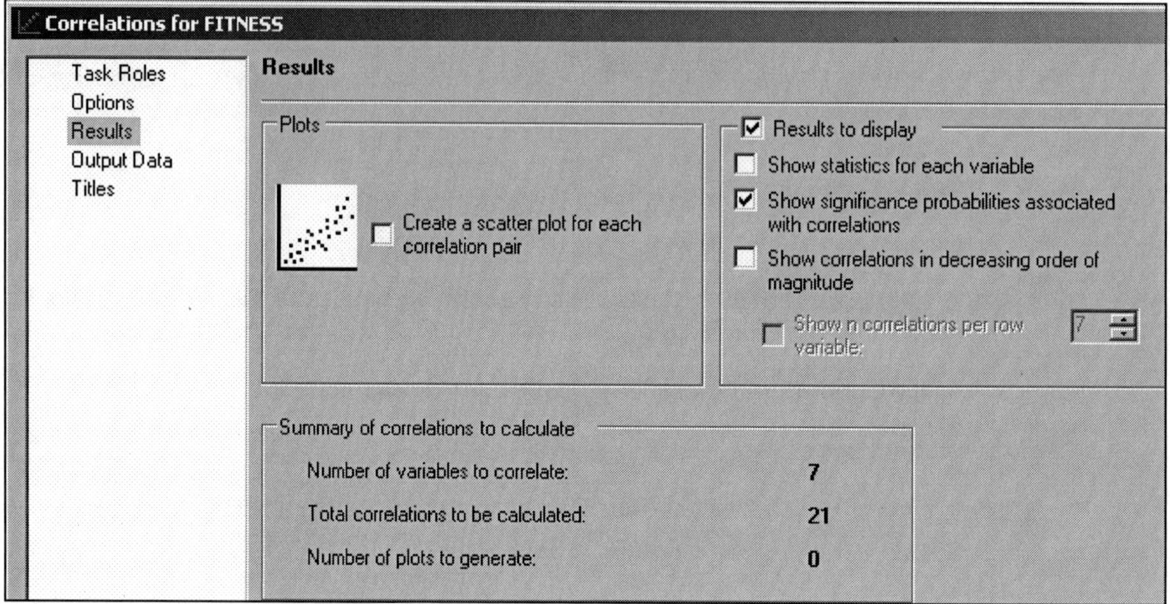

6. Select **Run**.

7. Select **No** to the pop-up window inquiry:

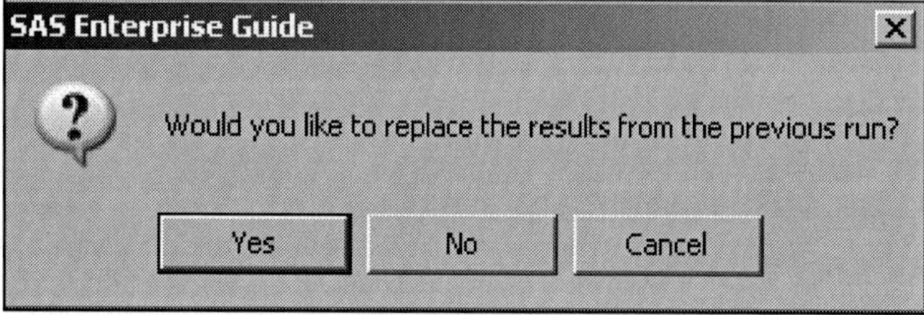

   Your choice will create separate results, and preserve the analysis with the dependent variable, `Oxygen_Consumption`, in the display tree. To avoid confusion, rename this latest task's results.

8. Make sure the second Correlations task is highlighted in the process flow.

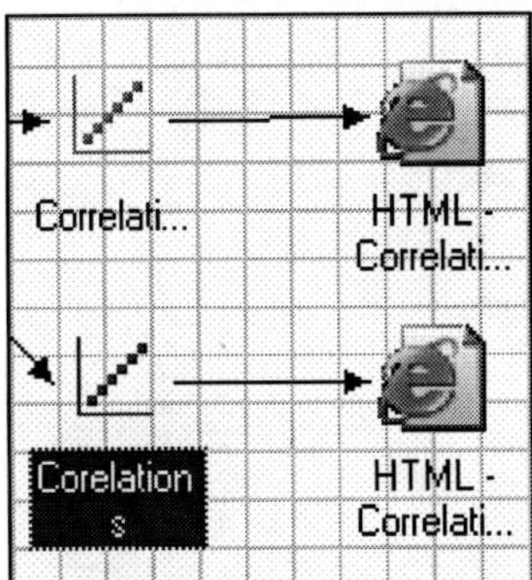

9. Select **Correlations** again. You can now rename this task `Corr IVs`.

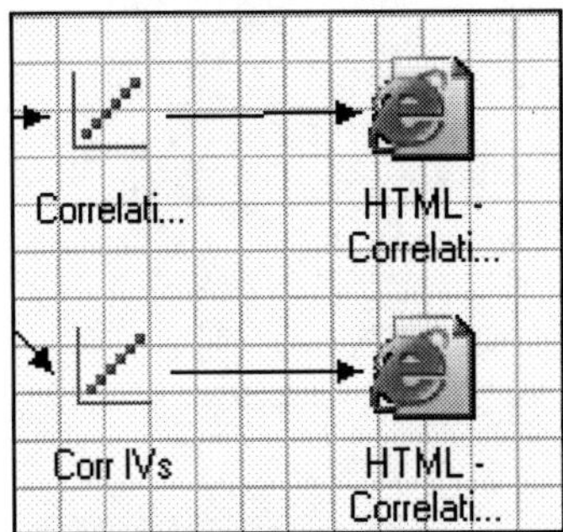

10. Return to the analysis by opening HTML.

Pearson Correlation Coefficients, N = 31 Prob > |r| under H0: Rho=0							
	Runtime	Age	Weight	Run_Pulse	Rest_Pulse	Maximum_Pulse	Performance
Runtime	1.00000	0.19523 0.2926	0.14351 0.4412	0.31365 0.0858	0.45038 0.0110	0.22610 0.2213	-0.98841 <.0001
Age	0.19523 0.2926	1.00000	-0.24050 0.1925	-0.31607 0.0832	-0.15087 0.4178	-0.41490 0.0203	-0.22943 0.2144
Weight	0.14351 0.4412	-0.24050 0.1925	1.00000	0.18152 0.3284	0.04397 0.8143	0.24938 0.1761	-0.10544 0.5724
Run_Pulse	0.31365 0.0858	-0.31607 0.0832	0.18152 0.3284	1.00000	0.35246 0.0518	0.92975 <.0001	-0.31369 0.0857
Rest_Pulse	0.45038 0.0110	-0.15087 0.4178	0.04397 0.8143	0.35246 0.0518	1.00000	0.30512 0.0951	-0.47957 0.0063
Maximum_Pulse	0.22610 0.2213	-0.41490 0.0203	0.24938 0.1761	0.92975 <.0001	0.30512 0.0951	1.00000	-0.22035 0.2336
Performance	-0.98841 <.0001	-0.22943 0.2144	-0.10544 0.5724	-0.31369 0.0857	-0.47957 0.0063	-0.22035 0.2336	1.00000

The correlations are displayed in matrix form, with diagonal values being equal. The value under the correlation is a p-value, testing the null hypothesis that Rho=0.

The following correlation table was created from the matrix by choosing small *p*-values. The table is in descending order, based on the absolute value of the correlation. It provides a summary of the correlation analysis of the independent variables.

Row Variable	Column Variable	Pearson's r	Prob > |r|
`Runtime`	`Performance`	-0.98841	<.0001
`Run_Pulse`	`Maximum_Pulse`	0.92975	<.0001
`Rest_Pulse`	`Performance`	-0.47957	0.0063
`Runtime`	`Rest_Pulse`	0.45038	0.0110
`Age`	`Maximum_Pulse`	-0.41490	0.0203
`Run_Pulse`	`Rest_Pulse`	0.35246	0.0518

3.2 Simple Linear Regression

Objectives

- Explain the concepts of simple linear regression.
- Fit a simple linear regression using the Linear Regression task.
- Produce predicted values and confidence intervals.

18

Overview

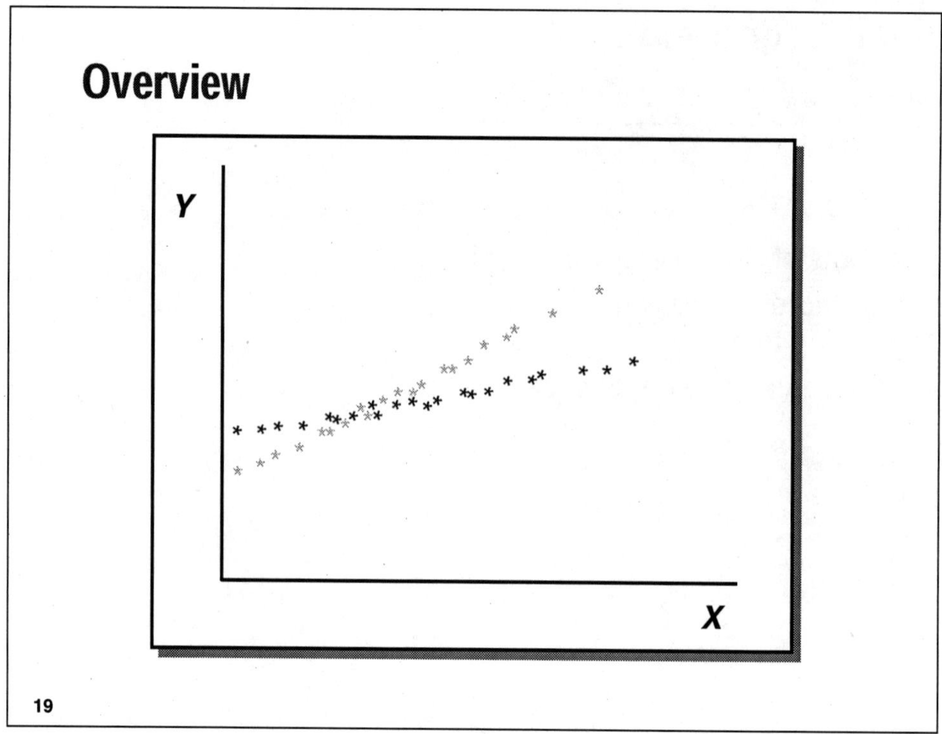

19

In the last section, you used correlation analysis to quantify the linear relationships between continuous response variables. Two pairs of variables can have the same correlation statistic, but the linear relationship can be different. In this section, you use simple linear regression to define the linear relationship between a response variable and a predictor variable.

The *response variable* is the variable of primary interest.

The *predictor variable* is used to explain the variability in the response variable.

Simple Linear Regression Analysis

The objectives of simple linear regression are to

- assess the significance of the predictor variable in explaining the variability or behavior of the response variable
- predict the values of the response variable given the values of the predictor variable.

20

In simple linear regression, the values of the predictor variable are assumed to be fixed. Thus, try to explain the variability of the response variable given the values of the predictor variable.

Fitness Example

PREDICTOR **RESPONSE**

`Performance` → `Oxygen_Consumption`

21

You noted that the performance measure has the highest correlation (-0.98841) with the oxygen consumption capacity of the club members. Consequently, you want to explore the relationship between `Oxygen_Consumption` and `Performance` using simple linear regression.

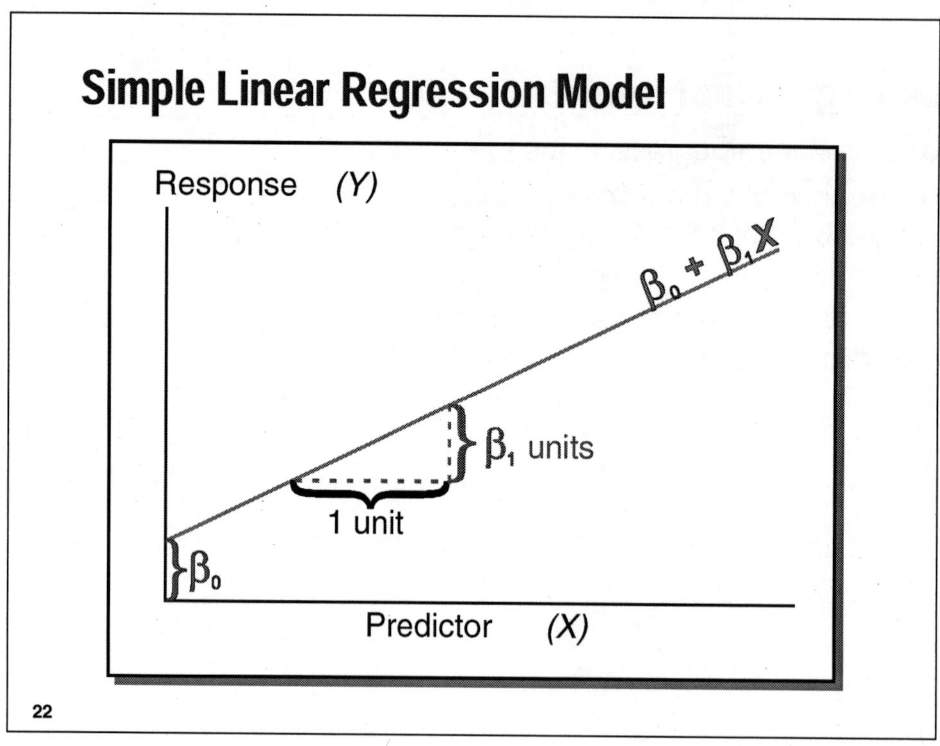

The relationship between the response variable and the predictor variable can be characterized by the equation $Y = \beta_0 + \beta_1 X + \varepsilon$

where

Y	response variable
X	predictor variable
β_0	intercept parameter, which corresponds to the value of the response variable when the predictor is 0
β_1	slope parameter, which corresponds to the magnitude of change in the response variable given a one-unit change in the predictor variable
ε	error term representing deviations of Y about $\beta_0 + \beta_1 X$.

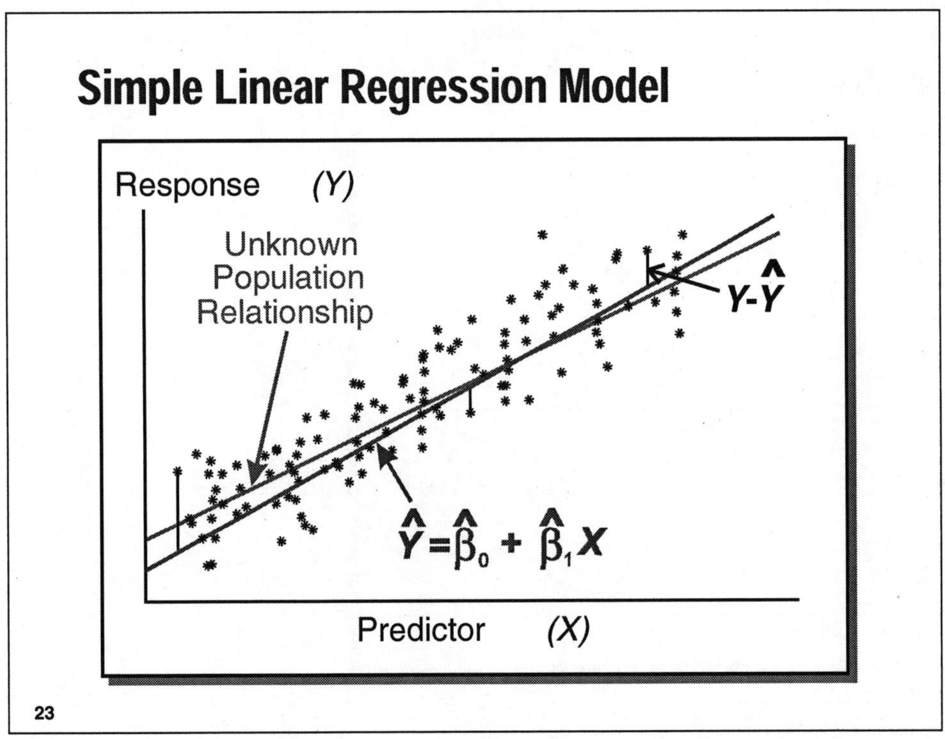

Because your goal in simple linear regression is usually to characterize the relationship between the response and predictor variables in your population, you begin with a sample of data. From this sample, you estimate the unknown population parameters (β_0, β_1) that define the assumed relationship between your response and predictor variables.

Estimates of the unknown population parameters β_0 and β_1 are obtained by the *method of least squares.* This method provides the estimates by determining the line that minimizes the sum of the squared vertical distances between the observations and the fitted line. In other words, the fitted or regression line is as close as possible to all the data points.

The method of least squares produces parameter estimates with certain optimum properties. If the assumptions of simple linear regression are valid, the least squares estimates are unbiased estimates of the population parameters and have minimum variance. The least squares estimators are often called BLUE (Best Linear Unbiased Estimators). The term *best* is used because of the minimum variance property.

Because of these optimum properties, the method of least squares is used by many data analysts to investigate the relationship between continuous predictor and response variables.

With a large and representative sample, the fitted regression line should be a good approximation of the relationship between the response and predictor variables in the population. The estimated parameters obtained using the method of least squares should be good approximations of the true population parameters.

The Baseline Model

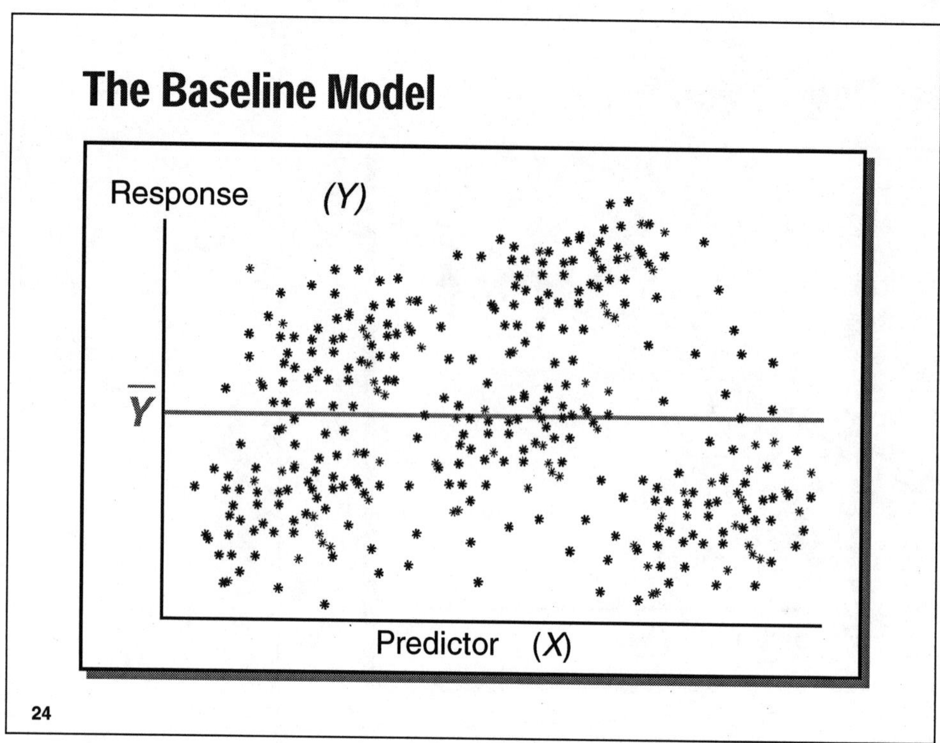

24

To determine whether the predictor variable explains a significant amount of variability in the response variable, the simple linear regression model is compared to the baseline model. The fitted regression line in a baseline model is a horizontal line across all values of the predictor variable. The slope of the regression line is 0 and the intercept is the sample mean of the response variable, ($\overline{Y}$).

In a baseline model, there is no association between the response variable and the predictor variable. Knowing the mean of the response variable is as good in predicting values in the response variable as knowing the values of the predictor variable.

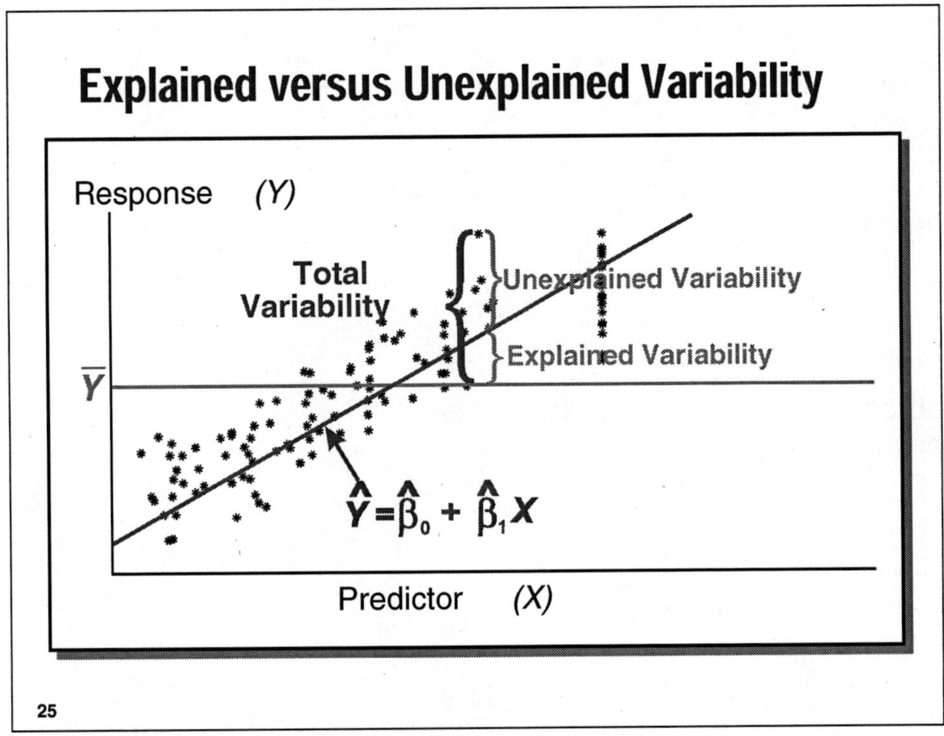

To determine whether a simple linear regression model is better than the baseline model, compare the explained variability to the unexplained variability.

Explained variability — is related to the difference between the regression line and the mean of the response variable. The model sum of squares (SSM) is the amount of variability explained by your model. The model sum of squares is equal to $\sum(\hat{Y}_i - \bar{Y})^2$.

Unexplained variability — is related to the difference between the observed values and the regression line. The error sum of squares (SSE) is the amount of variability unexplained by your model. The error sum of squares is equal to $\sum(Y_i - \hat{Y}_i)^2$.

Total variability — is related to the difference between the observed values and the mean of the response variable. The corrected total sum of squares is the sum of the explained and unexplained variability. The corrected total sum of squares is equal to $\sum(Y_i - \bar{Y})^2$.

Model Hypothesis Test

Null Hypothesis:

The simple linear regression model does not fit the data better than the baseline model.

$$\beta_1 = 0$$

Alternative Hypothesis:

The simple linear regression model does fit the data better than the baseline model.

$$\beta_1 \neq 0$$

26

If the estimated simple linear regression model does **not** fit the data better than the baseline model, you fail to reject the null hypothesis. Thus, you do **not** have enough evidence to say that the slope of the regression line in the population is **not** 0 and that the predictor variable explains a significant amount of variability in the response variable.

If the estimated simple linear regression model **does** fit the data better than the baseline model, you reject the null hypothesis. Thus, you **do** have enough evidence to say that the slope of the regression line in the population is **not** 0 and that the predictor variable explains a significant amount of variability in the response variable.

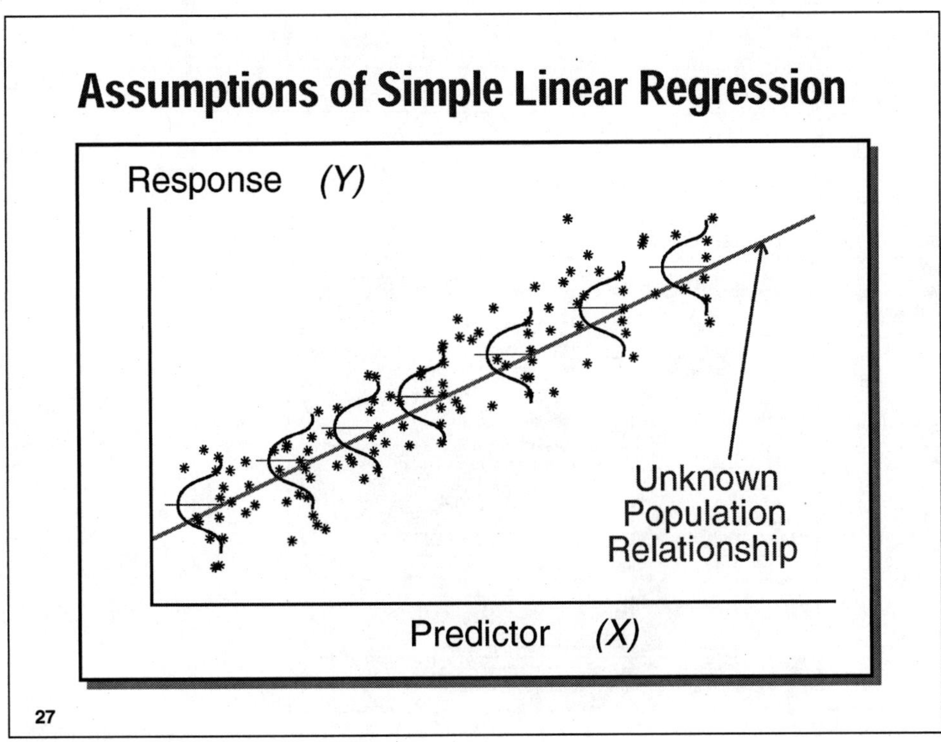

One of the assumptions of simple linear regression is that the mean of the response variable is linearly related to the value of the predictor variable. In other words, a straight line connects the means of the response variable at each value of the predictor variable.

The other assumptions are the same as the assumptions for ANOVA: the responses are normally distributed, have equal variances, and are independent at each value of the predictor variable.

The verification of these assumptions is discussed in a later chapter.

The Linear Regression Task

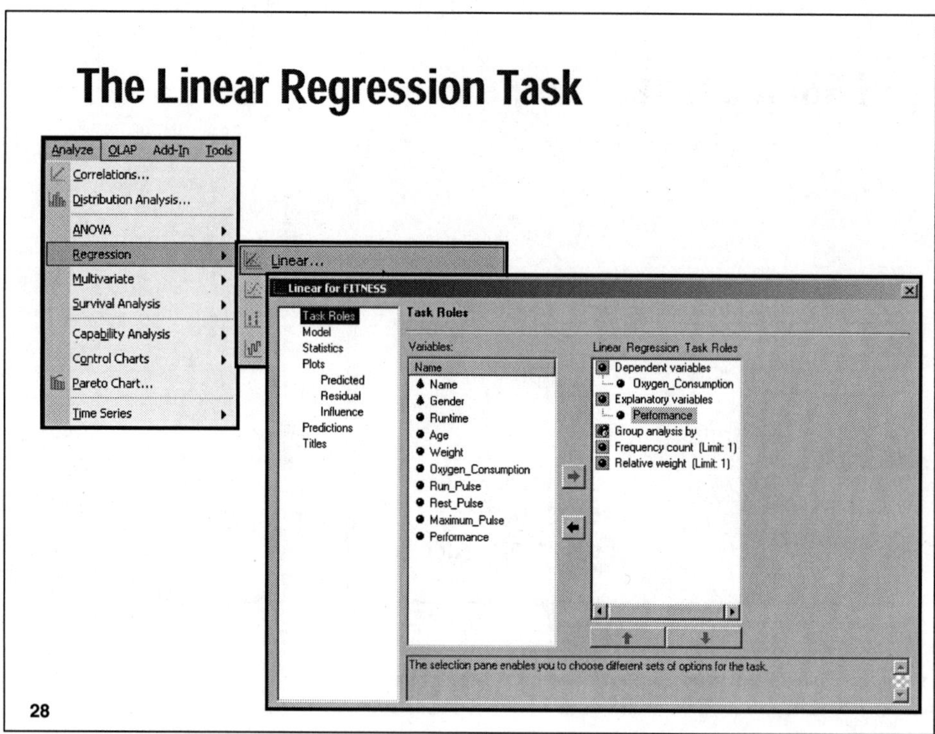

28

The Linear Regression task enables you to fit regression models to your data.

Performing Simple Linear Regression

Example: Because there is an apparent linear relationship between `Oxygen_Consumption` and `Performance`, perform a simple linear regression analysis with `Oxygen_Consumption` as the response variable.

1. Select **Analyze** ⇨ **Regression** ⇨ **Linear…**.
2. Assign the variable `Oxygen_Consumption` to the Dependent variables role. Assign `Performance` to the Explanatory variables role.

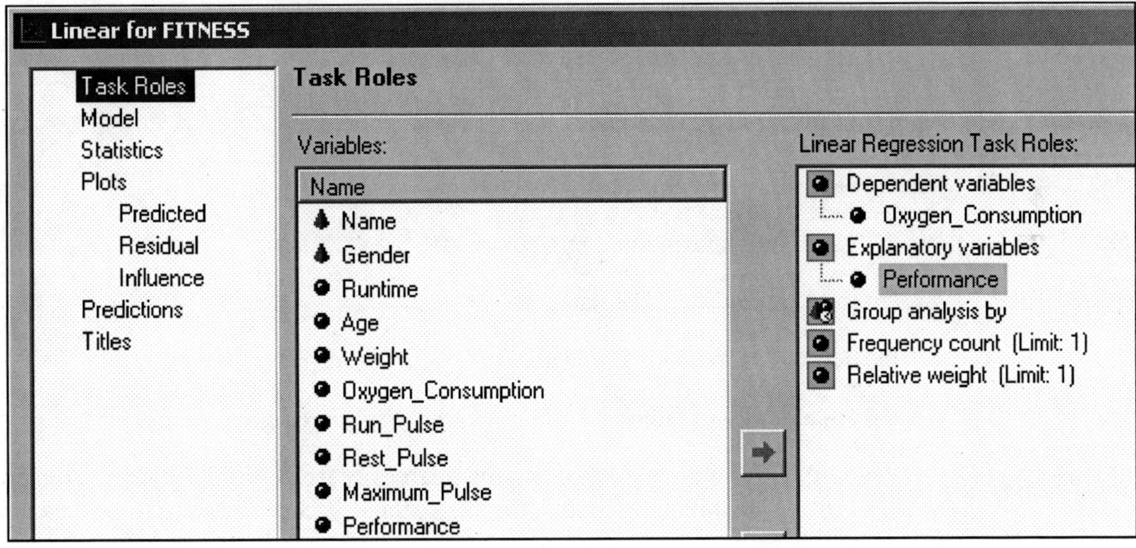

3. Select **Run**.

Analysis of Variance					
Source	DF	Sum of Squares	Mean Square	F Value	Pr > F
Model	1	635.34150	635.34150	85.22	<.0001
Error	29	216.21305	7.45562		
Corrected Total	30	851.55455			

The Analysis of Variance (ANOVA) table provides an analysis of the variability observed in the data and the variability explained by the regression line.

The ANOVA table for simple linear regression is divided into six columns, but all the contents are being explained.

Source	labels the source of variability.
Model	is the variability explained by your model.
Error	is the variability unexplained by your model.
Corrected Total	is the total variability in the data.
DF	is the degrees of freedom associated with each source of variability.
Sum of Squares	is the amount of variability associated with each source of variability.
Mean Square	is the ratio of the sum of squares and the degrees of freedom. This value corresponds to the amount of variability associated with each degree of freedom for each source of variation.
F Value	is the ratio of the mean square for the model and the mean square for the error. This ratio compares the variability explained by the regression line to the variability unexplained by the regression line.
Pr > F	is the *p*-value associated with the *F* value.

The *F* value tests whether the slope of the predictor variable is equal to 0. The *p*-value is small (less than .05), so you have enough evidence to reject the null hypothesis at the .05 significance level. Thus, you can conclude that the simple linear regression model fits the data better than the baseline model. In other words, `Performance` explains a significant amount of variability of `Oxygen_Consumption`.

The second part of the results provide summary measures of fit for the model.

Root MSE	2.73050	R-Square	0.7461
Dependent Mean	47.37581	Adj R-Sq	0.7373
Coeff Var	5.76349		

R-Square The coefficient of determination, usually referred to as the R^2 value.

This value is

- between 0 and 1.
- the proportion of variability observed in the data explained by the regression line. In this example, the value is 0.7461, which means that the regression line explains 75% of the total variation in the response values.
- the square of the Pearson correlation coefficient.

Root MSE The root mean square error is an estimate of the standard deviation of the response variable at each value of the predictor variable. It is the square root of the MSE.

Dependent Mean The overall mean of the response variable, $\overline{Y}$.

Coeff Var The coefficient of variation is the size of the standard deviation relative to the mean. The coefficient of variation is calculated as $\left(\frac{Root\ MSE}{\overline{Y}}\right) * 100$

The coefficient of variation is a unitless measure, so it can be used to compare data that has different units of measurement or different magnitudes of measurement.

Adj R-Sq The adjusted R^2 is the R^2 that is adjusted for the number of parameters in the model. This statistic is useful in multiple regression and is discussed in a later section.

The Parameter Estimates table defines the model for your data.

Parameter Estimates					
Variable	DF	Parameter Estimate	Standard Error	t Value	Pr > |t|
Intercept	1	35.57526	1.36917	25.98	<.0001
Performance	1	1.47507	0.15979	9.23	<.0001

DF — represents the degrees of freedom associated with each term in the model.

Parameter Estimate — is the estimated value of the parameters associated with each term in the model.

Standard Error — is the standard error of each parameter estimate.

t Value — is the *t* statistic, which is calculated by dividing the parameters by their corresponding standard errors.

Pr > |t| — is the *p*-value associated with the *t* statistic. It tests whether the parameter associated with each term in the model is different from 0. For this example, the slope for the predictor variable is statistically different from 0. Thus, you can conclude that the predictor variable explains a significant portion of variability in the response variable.

Because the estimate of β_0=35.58 and β_1=1.48, the estimated regression equation is given by Predicited **Oxygen_Consumption** = 35.58 + 1.48(**Performance**).

The model indicates that an increase of one unit for **Performance** amounts to a 1.48 increase in **Oxygen_Consumption**. However, this equation is appropriate only in the range of values you observed for the variable **Performance**.

The parameter estimates table also shows that the intercept parameter is not equal to 0. However, the test for the intercept parameter only has practical significance when the range of values for the predictor variable includes 0. In this example, the test may have practical significance because **Performance**=0 is inside the range of values you are considering (**Performance** ranges from 0 to 14).

Producing Predicted Values

What is `Oxygen_Consumption` when `Performance` is **1, 3, 5,** or **12**?

30

One objective in regression analysis is to predict values of the response variable given values of the predictor variables. You can obviously use the estimated regression equation to produce predicted values, but if you want a large number of predictions, this can be cumbersome.

To produce predicted values in the Linear Regression task, follow these steps:

1. Create a data set with the values of the independent variable for which you want to make predictions.

2. Fit a simple linear regression model to the original data and specify that predicted values be saved to the output data set for data from an additional source on the Results tab. Because the observations added in the previous step contain missing values for the response variable, SAS does not include these observations when fitting the regression model. However, it does produce predicted values for these observations.

Producing Predicted Values

Example: Produce predicted values of **`Oxygen_Consumption`** when the mean of **`Performance`** is 1, 3, 5, and 12.

The data set **`NEED_PREDICTION`** contains values for the predictor variable, **`Performance`**, but no values for **`Oxygen_Consumption`**. You can display predicted values based on the model you fit in the linear regression task.

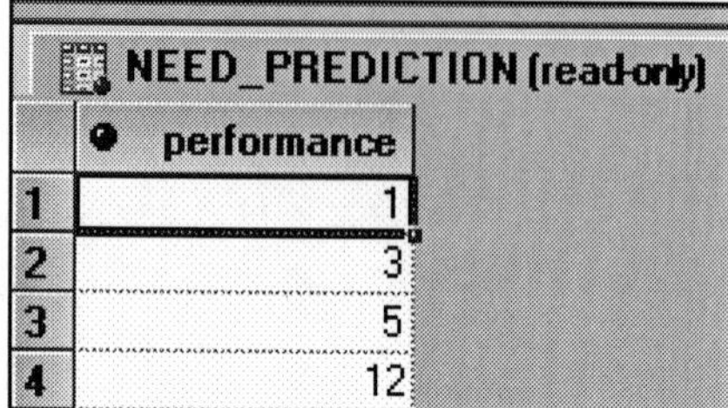

NEED_PREDICTION (read-only)

	performance
1	1
2	3
3	5
4	12

1. Double-click on the Linear task attached to **`FITNESS`** in the process flow.

2. Select the **Predictions** pane.

3. Select **<u>Additional data</u>** to read values of **`Performance`** from the data set **`NEED_PREDICTION`** to generate predictions for **`Oxygen_Consumption`**.

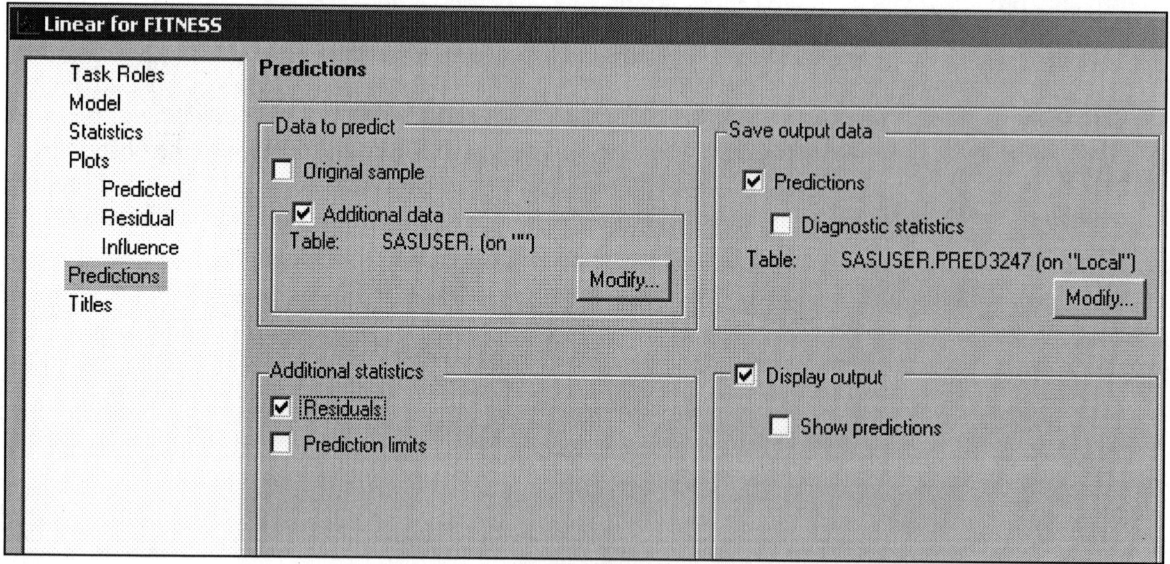

Notice that SAS Enterprise Guide selects a default location and name for an output data set. You can change this by selecting **<u>Modify</u>** next to the filename in the **Predictions** pane.

4. Select **Modify** to specify a data table from which `Performance` values are read.

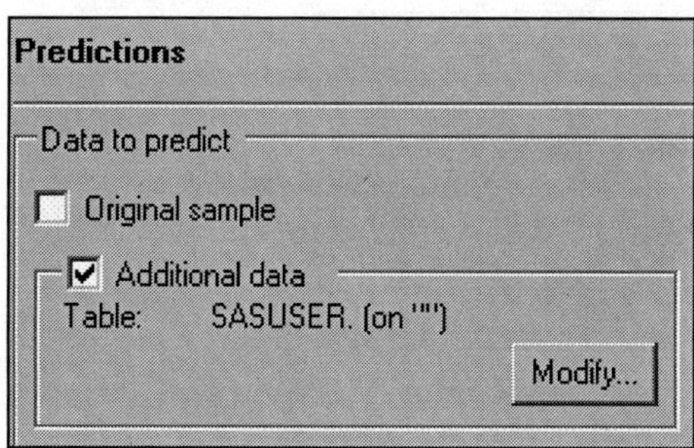

5. Select **Local** ⇨ **Libraries** ⇨ **SASUSER** if not already selected. Find the `NEED_PREDICTION` data set.

6. Select **Open**.

   The **Predictions** panel reflects the `SASUSER.NEED_PREDICTION` choice.

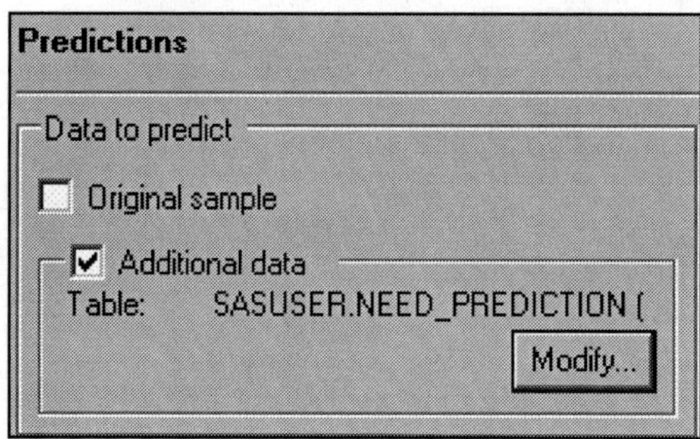

7. Select **Run**.

8. Select **Yes** to overwrite the results from the previous analysis.

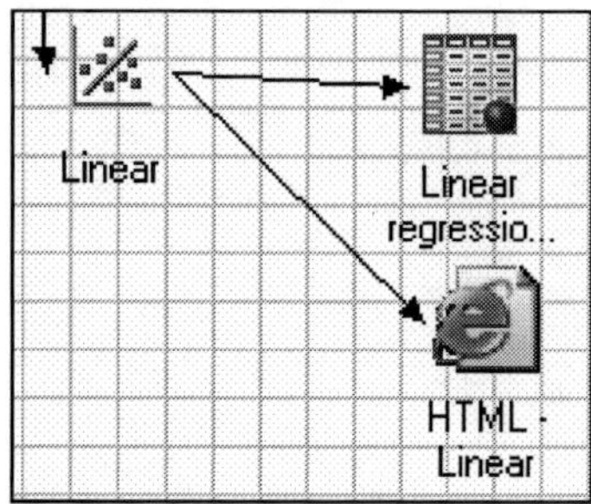

Predictions are saved to a data table in the project tree, beginning with the words Linear regression.

> If you have a large data set, a more efficient way to produce predicted values is to use the OUTEST= option in the REG procedure to generate a SAS data table with the regression coefficients. Next, generate a data set with the values of the independent variable. Finally, combine the coefficient and value data tables.

9. Double-click on the created table to view it. Scroll to the right to view the predictions.

Linear regression predictions and statistics for SASUSER.FITNESS (read-only)

	Performance	predicted_Oxygen_Consumption
1	1	37.050327
2	3	40.000463986
3	5	42.950600972
4	12	53.276080424

The table shows that the predicted value of **Oxygen_Consumption** is 37.05 when **Performance** equals 1. However, when **Performance** is 12, the predicted **Oxygen_Consumption** is 53.28.

Choose only values within or near the range of the predictor variable when you predict new values for the response variable. For this example, the observed values of the variable **Performance** range from 0 to 14. Therefore, it is unwise to predict the value of **Oxygen_Consumption** for when **Performance** is 100. The reason is that the relationship between the predictor variable and the response variable can be different beyond the range of your data.

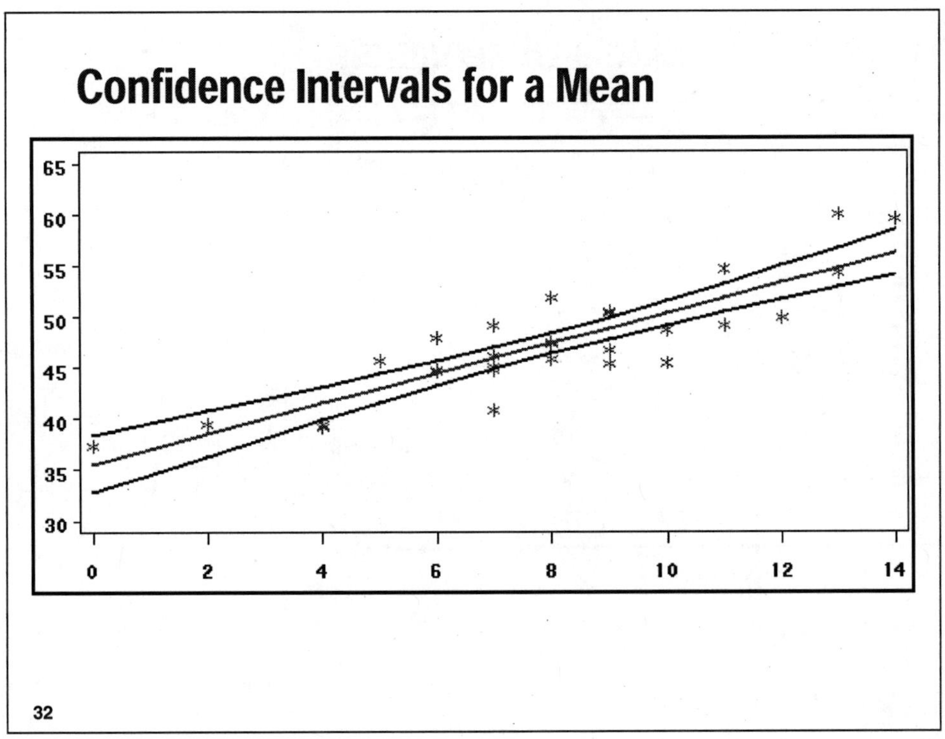

To assess the level of precision around the mean estimates of `Oxygen_Consumption`, you can produce confidence intervals around the means.

- A 95% confidence interval for the mean says that you are 95% confident your interval contains the population **mean** of Y for a particular X.
- Confidence intervals become wider as you move away from the mean of the independent variable. This reflects the fact that your estimates become more variable as you move away from the means of X and Y.

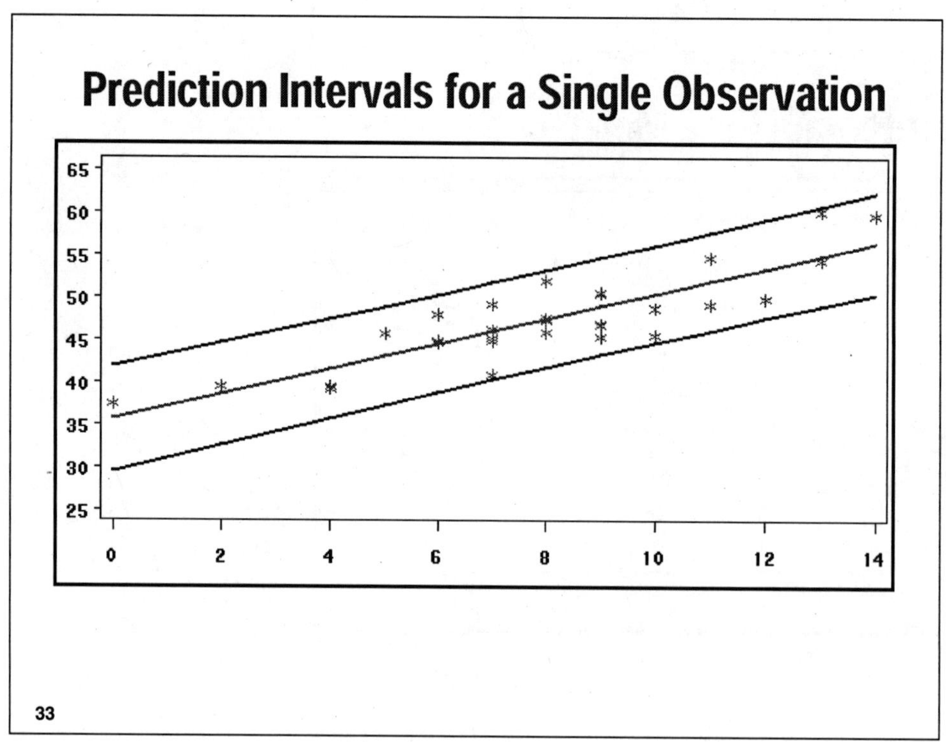

Suppose the mean **Oxygen_Consumption** at a fixed value of **Performance** is not the focus. If you are interested in establishing an inference on a future single observation, you need a prediction interval.

- A 95% prediction interval is one that you are 95% confident will contain a new observation.
- Prediction intervals are wider than confidence intervals because single observations have more variability than sample means.

Producing Confidence Intervals for the Mean and Prediction Intervals for New Values

Example: Use the Linear Regression task to produce plots of confidence intervals for the mean of `Performance` and on new values of `Performance`.

1. Locate the Linear task in the process flow.

2. Double-click on the task to open it.

3. Select the **Predicted** pane under Plots. Select **Observed vs. independents**. Select **Confidence limits** under **Show limits**.

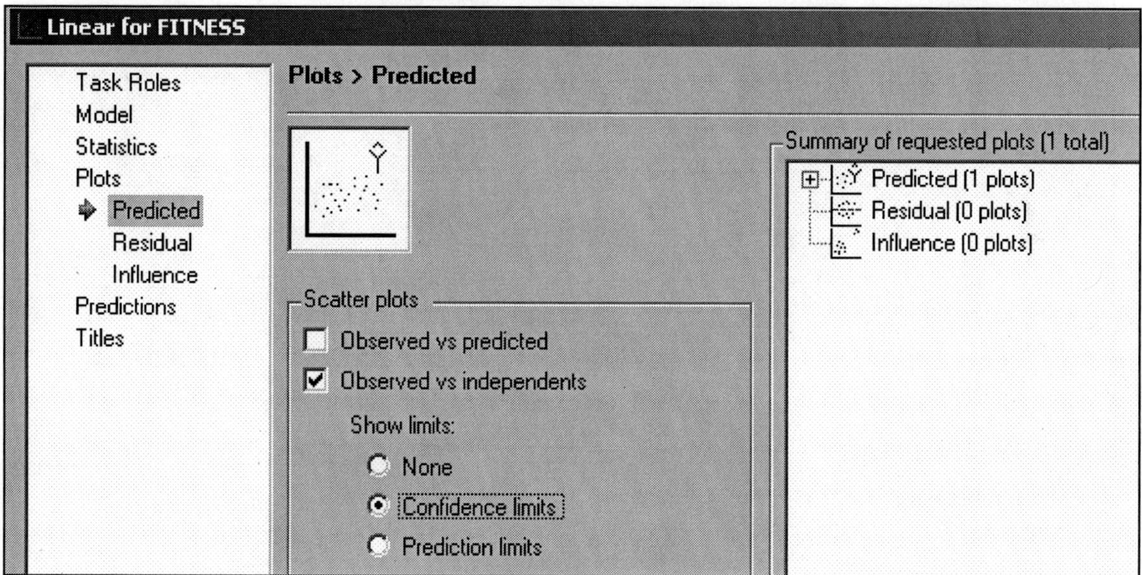

4. Select **Run**. Select **No** to create a new project node.

5. Rename this completed task `CIMean`.

6. Open the results and scroll to the graph at the end.

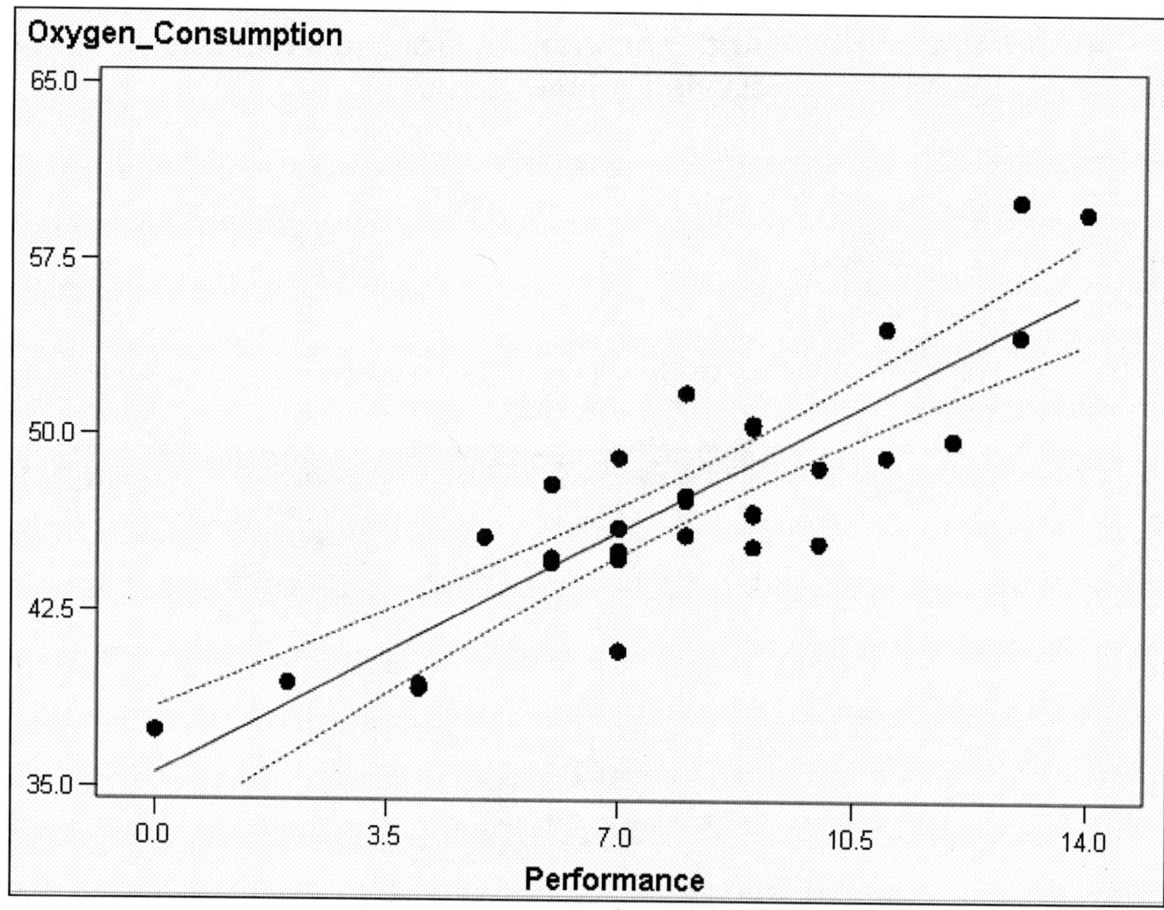

The data, regression line, and confidence intervals for the mean of `Performance` are plotted in the graph above

7. To obtain a plot of the prediction interval, double-click on the task to open it.

8. Select **Plots.**

9. Change the **Show limits** option to **Prediction limits**.

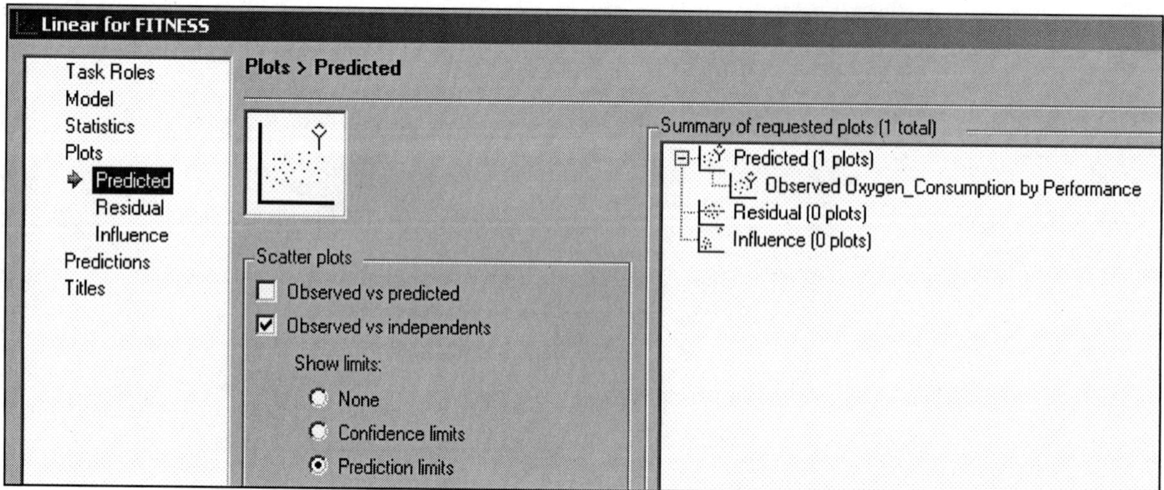

10. Select **Run** and **No** to prevent overwriting the previous results.

11. Rename the task **CIPred**.

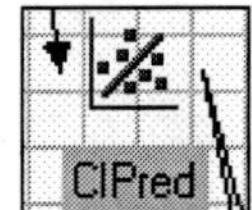

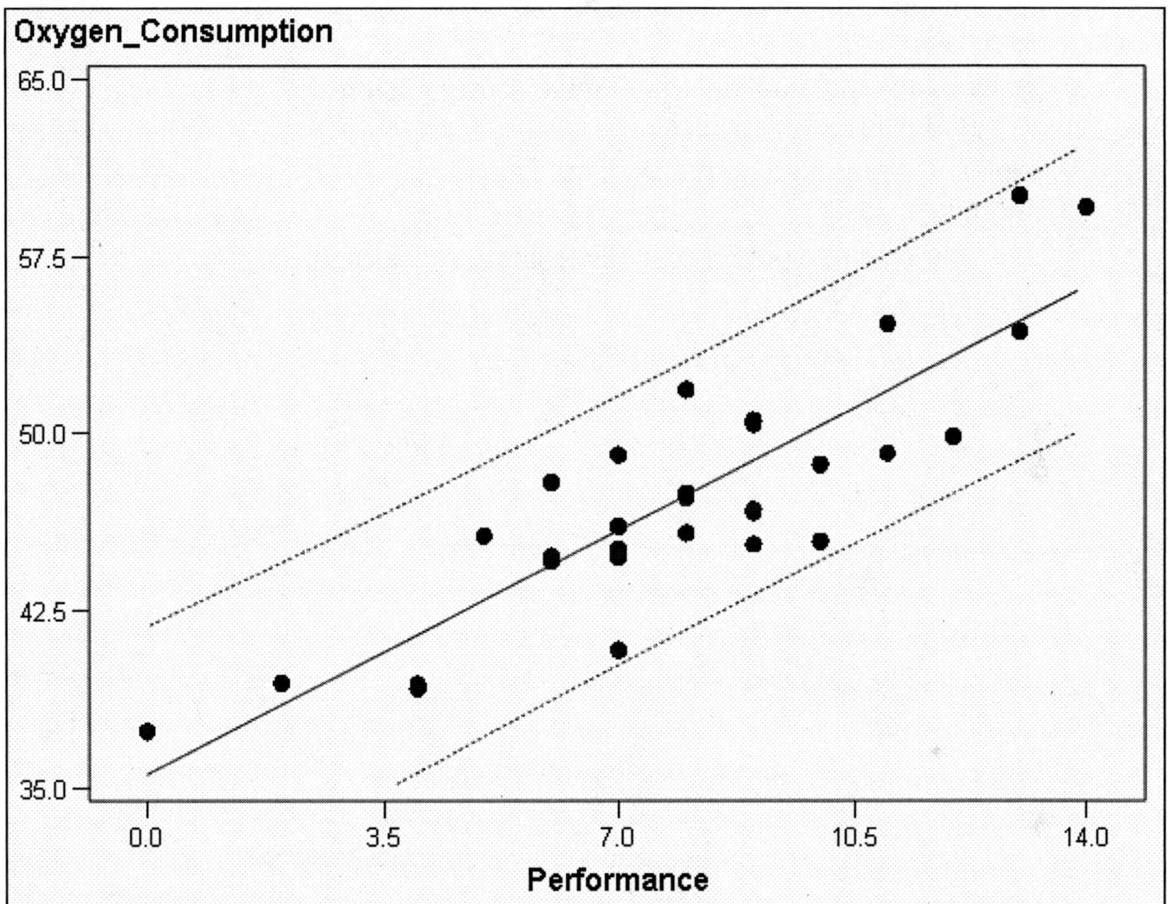

The data, regression line, and prediction intervals for the individual values of **Performance** are plotted in the graph above.

Notice that the prediction interval for an individual observation is wider than the confidence interval for the mean.

3.3 Concepts of Multiple Regression

Objectives

- Explain the mathematical model for multiple regression.
- Describe the main advantage of multiple regression versus simple linear regression.
- Explain the standard output from the Linear Regression task.
- Describe common pitfalls of multiple linear regression.

36

Multiple Linear Regression with Two Variables

Consider the two-variable model

$$Y = \beta_0 + \beta_1 X_1 + \beta_2 X_2 + \varepsilon$$

where

- Y is the dependent variable.
- X_1 and X_2 are the independent or predictor variables.
- ε is the error term.
- β_0, β_1, and β_2 are unknown parameters.

37

In simple linear regression, you can model the relationship between the two variables (two dimensions) with a line (one dimension).

For the two-variable model, you can model the relationship of three variables (three dimensions) with a plane (two dimensions).

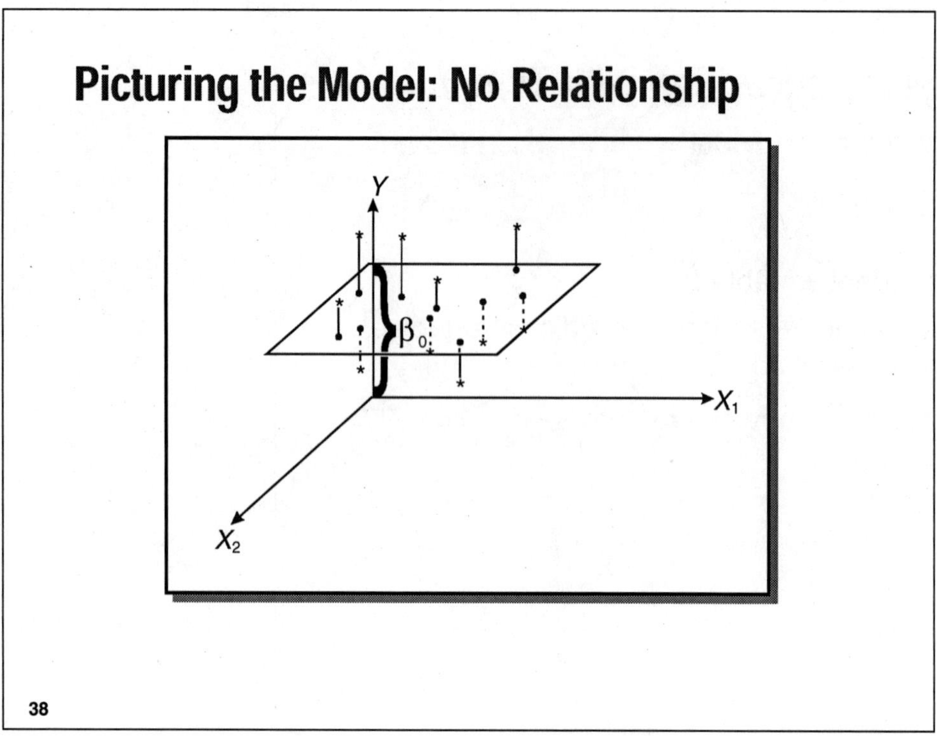

If there is no relationship among Y and X_1 and X_2, the model is a horizontal plane passing through the point ($Y = \beta_0$, $X_1 = 0$, $X_2 = 0$).

Picturing the Model: A Relationship

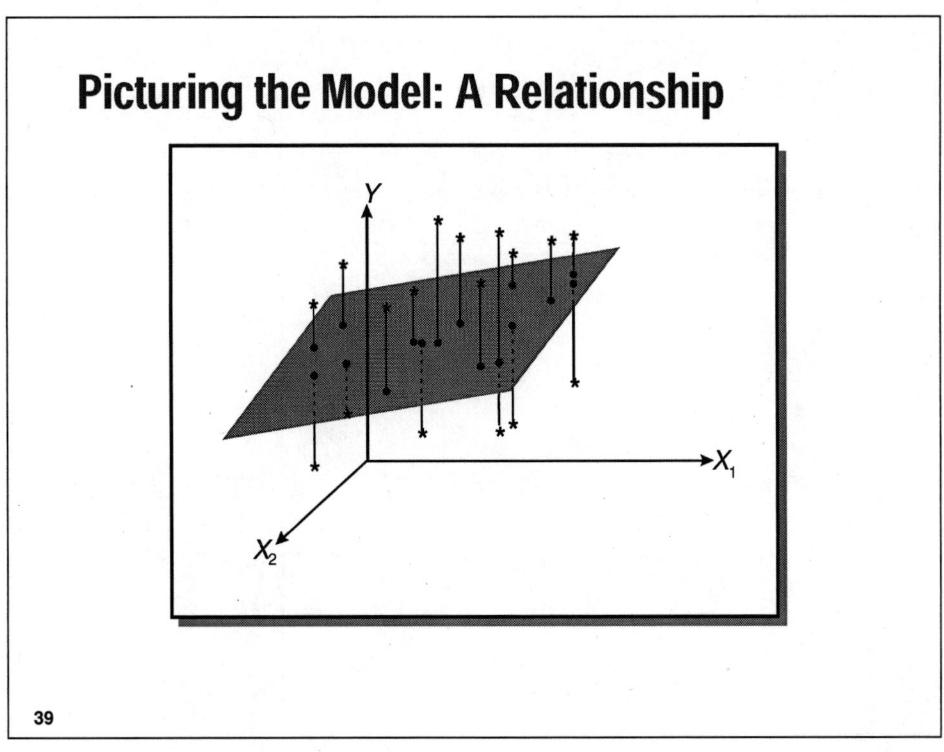

39

If there is a relationship among Y and X_1 and X_2, the model is a sloping plane passing through three points:

- $(Y = \beta_0, X_1 = 0, X_2 = 0)$
- $(Y = \beta_0 + \beta_1, X_1 = 1, X_2 = 0)$
- $(Y = \beta_0 + \beta_2, X_1 = 0, X_2 = 1)$.

The Multiple Linear Regression Model

In general, you model the dependent variable Y as a linear function of *k* independent variables (the Xs) as

$$Y = \beta_0 + \beta_1 X_1 + \ldots + \beta_k X_k + \varepsilon$$

40

You investigate the relationship of $k + 1$ variables ($k + 1$ dimensions) with a k-dimensional surface.

The multiple general linear model is not restricted to modeling only planes. By using higher order terms, such as quadratic or cubic powers of the Xs or cross products of one X with another, more complex surfaces than planes can be modeled.

In the examples, the models are limited to relatively simple surfaces, such as planes.

The model has $p = k + 1$ parameters (the βs) because of the intercept, β_0.

Model Hypothesis Test

Null Hypothesis:

- The regression model does not fit the data better than the baseline model.
- $\beta 1 = \beta 2 = \ldots = \beta k = 0$

Alternative Hypothesis:

- The regression model does fit the data better than the baseline model.
- Not all βis equal zero.

41

If the estimated linear regression model does **not** fit the data better than the baseline model, you fail to reject the null hypothesis. Thus, you do **not** have enough evidence to say that all of the slopes of the regression in the population are **not** 0 and that the predictor variables explain a significant amount of variability in the response variable.

If the estimated linear regression model **does** fit the data better than the baseline model, you reject the null hypothesis. Thus, you **do** have enough evidence to say that at least one slope of the regression in the population is **not** 0 and that at least one predictor variable explains a significant amount of variability in the response variable.

Assumptions for Linear Regression

- The mean of the Ys is accurately modeled by a linear function of the Xs.
- The random error term, ε, is assumed to have a normal distribution with a mean of zero and a constant variance, σ^2.
- The errors are independent.

42

Techniques to evaluate the validity of these assumptions are discussed in a later chapter.

Because of the central limit theorem, the assumption that the errors are normally distributed is not as restrictive as you might think.

 You also estimate σ^2 from the data.

Multiple Linear Regression versus Simple Linear Regression

Main Advantage

Multiple linear regression enables you to investigate the relationship among Y and several independent variables simultaneously.

Main Disadvantages

Increased complexity makes it more difficult to

- ascertain which model is "best"
- interpret the models.

43

The advantages far outweigh the disadvantages. In practice, many responses depend on multiple factors that may interact in some way.

SAS tools help you decide upon a "best" model, a choice that may depend upon the purposes of the analysis as well as subject matter expertise.

Common Applications

Multiple linear regression is a powerful tool for the following:

- Prediction – to develop a model to predict future values of a response variable (Y) based on its relationships with other predictor variables (Xs)
- Analytical or Explanatory Analysis – to develop an understanding of the relationships between the response variable and predictor variables.

44

The distinction between using multiple regression for an analytic analysis and prediction modeling is somewhat artificial. A model developed for an analytic study can be a good prediction model, and the reverse can also be true.

Myers actually refers to four applications of regression: prediction, variable screening, model specifications, and parameter estimation. The term analytical analysis is similar to Myers' parameter estimation application and variable screening.

Myers, R. H. (1990), *Classical and Modern Regression with Application, Second Edition,* Boston: Duxbury Press.

Prediction

The terms in the model, the values of their coefficients and their statistical significance are of secondary importance.

The focus is on producing a model that is the best at predicting future values of Y as a function of the Xs. The predicted value of Y is given by

$$\hat{Y} = \hat{\beta}_0 + \hat{\beta}_1 X_1 + \ldots + \hat{\beta}_k X_k$$

45

Most investigators do not ignore the terms in the model (the Xs), the values of their coefficients (the βs), or their statistical significance (the *p*-values). They use these statistics to help choose among models with different numbers of terms and predictive capability.

Analytical or Explanatory Analysis

The focus is on understanding the relationship between the dependent variable and the independent variables.

Consequently, the statistical significance of the coefficients is important as well as the magnitudes and signs of the coefficients.

46

Analytic Analysis Example

PREDICTORS		RESPONSE
Performance		
Runtime		
Age	→	Oxygen_Consumption
Weight		
Run_Pulse		
Rest_Pulse		
Maximum_Pulse		

47

An analyst knows from doing a simple linear regression that the measure of performance is an important variable in explaining the oxygen consumption capability of a club member.

The analyst is interested in investigating other information to ascertain whether other variables are important in explaining the oxygen consumption capability.

Recall that you did a simple linear regression on **Oxygen_Consumption** with **Performance** as the independent variable.

The R^2 for this model was 0.7461, which suggests that more of the variation in the oxygen consumption is still unexplained.

Consequently, adding other variables to the model, such as **Runtime** or **Age**, may provide a significantly better model.

Fitting a Multiple Linear Regression Model

Example: Use the Linear Regression task to perform multiple linear regression analysis of **Oxygen_Consumption** on **Performance** and **Runtime**. Interpret the results for the two-variable model.

1. Select **Fitness** as the active data set in the process flow.
2. Select **Analyze** ⇨ **Regression** ⇨ **Linear…**.
3. Assign **Oxygen_Consumption** as the Dependent variable. Assign **Performance** and **Runtime** as Explanatory variables.

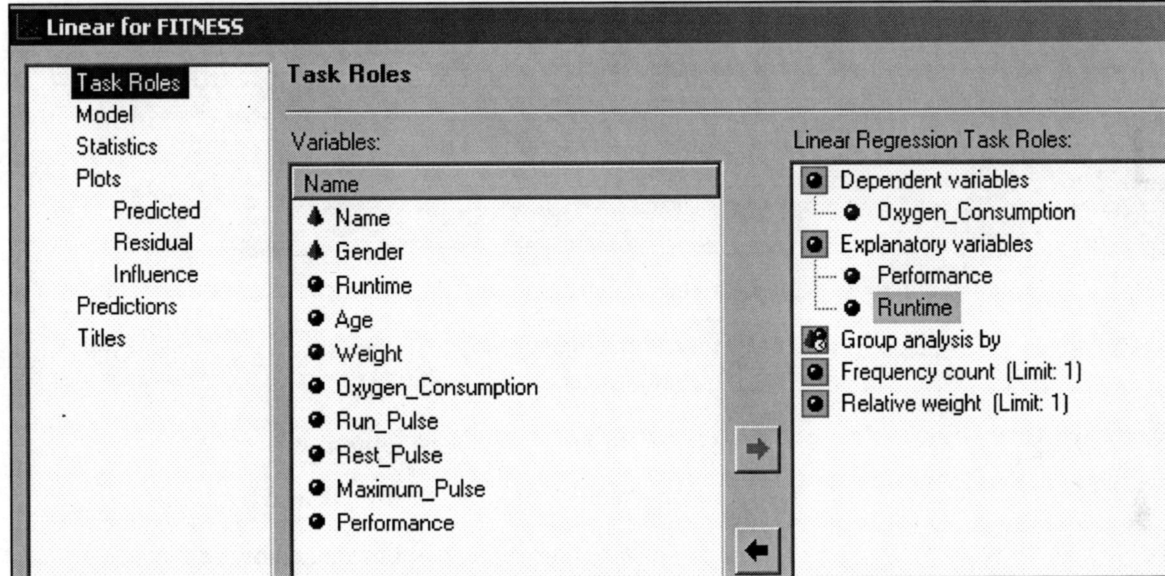

4. Select **Run**.

Examine the sections of the results separately.

The REG Procedure
Model: Linear_Regression_Model
Dependent Variable: Oxygen_Consumption

Number of Observations Read	31
Number of Observations Used	31

Analysis of Variance					
Source	DF	Sum of Squares	Mean Square	F Value	Pr > F
Model	2	637.96565	318.98283	41.82	<.0001
Error	28	213.58890	7.62818		
Corrected Total	30	851.55455			

Model DF is 2, the number of parameters minus one.

Error DF	is 28, the total numbers of observations (31) minus the number of parameters in the model (3).
Corrected Total DF	is 30, the number of observations minus one.
Model Sum of Squares	is the total variation in the Y explained by the model.
Error Sum of Squares	is the variation in the Y **not** explained by the model.
Corrected Total Sum of Squares	is the total variation in the Y.
Model Mean Square	is the Model Sum of Squares divided by the Model DF.
Mean Square Error	is the Error Sum of Squares divided by the Error DF and is an estimate of σ^2, the variance of the random error term.
F Value	is the (Mean Square Model)/(Mean Square Error).
Pr > F	is small; therefore, you reject H_0: $\beta_1 = \beta_2 = 0$ and conclude that at least one $\beta_i \neq 0$.

Root MSE	2.76192	R-Square	0.7492
Dependent Mean	47.37581	Adj R-Sq	0.7313
Coeff Var	5.82980		

The R^2 for this model, 0.7492, is only slightly larger than the R^2 for the model in which **`Performance`** is the only predictor variable, 0.7461.

The R^2 always increases as you include more terms in the model. However, choosing the best model is not as simple as making the R^2 as large as possible.

The adjusted R^2 is a measure similar to R^2, but it takes into account the number of terms in the model.

The adjusted R^2 for this model is 0.7313, which is smaller than the adjusted R^2 of 0.7373 for the **`Performance`** only model. This strongly suggests that the variable **`Runtime`** does not explain the oxygen consumption capacity if you know **`Performance`**.

Parameter Estimates

Variable	DF	Parameter Estimate	Standard Error	t Value	Pr > |t|
Intercept	1	55.37940	33.79380	1.64	0.1125
Performance	1	0.85780	1.06475	0.81	0.4272
Runtime	1	-1.40429	2.39427	-0.59	0.5622

Using the estimates for β_0, β_1, and β_2 above, this model can be written as
`Oxygen_Consumption` = 55.3794 + 0.8578***`Performance`** – 1.40429***`Runtime`**.

Both the *p*-values for **`Performance`** and **`Runtime`** are large, which suggests that neither slope is significantly different from 0.

The reason is that the test for β_i=0 is conditioned on the other terms in the model. So the test for β_1=0 is conditional on or adjusted for X_2 (**`Runtime`**). Similarly, the test for β_2=0 is conditional on X_1 (**`Performance`**).

`Performance` was significant when it was the only term in the model, but it is not significant when **`Runtime`** is included. This implies that the variables are correlated with each other.

The significance level of the test does **not** depend on the order in which you list the explanatory variables in the model, but it does depend upon which explanatory variables are actually included in the model.

Common Problems

Four common problems with regression are

- nonconstant variance
- correlated errors
- influential observations
- collinearity.

49

The first three problems can arise in simple linear regression or multiple regression. The first two problems are always violations of the assumptions. The third can be a violation of the assumptions, but not always.

The fourth problem, however, is unique to multiple linear regression. *Collinearity* is redundant information among the independent variables. Collinearity is **not** a violation of assumptions of multiple regression.

When the number of potential Xs is large, the likelihood of collinearity becoming a problem increases.

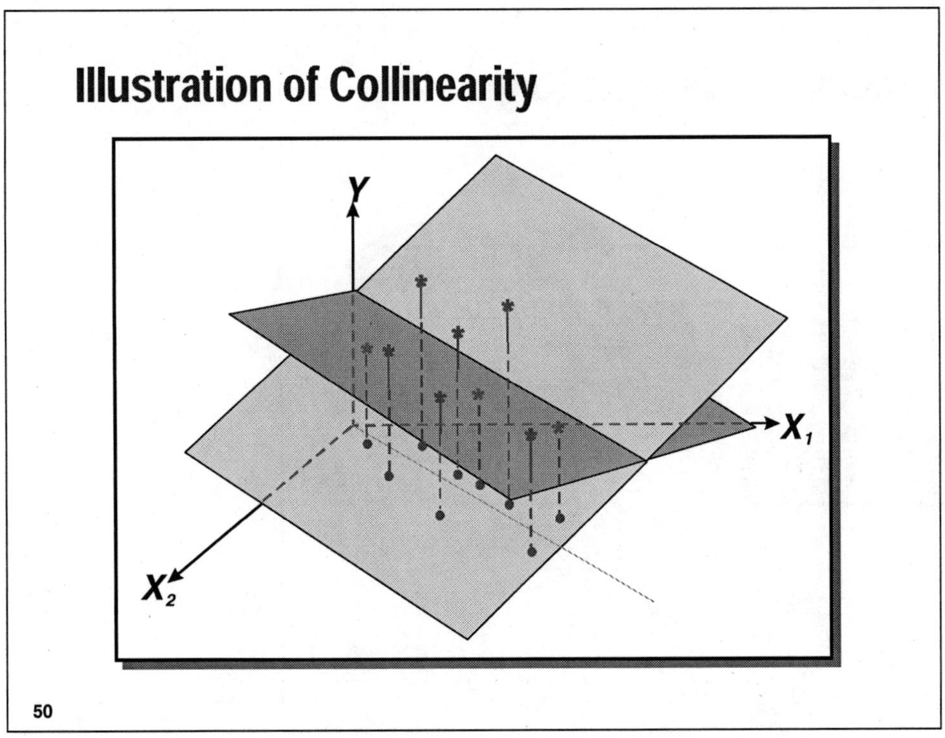

X_1 and X_2 almost follow a straight line $X_1 = X_2$ in the (X_1, X_2) plane.

Consequently, one variable provides nearly as much information as the other does. They are redundant.

Why is this a problem? Two reasons exist.

1. Neither can appear to be significant when both are in the model; however, both can be significant when only one is in the model. Thus, collinearity can hide significant variables.

2. Collinearity also increases the variance of the parameter estimates and consequently increases prediction error.

When collinearity is a problem, the estimates of the coefficients are unstable. This means they have a large variance. Consequently, the true relationship between Y and the Xs may be quite different from that suggested by the magnitude and sign of the coefficients.

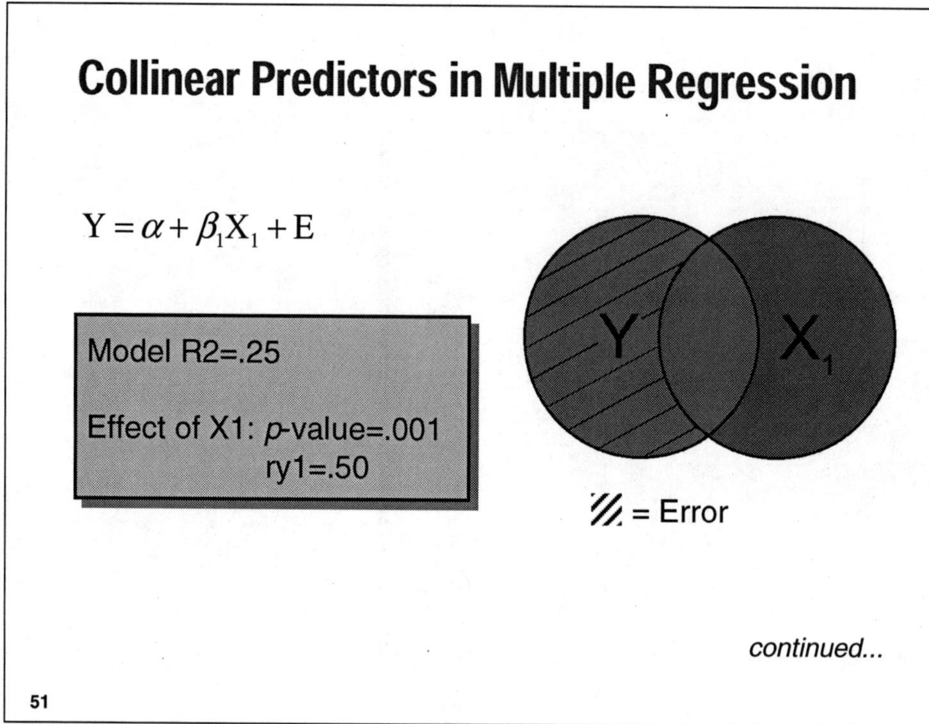

Collinear Predictors in Multiple Regression
$Y = \alpha + \beta_1 X_1 + E$
Model R2=.25
Effect of X1: p-value=.001
ry1=.50
Y
X_1
= Error
continued...
51

The following three slides using Venn diagrams show another visualization of collinearity.

The Venn diagram shows the variability of X and Y, and the extent to which variation in X explains variation in Y. The coefficient r_{y1} represents the correlation between Y and X_1. Consider the simple linear regression of X_1 on Y. X_1 accounts for 25% of the variance in Y, as shown by the dark blue area of overlap.

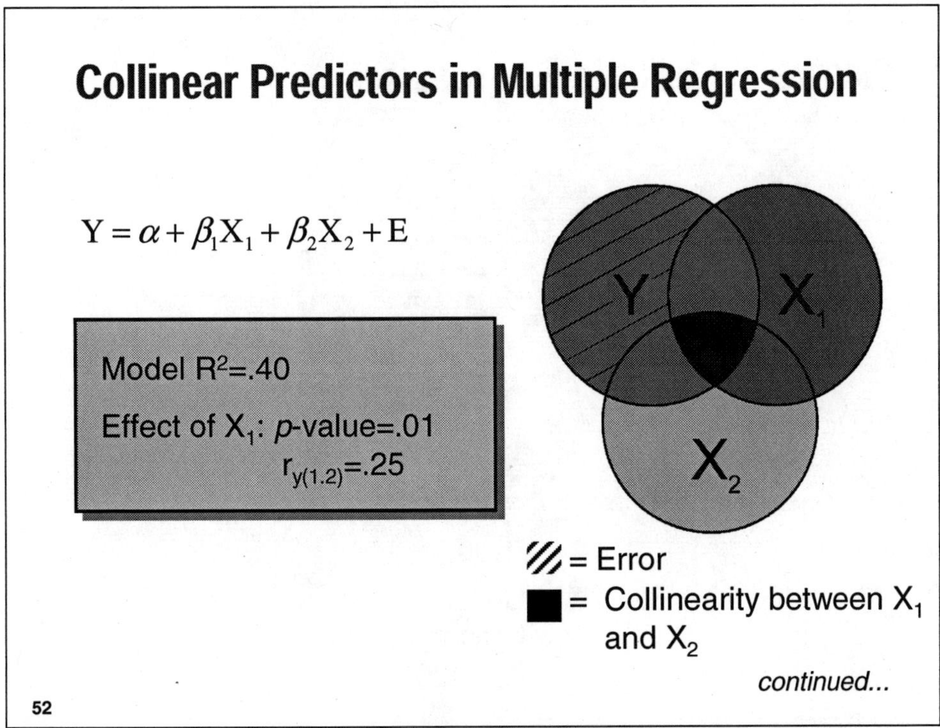

Collinear Predictors in Multiple Regression
$Y = \alpha + \beta_1 X_1 + \beta_2 X_2 + E$
Model R^2=.40
Effect of X_1: *p*-value=.01
$r_{y(1.2)}$=.25
Y
X_1
X_2
= Error
= Collinearity between X_1 and X_2
continued...
52

You suspect that X_2 is associated with Y and add it to the multiple regression model. However, X_1 and X_2 are correlated with one another. The coefficient $r_{y(1.2)}$ reflects the correlation of Y with X_1, controlling for the variable X_2. R^2 increases when X_2 is added to the model, but the individual effects of X_1 and X_2 appear smaller because the effects tests are based on partial correlation. In other words, only the unique variance accounted for by each variable is reflected in the effect tests.

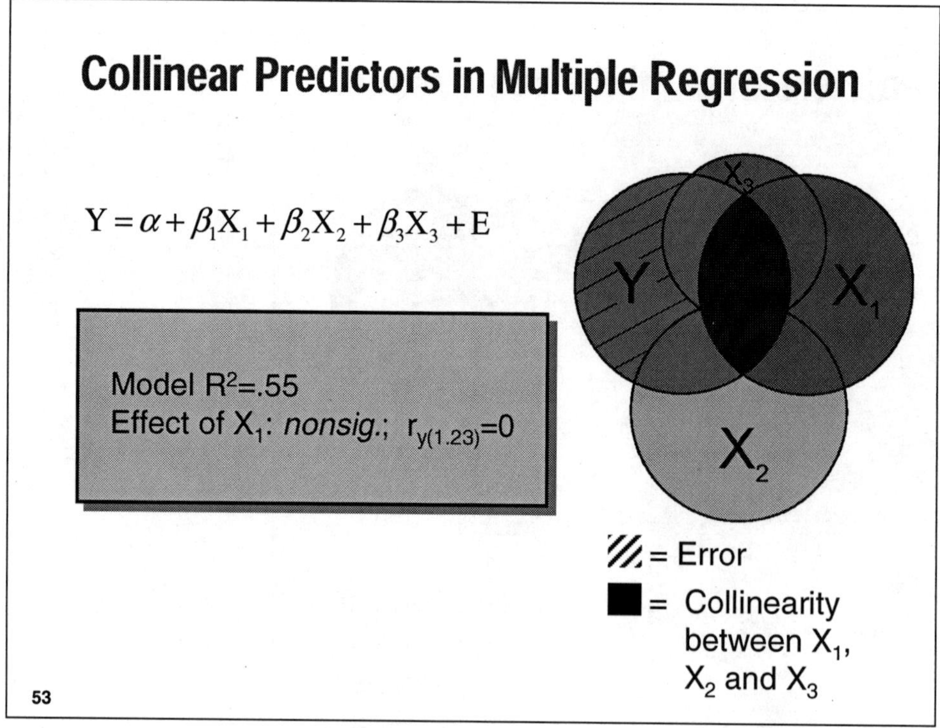

Add one more variable to the model, X_3, that is correlated with X_1. The coefficient $r_{y(1.23)}$ reflects the correlation between Y and X_1 controlling for the variables X_2 and X_3. Notice that the independent effect of X_1 is no longer statistically significant, as all the variance in Y accounted for by X_1 is also accounted for by other predictors in the model. The R^2 for this model has increased with each new term in the model, but the individual effects have decreased as terms are added to the model.

This example is extreme, but it illustrates the importance of planning your model carefully and checking for collinearity among predictors.

3.4 Model Building and Interpretation

Objectives

- Explain the Linear Regression task options for model selection.
- Describe model selection options and interpret output to evaluate the fit of several models.

55

Model Selection

Eliminating one variable at a time manually for

- a small number of independent variables is a reasonable approach
- a large number of independent variables can take an extreme amount of time.

56

The exercises are designed to walk you through a model selection process. You start with all the variables in the **FITNESS** data set and eliminate the least significant terms.

For this small example, a model can be developed in a reasonable amount of time. If you start with a large model, however, eliminating one variable at a time can take an extreme amount of time.

You continue this process until only terms with *p*-values less than some value, such as 0.10 or 0.05, remain.

Model Selection Options

The model selection options in the Model panel of the Linear Regression task support several model selection techniques including

All-possible regressions ranked using

- R-Squared, Adjusted R-Squared, or Mallows' C_p

Stepwise selection methods

- forward, backward, or stepwise.

The default is to use no selection criterion and fit only the full model.

57

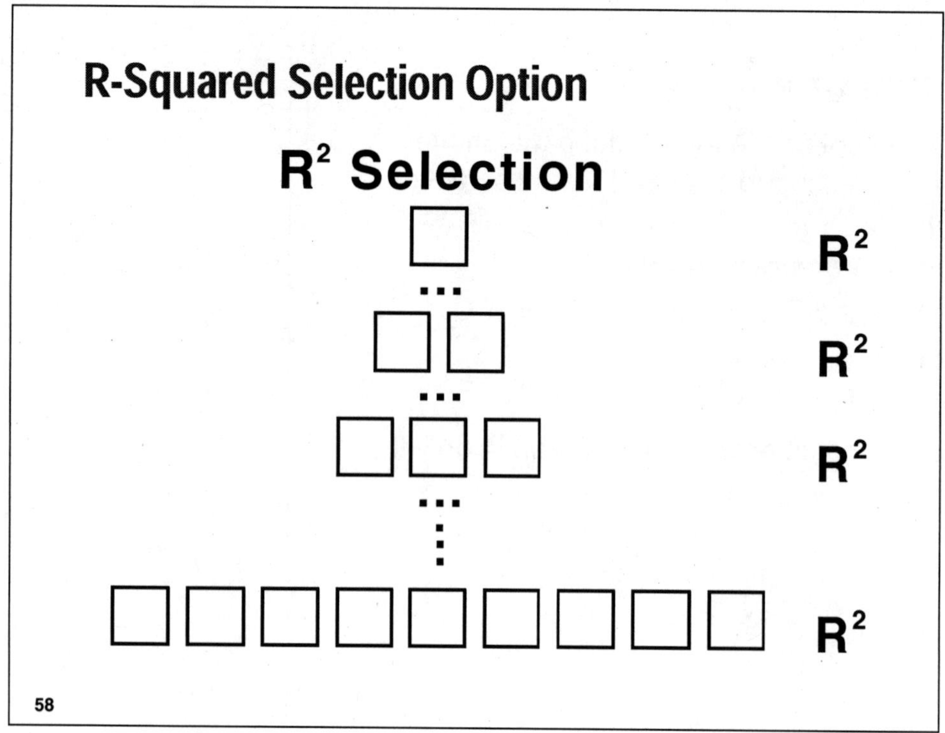

In the **FITNESS** data set, there are 7 possible independent variables. Therefore, there are $2^7 - 1=127$ possible regression models. There are 7 possible one-variable models, 21 possible two-variable models, 35 possible three-variable models, and so on.

You only look at the best four models as measured by the model R^2 for k=1, 2, 3, …, 7. This option only reduces the results. All regressions are still calculated.

If there were 20 possible independent variables, there would be over 1,000,000 models. In a later demonstration, you see another technique that does not have to examine all the models to help you choose a set of candidate models.

Mallows' C_p

- Mallows' C_p is a simple indicator of model bias. Models with a large C_p are biased.
- Look for models with $C_p \le p$, where *p* equals the number of parameters in the model including the intercept.

Mallows recommends choosing the first model where C_p approaches *p*.

59

Mallows' C_p is estimated by

$$C_p = p + \frac{(MSE_p - MSE_{full})(n-p)}{MSE_{full}}$$

where

MSE_p	the mean squared error for the model with *p* parameters
MSE_{full}	the mean squared error for the full model used to estimate the true residual variance
n	the number of observations.

Bias in this context refers to the model underfitting the sample. In other words, important variables are left out of the model.

Mallows, C. L. (1973), "Some Comments on C_p." *Technometrics*, 15: 661-675.

Hocking's Criterion

Hocking suggests using these criteria:

$C_p \leq p$ for prediction

$C_p \leq 2p - p_{full} + 1$ for parameter estimation.

60

Hocking, R. R. (1976), "The Analysis and Selection of Variables in Linear Regression," *Biometrics,* 32, 1-49.

Automatic Model Selection

Example: Use the Linear Regression task to produce a regression of `Oxygen_Consumption` on all the other variables in the `FITNESS` data set.

1. Select **Analyze** ⇨ **Regression** ⇨ **Linear…**.
2. Assign `Oxygen_Consumption` as the Dependent variable and assign the remaining numeric variables as the Explanatory variables as shown below.

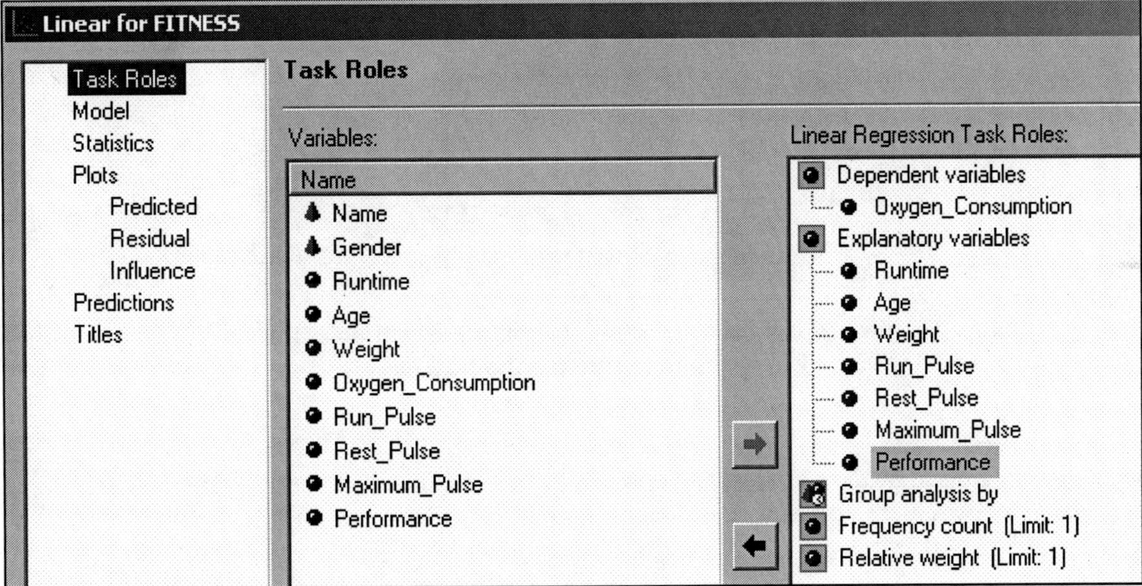

3. Select the **Model** pane. Under **Model selection method**, select the down-pointing arrow and select **R-squared selection** from the list that appears.

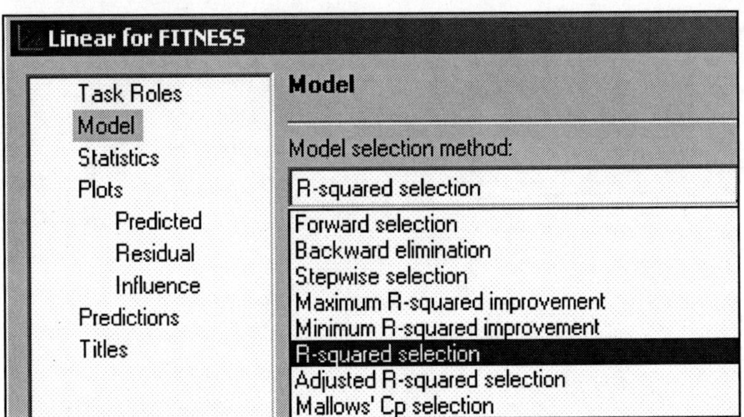

4. When you select a method, additional model fit statistics appear in a display box. From this list, select **Adjusted R-square** and **Mallows' Cp**.

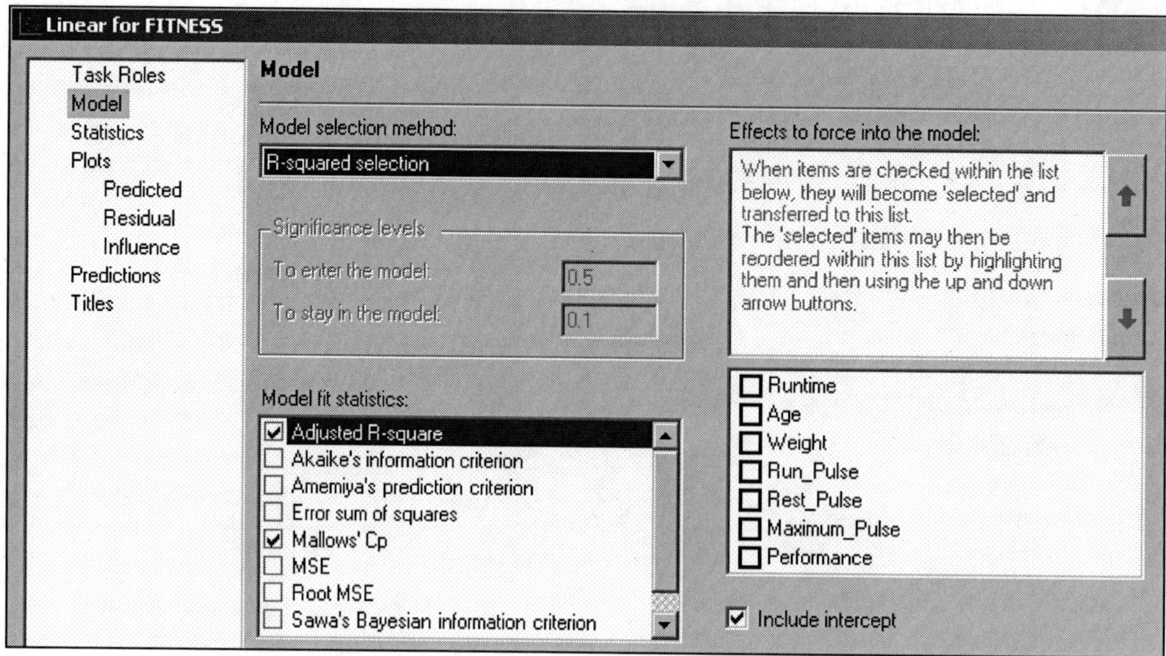

In this window you can make selections to control the variables that are forced to remain in the model with the **Effects to force into the model** pane.

5. Select **Run**.

The models are ranked by their R^2. The REG procedure has calculated all one-variable models, two-variable models, and so on, and ranked them from the largest to smallest R^2.

Partial results are shown below:

Number in Model	R-Square	Adjusted R-Square	C(p)	Variables in Model
1	0.7461	0.7373	11.3942	Performance
1	0.7434	0.7345	11.8074	Runtime
1	0.1595	0.1305	100.1000	Rest_Pulse
1	0.1585	0.1294	100.2529	Run_Pulse
1	0.0971	0.0660	109.5317	Age
1	0.0561	0.0235	115.7386	Maximum_Pulse
1	0.0265	-.0070	120.2033	Weight
2	0.7647	0.7479	10.5794	Runtime Age
2	0.7640	0.7472	10.6839	Run_Pulse Performance
2	0.7614	0.7444	11.0743	Runtime Run_Pulse
2	0.7597	0.7425	11.3400	Age Performance
2	0.7513	0.7335	12.6055	Weight Performance
2	0.7492	0.7313	12.9283	Runtime Performance
2	0.7484	0.7304	13.0516	Maximum_Pulse Performance
2	0.7464	0.7283	13.3507	Rest_Pulse Performance
2	0.7452	0.7270	13.5287	Runtime Maximum_Pulse
2	0.7449	0.7267	13.5707	Runtime Weight
2	0.7435	0.7252	13.7843	Runtime Rest_Pulse
2	0.3711	0.3261	70.1062	Age Run_Pulse
2	0.3010	0.2511	80.7018	Age Rest_Pulse
2	0.2896	0.2389	82.4171	Run_Pulse Maximum_Pulse

To control the number of candidate models displayed, insert the BEST= option in the MODEL statement.

To simplify the results from the Mallows' Cp statistics, create a plot of the Cp statistic by the number of parameters in the model.

6. Double-click on the Linear Regression task in the project tree. Select **Preview code** in the lower left of the window. The following window is presented. Select **Insert Code…**.

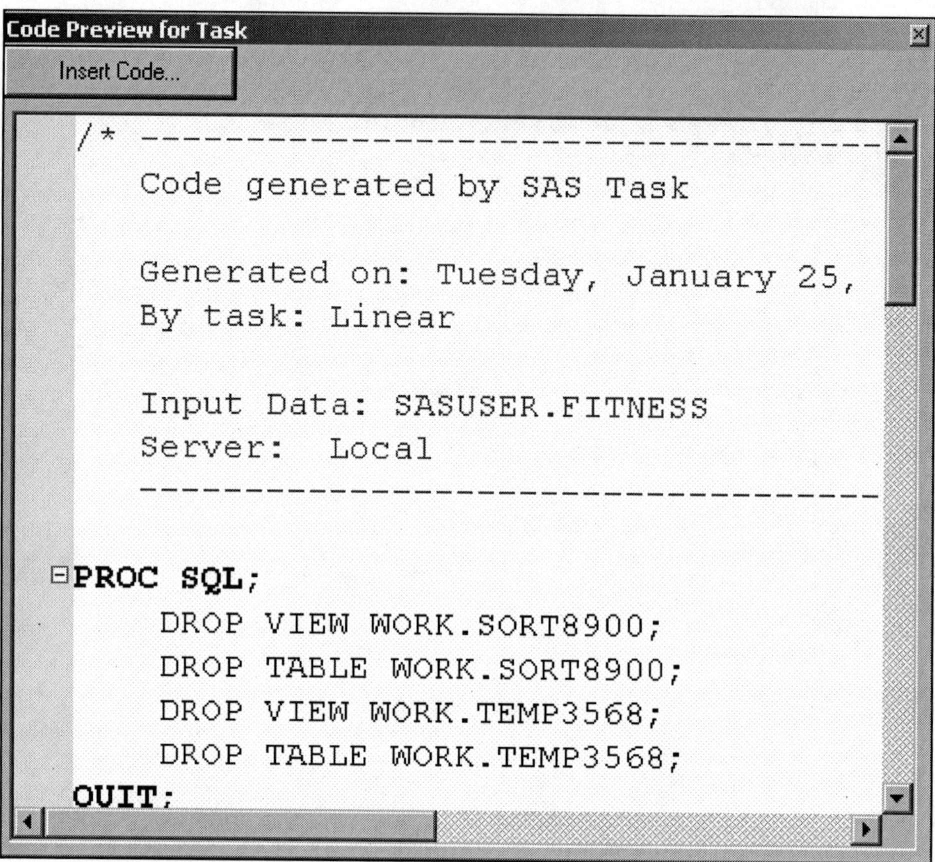

7. Locate and double-click the insertable code section in the MODEL statement after INCLUDE=0 and before the ending semicolon.

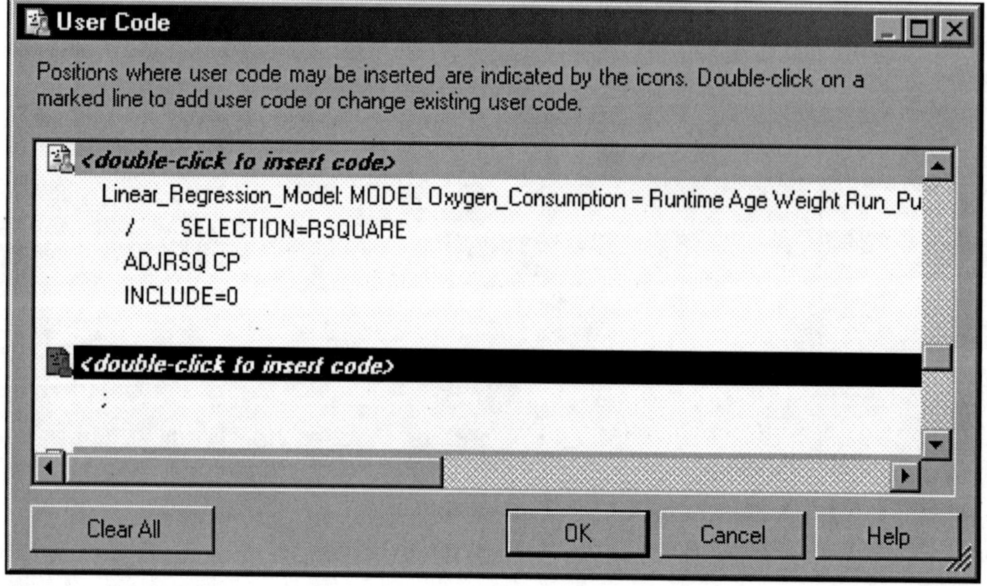

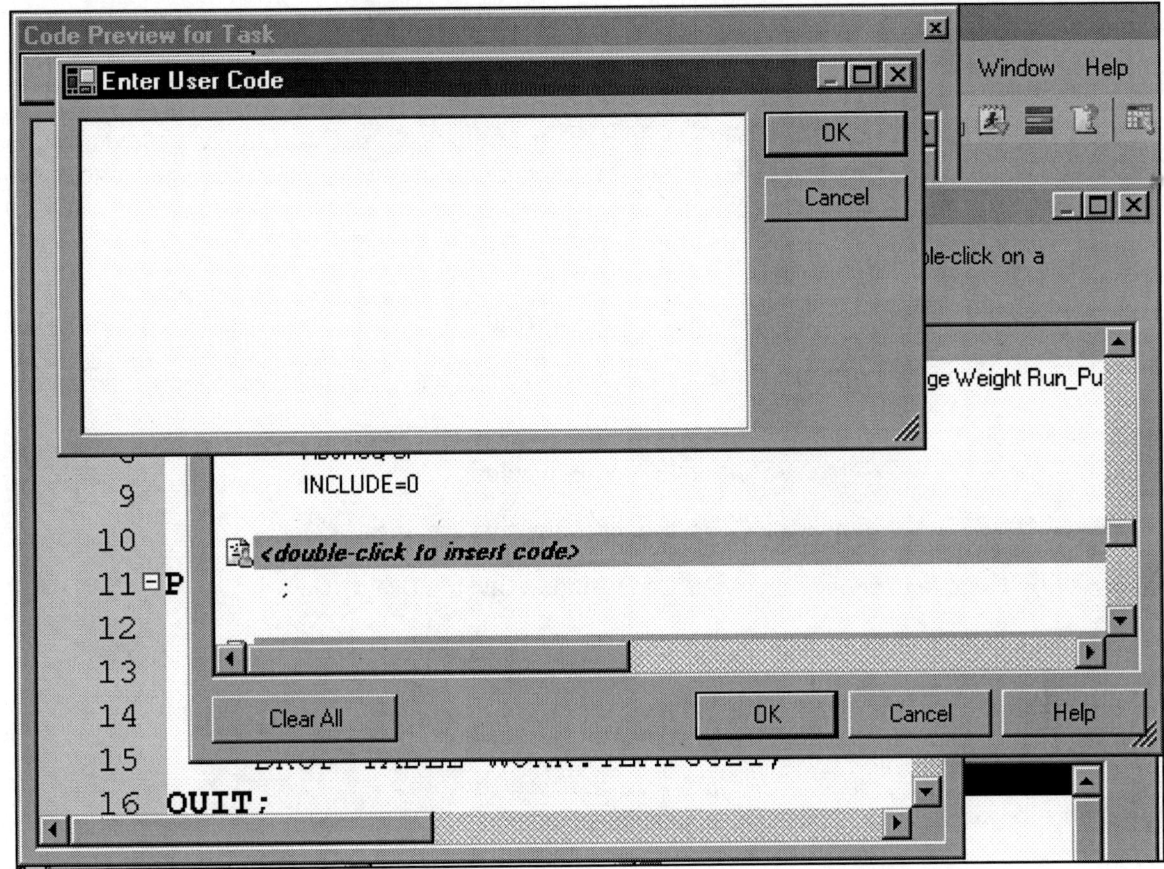

Using these steps will ensure that the code is inserted in the proper place.

8. Enter the following code in the resulting Enter User Code window:

```
best = 4;
plot cp. * np. /
vaxis = 0 to 30 by 5
haxis = 0 to 7 by 1
chocking = blue
cmallows = red;
```

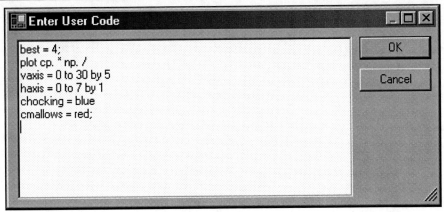

Summary of selected SAS options:

BEST=*n*	limits the results to only the best *n* models for a fixed number of variables.
PLOT statement	specifies that the values of the Mallows' C_p statistic (cp.) be plotted using the vertical axis and that the number of terms in the model (np.) be plotted using the horizontal axis.

Selected PLOT statement options:

VAXIS=	specifies the range for the vertical axis.
HAXIS=	specifies the range for the horizontal axis. Default is the range of the data.
CHOCKING=	requests a $2p - p_{full} + 1$ reference line in addition to the CMALLOWS reference line and specifies a color.
CMALLOWS=	requests a $C_p = p$ reference line and specifies a color.

9. Select **OK** twice to close the Enter User Code window and the User Code window.
10. Close the Code Preview window.
11. Select **Run**.
12. Select **Yes** to replace previous results.
13. Rename the task to `All Possible Reg=Rsquare`.

Locate and examine the graph first.

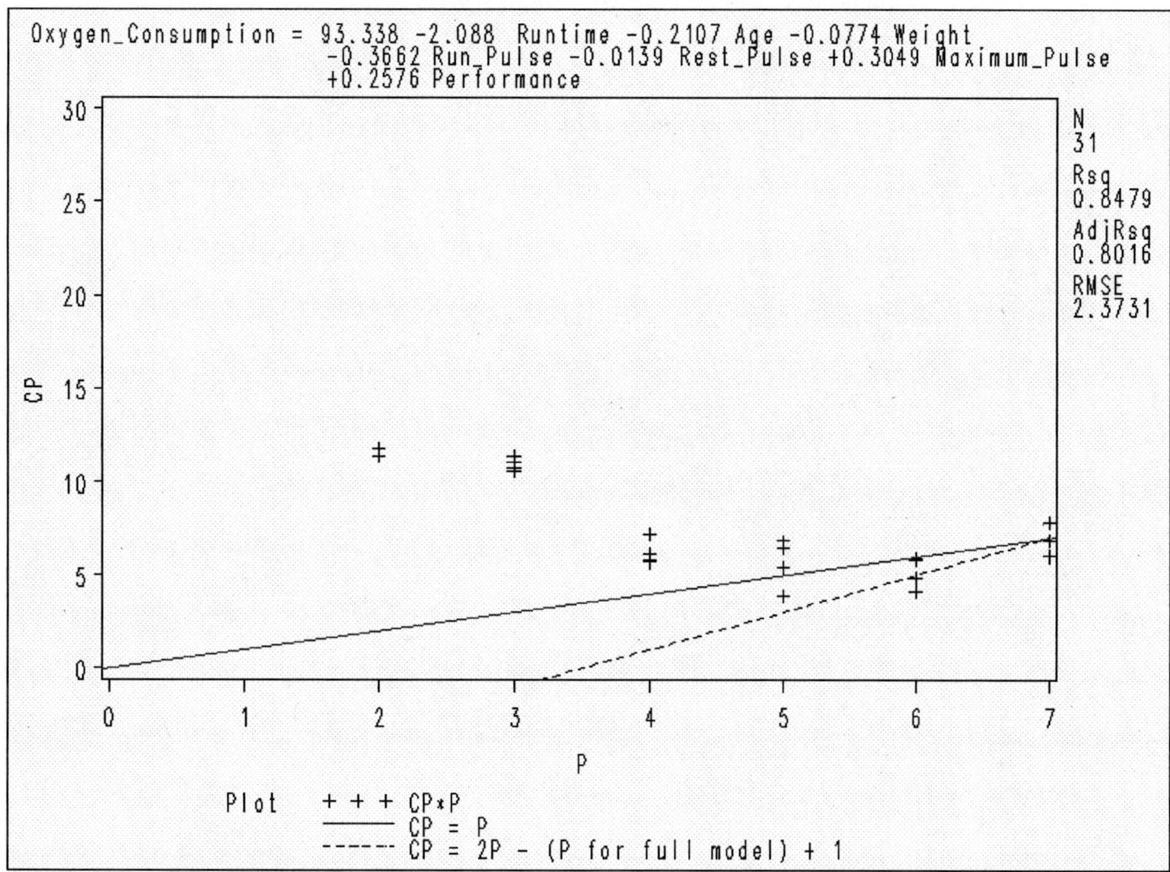

The line CP = P is plotted to help you identify models that satisfy the criterion $C_p \le p$ for prediction; it is the upper solid line in this graph and red in color. The lower dashed line (in blue) is plotted to help identify which models satisfy Hocking's criterion $C_p \le 2p - p_{full} + 1$ for parameter estimation, where p is the number of terms in the current model, including the intercept.

Use the graph and review the results to select a relatively short list of models that satisfy the criterion appropriate for your objective. The first model, which has its C_p fall below the line for Mallows' criterion, has five parameters. The first model to fall below Hocking's criterion has six parameters.

In the following table, the column **Number in Model** designates the number of independent variables in the current model; therefore, p is **Number in Model** + 1.

Number in Model	R-Square	Adjusted R-Square	C(p)	Variables in Model
1	0.7461	0.7373	11.3942	Performance
1	0.7434	0.7345	11.8074	Runtime
1	0.1595	0.1305	100.1000	Rest_Pulse
1	0.1585	0.1294	100.2529	Run_Pulse
2	0.7647	0.7479	10.5794	Runtime Age
2	0.7640	0.7472	10.6839	Run_Pulse Performance
2	0.7614	0.7444	11.0743	Runtime Run_Pulse
2	0.7597	0.7425	11.3400	Age Performance
3	0.8101	0.7890	5.7169	Runtime Run_Pulse Maximum_Pulse
3	0.8096	0.7884	5.7963	Runtime Age Run_Pulse
3	0.8072	0.7858	6.1523	Run_Pulse Maximum_Pulse Performance
3	0.8003	0.7781	7.2046	Age Run_Pulse Performance
4	0.8355	0.8102	3.8790	Runtime Age Run_Pulse Maximum_Pulse
4	0.8253	0.7984	5.4191	Age Run_Pulse Maximum_Pulse Performance
4	0.8181	0.7901	6.5036	Weight Run_Pulse Maximum_Pulse Performance
4	0.8160	0.7877	6.8265	Runtime Weight Run_Pulse Maximum_Pulse
5	0.8469	0.8163	4.1469	Runtime Age Weight Run_Pulse Maximum_Pulse
5	0.8421	0.8105	4.8787	Age Weight Run_Pulse Maximum_Pulse Performance
5	0.8356	0.8027	5.8571	Runtime Age Run_Pulse Rest_Pulse Maximum_Pulse
5	0.8355	0.8026	5.8738	Runtime Age Run_Pulse Maximum_Pulse Performance
6	0.8476	0.8096	6.0381	Runtime Age Weight Run_Pulse Maximum_Pulse Performance
6	0.8475	0.8094	6.0633	Runtime Age Weight Run_Pulse Rest_Pulse Maximum_Pulse
6	0.8421	0.8026	6.8779	Age Weight Run_Pulse Rest_Pulse Maximum_Pulse Performance
6	0.8356	0.7945	7.8565	Runtime Age Run_Pulse Rest_Pulse Maximum_Pulse Performance
7	0.8479	0.8016	8.0000	Runtime Age Weight Run_Pulse Rest_Pulse Maximum_Pulse Performance

In this example p_{full} equals 8, seven variables plus the intercept.

For $p = 5$ (Number in Model = 4), the "best" predictive model has a $C_p = 3.879 < 4$, satisfying Mallows' criterion (`Oxygen_Consumption` = `Runtime Age Weight Run_Pulse Maximum_Pulse`).

To determine the best explanatory model based on Hocking's criterion, the following table was created:

p=# terms in the current model, including the intercept	**Number in Model (k)**	**Minimum C_p with *p* terms**	**Hocking's Criterion : 2*p – 8 + 1 = 2*p – 7**	**C_p< Hocking's Criterion?**
2	1	11.3942	2*2 – 7 = –3	Not Applicable
3	2	10.5794	2*3 – 7 = –1	Not Applicable
4	3	5.7169	2*4 – 7 = 1	No
5	4	3.8790	2*5 – 7 = 3	No
6	5	4.1469	2*6 – 7 = 5	Yes

When *p*=6, the model
`Oxygen_Consumption = Runtime Age Weight Run_Pulse Maximum_Pulse`
had the smallest C_p and will be considered the "best" explanatory model.

For $p = 6$ (Number in Model=5), four models satisfy Mallows' criterion, but only two models also satisfy Hocking's criterion.

All Possible Regression Models

The two best candidate models for $p = 5$ and 6 include these independent variables:

$p = 5$ and $C_p = 3.88$: `Runtime`, `Age`, `Run_Pulse`, `Maximum_Pulse`

$p = 6$ and $C_p = 4.15$: `Runtime`, `Age`, `Weight`, `Run_Pulse`, `Maximum_Pulse`

62

In practice, you may not want to limit your subsequent investigation to only the best model for a given number of terms. Some models may be essentially equivalent based on their R^2 or other measures.

A limitation of the evaluation you have done thus far is that you do not know the magnitudes or signs of the coefficients of the candidate models or their statistical significance.

Estimating and Testing the Coefficients for the Selected Models

Example: Use the Linear Regression task to compare the ANOVA tables and parameter estimates for the two candidate models (the best 4-predictor and the best 5-predictor models) in the **FITNESS** data set. Create two different models, label them in the project tree, and compare the results.

1. Select **Analyze** ⇨ **Regression** ⇨ **Linear…**.
2. Assign **Oxygen_Consumption** as the Dependent variable and assign **Runtime**, **Age**, **Run_Pulse**, and **Maximum_Pulse** as the Explanatory variables.

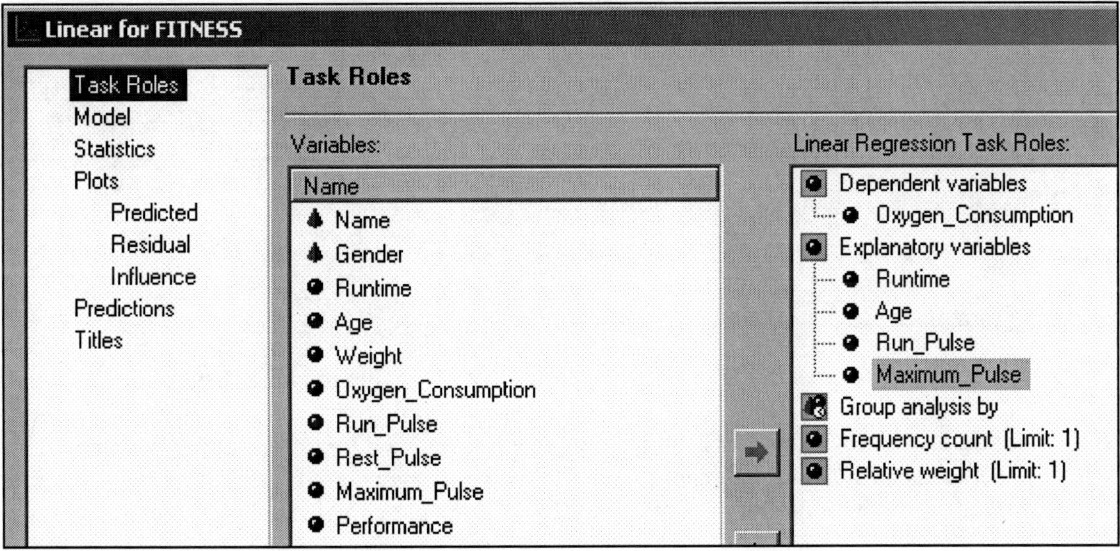

3. Select the **Titles** pane and change the title to **Best 4**.
4. Select **Run**.
5. Change the task label in the process flow to **Best 4**.

6. Double-click on the **`Best 4`**. Select the Columns tab. Add **`Weight`** to the list of Explanatory variables.

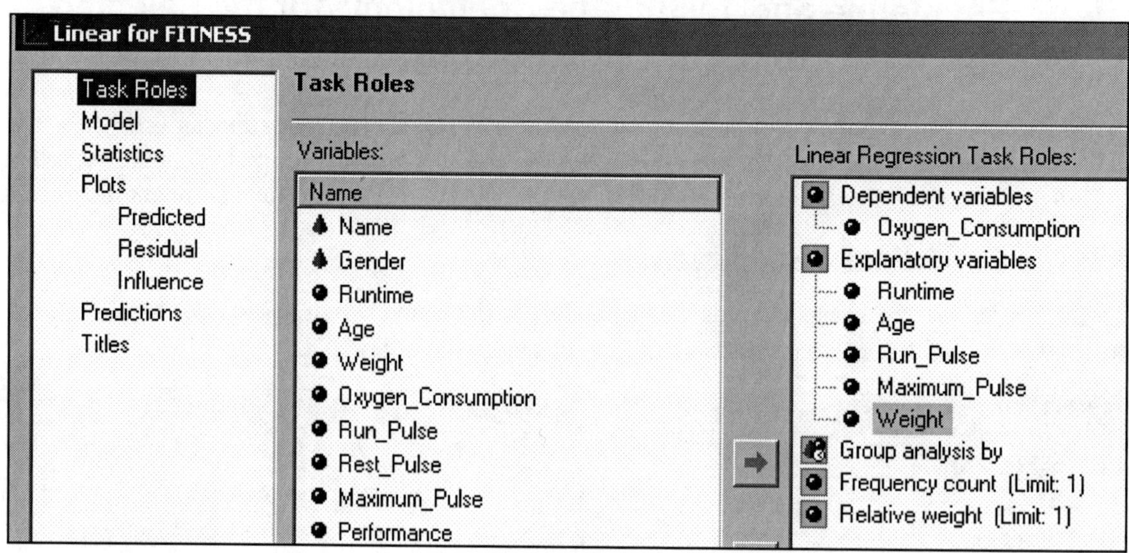

7. Select the **Titles** pane. Change the title to `Best 5`.

8. Select **Run**.

9. Select **No** to replace previous results.

10. Change the current task label in the project tree from best 4-variable model to **`Best 5`**.

✎ If you use code, PROC REG can have more than one MODEL statement. You can assign a label to each MODEL statement to identify the results generated for each model. This enables you to see both models in the same results window. An example is shown below:

```
proc reg data=sasuser.fitness;
   best4: model oxygen_consumption=runtime age
                run_pulse maximum_pulse;
   best5: model oxygen_consumption=runtime age
                run_pulse maximum_pulse weight;
   title 'Check "Best" Two Candidate Models';
run;
quit;
```

✎ Alternatively, you could use the Document Builder in SAS Enterprise Guide to place results from multiple analyses into the same report.

Results for the best 4-predictor model:

best 4

The REG Procedure
Model: Linear_Regression_Model
Dependent Variable: Oxygen_Consumption

Number of Observations Read	31
Number of Observations Used	31

Analysis of Variance					
Source	DF	Sum of Squares	Mean Square	F Value	Pr > F
Model	4	711.45087	177.86272	33.01	<.0001
Error	26	140.10368	5.38860		
Corrected Total	30	851.55455			

Root MSE	2.32134	R-Square	0.8355
Dependent Mean	47.37581	Adj R-Sq	0.8102
Coeff Var	4.89984		

Parameter Estimates					
Variable	DF	Parameter Estimate	Standard Error	t Value	Pr > |t|
Intercept	1	97.16952	11.65703	8.34	<.0001
Runtime	1	-2.77576	0.34159	-8.13	<.0001
Age	1	-0.18903	0.09439	-2.00	0.0557
Run_Pulse	1	-0.34568	0.11820	-2.92	0.0071
Maximum_Pulse	1	0.27188	0.13438	2.02	0.0534

The R^2 and adjusted R^2 are the same as calculated during the model selection program. If there are missing values in the data set, however, this may not always be true.

The model *F* is large and highly significant. `Age` and `Maximum_Pulse` are not significant at the 0.05 level of significance. However, all terms are significant at alpha=0.10.

The adjusted R^2 is close to the R^2, which suggests that there are not too many variables in the model.

Results for the best 5-predictor model:

best 5

The REG Procedure
Model: Linear_Regression_Model
Dependent Variable: Oxygen_Consumption

Number of Observations Read	31
Number of Observations Used	31

Analysis of Variance

Source	DF	Sum of Squares	Mean Square	F Value	Pr > F
Model	5	721.20532	144.24106	27.66	<.0001
Error	25	130.34923	5.21397		
Corrected Total	30	851.55455			

Root MSE	2.28341	R-Square	0.8469
Dependent Mean	47.37581	Adj R-Sq	0.8163
Coeff Var	4.81978		

Parameter Estimates

Variable	DF	Parameter Estimate	Standard Error	t Value	Pr > |t|
Intercept	1	101.33835	11.86474	8.54	<.0001
Runtime	1	-2.68846	0.34202	-7.86	<.0001
Age	1	-0.21217	0.09437	-2.25	0.0336
Run_Pulse	1	-0.37071	0.11770	-3.15	0.0042
Maximum_Pulse	1	0.30603	0.13452	2.28	0.0317
Weight	1	-0.07332	0.05360	-1.37	0.1836

The adjusted R^2 is slightly larger than in the best 4-variable model and very close to the R^2.

The model *F* is large, but smaller than in the best 4-variable model. However, it is still highly significant. All terms included in the model are significant except **`Weight`**. The *p*-values for **`Age`**, **`Run_Pulse`**, and **`Maximum_Pulse`** are smaller in this model than they were in the best 4-variable model.

Including the additional variable in the model changes the coefficients of the other terms and changes the *t* statistics for all.

Stepwise Selection Methods

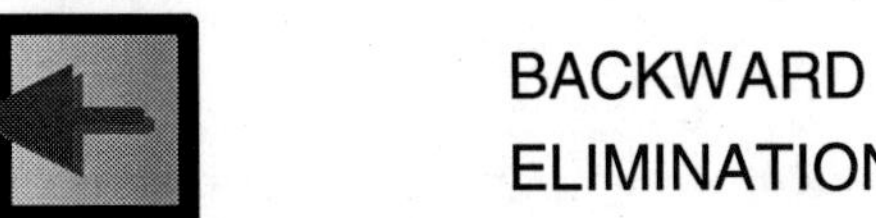

FORWARD SELECTION

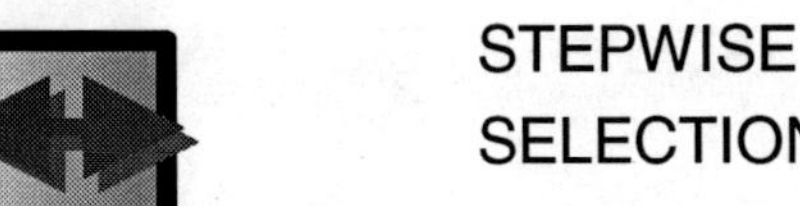

BACKWARD ELIMINATION

STEPWISE SELECTION

64

The all-possible regression technique that was discussed can be computer intensive, especially if there are a large number of potential independent variables.

The Linear Regression task also offers these stepwise selection options:

FORWARD first selects the best one-variable model, based on the smallest p-value for all independent variables. Then it selects the next smallest p-value of the remaining variables, producing a two-variable model. FORWARD continues this process, but stops when it reaches the point where no additional variables have a p-value level < 0.50.

BACKWARD begins with the full model. Next, the variable that is least significant, given the other variables, is removed from the model based on the largest p-value for all independent variables. BACKWARD continues this process until all of the remaining variables have a p-value < 0.10.

STEPWISE starts like FORWARD but allows the possibility of a variable being removed after it is in the model. The default entry p-value is 0.15 and the default stay p-value is also 0.15.

Special options can be used to change the default p-values.

Stepwise Regression

Example: Select a model for predicting `Oxygen_Consumption` in the `FITNESS` data set by using the FORWARD, BACKWARD and STEPWISE selection methods.

1. Select **Analyze** ⇨ **Regression** ⇨ **Linear…**.
2. Assign `Oxygen_Consumption` as the Dependent variable and the remaining numeric variables as the Explanatory variables, as shown below.

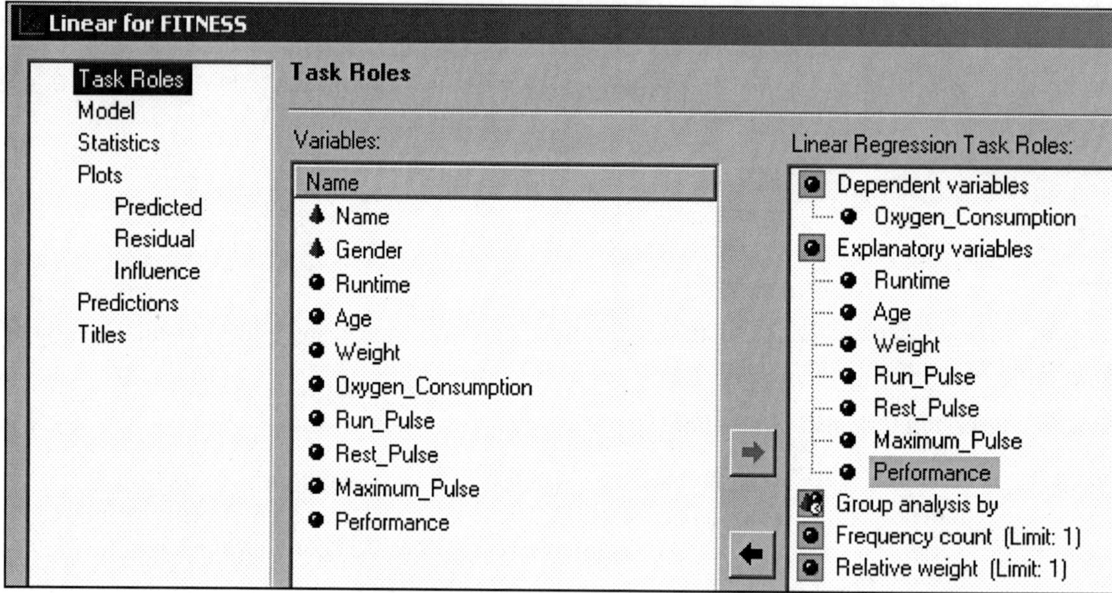

3. Select the **Model** pane.
4. Select **Forward selection** as the Model selection method.

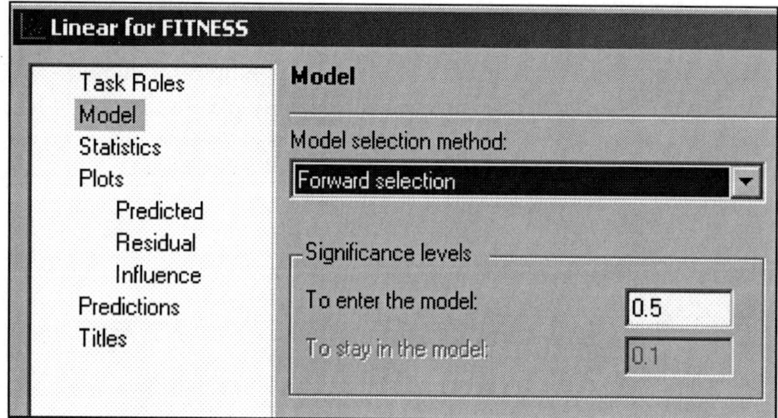

5. Select **Run**.
6. Change the task label in the process flow to `FORWARD Stepwise`.

The complete results follow:

Linear Regression Results

The REG Procedure
Model: Linear_Regression_Model
Dependent Variable: Oxygen_Consumption

Number of Observations Read	31
Number of Observations Used	31

Forward Selection: Step 1

Variable Performance Entered: R-Square = 0.7461 and C(p) = 11.3942

Analysis of Variance					
Source	DF	Sum of Squares	Mean Square	F Value	Pr > F
Model	1	635.34150	635.34150	85.22	<.0001
Error	29	216.21305	7.45562		
Corrected Total	30	851.55455			

Variable	Parameter Estimate	Standard Error	Type II SS	F Value	Pr > F
Intercept	35.57526	1.36917	5033.48080	675.13	<.0001
Performance	1.47507	0.15979	635.34150	85.22	<.0001

Bounds on condition number: 1, 1

Forward Selection: Step 2

Variable Run_Pulse Entered: R-Square = 0.7640 and C(p) = 10.6839

Analysis of Variance					
Source	DF	Sum of Squares	Mean Square	F Value	Pr > F
Model	2	650.60420	325.30210	45.33	<.0001
Error	28	200.95035	7.17680		
Corrected Total	30	851.55455			

Variable	Parameter Estimate	Standard Error	Type II SS	F Value	Pr > F
Intercept	48.60983	9.03851	207.58002	28.92	<.0001
Run_Pulse	-0.07327	0.05024	15.26270	2.13	0.1559
Performance	1.39954	0.16511	515.66060	71.85	<.0001

Bounds on condition number: 1.1091, 4.4366

Forward Selection: Step 3

Variable Maximum_Pulse Entered: R-Square = 0.8072 and C(p) = 6.1523

Analysis of Variance

Source	DF	Sum of Squares	Mean Square	F Value	Pr > F
Model	3	687.38657	229.12886	37.68	<.0001
Error	27	164.16798	6.08030		
Corrected Total	30	851.55455			

Variable	Parameter Estimate	Standard Error	Type II SS	F Value	Pr > F
Intercept	39.50427	9.10596	114.43553	18.82	0.0002
Run_Pulse	-0.35931	0.12515	50.11542	8.24	0.0079
Maximum_Pulse	0.33522	0.13629	36.78237	6.05	0.0206
Performance	1.32166	0.15524	440.73994	72.49	<.0001

Bounds on condition number: 8.1227, 50.931

Forward Selection: Step 4

Variable Age Entered: R-Square = 0.8253 and C(p) = 5.4191

Analysis of Variance					
Source	DF	Sum of Squares	Mean Square	F Value	Pr > F
Model	4	702.77828	175.69457	30.70	<.0001
Error	26	148.77627	5.72216		
Corrected Total	30	851.55455			

Variable	Parameter Estimate	Standard Error	Type II SS	F Value	Pr > F
Intercept	55.88849	13.33542	100.50593	17.56	0.0003
Age	-0.16144	0.09844	15.39171	2.69	0.1130
Run_Pulse	-0.33710	0.12216	43.56925	7.61	0.0105
Maximum_Pulse	0.26739	0.13854	21.31755	3.73	0.0646
Performance	1.23818	0.15897	347.15423	60.67	<.0001

Bounds on condition number: 8.4502, 77.481

Forward Selection: Step 5

Variable Weight Entered: R-Square = 0.8421 and C(p) = 4.8787

Analysis of Variance					
Source	DF	Sum of Squares	Mean Square	F Value	Pr > F
Model	5	717.08415	143.41683	26.66	<.0001
Error	25	134.47041	5.37882		
Corrected Total	30	851.55455			

Variable	Parameter Estimate	Standard Error	Type II SS	F Value	Pr > F
Intercept	62.17928	13.49230	114.23682	21.24	0.0001
Age	-0.18877	0.09690	20.41315	3.80	0.0627
Weight	-0.08827	0.05412	14.30587	2.66	0.1155
Run_Pulse	-0.36603	0.11976	50.24137	9.34	0.0053
Maximum_Pulse	0.30806	0.13661	27.35207	5.09	0.0331
Performance	1.19926	0.15596	318.04934	59.13	<.0001

Bounds on condition number: 8.7415, 105.27

Forward Selection: Step 6

Variable Runtime Entered: R-Square = 0.8476 and C(p) = 6.0381

Analysis of Variance					
Source	DF	Sum of Squares	Mean Square	F Value	Pr > F
Model	6	721.81791	120.30298	22.25	<.0001
Error	24	129.73665	5.40569		
Corrected Total	30	851.55455			

Variable	Parameter Estimate	Standard Error	Type II SS	F Value	Pr > F
Intercept	90.83022	33.47159	39.80699	7.36	0.0121
Runtime	-1.98433	2.12049	4.73376	0.88	0.3587
Age	-0.20470	0.09862	23.28867	4.31	0.0488
Weight	-0.07689	0.05560	10.33766	1.91	0.1794
Run_Pulse	-0.36818	0.12008	50.81482	9.40	0.0053
Maximum_Pulse	0.30593	0.13697	26.96687	4.99	0.0351
Performance	0.32048	0.95201	0.61258	0.11	0.7393

Bounds on condition number: 48.957, 700.99

No other variable met the 0.5000 significance level for entry into the model.

Summary of Forward Selection

Step	Variable Entered	Number Vars In	Partial R-Square	Model R-Square	C(p)	F Value	Pr > F
1	Performance	1	0.7461	0.7461	11.3942	85.22	<.0001
2	Run_Pulse	2	0.0179	0.7640	10.6839	2.13	0.1559
3	Maximum_Pulse	3	0.0432	0.8072	6.1523	6.05	0.0206
4	Age	4	0.0181	0.8253	5.4191	2.69	0.1130
5	Weight	5	0.0168	0.8421	4.8787	2.66	0.1155
6	Runtime	6	0.0056	0.8476	6.0381	0.88	0.3587

The model selected at each step is printed and a summary of the sequence of steps is given at the end of the results. In the summary, the variables are listed in the order in which they were selected. The partial R^2 shows the increase in the model R^2 as each term was added.

The model Forward stepwise selection selected has more variables than the models chosen using the all-regressions techniques.

In this example, only one variable was eliminated from the model. Remember that this is not always the case.

Now generate a model with BACKWARD elimination.

1. Open Forward Regression from the Process Flow.

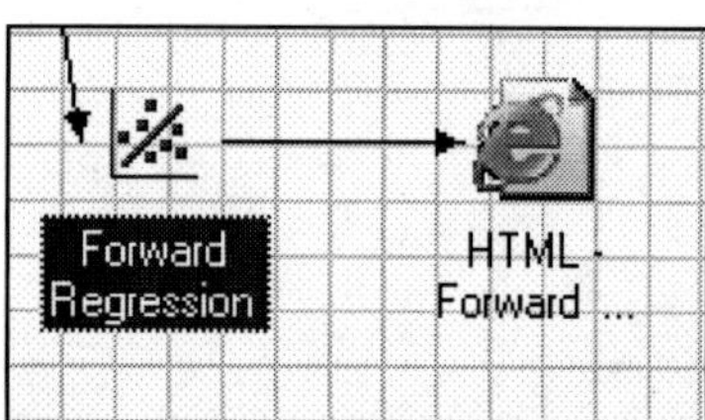

2. Select **Backward elimination** from the Model Selection method panel.

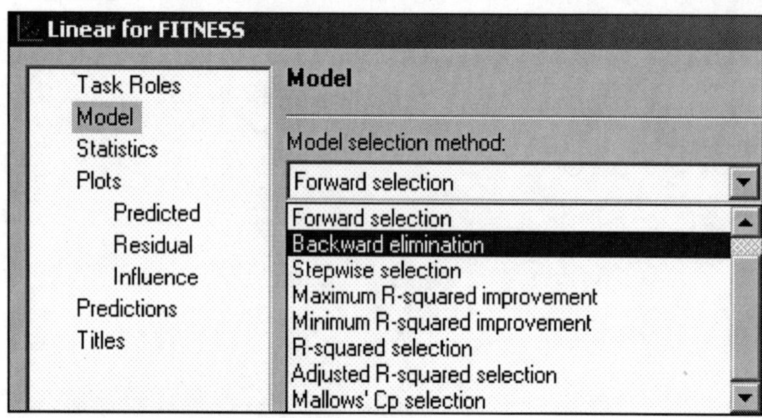

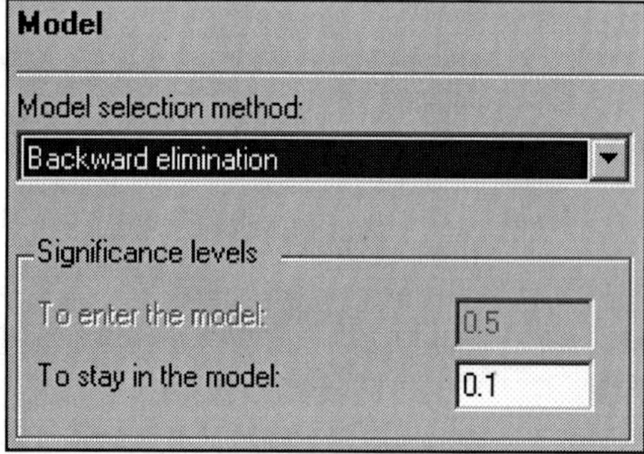

3. Select **Run**.

4. Select **No**.

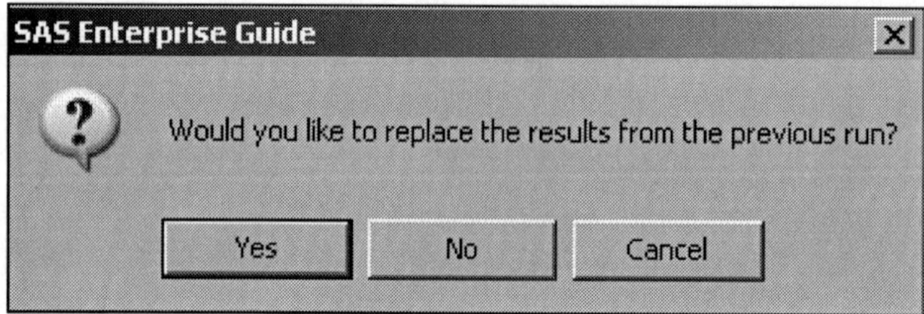

5. Rename the linear model node from Forward Regression to Backward Elimination.

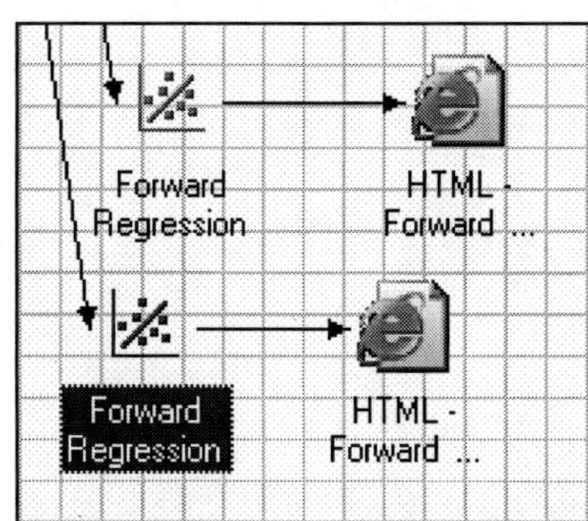

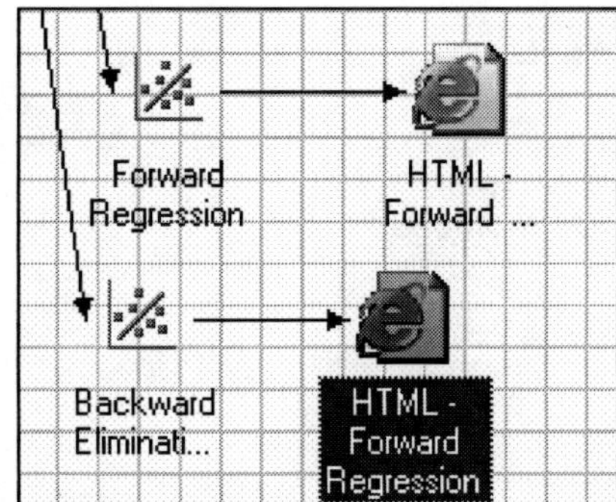

6. Delete the second occurrence of **HTML – Forward Regression**.

7. Select **Backward Elimination** and **Run This Task**.

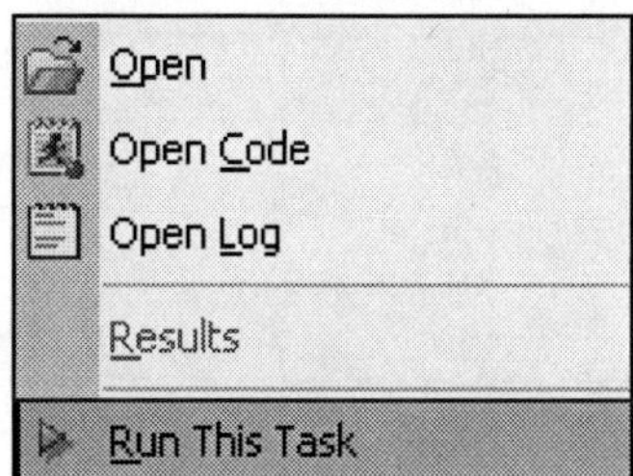

8. Select **Yes**.

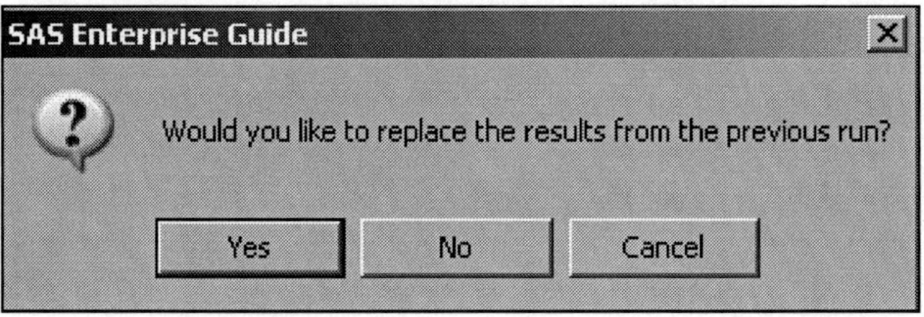

The complete results follow for backward elimination.

Linear Regression Results

The REG Procedure
Model: Linear_Regression_Model
Dependent Variable: Oxygen_Consumption

Number of Observations Read	31
Number of Observations Used	31

Backward Elimination: Step 0

All Variables Entered: R-Square = 0.8479 and C(p) = 8.0000

Analysis of Variance

Source	DF	Sum of Squares	Mean Square	F Value	Pr > F
Model	7	722.03251	103.14750	18.32	<.0001
Error	23	129.52204	5.63139		
Corrected Total	30	851.55455			

Variable	Parameter Estimate	Standard Error	Type II SS	F Value	Pr > F
Intercept	93.33753	36.49782	36.82939	6.54	0.0176
Runtime	-2.08804	2.22856	4.94363	0.88	0.3585
Age	-0.21066	0.10519	22.58631	4.01	0.0571
Weight	-0.07741	0.05681	10.45445	1.86	0.1862
Run_Pulse	-0.36618	0.12299	49.91978	8.86	0.0067
Rest_Pulse	-0.01389	0.07114	0.21460	0.04	0.8469
Maximum_Pulse	0.30490	0.13990	26.74945	4.75	0.0398
Performance	0.25756	1.02373	0.35646	0.06	0.8036

Backward Elimination (continued)

Backward Elimination: Step 1

Variable Rest_Pulse Removed: R-Square = 0.8476 and C(p) = 6.0381

Analysis of Variance					
Source	DF	Sum of Squares	Mean Square	F Value	Pr > F
Model	6	721.81791	120.30298	22.25	<.0001
Error	24	129.73665	5.40569		
Corrected Total	30	851.55455			

Variable	Parameter Estimate	Standard Error	Type II SS	F Value	Pr > F
Intercept	90.83022	33.47159	39.80699	7.36	0.0121
Runtime	-1.98433	2.12049	4.73376	0.88	0.3587
Age	-0.20470	0.09862	23.28867	4.31	0.0488
Weight	-0.07689	0.05560	10.33766	1.91	0.1794
Run_Pulse	-0.36818	0.12008	50.81482	9.40	0.0053
Maximum_Pulse	0.30593	0.13697	26.96687	4.99	0.0351
Performance	0.32048	0.95201	0.61258	0.11	0.7393

Bounds on condition number: 48.957, 700.99

Backward Elimination (continued)

Backward Elimination: Step 2

Variable Performance Removed: R-Square = 0.8469 and C(p) = 4.1469

Analysis of Variance					
Source	DF	Sum of Squares	Mean Square	F Value	Pr > F
Model	5	721.20532	144.24106	27.66	<.0001
Error	25	130.34923	5.21397		
Corrected Total	30	851.55455			

Variable	Parameter Estimate	Standard Error	Type II SS	F Value	Pr > F
Intercept	101.33835	11.86474	380.36418	72.95	<.0001
Runtime	-2.68846	0.34202	322.17052	61.79	<.0001
Age	-0.21217	0.09437	26.35286	5.05	0.0336
Weight	-0.07332	0.05360	9.75445	1.87	0.1836
Run_Pulse	-0.37071	0.11770	51.71988	9.92	0.0042
Maximum_Pulse	0.30603	0.13452	26.98596	5.18	0.0317

Bounds on condition number: 8.7438, 104.92

Backward Elimination (continued)

Backward Elimination: Step 3

Variable Weight Removed: R-Square = 0.8355 and C(p) = 3.8790

Analysis of Variance					
Source	DF	Sum of Squares	Mean Square	F Value	Pr > F
Model	4	711.45087	177.86272	33.01	<.0001
Error	26	140.10368	5.38860		
Corrected Total	30	851.55455			

Variable	Parameter Estimate	Standard Error	Type II SS	F Value	Pr > F
Intercept	97.16952	11.65703	374.42127	69.48	<.0001
Runtime	-2.77576	0.34159	355.82682	66.03	<.0001
Age	-0.18903	0.09439	21.61272	4.01	0.0557
Run_Pulse	-0.34568	0.11820	46.08558	8.55	0.0071
Maximum_Pulse	0.27188	0.13438	22.05933	4.09	0.0534

Bounds on condition number: 8.4426, 76.969

Backward Elimination (continued)

All variables left in the model are significant at the 0.1000 level.

Summary of Backward Elimination							
Step	Variable Removed	Number Vars In	Partial R-Square	Model R-Square	C(p)	F Value	Pr > F
1	Rest_Pulse	6	0.0003	0.8476	6.0381	0.04	0.8469
2	Performance	5	0.0007	0.8469	4.1469	0.11	0.7393
3	Weight	4	0.0115	0.8355	3.8790	1.87	0.1836

Now generate a model with STEPWISE.

1. Open Backward Elimination from the Process Flow.

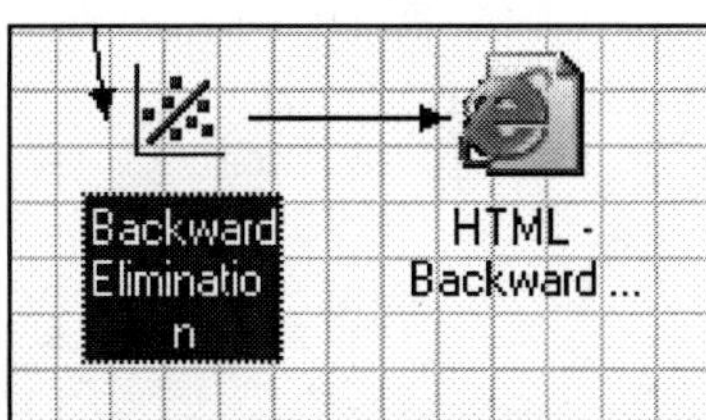

2. Select **Stepwise selection** from the Model Selection method panel.

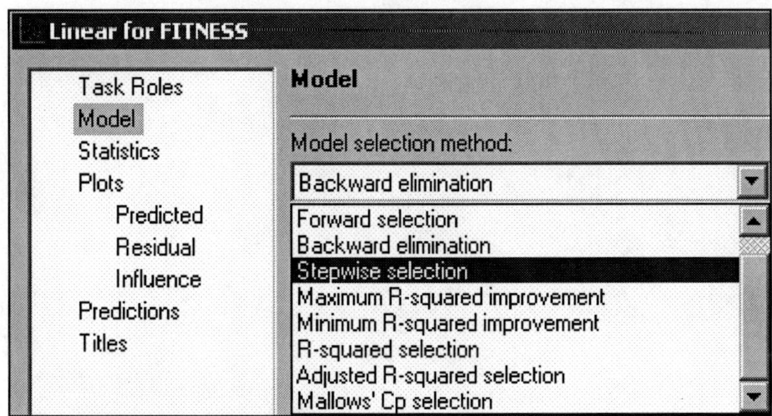

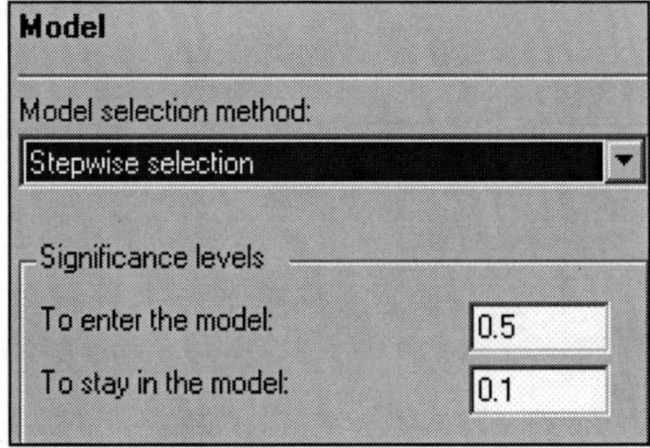

3. Select **Run**.

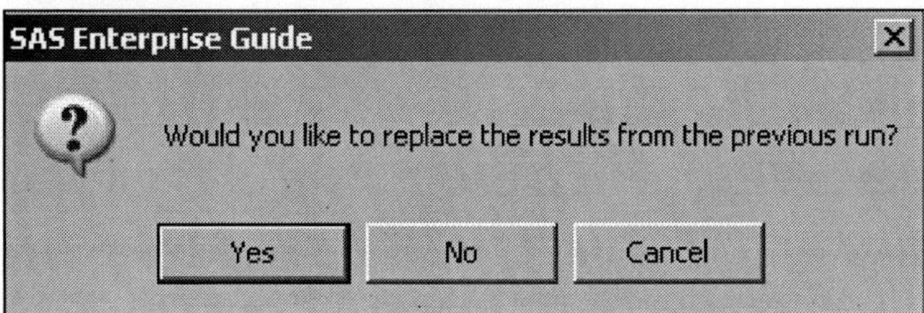

4. Select **No**.

5. Rename the linear model node from Backward Elimination to Stepwise Selection.

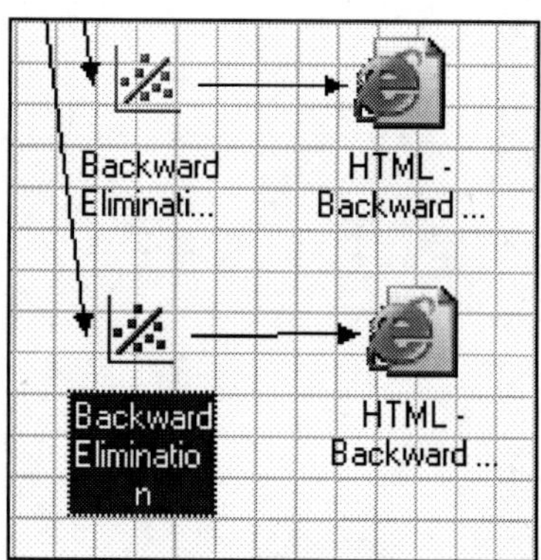

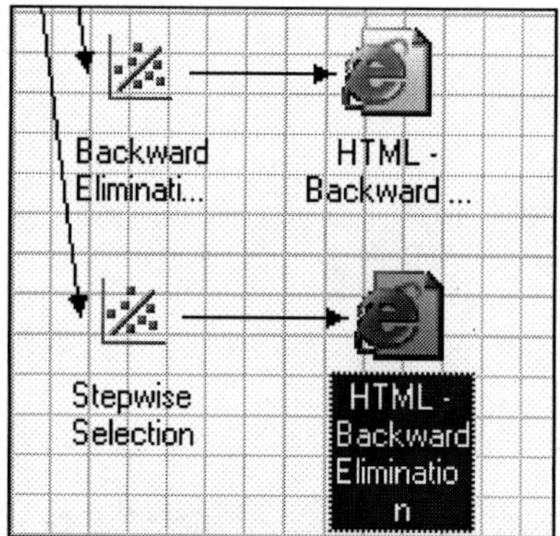

6. Delete the second occurrence of **HTML – Backward Elimination**.

7. Select **Stepwise Selection** and **Run This Task**.

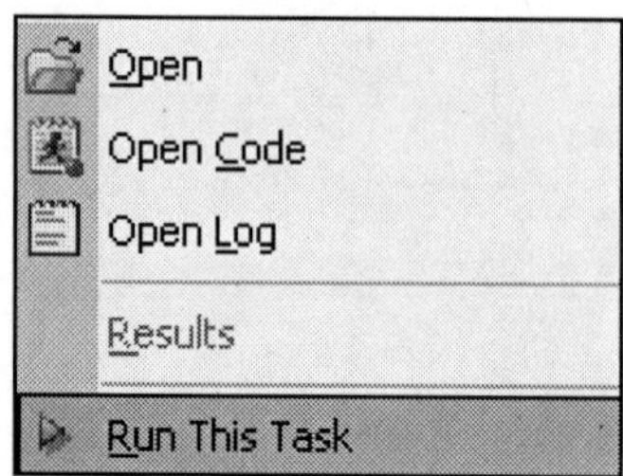

8. Select **Yes**.

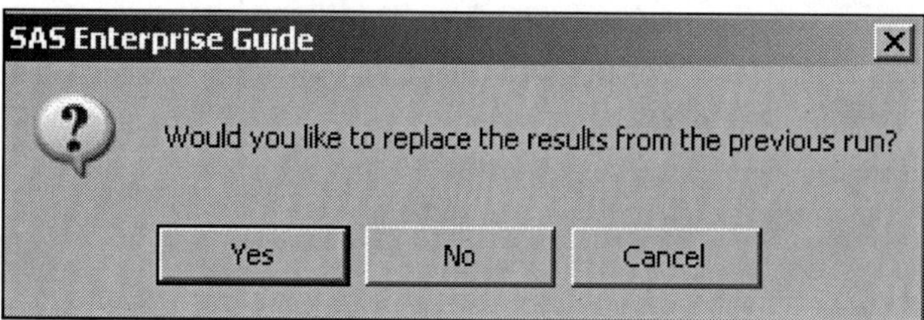

The complete results follow for stepwise selection.

Linear Regression Results

The REG Procedure
Model: Linear_Regression_Model
Dependent Variable: Oxygen_Consumption

Number of Observations Read	31
Number of Observations Used	31

Stepwise Selection: Step 1

Variable Performance Entered: R-Square = 0.7461 and C(p) = 11.3942

Analysis of Variance					
Source	DF	Sum of Squares	Mean Square	F Value	Pr > F
Model	1	635.34150	635.34150	85.22	<.0001
Error	29	216.21305	7.45562		
Corrected Total	30	851.55455			

Variable	Parameter Estimate	Standard Error	Type II SS	F Value	Pr > F
Intercept	35.57526	1.36917	5033.48080	675.13	<.0001
Performance	1.47507	0.15979	635.34150	85.22	<.0001

Bounds on condition number: 1, 1

Stepwise Selection (continued)

Stepwise Selection: Step 2

Variable Run_Pulse Entered: R-Square = 0.7640 and C(p) = 10.6839

Analysis of Variance					
Source	DF	Sum of Squares	Mean Square	F Value	Pr > F
Model	2	650.60420	325.30210	45.33	<.0001
Error	28	200.95035	7.17680		
Corrected Total	30	851.55455			

Variable	Parameter Estimate	Standard Error	Type II SS	F Value	Pr > F
Intercept	48.60983	9.03851	207.58002	28.92	<.0001
Run_Pulse	-0.07327	0.05024	15.26270	2.13	0.1559
Performance	1.39954	0.16511	515.66060	71.85	<.0001

Bounds on condition number: 1.1091, 4.4366

Stepwise Selection (continued)

Stepwise Selection: Step 3

Variable Run_Pulse Removed: R-Square = 0.7461 and C(p) = 11.3942

Analysis of Variance					
Source	DF	Sum of Squares	Mean Square	F Value	Pr > F
Model	1	635.34150	635.34150	85.22	<.0001
Error	29	216.21305	7.45562		
Corrected Total	30	851.55455			

Variable	Parameter Estimate	Standard Error	Type II SS	F Value	Pr > F
Intercept	35.57526	1.36917	5033.48080	675.13	<.0001
Performance	1.47507	0.15979	635.34150	85.22	<.0001

Bounds on condition number: 1, 1

Stepwise Selection (continued)

All variables left in the model are significant at the 0.1000 level.

The stepwise method terminated because the next variable to be entered was just removed.

Summary of Stepwise Selection								
Step	Variable Entered	Variable Removed	Number Vars In	Partial R-Square	Model R-Square	C(p)	F Value	Pr > F
1	Performance		1	0.7461	0.7461	11.3942	85.22	<.0001
2	Run_Pulse		2	0.0179	0.7640	10.6839	2.13	0.1559
3		Run_Pulse	1	0.0179	0.7461	11.3942	2.13	0.1559

Results from Stepwise Regression Techniques

FORWARD `Performance, Runtime, Age, Weight, Run_Pulse, Maximum_Pulse`

BACKWARD `Runtime, Age, Run_Pulse, Maximum_Pulse`

STEPWISE `Performance`

66

Comparison of Selection Methods

Stepwise regression	uses fewer computer resources.
All-possible regression	generates more candidate models which may have nearly equal R^2 statistics and C_p statistics.

67

The stepwise regression methods have an advantage when there is a large number of independent variables.

With the all-possible regressions techniques, you can compare essentially equivalent models and use your knowledge of the data set and subject area to select a model that is more easily interpreted.

Chapter 3 Modeling Summary				
Technique	**Model**	**R-Square**	**Adj R-Square**	**MSE**
Simple Linear Regression	`Performance`	0.7461	0.7373	7.45562

Stepwise: FORWARD	`Performance`
	`Runtime`
	`Age`
	`Weight`
	`Run_pulse`
	`Maximum_pulse`
		0.8476	0.8096	5.40569

Stepwise: BACKWARD	`Runtime`
	`Age`
	`Run_pulse`
	`Maximum_pulse`
		0.8355	0.8102	5.38860

Stepwise: STEPWISE	`Performance`	0.7461	0.7373	7.45562

Mallows (Prediction) BEST 4	`Runtime`
	`Age`
	`Run_pulse`
	`Maximum_pulse`
		0.8355	0.8102	5.38860

Hocking (Explanatory) BEST 5	`Runtime`
	`Age`
	`Weight`
	`Run_pulse`
	`Maximum_pulse`
		0.8469	0.8163	5.21397

3.5 Exercises

1. Describing the Relationship between Two Continuous Variables

The cost of tuition and graduation rates are recorded for the top 200 private and public colleges selected by *Money* magazine in 1991. Data is stored in the data set `USCOLLEGES1991`. The data set contains information for these variables:

`name`	name of the college or university
`rate`	graduation rate, excluding transfer students
`region`	school's geographical region
`state`	state where the college or university is located
`tuition`	tuition rate
`type`	type of school, either private or public.

a. Use the Distribution Analysis task to examine the distribution of the variables `rate` and `tuition`.

1) What conclusions can you draw about the distribution of these variables?

2) Do there appear to be any unusual observations?

b. Use the Correlations task to generate a correlation statistics and a plot for the variables `rate` versus `tuition`. Use the plot to answer the following questions.

1) Can a straight line adequately describe the data?

2) Are there any outliers you should investigate?

c. Use the correlation statistics from the previous exercise to answer the following questions.

1) What is the correlation coefficient for `rate` and `tuition`?

2) How would you interpret this coefficient?

3) What is the *p*-value for the coefficient?

4) Is it statistically significant at the 0.05 level?

2. Fitting a Simple Linear Regression

A college entrance exam is designed to predict freshman-year grade point averages. Twenty-five students take the exam, and the data is stored in a SAS data set named **GRADES**. The variables in the data set are

`score`	student's exam score
`gpa`	grade point average at the end of the freshman year.

a. Generate a scatter plot for the variables **gpa** versus **score**.

1) Can a straight line adequately describe the data?

2) What is the range of **score**?

3) Are there any outliers or influential observations you should investigate?

b. Perform a regression analysis by specifying **gpa** as the response variable and **score** as the predictor variable.

1) What is the value of the *F* statistic and the associated *p*-value? How would you interpret this with regard to the model?

2) Write out the predicted regression equation. How would you interpret this?

3) What is the value of the R^2 statistic? How would you interpret this?

4) What is the parameter estimate for **score**? What is the interpretation of the estimate?

c. Produce predicted values for **gpa** when **score** is 40, 60, and 80.

1) What are the predicted values?

2) Is it appropriate to predict **gpa** when **score** is 200?

> When typing values into a data table, there is no need to use the save icon to save the data. Entries are automatically saved.

d. Produce confidence and prediction intervals around these predictions and generate plots of these intervals.

1) What is the 95% confidence interval for the predicted mean of **gpa** when **score** is 60? How would you interpret this?

2) What is the 95% prediction interval for the predicted value of **gpa** when **score** is 60? How would you interpret this?

3. **Performing a Multiple Regression**

   Using the `FITNESS` data set, run a regression of `Oxygen_Consumption` on the independent variables `Performance`, `Runtime`, `Age`, `Weight`, `Run_Pulse`, `Rest_Pulse`, and `Maximum_Pulse`.

   a. Compare the ANOVA table with the `Oxygen_Consumption` and `Performance` regression ANOVA table in the demonstration. What is different?

   b. How do the R^2 and the adjusted R^2 compare with these statistics for the `Oxygen_Consumption` and `Performance` regression demonstration?

   c. Did the estimate for the intercept change? Did the estimate for the slope of `Performance` change?

4. **Simplifying the Model**

   a. Rerun the model in Exercise **3**, but eliminate the variable with the highest *p*-value. Compare the results with the Exercise **3** model.

   b. Did the *p*-value for the model change?

   c. Did the R^2 and adjusted R^2 change?

   d. Did the parameter estimates and their *p*-values change?

5. **More Simplifying of the Model**

   a. Rerun the model in Exercise **4**, but drop the variable with the highest *p*-value.

   b. How did the results change from the previous model?

   c. Did the number of parameters with a *p*-value less than 0.05 change?

6. **Using All-Regression Techniques**

   The data set `CARS1993` contains information about the median price (`MIDPRICE`) of 92 different makes and models of cars. The data set also contains data about the cars' miles per gallon, city and highway (`CITYMPG` and `HWYMPG`), engine size and other characteristics (`EGNSIZE`, `HRSPOWER`, `RPM`, `REVLTNS`), fuel tank capacity (`FUELTNK`), and weight (`WEIGHT`).

   a. Use an all-regressions technique to identify a set of candidate models. Make sure the C_p is printed to aid in model selection. If desired, add code to create a graph of the number of parameters versus the MALLOWS and HOCKING criteria.

   b. Use a stepwise regression method to select a candidate model; try STEPWISE and BACKWARD. Compare the selected candidate models and use the two different approaches.

3.6 Chapter Summary

Before you perform an analysis, it is important to examine scatter plots and calculate correlation statistics. Scatter plots describe the relationship between two continuous variables. The Pearson correlation statistic measures the degree of linear relationship between two variables.

Simple linear regression defines the linear relationship between a continuous response variable and a continuous predictor variable. The assumptions of a linear regression analysis are

- the mean of the response variable is linearly related to the value of the predictor variable
- the observations are independent
- the error terms for each value of the predictor variable are normally distributed
- the error variances for each value of the predictor variable are equal.

You can verify these assumptions by

- examining a plot of the residuals versus the predicted values
- checking the residuals for normality.

When you perform a simple linear regression, the null hypothesis is that the simple linear regression does not fit the data better than the baseline model ($\beta_1 = 0$). The alternative hypothesis is that the simple linear regression model does fit the data better than the baseline model ($\beta_1 \neq 0$).

Multiple regression enables you to investigate the relationship between a response variable and several predictor variables simultaneously. The null hypothesis is that the slopes for all of the predictor variables are equal to zero ($\beta_1 = \beta_2 = \ldots = \beta_k = 0$). The alternative hypothesis is that at least one slope is not equal to zero. If you reject the null hypothesis, you must determine which of the independent variables have non-zero slopes and are, therefore, useful in the model.

The tests of the parameter estimates help you determine which slopes are nonzero, but they must be considered carefully. They test the significance of each variable when it is added to a model that already contains all of the other independent variables. Therefore, if independent variables in the model are correlated with one another, the significance of both variables can be hidden in these tests.

There are different model selection options. They can generally be divided into two types: all-possible regression options and stepwise options. With the all-possible regression options, regressions using all possible combinations of variables are calculated. All of the regressions are then ranked either by R^2, adjusted R^2, or Mallows' C_p. All-possible regression techniques can be computer intensive, especially if there are a large number of potential independent variables. Stepwise selection procedures help choose the independent variables that are most useful in explaining or predicting your dependent variable. Some of the stepwise selection methods are FORWARD, BACKWARD, and STEPWISE.

Four common problems with regression are nonconstant variance, correlated errors, influential observations, and collinearity. Collinearity is a problem unique to multiple regression. It can hide significant variables and increase the variance of the parameter estimates resulting in an unstable model.

The Correlations task and Regression task were introduced in this chapter: The Correlations task uses the CORR procedure from Base SAS to generate the Pearson correlation coefficient/ Scatter plots were also generated.

The Linear task from the REG procedure from SAS/STAT software was used to perform simple and multiple linear regression; all possible regression techniques and the three stepwise techniques were invoked using this task as well.

3.7 Solutions to Exercises

1. Describing the Relationship between Two Continuous Variables

a. Use the Distribution Analysis task on the **USCOLLEGES1991** data set. Assign **rate** and **tuition** as Analysis variables. Select the tables and plots you think will give you the best picture of the two distributions.

Partial results for **rate**

The UNIVARIATE Procedure
Variable: rate

Moments			
N	196	Sum Weights	196
Mean	66.1989796	Sum Observations	12975
Std Deviation	11.3506443	Variance	128.837127
Skewness	0.23195477	Kurtosis	0.34296403
Uncorrected SS	884055	Corrected SS	25123.2398
Coeff Variation	17.1462527	Std Error Mean	0.81076031

Basic Statistical Measures			
Location		Variability	
Mean	66.19898	Std Deviation	11.35064
Median	65.00000	Variance	128.83713
Mode	60.00000	Range	67.00000
		Interquartile Range	13.50000

Missing Values			
		Percent Of	
Missing Value	Count	All Obs	Missing Obs
.	4	2.00	100.00

Partial results for **`rate`**

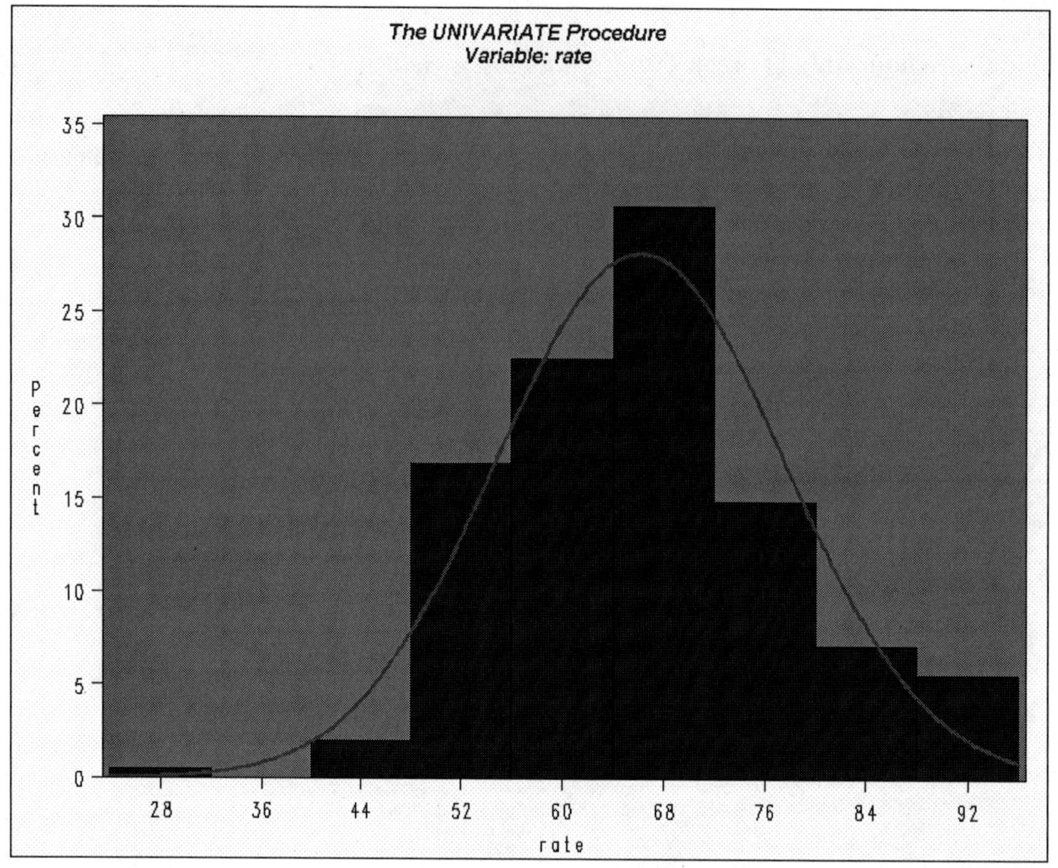

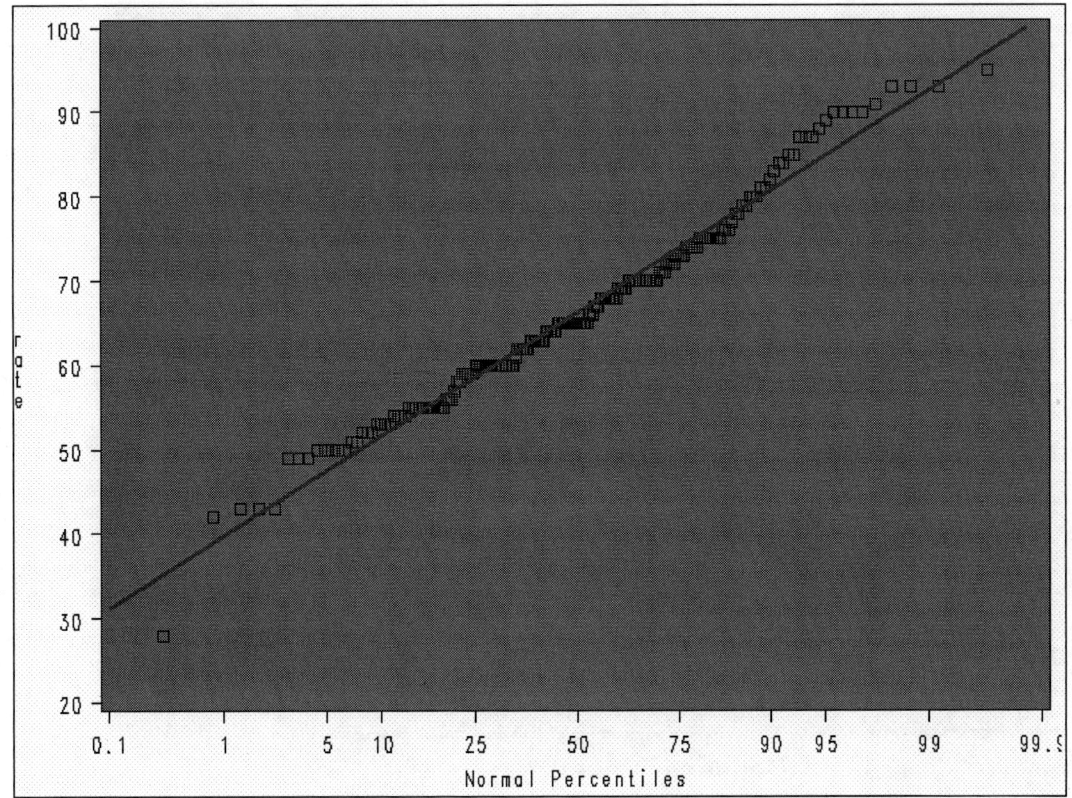
100
90
80
70
60
50
40
30
20
rate
0.1
1
5
10
25
50
75
90
95
99
Normal Percentiles

Partial results for `tuition`

The UNIVARIATE Procedure
Variable: tuition

Moments			
N	199	Sum Weights	199
Mean	7152.34673	Sum Observations	1423317
Std Deviation	2762.1446	Variance	7629442.79
Skewness	1.195457	Kurtosis	2.06346036
Uncorrected SS	1.16907E10	Corrected SS	1510629673
Coeff Variation	38.6187178	Std Error Mean	195.803239

Basic Statistical Measures			
Location		Variability	
Mean	7152.347	Std Deviation	2762
Median	6685.000	Variance	7629443
Mode	4622.000	Range	15390
		Interquartile Range	2900

Note: The mode displayed is the smallest of 4 modes with a count of 2.

Missing Values			
		Percent Of	
Missing Value	Count	All Obs	Missing Obs
.	1	0.50	100.00

Partial results for **`tuition`**

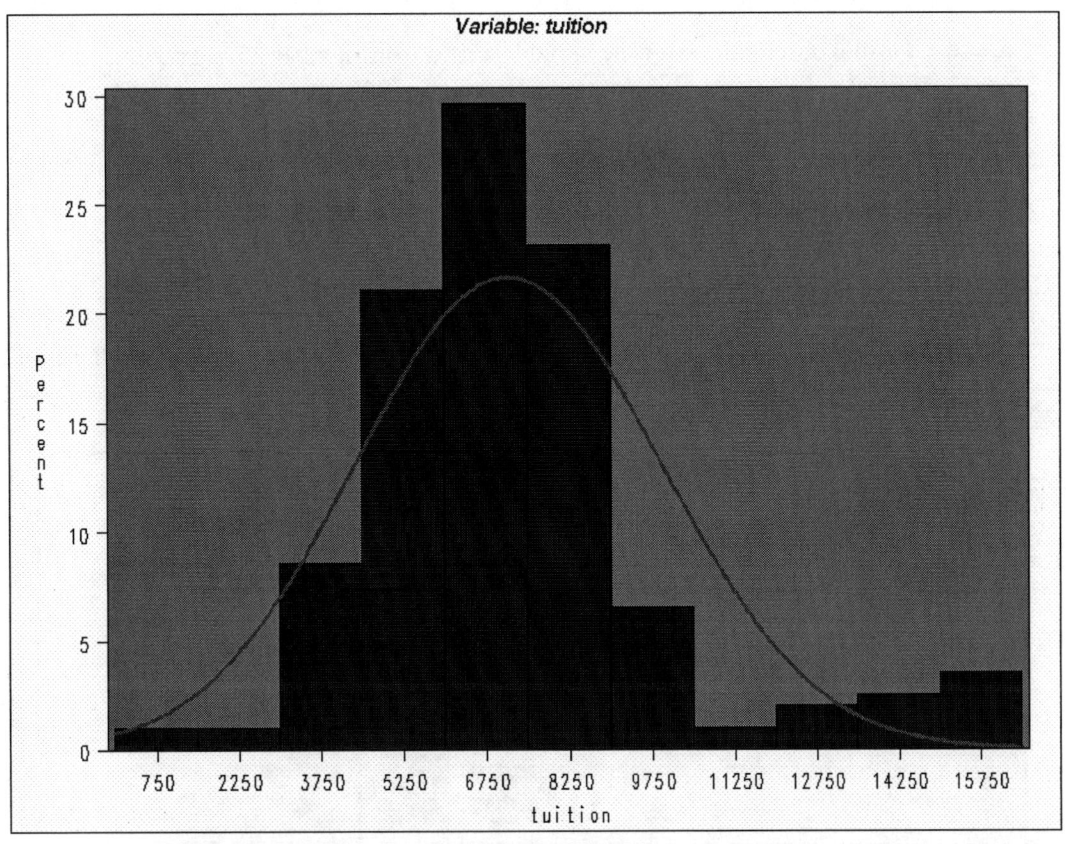

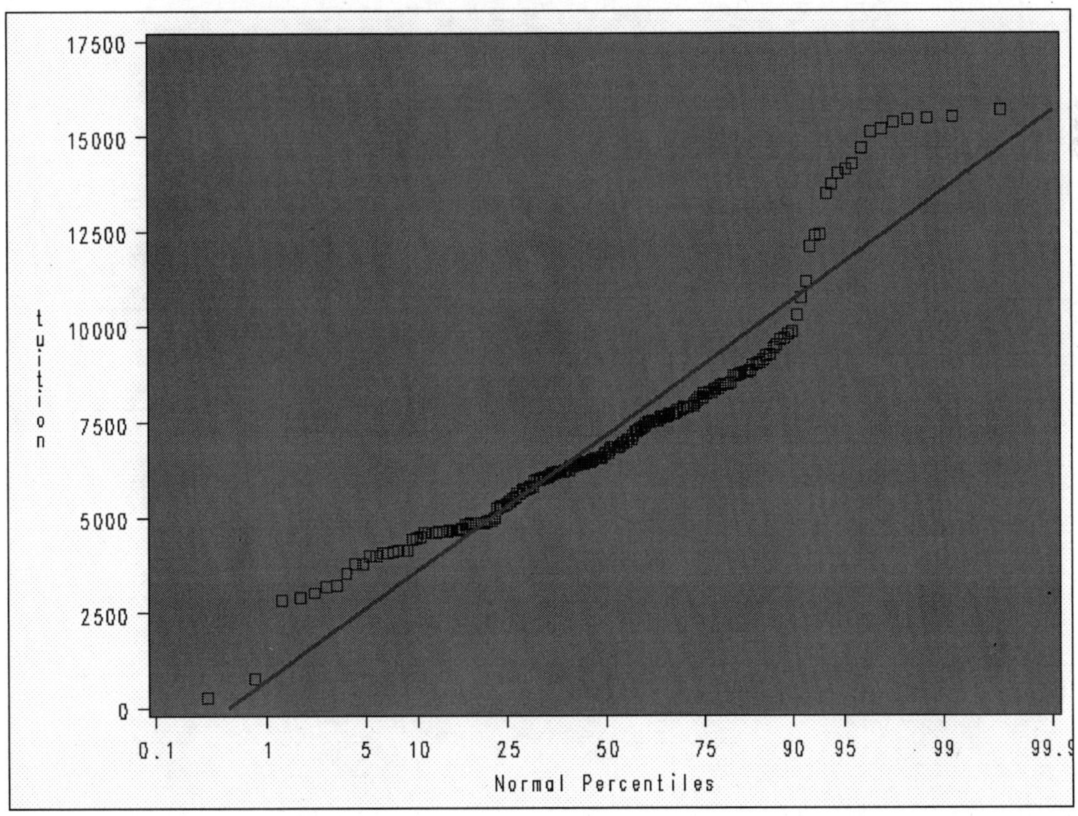

1) The variable **rate** is skewed slightly to the right with slightly heavy tails. The variable **tuition** is skewed to the right.

2) There are two unusual observations for the variable **rate**: row number 25, `City College-City U. of N.Y.` with a graduation rate of 28% and row number 54, `Harvard`, with a graduation rate of 95%. The variable **tuition** has several unusual observations: those colleges with tuition below $1000 and those with tuition above $13,000.

b. Use the Correlations task (located under the Analyze pull-down menu) to investigate the relationship between **rate** and **tuition**. Select **tuition** as the Analysis variable and **rate** as the Correlate with variable. Use the **Plots** pane to request a scatter plot.

Selecting **tuition** as the Analysis variable puts it on the Y-axis in the resulting scatter plot.

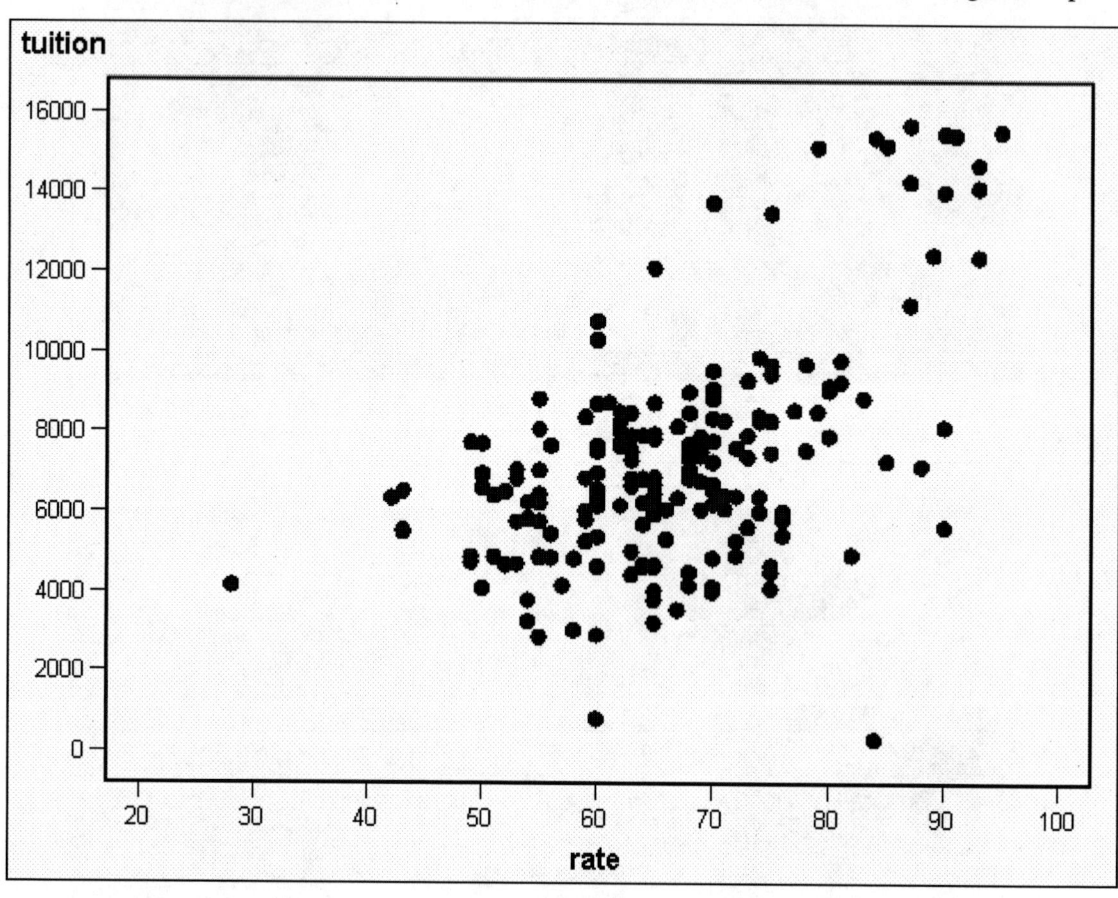

1) A straight line can adequately describe the data.

2) If you examine the plot from left to right, there appear to be three outliers that warrant investigation:

   - `rate=28 and tuition=4145`
   - `rate=60 and tuition=800`
   - `rate=84 and tuition=300`

Correlation Analysis

The CORR Procedure

1 With Variables:	rate
1 Variables:	tuition

Simple Statistics

Variable	N	Mean	Std Dev	Sum	Minimum	Maximum
rate	196	66.19898	11.35064	12975	28.00000	95.00000
tuition	199	7152	2762	1423317	300.00000	15690

Pearson Correlation Coefficients
Prob > |r| under H0: Rho=0
Number of Observations

	tuition
rate	0.55385 <.0001 196

c.

1) The correlation coefficient is 0.55385.

2) The correlation indicates a moderately strong positive linear relationship between **`rate`** and **`tuition`**.

3) The *p*-value is less than 0.0001.

4) The correlation coefficient is statistically significant at the .05 level.

2. Fitting a Simple Linear Regression

a. Open the **GRADES** data table and use the Correlations task to investigate the relationship between **score** and **gpa**. Assign **gpa** as the Analysis variable and assign **score** as the Correlate with variable. Check the box on the **Plots** pane to get a scatter plot.

> Selecting **score** as the Analysis variable puts it on the Y-axis in the resulting scatter plot.

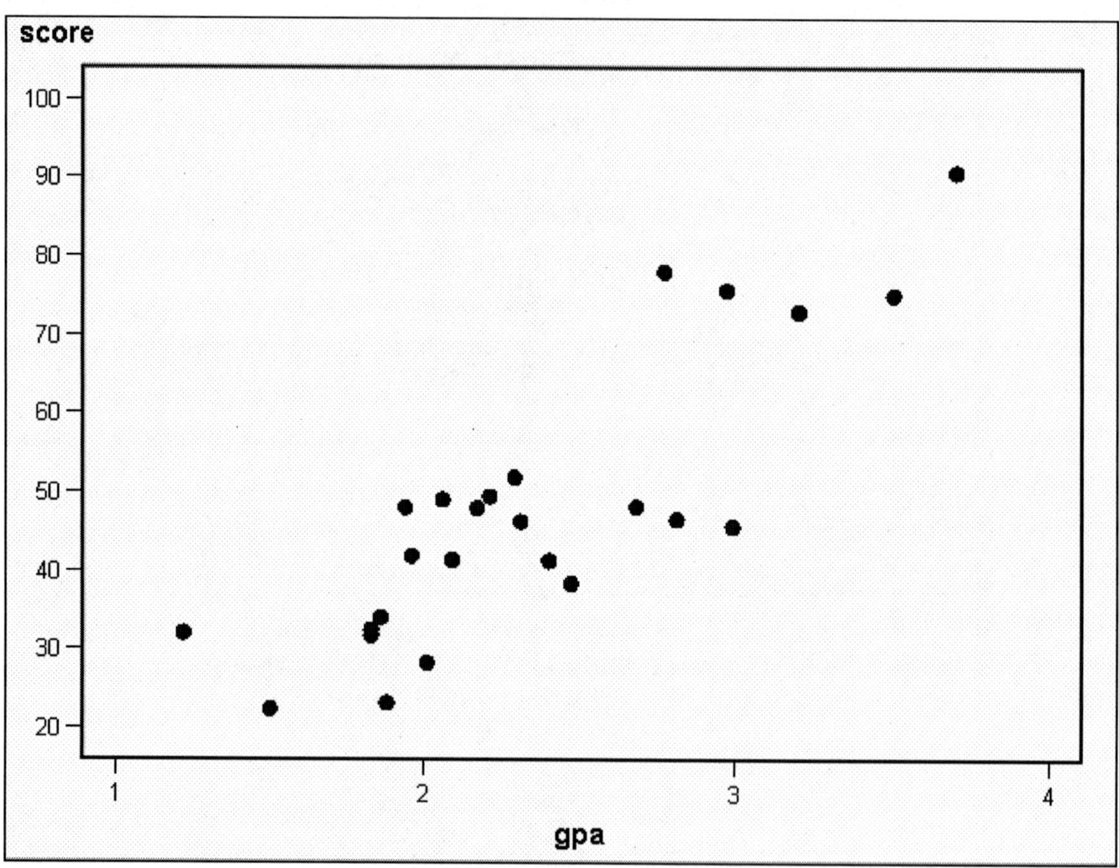

1) A straight line can adequately describe the data.

2) The range of **score** is approximately 22 to 91.

3) There are no outliers that warrant investigation.

b. Use the Regression task to perform a regression analysis where `gpa` is the dependent variable and `score` is the explanatory variable. Use the task defaults.

Linear Regression Results

The REG Procedure
Model: Linear_Regression_Model
Dependent Variable: gpa

Number of Observations Read	25
Number of Observations Used	25

Analysis of Variance

Source	DF	Sum of Squares	Mean Square	F Value	Pr > F
Model	1	6.33971	6.33971	58.77	<.0001
Error	23	2.48109	0.10787		
Corrected Total	24	8.82080			

Root MSE	0.32844	R-Square	0.7187
Dependent Mean	2.34600	Adj R-Sq	0.7065
Coeff Var	14.00003		

Parameter Estimates

Variable	DF	Parameter Estimate	Standard Error	t Value	Pr > |t|
Intercept	1	0.98051	0.18985	5.16	<.0001
score	1	0.02866	0.00374	7.67	<.0001

1) The value of the *F* statistic is 58.77 and the corresponding *p*-value is less than 0.0001. With this result, you can reject the null hypothesis and conclude that at least one of the parameter estimates is not equal to 0. Because this is a simple linear regression, this means the parameter estimate for **`score`** is not equal to 0.

2) The predicted regression equation is **`gpa`** = 0.98051 + 0.02866 * **`score`**. The model indicates the predicted grade point average at the end of the freshman year is equal to 0.98051 + (0.02866 * the student's exam score).

3) The R^2 statistic is 0.7187. This means the regression line explains 71.87% of the total variation in the data.

4) The parameter estimate for **`score`** is 0.02866. This means that a one-point increase in the exam score would amount to a 0.02866 increase in the grade point average at the end of the freshman year.

c. Create a new data table, named **`predict_score`**, and enter the values of **`40`**, **`60`**, and **`80`** into a column entitled **`Score`**. Close **`predict_score`**. Re-open the Regression task in step **b.** and add **`predict_score`** as the data table to generate predicted values.

1) Because creating a new data table is not demonstrated in this class, use the following steps:

a) Select **File** ⇨ **New** ⇨ **Data...**.

b) Use the default location of WORK and type **`predict_score`** as the data set name (spaces are not allowed in SAS data set names.) Select **Save**.

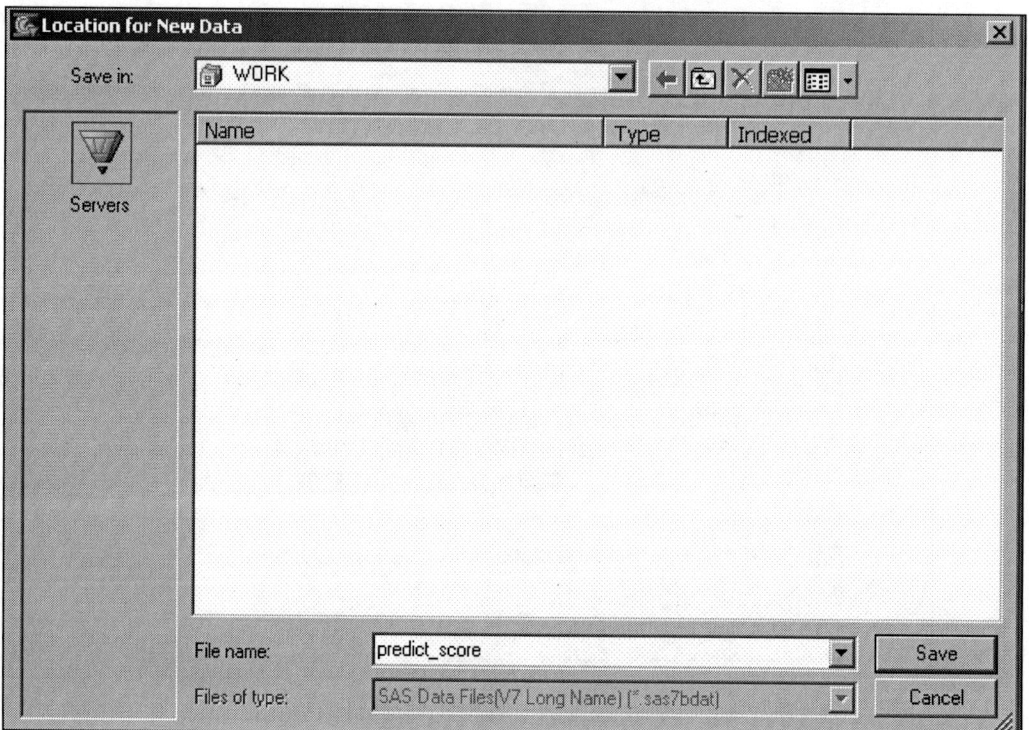

c) The data set **`predict_score`** is added to the project tree. Double-click to open it.

predict_score

	A	B	C	D	E	F
1						
2						
3						
4						
5						
6						
7						
8						
9						
10						
11						
12						

SAS Enterprise Guide presents an empty data table. You need to change the first column's name from **`A`** to **`Score`** and add the values of `40`, `60`, and `80`.

d) Select the **A**, column, right click, and select **Properties…**.

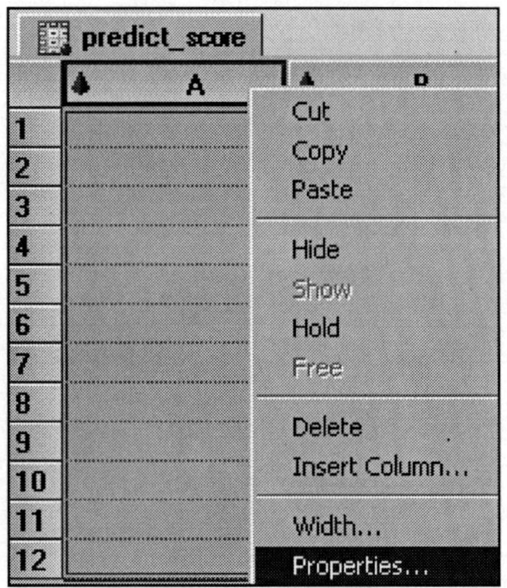

e) Highlight the default column name of **A** and type **Score**.

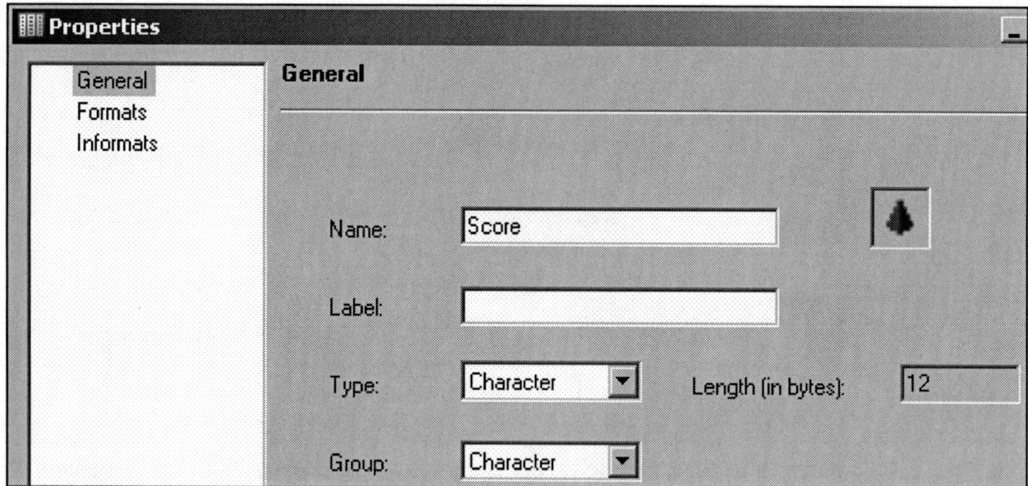

f) Click beside the black triangle in the Type field and select **Numeric**. Note that the symbol changes from a red triangle to a blue dot.

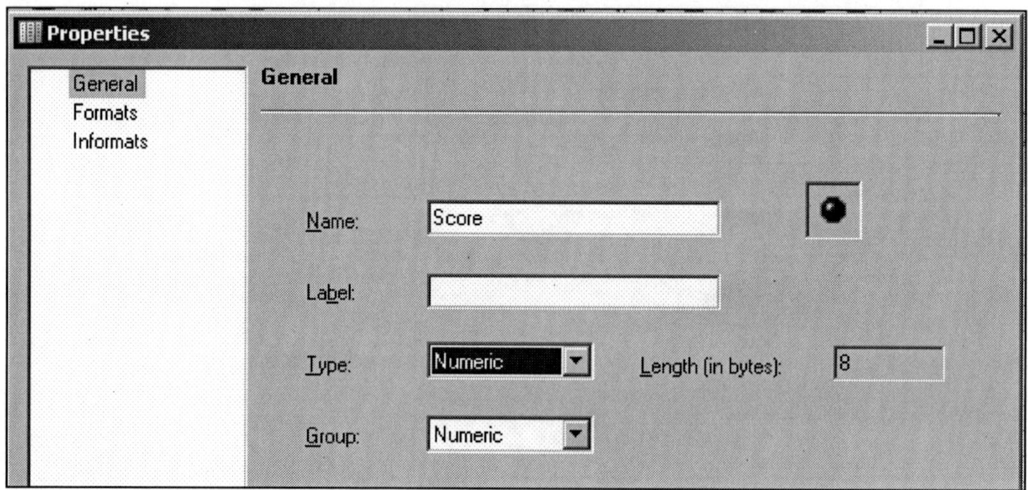

g) Select **OK**.

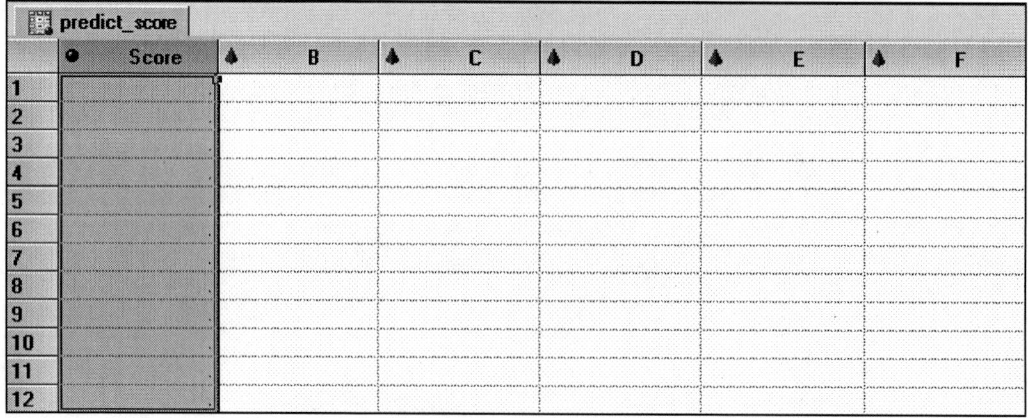

h) Select the first row of **Score**. Type `40` and press Enter. With the cursor in the second row, type `60` and press Enter. Repeat the same steps for the third row and type `80`.

predict_score

	Score	B	C	D	E	F
1	40					
2	60					
3	80					

i) Select the remaining empty columns. Right-click and select **Delete**.

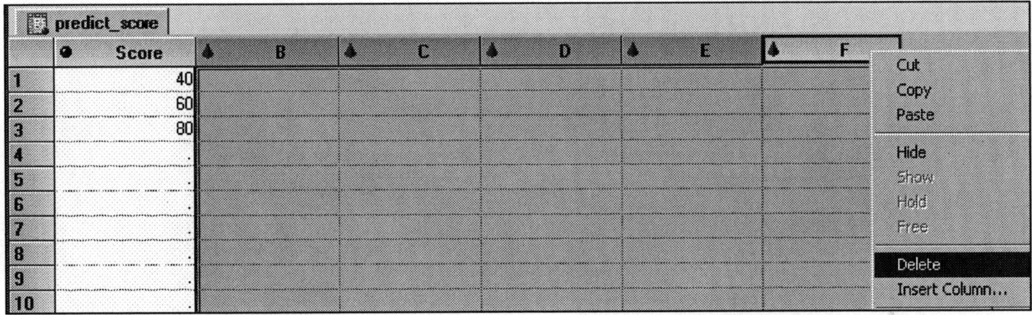

j) Select **Yes**.

Entries in the data table are automatically saved. There is no need to save the table.

k) Select rows 4 through 12, right click and select **Delete rows**.

l) Select **Yes**.

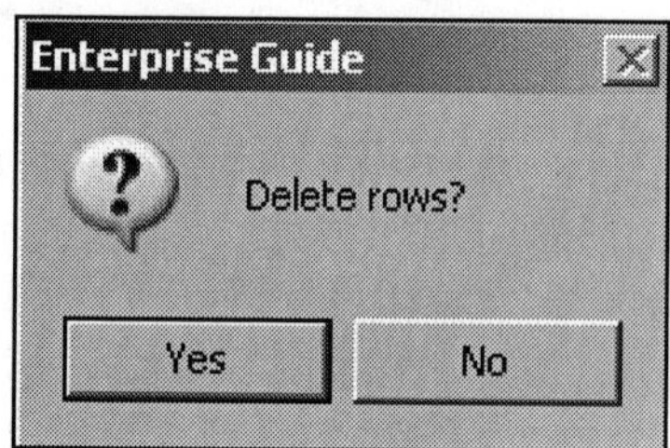

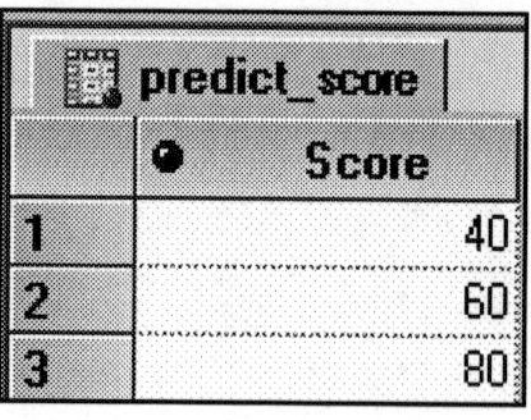

m) Close `predict_score`.

Find and open the Linear Regression node that you created in part **b**.

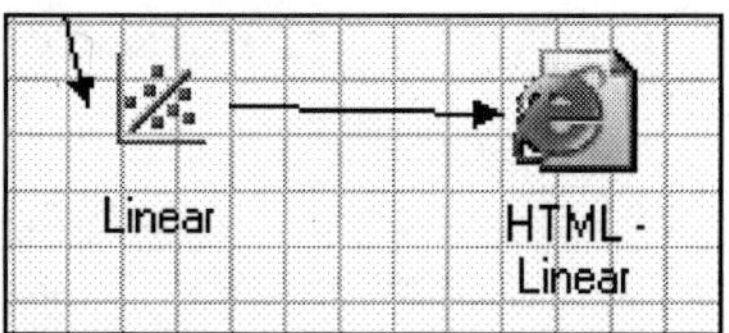

Use the **Predictions** pane to request predicted values. Check **Additional Data** under Data to predict, and use the Modify button to locate **WORK.PREDICT_SCORE**. (Do not forget to change the library. SAS opens SASUSER by default).

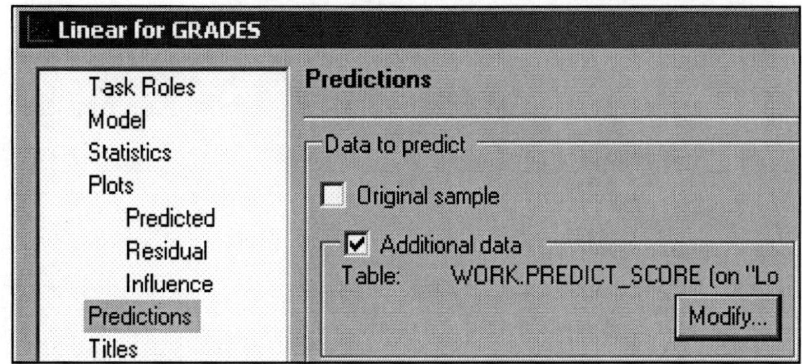

Select **Run** to run the analysis, and select **Yes** at the pop-up window to replace the results of the previous run.

The regression results are the same as Exercise **2**, part **b**. Select and open the data table `Predictions for "gpa=score"`.

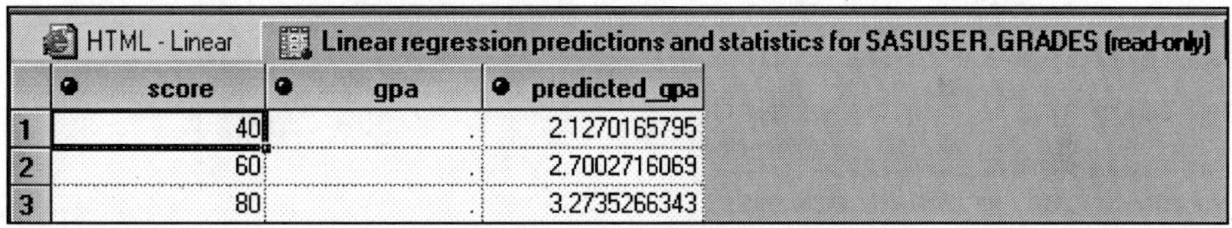

HTML - Linear | Linear regression predictions and statistics for SASUSER.GRADES (read-only)

	score	gpa	predicted_gpa
1	40	.	2.1270165795
2	60	.	2.7002716069
3	80	.	3.2735266343

The predicted values are 2.1270, 2.700, and 3.2735, respectively.

2) Because the values of `score` range from 22 to 92, it would be inappropriate to predict `gpa` when `score` is 200.

d. Open the Linear Regression node that you just completed, and add the options to request confidence intervals around the mean and prediction intervals for a given value of the predictor variable. Generate the requested plots for these intervals.

Use the Predicted selection under Plots. Check the box next to **Observed vs Independents** and select **Confidence limits**. Select **Predictions** on the left and check the boxes next to **Residuals** and **Prediction limits** under **Additional Statistics**.

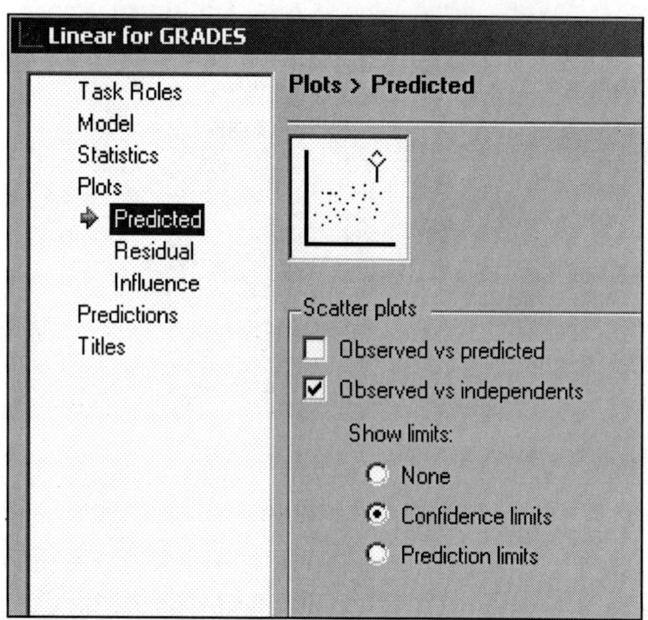

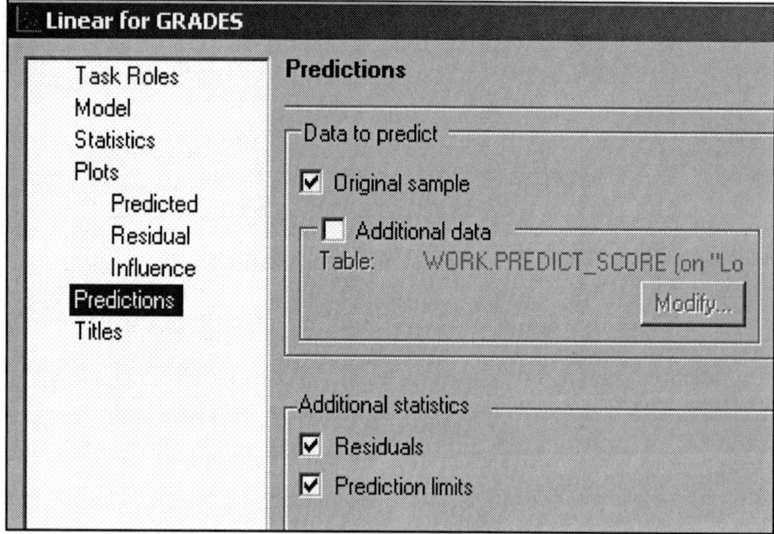

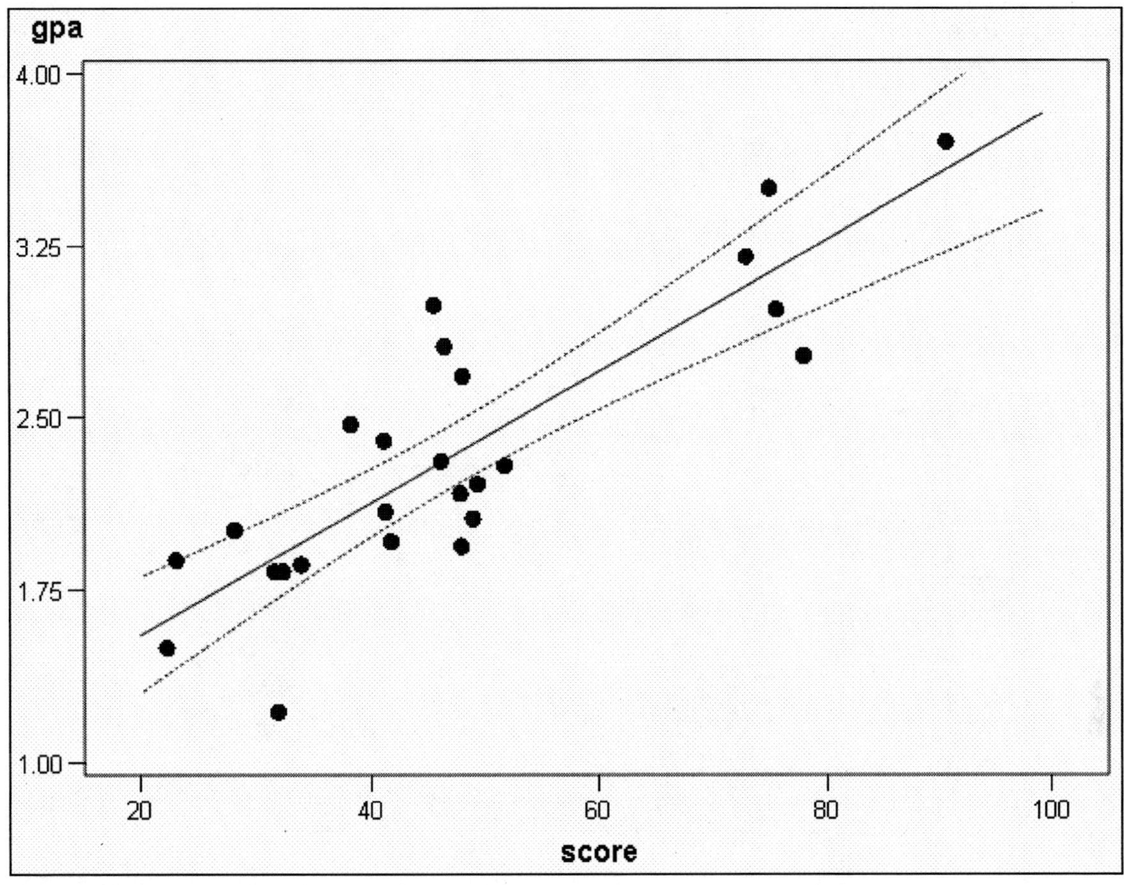

This plot represents the confidence interval for the mean of `gpa`.

To generate the plot for individual predicted value, you must open the last linear regression task and select `Prediction limits` in the **Plots** panel.

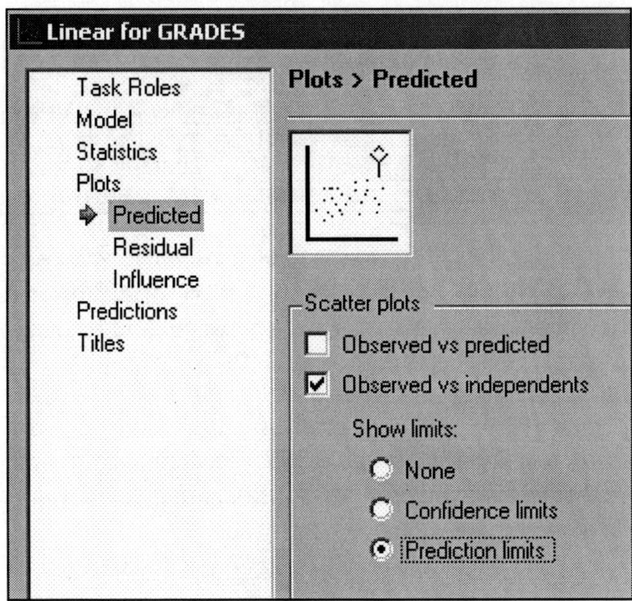

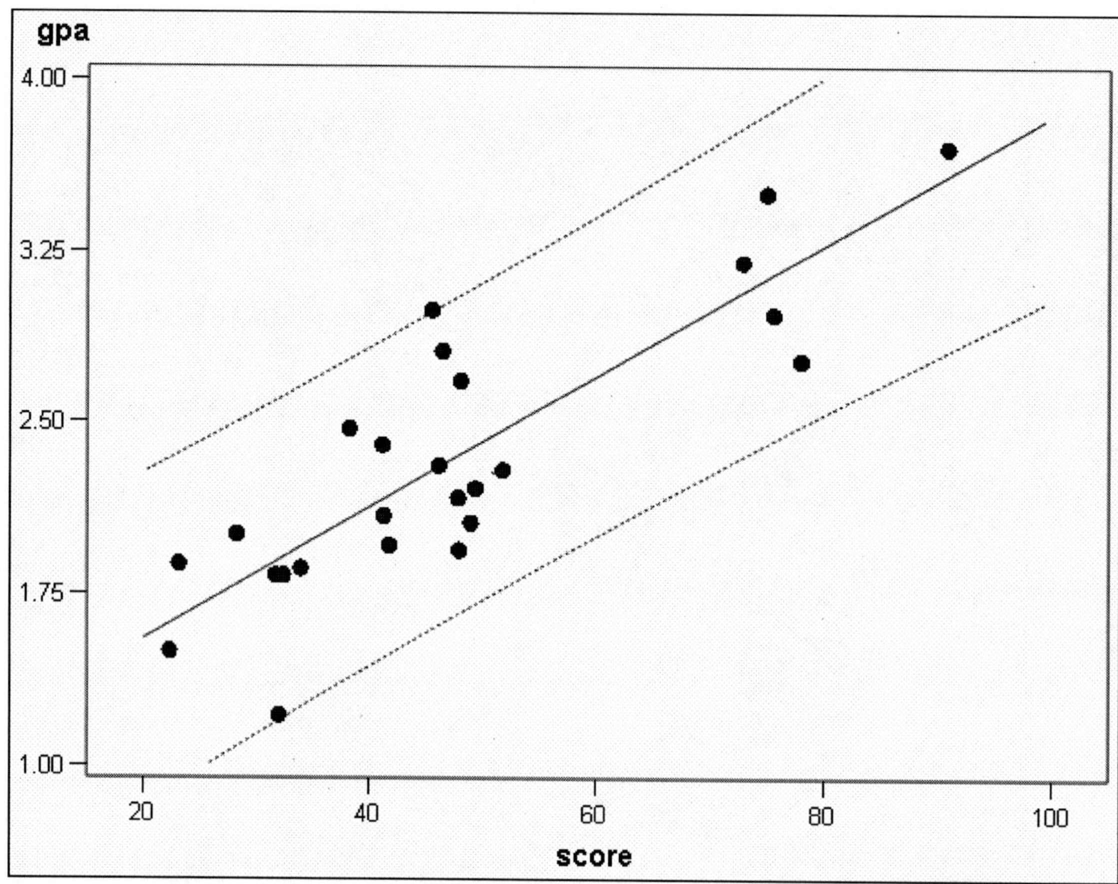

This plot is for the prediction interval for an individual value of `gpa`.

The most convenient place to find the values of `gpa`, `predicted_gpa`, and the confidence intervals for the mean is in the data table resulting from the Linear Models task. Double-click the table to open it.

Linear regression predictions and statistics for SASUSER.GRADES (read-only)

	score	predicted_gpa	lclm_gpa	uclm_gpa	lcl_gpa	ucl_gpa
26	40	2.1270165795	1.978838161	2.2751949981	1.4316145531	2.8224186059
27	60	2.7002716069	2.5341271053	2.8664161086	2.0008210154	3.3997221985
28	80	3.2735266343	2.9887313305	3.5583219381	2.5368207909	4.0102324777

1) The 95% predicted confidence interval for the predicted mean of `gpa` when `score` is 60 is 2.5341 through 2.8664, located in the columns `uclm_gpa` and `lclm_gpa`. This indicates that you are 95% confident that the population mean of `gpa` is between 2.5341 and 2.8664 when `score` is 60.

2) Using the same table but the last two columns, when `score` is 60, the predicted prediction interval for the predicted value of `gpa` is 2.0008 through 3.3997, located in columns `ucl_gpa` and `lcl_gpa`. This indicates that you are 95% confident that a new value of `gpa` falls between 2.0008 and 3.3997 when `score` is 60.

3. Performing a Multiple Regression

Open **FITNESS**. Use the Regression task to perform the requested multiple linear regression. Assign **Oxygen_Consumption** as the Dependent variable and the rest of the numeric variables in the data set as Independent variables.

Analysis of Variance

Source	DF	Sum of Squares	Mean Square	F Value	Pr > F
Model	7	722.03251	103.14750	18.32	<.0001
Error	23	129.52204	5.63139		
Corrected Total	30	851.55455			

Root MSE	2.37306	R-Square	0.8479
Dependent Mean	47.37581	Adj R-Sq	0.8016
Coeff Var	5.00900		

Parameter Estimates

Variable	DF	Parameter Estimate	Standard Error	t Value	Pr > |t|
Intercept	1	93.33753	36.49782	2.56	0.0176
Runtime	1	-2.08804	2.22856	-0.94	0.3585
Age	1	-0.21066	0.10519	-2.00	0.0571
Weight	1	-0.07741	0.05681	-1.36	0.1862
Run_Pulse	1	-0.36618	0.12299	-2.98	0.0067
Rest_Pulse	1	-0.01389	0.07114	-0.20	0.8469
Maximum_Pulse	1	0.30490	0.13990	2.18	0.0398
Performance	1	0.25756	1.02373	0.25	0.8036

a. There are key differences between the ANOVA table for this expanded model and the Simple Linear Regression model:

- The degrees of freedom for the model are much higher, 7 versus 1.
- The Mean Square Model and the *F* ratio are much smaller.

b. Both the R^2 and adjusted R^2 for the full models are larger than the simple linear regression. Consequently, the full model explains over 80 percent of the variation in the **`Oxygen_Consumption`** variable versus only about 75 percent explained by the simple linear regression.

c. Yes, including the other variables in the model changed both the estimate of the intercept and the slope for **`Performance`**. Also, the *p*-values for both changed dramatically. The slope of **`Performance`** is now not significantly different from zero.

4. Simplifying the Model

Examine the Parameter Estimates table from the previous exercise.

Parameter Estimates					
Variable	DF	Parameter Estimate	Standard Error	t Value	Pr > |t|
Intercept	1	93.33753	36.49782	2.56	0.0176
Runtime	1	-2.08804	2.22856	-0.94	0.3585
Age	1	-0.21066	0.10519	-2.00	0.0571
Weight	1	-0.07741	0.05681	-1.36	0.1862
Run_Pulse	1	-0.36618	0.12299	-2.98	0.0067
Rest_Pulse	1	-0.01389	0.07114	-0.20	0.8469
Maximum_Pulse	1	0.30490	0.13990	2.18	0.0398
Performance	1	0.25756	1.02373	0.25	0.8036

a. Open the Linear Regression task from the previous exercise by double-clicking it in the process flow. Because **`Rest_Pulse`** has the largest *p*-value (0.8469) in the above model, delete it from the list of explanatory variables and re-run the analysis. Do not replace the results of the previous run.

Analysis of Variance					
Source	DF	Sum of Squares	Mean Square	F Value	Pr > F
Model	6	721.81791	120.30298	22.25	<.0001
Error	24	129.73665	5.40569		
Corrected Total	30	851.55455			

Root MSE	2.32501	R-Square	0.8476
Dependent Mean	47.37581	Adj R-Sq	0.8096
Coeff Var	4.90760		

Parameter Estimates					
Variable	DF	Parameter Estimate	Standard Error	t Value	Pr > |t|
Intercept	1	90.83022	33.47159	2.71	0.0121
Runtime	1	-1.98433	2.12049	-0.94	0.3587
Age	1	-0.20470	0.09862	-2.08	0.0488
Weight	1	-0.07689	0.05560	-1.38	0.1794
Run_Pulse	1	-0.36818	0.12008	-3.07	0.0053
Maximum_Pulse	1	0.30593	0.13697	2.23	0.0351
Performance	1	0.32048	0.95201	0.34	0.7393

b. No, the *p*-value for the over model F test did not change.

c. The R^2 only dropped by 0.0003, essentially no change. The adjusted R^2 increased from 0.8016 to 0.8096. When an adjusted R^2 increases by removing a variable from the models, it strongly implies that the removed variable was not necessary.

d. All the parameter estimates and their *p*-values changed; some only changed a little.

5. **More Simplifying of the Model**

Examine the Parameter Estimates table from the previous exercise.

Parameter Estimates					
Variable	DF	Parameter Estimate	Standard Error	t Value	Pr > |t|
Intercept	1	90.83022	33.47159	2.71	0.0121
Runtime	1	-1.98433	2.12049	-0.94	0.3587
Age	1	-0.20470	0.09862	-2.08	0.0488
Weight	1	-0.07689	0.05560	-1.38	0.1794
Run_Pulse	1	-0.36818	0.12008	-3.07	0.0053
Maximum_Pulse	1	0.30593	0.13697	2.23	0.0351
Performance	1	0.32048	0.95201	0.34	0.7393

a. Because **Performance** has the largest *p*-value (0.7393) in the above model, delete it from the list of explanatory variables and rerun the analysis. Select **Run** and **No** to replace the previous results.

Analysis of Variance

Source	DF	Sum of Squares	Mean Square	F Value	Pr > F
Model	5	721.20532	144.24106	27.66	<.0001
Error	25	130.34923	5.21397		
Corrected Total	30	851.55455			

Root MSE	2.28341	R-Square	0.8469
Dependent Mean	47.37581	Adj R-Sq	0.8163
Coeff Var	4.81978		

Parameter Estimates

Variable	DF	Parameter Estimate	Standard Error	t Value	Pr > |t|
Intercept	1	101.33835	11.86474	8.54	<.0001
Runtime	1	-2.68846	0.34202	-7.86	<.0001
Age	1	-0.21217	0.09437	-2.25	0.0336
Weight	1	-0.07332	0.05360	-1.37	0.1836
Run_Pulse	1	-0.37071	0.11770	-3.15	0.0042
Maximum_Pulse	1	0.30603	0.13452	2.28	0.0317

b. The ANOVA table did not change significantly. The R^2 decreased slightly. The adjusted R^2 increased again, confirming that the variable **Performance** did not contribute to explaining the variation in **Oxygen_Consumption** when the other variables are in the model.

c. The *p*-value for **Runtime** changed dramatically and is now less than 0.05. **Age**, **Run_Pulse**, and **Maximum_Pulse** also have *p*-values less than 0.05, as they did in the previous model. **Weight** has about the same *p*-value.

6. Using All-Regression Techniques

Open `CARS1993`. Use the Linear Regression task, assigning `MIDPRICE` as the dependent variable and the other numeric variables as independent variables. On the **Model** pane, change the **Model selection method** to **R-squared selection**. Check the boxes next to **Adjusted R-square** and **Mallows' Cp.**

Use the **Preview Code** checkbox and click the **Insert Code** button to add code for the graph. Be sure to add the code before the semicolon on the MODEL statement.

```
/* Start of custom user code. */
BEST=4;
PLOT CP.*NP./
            VAXIS=0 TO 30 BY 5
            HAXIS=2 TO 8
            CMALLOWS=RED
            CHOCKING=BLUE
/* End of custom user code. */
    ;
RUN;
QUIT;
```

The starting value of the HAXIS was changed to 2, since the values of 0 and 1 are not meaningful.

Select **Run** to run the task.

Linear Regression Results

The REG Procedure
Model: Linear_Regression_Model
Dependent Variable: MIDPRICE

R-Square Selection Method

Number of Observations Read	92
Number of Observations Used	92

Number in Model	R-Square	Adjusted R-Square	C(p)	Variables in Model
1	0.6735	0.6699	7.4674	HRSPOWER
1	0.4754	0.4696	65.4143	WEIGHT
1	0.4468	0.4407	73.7725	FUELTNK
1	0.4172	0.4107	82.4296	EGNSIZE
2	0.6891	0.6821	4.9076	HRSPOWER WEIGHT
2	0.6879	0.6809	5.2786	HRSPOWER FUELTNK
2	0.6873	0.6803	5.4456	CITYMPG HRSPOWER
2	0.6855	0.6785	5.9588	HWYMPG HRSPOWER
3	0.7037	0.6936	2.6456	HRSPOWER REVLTNS WEIGHT
3	0.6984	0.6881	4.1941	CITYMPG HRSPOWER REVLTNS
3	0.6937	0.6833	5.5609	HRSPOWER REVLTNS FUELTNK
4	0.7095	0.6962	2.9396	CITYMPG EGNSIZE HRSPOWER REVLTNS
4	0.7082	0.6948	3.3271	CITYMPG HRSPOWER REVLTNS WEIGHT
4	0.7063	0.6928	3.8831	EGNSIZE HRSPOWER REVLTNS WEIGHT
4	0.7047	0.6912	4.3478	HWYMPG HRSPOWER REVLTNS WEIGHT
5	0.7125	0.6958	4.0724	CITYMPG EGNSIZE HRSPOWER REVLTNS WEIGHT
5	0.7108	0.6940	4.5675	CITYMPG EGNSIZE HRSPOWER RPM REVLTNS
5	0.7105	0.6937	4.6468	CITYMPG HWYMPG HRSPOWER REVLTNS WEIGHT
5	0.7101	0.6933	4.7720	CITYMPG HWYMPG EGNSIZE HRSPOWER REVLTNS
6	0.7143	0.6941	5.5443	CITYMPG EGNSIZE HRSPOWER RPM REVLTNS WEIGHT
6	0.7141	0.6939	5.6047	CITYMPG HWYMPG EGNSIZE HRSPOWER REVLTNS WEIGHT
6	0.7127	0.6924	6.0158	CITYMPG EGNSIZE HRSPOWER REVLTNS FUELTNK WEIGHT
6	0.7114	0.6910	6.4109	CITYMPG HWYMPG EGNSIZE HRSPOWER RPM REVLTNS
7	0.7159	0.6923	7.0665	CITYMPG HWYMPG EGNSIZE HRSPOWER RPM REVLTNS WEIGHT
7	0.7146	0.6908	7.4741	CITYMPG EGNSIZE HRSPOWER RPM REVLTNS FUELTNK WEIGHT
7	0.7143	0.6905	7.5515	CITYMPG HWYMPG EGNSIZE HRSPOWER REVLTNS FUELTNK WEIGHT
7	0.7119	0.6879	8.2551	CITYMPG HWYMPG EGNSIZE HRSPOWER RPM REVLTNS FUELTNK
8	0.7162	0.6888	9.0000	CITYMPG HWYMPG EGNSIZE HRSPOWER RPM REVLTNS FUELTNK WEIGHT

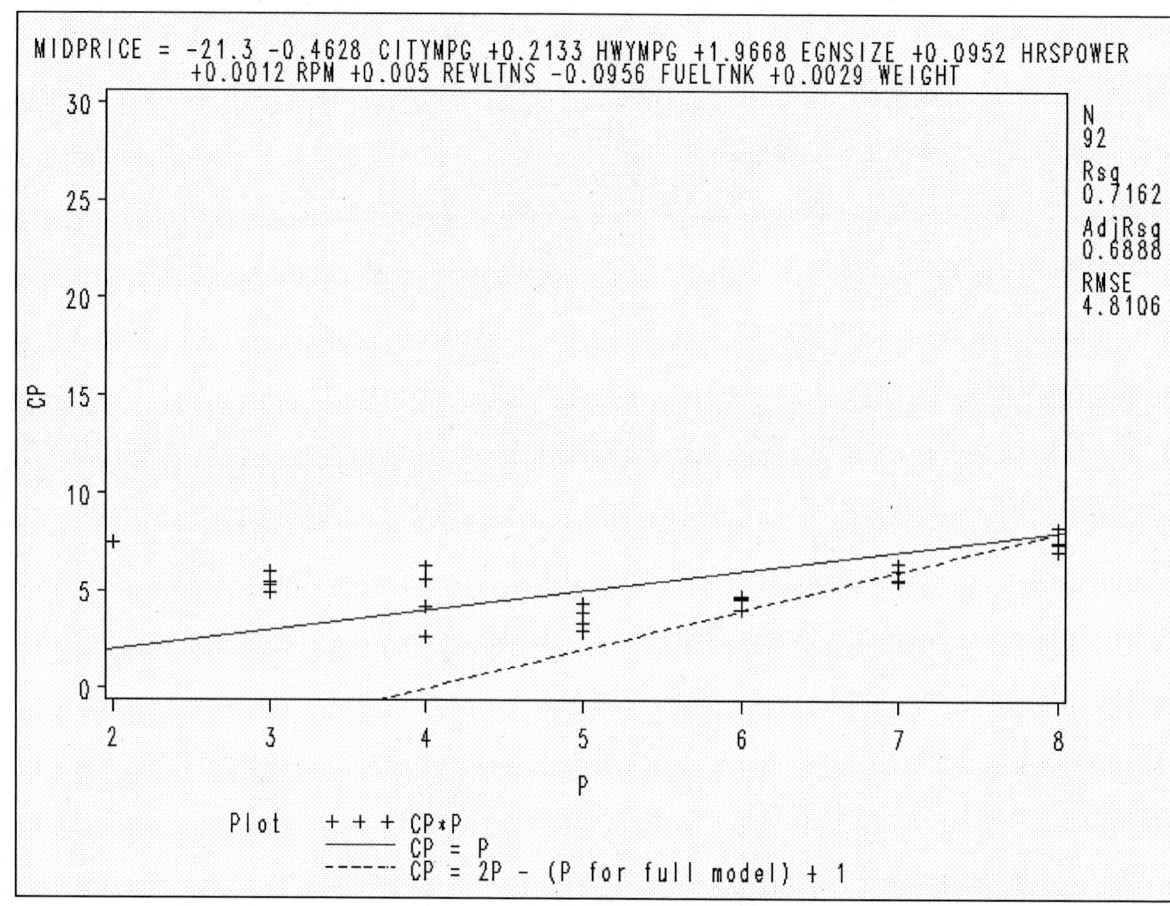

a. Using the graph above, Cp < *p* first occurs when *p*=4. Examine the results table when **Number in Model**=3 and you will find **MIDPRICE=HRSPOWER REVLTNS WEIGHT**. This model would be the best for prediction.

3	0.7037	0.6936	2.6456	HRSPOWER REVLTNS WEIGHT
3	0.6984	0.6881	4.1941	CITYMPG HRSPOWER REVLTNS
3	0.6937	0.6833	5.5609	HRSPOWER REVLTNS FUELTNK
3	0.6914	0.6809	6.2491	HWYMPG HRSPOWER REVLTNS

In this example p_{full} equals 9, 8 variables plus the intercept.

p=# terms in the current model, including the intercept	**Number in Model (k)**	**Minimum C_p with *p* terms**	**Hocking's Criterion : 2*p – 9 + 1 = 2*p – 8**	**C_p< Hocking's Criterion?**
4	3	2.6456	2*4 – 8 = 0	No
5	4	2.9396	2*5 – 8 = 2	No
6	5	4.0724	2*6 – 8 = 4	No
7	6	5.5443	2*7 – 8 = 6	Yes

`MidPrice=CityMPG EngineSize HorsePower RPM Revolutions Weight` is the smallest model that satisfies Hocking's criterion (5.5443 < 6).

b. Open the Linear Regression under the **`CARS1993`** data table. Use the options found in the **Model** pane to change the selection criteria. You can only use one selection criterion at a time, so you will have to re-run the task using stepwise and then again using backward elimination. Select **Run** and **No** so you do not replace the previous results.

Stepwise selection results:

Stepwise Selection: Step 1

Variable HRSPOWER Entered: R-Square = 0.6735 and C(p) = 7.4674

Analysis of Variance					
Source	DF	Sum of Squares	Mean Square	F Value	Pr > F
Model	1	4558.23301	4558.23301	185.69	<.0001
Error	90	2209.31688	24.54797		
Corrected Total	91	6767.54989			

Variable	Parameter Estimate	Standard Error	Type II SS	F Value	Pr > F
Intercept	-0.38356	1.51673	1.56985	0.06	0.8009
HRSPOWER	0.13586	0.00997	4558.23301	185.69	<.0001

Bounds on condition number: 1, 1

Stepwise selection results (continued)

Stepwise Selection: Step 2

Variable WEIGHT Entered: R-Square = 0.6891 and C(p) = 4.9076

Analysis of Variance					
Source	DF	Sum of Squares	Mean Square	F Value	Pr > F
Model	2	4663.75669	2331.87835	98.65	<.0001
Error	89	2103.79320	23.63813		
Corrected Total	91	6767.54989			

Variable	Parameter Estimate	Standard Error	Type II SS	F Value	Pr > F
Intercept	-5.42859	2.81367	87.99160	3.72	0.0569
HRSPOWER	0.11330	0.01448	1446.53699	61.20	<.0001
WEIGHT	0.00270	0.00128	105.52368	4.46	0.0374

Bounds on condition number: 2.1914, 8.7656

Stepwise selection results (continued)

Stepwise Selection: Step 3

Variable REVLTNS Entered: R-Square = 0.7037 and C(p) = 2.6456

Analysis of Variance					
Source	DF	Sum of Squares	Mean Square	F Value	Pr > F
Model	3	4762.38708	1587.46236	69.67	<.0001
Error	88	2005.16281	22.78594		
Corrected Total	91	6767.54989			

Variable	Parameter Estimate	Standard Error	Type II SS	F Value	Pr > F
Intercept	-18.38406	6.81229	165.94481	7.28	0.0083
HRSPOWER	0.11727	0.01435	1522.31498	66.81	<.0001
REVLTNS	0.00311	0.00149	98.63038	4.33	0.0404
WEIGHT	0.00437	0.00149	196.26395	8.61	0.0043

Bounds on condition number: 3.0942, 22.638

Stepwise selection results (continued)

Stepwise Selection: Step 4

Variable CITYMPG Entered: R-Square = 0.7082 and C(p) = 3.3271

Analysis of Variance					
Source	DF	Sum of Squares	Mean Square	F Value	Pr > F
Model	4	4792.90119	1198.22530	52.79	<.0001
Error	87	1974.64870	22.69711		
Corrected Total	91	6767.54989			

Variable	Parameter Estimate	Standard Error	Type II SS	F Value	Pr > F
Intercept	-10.70429	9.49190	28.86552	1.27	0.2625
CITYMPG	-0.19618	0.16919	30.51411	1.34	0.2494
HRSPOWER	0.11534	0.01442	1453.00636	64.02	<.0001
REVLTNS	0.00345	0.00152	116.88330	5.15	0.0257
WEIGHT	0.00313	0.00183	66.34802	2.92	0.0909

Bounds on condition number: 4.6961, 51.657

Stepwise selection results (continued)

Stepwise Selection: Step 5

Variable CITYMPG Removed: R-Square = 0.7037 and C(p) = 2.6456

Analysis of Variance					
Source	DF	Sum of Squares	Mean Square	F Value	Pr > F
Model	3	4762.38708	1587.46236	69.67	<.0001
Error	88	2005.16281	22.78594		
Corrected Total	91	6767.54989			

Variable	Parameter Estimate	Standard Error	Type II SS	F Value	Pr > F
Intercept	-18.38406	6.81229	165.94481	7.28	0.0083
HRSPOWER	0.11727	0.01435	1522.31498	66.81	<.0001
REVLTNS	0.00311	0.00149	98.63038	4.33	0.0404
WEIGHT	0.00437	0.00149	196.26395	8.61	0.0043

Bounds on condition number: 3.0942, 22.638

Stepwise selection results (continued)

All variables left in the model are significant at the 0.1000 level.

The stepwise method terminated because the next variable to be entered was just removed.

Summary of Stepwise Selection								
Step	Variable Entered	Variable Removed	Number Vars In	Partial R-Square	Model R-Square	C(p)	F Value	Pr > F
1	HRSPOWER		1	0.6735	0.6735	7.4674	185.69	<.0001
2	WEIGHT		2	0.0156	0.6891	4.9076	4.46	0.0374
3	REVLTNS		3	0.0146	0.7037	2.6456	4.33	0.0404
4	CITYMPG		4	0.0045	0.7082	3.3271	1.34	0.2494
5		CITYMPG	3	0.0045	0.7037	2.6456	1.34	0.2494

The stepwise selection method generated the model **MIDPRICE=HRSPOWER WEIGHT REVLTNS**.

Backward elimination results

Backward Elimination: Step 0

All Variables Entered: R-Square = 0.7162 and C(p) = 9.0000

Analysis of Variance					
Source	DF	Sum of Squares	Mean Square	F Value	Pr > F
Model	8	4846.75465	605.84433	26.18	<.0001
Error	83	1920.79524	23.14211		
Corrected Total	91	6767.54989			

Variable	Parameter Estimate	Standard Error	Type II SS	F Value	Pr > F
Intercept	-21.30023	13.86601	54.60955	2.36	0.1283
CITYMPG	-0.46278	0.33213	44.93125	1.94	0.1672
HWYMPG	0.21335	0.30985	10.97213	0.47	0.4930
EGNSIZE	1.96681	1.54127	37.68488	1.63	0.2055
HRSPOWER	0.09518	0.02534	326.62826	14.11	0.0003
RPM	0.00125	0.00168	12.76225	0.55	0.4598
REVLTNS	0.00501	0.00199	146.56253	6.33	0.0138
FUELTNK	-0.09563	0.37077	1.53946	0.07	0.7971
WEIGHT	0.00292	0.00261	29.04458	1.26	0.2658

Bounds on condition number: 13.795, 517.18

Backward Elimination: Step 1

Variable FUELTNK Removed: R-Square = 0.7159 and C(p) = 7.0665

Analysis of Variance					
Source	DF	Sum of Squares	Mean Square	F Value	Pr > F
Model	7	4845.21519	692.17360	30.25	<.0001
Error	84	1922.33471	22.88494		
Corrected Total	91	6767.54989			

Variable	Parameter Estimate	Standard Error	Type II SS	F Value	Pr > F
Intercept	-21.54301	13.75694	56.12017	2.45	0.1211
CITYMPG	-0.44933	0.32618	43.42806	1.90	0.1720
HWYMPG	0.21416	0.30810	11.05737	0.48	0.4889
EGNSIZE	1.91594	1.52009	36.35611	1.59	0.2110
HRSPOWER	0.09486	0.02516	325.20857	14.21	0.0003
RPM	0.00123	0.00167	12.45546	0.54	0.4627
REVLTNS	0.00487	0.00191	149.11596	6.52	0.0125
WEIGHT	0.00257	0.00220	31.11140	1.36	0.2469

Bounds on condition number: 13.455, 387.6

Backward elimination results (continued)

Backward Elimination: Step 2

Variable HWYMPG Removed: R-Square = 0.7143 and C(p) = 5.5443

Analysis of Variance					
Source	DF	Sum of Squares	Mean Square	F Value	Pr > F
Model	6	4834.15781	805.69297	35.42	<.0001
Error	85	1933.39208	22.74579		
Corrected Total	91	6767.54989			

Variable	Parameter Estimate	Standard Error	Type II SS	F Value	Pr > F
Intercept	-17.93412	12.70083	45.35203	1.99	0.1616
CITYMPG	-0.25861	0.17585	49.19572	2.16	0.1451
EGNSIZE	2.01499	1.50878	40.56890	1.78	0.1853
HRSPOWER	0.09549	0.02507	329.99320	14.51	0.0003
RPM	0.00122	0.00167	12.22170	0.54	0.4656
REVLTNS	0.00458	0.00186	138.48985	6.09	0.0156
WEIGHT	0.00216	0.00211	23.67836	1.04	0.3105

Bounds on condition number: 9.8797, 205.92

Backward elimination results (continued)

Backward Elimination: Step 3

Variable RPM Removed: R-Square = 0.7125 and C(p) = 4.0724

Analysis of Variance					
Source	DF	Sum of Squares	Mean Square	F Value	Pr > F
Model	5	4821.93612	964.38722	42.63	<.0001
Error	86	1945.61377	22.62342		
Corrected Total	91	6767.54989			

Variable	Parameter Estimate	Standard Error	Type II SS	F Value	Pr > F
Intercept	-11.79750	9.52549	34.70274	1.53	0.2189
CITYMPG	-0.23444	0.17226	41.90233	1.85	0.1771
EGNSIZE	1.29829	1.14602	29.03493	1.28	0.2604
HRSPOWER	0.11013	0.01511	1201.97296	53.13	<.0001
REVLTNS	0.00465	0.00185	142.84618	6.31	0.0138
WEIGHT	0.00197	0.00209	20.06682	0.89	0.3489

Bounds on condition number: 6.1645, 108.04

Backward elimination results (continued)

Backward Elimination: Step 4

Variable WEIGHT Removed: R-Square = 0.7095 and C(p) = 2.9396

Analysis of Variance					
Source	DF	Sum of Squares	Mean Square	F Value	Pr > F
Model	4	4801.86930	1200.46732	53.13	<.0001
Error	87	1965.68060	22.59403		
Corrected Total	91	6767.54989			

Variable	Parameter Estimate	Standard Error	Type II SS	F Value	Pr > F
Intercept	-5.51825	6.79871	14.88484	0.66	0.4192
CITYMPG	-0.33106	0.13829	129.48763	5.73	0.0188
EGNSIZE	1.82506	0.99961	75.31613	3.33	0.0713
HRSPOWER	0.11240	0.01491	1284.67376	56.86	<.0001
REVLTNS	0.00473	0.00185	148.79669	6.59	0.0120

Bounds on condition number: 4.3657, 50.637

Backward elimination results (continued)

All variables left in the model are significant at the 0.1000 level.

Summary of Backward Elimination

Step	Variable Removed	Number Vars In	Partial R-Square	Model R-Square	C(p)	F Value	Pr > F
1	FUELTNK	7	0.0002	0.7159	7.0665	0.07	0.7971
2	HWYMPG	6	0.0016	0.7143	5.5443	0.48	0.4889
3	RPM	5	0.0018	0.7125	4.0724	0.54	0.4656
4	WEIGHT	4	0.0030	0.7095	2.9396	0.89	0.3489

The backward elimination model is **`MIDPRICE=CITYMPG EGNSIZE HRSPOWER REVLTNS`**.

Method	Model
Mallows	**`MIDPRICE=HRSPOWER REVLTNS WEIGHT`**
Hocking	**`MIDPRICE=CITYMPG EGNSIZE HRSPOWER REVLTNS WEIGHT`**
STEPWISE	**`MIDPRICE=HRSPOWER REVLTNS WEIGHT`**
BACKWARD	**`MIDPRICE=CITYMPG EGNSIZE HRSPOWER REVLTNS`**

Chapter 4 Regression Diagnostics

4.1 Examining Residuals

Objectives

- Review the assumptions of linear regression.
- Examine the assumptions with scatter plots and residual plots.

3

Assumptions for Regression

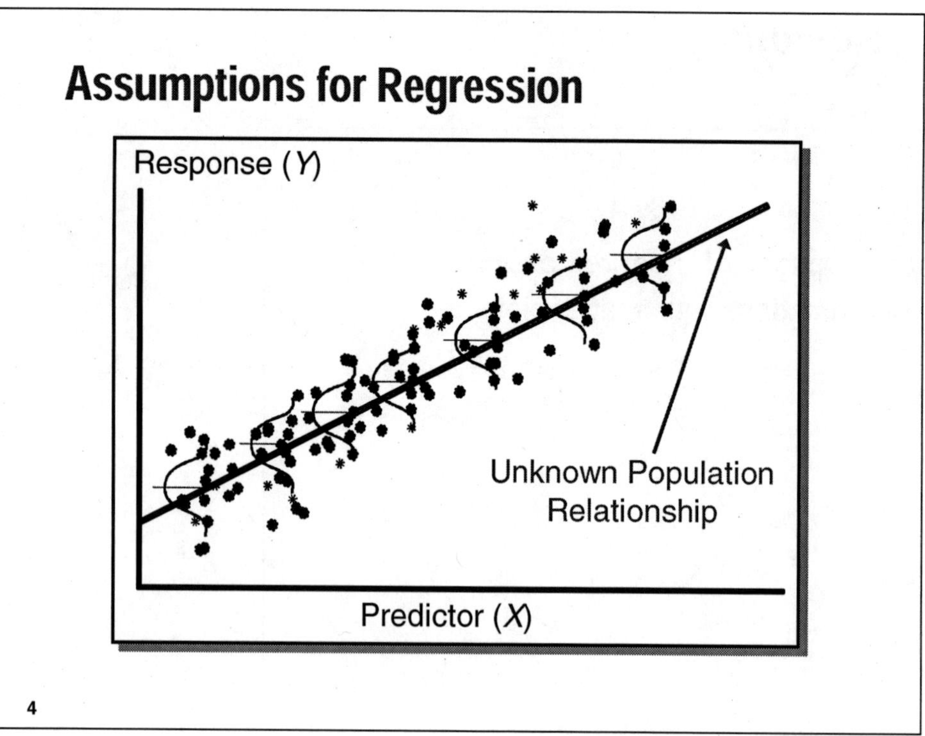

4

Recall that the model for the linear regression has the form $Y=\beta_0+\beta_1X+\varepsilon$. When you perform a regression analysis, several assumptions about the error terms must be met to provide valid tests of hypothesis and confidence intervals. The assumptions are that the error terms

- have a mean of 0 at each value of the predictor variable
- are normally distributed at each value of the predictor variable
- have the same variance at each value of the predictor variable
- are independent.

You can use scatter plots and residual plots to help verify these assumptions.

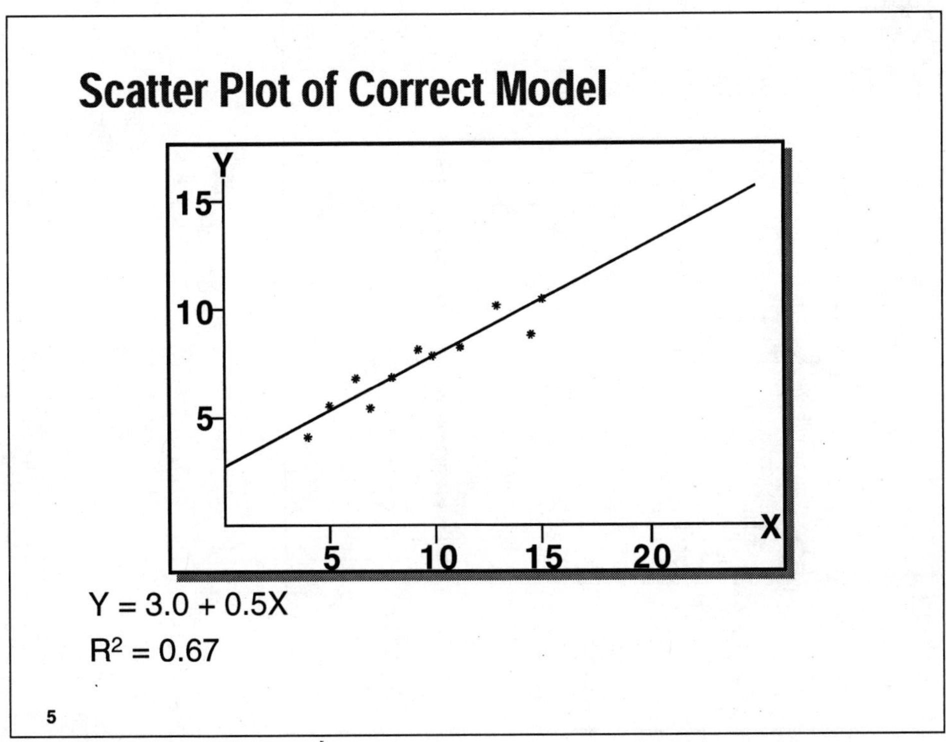

To illustrate the importance of plotting data, four examples were developed by Anscombe. In each example, the scatter plot of the data values is different. However, the regression equation and the R^2 statistic are the same.

In the first plot, a regression line adequately describes the data.

Anscombe, F. (1973) “Graphs in Statistical Analysis,” *The American Statistician*, 27: 17-21.

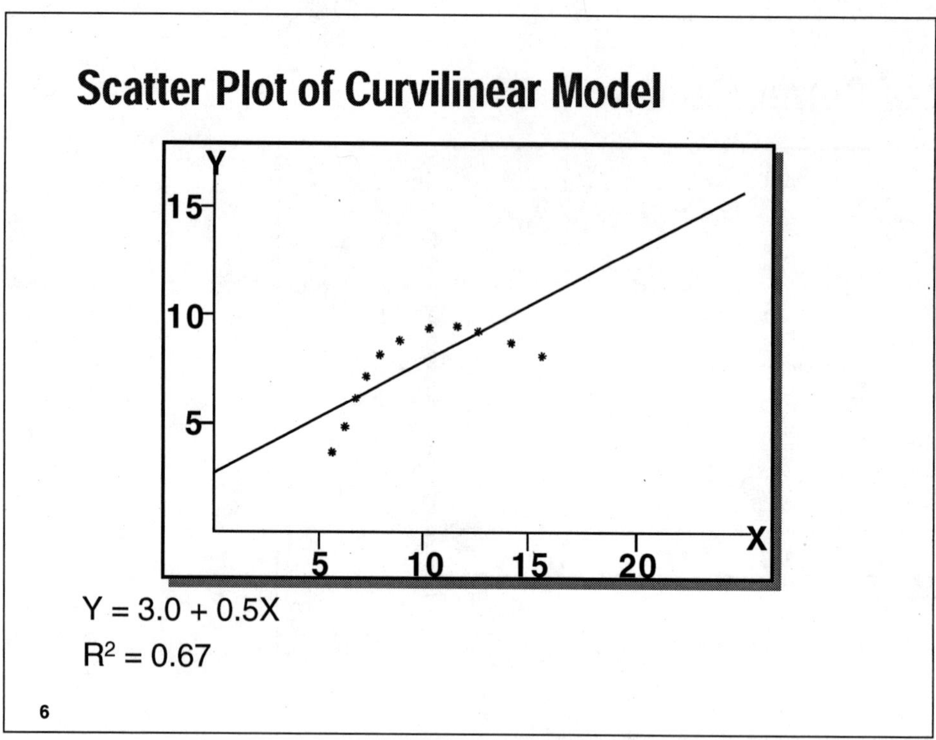

In the second plot, a simple linear regression model is not appropriate because you fit a straight line through a curvilinear relationship.

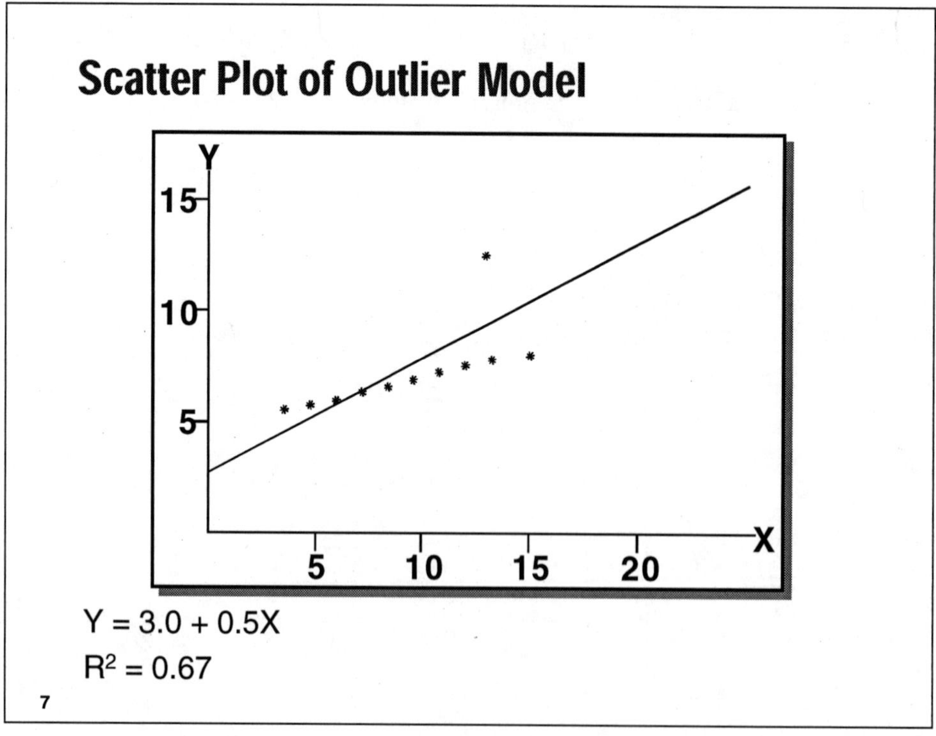

In the third plot, there seems to be an outlying data value that is affecting the regression line. This outlier is an influential data value in that it substantially changes the fit of the regression line.

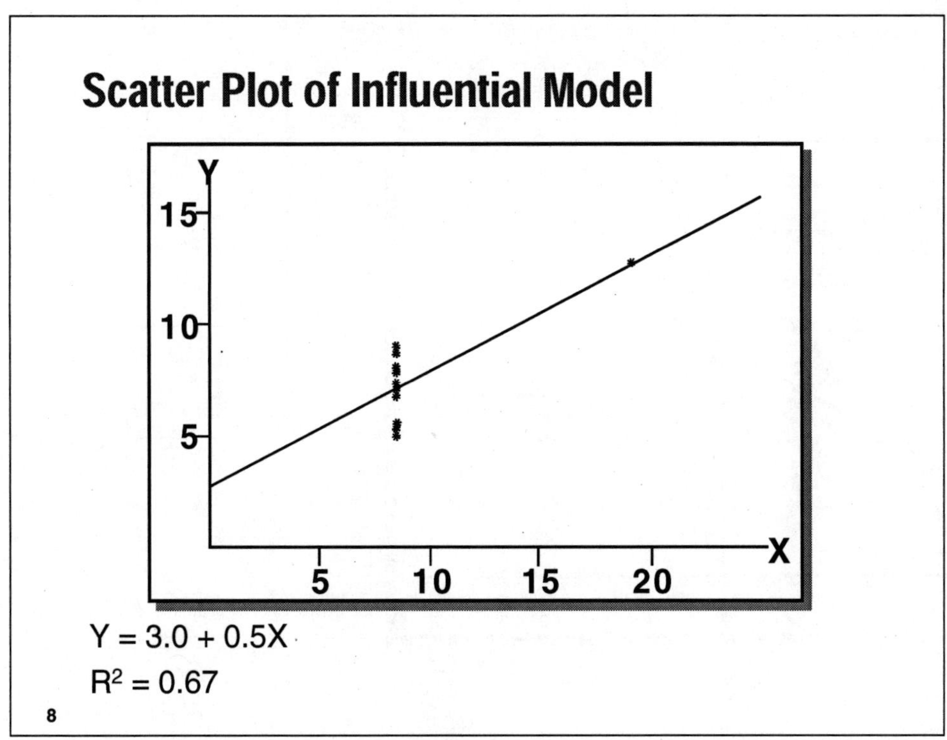

In the fourth plot, the outlying data point dramatically changes the fit of the regression line. In fact, the slope would be undefined without the outlier.

The four plots illustrate that relying on the regression output to describe the relationship between your variables could be misleading. The regression equations and the R^2 statistics are the same even though the relationships between the two variables are different. Always produce a scatter plot before you conduct a regression analysis.

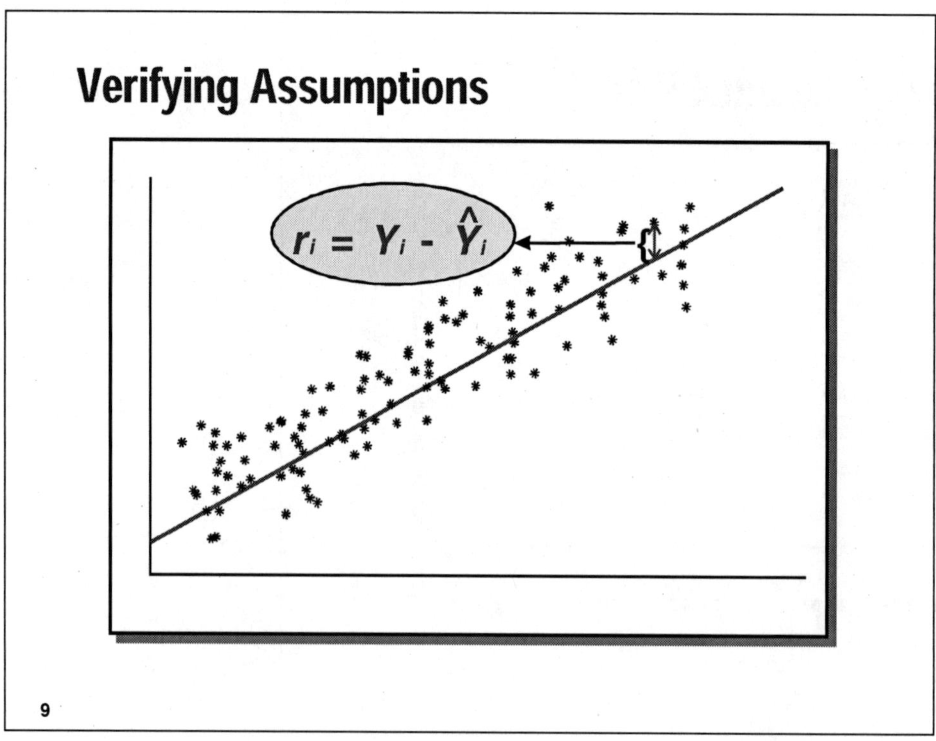

To verify the assumptions for regression, you can use the residual values from the regression analysis. Residuals are defined as

$$r_i = Y_i - \hat{Y}_i$$

where $\hat{Y}_i$ is the predicted value for the ith value of the dependent variable.

You can examine two types of plots when verifying assumptions:

- the residuals versus the predicted values
- the residuals versus the values of the independent variable.

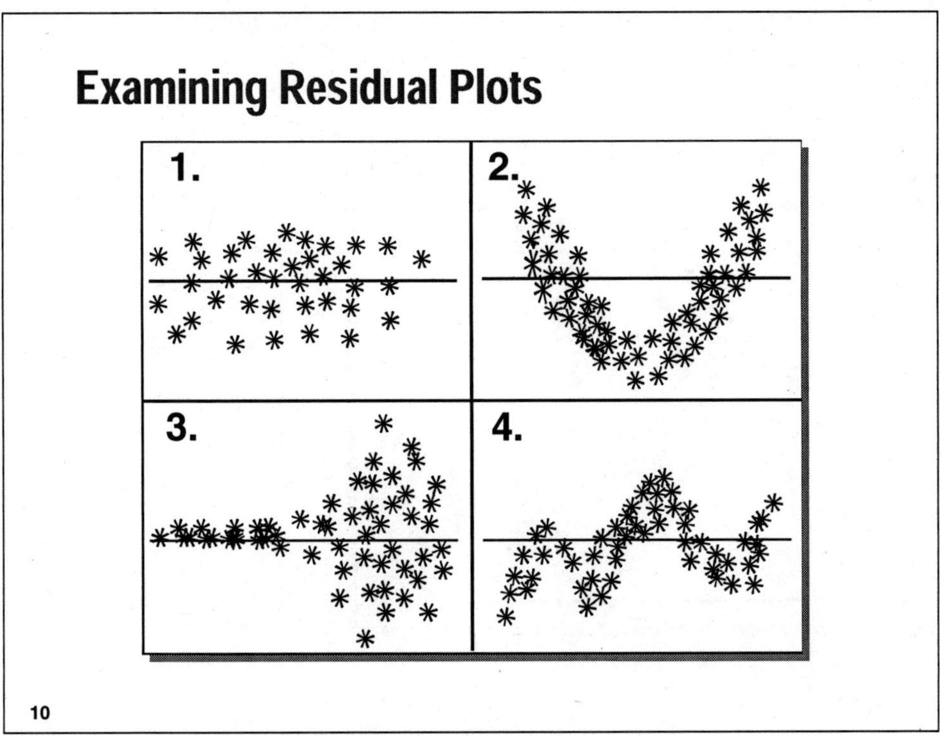

The graphs above are plots of residual values versus predicted values or predictor variable values for four models fit to different sets of data. If model assumptions are valid, then the residual values should be randomly scattered about a reference line at 0. Any patterns or trends in the residuals may indicate problems in the model.

1. The model form appears to be adequate and the assumption of equal variances appears to be valid because the residuals are randomly scattered about a reference line at 0 and no patterns appear in the residual values.

2. The model form is incorrect. The plot indicates that the model should take into account curvature in the data. One possible solution is to add a quadratic term as one of the predictor variables.

3. The variance is not constant. As you move from left to right, the variance increases. One possible solution is to transform your dependent variable.

4. The observations are not independent. For this graph, the residuals tend to be followed by residuals with the same sign, which is called *autocorrelation*. This problem can occur when you have observations that were collected over time. A possible solution is to use the Regression Analysis with Autoregressive Errors task in SAS Enterprise Guide.

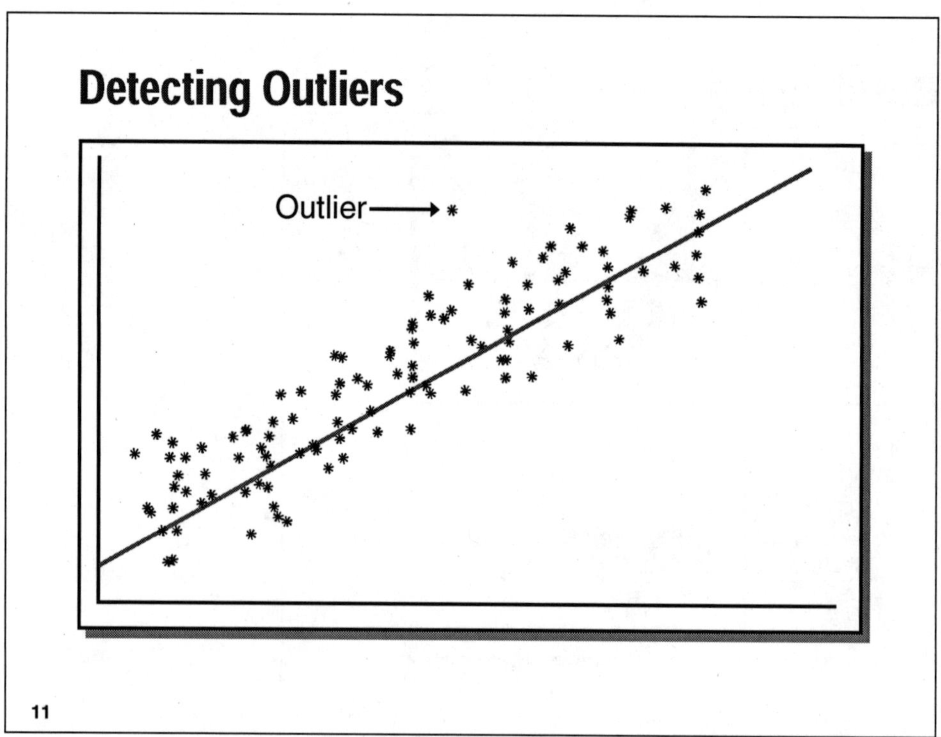

Besides verifying assumptions, it is also important to check for outliers. Observations that are outliers are far away from the bulk of your data. These observations are often data errors or reflect unusual circumstances. In either case, it is good statistical practice to detect these outliers and find out why they occurred.

Studentized Residual

Studentized residuals (SR) are obtained by dividing the residuals by their standard errors.

Suggested cutoffs are

- |SR| > 2 for data sets with a relatively small number of observations
- |SR| > 3 for data sets with a relatively large number of observations.

12

One way to check for outliers is to use the studentized residuals, which are calculated by dividing the residual values by their standard errors. For a model that fits the data well and has no outliers, most of the studentized residuals should be close to 0. In general, studentized residuals that have an absolute value less than 2.0 could have easily occurred by chance. Studentized residuals that are between an absolute value of 2.0 to 3.0 occur infrequently and may be outliers. Studentized residuals that are larger than an absolute value of 3.0 occur rarely by chance alone and should be investigated.

Residual and Outlier Plots

Example: Use the Linear Regression task to generate studentized residuals. Verify the assumption of equal variance and inspect a graph to validate the assumption of normal studentized residuals. Use the Graph task to generate a simple plot to identify potential outliers. Use the best 4-variable model generated in the previous chapter.

With SAS Enterprise Guide, many of the plots that are used in regression analysis are available in the **Plots** pane of the Linear Regression task, or they can be created with an output data set. However, sometimes you want plots that are not in the point-and-click environment. In this demonstration, you will learn to create plots beyond simply those available in the tasks.

1. Locate **`FITNESS`** in the process flow.

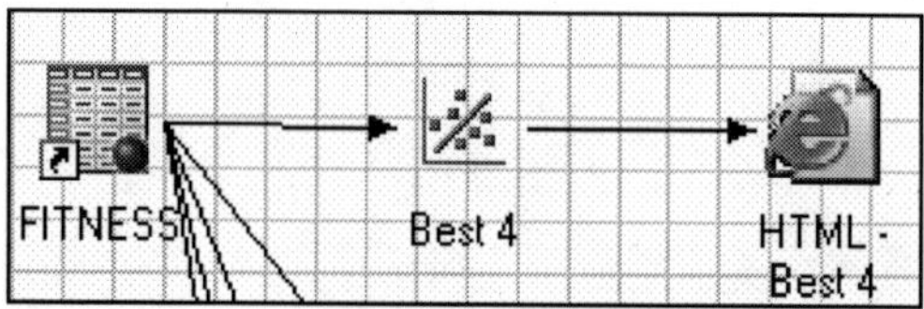

2. Double-click on **Best 4** in the display to open it.

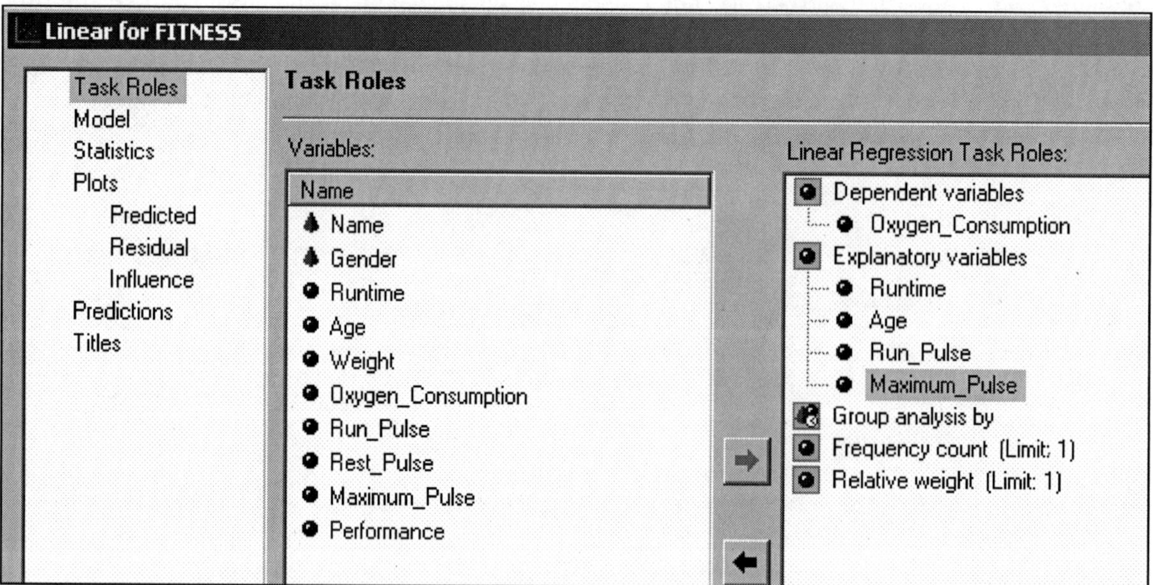

3. Select **Residual** under Plots.

4. Select **Ordinary vs predicted Y** and **Ordinary vs independents**.

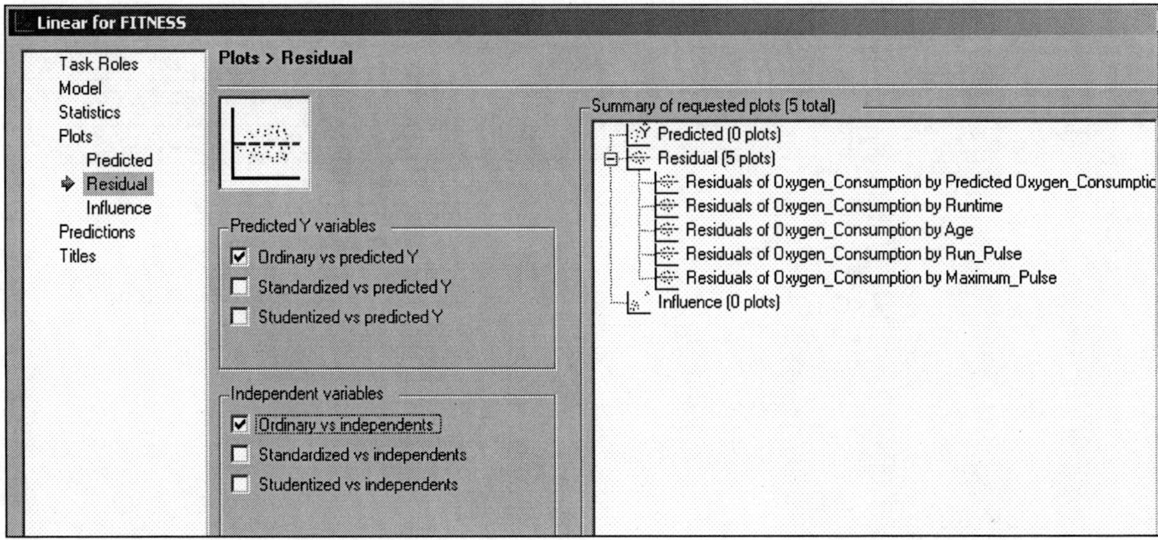

5. Select **Predictions**.

6. Select **Original sample**. Select **Residuals** from **Additional statistics**. SAS Enterprise Guide will also generate a Predictions data table by default.

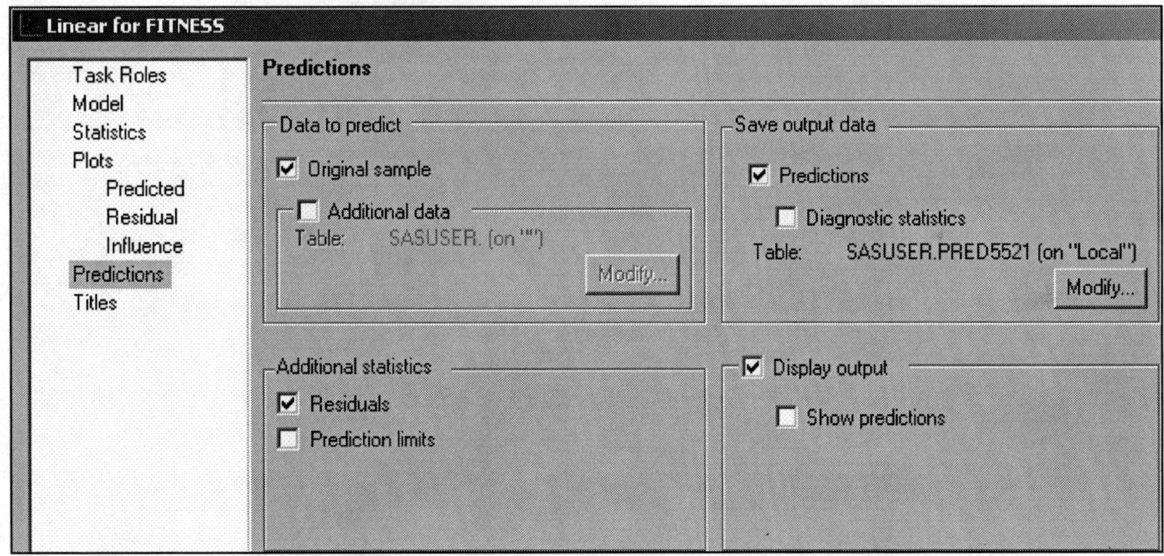

Change the name of the data table used to save the residuals. SAS Enterprise Guide uses the default library, SASUSER, to save this new data set. SASUSER is a permanent SAS library.

7. Select **Modify…**.

8. Name the data set **`ck4outliers`**.

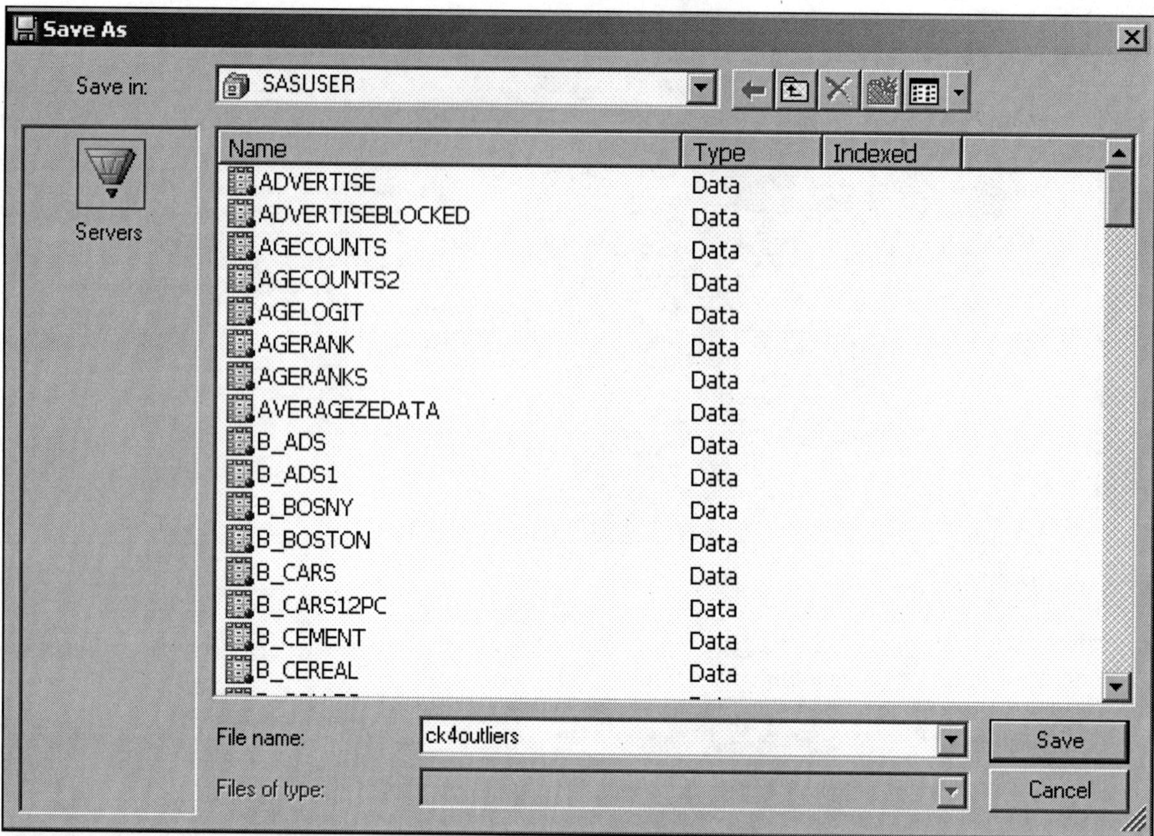

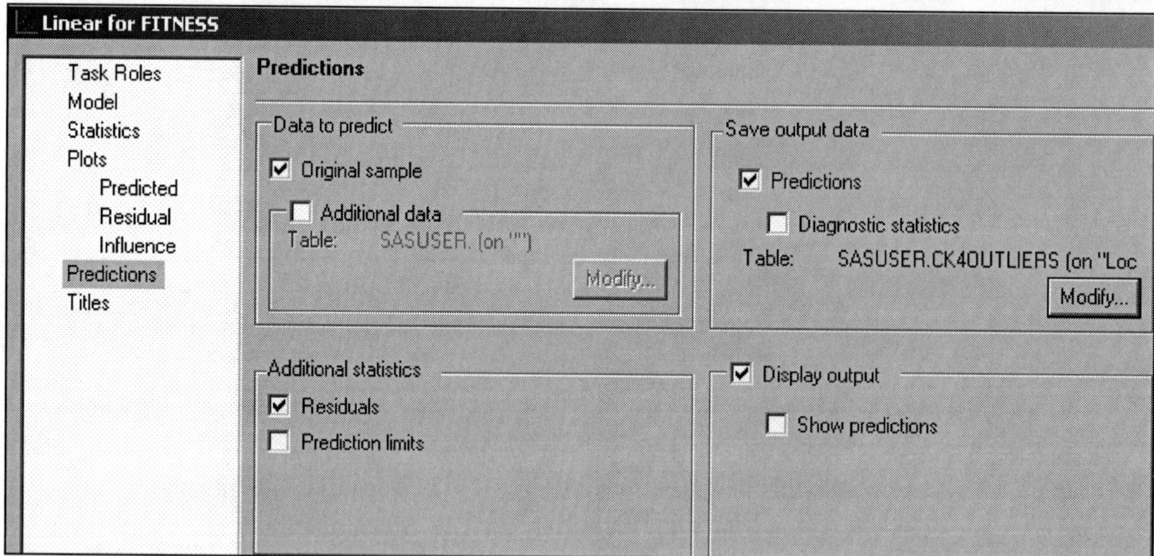

You will use the output table created in this step later to create a normal quantile plot of studentized residuals and to check for outliers.

9. Select **Save**.

10. Select **Run**.

11. Select **No** to create a new node in the process flow with the same name, Best 4.

12. Rename this latest node `Ck Assumptions Best 4`.

13. Make the `Linear Regression...` output data set the active table by selecting it in the process flow. This is the **CK4OUTLIER** data set.

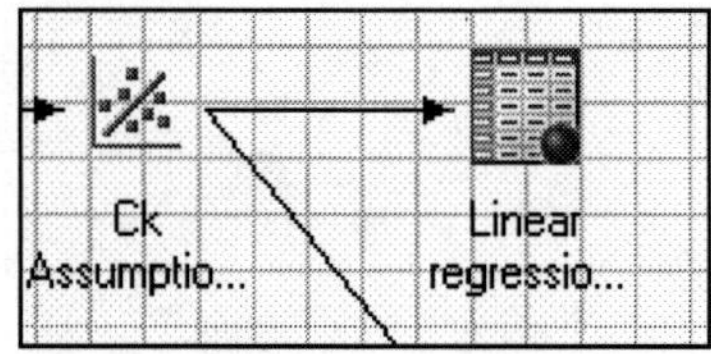

Select the html task results. Examine the residual plot to verify visually that the variance is approximately equal across the predicted values of the model.

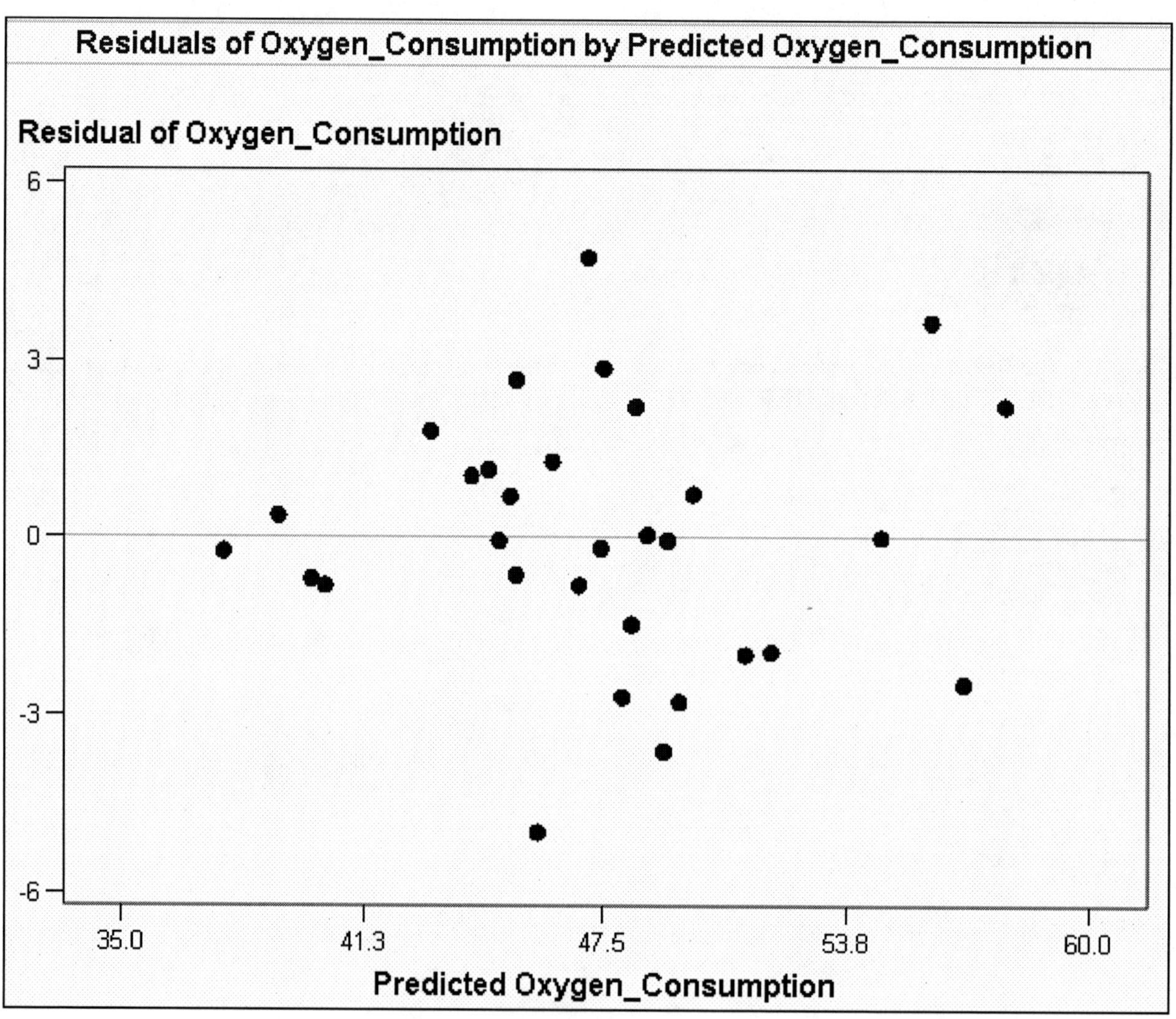

The plot of the residuals by predicted values of `Oxygen_Consumption` is shown above. The residual values appear to be randomly scattered about the reference line at 0. There are no apparent trends or patterns in the residuals.

To verify the assumption of independent observations, you must ensure that you take a random sample from your identified population. The plot of the residuals versus the values of the independent variables, `Runtime`, `Age`, `Run_Pulse`, and `Maximum_Pulse` are show below. There is also no apparent trend or pattern in the residuals.

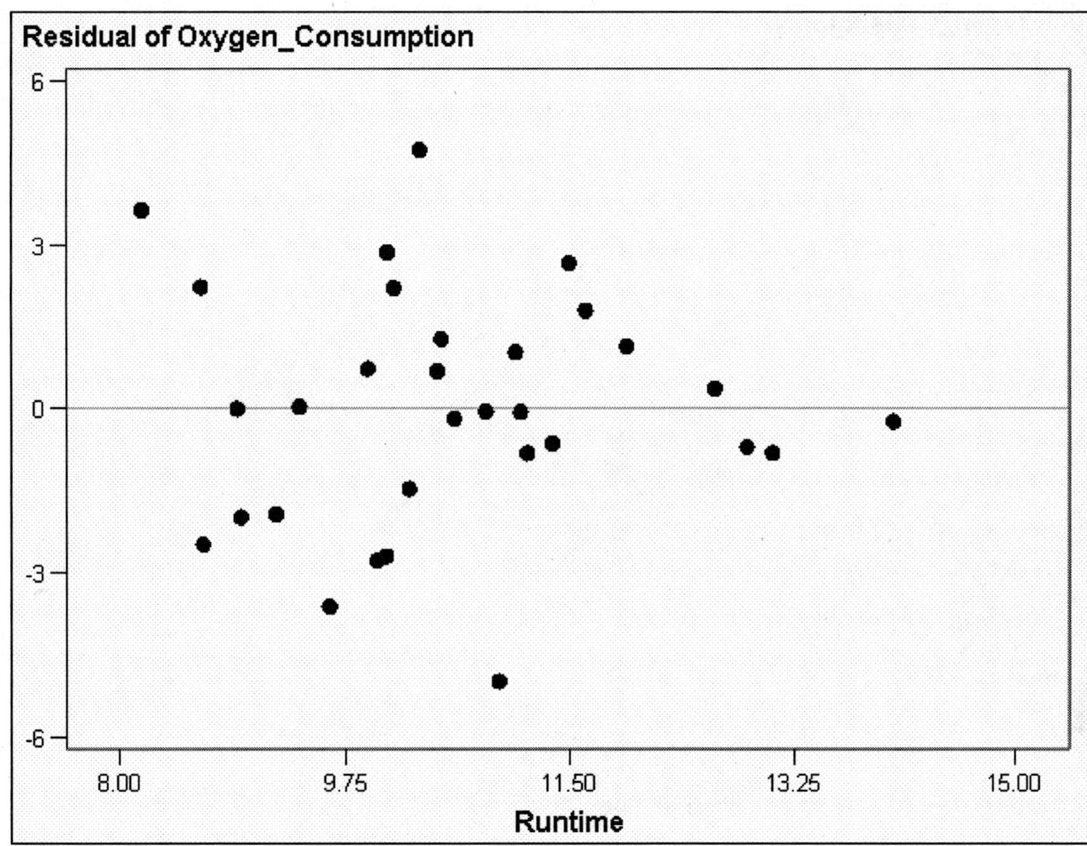
Residual of Oxygen_Consumption
6
3
0
-3
-6
8.00
9.75
11.50
13.25
15.00
Runtime

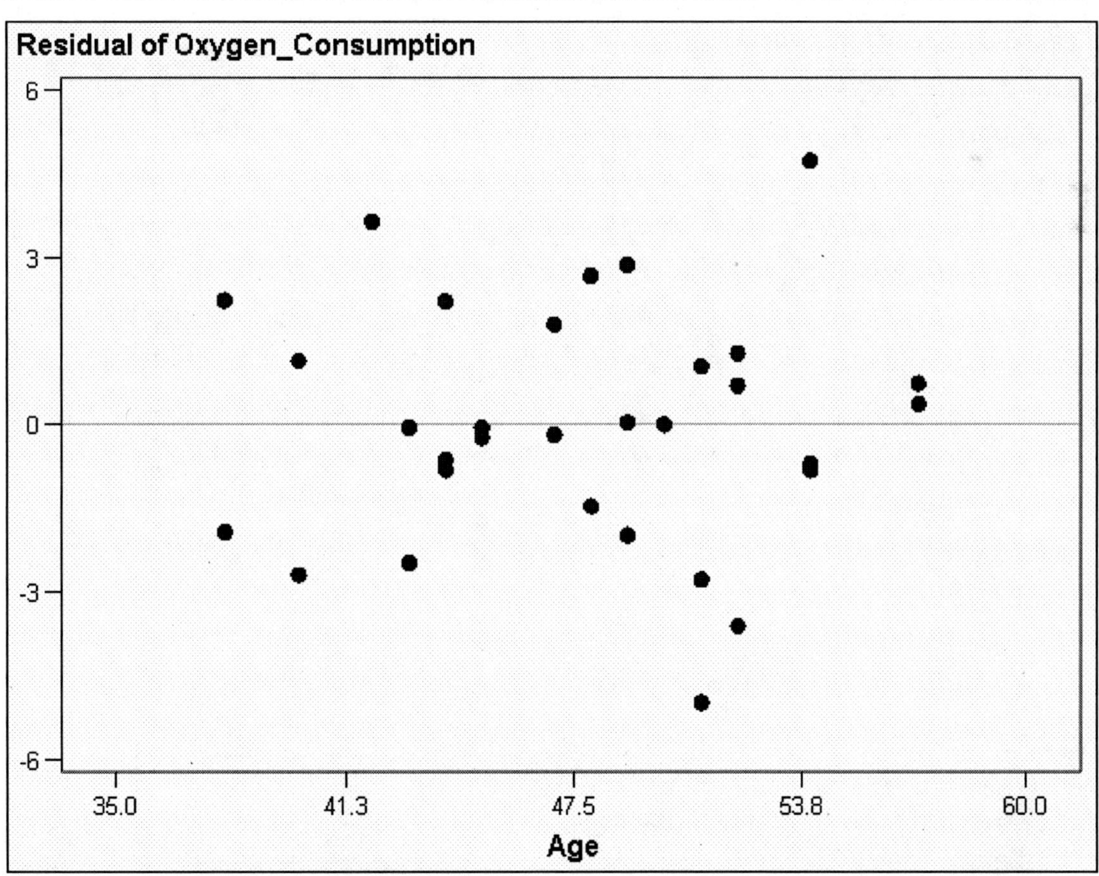
Residual of Oxygen_Consumption
6
3
0
-3
-6
35.0
41.3
47.5
53.8
60.0
Age

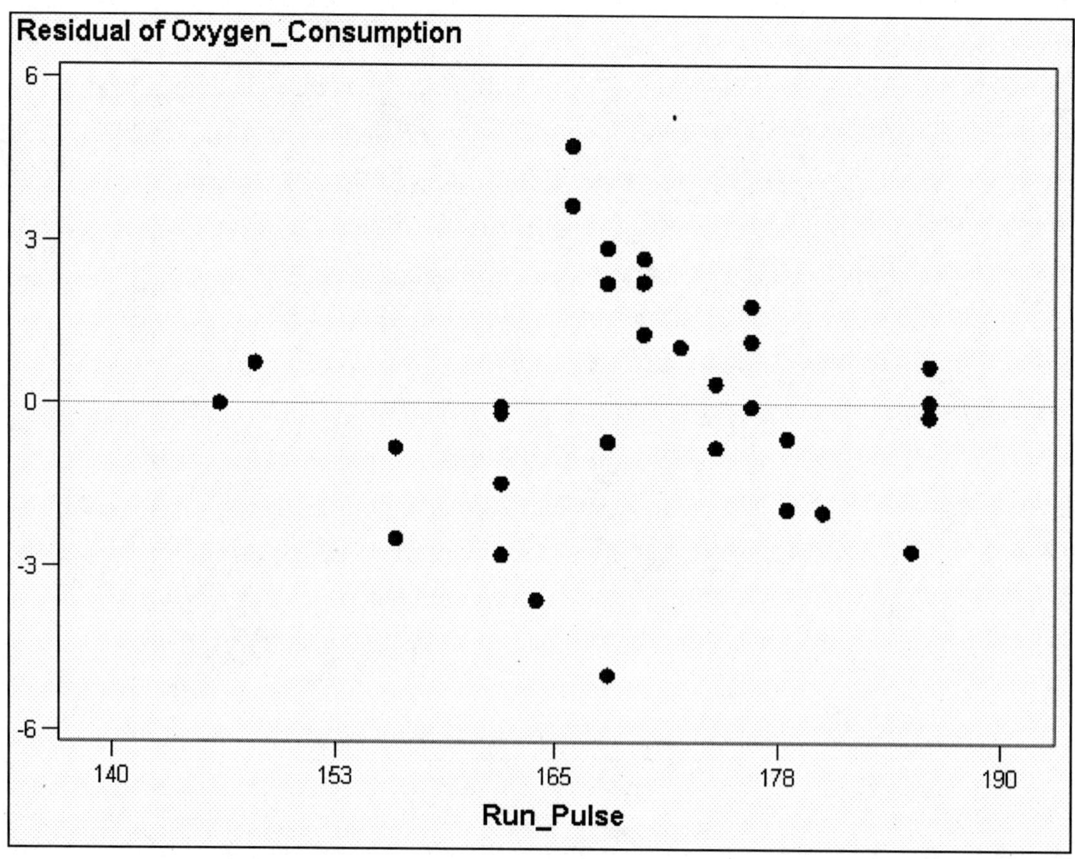
Residual of Oxygen_Consumption
6
3
0
-3
-6
140
153
165
178
190
Run_Pulse

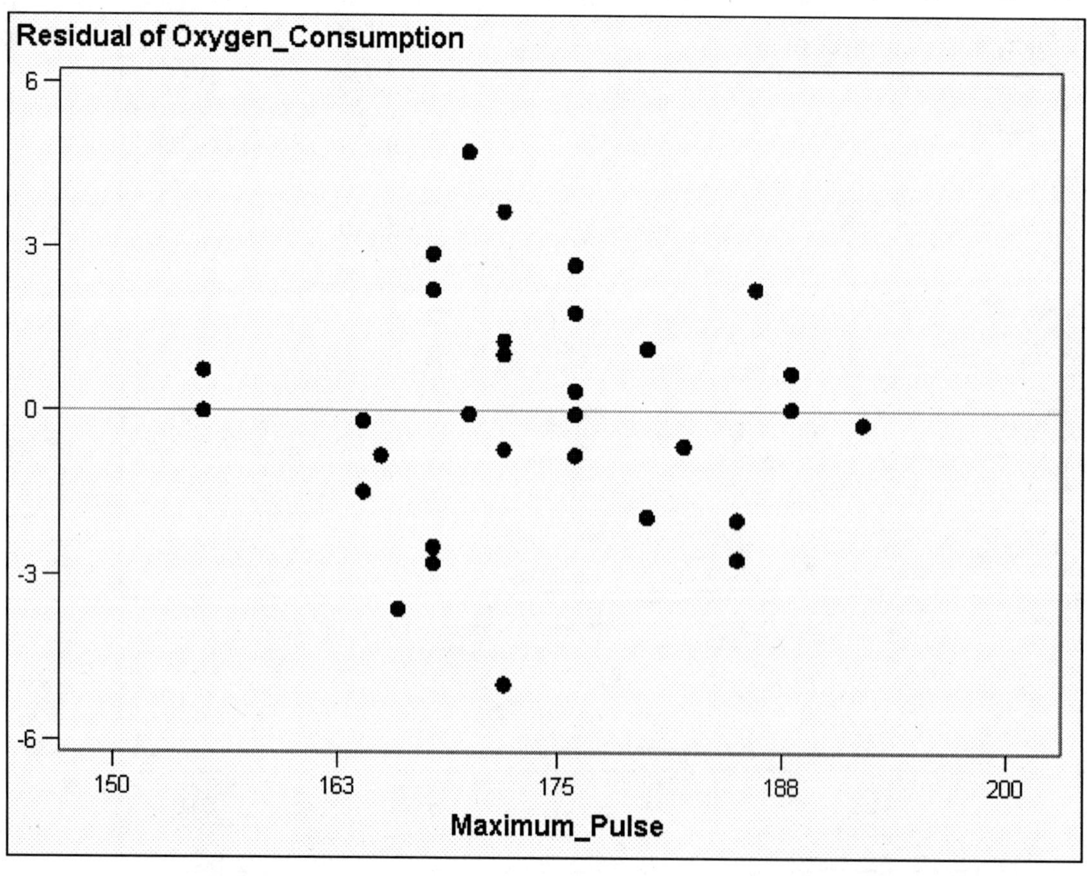
Residual of Oxygen_Consumption
6
3
0
-3
-6
150
163
175
188
200
Maximum_Pulse

You can look for potential outliers by using the studentized residual and a variable in the data that will uniquely identify each data point.

14. Select **Graph** ⇨ **Scatter Plot…**.

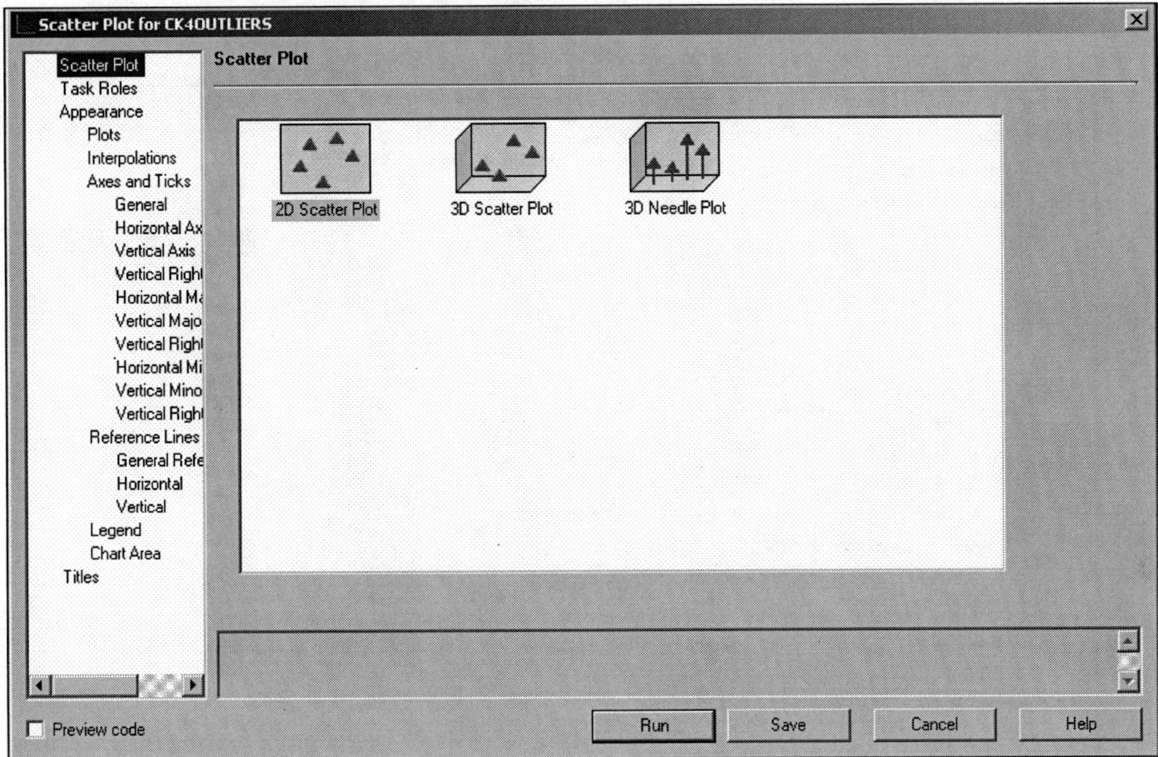

15. Select **2D Scatter Plot**. Select **Task Roles** to assign columns to roles.

16. Drag `Name` to the Horizontal axis and `student_Oxygen_Consumption` to the Vertical axis.

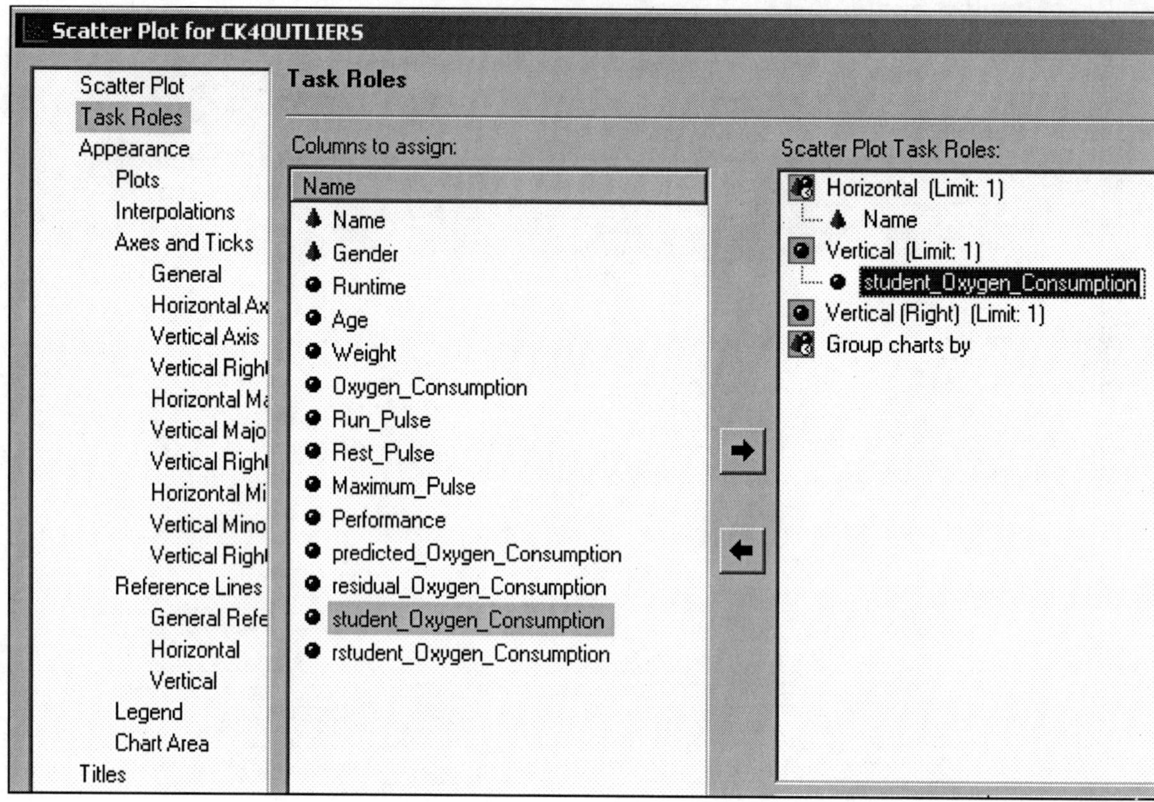

17. Select **Horizontal** under Reference Lines.

18. Select **Use reference lines** and then select **Specify values for lines**.

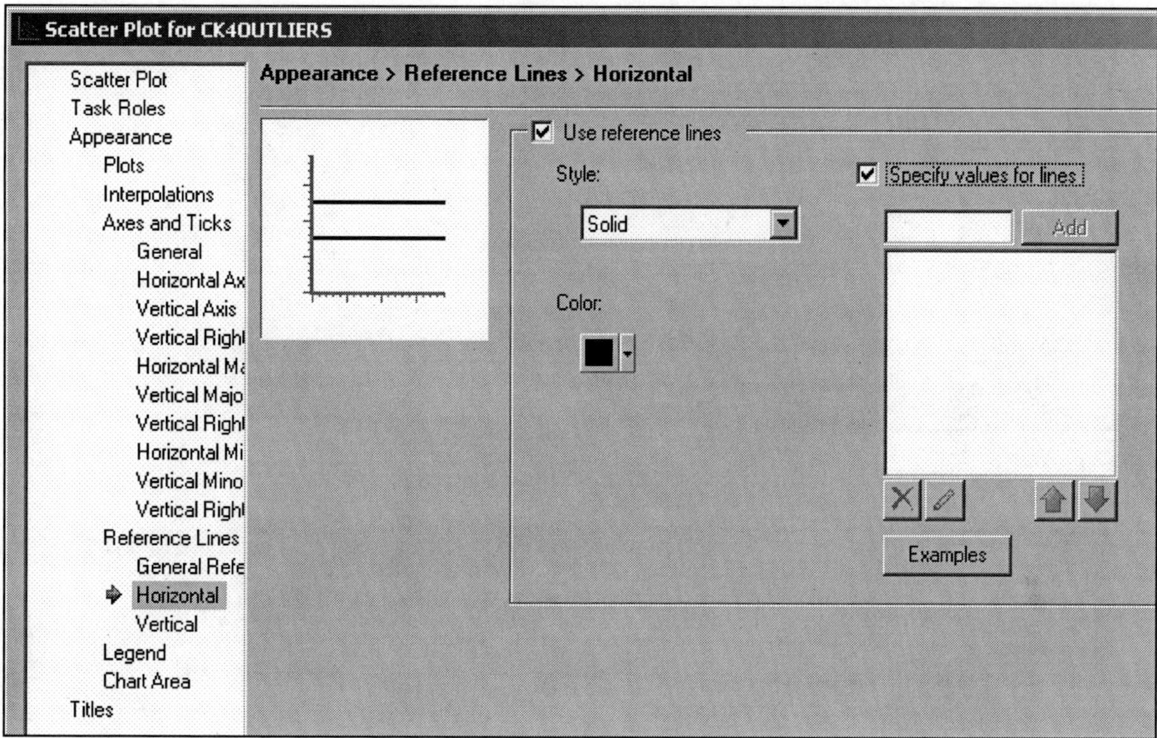

19. Type the value `3` in **Specify values for lines**:

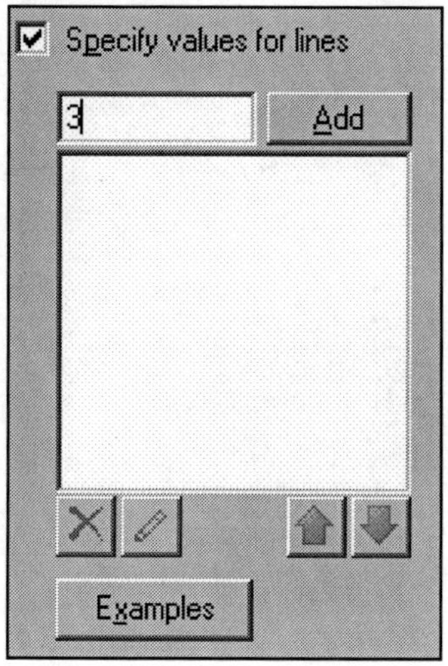

20. Select **Add**. Repeat these steps to add the values of `2`, `-2`, and `-3`.

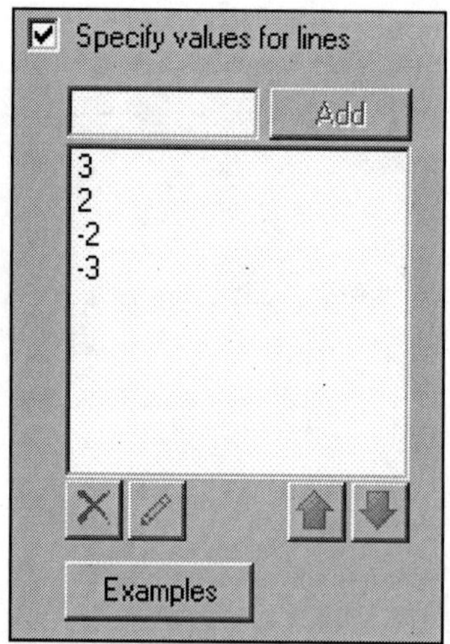

21. Select **Titles**. Enter `Visually Look for Outliers in Best 4 Model` as the title.

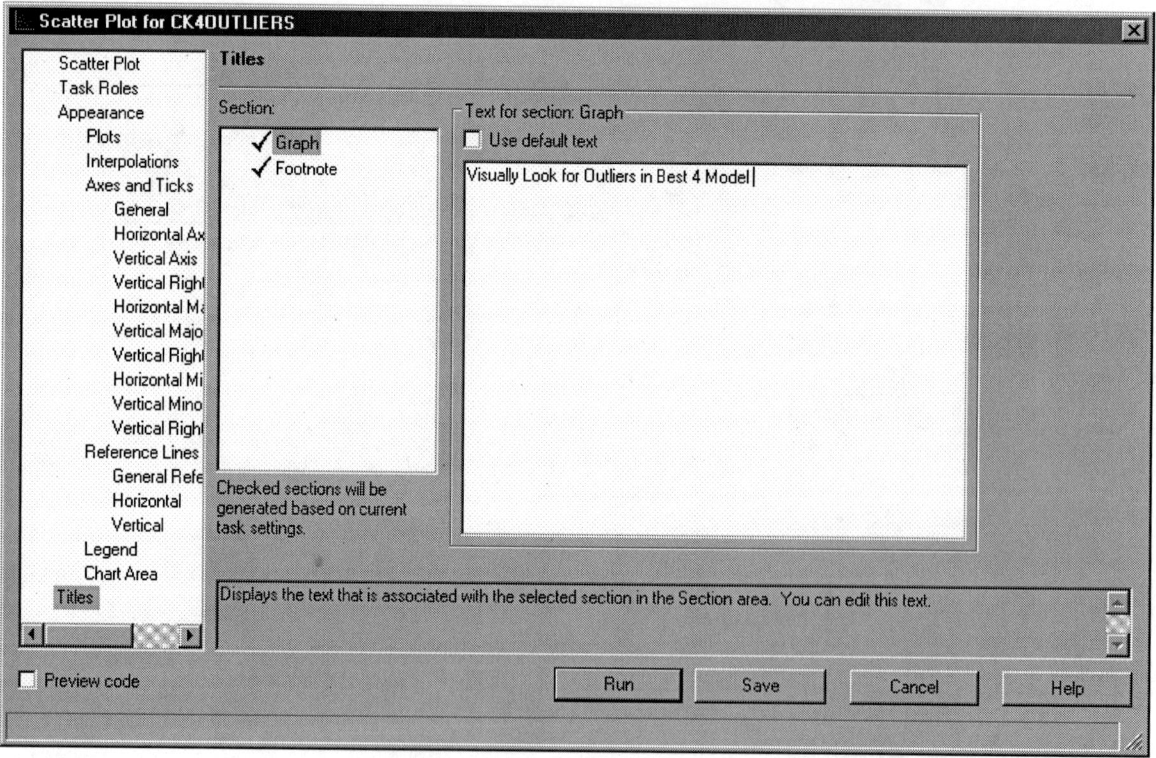

22. Select **Run**.

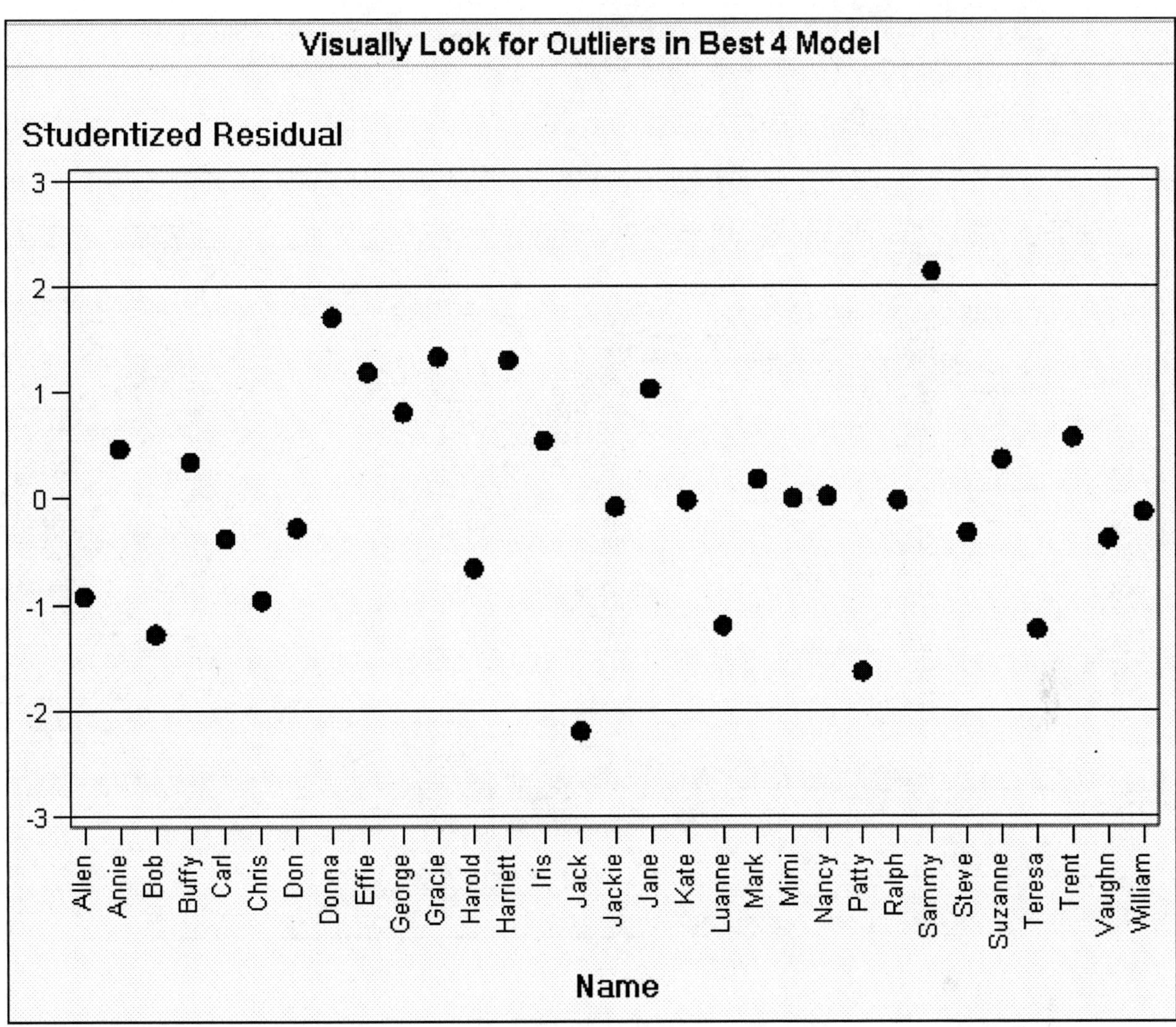

Remember that studentized residuals that have absolute values greater than 2 or 3 may be outliers and should be investigated. The reference lines added to the graph help to identify the observations visually.

It appears that Jack and Sammy may be potential outliers in this model because they both fall outside the values of 2 and –2.

To evaluate the assumption of the normality of the studentized residuals, generate a plot of the studentized residuals against the normal quartiles using the Distribution Analysis task.

23. Select **Analyze** ⇨ **Distribution Analysis…**.

24. Assign `student_Oxygen_Consumption` as the Analysis variable.

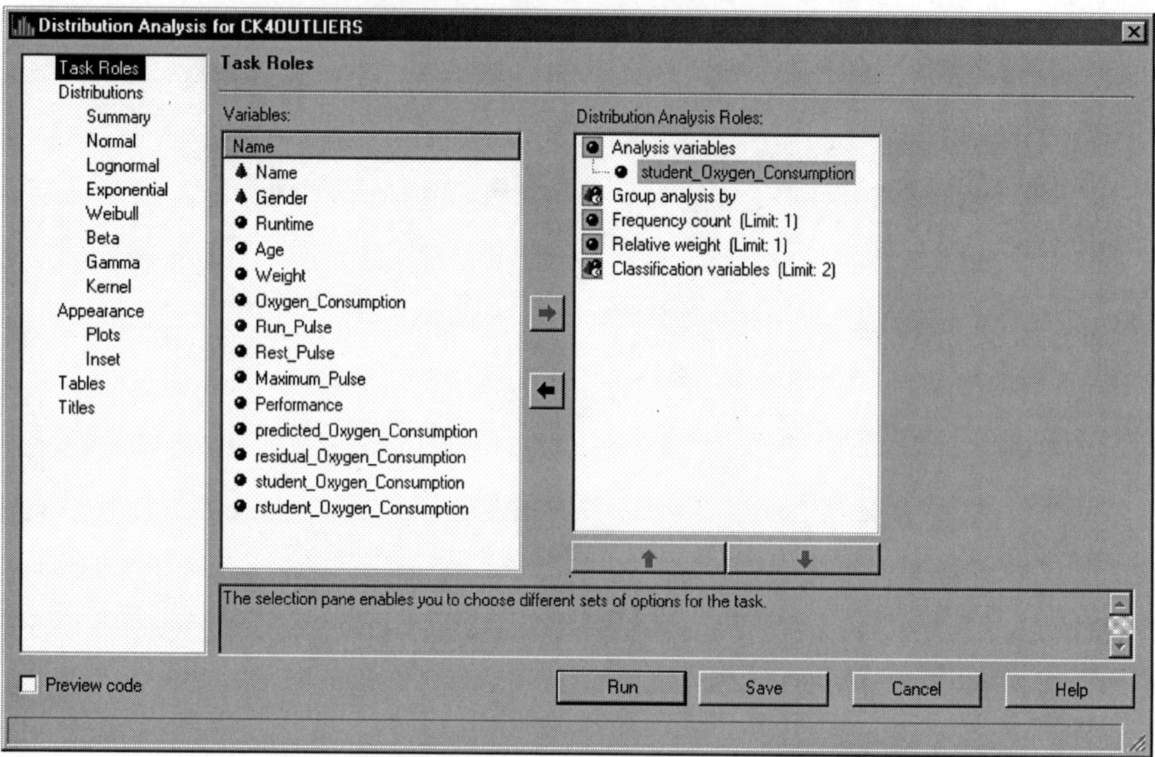

25. Select **Plots**.

26. Select **Probability Plot** from the list of graphics. Set the Background color to white.

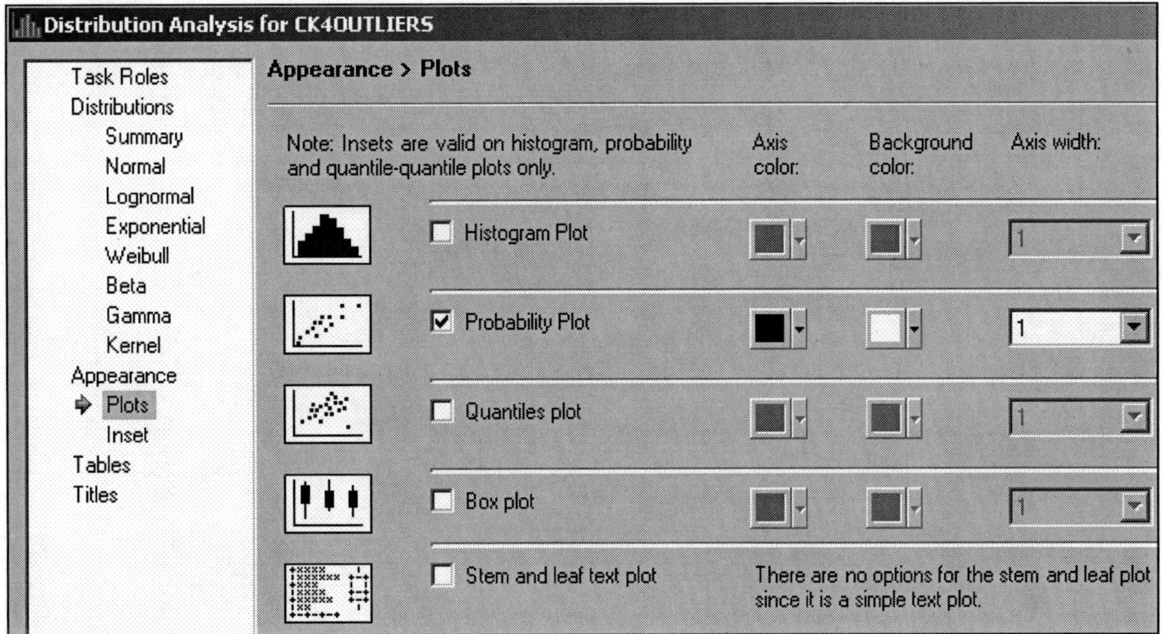

27. Select **Normal** under Distributions. Select **Normal** for the fitted distribution, red for the line color, and a width of 2.

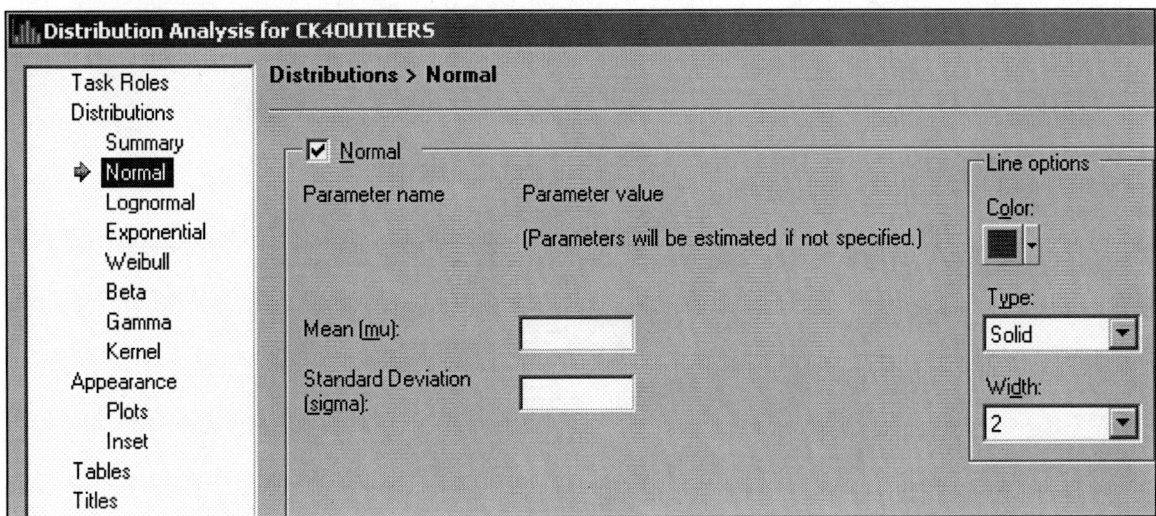

28. Select **Tables** and **Suppress all tables**.

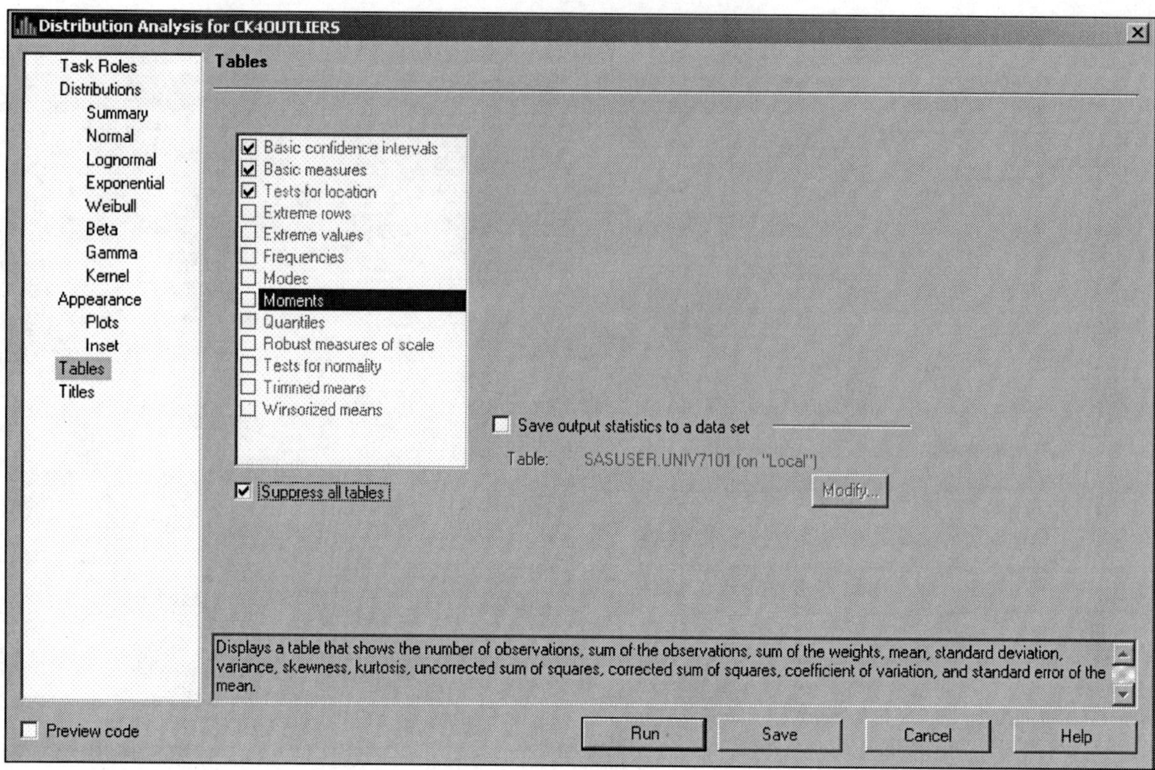

29. Select **Run**.

The plot of the student residuals versus the normal percentiles is shown below. If the residuals are normally distributed, the plot should appear to be a straight line with a slope of about 1. If the plot deviates substantially from the ideal, then there is evidence against normality.

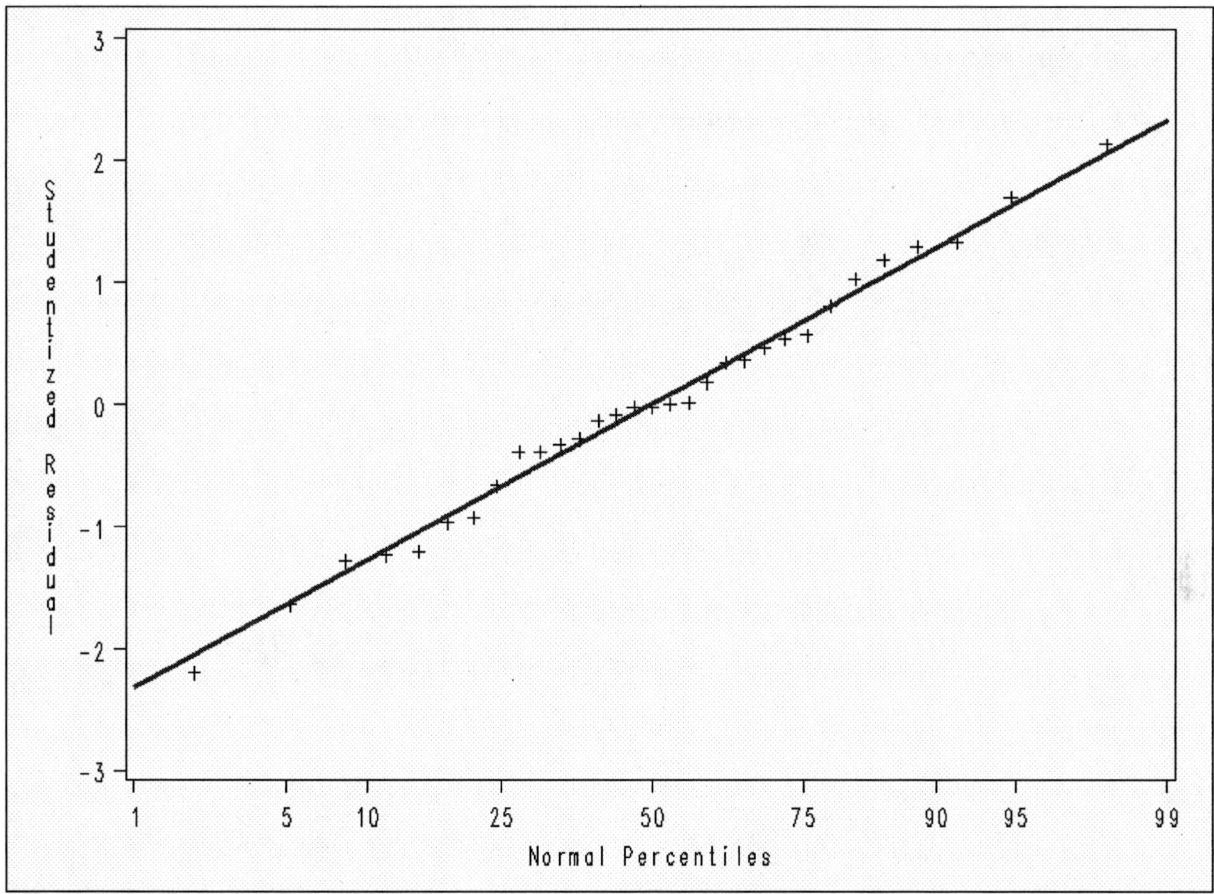

The plot above shows no substantial deviation from the expected pattern. Thus, you can conclude that the residuals do not significantly violate the normality assumption. If the residuals did violate the normality assumption, then a transformation of the response variable may be warranted.

4.2 Influential Observations

Objectives

- Use statistics to identify potential influential observations.

15

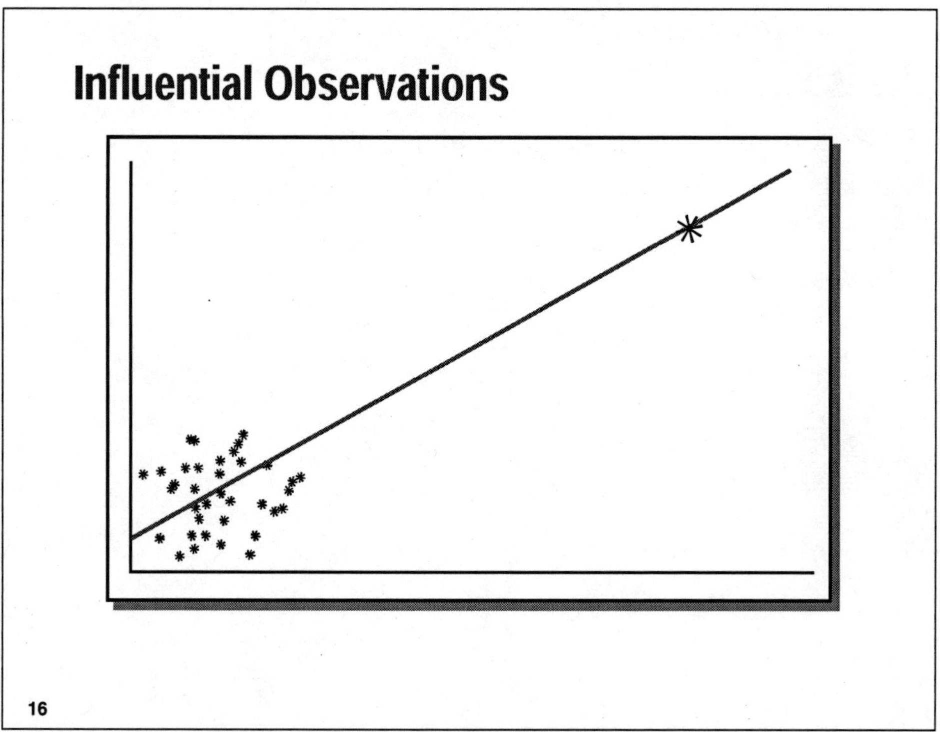

Recall in the previous section that you saw examples of data sets where the simple linear regression model fits were essentially the same. However, plotting the data revealed that the model fits were different.

One of the examples showed a highly influential observation like the example above.

Identifying influential observations in a multiple linear regression is more complex because you have more predictors to consider.

The Linear Regression task has options to calculate statistics to identify influential observations.

Diagnostic Statistics

Four statistics that help identify influential observations are

- STUDENT residual
- Cook's D
- RSTUDENT residual
- DFFITS.

17

You learned earlier how to save residual and predicted values in SAS Enterprise Guide. The Diagnostic statistics check box produces the Cook's D and DFFITS statistics shown above.

Cook's D Statistic

The Cook's D statistic is a measure of the simultaneous change in the parameter estimates when an observation is deleted from the analysis.

A suggested cutoff is $D_i > \frac{4}{n}$, where *n* is the sample size.

If the above condition is true, then the observation might have an adverse effect on the analysis.

18

To detect influential observations, you can use the Cook's D statistic. This statistic measures the change in the parameter estimates that results from deleting each observation.

Identify observations above the cutoff and investigate the reasons they occurred.

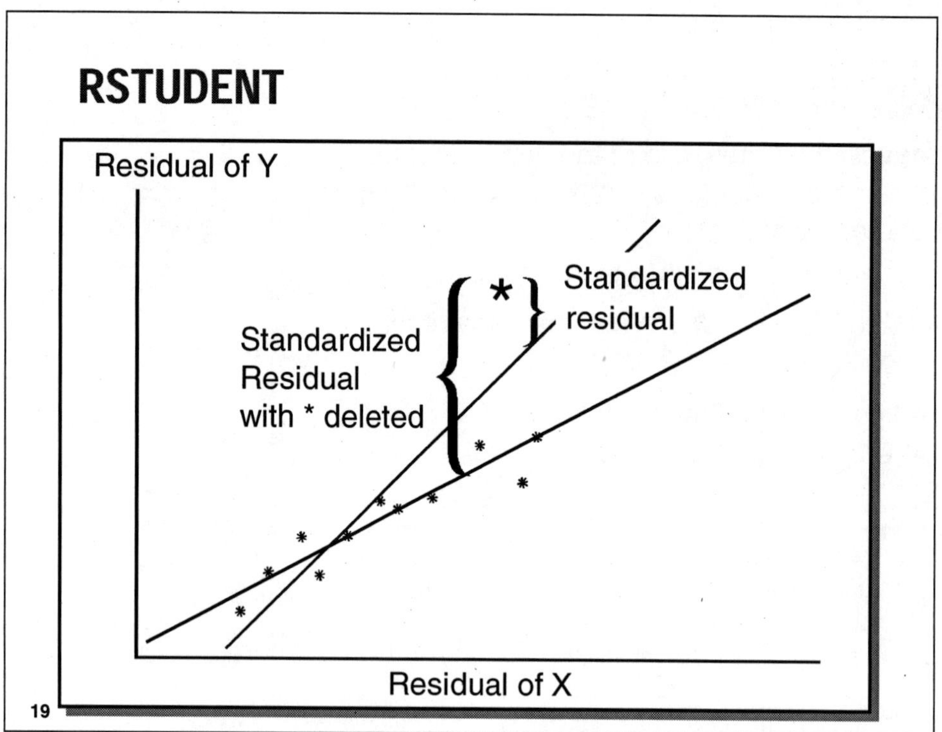

Recall that STUDENT residuals are the ordinary residuals divided by their standard errors. The RSTUDENT residuals are similar to the STUDENT residuals except that they are calculated after deleting the ith observation. In other words, the RSTUDENT is the difference between the observed Y and the predicted value of Y excluding this observation from the regression.

If the RSTUDENT is different from the STUDENT residual for a specific observation, that observation is likely to be influential.

DFFITS

The DFFITS$_i$ measures the impact that the ith observation has on the predicted value.

$$DFFITS_i = \frac{\hat{Y}_i - \hat{Y}_{(i)}}{s(\hat{Y}_i)}$$

$\hat{Y}_i$ is the ith predicted value.

$\hat{Y}_{(i)}$ is the ith predicted value when the ith observation is deleted.

$s(\hat{Y}_i)$ is the standard error of the ith predicted value.

20

The suggested cutoff is $|\text{DFFITS}_i| > 2\sqrt{\frac{p}{n}}$.

See Belsey, D. A., Kuh, E., and Welsch, R. E. 1980. *Regression Diagnostics: Identifying Influential Data and Sources of Collinearity*. New York: Wiley.

Looking for Influential Observations

Example: Generate the RSTUDENT and DFFITS influence statistics for the best 4-variable model. Save the influence statistics to an output data set. Then create a data set with only observations that exceed the suggested cutoffs of the influence statistics.

1. Double-click **Ck Assumptions Best 4** that you created earlier.

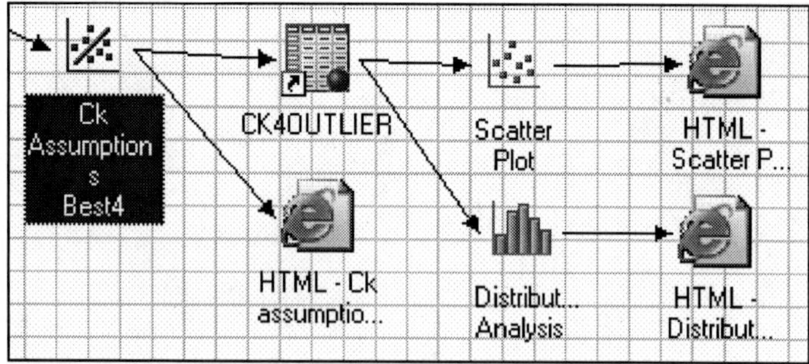

2. Select **Predictions**.

3. Ensure that **Original sample** and **Residuals** are selected. Select **Diagnostic statistics** from **Save output data**.

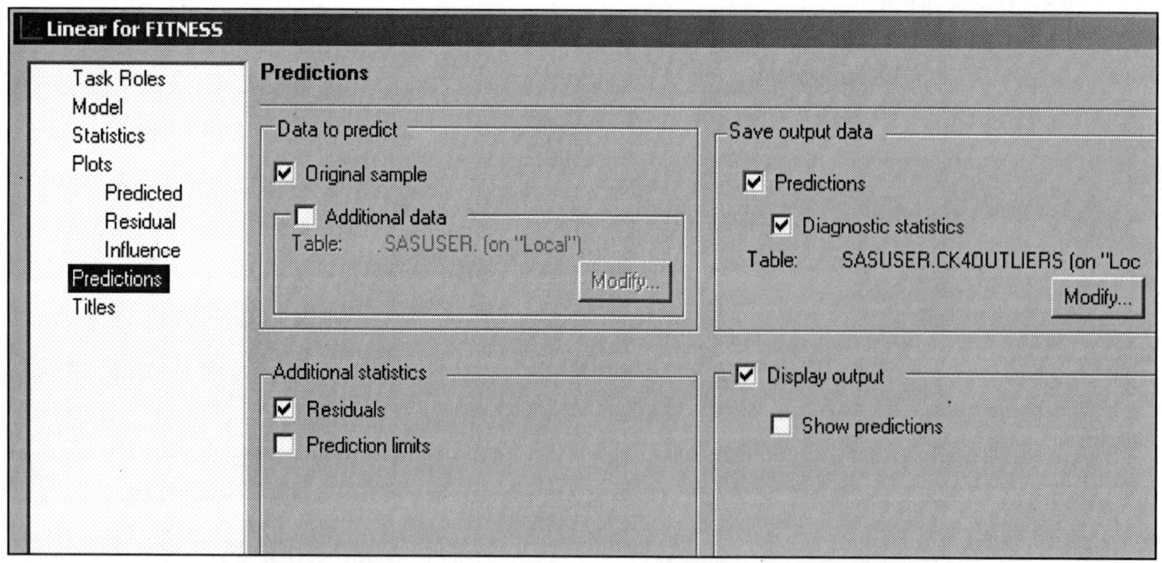

By adding the diagnostic statistics from this dialog window, SAS Enterprise Guide generates the statistics to identify influential data points in the current model.

4. Select the titles and type **`Look for Influential Observations`** as the second line of the title.

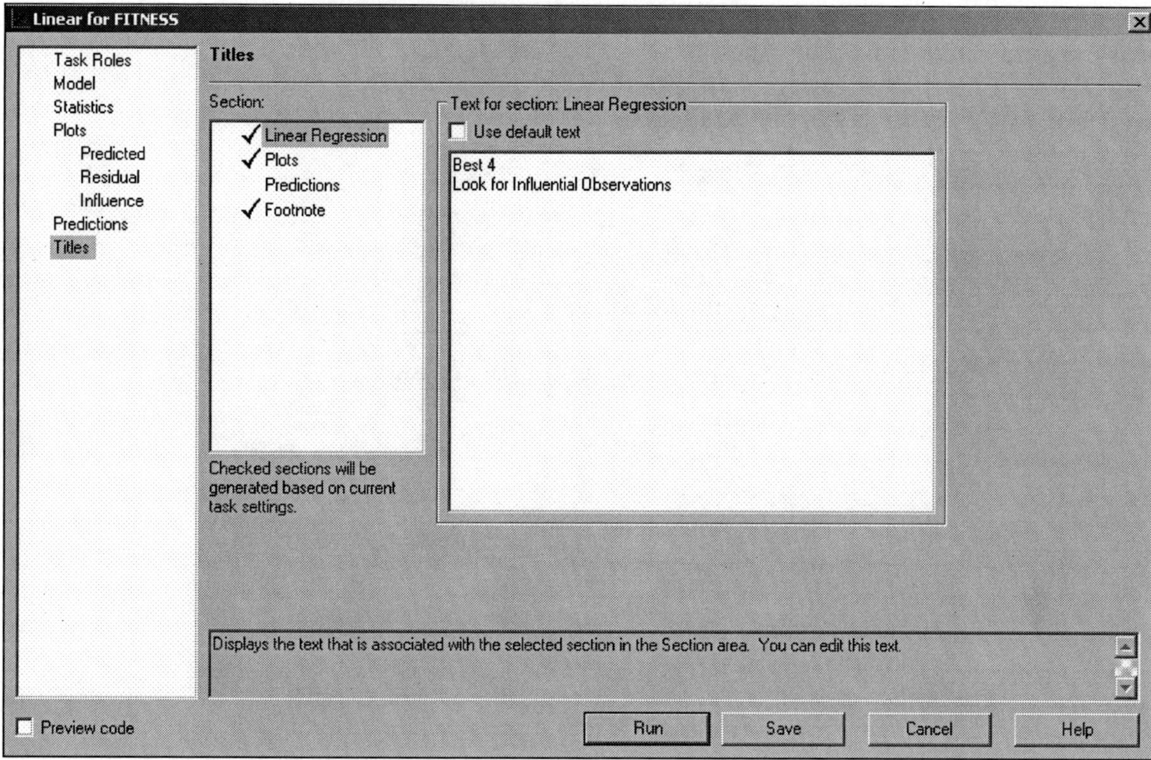

5. Select **Run**. Select **Yes** to replace the existing results.

Inspect the results. The ANOVA table and the Parameter Estimates table are identical to the previous example, so they are not shown.

To determine which, if any, of the observations are beyond their cutoffs for any of the diagnostic statistics, you would calculate the cutoffs and physically examine the **`CK4OUTLIERS`** table. Partial results for the Output Statistics table is shown:

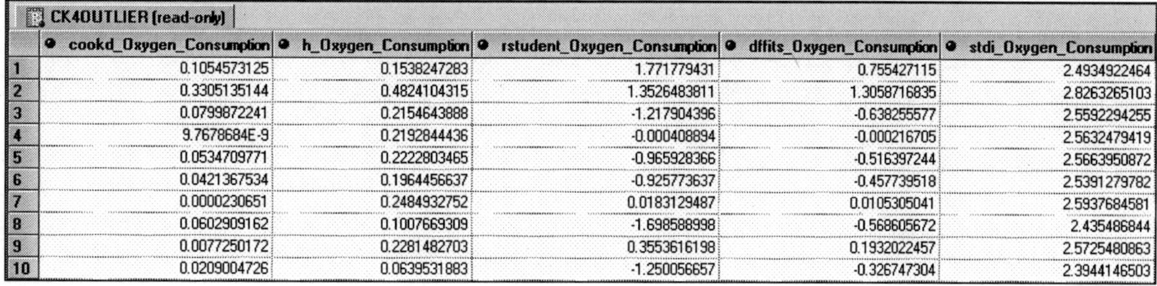
CK4OUTLIER (read-only)

	cookd_Oxygen_Consumption	h_Oxygen_Consumption	rstudent_Oxygen_Consumption	dffits_Oxygen_Consumption	stdi_Oxygen_Consumption
1	0.1054573125	0.1538247283	1.771779431	0.755427115	2.4934922464
2	0.3305135144	0.4824104315	1.3526483811	1.3058716835	2.8263265103
3	0.0799872241	0.2154643888	-1.217904396	-0.638255577	2.5592294255
4	9.7678684E-9	0.2192844436	-0.000408894	-0.000216705	2.5632479419
5	0.0534709771	0.2222803465	-0.965928366	-0.516397244	2.5663950872
6	0.0421367534	0.1964456637	-0.925773637	-0.457739518	2.5391279782
7	0.0000230651	0.2484932752	0.0183129487	0.0105305041	2.5937684581
8	0.0602909162	0.1007669309	-1.698588998	-0.568605672	2.435486844
9	0.0077250172	0.2281482703	0.3553616198	0.1932022457	2.5725480863
10	0.0209004726	0.0639531883	-1.250056657	-0.326747304	2.3944146503

You could sort this table by each of the diagnostic statistics and manually generate a list of those observations that exceed their respective cutoffs. What if your data numbered in the tens of thousands?

✎ You could use a query to create this report, but the program included may be more efficient.

To provide a more efficient solution, use a program to set 0/1 indicator variables (**rstud_i**, **dfits_i**, and **cookd_i**) that compare the diagnostic statistics with their suggested cutoffs.

Insert the SAS program **influential_fitness.sas** into the current project. (Your instructor will help you located the file on your computer.)

1. Select **File** ⇨ **Open**⇨**From My Computer**.

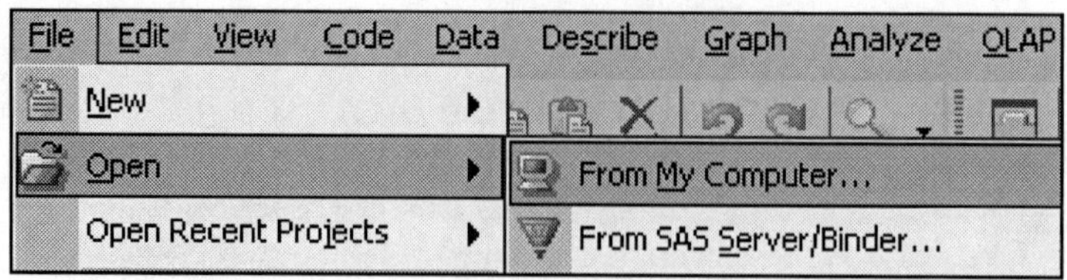

2. Locate the file **influential_fitness.sas**. Select **Open**.

The program is shown below:

influential_fitness.sas

```
/*******************************************/
/* inserted code: influential_fitness.sas */
/*******************************************/

/*  set the values of these macro variables,
    based on your model.
*/
%let numparms = 5; /* # of predictor variables + 1 */
%let numobs = 31;  /* # of observations */

data influential;
/* Below is a reference to the data set that SAS
   Enterprise Guide created with the diagnostic
   statistics. You should change this to your
   data set name, if it is different. */
   set SASUSER.CK4OUTLIERS;

   cutdifts = 2*(sqrt(&numparms/&numobs));
   cutcookd = 4/&numobs;

/* You should also change the names of the
   dependent variable names used below from
       xxxxxx_Oxygen_Consumption   --to--
       xxxxxx_Your_Dependent_Variable_Name
   if you use this program outside of class.
*/ rstud_i = (abs(rstudent_Oxygen_Consumption)>3);
   dfits_i = (abs(dffits_Oxygen_Consumption)>cutdifts);
   cookd_i = (cookd_Oxygen_Consumption>cutcookd);
   sum_i = rstud_i + dfits_i + cookd_i;
   if sum_i > 0;
run;
```

The variables **numparms** and **numobs** are the number of parameters in your model and your sample size, respectively. If you use this program with your data, change these two values to reflect your number of parameters and sample size. The remaining lines in the program create cutoff variables for the diagnostic statistics.

The **sum_i** variable is the total number of diagnostic statistics that exceed the cutoffs for the observation.

The last line subsets the file so the data set **`INFLUENTIAL`** includes only those observations that have at least one statistic that exceeds the cutoff. If the number of influential observations is large, you may not have the proper model.

Submit the program by selecting **Submit**, , on the toolbar.

The resulting data table, WORK.INFLUENCE is shown below. Only one observation, Gracie, exceeded the cutoffs you specified.

Partial Output

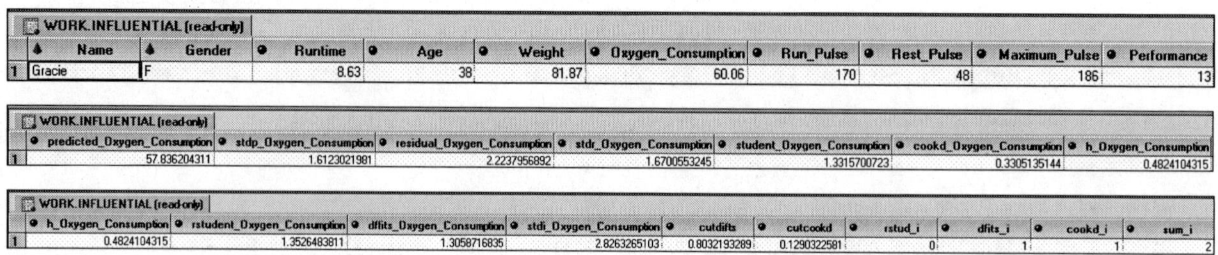

WORK.INFLUENTIAL (read-only)

	Name	Gender	Runtime	Age	Weight	Oxygen_Consumption	Run_Pulse	Rest_Pulse	Maximum_Pulse	Performance
1	Gracie	F	8.63	38	81.87	60.06	170	48	186	13

WORK.INFLUENTIAL (read-only)

	predicted_Oxygen_Consumption	stdp_Oxygen_Consumption	residual_Oxygen_Consumption	stdr_Oxygen_Consumption	student_Oxygen_Consumption	cookd_Oxygen_Consumption	h_Oxygen_Consumption
1	57.836204311	1.6123021981	2.2237956892	1.6700553245	1.3315700723	0.3305135144	0.4824104315

WORK.INFLUENTIAL (read-only)

	h_Oxygen_Consumption	rstudent_Oxygen_Consumption	dffits_Oxygen_Consumption	stdi_Oxygen_Consumption	cutdifts	cutcookd	rstud_i	dfits_i	cookd_i	sum_i
1	0.4824104315	1.3526483811	1.3058716835	2.8263265103	0.8032193289	0.1290322581	0	1	1	2

For easier legibility, this data table was displayed using **Describe** ⇨ **List Data …** and moving all the variables to **List Data Task Roles**:

Row number	Name	Gender	Runtime	Age	Weight	Oxygen_Consumption	Run_Pulse	Rest_Pulse	Maximum_Pulse
1	Gracie	F	8.63	38	81.87	60.06	170	48	186

Performance	predicted_Oxygen_Consumption	stdp_Oxygen_Consumption	residual_Oxygen_Consumption	stdr_Oxygen_Consumption
13	57.8362	1.61230	2.22380	1.67006

student_Oxygen_Consumption	cookd_Oxygen_Consumption	h_Oxygen_Consumption	rstudent_Oxygen_Consumption
1.33157	0.33051	0.48241	1.35265

dffits_Oxygen_Consumption	stdi_Oxygen_Consumption	cutdifts	cutcookd	rstud_i	dfits_i	cookd_i	sum_i
1.30587	2.82633	0.80322	0.12903	0	1	1	2

How to Handle Influential Observations

1. Recheck the data to ensure that no transcription or data entry errors occurred.
2. If the data is valid, one possible explanation is that the model is not adequate.
3. A model with higher order terms, such as polynomials and interactions between the variables, may be necessary to fit the data well.

22

If the unusual data is erroneous, correct the errors and reanalyze the data.

In this course, time does not permit discussion of higher order models in any depth.

Another possibility is that the observation, though valid, may be unusual. If you had a larger sample size, there might be more observations like the unusual ones.

You may have to collect more data to confirm the relationship suggested by the influential observation.

In general, do not exclude data. In many circumstances, some of the unusual observations contain important information.

If you do choose to exclude some observations, include a description of the types of observations you exclude and provide an explanation. Also discuss the limitation of your conclusions, given the exclusions, as part of your report or presentation.

4.3 Collinearity

Objectives

- Determine if collinearity exists in a model.
- Generate output to evaluate the strength of the collinearity and what variables are involved in the collinearity.
- Determine methods to minimize collinearity in a model.

24

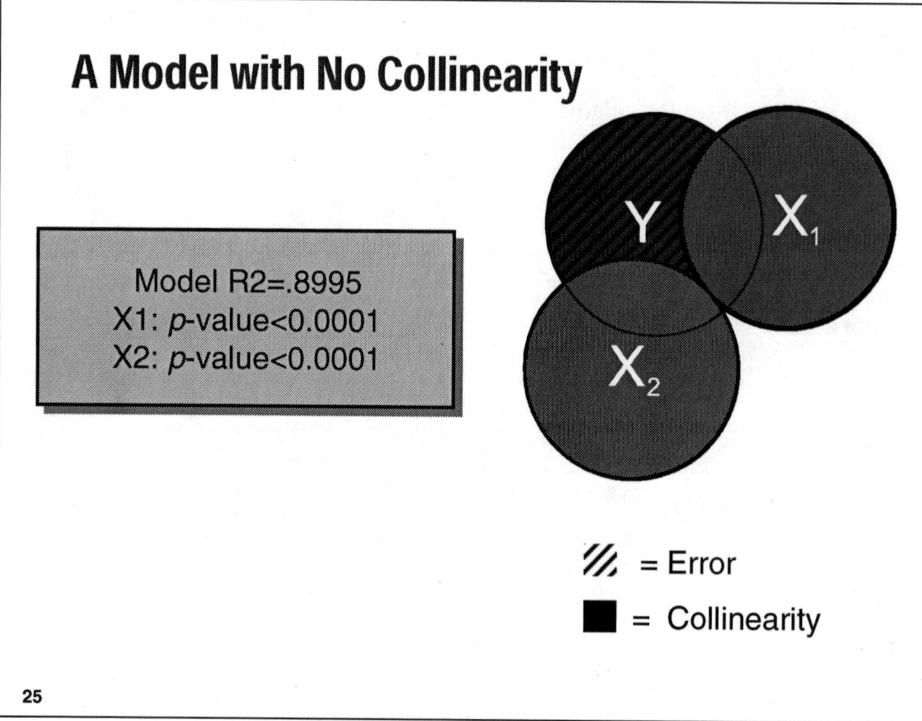

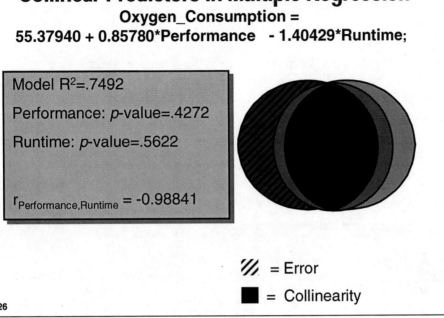

Collinear Predictors in Multiple Regression

Oxygen_Consumption =
55.37940 + 0.85780*Performance - 1.40429*Runtime;

Model R^2=.7492

Performance: *p*-value=.4272

Runtime: *p*-value=.5622

$r_{Performance,Runtime}$ = -0.98841

= Error

= Collinearity

26

Recall that collinearity arises when the Xs contain redundant information; for example, `Performance` and `Runtime` are highly correlated with each other.

Collinearity can cause these problems in your model:

- truly significant terms may be hidden
- the variances of the coefficients are increased, which results in less precise estimates of the parameters and the predicted values.

Collinearity is **not** a violation of the assumptions.

Example of Collinearity

Example: Generate a regression with **Oxygen_Consumption** as the dependent variable and **Performance**, **Runtime**, **Age**, **Weight**, **Run_Pulse**, **Rest_Pulse**, and **Maximum_Pulse** as the explanatory variables. Compare this model with the Best 4 model from the previous section.

1. Select **FITNESS** as the active data source.
2. Select **Analyze** ⇨ **Regression** ⇨ **Linear…**.
3. Assign the Dependent and Explanatory variables to fit the model described above.

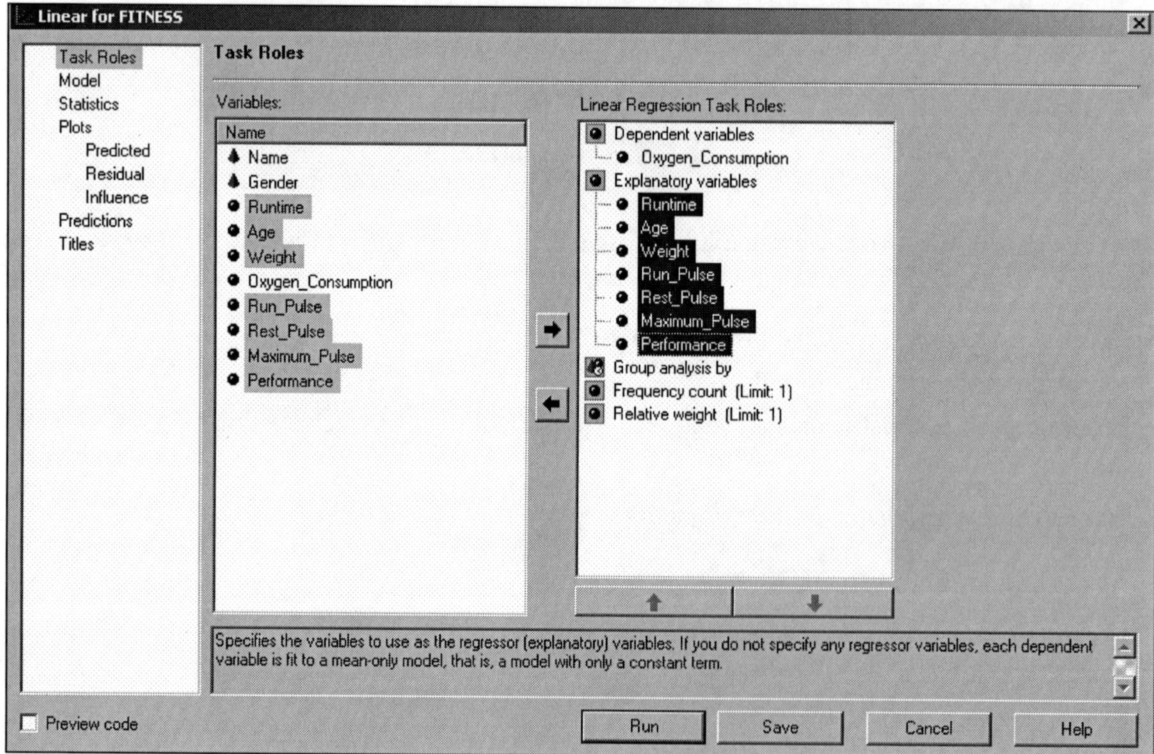

4. Select **Titles**. Change the title to `Collinearity -- Full Model`.

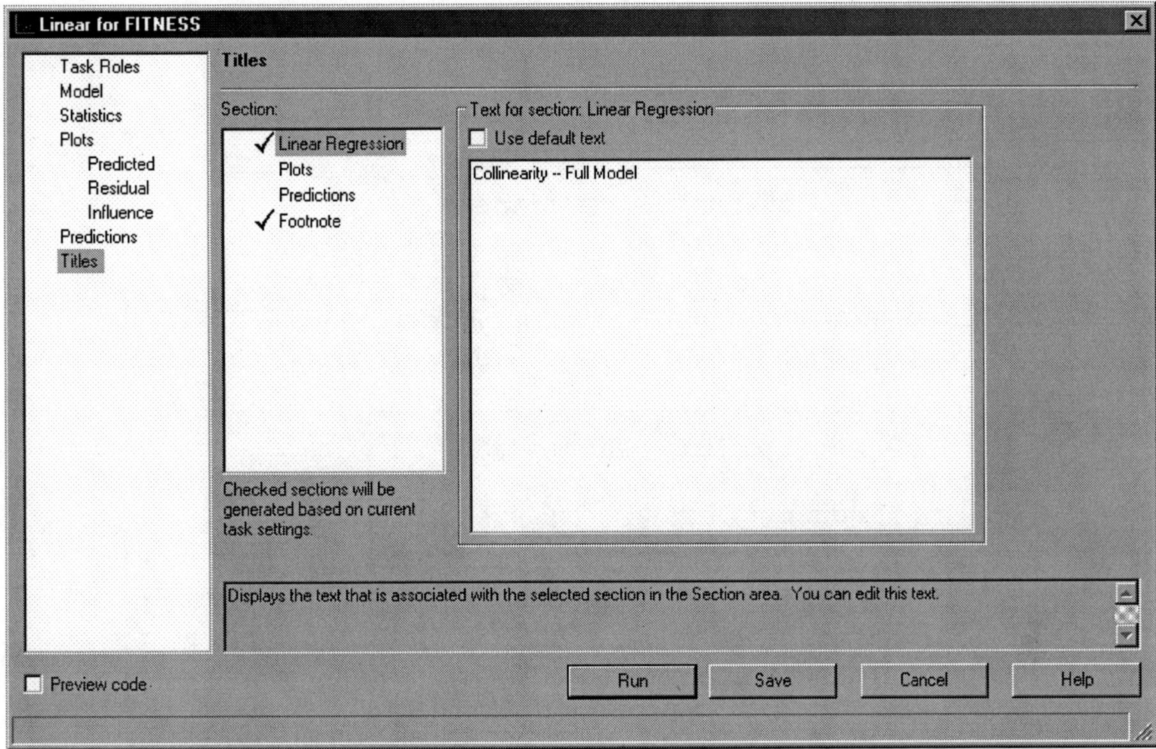

5. Select **Run**.

6. Rename the task node from **Linear** to `FullModel`.

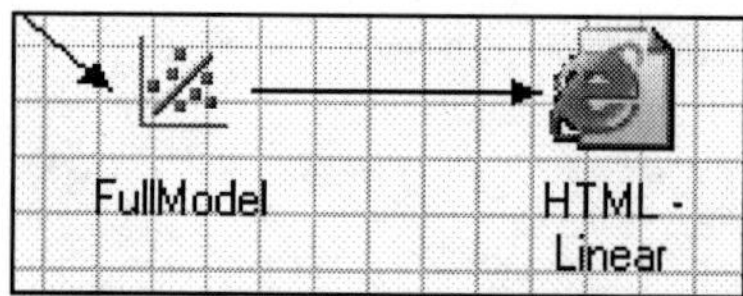

Collinearity -- Full Model

The REG Procedure
Model: Linear_Regression_Model
Dependent Variable: Oxygen_Consumption

Number of Observations Read	31
Number of Observations Used	31

Analysis of Variance					
Source	DF	Sum of Squares	Mean Square	F Value	Pr > F
Model	7	722.03251	103.14750	18.32	<.0001
Error	23	129.52204	5.63139		
Corrected Total	30	851.55455			

Root MSE	2.37306	R-Square	0.8479
Dependent Mean	47.37581	Adj R-Sq	0.8016
Coeff Var	5.00900		

The Model *F* is highly significant and the R^2 is large. These statistics suggest that the model fits the data well.

Parameter Estimates					
Variable	DF	Parameter Estimate	Standard Error	t Value	Pr > |t|
Intercept	1	93.33753	36.49782	2.56	0.0176
Runtime	1	-2.08804	2.22856	-0.94	0.3585
Age	1	-0.21066	0.10519	-2.00	0.0571
Weight	1	-0.07741	0.05681	-1.36	0.1862
Run_Pulse	1	-0.36618	0.12299	-2.98	0.0067
Rest_Pulse	1	-0.01389	0.07114	-0.20	0.8469
Maximum_Pulse	1	0.30490	0.13990	2.18	0.0398
Performance	1	0.25756	1.02373	0.25	0.8036

However, when you examine the *p*-values of the parameters, only **`Run_Pulse`** and **`Maximum_Pulse`** are statistically significant.

Recall that the best 4-variable model included **`Runtime`**; however, in the full model, this variable is not statistically significant (*p*-value=0.3585).

Including all the terms in the model hid at least one significant term.

When you have a significant Model *F* but no highly significant terms, collinearity is a likely problem.

Collinearity Diagnostics

The Linear Regression task offers the following tools that help quantify the magnitude of the collinearity problems and identify the sets of Xs that are collinear:

- variance inflation factor
- collinearity statistics
- collinearity statistics without intercept.

28

Selected collinearity tools are

- variance inflation factor, which provides a measure of the magnitude of the collinearity
- collinearity statistics, which include the intercept vector when analyzing the X′X matrix for collinearity
- collinearity statistics without the intercept, which exclude the intercept vector.

Statistics are also generated to provide a measure of the magnitude of the collinearity as well as give information that can be used to identify the sets of Xs that are the source of the collinearity.

Variance Inflation Factor (VIF)

The VIF is a relative measure of the increase in the variance because of collinearity. It can be thought of as the ratio:

$$VIF_i = \frac{1}{1 - R_i^2}$$

A $VIF_i > 10$ indicates that collinearity is a problem.

29

You can calculate a VIF for each term in the model.

Marquardt suggests that a VIF > 10 indicates the presence of strong collinearity in the model.

$VIF_i = 1/(1 - R_i^2)$, where R_i^2 is the R^2 of X_i, regressed on all the other Xs in the model.

For example, if the model is Y = X1 X2 X3 X4, i = 1 to 4.

To calculate the R^2 for X3, fit the model X3 = X1 X2 X4. Take the R^2 from the model with X_3 as the dependent variable and replace it in the formula $VIF_3 = 1/(1 - R_3^2)$. If VIF_3 is greater than 10, X3 is possibly involved in collinearity.

Marquardt, D. W. 1980. "You Should Standardize the Predictor Variables in Your Regression Models." *Journal of the American Statistical Association*, 75: 74-103.

Collinearity Statistics

- Some collinearity statistics include the intercept, while others adjust (eliminate) the intercept.
- Condition indices indicate the relative strength of the collinearity in the model.
- Variance proportions are statistics that identify the subset of the Xs that are collinear.

30

Collinearity statistics include

- eigenvalues
- condition index
- variance proportion.

Eigenvalues are also called characteristic roots. Eigenvalues near zero indicate strong collinearity. A value λ is called an eigenvalue if there exists a nonzero vector z such that $(\mathbf{X'X})\mathbf{z} = \lambda\mathbf{z}$. The *condition index*, η_i, is the square root of the largest eigenvalue divided by λ_i.

The *variance proportions* used in combination with the condition index can be used to identify the sets of Xs that are collinear. Variance proportions greater than 0.50 indicate which terms are correlated. The variance proportions are calculated for each term in the model.

The variance proportions for each term sum to 1.

Guidelines Including the Intercept

Condition index values

- between 10 and 30 suggest weak dependencies
- between 30 and 100 indicate moderate dependencies
- greater than 100 indicate strong collinearity.

31

Variance Proportions

Those predictors with variance proportions greater than 0.50 associated with a large condition index identify the subsets of the collinear predictors.

32

Guidelines Excluding the Intercept

There are no published guidelines for these statistics.

However, using the guidelines that include the intercept in conjunction with the statistics excluding the intercept enables you to evaluate the severity of the collinearity when the intercept is part of the collinearity.

33

Collinearity Diagnostics

Example: Using the Linear Regression task, generate the VIF statistics as well as the collinearity statistics that include and exclude the intercept to assess the magnitude of the collinearity problem and identify the terms involved in the collinearity.

1. Reopen the dialog **`FullModel`**.
2. Select **Statistics**.
3. Select **Collinearity analysis**, **Collinearity analysis without the intercept**, and **Variance inflation values** from the list of Diagnostics.

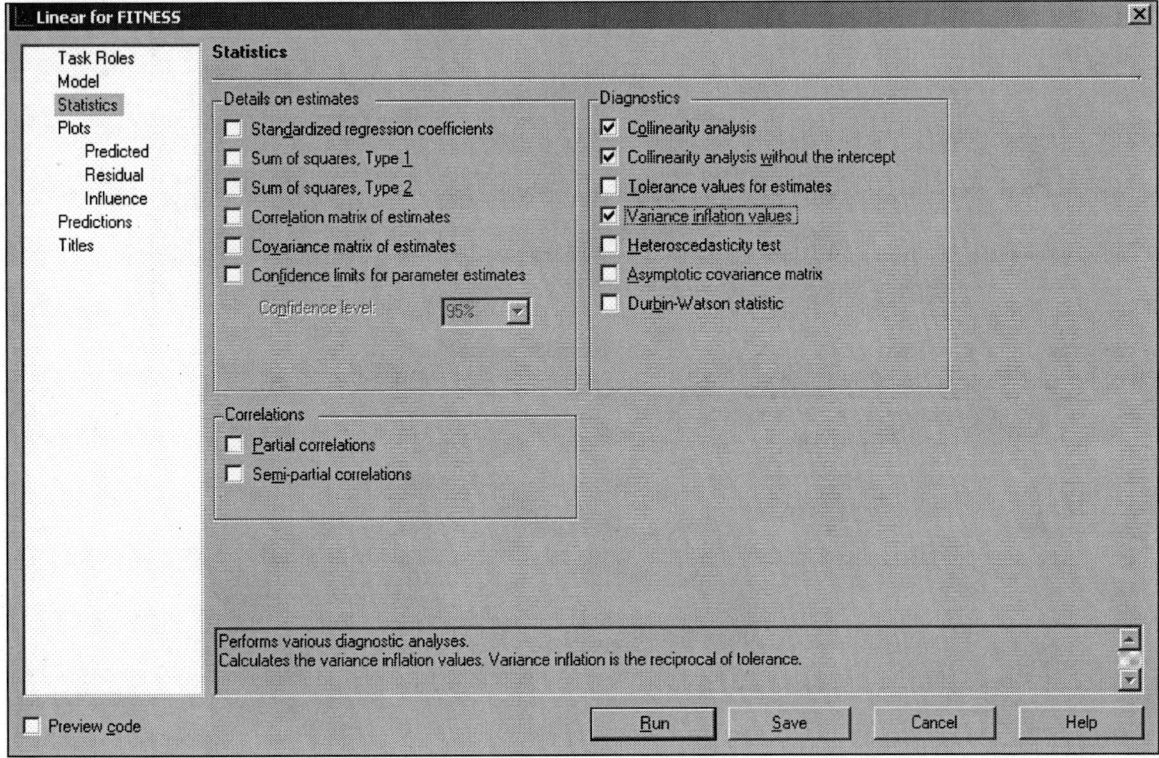

4. Select **Titles**. Enter `Using VIF and Collinearity Stats` as the title's second line.

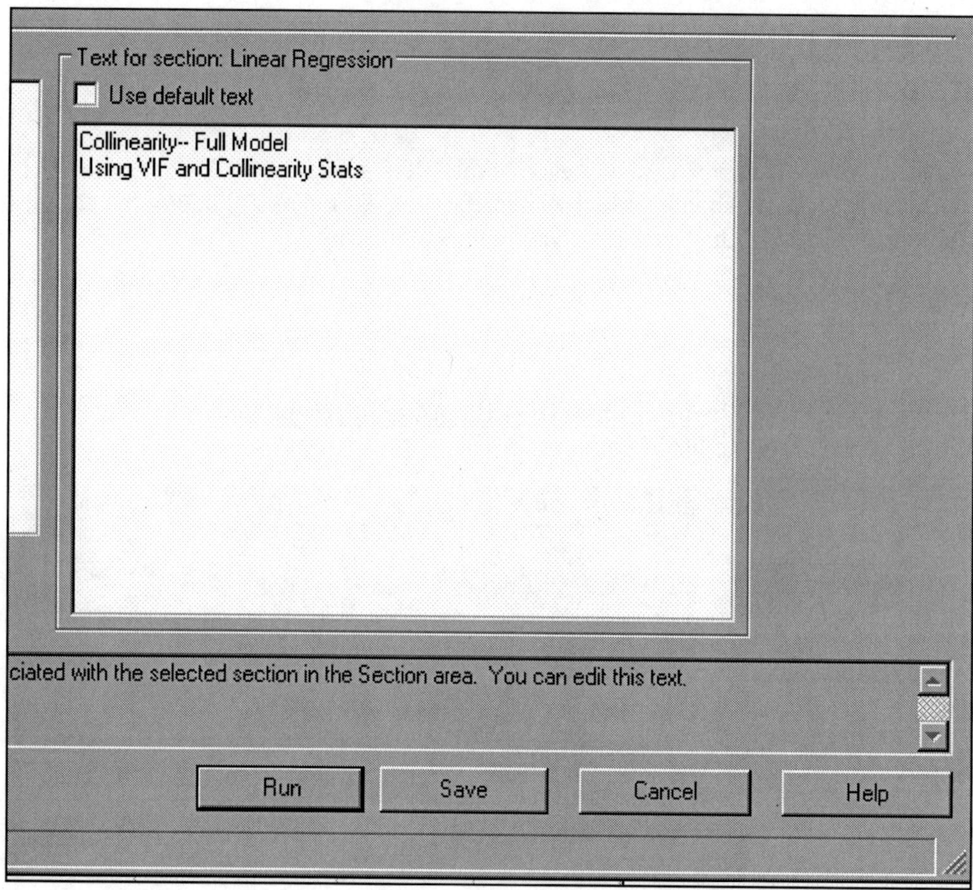

5. Select **Run**. Select **Yes** to replace the results from the previous run.

Examine the results.

Parameter Estimates						
Variable	DF	Parameter Estimate	Standard Error	t Value	Pr > |t|	Variance Inflation
Intercept	1	93.33753	36.49782	2.56	0.0176	0
Runtime	1	-2.08804	2.22856	-0.94	0.3585	50.92913
Age	1	-0.21066	0.10519	-2.00	0.0571	1.63228
Weight	1	-0.07741	0.05681	-1.36	0.1862	1.19280
Run_Pulse	1	-0.36618	0.12299	-2.98	0.0067	8.46965
Rest_Pulse	1	-0.01389	0.07114	-0.20	0.8469	1.56516
Maximum_Pulse	1	0.30490	0.13990	2.18	0.0398	8.75615
Performance	1	0.25756	1.02373	0.25	0.8036	54.34236

Some of the VIFs are much larger than 10. A severe collinearity problem is present.

Collinearity diagnostics results, including the intercept in the model, follows:

Collinearity Diagnostics											
			Proportion of Variation								
Number	Eigenvalue	Condition Index	Intercept	Runtime	Age	Weight	Run_Pulse	Rest_Pulse	Maximum_Pulse	Performance
1	7.81224	1.00000	0.00000223	0.00000516	0.00011543	0.00015063	0.00000679	0.00019829	0.00000501	0.00003396
2	0.14978	7.22204	4.610439E-7	0.00026016	0.00032355	0.00018997	0.00001537	0.00374	0.00000627	0.01283
3	0.01739	21.19723	0.00006157	0.00028745	0.24299	0.00908	0.00032301	0.24059	0.00022961	0.00023609
4	0.01246	25.03710	0.00000120	0.00016004	0.05498	0.39864	0.00016217	0.33791	0.00022890	0.00120
5	0.00606	35.90012	0.00027949	0.00149	0.09288	0.45536	0.01695	0.29325	0.00969	0.00007171
6	0.00179	66.03652	0.01276	0.07620	0.38685	0.10219	0.04272	0.01670	0.01335	0.03405
7	0.00018592	204.98810	0.00326	0.02721	0.01651	0.01929	0.92679	0.00001297	0.92625	0.03584
8	0.00009415	288.05165	0.98363	0.89439	0.20535	0.01510	0.01303	0.10759	0.05024	0.91573

Two condition indices are well above 100. For the largest (288.05165), the variance proportions for **`Intercept`**, **`Runtime`**, and **`Performance`** are greater than 0.50, indicating that these three terms are involved in collinearity. Because the **`Intercept`** is involved in collinearity, examine the variance proportion statistics that exclude the intercept.

Collinearity diagnostics, excluding the intercept in the model, follows:

Collinearity Diagnostics (intercept adjusted)										
			Proportion of Variation							
Number	Eigenvalue	Condition Index	Runtime	Age	Weight	Run_Pulse	Rest_Pulse	Maximum_Pulse	Performance
1	2.92687	1.00000	0.00133	0.00328	0.00953	0.00870	0.03205	0.00750	0.00124
2	1.87356	1.24988	0.00194	0.10087	0.01834	0.00620	0.00309	0.00967	0.00196
3	0.94035	1.76424	0.00035679	0.00167	0.74750	0.00695	0.03473	0.00343	0.00014220
4	0.74998	1.97550	0.00003187	0.20986	0.00001480	0.02020	0.43182	0.01612	0.00001910
5	0.43947	2.58069	0.00519	0.57367	0.16190	0.00433	0.41363	0.00220	0.00329
6	0.06022	6.97181	0.00012410	0.03802	0.02856	0.95340	0.00431	0.96071	0.00019461
7	0.00955	17.50829	0.99103	0.07263	0.03416	0.00023243	0.08038	0.00036791	0.99315

A similar pattern of collinearity appears when you use the intercept adjusted results. Examining the last row of the above table reveals that `Performance` (0.99315) and `Runtime` (0.99103) possess variance proportions greater than 0.50. You can conclude that these two variables are involved in the collinearity.

Begin the process of eliminating collinear terms by returning to the Parameter Estimates table and recording the p-values of the identified subset of the independent variables:

`Performance` p-value=0.8036

`Runtime` p-value=0.3585

With this subset of collinear variables, eliminate **`Performance`** from the model. Notice that this variable also has a high VIF.

6. Reopen the **`FullModel`** dialog.

7. Remove the variable **`Performance`** from the Explanatory variables list.

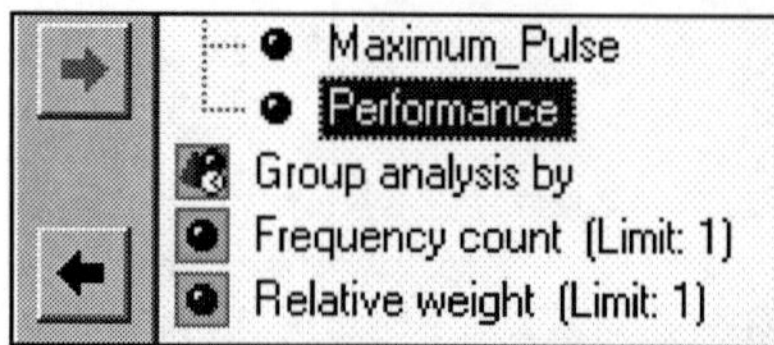

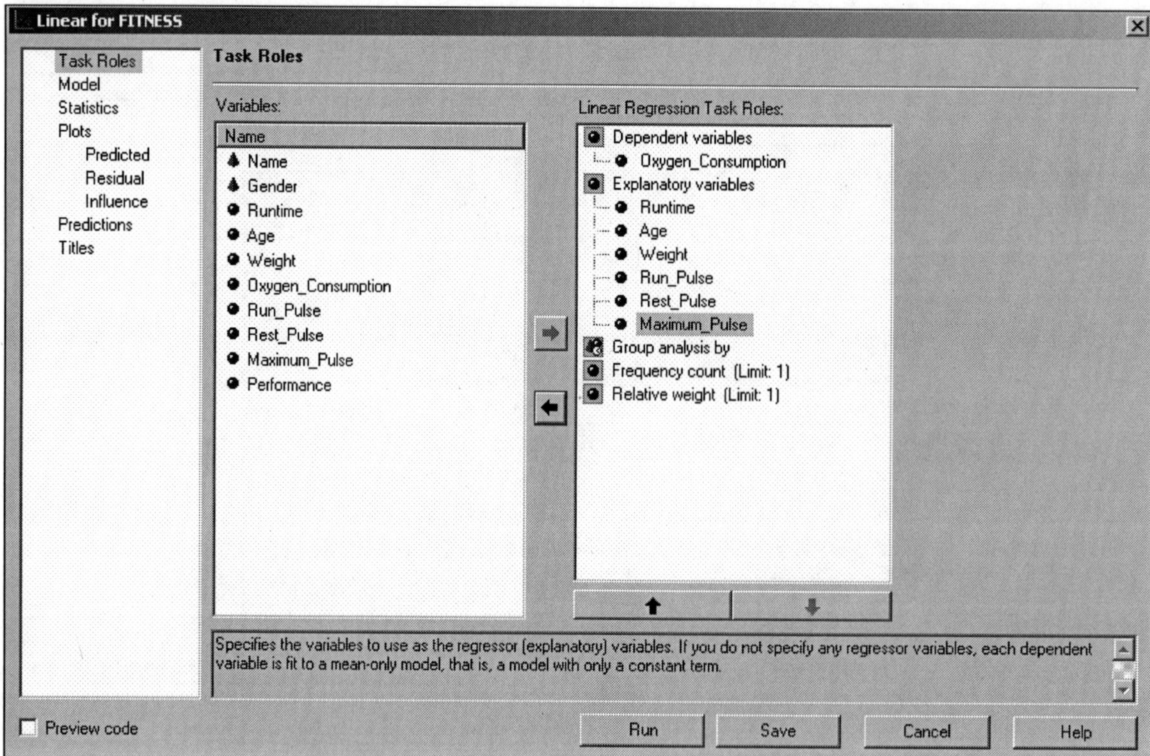

8. Change the title to **`Collinearity -- Performance removed`**.

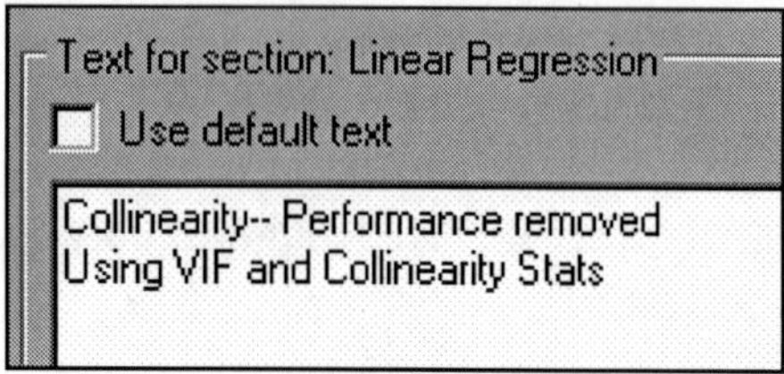

9. Select **Run**. Select **No** to create a new node in the process flow.

10. Change the name of the node in the process flow to **NoPerf**.

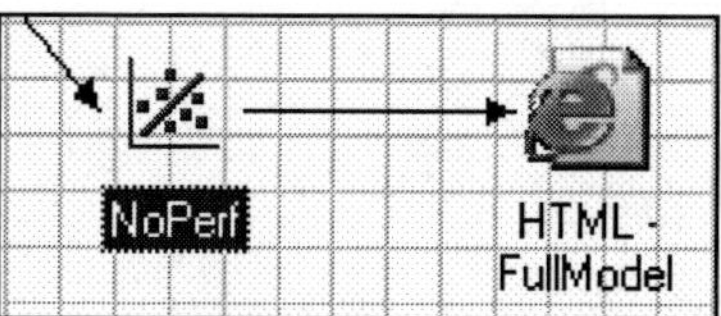

Partial results

Parameter Estimates						
Variable	DF	Parameter Estimate	Standard Error	t Value	Pr > |t|	Variance Inflation
Intercept	1	101.96313	12.27174	8.31	<.0001	0
Runtime	1	-2.63994	0.38532	-6.85	<.0001	1.58432
Age	1	-0.21848	0.09850	-2.22	0.0363	1.48953
Weight	1	-0.07503	0.05492	-1.37	0.1845	1.15973
Run_Pulse	1	-0.36721	0.12050	-3.05	0.0055	8.46034
Rest_Pulse	1	-0.01952	0.06619	-0.29	0.7706	1.41004
Maximum_Pulse	1	0.30457	0.13714	2.22	0.0360	8.75535

Run_Pulse and **Maximum_Pulse** are significant in this model as they were in the previous model, but now both **Runtime** and **Age** are significant in this model.

The VIFs are now all less than 10.

Scroll forward to find the Collinearity Diagnostics table:

Collinearity Diagnostics

			Proportion of Variation						
Number	Eigenvalue	Condition Index	Intercept	Runtime	Age	Weight	Run_Pulse	Rest_Pulse	Maximum_Pulse
1	6.94983	1.00000	0.00002395	0.00021174	0.00015997	0.00019576	0.00000860	0.00027961	0.00000633
2	0.01856	19.35297	0.00224	0.02439	0.15550	0.00878	0.00000185	0.39351	0.00000723
3	0.01521	21.37532	0.00069190	0.12332	0.15174	0.23637	0.00113	0.03259	0.00121
4	0.00914	27.57505	0.00635	0.61945	0.03075	0.17375	0.00152	0.19195	0.00125
5	0.00603	33.94799	0.00139	0.12581	0.11951	0.45090	0.01510	0.35859	0.00840
6	0.00105	81.17086	0.79602	0.09233	0.47800	0.10834	0.06682	0.01756	0.00556
7	0.00017900	197.04044	0.19329	0.01449	0.06435	0.02167	0.91542	0.00552	0.98356

The largest condition index is still greater than 100, indicating that there is still collinearity in this model. For the largest condition index, the variance proportions for **Run_Pulse** (0.91542) and **Maximum_Pulse** (0.98356) are greater than 0.5. Note that the **Intercept** is not involved in collinearity, so there is no need to examine the COLLINOINT output.

Because the variable **Maximum_Pulse** (0.0360) has a higher *p*-value than **Run_Pulse** (0.0055), generate another model and eliminate the variable **Maximum_Pulse** from the model.

11. Reopen the **`NoPerf`** node in the project tree.

12. Remove the variable **`Maximum_Pulse`** from the Explanatory variables list.

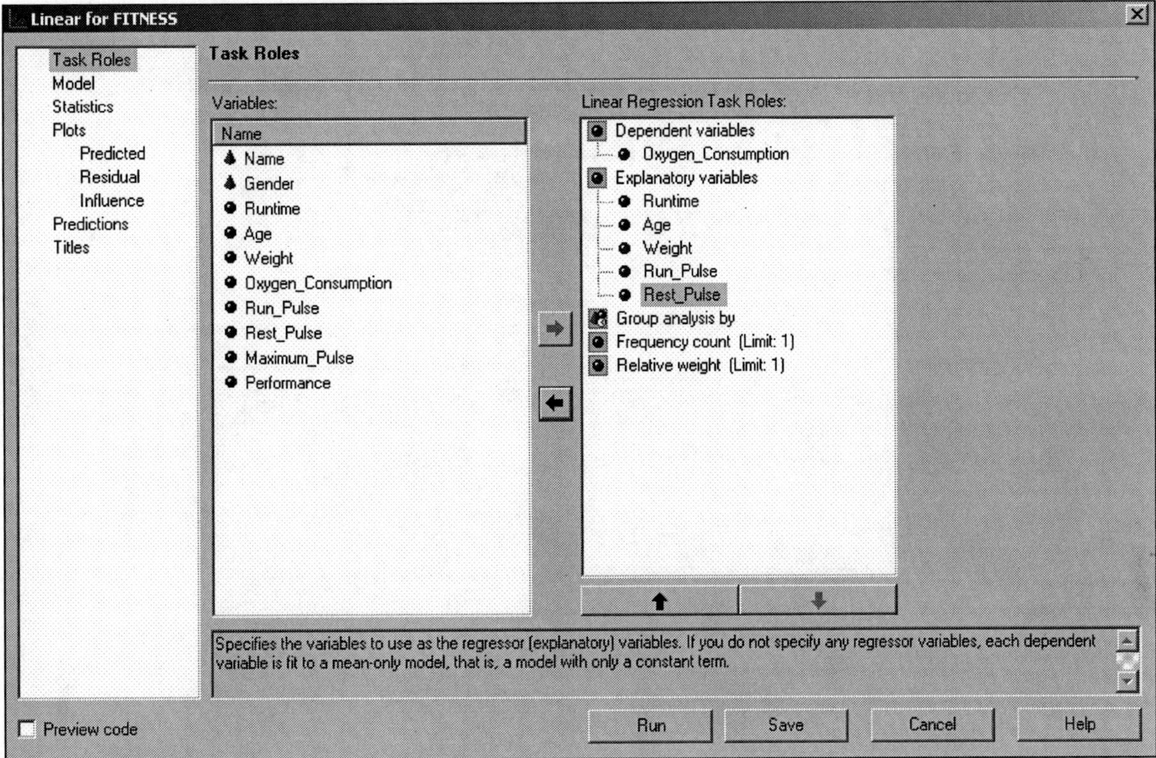

13. Change the title to **`Collinearity -- Performance and Maximum_Pulse removed`**.

14. Select **<u>Run</u>**. Select **<u>No</u>** to create a new node in the project tree.

15. Rename the node **`NoPerfNoMax`**.

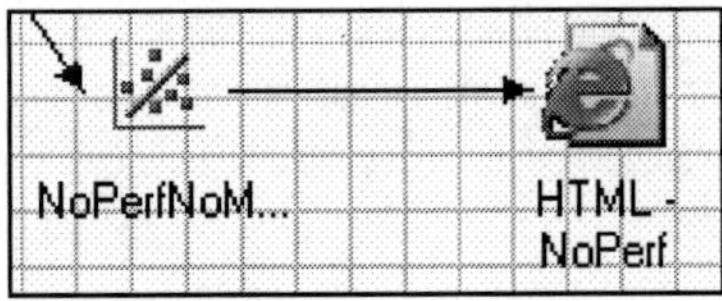

Examine the results.

Analysis of Variance					
Source	DF	Sum of Squares	Mean Square	F Value	Pr > F
Model	5	694.98323	138.99665	22.19	<.0001
Error	25	156.57132	6.26285		
Corrected Total	30	851.55455			

Root MSE	2.50257	R-Square	0.8161
Dependent Mean	47.37581	Adj R-Sq	0.7794
Coeff Var	5.28238		

Parameter Estimates						
Variable	DF	Parameter Estimate	Standard Error	t Value	Pr > |t|	Variance Inflation
Intercept	1	115.46115	11.46893	10.07	<.0001	0
Runtime	1	-2.71594	0.41288	-6.58	<.0001	1.57183
Age	1	-0.27650	0.10217	-2.71	0.0121	1.38477
Weight	1	-0.05300	0.05811	-0.91	0.3704	1.12190
Run_Pulse	1	-0.12213	0.05207	-2.35	0.0272	1.36493
Rest_Pulse	1	-0.02485	0.07116	-0.35	0.7298	1.40819

The variables **`Weight`** and **`Rest_Pulse`** are not statistically significant, indicating that they might be removed from the model. All VIFs are relatively small.

Collinearity Diagnostics								
			Proportion of Variation					
Number	Eigenvalue	Condition Index	Intercept	Runtime	Age	Weight	Run_Pulse	Rest_Pulse
1	5.95261	1.00000	0.00004324	0.00029113	0.00023471	0.00027579	0.00007258	0.00038178
2	0.01855	17.91390	0.00296	0.02190	0.17447	0.00826	0.00002193	0.38754
3	0.01434	20.37297	0.00139	0.09587	0.14694	0.36846	0.00674	0.02990
4	0.00882	25.97155	0.01086	0.75407	0.04148	0.06095	0.00710	0.27246
5	0.00465	35.78017	0.02723	0.02828	0.18069	0.46144	0.26977	0.29881
6	0.00102	76.21454	0.95752	0.09958	0.45619	0.10061	0.71629	0.01090

Collinearity Diagnostics (intercept adjusted)							
			Proportion of Variation				
Number	Eigenvalue	Condition Index	Runtime	Age	Weight	Run_Pulse	Rest_Pulse
1	1.86111	1.00000	0.07701	0.02981	0.04373	0.12341	0.11184
2	1.28404	1.20392	0.14039	0.27964	0.09841	0.01037	0.03290
3	0.89216	1.44433	0.04970	0.07934	0.68711	0.03614	0.08003
4	0.59808	1.76404	0.00449	0.05979	0.03567	0.66283	0.45266
5	0.36462	2.25927	0.72841	0.55142	0.13508	0.16726	0.32257

The largest condition index is now approximately 76. This indicates that there are some moderate dependencies between the predictor variables in this model. Examination of the variance proportions indicates that the **Intercept** and **Run_Pulse** are involved in collinearity.

When you use the intercept adjusted results, **Runtime** (variance proportion=0.72841) and **Age** (variance proportion=0.55142) are involved in collinearity.

Now return to the Parameter Estimates table and record the *p*-values of **Runtime** (<0.0001) and **Age** (0.0121).

Options include the following:

- Accept the current model without deleting any more variables, because **Runtime** and **Age** are both statistically significant. Furthermore, remember that the maximum Condition Index is approximately 76 for this model and that falls into the moderate range of collinearity.
- As noted earlier, the variables **Weight** (*p*-value=0.3704) and **Rest_Pulse** (*p*-value=0.7298) are not statistically significant; you may want to eliminate **Rest_Pulse** from the model and re-execute the reduced model.

Guidelines for Eliminating Terms

1. Determine the set of Xs using the variance proportions associated with the largest condition index.
2. Drop the variable among the set with the largest *p*-value that also has a large VIF.
3. Rerun the regression and repeat, if necessary.

35

In the previous demonstration you saw how to identify the sets of Xs that were collinear.

The natural question is, "Which terms should be dropped?" Subject-matter expertise should be used as well as the suggested guidelines above.

There are other approaches to dealing with collinearity. Two techniques are ridge regression and principle components regression. In addition, recentering the predictor variables can sometimes eliminate collinearity problems, especially in a polynomial regression.

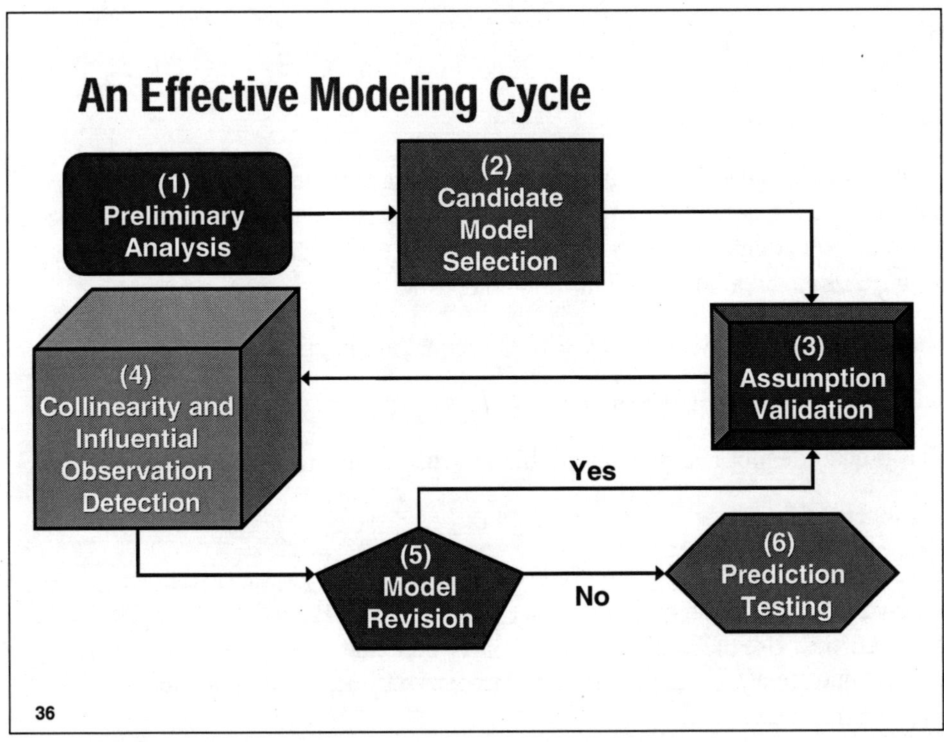

(1) Preliminary Analysis: This step includes the use of descriptive statistics, graphs, and correlation analysis.

(2) Candidate Model Selection: This step uses the numerous selection options in linear regression to identify one or more candidate models.

(3) Assumption Validation: This step includes the plots of residuals and graphs of the residuals versus the predicted values. It also includes a test for equal variances.

(4) Collinearity and Influential Observation Detection: The former includes the use of the VIF statistic, condition indices, and variation proportions; the latter includes the examination of RSTUDENT residuals, Cook's D statistic, and DFFITS statistics and their respective cutoffs.

(5) Model Revision: If steps (3) and (4) indicate the need for model revision, generate a new model by returning to these two steps.

(6) Prediction Testing: If possible, validate the model with data not used to build the model.

4.4 Exercises

1. Examining Residuals

a. A college entrance exam is designed to predict freshman-year grade point averages. Twenty-five students take the exam, and the data is stored in the **GRADES** data set. Run a regression of **gpa** on **score**. Create residual plots of the residuals by **score** and by the predicted values, a plot of student residuals by **score**, and a normal quantile-quantile plot.

1) Do the residual plots indicate any problems with the model assumptions?

2) Are there any outliers indicated by the student residuals?

3) Does the quantile-quantile plot indicate any problems with the normality assumption?

2. Detecting Influential Observations

a. Using the **CARS1993** data set, run a regression of **midprice** on **citympg**, **egnsize**, **hrspower**, and **revltns**. Create an output data set with the RSTUDENT, COOKD, and DFFITS diagnostic statistics. Use these statistics to identify potential influential observations based on the suggested cutoff values. (Hint: Use **influential_cars.sas** and change its parameters to complete this task.)

3. Ascertaining Collinearity

a. Using the **CARS1993** data set, run a regression of **midprice** on all the other variables in the file.

1) Determine whether there is a collinearity problem.

2) If so, identify the sets of Xs that are collinear with each other, and eliminate one term from the model. Reassess the need to continue this process.

4.5 Chapter Summary

The four assumptions of linear regression analysis are

- the mean of the response variable is linearly related to the value of the predictor variable(s)
- the observations are independent
- the error terms for each value of the predictor variable are normally distributed
- the error variances for each value of the predictor variable are equal.

If these assumptions are not valid, the probability of drawing incorrect conclusions from the analysis may be increased.

It is important to be aware of influential observations in any regression model even though their existence does not violate the regression assumptions. For multiple regression, scatter plots do not necessarily identify influential observations. However, some statistics that can help identify influential observations are studentized residuals, RSTUDENT residuals, Cook's D, and DFFITS.

If more than one percent of the observations are identified as influential observations, it is possible that you do not have an adequate model; you may want to add higher-level terms, such as polynomial and interaction terms. In general, do not exclude data.

Collinearity is a problem unique to multiple regression. It can hide significant variables and increase the variance of the parameter estimates, resulting in an unstable model. Statistics useful in identifying collinearity are the variance inflation factor (VIF) and condition indices combined with variance proportions. From a statistical perspective, after you have identified the subset of independent variables that are collinear, one solution is to remove variables, only one at a time, from the model to eliminate the collinearity.

4.6 Solutions Exercises

1. Examining Residuals

a. Locate the **GRADES** data set. Previous results provide an easy starting point to generate residual plots.

1) Locate **Grades** and select the Linear task used in Exercise **3.b**.

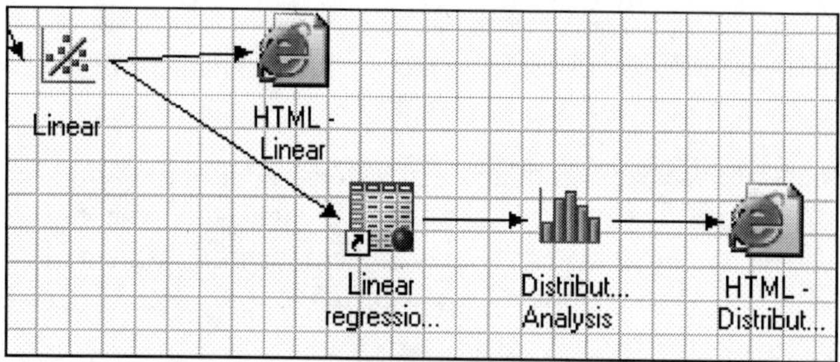

a) Select **Residual** on the left and check the boxes next to **Ordinary vs predicted Y** and **Ordinary vs Independents**.

b) Select **Predictions** on the left. Check the box next to **Original Sample**. Make sure the box next to **Predictions** and the box next to **Display output** are checked. You can change the name of the output data table to something easier to remember if you wish.

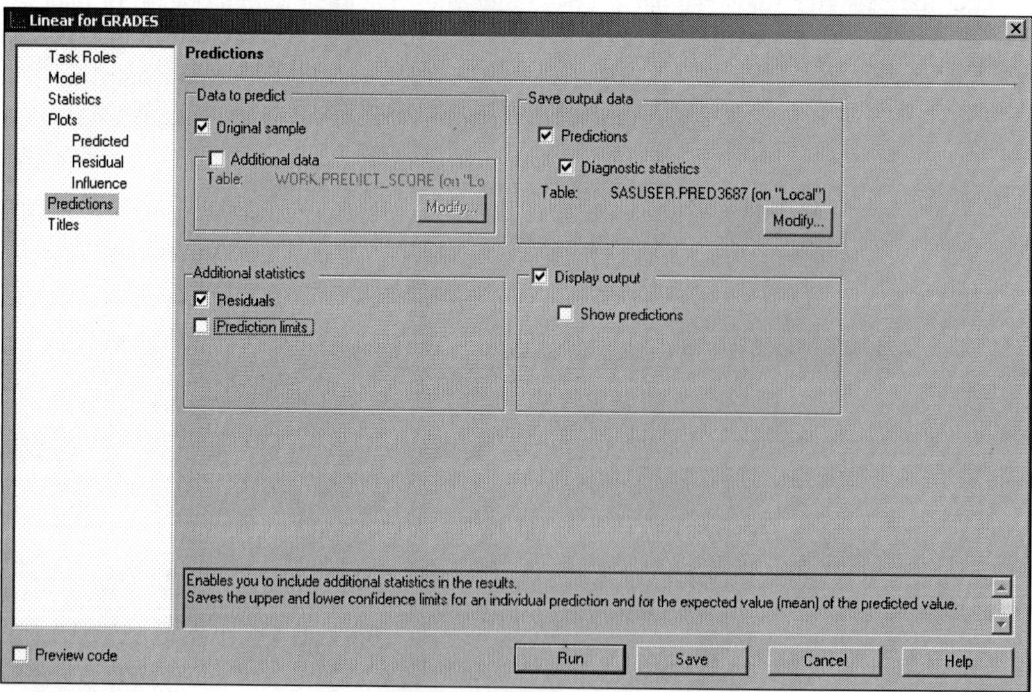

c) Select **Run**.

d) Select **No** in the pop-up window that opens to keep from replacing the results of the previous run.

e) For clarity, you may want to rename the latest Linear Regression results.

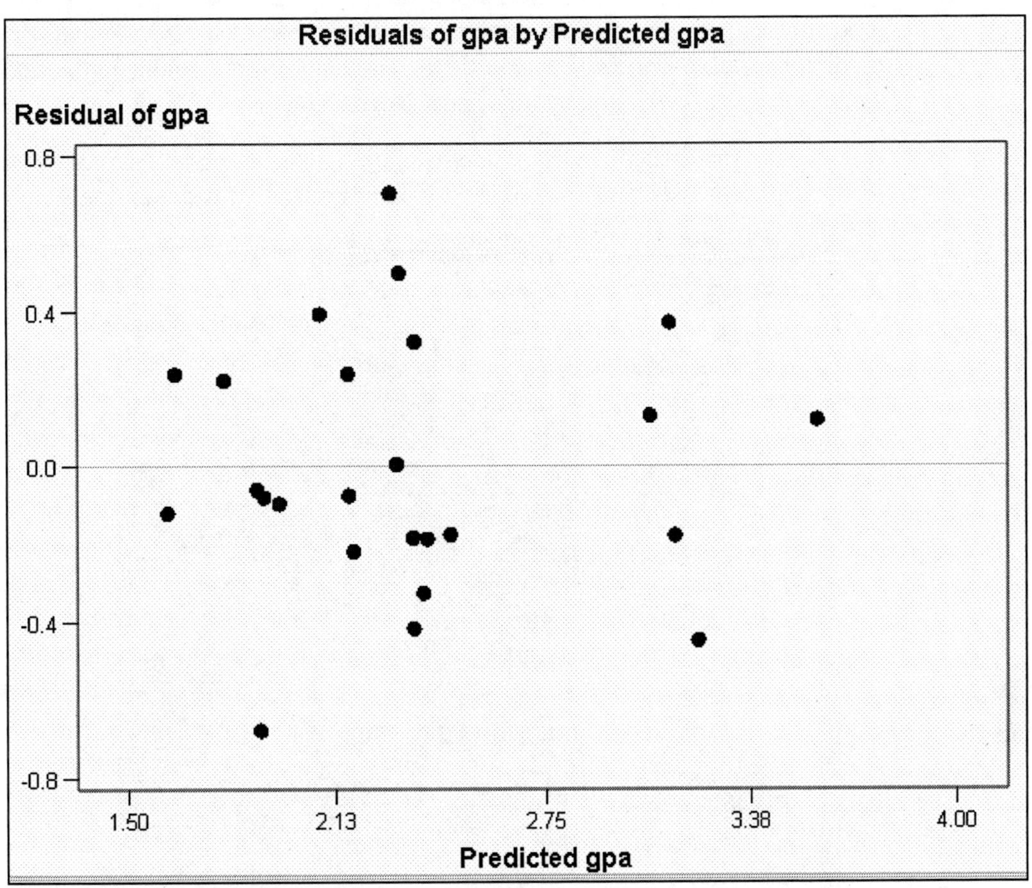

There appears to be an equal spread of the data above and below the zero reference line, as indicated by the vertical maximum and minimum values, 0.702 and –0.678, respectively. Visually, it appears that the assumption of equal variance is not violated.

2) To locate any potential outliers, generate a plot of the studentized residuals of `gpa` and the predictor variable `score`. Because there is no identifying variable in the `GRADES` table, you can use the plots generated by the Linear Regression task.

   a) Re-Open the Linear Models task created in the last exercise. Go to the **Residuals** pane under Plots and check the box next to **Studentized vs Independents**.

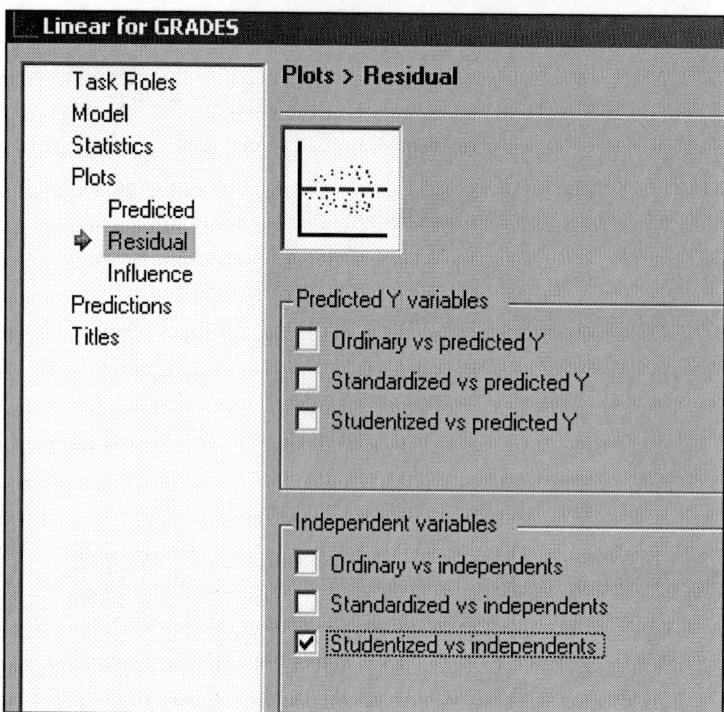

   b) Select **Run**.

c) Select <u>**Yes**</u> to replace the results of the previous run.

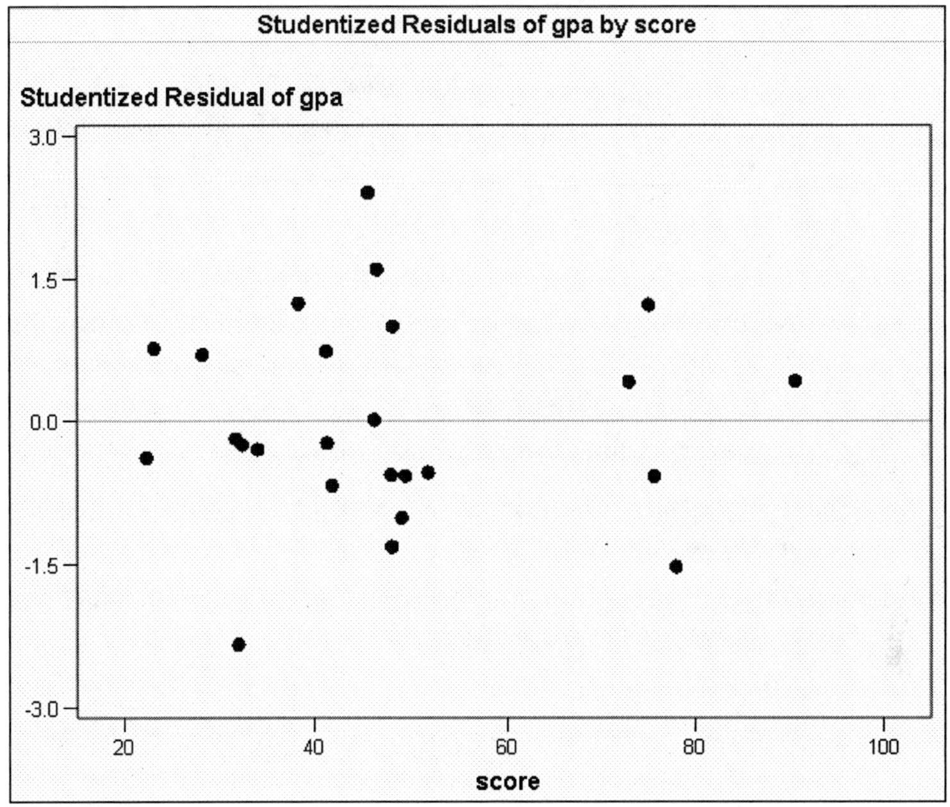

When `score=32`, the studentized residual is less than the cutoff of –2.

When `score=45.6`, the studentized residual is greater than the cutoff of 2.

These two data points should be investigated as possible outliers.

3) Use the Distribution task to investigate the normality of the residuals of `gpa`.

   a) Re-open the Linear Models task used in the previous exercise.

   b) Select the **Predictions** pane. Uncheck the box next to **Additional data** and check the boxes next to **Original sample** and **Residuals.**

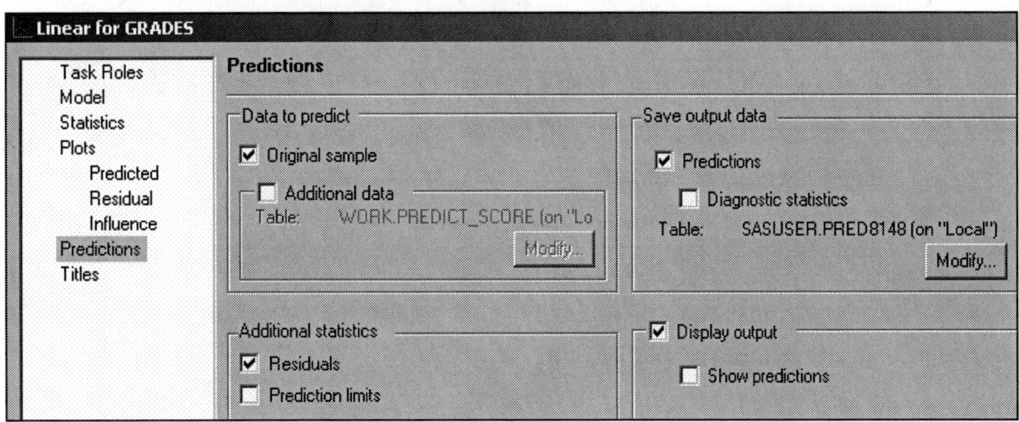

c) Select **Run**.

d) Double-click the resulting data table to view it.

Linear regression predictions and statistics for SASUSER.GRADES (read-only)

	score	gpa	predicted_gpa	residual_gpa	student_gpa	rstudent_gpa
1	49.4	2.21	2.3964464424	-0.186446442	-0.579498414	-0.570944077
2	41.3	2.09	2.1642781563	-0.074278156	-0.231446108	-0.226622816
3	31.7	1.83	1.8891157432	-0.059115743	-0.186934289	-0.182964385
4	32.4	1.83	1.9091796691	-0.079179669	-0.249998854	-0.244836584
5	78	2.77	3.2162011316	-0.446201132	-1.481803685	-1.523792729

e) Use the Distribution Analysis task to examine the distribution for the `residual_gpa` variable. Make sure that the output data table is the active data source, and go to **Analyze** ⇨ **Distribution Analysis…**.

f) Assign `gpa_residual` to the Analysis variable role.

g) Select **Normal** under Distributions and check the box next to **Normal**. Make any desired changes to the line width and color.

h) Select **Plots** under Appearance and check the box next to **Probability Plot**. Make any desired changes to the axis and background colors.

i) Select **Run**.

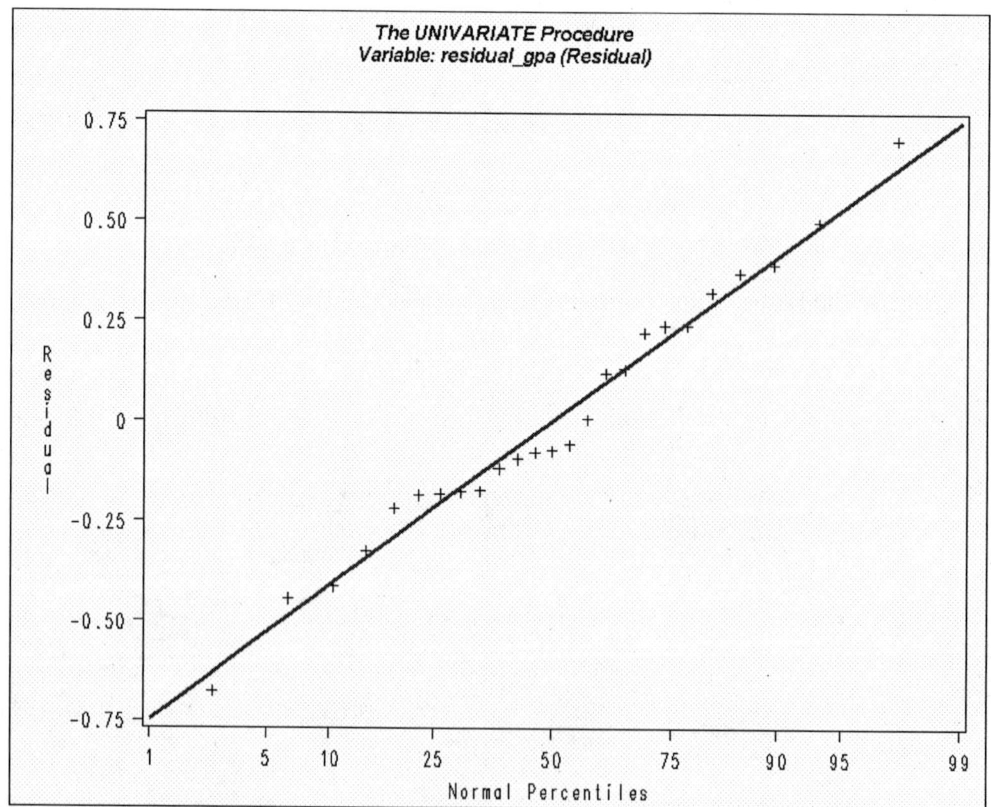

The normal probability plot shows no serious departure from normality.

2. Detecting Influential Observations

a. Locate and select **CARS1993** as the active data source. Generate influence statistics for this model to determine if any influential observations exist.

1) Select the Linear Regression task under **Analyze** ⇨ **Regression** ⇨ **Linear…**.

2) Assign **midprice** to the Dependent variable role. Assign **citympg**, **egnsize**, **hrspower**, and **revltns** to the Explanatory variables role.

3) Select **Predictions** on the left. Check the boxes next to **Original sample**, **Predictions**, and **Diagnostic statistics**.

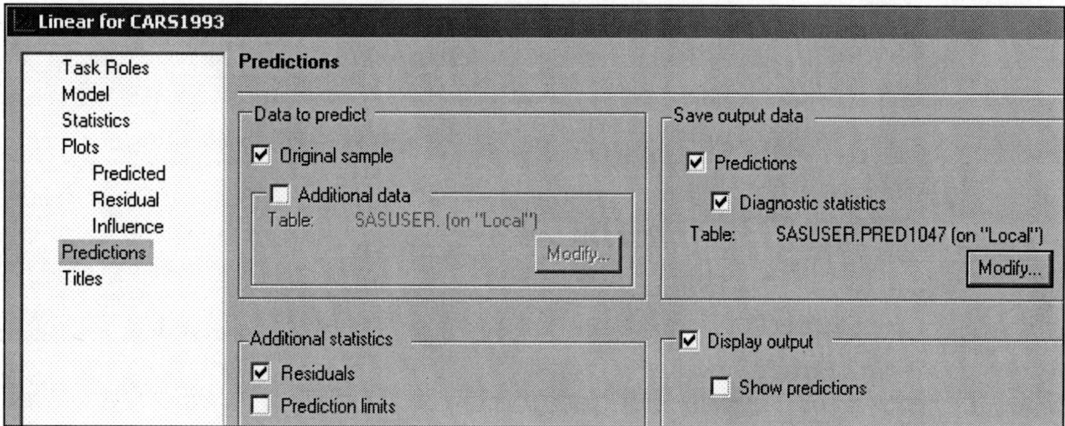

4) Select **Run**.

5) Investigate the contents of the new data table. Right-click and select **Properties**.

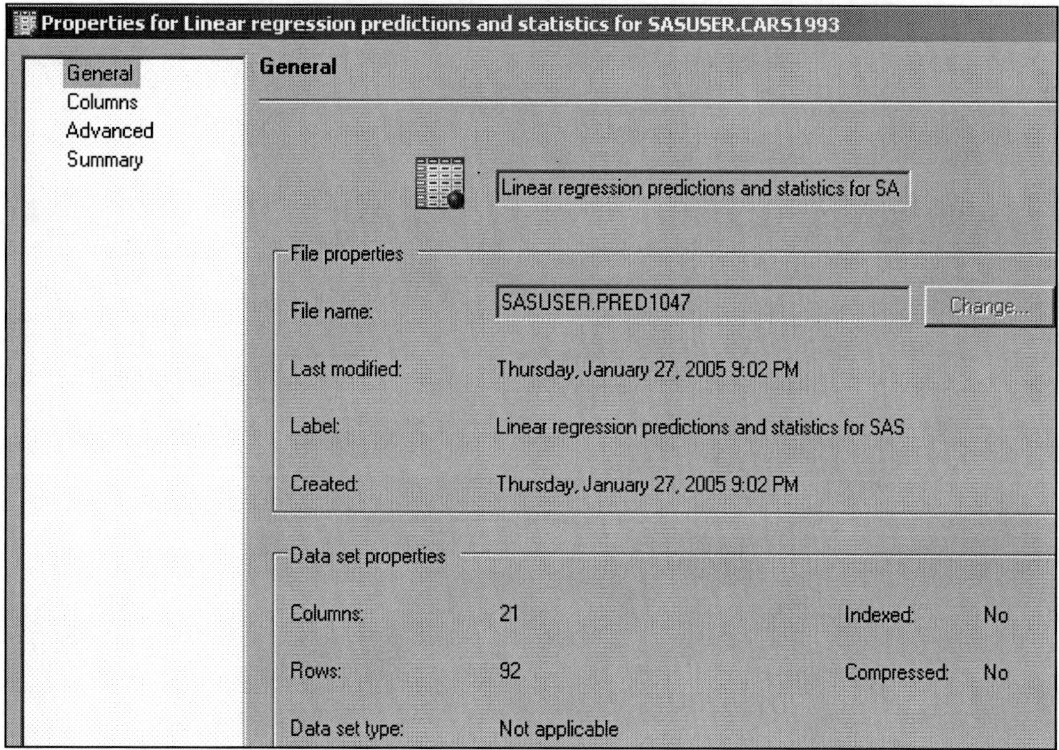

6) Select **Columns** to familiarize yourself with the statistics and their labels.

Columns

Name	Type	Length	Format	Informat	Label
MANUFAC	Character	14	$14.0	$12.0	
MODEL	Character	16	$16.0	$12.0	
MIDPRICE	Numeric	8	BEST12.0	F12.0	
CITYMPG	Numeric	8	BEST12.0	F12.0	
HWYMPG	Numeric	8	BEST12.0	F12.0	
EGNSIZE	Numeric	8	BEST12.0	F12.0	
HRSPOWER	Numeric	8	BEST12.0	F12.0	
RPM	Numeric	8	BEST12.0	F12.0	
REVLTNS	Numeric	8	BEST12.0	F12.0	
FUELTNK	Numeric	8	BEST12.0	F12.0	
WEIGHT	Numeric	8	BEST12.0	F12.0	
predicted_MIDPRICE	Numeric	8	BEST12.0	F12.0	Predicted Value of MIDPRICE
stdp_MIDPRICE	Numeric	8	BEST12.0	F12.0	Standard Error of Mean Predicted Value
residual_MIDPRICE	Numeric	8	BEST12.0	F12.0	Residual
stdr_MIDPRICE	Numeric	8	BEST12.0	F12.0	Standard Error of Residual
student_MIDPRICE	Numeric	8	BEST12.0	F12.0	Studentized Residual
cookd_MIDPRICE	Numeric	8	BEST12.0	F12.0	Cook's D Influence Statistic
h_MIDPRICE	Numeric	8	BEST12.0	F12.0	Leverage
rstudent_MIDPRICE	Numeric	8	BEST12.0	F12.0	Studentized Residual without Current Obs
dffits_MIDPRICE	Numeric	8	BEST12.0	F12.0	Standard Influence on Predicted Value
stdi_MIDPRICE	Numeric	8	BEST12.0	F12.0	Standard Error of Individual Prediction

7) To insert the program **influential_cars.sas**, select **Open ⇨ From My Computer**.

influential_cars.sas

```
/****************************************/
/* inserted code: influential_cars.sas    */
/****************************************/

/*   set the values of these macro variables,
     based on your model.
*/
%let numparms = 5; /* # of predictor variables + 1 */
%let numobs = 92;  /* # of observations */

data influential;
/* Below is a reference to the data set that SAS
   Enterprise Guide created with the diagnostic
   statistics. You should change this to your
   data set name, if it is different. */
   set SASUSER.PREDXXXX;

   cutdifts = 2*(sqrt(&numparms/&numobs));
   cutcookd = 4/&numobs;

/* You should also change the names of the
   dependent variable names used below from
       xxxxxx_Midprice    --to--
       xxxxxx_Your_Dependent_Variable_Name
   if you use this program outside of class.
*/ rstud_i = (abs(rstudent_Midprice)>3);
   dfits_i = (abs(dffits_Midprice)>cutdifts);
   cookd_i = (cookd_Midprice>cutcookd);
   sum_i = rstud_i + dfits_i + cookd_i;
   if sum_i > 0;
run;
```

8) You must make only one change in **influential_cars.sas**, the name of your prediction data table.

9) Change the XXXX found in the SAS statement **set SASUSER.PREDXXXX** to the name of your prediction table. In the current example, XXXX is changed to 1047. The changed statement now reads

set SASUSER.PRED1047

```
data influential;
/* Below is a reference to the data set that SAS
   Enterprise Guide created with the diagnostic
   statistics. You should change this to your
   data set name, if it is different. */
   set SASUSER.PRED1047;
```

10) Right-click in the window and select **Run on Local**.

11) The data table **INFLUENTIAL** has seven rows and displays only the observations that exceed one or more of the cutoffs.

Only a portion of the table **WORK.INFLUENTIAL** is displayed below.

WORK.INFLUENTIAL (read-only)

	MANUFAC	MODEL	MIDPRICE	CITYMPG	HWYMPG
1	Audi	100	37.7	19	26
2	Dodge	Stealth	25.8	18	24
3	Geo	Metro	8.4	46	50
4	Honda	Civic	12.1	42	46
5	Infiniti	Q45	47.9	17	22
6	Lincoln	Continental	34.3	17	26
7	Mercedes-Benz	190E	31.9	20	29

12) Hide all the columns between `MODEL` and `rstud_i`. Select **MIDPRICE** and SHIFT-click on **rstud_i**, ALT-click and select **Hide**.

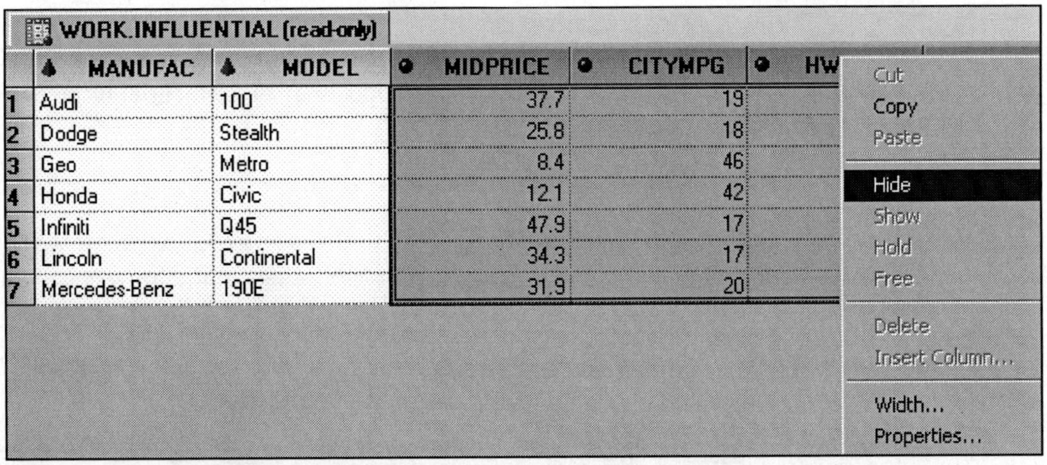

WORK.INFLUENTIAL (read-only)

	MANUFAC	MODEL	MIDPRICE	CITYMPG	HW
1	Audi	100	37.7	19	
2	Dodge	Stealth	25.8	18	
3	Geo	Metro	8.4	46	
4	Honda	Civic	12.1	42	
5	Infiniti	Q45	47.9	17	
6	Lincoln	Continental	34.3	17	
7	Mercedes-Benz	190E	31.9	20	

Cut
Copy
Paste
Hide
Show
Hold
Free
Delete
Insert Column...
Width...
Properties...

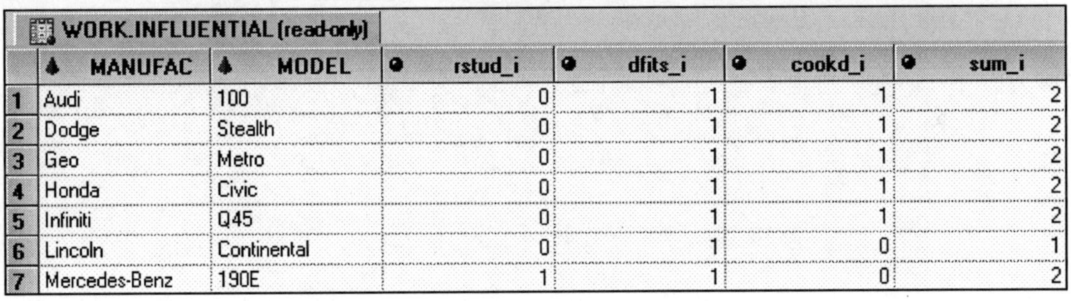

WORK.INFLUENTIAL (read-only)

	MANUFAC	MODEL	rstud_i	dfits_i	cookd_i	sum_i
1	Audi	100	0	1	1	2
2	Dodge	Stealth	0	1	1	2
3	Geo	Metro	0	1	1	2
4	Honda	Civic	0	1	1	2
5	Infiniti	Q45	0	1	1	2
6	Lincoln	Continental	0	1	0	1
7	Mercedes-Benz	190E	1	1	0	2

13) The `dfits_i` variable is one for all seven observations, indicating that the DFFITS statistic is greater than its cutoff. These observations may be influential if the model is to be used for predictive purposes.

14) The `cookd_i` variable is one for the first five observations, indicating that the Cook's D statistic is greater than its cutoff. These observations may be influential if the model is to be used for explanatory purposes.

15) The Mercedes-Benz 190E is an influential observation in regard to its studentized residual.

16) In summary, analysis of the output above reveals two basic **types** of cars that appear to be influential: most are luxury cars, such as the Mercedes-Benz, but a few are economy cars, such as the Geo Metro.

When you choose to close your current project, you receive the following SAS Enterprise Guide warning message:

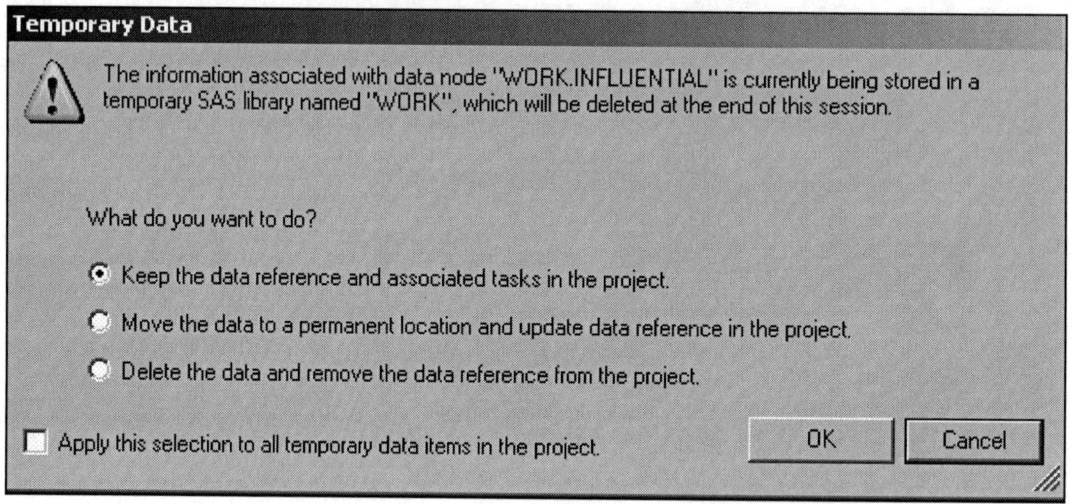

Select **Keep** to retain the data reference. If you close the project and come back to it, you would have to run this code again to see the resulting data table.

3. **Ascertaining Collinearity**

a. Use the Regression task to generate a model on the `CARS1993` data set. The variable `MIDPRICE` is the dependent variable and all the other numeric variables are independent variables.

1) Request collinearity statistics on this model.

a) Make sure the `CARS1993` data set is the active data source, and then select **Analyze** ⇨ **Regression** ⇨ **Linear…**.

b) Assign `MIDPRICE` to the Analysis variables role. Assign the other numeric variables in the data set to the Explanatory variables role.

c) Select Statistics on the left. Check the boxes next to Collinearity **analysis, Collinearity analysis without the intercept**, and **Variance inflation values**.

d) Select **Run**.

Full Model - 8 Explanatory Variables

The REG Procedure
Model: Linear_Regression_Model
Dependent Variable: MIDPRICE

Number of Observations Read	92
Number of Observations Used	92

Analysis of Variance					
Source	DF	Sum of Squares	Mean Square	F Value	Pr > F
Model	8	4846.75465	605.84433	26.18	<.0001
Error	83	1920.79524	23.14211		
Corrected Total	91	6767.54989			

Root MSE	4.81062	R-Square	0.7162
Dependent Mean	19.04891	Adj R-Sq	0.6888
Coeff Var	25.25406		

Parameter Estimates						
Variable	DF	Parameter Estimate	Standard Error	t Value	Pr > |t|	Variance Inflation
Intercept	1	-21.30023	13.86601	-1.54	0.1283	0
CITYMPG	1	-0.46278	0.33213	-1.39	0.1672	13.79500
HWYMPG	1	0.21335	0.30985	0.69	0.4930	10.77958
EGNSIZE	1	1.96681	1.54127	1.28	0.2055	10.13323
HRSPOWER	1	0.09518	0.02534	3.76	0.0003	6.84937
RPM	1	0.00125	0.00168	0.74	0.4598	4.00125
REVLTNS	1	0.00501	0.00199	2.52	0.0138	3.87621
FUELTNK	1	-0.09563	0.37077	-0.26	0.7971	5.85717
WEIGHT	1	0.00292	0.00261	1.12	0.2658	9.35541

Based on the VIFs for the variables in this full model, it appears collinearity does exist, with **`CITYMPG`**, **`HWYMPG`**, and **`EGNSIZE`** possibly involved in collinearity because their individual VIFs are all greater than the cutoff of 10.

Collinearity Diagnostics

Number	Eigenvalue	Condition Index	Proportion of Variation								
			Intercept	CITYMPG	HWYMPG	EGNSIZE	HRSPOWER	RPM	REVLTNS	FUELTNK	WEIGHT
1	8.56748	1.00000	0.00001775	0.00005398	0.00003896	0.00015826	0.00021121	0.00004222	0.00014346	0.00008444	0.00005034
2	0.34165	5.00766	0.00002040	0.00242	0.00092131	0.00981	0.00891	0.00021349	0.00447	0.00086107	0.00057418
3	0.04238	14.21803	0.00010723	0.00597	0.00440	0.10287	0.14274	0.00911	0.01386	0.00006764	0.00054570
4	0.02959	17.01556	0.00094549	0.01676	0.00979	0.01302	0.14581	0.00012552	0.04576	0.04919	0.01662
5	0.00825	32.22765	0.00488	0.00056451	0.01389	0.21469	0.03055	0.04123	0.75147	0.02732	0.03674
6	0.00453	43.50895	0.03842	0.10194	0.01032	0.16026	0.12733	0.16212	0.00664	0.56496	0.01328
7	0.00314	52.20546	0.00151	0.09013	0.01363	0.19335	0.12317	0.14514	0.01017	0.33940	0.63917
8	0.00206	64.55296	0.01999	0.67656	0.69449	0.12445	0.10002	0.18080	0.04987	0.01478	0.00292
9	0.00091723	96.64673	0.93411	0.10559	0.25253	0.18141	0.32126	0.46122	0.11761	0.00334	0.29009

The largest condition index in the Collinearity Diagnostics table (96.64673) indicates moderate to strong collinearity. You decide that value is considered unacceptable, based on your subject matter knowledge. Examining the Proportion of Variation columns associated with the largest condition index reveals that the intercept (0.93411) is involved in collinearity.

2) Because the intercept is involved in collinearity, find the results table entitled Collinearity Diagnostics (intercept adjusted). Examine closely the last line of the Collinearity Diagnostics (intercept adjusted) and notice that **CITYMPG** (0.90626) and **HWYMPG** (0.81460) are collinear.

Collinearity Diagnostics (ir					
Number	Eigenvalue	Condition Index	CITYMPG	HWYMPG	EGNSIZE
1	5.65062	1.00000	0.00191	0.00218	0.00252
2	1.08877	2.27814	0.00056273	0.00157	0.00228
3	0.59825	3.07332	0.01721	0.04653	0.02786
4	0.32062	4.19809	0.02442	0.02101	0.00969
5	0.15553	6.02764	0.00796	0.02836	0.06053
6	0.08466	8.16953	0.03582	0.00864	0.00365
7	0.05925	9.76544	0.00586	0.07711	0.86581
8	0.04229	11.55856	0.90626	0.81460	0.02766

ntercept adjusted)				
Proportion of Variation				
HRSPOWER	RPM	REVLTNS	FUELTNK	WEIGHT
0.00280	0.00177	0.00554	0.00433	0.00304
0.02868	0.15485	0.01003	0.00259	0.00006437
0.04183	0.00513	0.07715	0.00730	0.00015755
0.00275	0.02437	0.30840	0.15850	0.02322
0.19789	0.12978	0.38994	0.28363	0.03776
0.01637	0.02221	0.01514	0.49895	0.85564
0.63997	0.61231	0.03598	0.00109	0.02267
0.06970	0.04957	0.15782	0.04361	0.05744

Return to the Parameter Estimates table, and observe:

Variable	p-value	Variance Inflation (VIF)
`CITYMPG`	0.1672	13.79500
`HWYMPG`	0.4930	10.77958

`HWYMPG` has a larger *p*-value than **`CITYMPG`** but both variables have high variance inflation factors (VIFs).

Based on the statistical methods you have studied thus far, generate another model, but remove **`HWYMPG`**. For clarity, you may want to rename the current task in the process flow.

a) Re-open the Linear Regression task from the previous portion of the exercise.

b) On the **Task Roles** pane, select **HWYMPG** and remove it as an explanatory variable.

c) Select **Finish** and **No** to retain the results of the previous run.

Reduced Model - 7 Explanatory Variables - Removed Hwympg

The REG Procedure
Model: Linear_Regression_Model
Dependent Variable: MIDPRICE

Number of Observations Read	92
Number of Observations Used	92

Analysis of Variance

Source	DF	Sum of Squares	Mean Square	F Value	Pr > F
Model	7	4835.78252	690.82607	30.04	<.0001
Error	84	1931.76738	22.99723		
Corrected Total	91	6767.54989			

Based on the Variance Inflations for the variables in this reduced model, it appears collinearity does exist with **EGNSIZE** (VIF=10.04317) and possibly **WEIGHT** (VIF=8.89700).

Parameter Estimates						
Variable	DF	Parameter Estimate	Standard Error	t Value	Pr > |t|	Variance Inflation
Intercept	1	-17.69884	12.80148	-1.38	0.1705	0
CITYMPG	1	-0.27318	0.18511	-1.48	0.1438	4.31235
EGNSIZE	1	2.06686	1.52960	1.35	0.1802	10.04317
HRSPOWER	1	0.09582	0.02524	3.80	0.0003	6.84018
RPM	1	0.00124	0.00168	0.74	0.4624	4.00087
REVLTNS	1	0.00472	0.00194	2.43	0.0171	3.70630
FUELTNK	1	-0.09824	0.36959	-0.27	0.7910	5.85656
WEIGHT	1	0.00253	0.00254	1.00	0.3223	8.89700

Examine the Collinearity Diagnostics table to determine the strength of the collinearity.

Collinearity Diagnostics											
			Proportion of Variation								
Number	Eigenvalue	Condition Index	Intercept	CITYMPG	EGNSIZE	HRSPOWER	RPM	REVLTNS	FUELTNK	WEIGHT
1	7.61605	1.00000	0.00002612	0.00021510	0.00020476	0.00027108	0.00005320	0.00018792	0.00010759	0.00006743
2	0.30210	5.02100	0.00007627	0.01143	0.01113	0.00917	0.00046346	0.00766	0.00067031	0.00049675
3	0.03995	13.80774	0.00055015	0.01974	0.09259	0.21419	0.00799	0.00253	0.00101	0.00245
4	0.02542	17.31005	0.00032418	0.17086	0.05873	0.07367	0.00000799	0.03733	0.06339	0.01849
5	0.00784	31.15814	0.00879	0.05756	0.16307	0.03900	0.05858	0.84689	0.01110	0.03942
6	0.00445	41.35372	0.04200	0.59807	0.16037	0.11615	0.14065	0.02284	0.54309	0.00868
7	0.00311	49.46543	0.00118	0.09180	0.21365	0.13885	0.17198	0.02496	0.37842	0.68907
8	0.00107	84.35927	0.94706	0.05033	0.30025	0.40869	0.62027	0.05760	0.00221	0.24133

The largest condition index (84.35927) is less than 100, indicating moderate collinearity. The values on the last line of the Proportion of Variation columns indicate that the intercept (0.94706) and **RPM** (0.62027) are collinear. Because the intercept is involved, the Collinearity Diagnostics (intercept adjusted) table is used.

Collinearity Diagnostics (intercept adjusted)										
			Proportion of Variation							
Number	Eigenvalue	Condition Index	CITYMPG	EGNSIZE	HRSPOWER	RPM	REVLTNS	FUELTNK	WEIGHT
1	4.94069	1.00000	0.00745	0.00352	0.00373	0.00250	0.00798	0.00558	0.00417
2	1.07301	2.14582	0.00140	0.00112	0.03533	0.15661	0.00677	0.00330	0.00022938
3	0.43562	3.36776	0.07248	0.02392	0.02994	0.00748	0.22143	0.09707	0.01337
4	0.26828	4.29143	0.37285	0.06201	0.03654	0.03214	0.23332	0.03586	0.00489
5	0.14145	5.91010	0.35903	0.01946	0.18615	0.13785	0.39102	0.28337	0.04411
6	0.08382	7.67742	0.01982	0.01150	0.00706	0.01057	0.02931	0.55418	0.93114
7	0.05715	9.29827	0.16697	0.87847	0.70125	0.65287	0.11017	0.02063	0.00209

Based on the Proportion of Variation, **EGNSIZE** (0.87847), **HRSPOWER** (0.70125), and **RPM** (0.65287) are all involved in collinearity.

Returning to the Parameter Estimates table, you record the *p*-value and variance inflation factor for the three variables:

Variable	p-value	Variance Inflation (VIF)
EGNSIZE	0.1802	10.04317
HRSPOWER	0.0003	6.84018
RPM	0.4624	4.00087

It is clear that **HRSPOWER** should stay in the model. It is your decision as to whether to delete **EGNSIZE** (large variance inflation factor) or **RPM** (largest *p*-value) from the model.

Because **EGNSIZE** has a large VIF, you decide to remove this term from the model. You may want to rename the last linear regression node in the process flow.

d) Re-open the Linear Regression task.

e) Remove **EGNSIZE** from the model.

f) Select **Run** and **No**.

Reduced Model - 6 Explanatory Variables - Removed Hwympg, Engsize

The REG Procedure
Model: Linear_Regression_Model
Dependent Variable: MIDPRICE

Number of Observations Read	92
Number of Observations Used	92

Analysis of Variance

Source	DF	Sum of Squares	Mean Square	F Value	Pr > F
Model	6	4793.79294	798.96549	34.41	<.0001
Error	85	1973.75696	23.22067		
Corrected Total	91	6767.54989			

Root MSE	4.81878	R-Square	0.7083
Dependent Mean	19.04891	Adj R-Sq	0.6878
Coeff Var	25.29689		

Based on the Variance Inflations for the variables in this second reduced model, it does not appear that collinearity would be considered in this model, based on the VIFs. Notice that **WEIGHT** (VIF=8.63129) is still relatively close to the cutoff of 10.

Parameter Estimates						
Variable	DF	Parameter Estimate	Standard Error	t Value	Pr > |t|	Variance Inflation
Intercept	1	-9.54750	11.34573	-0.84	0.4024	0
CITYMPG	1	-0.20017	0.17791	-1.13	0.2637	3.94503
HRSPOWER	1	0.11778	0.01940	6.07	<.0001	4.00345
RPM	1	-0.00022801	0.00128	-0.18	0.8596	2.32607
REVLTNS	1	0.00362	0.00177	2.05	0.0438	3.05430
FUELTNK	1	-0.03453	0.36835	-0.09	0.9255	5.76125
WEIGHT	1	0.00312	0.00251	1.24	0.2177	8.63129

Examine the Collinearity Diagnostics table to determine the strength of the collinearity.

			Collinearity Diagnostics							
			Proportion of Variation							
Number	Eigenvalue	Condition Index	Intercept	CITYMPG	HRSPOWER	RPM	REVLTNS	FUELTNK	WEIGHT
1	6.72190	1.00000	0.00004323	0.00030759	0.00058441	0.00011859	0.00029844	0.00013912	0.00008829
2	0.22126	5.51186	0.00004223	0.01904	0.04404	0.00049266	0.01164	0.00248	0.00168
3	0.03058	14.82522	0.00186	0.01761	0.42508	0.01247	0.00015309	0.04620	0.02642
4	0.01539	20.89865	0.00258	0.40888	0.00016084	0.01463	0.43880	0.00207	0.00954
5	0.00583	33.95555	0.02627	0.20025	0.33555	0.54320	0.38389	0.03548	0.00129
6	0.00365	42.93686	0.02604	0.07935	0.03019	0.06185	0.16266	0.91265	0.37173
7	0.00140	69.40996	0.94315	0.27456	0.16439	0.36723	0.00256	0.00096836	0.58925

The largest condition index (69.40996) is less than 100, indicating moderate collinearity.

You could continue this process of eliminating one predictor variable at a time until the largest Condition Index falls below a specific value or the VIFs fall below their cutoff.

To complete the documentation of this process, rename the last linear regression node **`Reduce 2`**.

Chapter 5 Categorical Data Analysis

5.1 Describing Categorical Data

Objectives

- Recognize the differences between categorical data and continuous data.
- Identify a variable's scale of measurement.
- Examine the distribution of categorical variables.
- Do preliminary examinations of associations between variables.

3

Overview

	Type of Predictors		
Type of Response	**Categorical**	**Continuous**	**Categorical and Continuous**
Continuous	Analysis of Variance	Linear Regression	Analysis of Covariance (Regression with dummy variables)
Categorical	Logistic Regression or Contingency Tables	Logistic Regression	Logistic Regression

4

Categorical data analysis is concerned with categorical responses, regardless of whether the predictor variables are categorical or continuous. Categorical responses have a measurement scale consisting of a set of categories. *Continuous data analysis* is concerned with the analysis of continuous responses, regardless of whether the predictor variables are categorical or continuous.

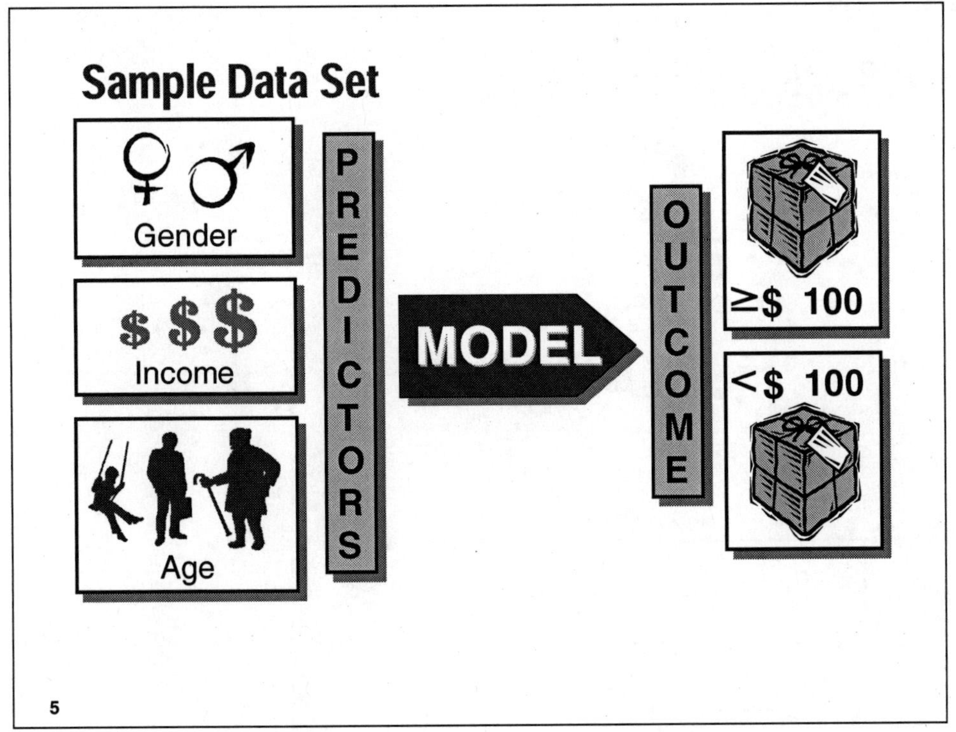

Example: A company that sells its products via a catalog wants to identify those customers to whom advertising efforts should be directed. It was decided that customers who spend 100 dollars or more are the target group. Based on the orders received over the last six months, the company wants to characterize this group of customers. The data is stored in the **CATALOGSALES** data set.

The variables in the data set are

purchase	purchase price (1=$100 or more, 0=under $100)
age	age of customer in years
gender	gender of customer (`Male`, `Female`)
income	annual income (`Low`, `Middle`, `High`).

✎ This is a hypothetical data set.

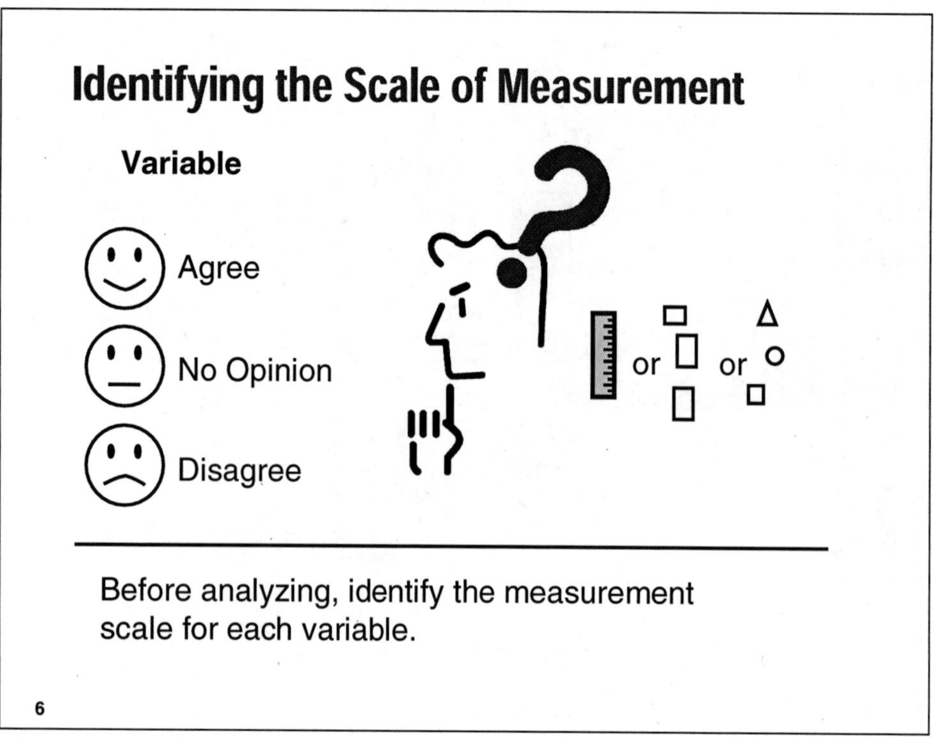

There are a variety of statistical methods for analyzing categorical data. To choose the appropriate method, you must determine the scale of measurement for your response variable.

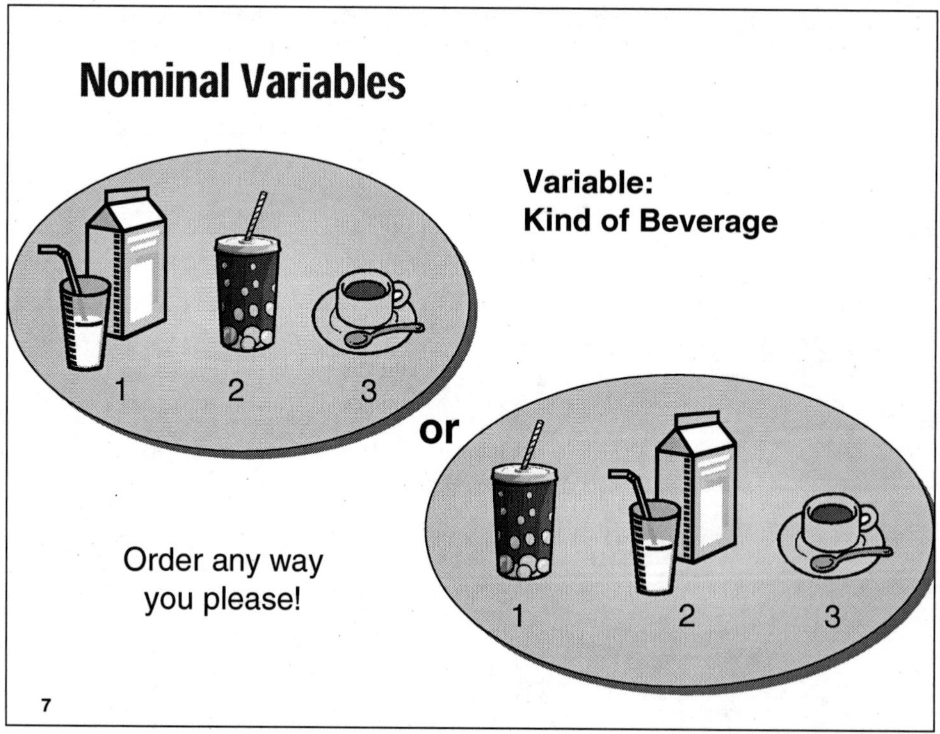

Nominal variables have values with no logical ordering. In the **CATALOGSALES** data set, **gender** is a nominal variable.

Ordinal Variables

Variable: Size of Beverage

Small Medium Large

8

Ordinal variables have values with a logical order. However, the relative distances between the values are not clear. In the **CATALOGSALES** data set, **income** is an ordinal variable.

After you choose the appropriate scale of measurement, you can describe the relationship between categorical variables with the use of frequency tables.

Examining Categorical Variables

By examining the distribution of categorical variables, you can

- screen for unusual data values
- determine the frequency of data values
- recognize possible associations among variables.

9

Association

- An association exists between two variables if the distribution of one variable changes when the level (or values) of the other variable change.
- If there is no association, the distribution of the first variable is the same regardless of the level of the other variable.

10

No Association

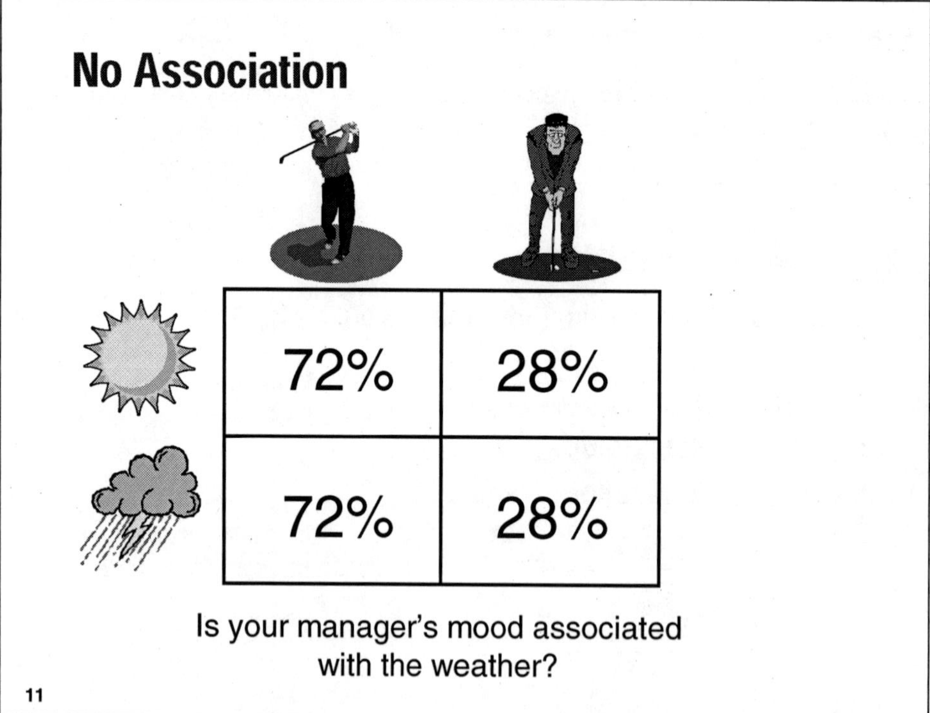

Is your manager's mood associated with the weather?

11

There appears to be no association here because the row percentages are the **same** in each column.

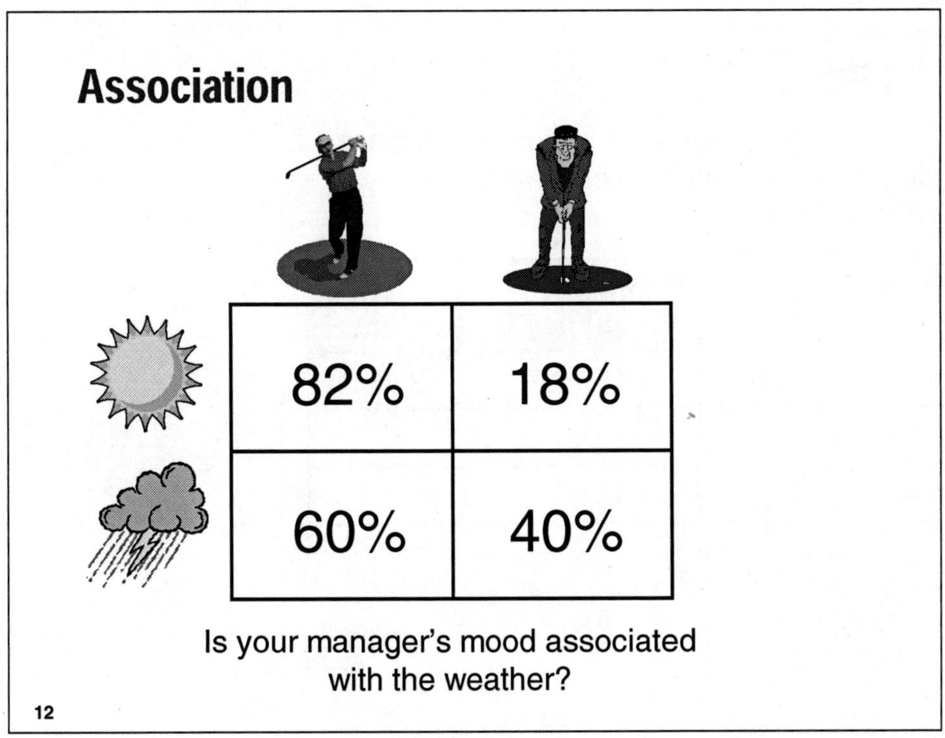

There appears to be an association here because the row percentages are **different** in each column.

Frequency Tables

A frequency table shows the number of observations that fall in certain categories or intervals. A one-way frequency table examines one variable.

Income	Frequency	Percent	Cumulative Frequency	Cumulative Percent
High	155	36	155	36
Low	132	31	287	67
Medium	144	33	431	100

13

Typically, there are four types of frequency measures included in a frequency table:

frequency — is the number of times the value appears in the data set.

percent — is 100 times the relative frequency. This represents the percent of the data that has this value.

cumulative frequency — accumulates the frequency of each of the values by adding the second frequency to the first and so on.

cumulative percent — accumulates the percent each value represents by adding the second percent to the first and so on.

Crosstabulations

A *crosstabulation* shows the number of observations for each combination of the row and column variables.

	column 1	column 2	...	column c
row 1	$cell_{11}$	$cell_{12}$	...	$cell_{1c}$
row 2	$cell_{21}$	$cell_{22}$	...	$cell_{2c}$
...	...	...	...	...
row r	$cell_{r1}$	$cell_{r2}$	...	$cell_{rc}$

14

The One-Way Frequencies Task

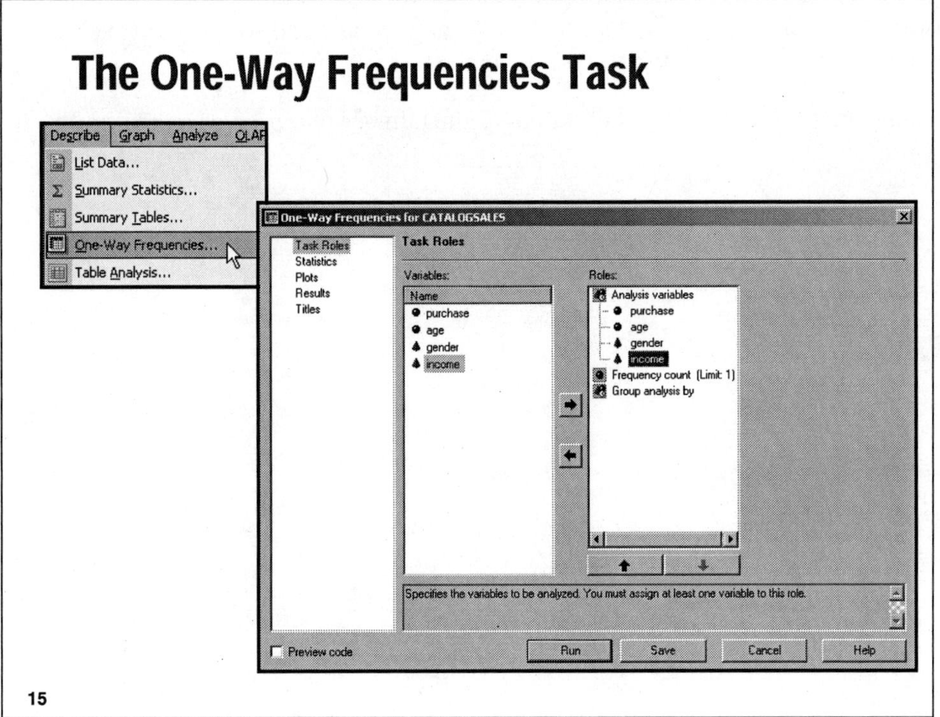

15

The One-Way Frequencies task calls the FREQ procedure to create one-way tables showing frequencies of observations at each level of an (usually categorical) analysis variable and to produce statistical tests.

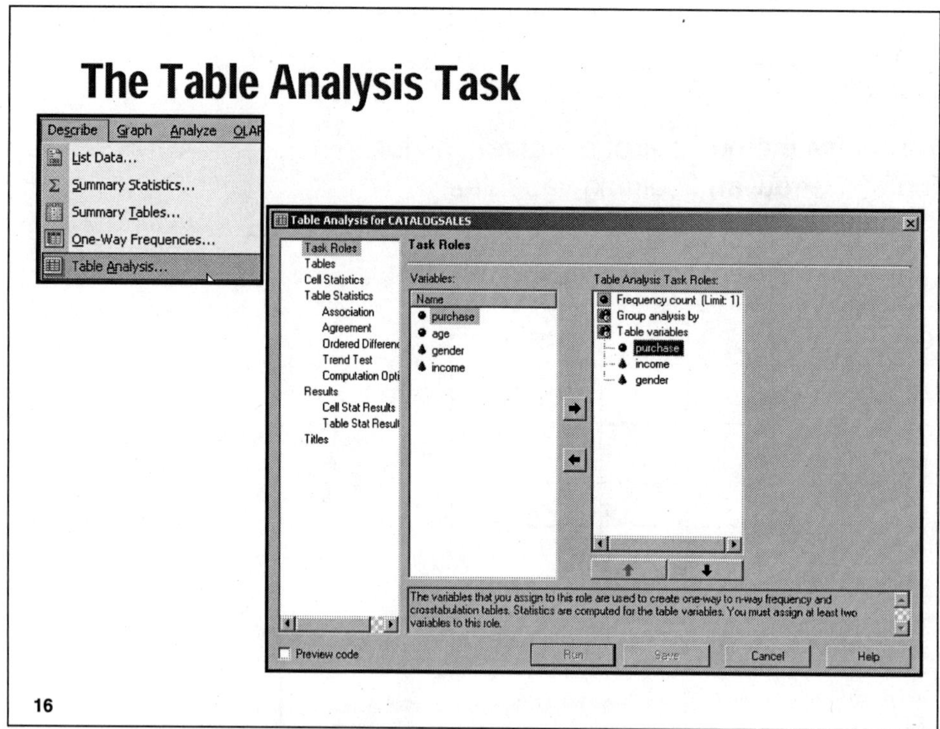

The Table Analysis task also calls the FREQ procedure but is designed for generating *n*-way frequency tables. A variety of statistical tests for association, expected frequency, trends, and so on are available in the task. You can specify more than one *n*-way table at a time in the task.

The Table Analysis task can generate large volumes of output as the number of variables increases.

Examining Distributions

Example: Examine the **CATALOGSALES** data.

1. Locate **CATALOGSALES** in the process flow.
2. Open **CATALOGSALES** by double-clicking on it.

CATALOGSALES (read-only)

	purchase	age	gender	income
1	0	41	Female	Low
2	0	47	Female	Low
3	1	41	Female	Low
4	1	39	Female	Low
5	0	32	Female	Low

The variable **age** is a continuous variable expressed as integers, **gender** is nominal with values of `Female` and `Male`, **income** has values of `Low`, `Medium`, and `High`, and **purchase** is coded with the values of `1` or `0`. To avoid confusion in the analyses, generate a SAS format for **purchase**; a 1 represents the customer who purchased over 100 dollars and a 0 represents the customer who purchased under 100 dollars.

Example: Use the Create Format task to create a format to apply to the values of **purchase**. Then use the One-Way Frequencies task to create one-way frequency tables for the variables **gender**, **age**, **income**, and **purchase**.

Create a format named **Purfmt.** that applies a label of $100 + when **purchase**=1, and a label of < $100 when **purchase**=0.

1. Select **Data** ⇨ **Create Format…**.

Formats are created independently of the data. You do not need to select a data set before you create a format.

2. Enter `Purfmt` as the **Format name**. Select **Numeric** because this format will be applied to a numeric variable. Select **WORK** as the library where you would like to save your format.

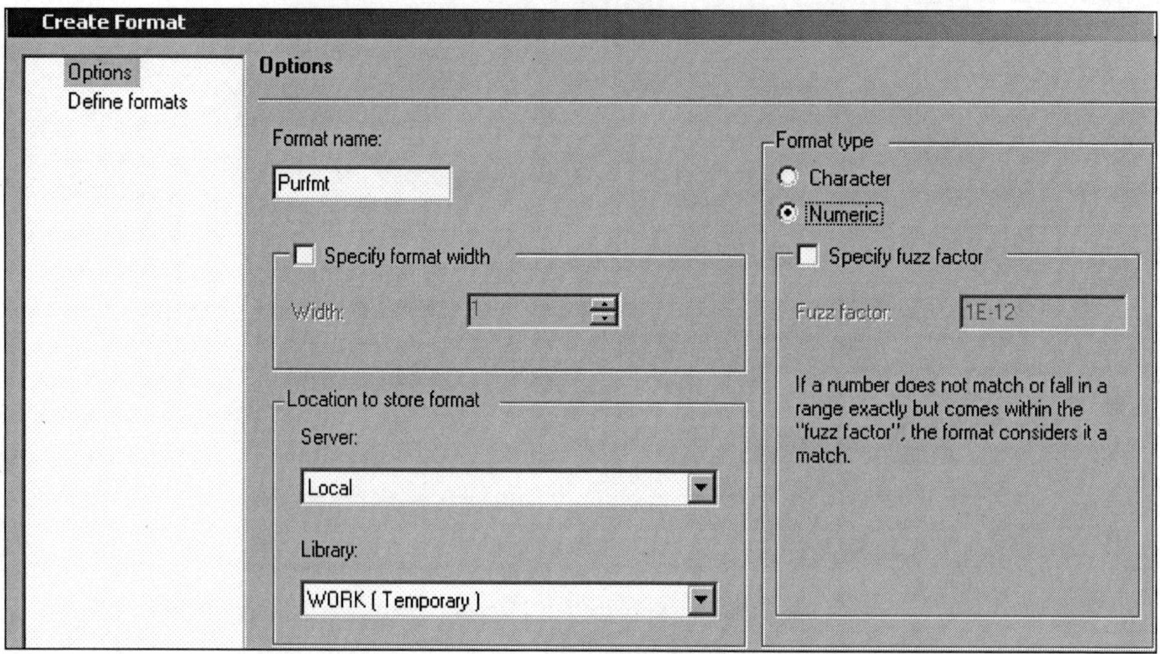

3. Select **Define formats** from the left pane.

4. To add the first label, select **New Label**. For the Label definition, enter `$100 +`. To specify the value for the label, select **New Range**. Enter `1` in Discrete Values as shown below.

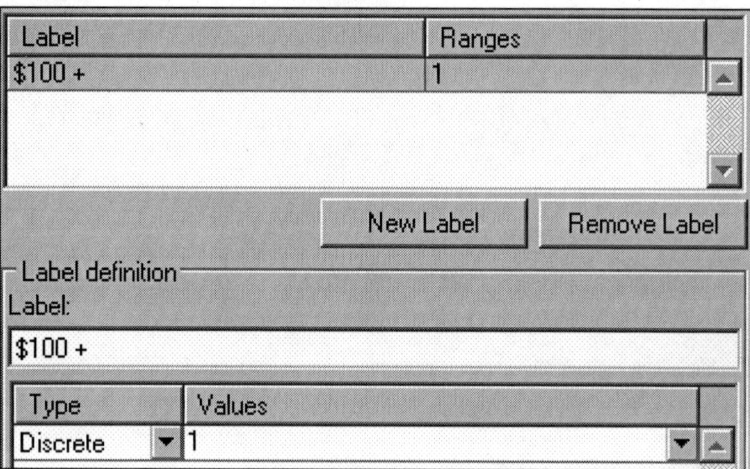

5. To add the second label, select **New Label**. In Label definition, enter `< $100`. To specify the value, select **New Range**. Enter `0` in Discrete Values.

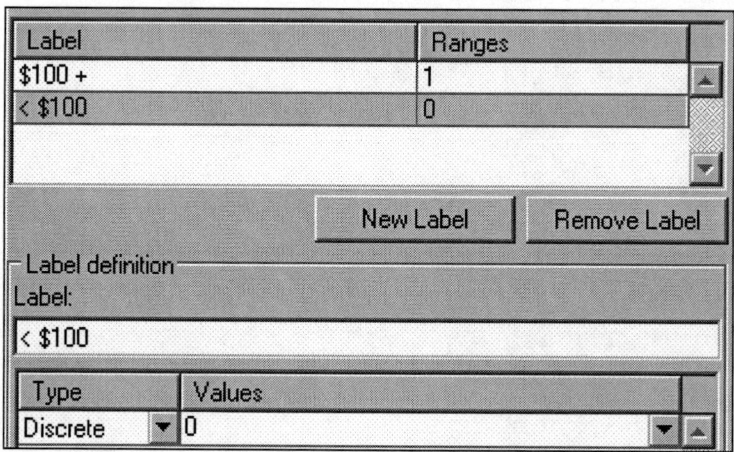

6. Select **Run**.

   SAS Enterprise Guide places a Create Format node at the bottom of the process flow. This node is not linked to any data sources because formats are stored and function independently of data.

Next, create the one-way frequency tables for `gender`, `age`, and `purchase`.

1. Locate and open the `CATALOGSALES` data table.
2. Select **Describe** ⇨ **One-way Frequencies**.
3. Assign `gender`, `age`, and `purchase` as the Analysis variables.
4. To assign the format you created, right-click on the variable `purchase`. Select **Properties**.

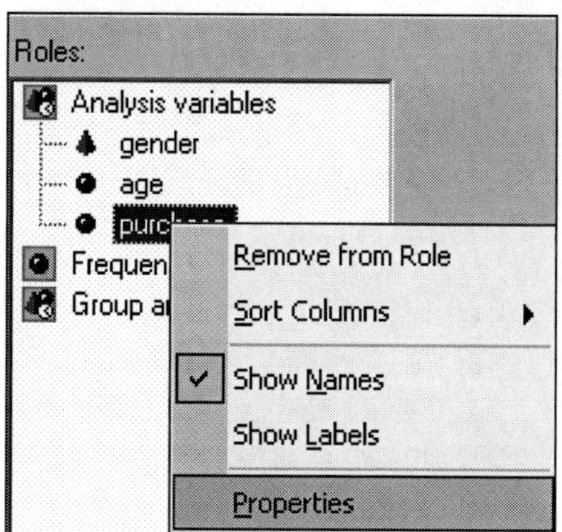

5. Select **Change…** next to the Format field to apply a format.

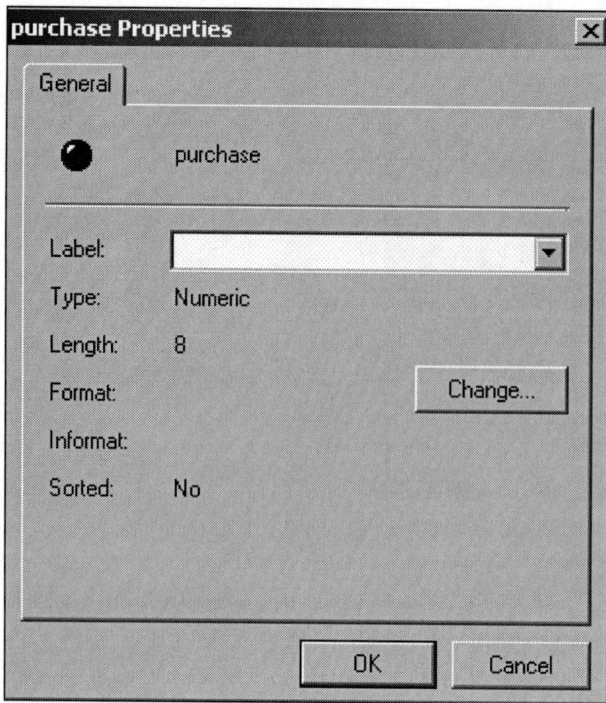

6. From the Categories list, select **User Defined**. Select **PURFMT** on the right.

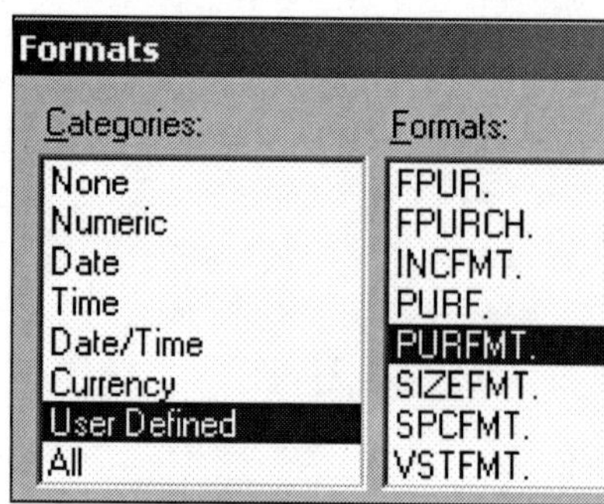

7. Select **OK** ⇨ **OK**.

8. Select **Run**.

One-Way Frequencies
Results

The FREQ Procedure

gender	Frequency	Percent	Cumulative Frequency	Cumulative Percent
Female	240	55.68	240	55.68
Male	191	44.32	431	100.00

age	Frequency	Percent	Cumulative Frequency	Cumulative Percent
23	1	0.23	1	0.23
24	1	0.23	2	0.46
25	2	0.46	4	0.93
26	5	1.16	9	2.09
28	3	0.70	12	2.78
29	6	1.39	18	4.18
30	6	1.39	24	5.57
31	11	2.55	35	8.12
32	11	2.55	46	10.67
33	25	5.80	71	16.47
34	23	5.34	94	21.81
35	28	6.50	122	28.31
36	19	4.41	141	32.71
37	29	6.73	170	39.44
38	37	8.58	207	48.03
39	30	6.96	237	54.99

40	31	7.19	268	62.18
41	35	8.12	303	70.30
42	19	4.41	322	74.71
43	18	4.18	340	78.89
44	19	4.41	359	83.29
45	17	3.94	376	87.24
46	12	2.78	388	90.02
47	13	3.02	401	93.04
48	8	1.86	409	94.90
49	7	1.62	416	96.52
50	5	1.16	421	97.68
51	4	0.93	425	98.61
52	2	0.46	427	99.07
55	2	0.46	429	99.54
56	1	0.23	430	99.77
58	1	0.23	431	100.00

purchase	Frequency	Percent	Cumulative Frequency	Cumulative Percent
< $100	269	62.41	269	62.41
$100 +	162	37.59	431	100.00

There seems to be no unusual data values that might be due to coding errors for any of the variables. Notice that **`purchase`** displays the formatted values.

Two-Way Tables

Example: Use the Table Analysis task to create two-way frequency tables for the variables **purchase** and **gender**, and **purchase** and **income**. Apply the **PURFMT.** format you created earlier to the variable **purchase**.

1. Select **Describe** ⇨ **Table Analysis…**.

2. Assign **income**, **gender**, and **purchase** as Table variables.

   ✎ You can also create simple one-way tables in the Table Analysis task.

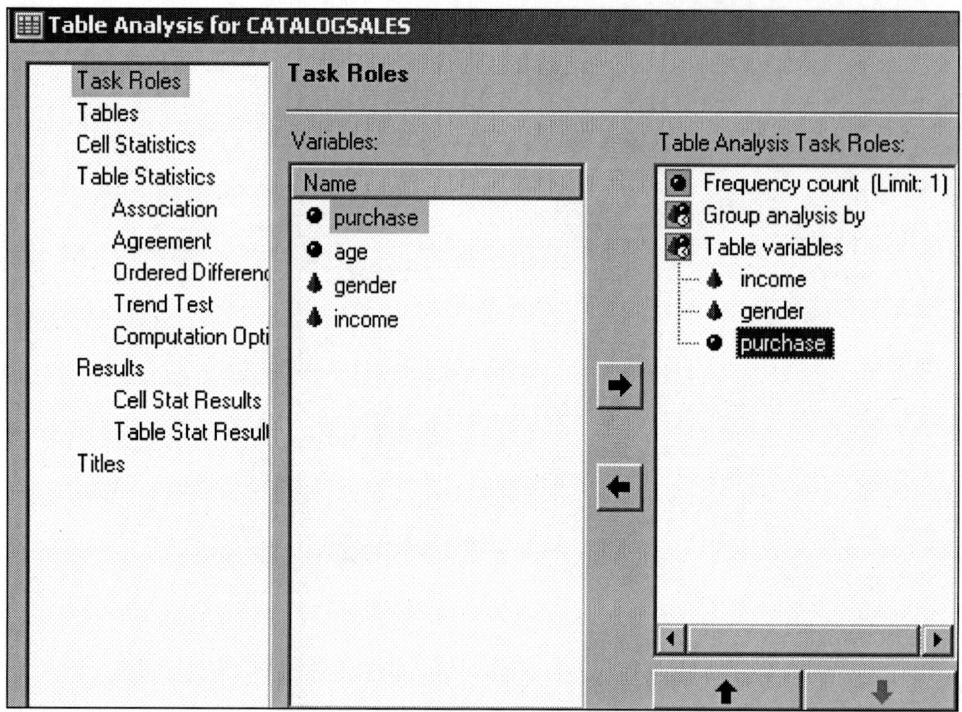

3. Assign the **PURFMT.** format to **purchase**. Right-click on the variable name **purchase**. Select **Properties**. Select **Change…** next to Format and apply the User Defined format **PURFMT.** to the **purchase** variable. Select **OK** ⇨ **OK**.

4. Select the **Tables** pane. Drag the variable `purchase` to the columns area of the Preview window.

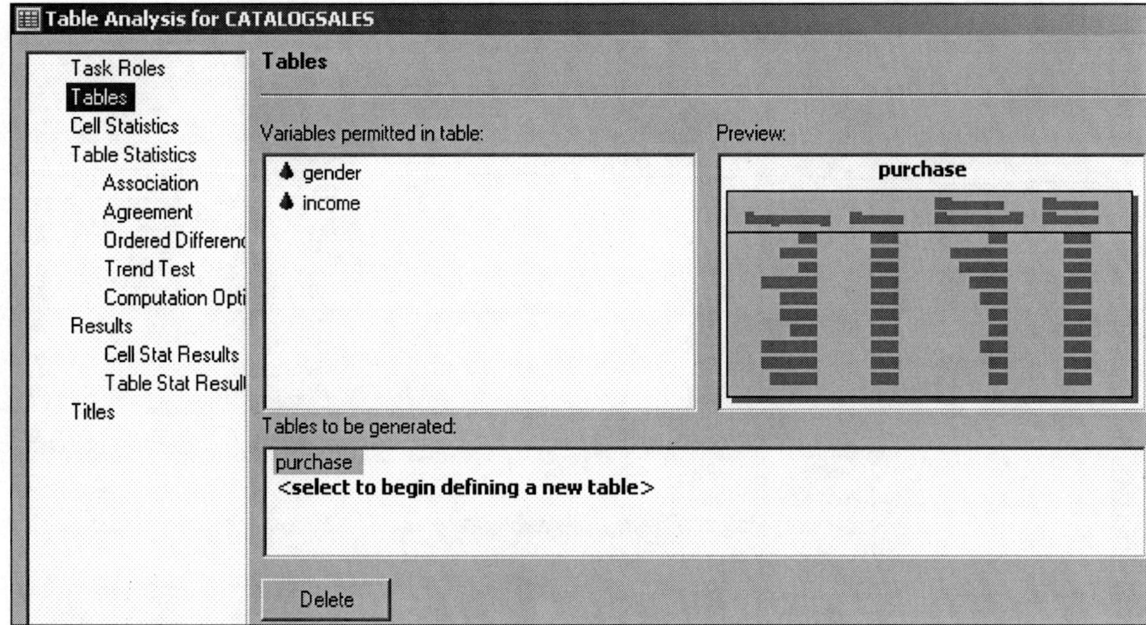

5. Drag the variable `gender` to the rows area of the Preview window.

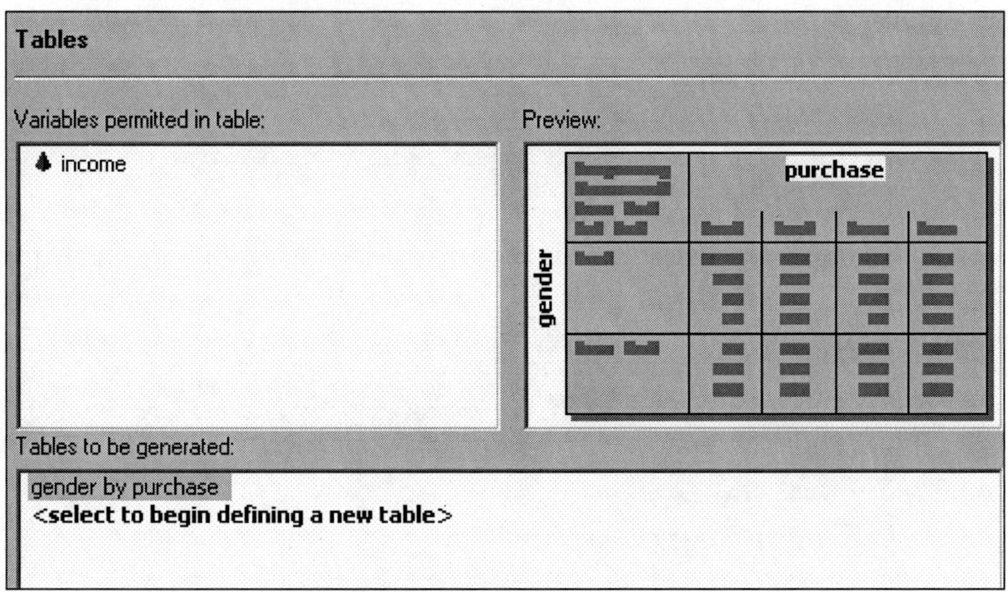

6. At the bottom, select **<select to begin defining a new table>**.

7. Drag and drop `purchase` to the rows and `income` to the columns.

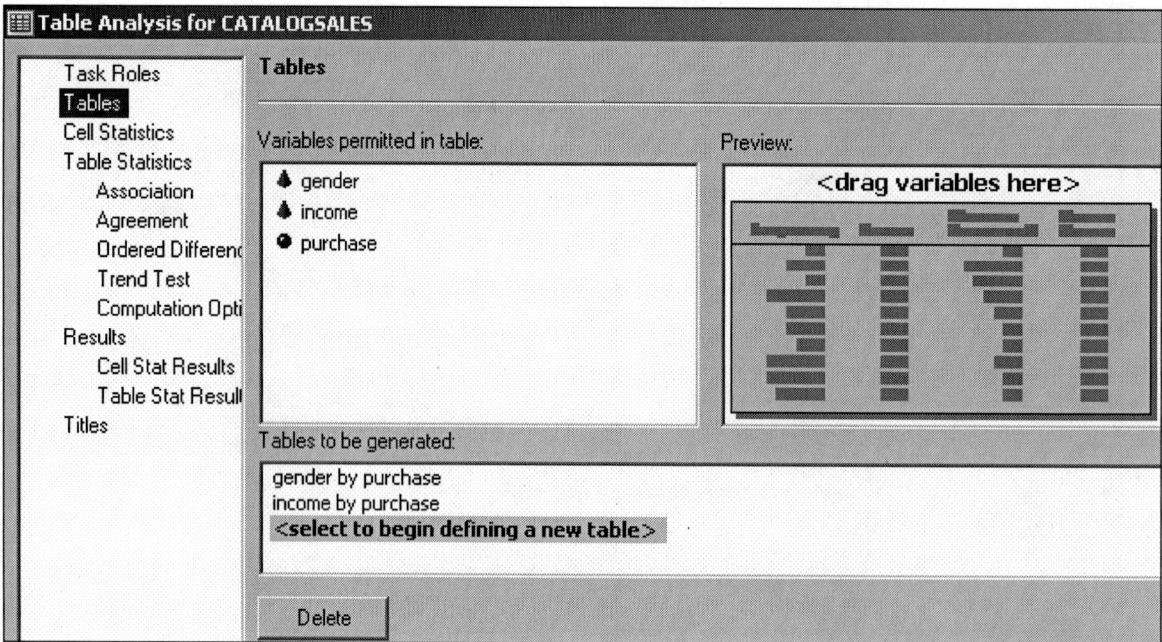

8. Select the **Cell Statistics** pane. Select **Row percentages**, **Column percentages**, **Cell frequencies**, and **Cell percentages**.

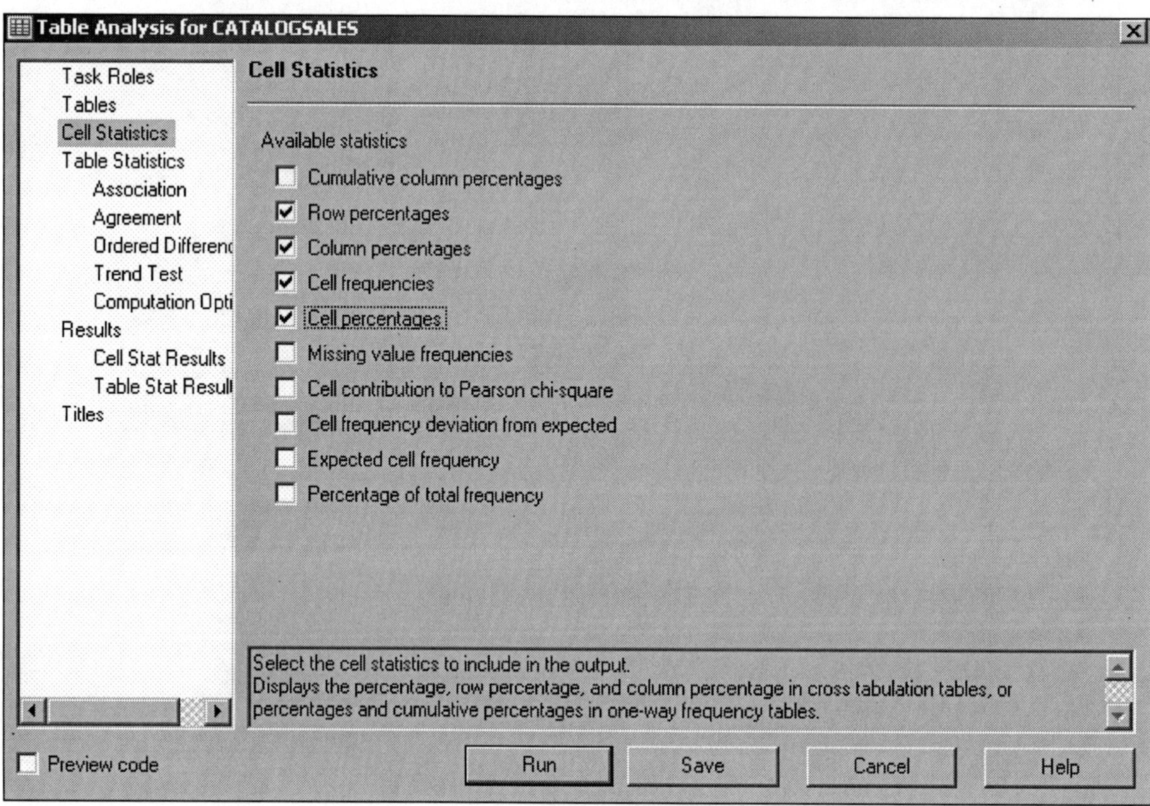

9. Select **Run**.

   The requested two-way frequency tables are shown below. You can get a preliminary idea whether there are associations between the outcome variable, `purchase`, and the predictor variables, `gender` and `income`, by examining the distribution of `purchase` for each value of the predictors.

   Examine the two tables in the results.

Table Analysis

Results

The FREQ Procedure

Frequency Percent Row Pct Col Pct	Table of gender by purchase		
	purchase		
gender	< $100	$100 +	Total
Female	139 32.25 57.92 51.67	101 23.43 42.08 62.35	240 55.68
Male	130 30.16 68.06 48.33	61 14.15 31.94 37.65	191 44.32
Total	269 62.41	162 37.59	431 100.00

By examining the row percentages, you see that `purchase` is associated with `gender` and `income`. For example, 48% of the high-income customers made purchases of 100 dollars or more compared to 32% of the low-income customers and 32% of the medium-income customers.

Frequency Percent Row Pct Col Pct	Table of income by purchase			
		purchase		
	income	< $100	$100 +	Total
	High	81 18.79 52.26 30.11	74 17.17 47.74 45.68	155 35.96
	Low	90 20.88 68.18 33.46	42 9.74 31.82 25.93	132 30.63
	Medium	98 22.74 68.06 36.43	46 10.67 31.94 28.40	144 33.41
	Total	269 62.41	162 37.59	431 100.00

When you examine the row percentages, it appears that **`income=Low`** (31.82%) and **`income=Medium`** (31.94) have approximately the same percentage of purchasing 100 dollars or more; **`income=High`** appears larger (47.74%).

Ordering Values

When you have an ordinal variable such as `income`, it is important to put the values in a logical order for analysis purposes.

Present Order	Logical Order
High	Low
Low	Medium
Medium	High

18

Treating an ordinal variable as nominal can reduce the power of your statistical tests. In other words, statistical tests detecting linear associations have more power than statistical tests detecting general associations.

Ordering Values in the Frequency Table

Example: Use a query to recode `income` as a variable called `inclevel` so that the sorted order corresponds to its logical order.

1. Select **Data** ⇨ **Filter and Query Active Data…**.

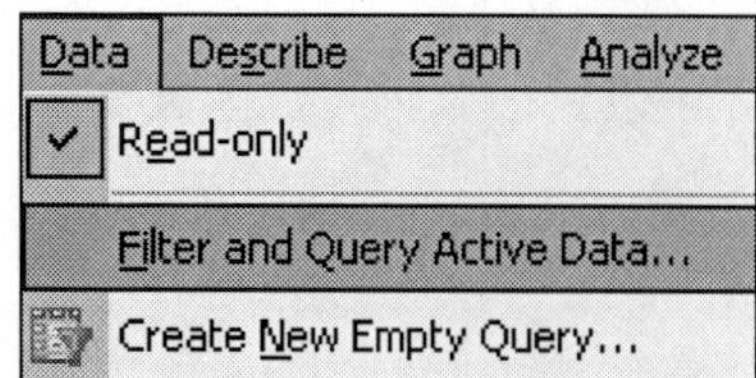

2. Select the Select and Sort tab. Select **income** and then select **Properties…**.

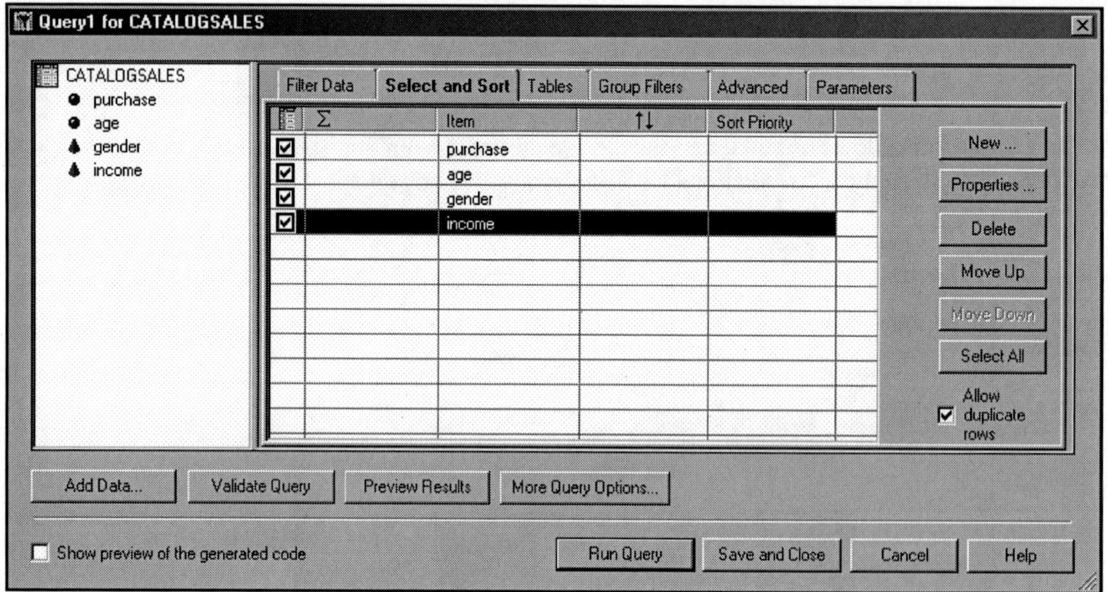

3. Rename the recoded variable by typing `inclevel` in the alias field.

4. Select the Replace Values tab.

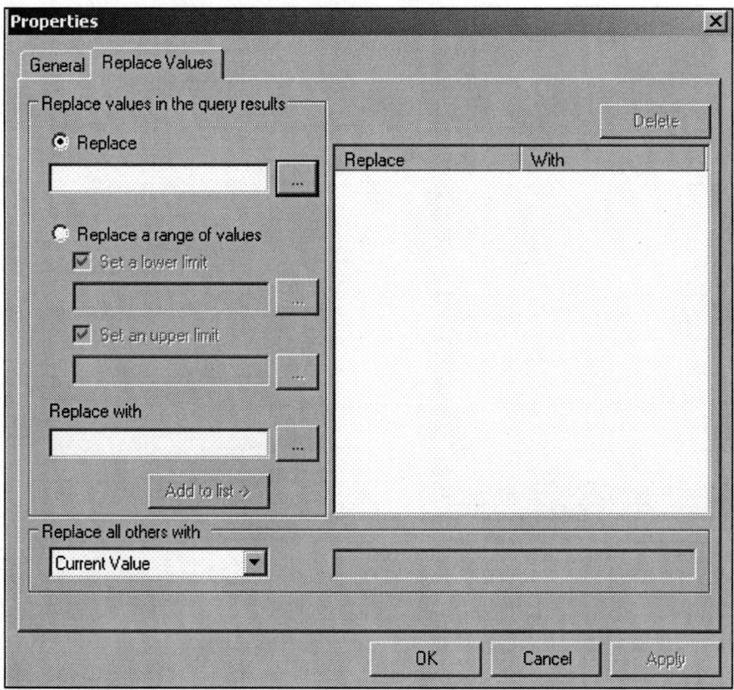

5. Next to the box under the **Replace** radio button, select **...** to get a list of values.

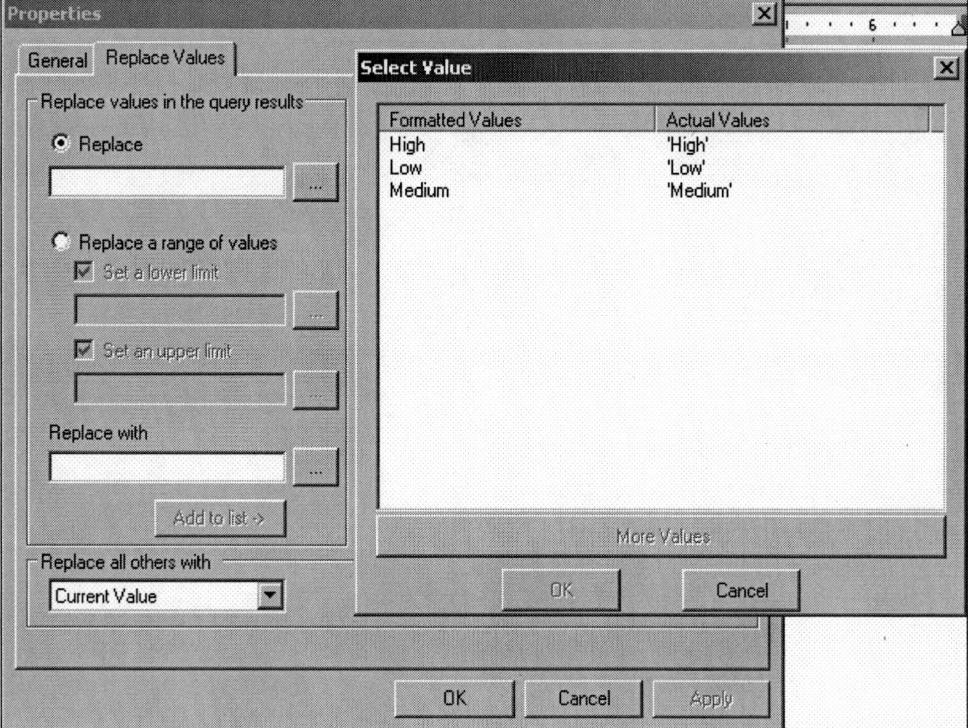

6. Select **Low** as the value to replace. Enter `1` under **Replace with.**

7. Select **Add to List->**.

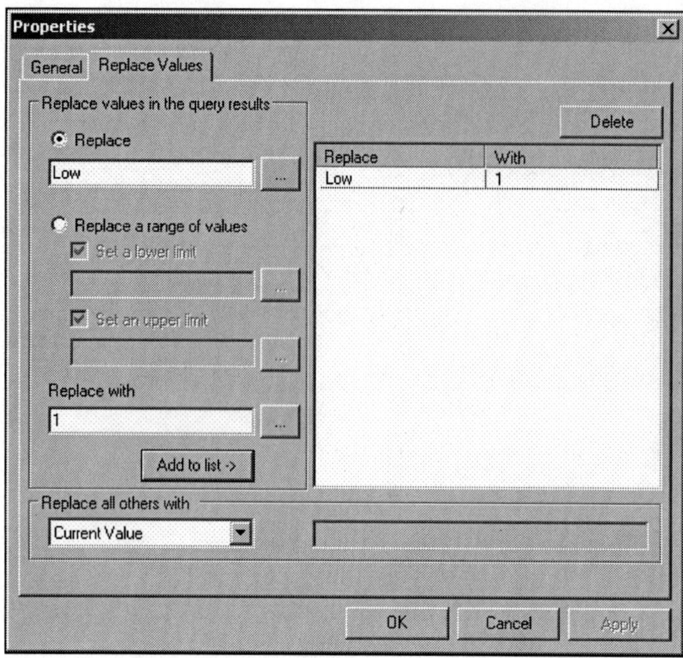

8. Select **...** next to the white box under **Replace**. Select **Medium** from the resulting list of values. Enter `2` in **Replace with.**

9. Select **Add to list->**.

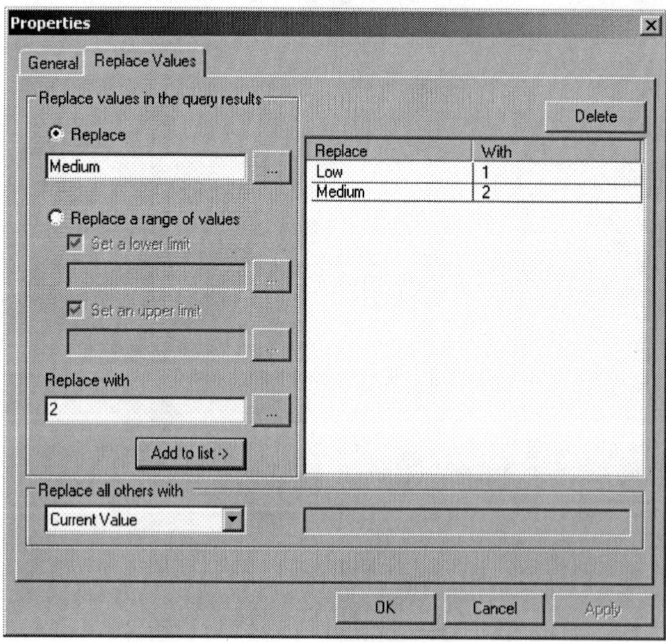

10. Select **...** next to the white box under **Replace**. Select **High** from the resulting list of values. Enter `3` in **Replace with.**

11. Select **Add to list->**.

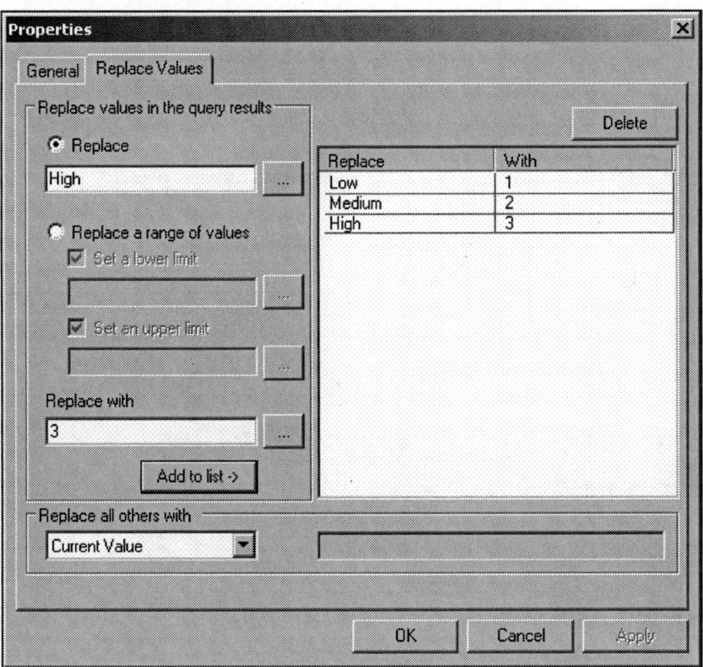

12. Change the **Replace all others with** option to **Missing Value**.

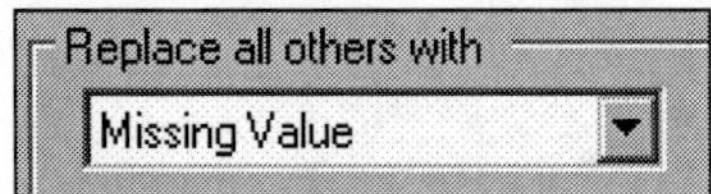

13. Select **OK**.

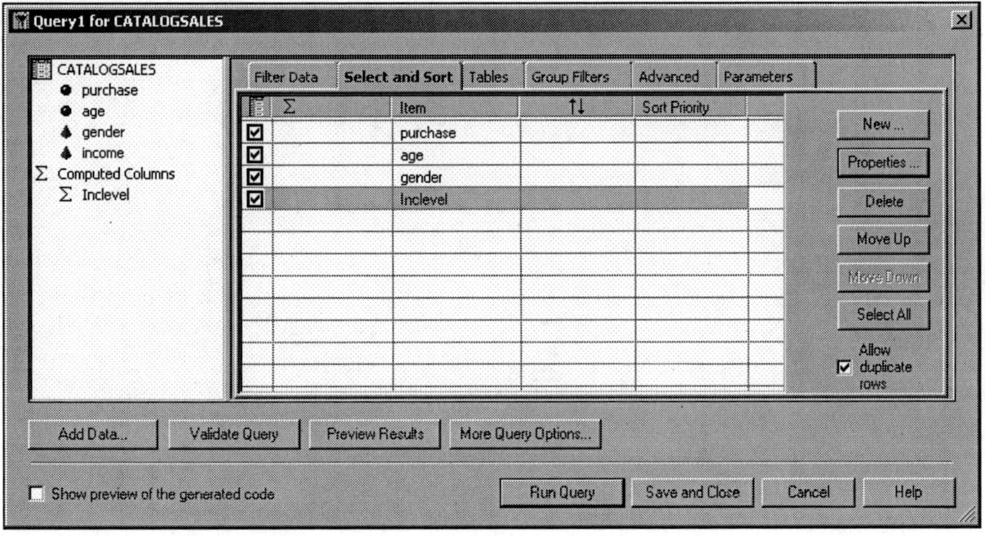

The original variable `income` is no longer in the item list.

14. Add the original variable `income` to `CATALOGSALES` by dragging it from the variable list on the left to the Select and Sort list of variables.

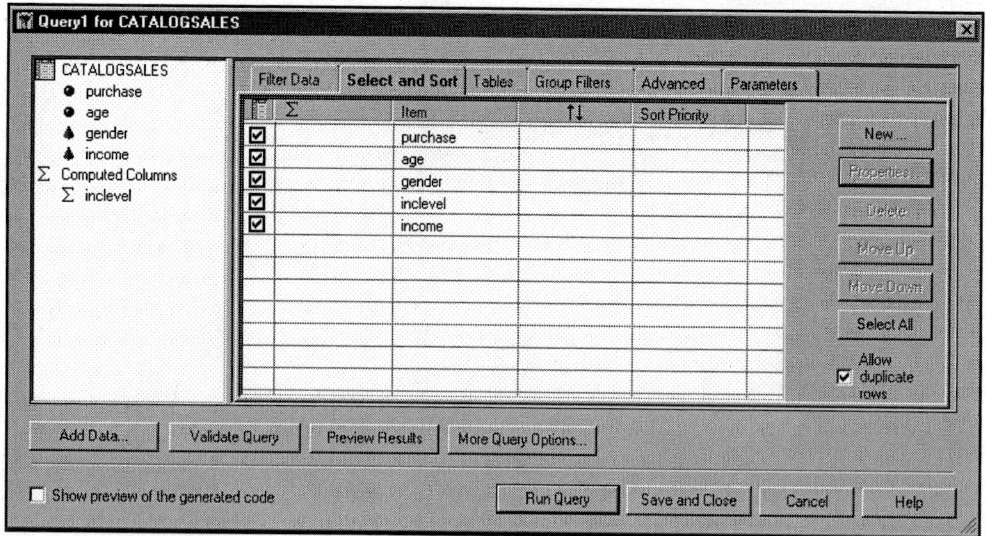

15. Select the Advanced tab. And select **Change...** to change the name of the data set.

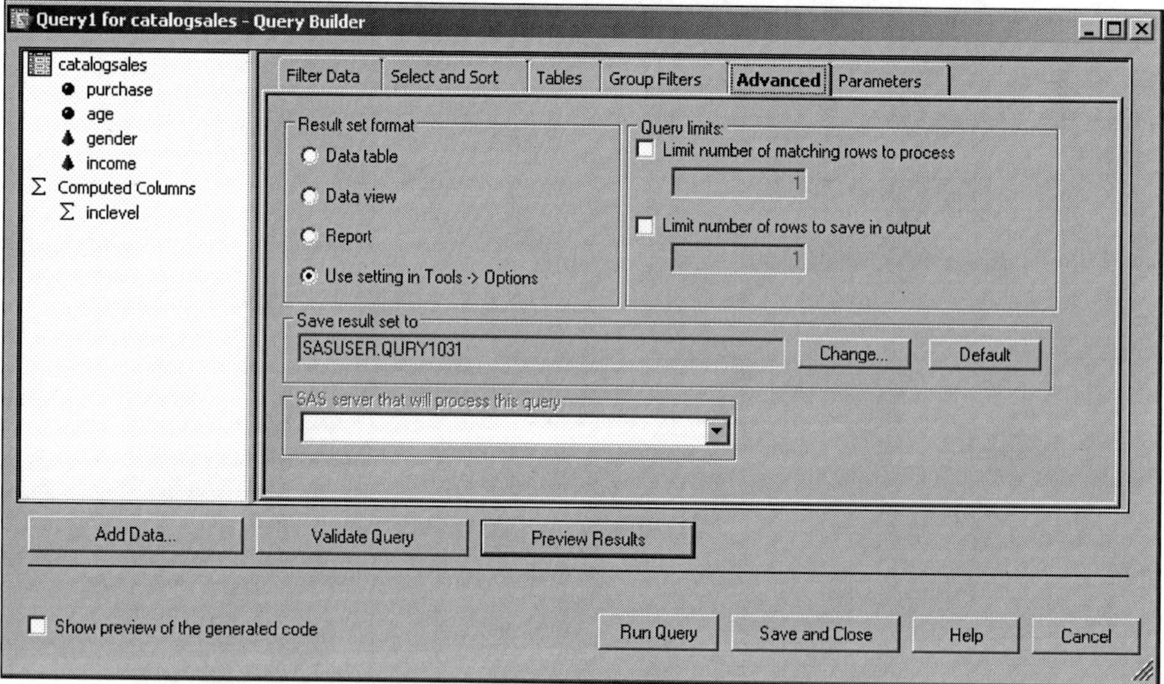

16. Leave the table in the SASUSER library, but change the name to **`catalogsalesinclevel`**.

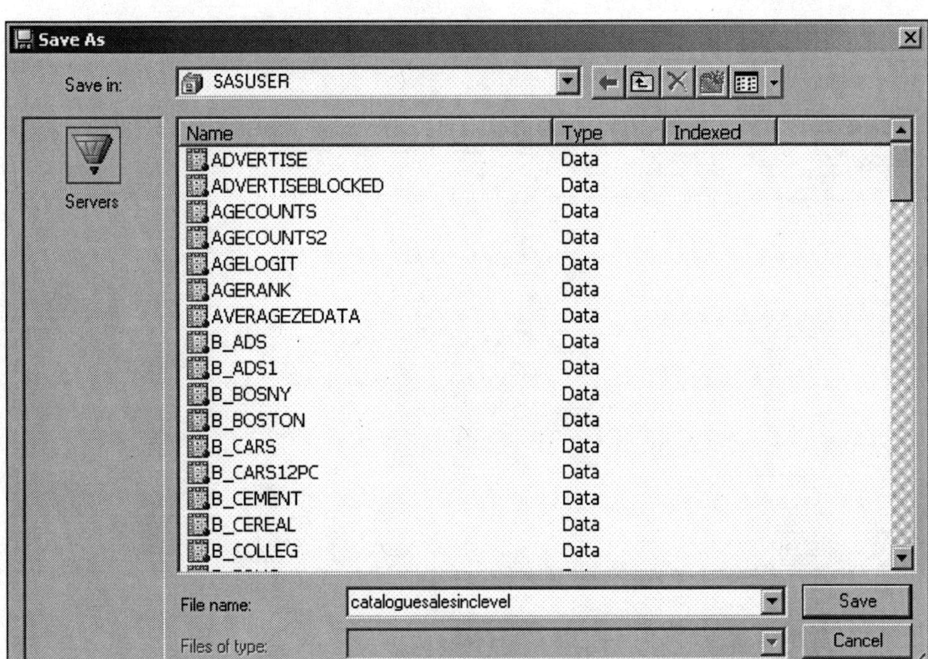

A new node is added to the project. You can specify whether you want query results to be views or data tables in **Tools** ⇨ **Options** or at the time that the query is created.

17. Select **Save** to change the name of the table.

18. Select **Run Query**.

A new node is added the process flow.

SASUSER.catalogsalesinclevel (read-only)

	purchase	age	gender	inclevel	income
1	0	41	Female	1	Low
2	0	47	Female	1	Low
3	1	41	Female	1	Low
4	1	39	Female	1	Low
5	0	32	Female	1	Low
6	0	32	Female	1	Low
7	0	33	Female	1	Low
8	0	45	Female	1	Low
9	0	43	Female	1	Low
10	0	40	Female	1	Low

A portion of the resulting table is shown above.

19. For clarity, you can change the query label to something more descriptive by right-clicking in the process flow and selecting **Rename**.

Next, create a format, **`incfmt.`**, to provide more descriptive values than the numeric values of the new variable **`inclevel`** in **CATALOGSALESINCOME**.

20. Select **Data** ⇨ **Create format**.

21. Enter `incfmt` as the **Format name**. Select **Numeric** as the **Format type** and specify that the format be saved in the WORK library.

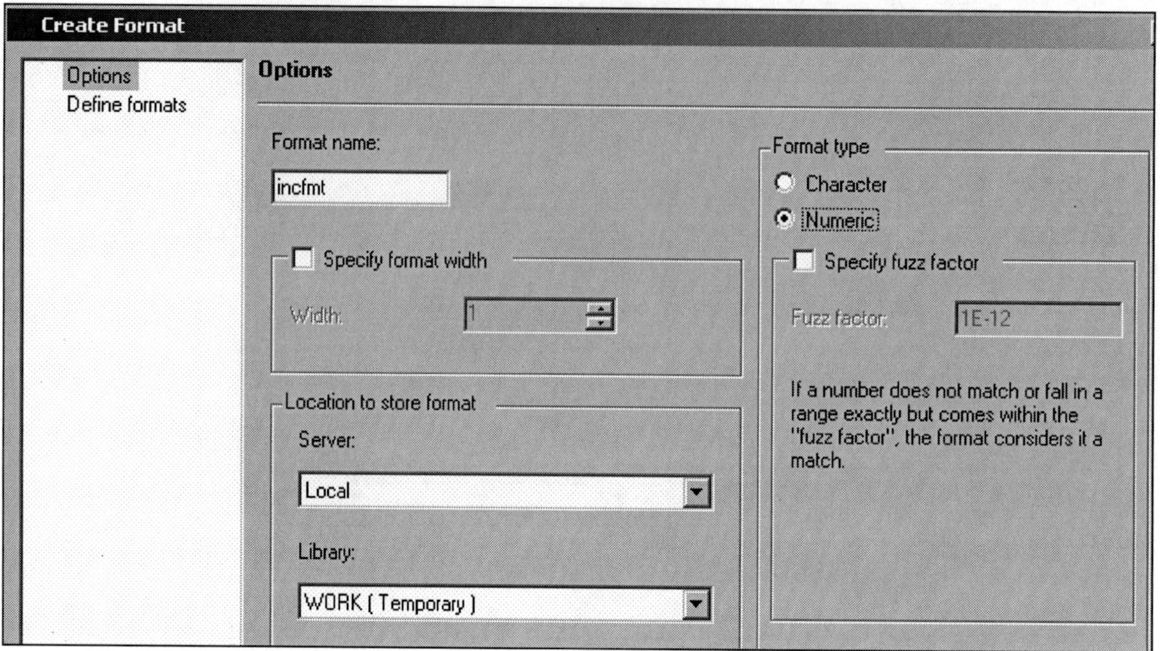

Saving a format in the WORK library saves it only for that session. It is deleted when you exit SAS Enterprise Guide. If you wish to use the format again, you must re-run the format task the next time you open SAS Enterprise Guide.

22. Select **Define formats**.

Create the Labels and Values for the new format `incfmt`.

23. Select **New Label**. Enter `Low Income` as the Label. Select **New Range**. Enter `1` as the Discrete Value.

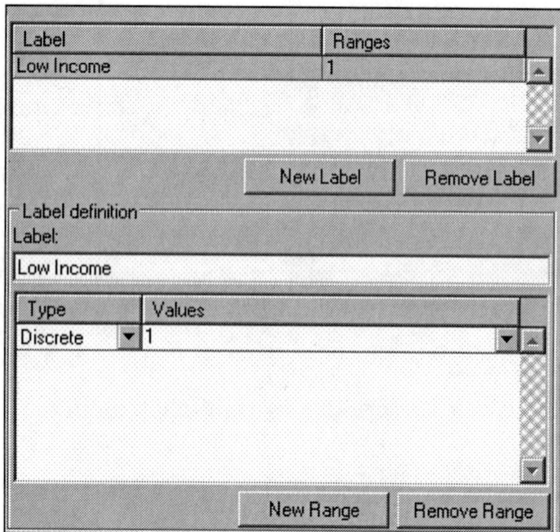

24. Complete the format definition for medium and high income. Your **Define Format** pane should appear as shown below:

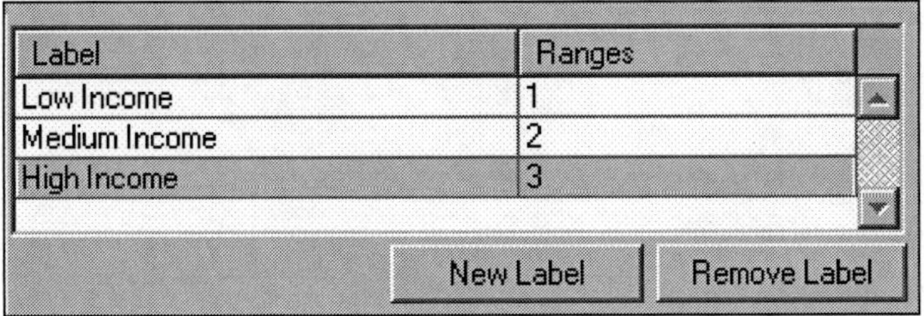

25. Select **Run**.

Create the two-way table of **`inclevel`** by **`purchase`**.

1. Select **Describe** ⇨ **Table Analysis**.
2. Assign **`purchase`** and **`inclevel`** to the Table variables role.
3. Right-click on **`purchase`**, select **Properties**, and apply **`PURFMT.`** from the list of formats.
4. Right-click on **`inclevel`**, select **Properties**, and apply **`INCFMT`**. from the list of formats.
5. Select and drag **`purchase`** to the columns area of the Table Preview window.
6. Select and drag **`inclevel`** to the rows area of the Table Preview window.

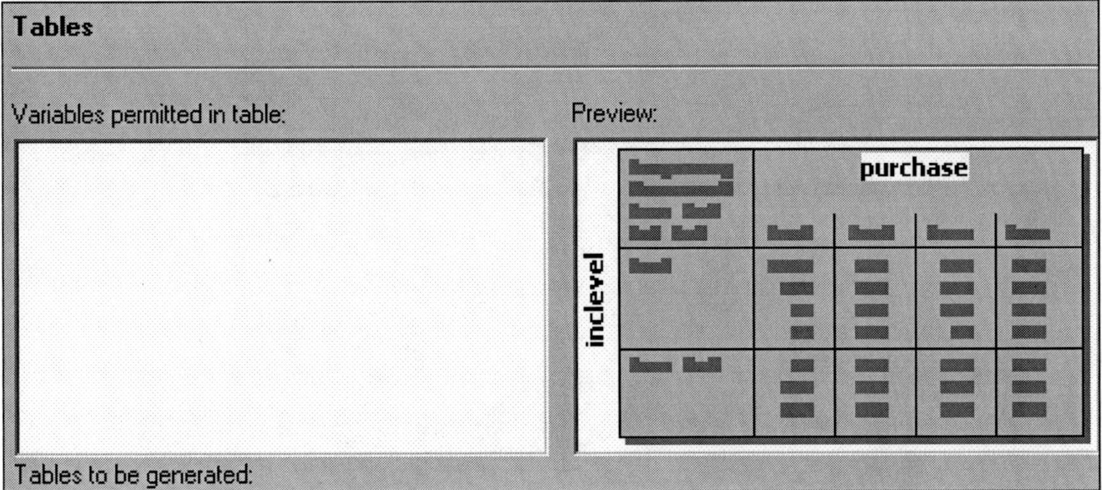

7. Select the Cell Statistics tab. Use the check boxes to select the statistics shown below:

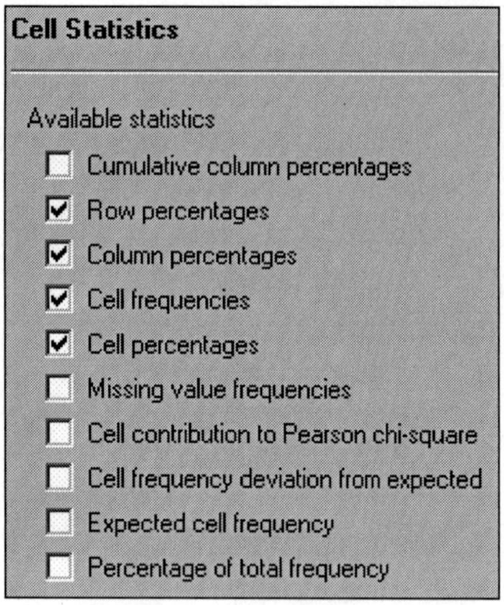

Cell Statistics

Available statistics

- [ ] Cumulative column percentages
- [x] Row percentages
- [x] Column percentages
- [x] Cell frequencies
- [x] Cell percentages
- [ ] Missing value frequencies
- [ ] Cell contribution to Pearson chi-square
- [ ] Cell frequency deviation from expected
- [ ] Expected cell frequency
- [ ] Percentage of total frequency

8. Select **Run**.

The crosstabulation of **inclevel** and **purchase** is shown below. The values of **inclevel** are now in a logical order.

Frequency Percent Row Pct Col Pct	Table of inclevel by purchase			
		purchase		
	inclevel	< $100	$100 +	Total
	Low Income	90 20.88 68.18 33.46	42 9.74 31.82 25.93	132 30.63
	Medium Income	98 22.74 68.06 36.43	46 10.67 31.94 28.40	144 33.41
	High Income	81 18.79 52.26 30.11	74 17.17 47.74 45.68	155 35.96
	Total	269 62.41	162 37.59	431 100.00

5.2 Tests of Association

Objectives

- Perform a chi-square test for association.
- Examine the strength of the association.
- Produce exact *p*-values for the chi-square test for association.
- Perform a Mantel-Haenszel chi-square test.

21

Introduction

purchase

gender		< $100	$100 +
	Female	0.58	0.42
	Male	0.68	0.32

Row probabilities of `gender` by `purchase`

22

There appears to be an association between **`gender`** and **`purchase`** because the row probabilities are different in each column. To test for this association, you assess whether the probability of females purchasing items of 100 dollars or more (0.42) is significantly different from the probability of males purchasing items of 100 dollars or more (0.32).

Null Hypothesis

- There is no association between `gender` and `purchase`.
- The probability of purchasing items of 100 dollars or more is the same whether you are male or female.

23

Alternative Hypothesis

- There is an association between `gender` and `purchase`.
- The probability of purchasing items over 100 dollars is different between males and females.

24

Chi-Square Test

NO ASSOCIATION

observed frequencies = expected frequencies

ASSOCIATION

observed frequencies ≠ expected frequencies

25

The Pearson chi-square test is a commonly used test that examines whether there is an association between two categorical variables. The chi-square test measures the difference between the observed cell frequencies and the cell frequencies that are expected if there is no association between the variables. If you have a significant chi-square statistic, there is strong evidence an association exists between your variables.

 The expected frequencies are calculated by the formula (row total * column total) / sample size.

p-Value for Chi-Square Test

This *p*-value is the

- probability of observing a chi-square statistic at least as large as the one actually observed, given that there is no association between the variables
- probability of the association you observe in the data occurring by chance.

26

In general, the larger the chi-square values are, the smaller the *p*-values are, which means you have more evidence against the null hypothesis.

Chi-Square Tests

Chi-square tests and the corresponding *p*-values

- determine whether an association exists
- do not measure the strength of an association
- depend on and reflect the sample size.

27

If you double the size of your sample by copying each observation, you double the chi-square statistic even though the strength of the association does not change.

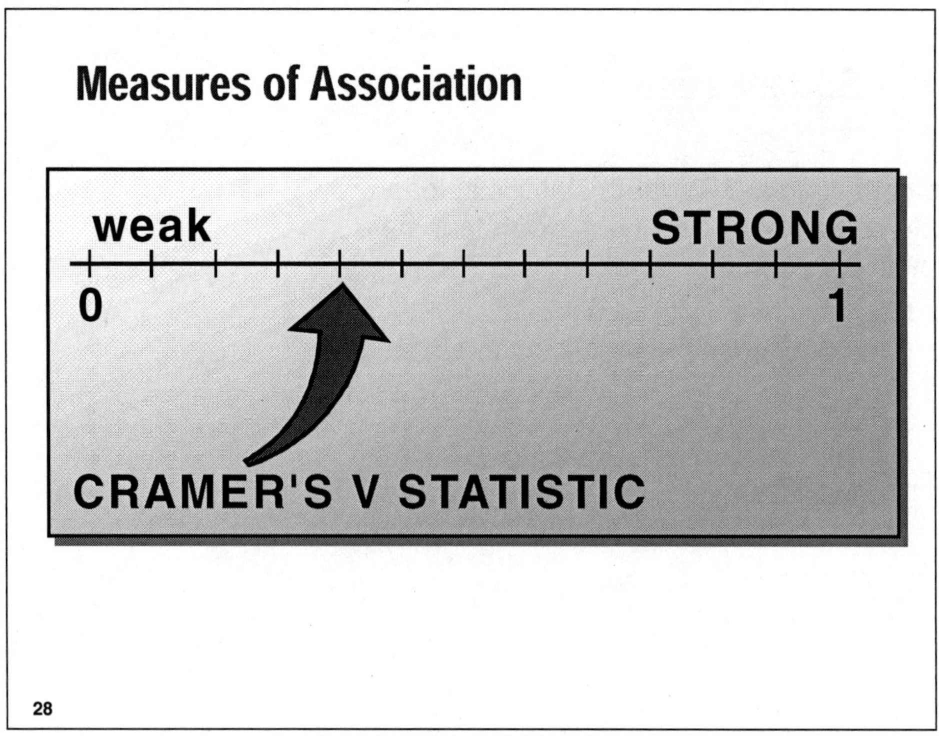

One measure of the strength of the association between two nominal variables is Cramer's V statistic. It is in the range of -1 to 1 for 2-by-2 tables and 0 to 1 for larger tables. Values further away from 0 indicate the presence of a relatively strong association.

Cramer's V statistic is derived from the Pearson chi-square statistic.

Chi-Square Test

Example: Use the Table Analysis task to test for an association between the variables **`gender`** and **`purchase`**. Also generate the expected cell frequencies and the cell's contribution to the total chi-square statistic.

1. Double-click the Table Analysis task created for **`gender`** by **`purchase`**.

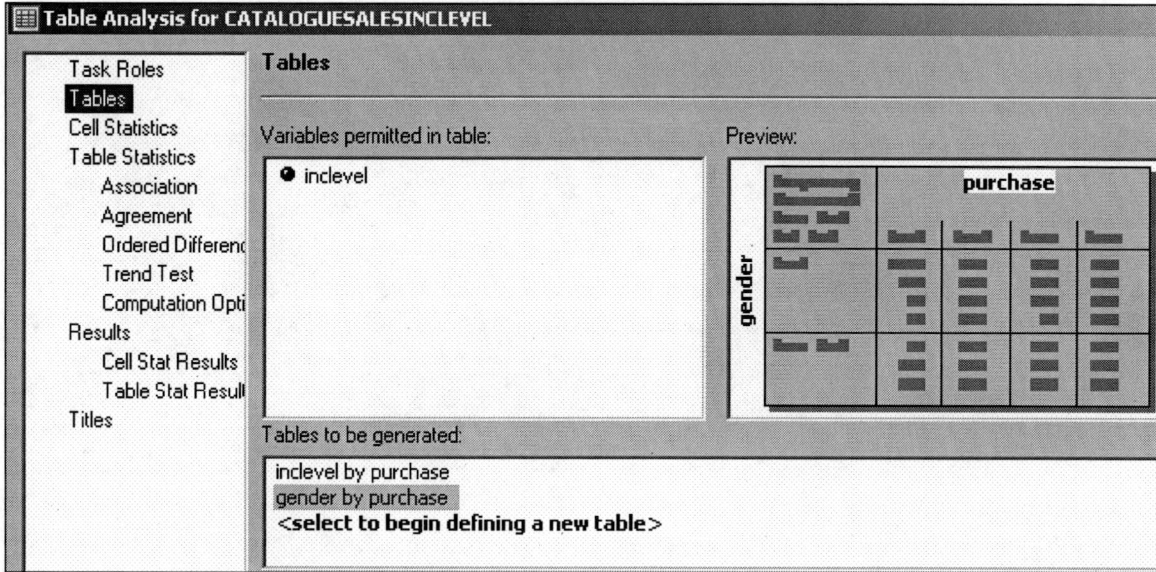

2. Select the **Cell Statistics** tab.

3. Select **Row percentages**, **Cell frequencies**, **Cell contribution to Pearson chi-square**, and **Expected cell frequency** as shown.

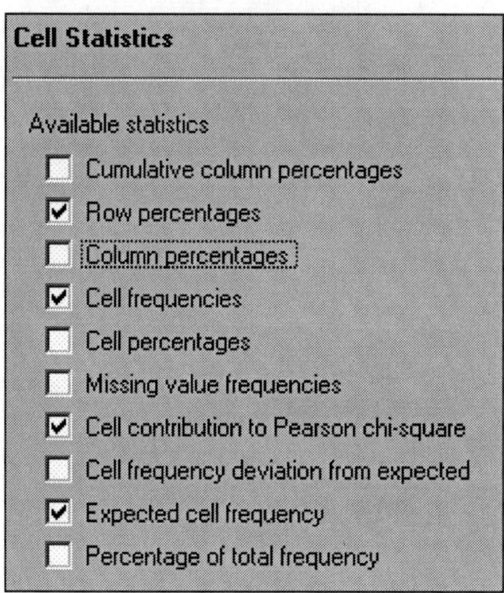

4. On the left, select **Association** under Table Statistics and check the box next to **Chi-square tests**.

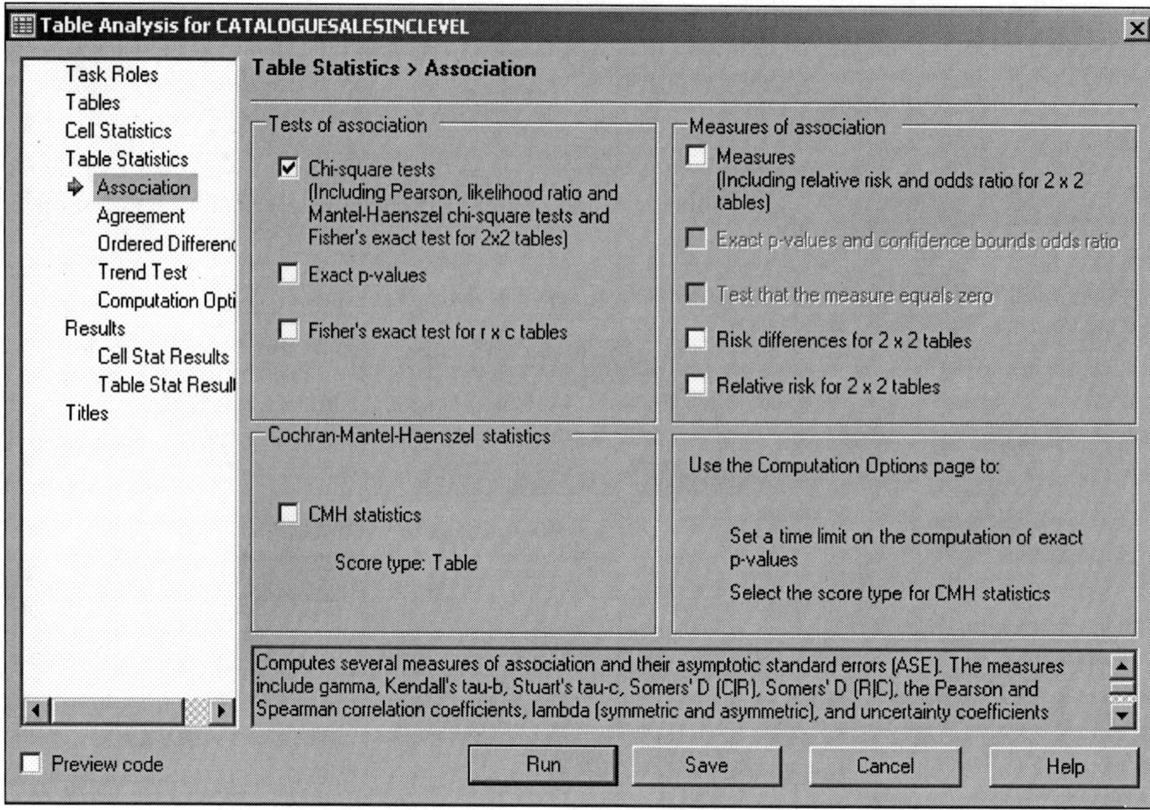

5. Select **Run**.

Two tables make up the results of this task.

Frequency Expected Cell Chi-Square Row Pct	Table of gender by purchase		
	purchase		
gender	< $100	$100 +	Total
Female	139 149.79 0.7774 57.92	101 90.209 1.2909 42.08	240
Male	130 119.21 0.9769 68.06	61 71.791 1.6221 31.94	191
Total	269	162	431

It appears that the cell for `purchase=1` (100 dollars or more) and `gender=Male` (1.6221) contributes the most to the chi-square statistic (4.6672).

The cell chi-square is calculated using this formula:
(observed frequency – expected frequency)^2 / expected frequency

Statistics for Table of gender by purchase

Statistic	DF	Value	Prob
Chi-Square	1	4.6672	0.0307
Likelihood Ratio Chi-Square	1	4.6978	0.0302
Continuity Adj. Chi-Square	1	4.2447	0.0394
Mantel-Haenszel Chi-Square	1	4.6564	0.0309
Phi Coefficient		-0.1041	
Contingency Coefficient		0.1035	
Cramer's V		-0.1041	

Because the *p*-value for the chi-square statistic is 0.0307 and is below .05, you reject the null hypothesis at the 0.05 level and conclude that there is evidence of an association between **`gender`** and **`purchase`**. However, Cramer's V indicates that the association detected with the chi-square test is relatively weak. This means that the association was detected because of the large sample size, not because of its strength.

The chi-square statistic is calculated by summing the cell chi-square values. It exploits the property that the frequency distributions tend toward a normal distribution in very large samples. The formula is Σ(observed – expected)^2 / expected.

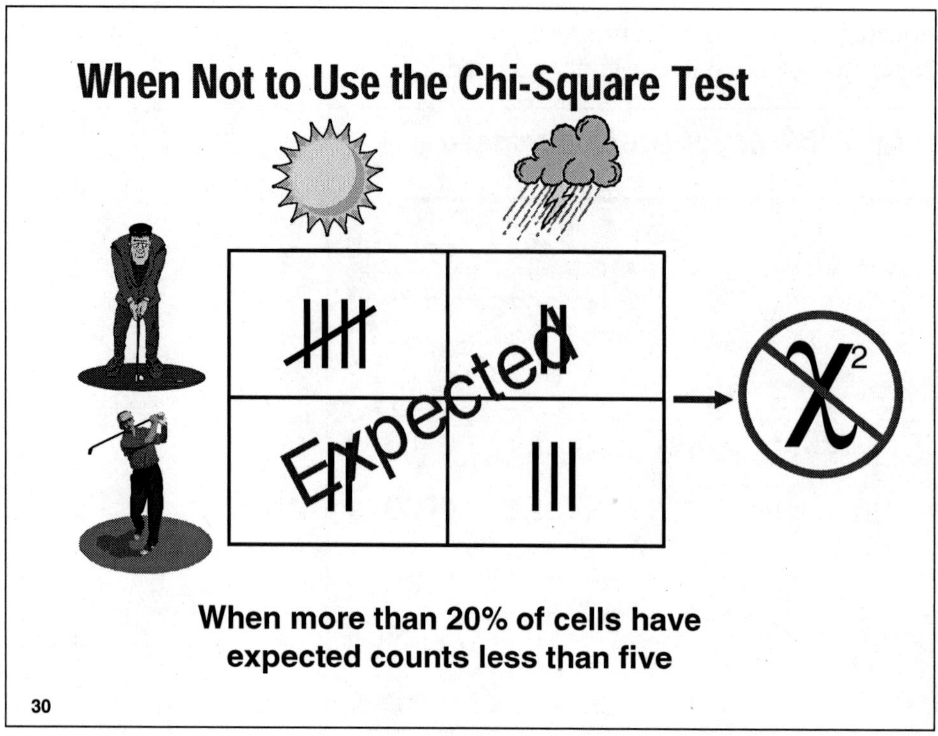

When Not to Use the Chi-Square Test
Expected
2
When more than 20% of cells have
expected counts less than five
30

There are times when the chi-square test may not be appropriate. In fact, when more than 20% of the cells have an expected cell frequency of less than 5, the chi-square test may not be valid. This is because the *p*-values are based on the assumption that the test statistic follows a particular distribution when the sample size is sufficiently large. Therefore, when the sample sizes are small, the asymptotic (large sample) *p*-values may not be valid.

Observed versus Expected Values

Observed Values

1	5	8
5	6	7
6	5	6

Expected Values

3.43	4.57	6.00
4.41	5.88	7.71
4.16	5.55	7.29

31

The criterion for the chi-square test is based on the expected values, not the observed values. In the slide above, 1 out of 9, or 11%, have observed values less than 5. However, 4 out of 9, or 44%, have expected values of less than 5. Therefore, the chi-square test may not be valid.

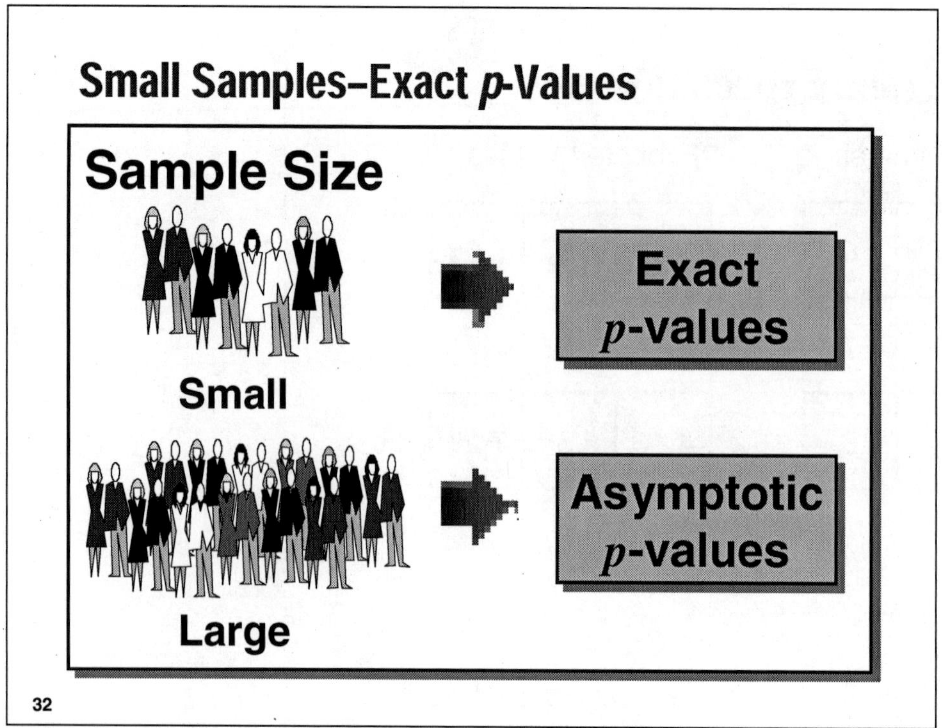

You can obtain exact p-values for many tests in the Frequency Analysis tasks. Exact p-values are useful when the sample size is small; in which case, the asymptotic p-values may not be useful.

However, large data sets (in terms of sample size, number of rows, and number of columns) may require a prohibitive amount of time and memory for computing exact p-values. For large data sets, consider whether exact p-values are needed or whether asymptotic p-values might be quite close to the exact p-values.

Exact *p*-Values for Pearson Chi-Square

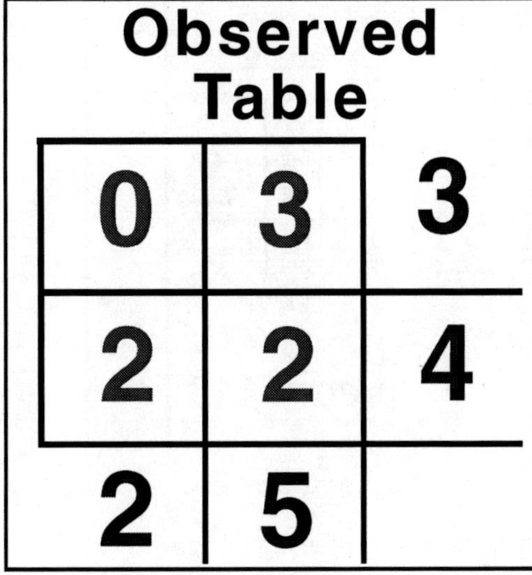

33

Exact *p*-values reflect the probability of observing a table with at least as much evidence of an association as the one actually observed, given there is no association between the variables. If your significance level is .05, exact *p*-values below .05 reflect significant associations.

For example, consider the table above. With such a small sample size, the asymptotic *p*-values would not be valid.

Exact *p*-Values for Pearson Chi-Square

Observed Table

0	3	3
2	2	4
2	5	

$\chi^2 = 2.100$
prob = .286

Possible Table 1

1	2	3
1	3	4
2	5	

$\chi^2 = 0.058$
prob = .571

Possible Table 2

2	1	3
0	4	4
2	5	

$\chi^2 = 3.733$
prob = .143

34

A key assumption behind the computation of exact *p*-values is that the column totals and row totals are fixed. Thus, there are only three possible tables.

To compute an exact *p*-value for this example, examine the chi-square value for each table and the probability that the table occurs given the three tables (the probabilities add up to 1). The Observed Table has a chi-square value of 2.100, so any table with a chi-square value of 2.100 or higher would be used to compute the exact *p*-value. Thus, the exact *p*-value would be 0.286 (Observed Table)+0.143 (Possible Table 2) = .429. This means that you have a 43% chance of obtaining a table with at least as much of an association as the observed table simply by random chance.

Exact *p*-Values for Pearson Chi-Square Test

Example: Use the Table Analysis task to produce exact *p*-values for the Pearson chi-square test. Use the data set **`EXACT`**.

1. Select **`EXACT`** as the active data source in the project tree.
2. Select **Analysis** ⇨ **Table Analysis**.
3. Select and drag **`b`** to the column area of the Preview: window.
4. Select and drag **`a`** to the row area of the Preview: window.

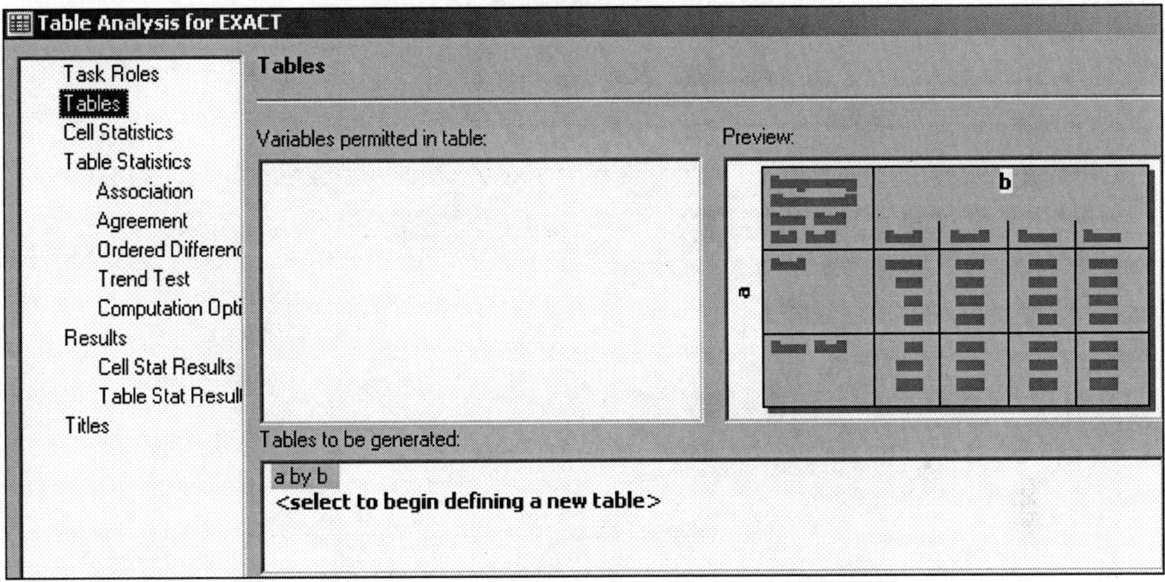

5. Select **Cell Statistics** on the left. Select the statistics shown below:

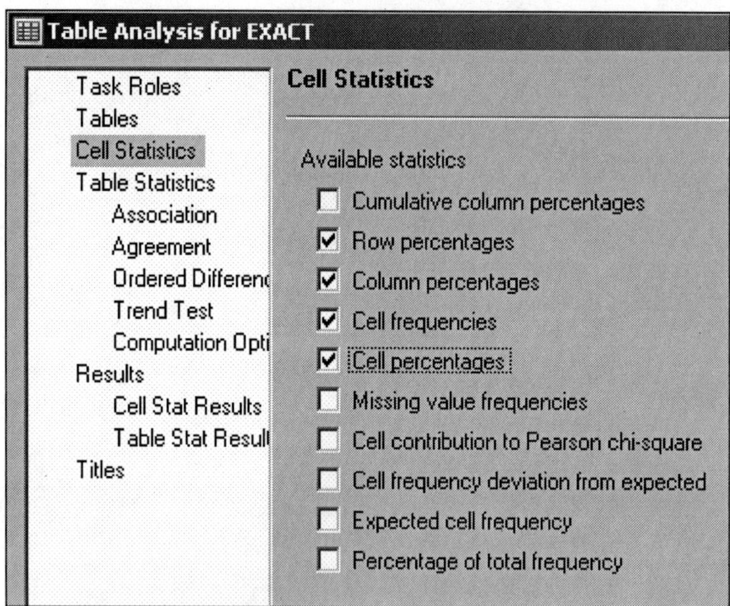

6. Select the **Association** pane under Table Statistics. Select **Chi-square tests** and **Exact p-values**.

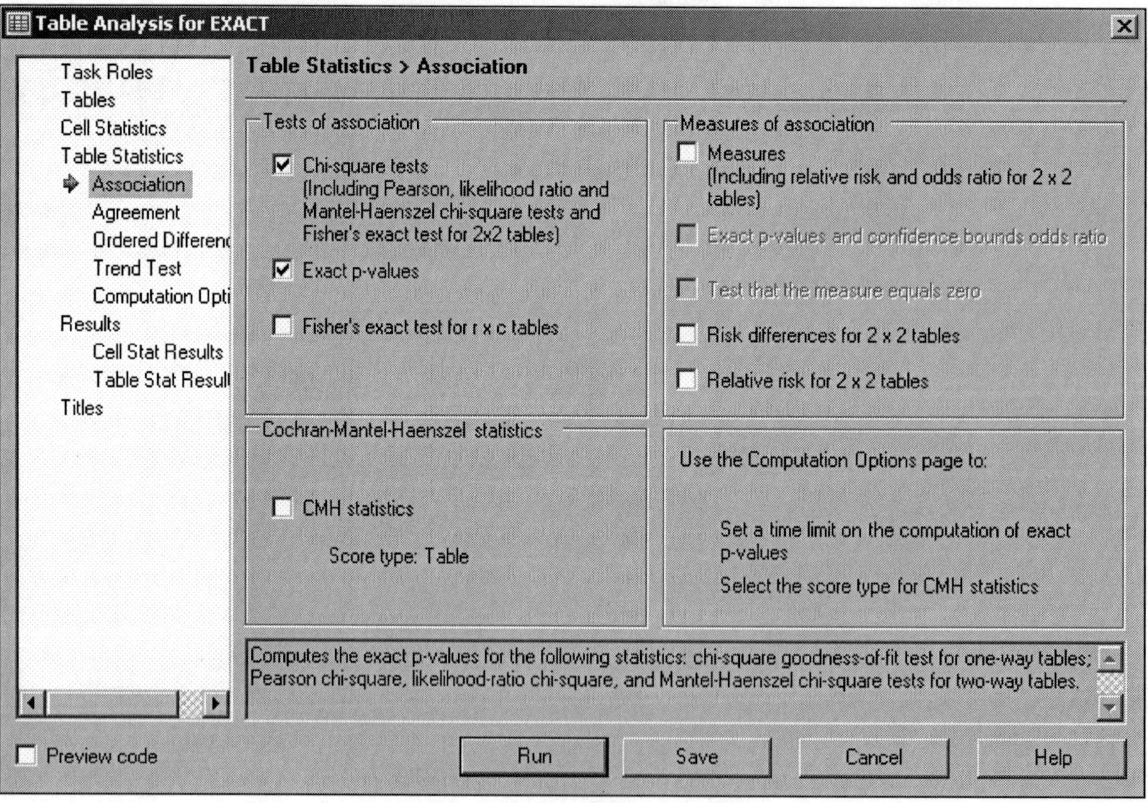

7. Select **Run**.

The two default result tables are shown below.

Frequency Percent Row Pct Col Pct	Table of a by b		
	b		
a	1	2	Total
1	0 0.00 0.00 0.00	3 42.86 100.00 60.00	3 42.86
2	2 28.57 50.00 100.00	2 28.57 50.00 40.00	4 57.14
Total	2 28.57	5 71.43	7 100.00

Statistics for Table of a by b

Statistic	DF	Value	Prob
Chi-Square	1	2.1000	0.1473
Likelihood Ratio Chi-Square	1	2.8306	0.0925
Continuity Adj. Chi-Square	1	0.3646	0.5460
Mantel-Haenszel Chi-Square	1	1.8000	0.1797
Phi Coefficient		-0.5477	
Contingency Coefficient		0.4804	
Cramer's V		-0.5477	

WARNING: 100% of the cells have expected counts less than 5.
(Asymptotic) Chi-Square may not be a valid test.

The warning message informs you that because of the small sample size, the asymptotic chi-square may not be a valid test.

Partial Output

Pearson Chi-Square Test	
Chi-Square	2.1000
DF	1
Asymptotic Pr > ChiSq	0.1473
Exact Pr >= ChiSq	0.4286

Notice the difference between the exact *p*-value (0.4286) and the asymptotic *p*-value (0.1473) in the Pearson Chi-Square Test table. Exact *p*-values tend to be larger than asymptotic *p*-values because the exact tests are more conservative.

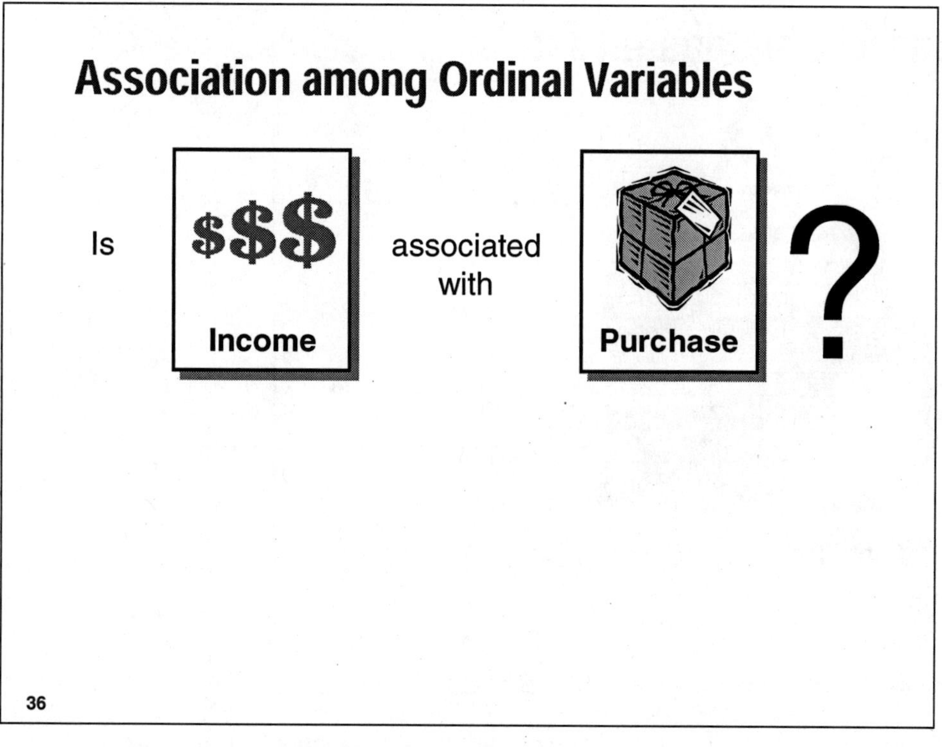
Association among Ordinal Variables
Is
$$$
Income
associated
with
Purchase
?
36

You have already seen that **purchase** and **gender** have a significant association. Another question you can ask is whether **purchase** and **income** have a significant association. You can use the chi-square test, but because **income** is ordinal and **purchase** can be considered ordinal, you may want to test for an ordinal association. The appropriate test for ordinal associations is the Mantel-Haenszel chi-square test.

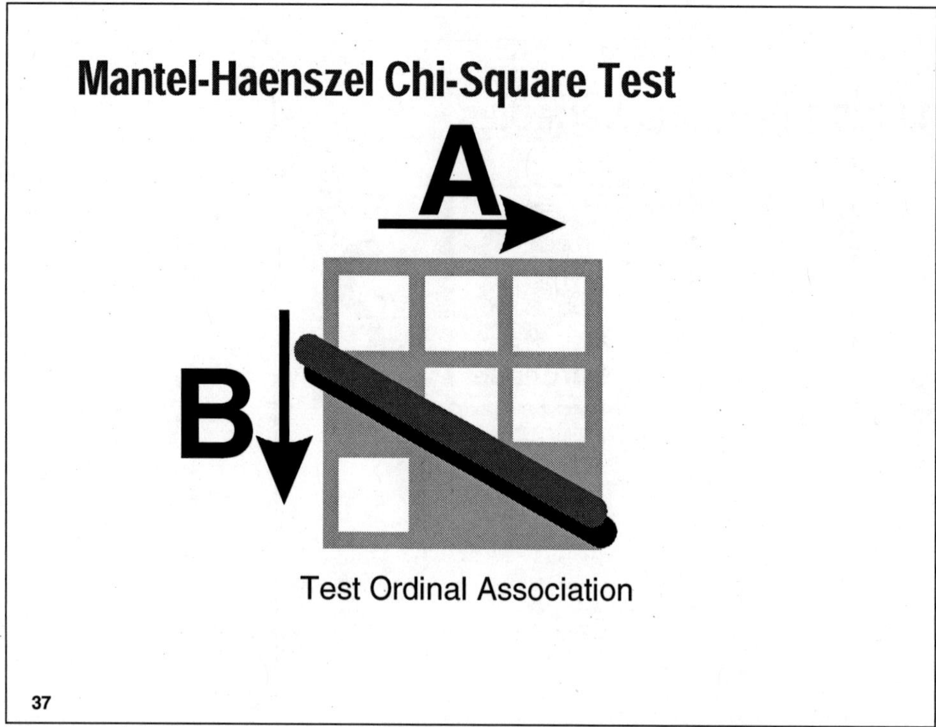

The Mantel-Haenszel chi-square test is particularly sensitive to ordinal associations. An *ordinal association* implies that as one variable increases, the other variable tends to increase or decrease. For the test results to be meaningful when there are variables with more than two levels, the levels must be in a logical order.

Null hypothesis: There is no ordinal association between the row and column variables.

Alternative hypothesis: There is an ordinal association between the row and column variables.

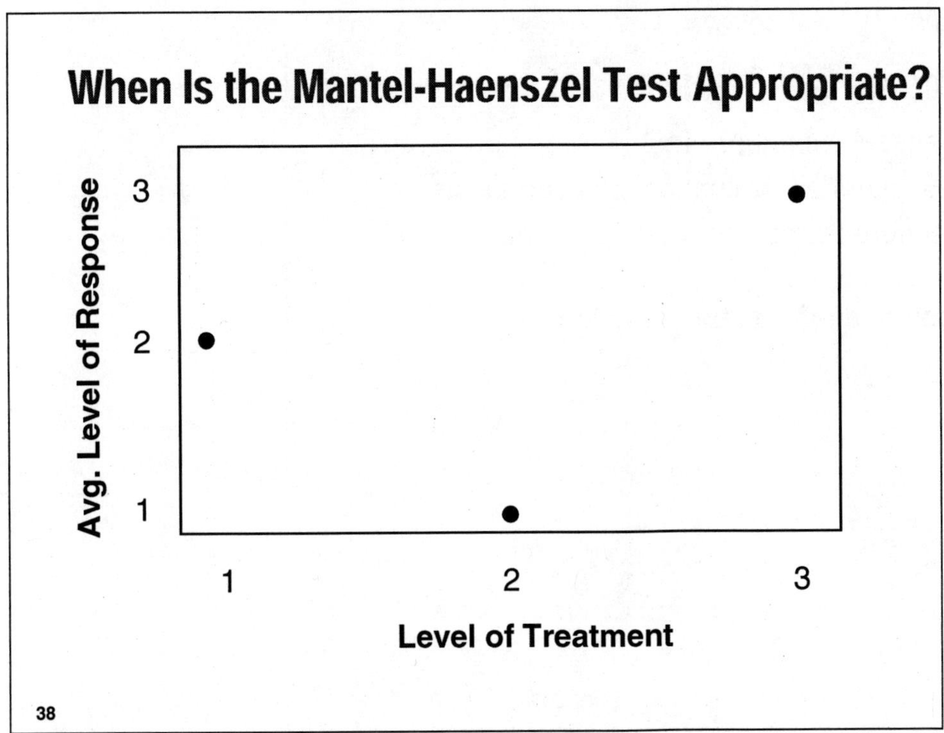

The Mantel-Haenszel test expects the effect of the predictor to be constant. That is, if the average value of the response decreases from the first level to the second level, it expects the average level of the response to decrease from the second level to the third. The above relationship would not be statistically significant under Mantel-Haenszel.

Mantel-Haenszel Chi-Square Test

The Mantel-Haenszel chi-square test

- determines whether an ordinal association exists
- does not measure the strength of the ordinal association
- depends upon and reflects the sample size.

39

The Mantel-Haenszel chi-square statistic is more powerful than the general association chi-square statistic for detecting an ordinal association. The reasons are that

- all of the Mantel-Haenszel statistic's power is concentrated toward that objective
- the power of the general association statistic is dispersed over a greater number of alternatives.

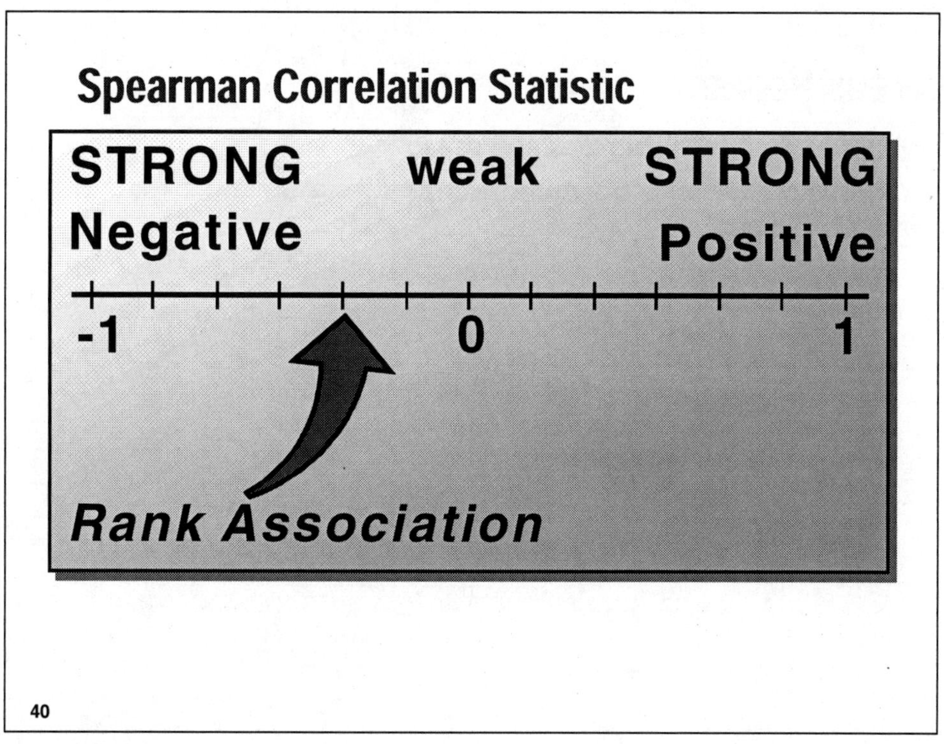

To measure the strength of the ordinal association, you can use the Spearman correlation statistic. This statistic

- has a range between -1 and 1
- has values close to 1 if there is a relatively high degree of positive correlation
- has values close to -1 if there is a relatively high degree of negative correlation
- is appropriate only if both variables are ordinally scaled and the values are in a logical order.

Spearman versus Pearson

- The Spearman correlation uses ranks of the data.
- The Pearson correlation uses the observed values when the variable is numeric.

41

The Spearman statistic can be interpreted as the Pearson correlation between the ranks on variable X and the ranks on variable Y.

Detecting Ordinal Associations

Example: Use the Table Analysis task to test whether an ordinal association exists between **purchase** and **income**. Use the variable **inclevel** and the appropriate format to ensure that the income levels are in a logical order. Use custom code to request confidence bounds for the measures of association in the output.

1. Make sure that **CATALOGSALESINCOME** is the active data table.
2. Select **Describe** ⇨ **Table Analysis**.
3. Right-click **purchase** and select **Properties**.
4. Select **Change…** beside Format.
5. Select **OK** ⇨ **OK**.
6. Format the variable **inclevel** using the same method.
7. Select **User Defined** ⇨ **INCFMT.**.
8. Select **OK** ⇨ **OK**.
9. Assign **purchase** and **inclevel** to the Table variables role.

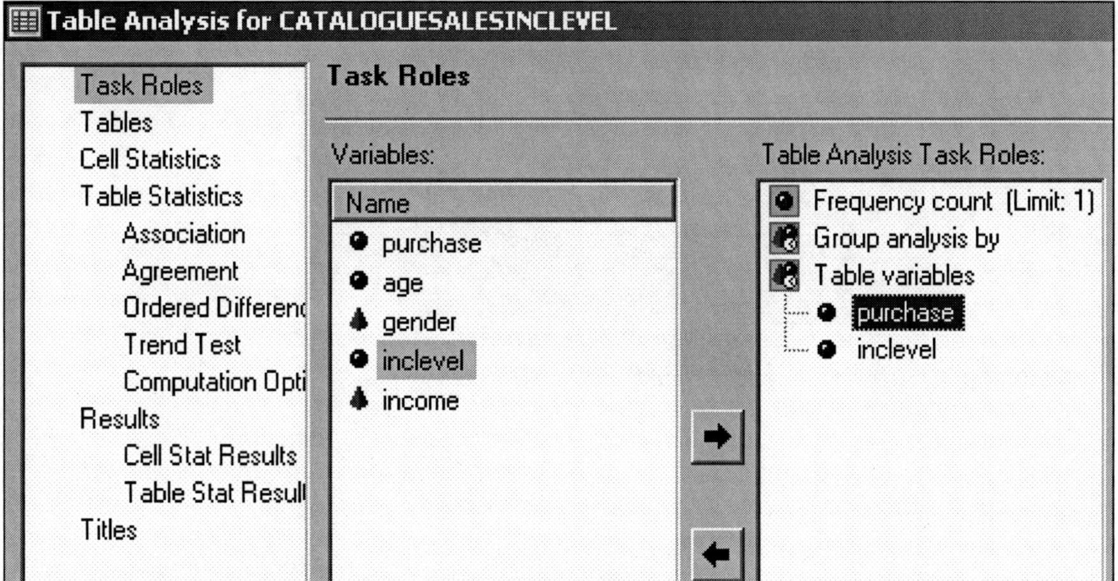

10. Select **Tables** on the left. Drag and drop `purchase` to the column area and `inclevel` to the row area.

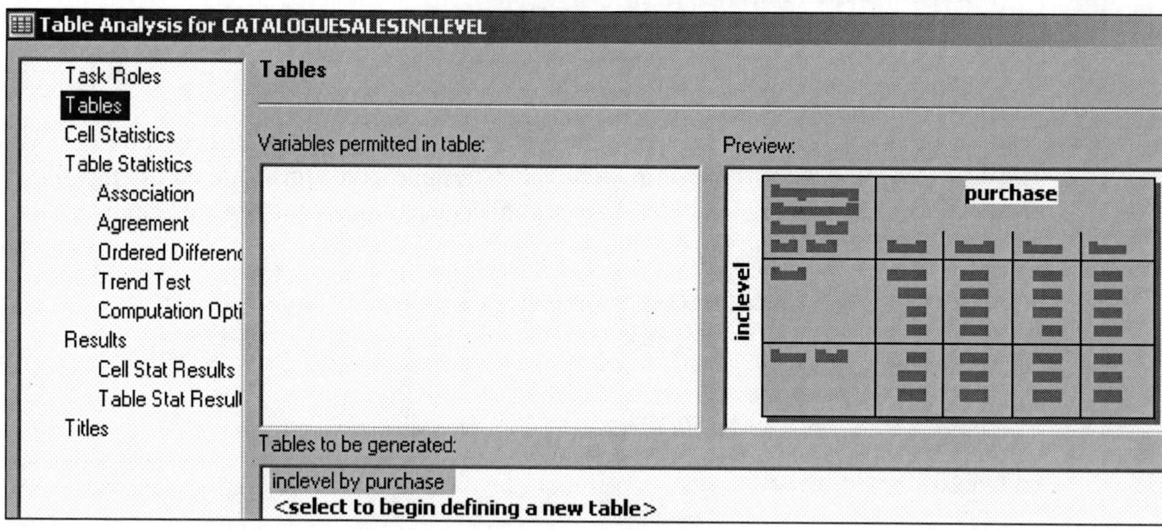

11. Select **Cell Statistics** on the left. Check the boxes as shown below:

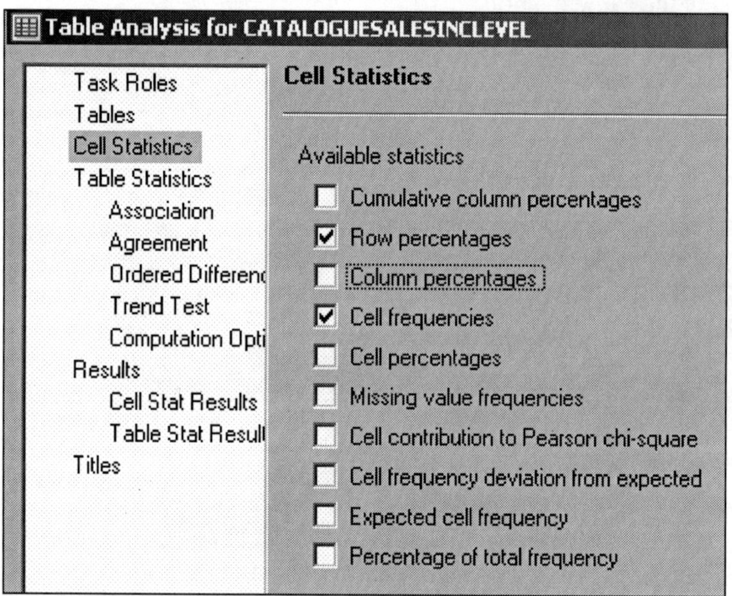

12. Select **Association** under Table Statistics on the left. Select **Chi-square tests** from **Tests of association**. Select **Measures** from **Measures of association**.

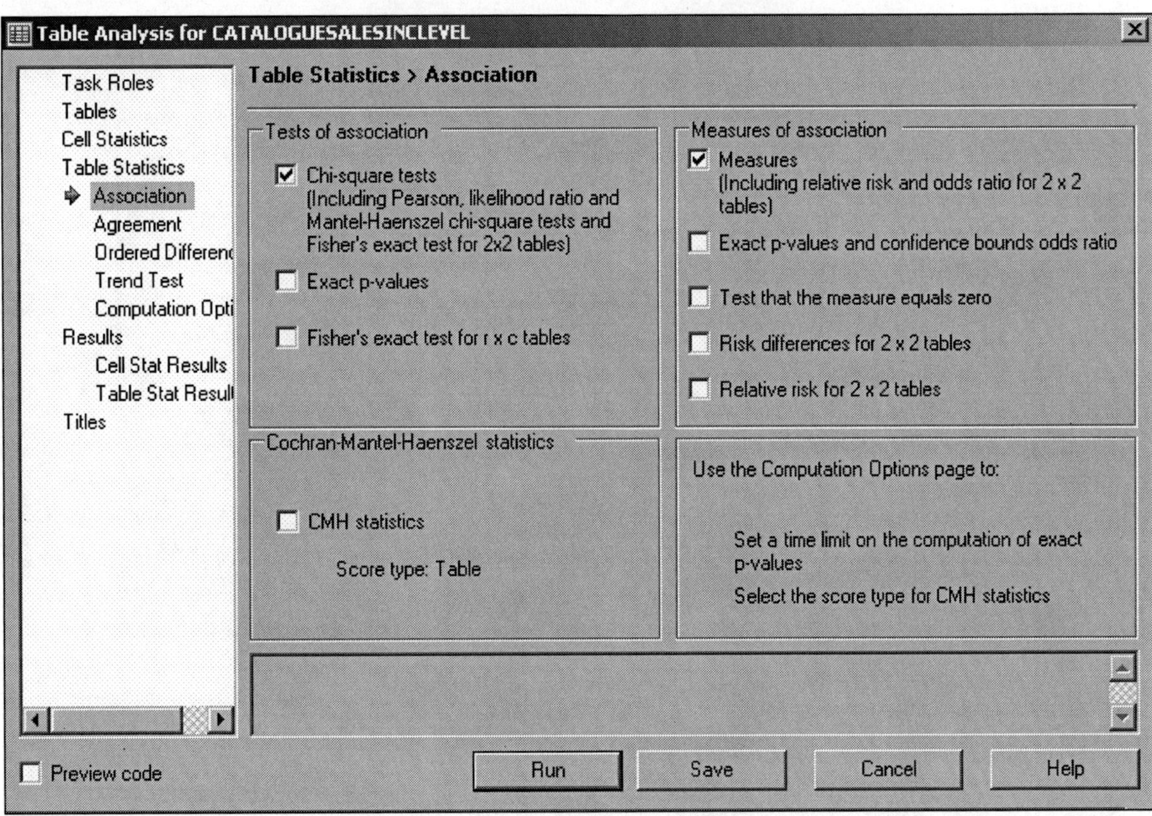

13. Add an option to generate confidence intervals. Select **Preview code**.

14. Select **Insert Code...** from the Code Preview for Task window.

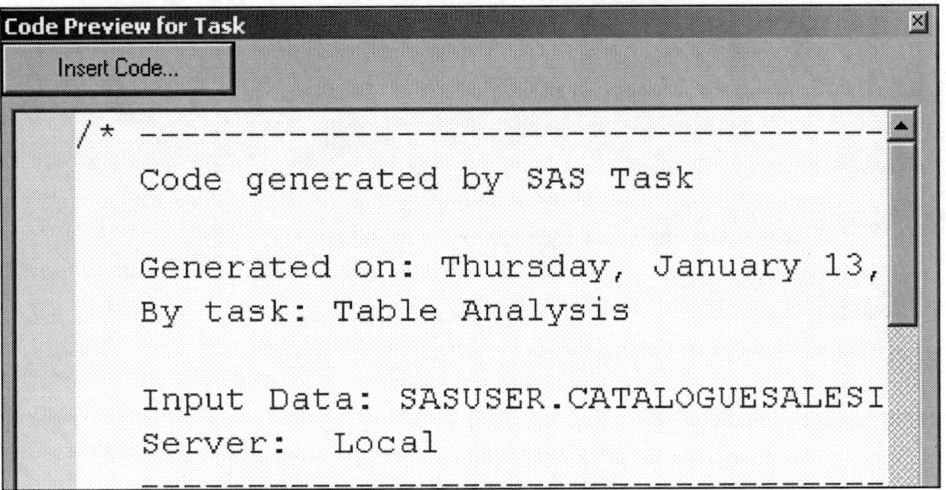

15. Scroll down the User Code window and find the PROC FREQ statement. Double-click on the ***<double-click to insert code>*** area under the TABLES statement.

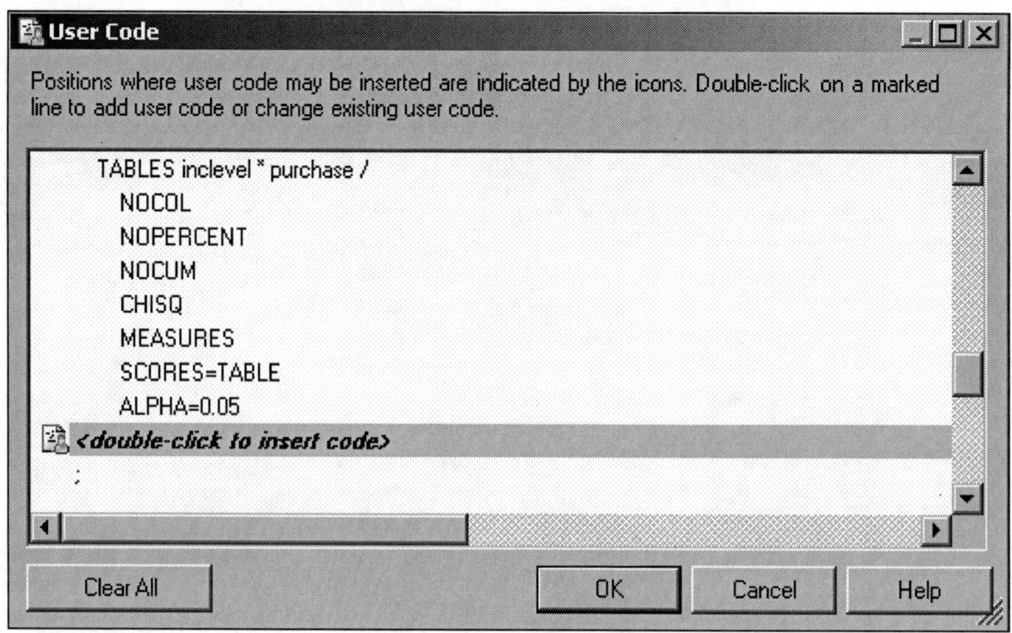

Make sure the code you insert is *before* the semi-colon.

16. Type `CL` in the Enter User Code window that appears.

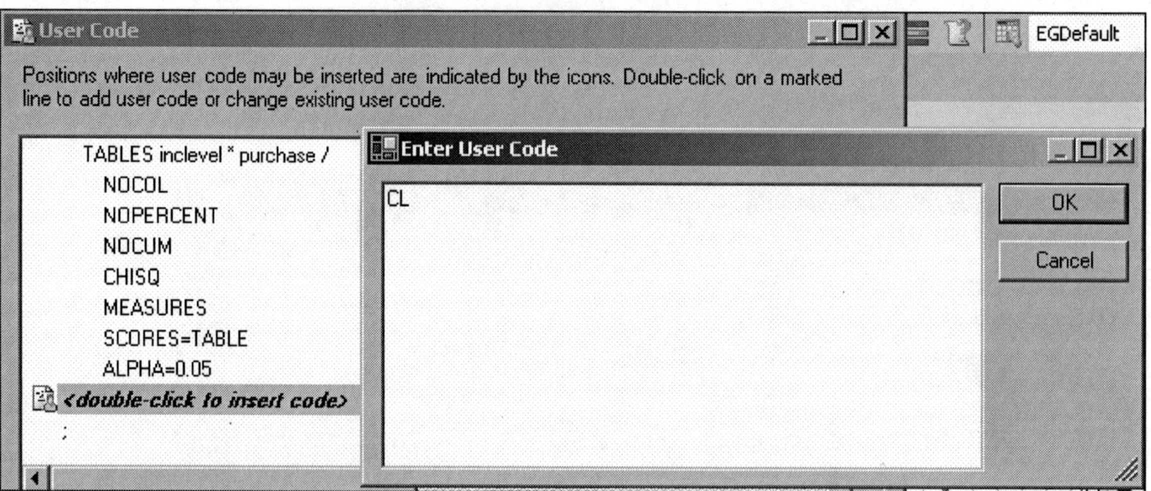

17. Select **OK** ⇨ **OK**.

18. Close the Code Preview for Task window.

19. Select **Run.**

The crosstabulation is shown below:

Frequency Row Pct	Table of inclevel by purchase		
	purchase		
inclevel	< $100	$100 +	Total
LOW INCOME	90 68.18	42 31.82	132
MEDIUM INCOME	98 68.06	46 31.94	144
HIGH INCOME	81 52.26	74 47.74	155
Total	269	162	431

The results of the Mantel-Haenszel chi-square test are shown below:

Statistics for Table of inclevel by purchase

Statistic	DF	Value	Prob
Chi-Square	2	10.6404	0.0049
Likelihood Ratio Chi-Square	2	10.5425	0.0051
Mantel-Haenszel Chi-Square	1	8.1174	0.0044
Phi Coefficient		0.1571	
Contingency Coefficient		0.1552	
Cramer's V		0.1571	

Because the p-value of the Mantel-Haenszel chi-square is 0.0044, you can conclude at the 0.05 significance level that there is evidence of an ordinal association between `purchase` and `inclevel`.

The Spearman correlation statistic is included in the table below, as well as many others. Also included in the table are the ASE and the 95% confidence bounds.

Statistic	Value	ASE	95% Confidence Limits	
Gamma	0.2324	0.0789	0.0777	0.3871
Kendall's Tau-b	0.1312	0.0454	0.0423	0.2201
Stuart's Tau-c	0.1466	0.0508	0.0471	0.2461
Somers' D C|R	0.1102	0.0382	0.0353	0.1850
Somers' D R|C	0.1562	0.0540	0.0505	0.2620
Pearson Correlation	0.1374	0.0480	0.0433	0.2315
Spearman Correlation	0.1391	0.0481	0.0449	0.2334
Lambda Asymmetric C|R	0.0000	0.0000	0.0000	0.0000
Lambda Asymmetric R|C	0.0616	0.0470	0.0000	0.1536
Lambda Symmetric	0.0388	0.0300	0.0000	0.0976
Uncertainty Coefficient C|R	0.0185	0.0114	0.0000	0.0408
Uncertainty Coefficient R|C	0.0112	0.0069	0.0000	0.0246
Uncertainty Coefficient Symmetric	0.0139	0.0086	0.0000	0.0307

Sample Size = 431

The Spearman correlation statistic indicates that there is a relatively small positive ordinal relationship between **`inclevel`** and **`purchase`**. (As **`inclevel`** levels increase, **`purchase`** levels increase.)

The ASE is the Asymptotic Standard Error, which is what the standard error approaches as your sample size increases to infinity.

Because the 95% confidence interval for the Spearman correlation statistic does not contain 0, the relationship is significant at the 0.05 significance level.

The confidence bounds are valid only if your sample size is large. A general guideline is to have a sample size of at least 25 for each degree of freedom in the Pearson chi-square statistic.

5.3 Introduction to Logistic Regression

Objectives

- Explain the concepts of logistic regression.
- Fit a binary logistic regression model using the Logistic Regression task.
- Explain effect and cell coding.
- Define and explain the odds ratio.

44

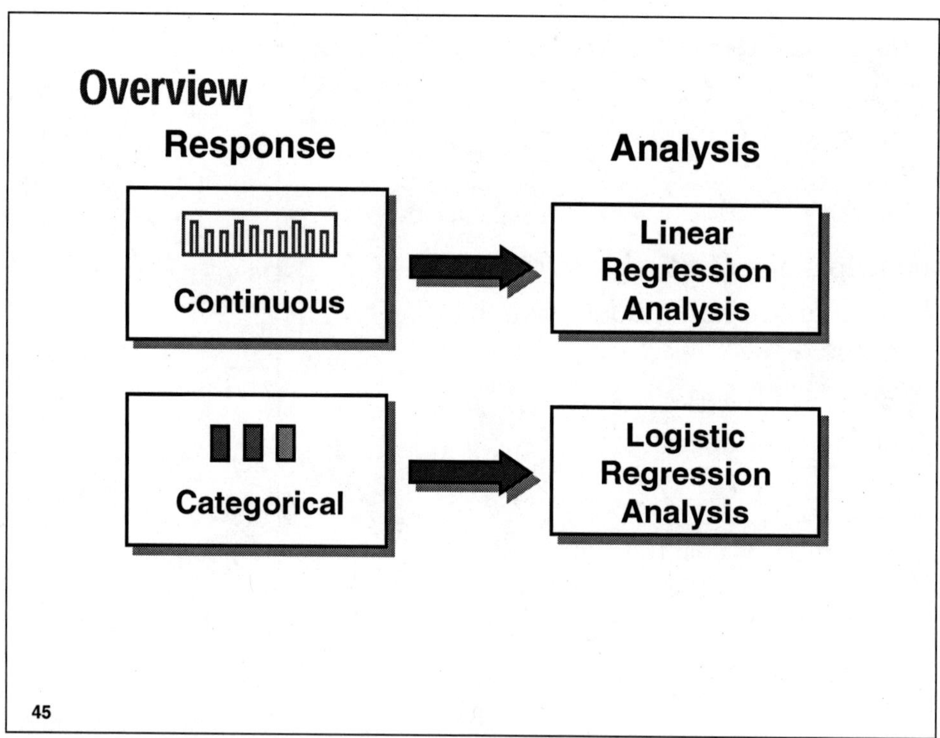

Regression analysis enables you to characterize the relationship between a response variable and one or more predictor variables. In linear regression, the response variable is continuous. In *logistic regression*, the response variable is categorical.

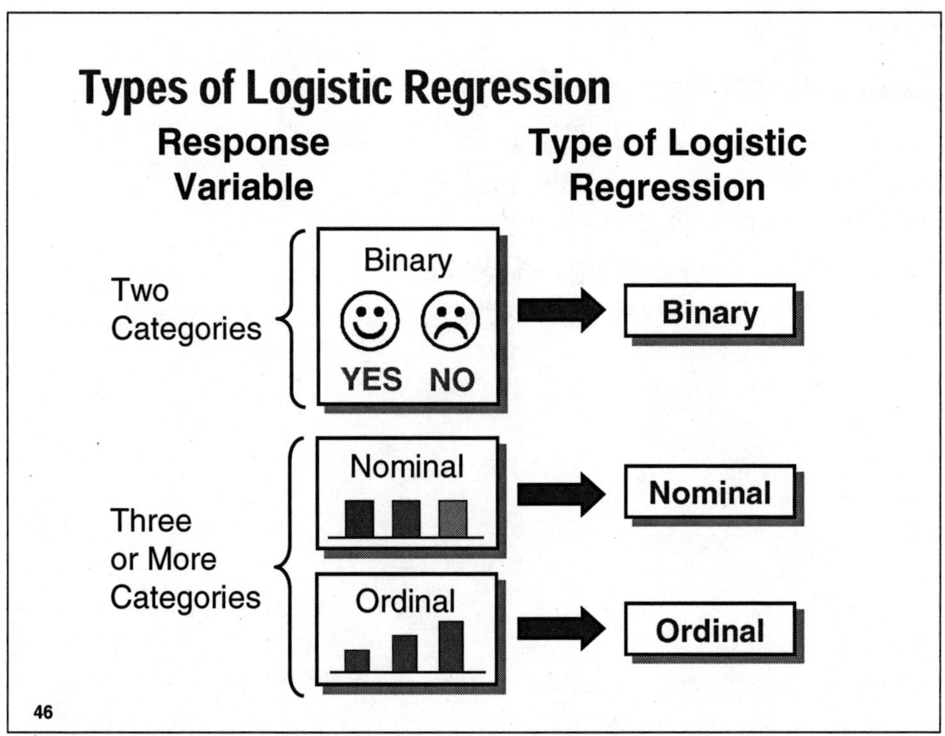

If the response variable is dichotomous (two categories), the appropriate logistic regression model is binary logistic regression.

If you have more than two categories (levels) within the response variable, then there are two possible logistic regression models:

1. If the response variable is nominal, you fit a nominal logistic regression.
2. If the response variable is ordinal, you fit an ordinal logistic regression.

What Does Logistic Regression Do?

The logistic regression model uses the predictor variables, which can be categorical or continuous, to predict the probability of specific outcomes.

In other words, logistic regression is designed to describe probabilities associated with the values of the response variable.

47

Because you are modeling probabilities, a continuous linear regression model would not be appropriate. One problem is that the predicted values from a linear model can assume, theoretically, any value. However, probabilities are by definition bounded between 0 and 1. Logistic regression models ensure that the estimated probabilities are between 0 and 1.

Another problem is that the relationship between the probability of the outcome and a predictor variable is usually nonlinear rather than linear. In fact, the relationship often resembles an S-shaped curve.

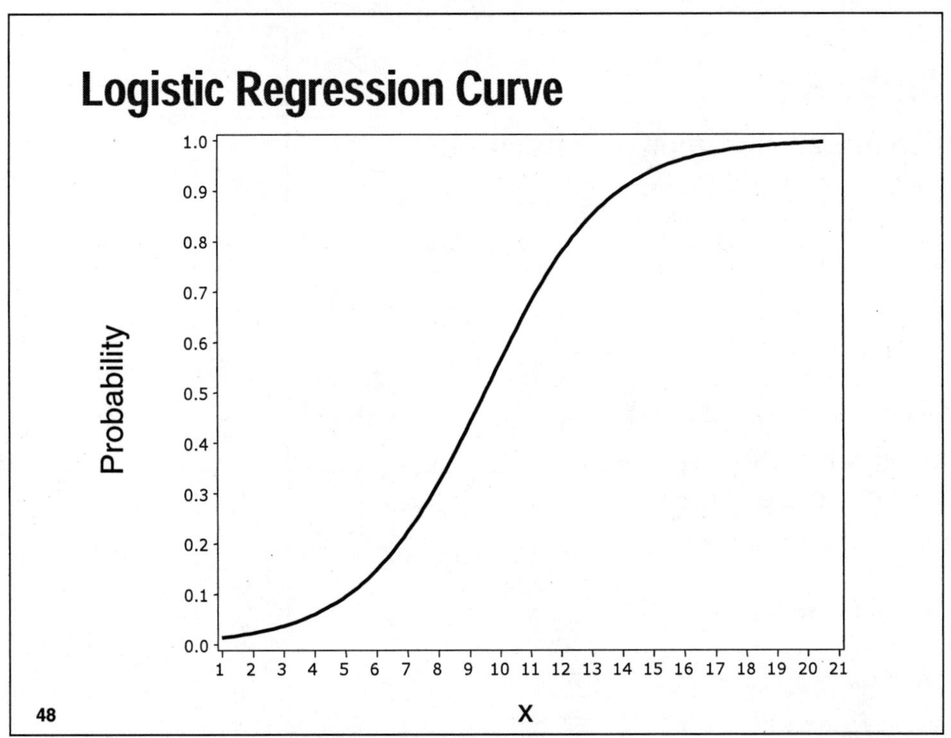

The nonlinear relationship between the probability of the outcome and the predictor variables is solely due to the constrained scale of the probabilities. Furthermore, the relationship is fairly linear in the middle of the range of the probabilities (.20 to .80) and fairly nonlinear at the end of the range (0 to .20 and .80 to 1).

The parameter estimate of this curve determines the rate of increase or decrease of the estimated curve. When the parameter estimate is greater than 0, the probability of the outcome increases as the predictor variable values increase. When the parameter estimate is less than 0, the probability decreases as the predictor variable values increase. As the absolute value of the parameter estimate increases, the curve has a steeper rate of change. When the parameter estimate is equal to 0, the curve resembles a straight line.

Logit Transformation

Logistic regression models transform probabilities to values called *logits*.

$$\text{logit}(p_i) = \log\left(\frac{p_i}{1-p_i}\right)$$

where

i indexes all cases (observations)

p_i is the probability the event (a sale, for example) occurs in the ith case

log is the natural log (to the base e).

49

A logistic regression model applies a transformation to the probabilities. The probabilities are transformed because the relationship between the probabilities and the predictor variable is nonlinear.

The logit transformation ensures the model generates estimated probabilities between 0 and 1.

The ratio [p / (1 – p)] is also known as odds, which is discussed later in this chapter. In the current example using **CATALOGSALESINCOME**, the probability of interest is whether the customer purchased 100 dollars or more.

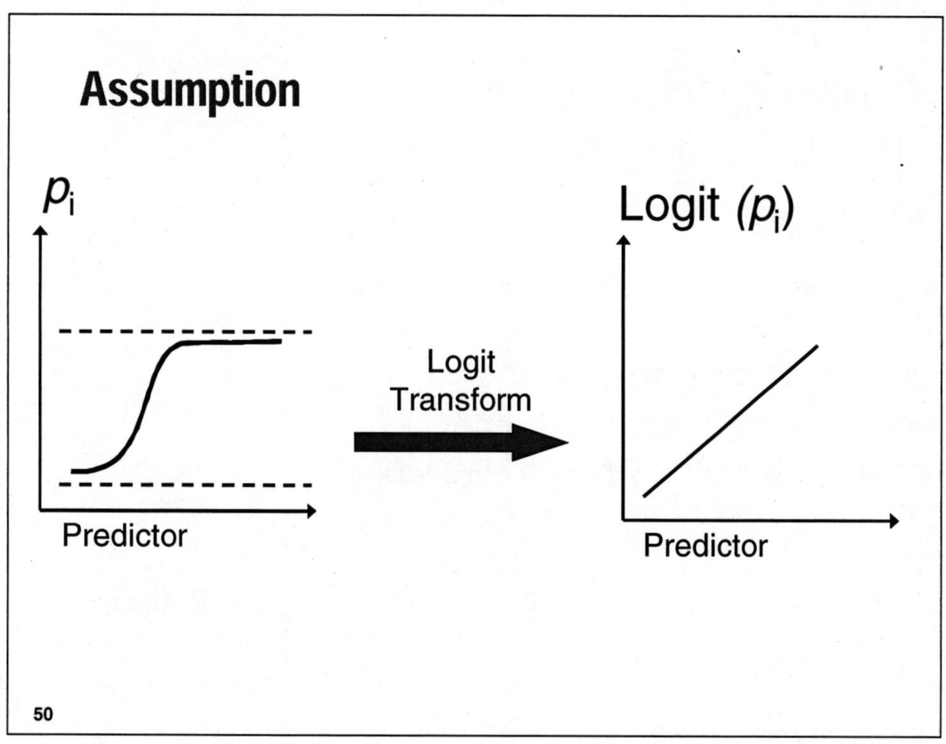

Assumption in logistic regression: The logit transformation of the probabilities results in a linear relationship with the predictor variables.

To verify this assumption, it would be useful to plot the logits by the predictor variable. Logit plots are illustrated in a later section.

Logistic Regression Model

$$\text{logit}(p_i) = \beta_0 + \beta_1 X_1 + \varepsilon_i$$

where

$\text{logit}(p_i)$	is the logit transformation of the probability of the event.
β_0	is the intercept of the regression line.
β_1	is the slope of the regression line.
ε_i	error (residual) associated with each observation.

51

For a binary outcome variable, the linear logistic model with one predictor variable has the form above.

Unlike linear regression, the categorical response is not normally distributed and the variances are not the same. Also, logistic regression usually requires a more complex iterative estimation method called maximum likelihood to estimate the parameters than linear regression does. This method finds the parameter estimates that are most likely to occur given the data. It accomplishes this by maximizing the likelihood function that expresses the probability of the observed data as a function of the unknown parameters.

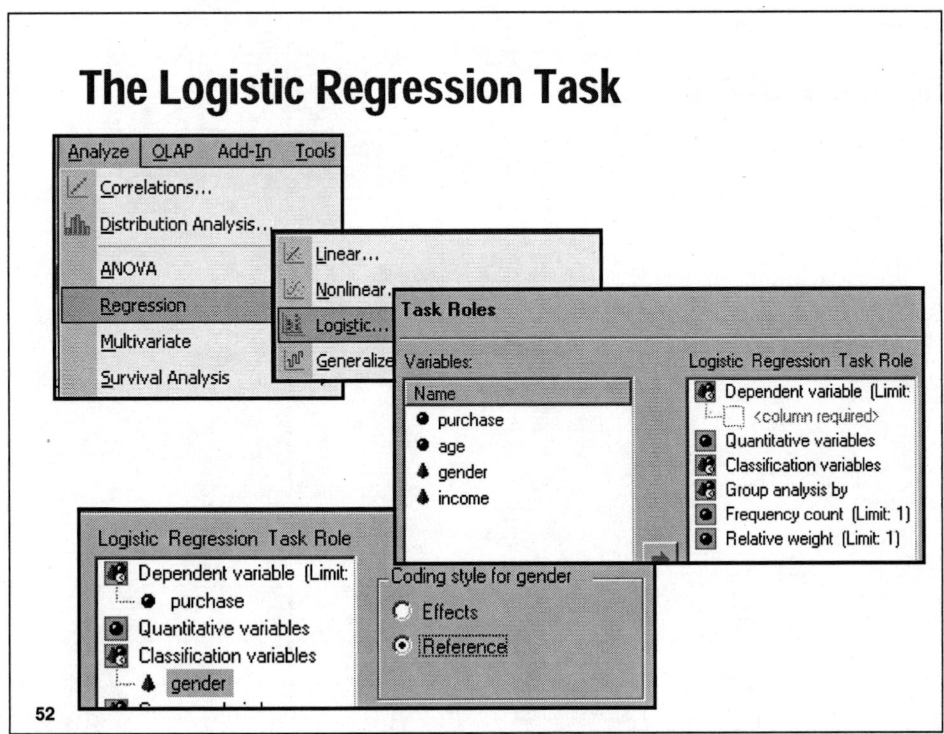

In the Logistic Regression task, you specify the proposed relationship between the categorical dependent variable and the independent variables.

Effect Coding: Two Levels

Class	Value	Design Variables 1
gender	Female	1
	Male	-1

53

Effect Coding: Three Levels

Class	Value	Label	Design Variables 1	2
inclevel	1	Low Income	1	0
	2	Medium Income	0	1
	3	High Income	-1	-1

54

For *effect coding* (also called *deviation from the mean coding*), the number of design variables created is the number of levels of the class variable minus 1. For example, because the variable **`inclevel`** has three levels, two design variables were created. For the last level of the class variable (`High`), all the design variables have a value of –1. Parameter estimates of the CLASS main effects using this coding scheme estimate the difference between the effect of each level and the average effect over all levels.

Effect Coding: An Example

$$\text{logit}(p) = \beta_0 + \beta_1 * D_{\text{Low income}} + \beta_2 * D_{\text{Medium income}}$$

$\beta_0 =$	the average value of the logit across all categories
$\beta_1 =$	the difference between the average logit and the logit for Low income
$\beta_2 =$	the difference between the average logit and the logit for Medium income
$-(\beta_1+\beta_2) =$	the difference between the average logit and the logit for High income

55

Because the sum of the deviations around the mean must equal zero, the effect for High income must be the negative of the sum of the effects for Low and Medium income.

Reference Cell Coding: Two Levels

		Design Variables
Class	Value	1
gender	Female	1
	Male	0

56

Reference Cell Coding: Three Levels

			Design Variables	
Class	Value	Label	1	2
inclevel	1	Low Income	1	0
	2	Medium Income	0	1
	3	High Income	0	0

57

For *reference cell coding*, parameter estimates of the CLASS main effects estimate the difference between the effect of each level and the last level, called the *reference level.* For example, the effect for the level `Low` estimates the difference between `Low` and `High`. You can choose the reference level in the CLASS statement.

Reference Cell Coding: An Example

$$\text{logit}(p) = \beta_0 + \beta_1 * D_{\text{Low income}} + \beta_2 * D_{\text{Medium income}}$$

$\beta_0 =$ the value of the logit when income is High

$\beta_1 =$ the difference between the logits for Low and High income

$\beta_2 =$ the difference between the logits for Medium and High income

58

Binary Logistic Regression

Example: Fit a binary logistic regression model in the Logistic Regression task using **CATALOGSALESINCLEVEL**. Select **purchase** as the outcome variable and **gender** as the predictor variable. Specify reference cell coding and select **Male** as the reference group. Model the probability of spending 100 dollars or more and request confidence intervals around the estimated odds ratios.

1. Select **Analyze** ⇨ **Regression** ⇨ **Logistic...**.

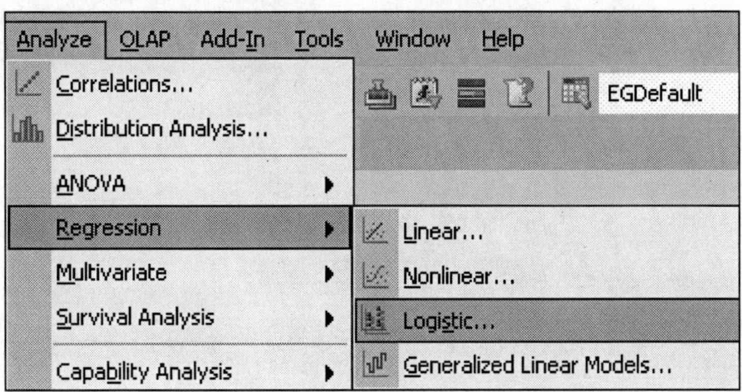

2. Assign `purchase` as the Dependent variable. In the **Response variable** pane, change the Sort order option from Ascending to Descending.

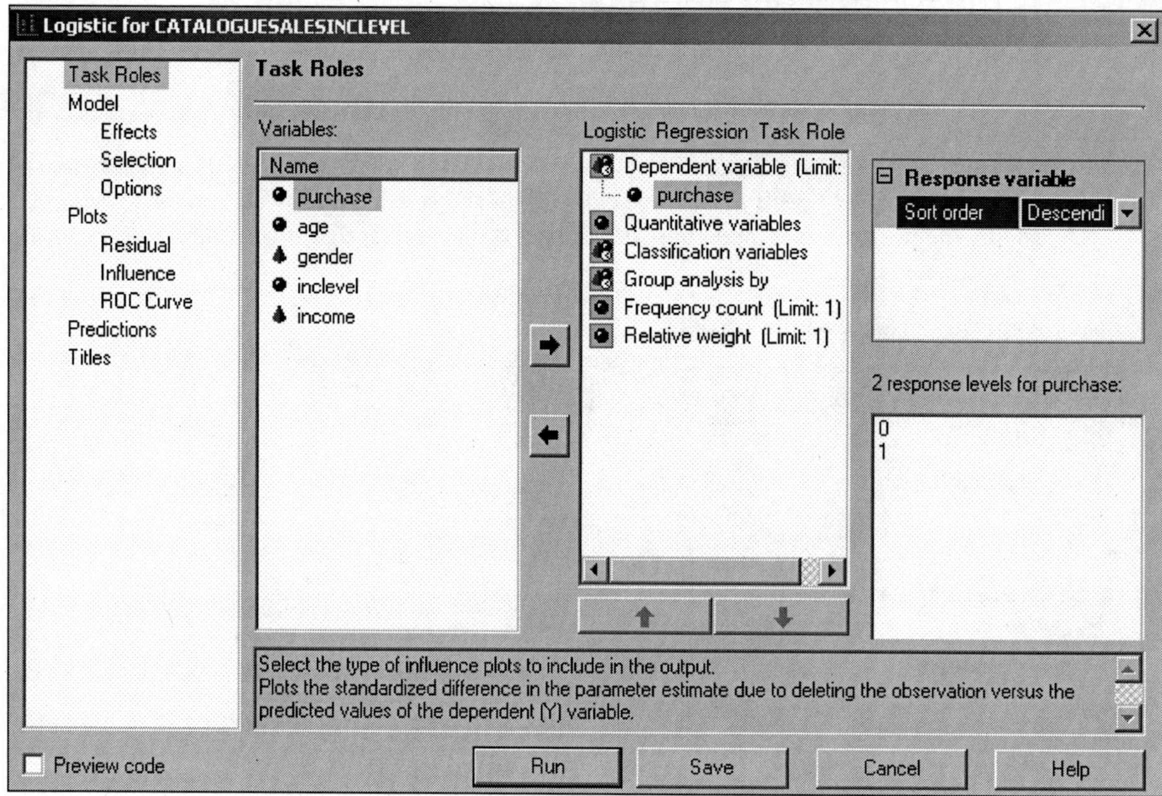

3. Assign **gender** as the Classification variable. Change the Coding style from Effects to Reference.

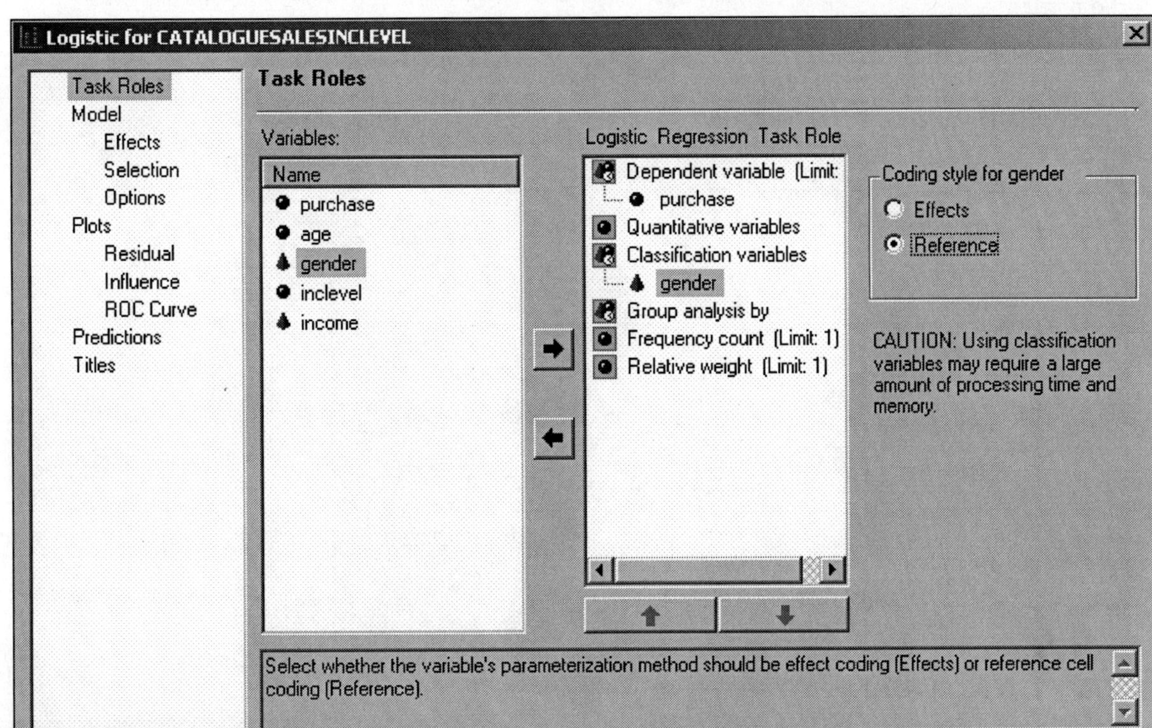

The reference cell is always the last group, alphanumerically, in the class variable. In this case, `Male` will be the reference group. You can specify the reference group in the code with a REF= option in the CLASS statement.

If there are numerous levels in the Classification variable, you may want to reduce the number of levels using subject matter knowledge. This is especially important when the levels have few or no observations. This can easily be done in a query.

4. Select **Effects** under Model in the left-side pane. Select **gender** and **Main** to add the gender effect to the model.

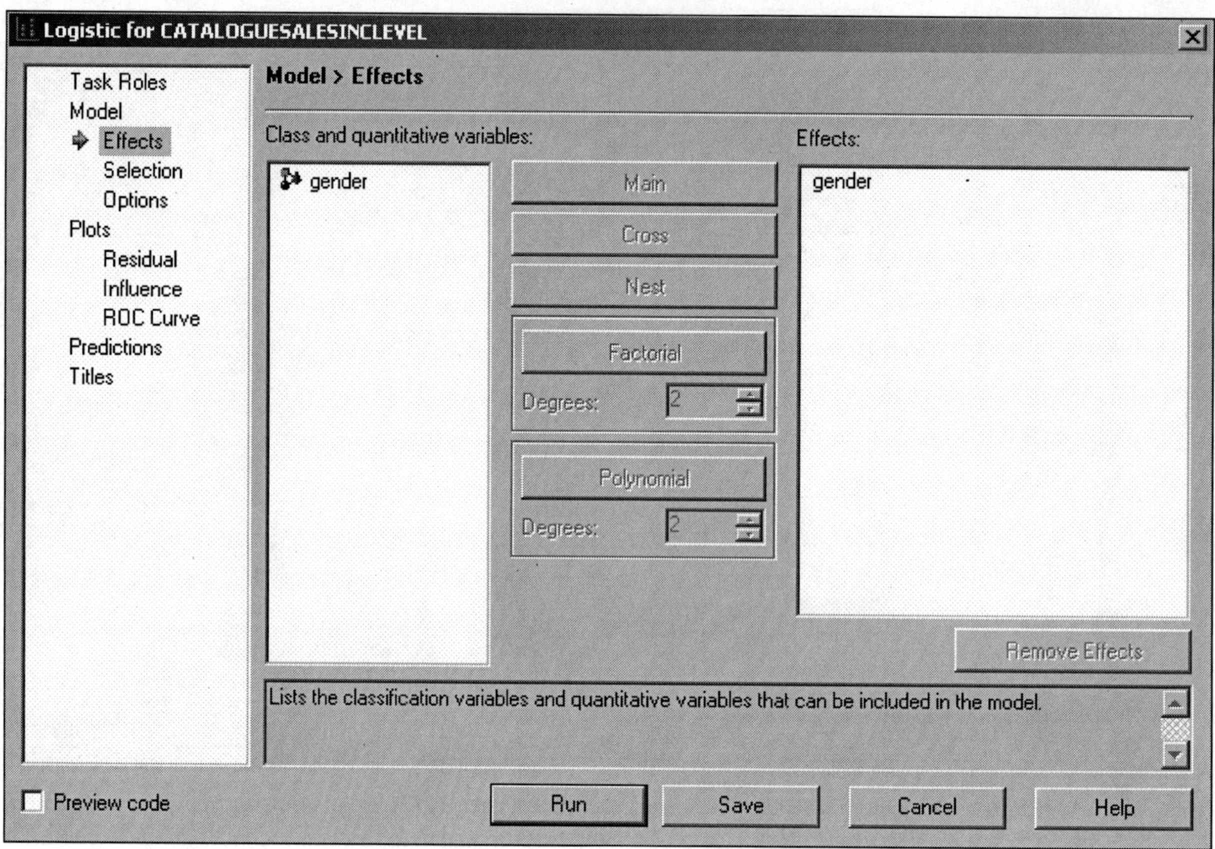

5. Select **Run**.

Examine the results.

Model Information	
Data Set	WORK.SORT7646
Response Variable	purchase
Number of Response Levels	2
Model	binary logit
Optimization Technique	Fisher's scoring

Number of Observations Read	431
Number of Observations Used	431

The Model Information table describes the data set, the response variable, the number of observations, and the link function. The *link function* is the term used to describe the transformation applied to the probabilities. For this example, the logit transformation is used. Other link functions in the LOGISTIC procedure include PROBIT or NORMIT (inverse standard normal distribution function) and CLOGLOG (complementary log-log function). These can be requested on the Statistics tab in the Logistic Regression task.

Response Profile		
Ordered Value	purchase	Total Frequency
1	1	162
2	0	269

Probability modeled is purchase=1.

The Response Profile table shows the response variable values, listed according to their ordered values. By default, SAS orders the response variable alphanumerically so that it bases the logistic regression model on the probability of the smallest value. Because you changed the value to be modeled in this example, the model is based on the probability of purchasing items of 100 dollars or more (**`purchase=1`**). The Response Profile table also shows the value of the response variable and the frequency.

Class Level Information		
Class	**Value**	**Design Variables**
gender	Female	1
	Male	0

The Class Level Information table includes the Classification variables in the model. Because you used reference cell coding and `Male` is the reference cell, the design variable is 1 when **`gender='Female'`** and 0 when **`gender='Male'`**.

Model Convergence Status
Convergence criterion (GCONV=1E-8) satisfied.

Model Fit Statistics		
Criterion	**Intercept Only**	**Intercept and Covariates**
AIC	572.649	569.951
SC	576.715	578.084
-2 Log L	570.649	565.951

The Model Convergence Status informs you that the convergence criterion was met. There are a number of options to control the convergence criterion, but the default is the gradient convergence criterion with a default value of 1.0E-8 (0.00000001).

The Model Fit Statistics table provides three tests:

- AIC is Akaike's 'A' information criterion
- SC is the Schwarz criterion
- –2Log L is the –2 log likelihood.

These are goodness-of-fit measures that you can use to compare one model to another. Lower values indicate a more desirable model. AIC and SC adjust for the number of predictor variables and the number of observations.

You can use the Model Fit Statistics table to compare models, only if you use the same data.

Testing Global Null Hypothesis: BETA=0			
Test	Chi-Square	DF	Pr > ChiSq
Likelihood Ratio	4.6978	1	0.0302
Score	4.6672	1	0.0307
Wald	4.6436	1	0.0312

Type 3 Analysis of Effects			
Effect	DF	Wald Chi-Square	Pr > ChiSq
gender	1	4.6436	0.0312

The Testing Global Null Hypothesis: BETA=0 table provides three statistics to test the null hypothesis that all regression coefficients of the model are 0.

Using the Likelihood Ratio test, a significant *p*-value for the Likelihood Ratio test provides evidence that at least one of the regression coefficients for an explanatory variable is nonzero (in this example the *p*-value is 0.0302, which is significant at the .05 level). This statistic is similar to the overall *F* test in linear regression. The Score and Wald tests are also used to test whether all the regression coefficients are 0.

The Type 3 Analysis of Effects table is generated when Classification variables are specified for the model. The listed effect (variable) is tested using the Wald chi-square statistic (in this example, 4.6436 with a *p*-value of 0.0312). This analysis is similar to the individual *t*-test you saw in Linear Regression output. Because `gender` is the only Classification variable in the model, the value listed in the table will be identical to the Wald test in the Testing Global Null Hypothesis table.

A reference for AIC can be found in Findley, D.F. and Parzen, E. 1995. "A Conversation with Hirotugu Akaike," *Statistical Science*, Vol. 10. No. 1: 104-117.

Analysis of Maximum Likelihood Estimates						
Parameter		DF	Estimate	Standard Error	Wald Chi-Square	Pr > ChiSq
Intercept		1	-0.7566	0.1552	23.7700	<.0001
gender	Female	1	0.4373	0.2029	4.6436	0.0312

The Analysis of Maximum Likelihood Estimates table lists the estimated model parameters, their standard errors, Wald chi-square statistics, and their *p*-values.

The parameter estimates are the estimated coefficients of the fitted logistic regression model. The logistic regression equation is logit($\hat{p}$) = –0.7566 + 0.4373***gender**.

The Wald chi-square, and its associated *p*-value, tests whether the parameter estimate is significantly different from 0. For this example, both the *p*-values for the intercept and the variable **gender** are significant at the 0.05 significance level.

The next table of output is the Odds Ratio Estimates. A number of terms need to be introduced.

Odds Ratio Estimates			
Effect	Point Estimate	95% Wald Confidence Limits	
gender Female vs Male	1.549	1.040	2.305

What Is an Odds Ratio?

An *odds ratio* indicates how much more likely, with respect to odds, a certain event occurs in one group relative to its occurrence in another group.

Example: How much more likely are females to purchase 100 dollars or more in items compared to males?

60

Probability of Outcome

	Outcome		
	Yes	**No**	**Total**
Group A	20	60	80
Group B	10	90	100
Total	30	150	180

Probability of a **Yes outcome** in Group A = 20/80 **(0.25)**

Probability of a **No outcome** in Group A = 60/80 **(0.75)**

61

You have a 25% chance of getting the outcome in group A.

What is the chance of getting the outcome in group B?

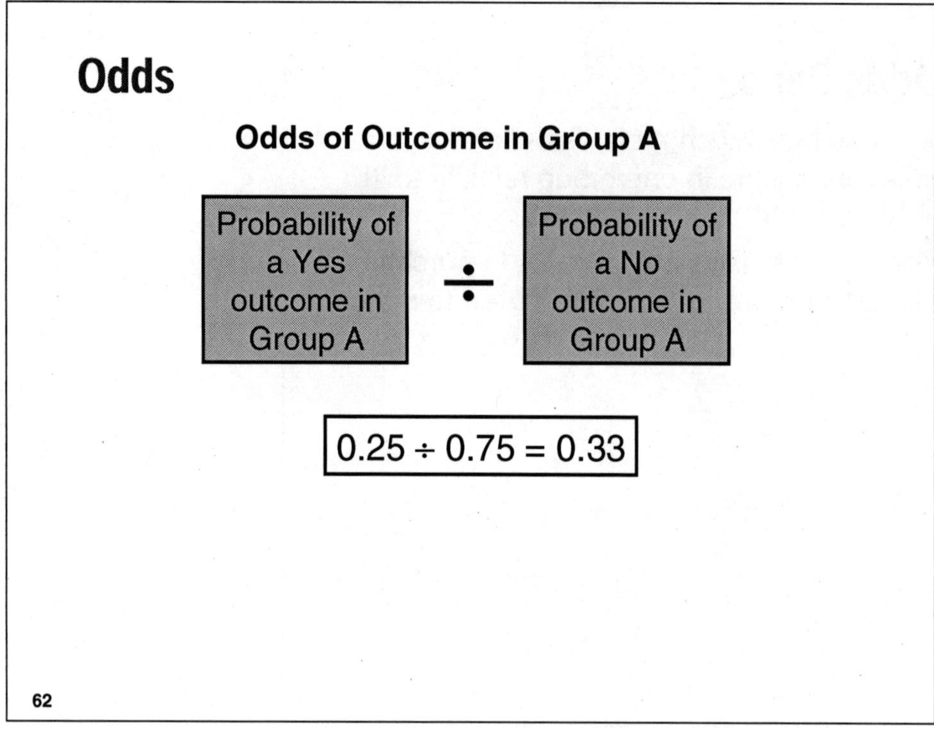

	Outcome		Total
	YES	NO	
Group A	20	60	80
Group B	10	90	100
	30	150	180

The odds of an outcome is the ratio of the expected number of times that the outcome will occur to the expected number of times the outcome will **not** occur. In other words, the odds is simply the ratio of the probability of the outcome to the probability of no outcome. The odds for group A equals 0.33, indicating that you expect only 1/3 as many occurrences as nonoccurrences in group A.

What is the odds of getting the outcome in group B?

Odds Ratio

Odds Ratio of Group A to Group B

Odds of outcome in Group A ÷ Odds of outcome in Group B

$0.33 \div 0.11 = \mathbf{3}$

63

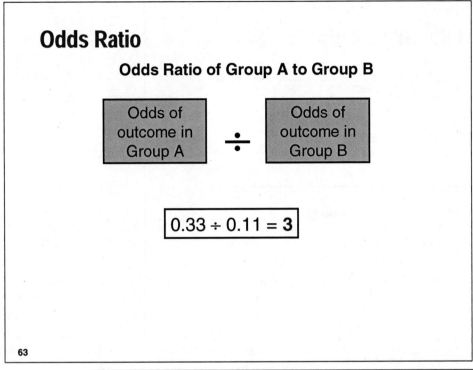

	Outcome		Total
	YES	NO	
Group A	20	60	80
Group B	10	90	100
	30	150	180

The odds ratio of group A to B equals 3, indicating the odds of getting the outcome in group A are 3 times those in group B.

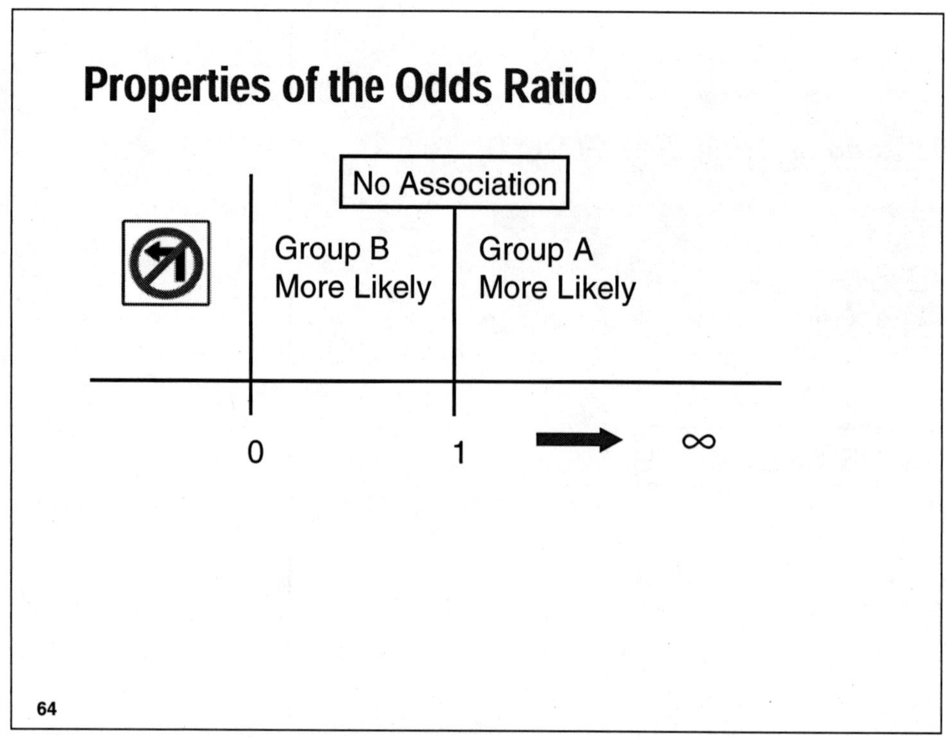

The odds ratio shows the strength of the association between the predictor variable and the outcome variable. If the odds ratio is 1, then there is no association between the predictor variable and the outcome. If the odds ratio is greater than 1, then group A is more likely to have the outcome. If the odds ratio is less than 1, then group B is more likely to have the outcome. For example, an odds ratio of 3 indicates that the odds of getting the outcome in group A is 3 times that in group B.

Odds Ratio Calculation from the Current Logistic Regression Model

Logistic regression model:

$$\text{logit}(\hat{p}) = \log(\textit{odds}) = \beta_0 + \beta_1 * (\text{gender})$$

Odds ratio (females to males):

$$\text{odds}_{\text{females}} = e^{\beta_0 + \beta_1}$$

$$\text{odds}_{\text{males}} = e^{\beta_0}$$

$$\text{odds ratio} = \frac{e^{\beta_0 + \beta_1}}{e^{\beta_0}} = e^{\beta_1}$$

65

The odds ratio is computed by exponentiating the parameter estimate for the predictor variable. For this example, the odds ratio for `gender` (coded 1 for female and 0 for male) compares the predicted odds of females to purchase 100 dollars or more in items compared to males.

Odds Ratio

Wald

Odds Ratio Estimates			
Effect	Point Estimate	95% Wald Confidence Limits	
gender Female vs Male	1.549	1.040	2.305

Profile likelihood

Odds Ratio Estimates			
Effect	Point Estimate	95% Wald Confidence Limits	
gender Female vs Male	1.549	1.040	2.305

66

The Odds Ratio Estimates table previously displayed was copied in the slide above. The 95% Wald Confidence Limits do not include 1.000 (1.040, 2.305), indicating the odds ratio is significant at the 0.05 significance level.

If you want a different significance level for the confidence intervals, you can change the confidence level on the Statistics tab in the Logistic Regression task.

The point estimate for the odds ratio estimates can also be computed manually.

Model Assessment: Comparing Pairs

- Counting concordant, discordant, and tied pairs is a way to assess how well the model predicts its own data and therefore how well the model fits.
- In general, you want a high percentage of concordant pairs and low percentages of discordant and tied pairs.

67

Comparing Pairs

To find concordant, discordant, and tied pairs, compare everyone who had the outcome of interest against everyone who did not.

< $100 $100 +

68

Concordant Pair

Compare a woman who bought more than $100 worth of goods from the catalog and a man who did not.

< $100 $100 +

P(100+) = .32 P(100+) = .42

The actual sorting agrees with the model.
This is a **concordant** pair.

69

For all pairs of observations with different values of the response variable, a pair is *concordant* if the observation with the outcome has a **higher** predicted outcome probability (based on the model) than the observation without the outcome.

Discordant Pair

Compare a man who bought more than $100 worth of goods from the catalog and a woman who did not.

< $100 $100 +

P(100+) = .42 P(100+) = .32

The actual sorting disagrees with the model.
This is a **discordant** pair.

70

A pair is *discordant* if the observation with the outcome has a **lower** predicted outcome probability than the observation without the outcome.

Tied Pair

Compare two woman. One bought more than $100 worth of goods from the catalog, but the other did not.

< $100	$100 +

P(100+) = .42	P(100+) = .42

The model cannot distinguish between the two.
This is a **tied** pair.

71

A pair is *tied* if it is neither concordant nor discordant (the probabilities are the same).

Concordant versus Discordant

	Customer Purchasing Over $100		
	Predicted Outcome Probability	Females (0.42)	Males (0.32)
Customer Purchasing Less Than $100	Females (0.42)	Tie	Discordant Pair
	Males (0.32)	Concordant Pair	Tie

72

This table shows the difference between discordant and concordant pairs. Because the predictor variable (**`gender`**) has only two levels, there are only two predicted outcome probabilities for purchasing items of 100 dollars or more (`Female`=0.42 and `Male`=0.32). For all pairs of observations with different outcomes (making purchases of 100 dollars or more versus making purchases of less than 100 dollars), a comparison is made of the predicted outcome probabilities. If the observation with the outcome (in this case making purchases of 100 dollars or more) has a higher predicted outcome probability compared to an observation without the outcome, the pair is concordant. However, if the observation with the outcome has a lower predicted outcome probability compared to the predicted outcome probability of an observation without the outcome, the pair is discordant. If the predicted outcome probabilities are tied, then the pair is tied.

In more complex models, there are more than two predicted outcome probabilities. However, the same comparisons are made across all pairs of observations with different outcomes.

Model: Concordant, Discordant, and Tied Pairs

Association of Predicted Probabilities and Observed Responses			
Percent Concordant	30.1	Somers' D	0.107
Percent Discordant	19.5	Gamma	0.215
Percent Tied	50.4	Tau-a	0.050
Pairs	43578	c	0.553

73

The Association of Predicted Probabilities and Observed Responses table shows the number of observation pairs upon which the percentages are based. For this example, there are 162 observations with an outcome of 100 dollars or more and 269 observations with an outcome of under 100 dollars. This creates 162*269 = 43,578 pairs of observations with different outcome values.

The four rank correlation indices (Somer's D, Gamma, Tau-a, and *c*) are computed from the numbers of concordant, discordant, and tied pairs of observations. The difference between them is how they treat the tied pairs. In general, a model with higher values for these indices has better predictive ability than a model with lower values for these indices.

5.4 Multiple Logistic Regression

Objectives

- Define and explain the adjusted odds ratio.
- Fit a multiple logistic regression model using the backward elimination method.
- Fit a multiple logistic regression model with interactions.

75

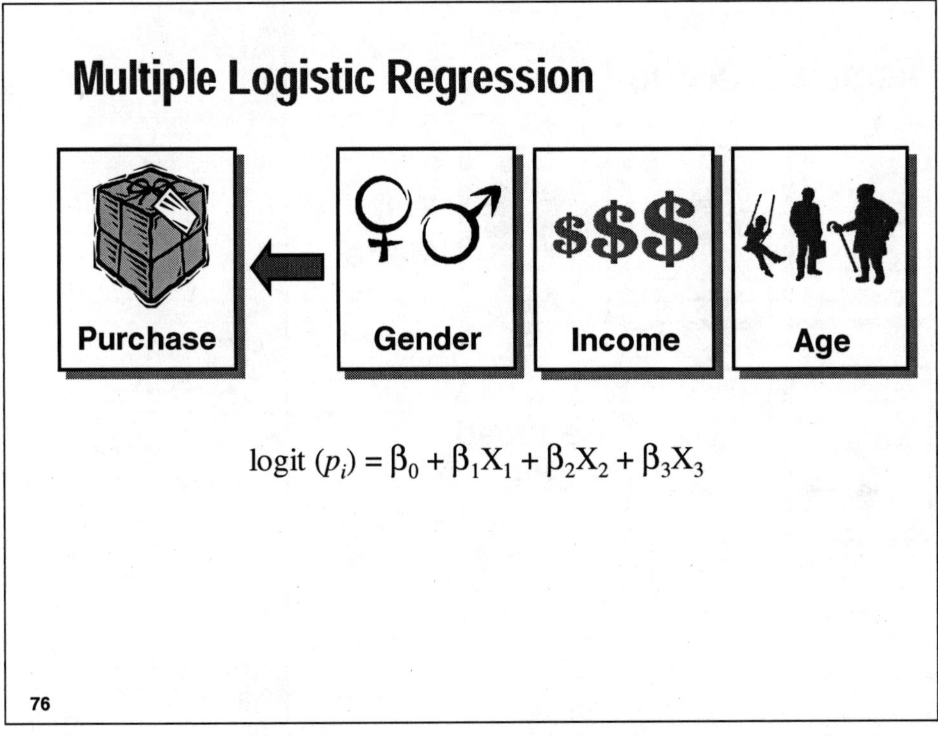

In multiple logistic regression models, several continuous or categorical predictor variables are trying to explain the variability of the response variable. The goal in multiple logistic regression is similar to that in linear multiple regression. Find the best subset of variables by eliminating unnecessary ones. Models that are parsimonious, or simple, are more likely to be numerically stable and easier to generalize.

If you have a large number of variables, you may need to try a variable reduction method such as variable clustering before modeling with logistic regression.

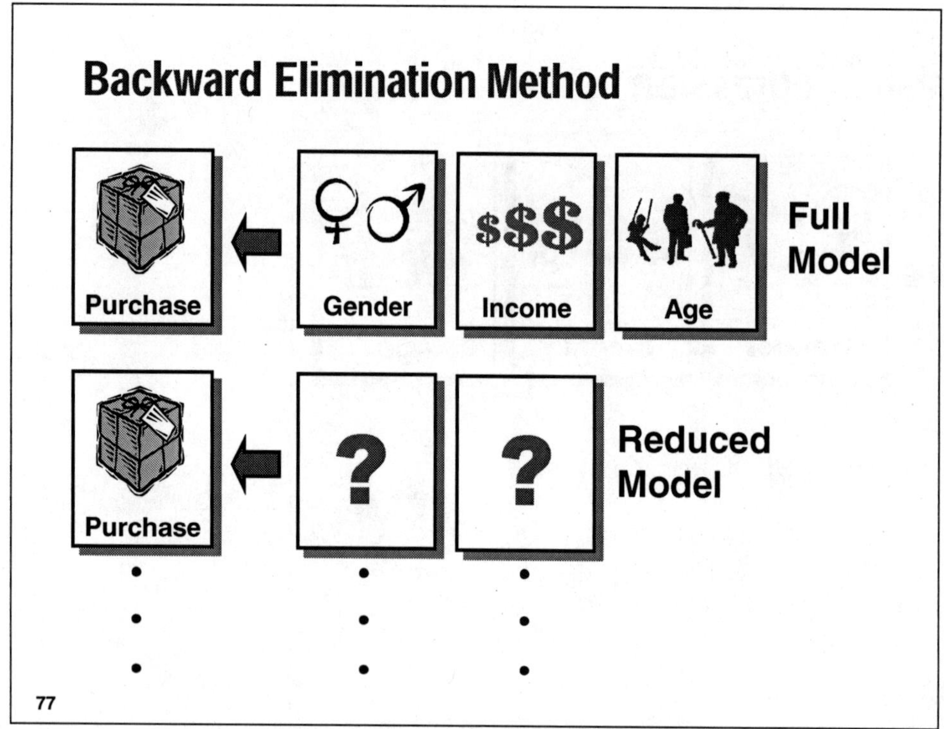

One way to eliminate unnecessary terms in a model is the *backward elimination method*. Backward logistic regression in SAS begins by fitting the full model with all the main effects. It then eliminates the nonsignificant parameter estimates one at a time, starting with the least significant term (the one with the largest *p*-value). The final model should only have significant main effects.

The significance level you choose depends on how much evidence you need in the significance of the predictor variables. The smaller your significance level, the more evidence you need to keep the predictor variable. In other words, the smaller your significance level is, the smaller the *p*-value has to be to keep the predictor variable.

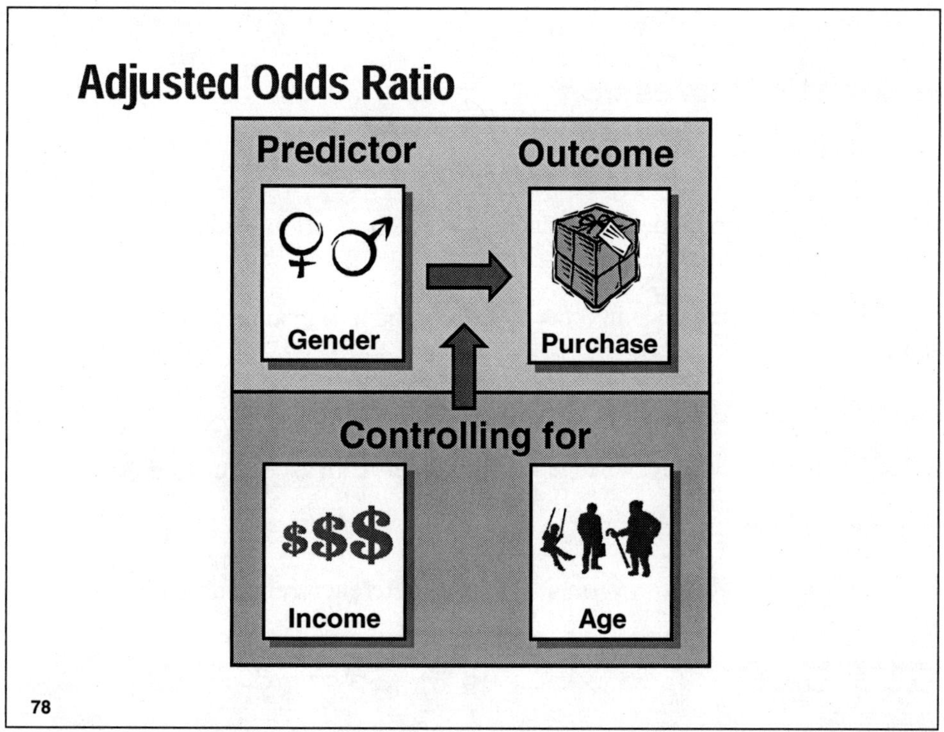

One major difference between a model with one predictor variable and a model with more than one predictor variable is that the reported odds ratios are now adjusted odds ratios.

Adjusted odds ratios measure the effect between a predictor variable and a response variable, while holding all the other predictor variables constant. In other words, the levels of the predictor variables would remain the same across the observations.

For example, the odds ratio for the variable **`gender`** would measure the effect of **`gender`** on **`purchase`** while holding **`income`** and **`age`** constant. (All observations are held at the same income and at the same age.)

The assumption is that the odds ratio for **`gender`** is the same regardless of the level of **`income`** or **`age`**. If that assumption is not true, you have an interaction. This is discussed later in the chapter.

Multiple Logistic Regression

Example: Fit a multiple logistic regression model using the backward elimination method. The full model should include all the main effects.

Set up the analysis and then edit the generated code in order to specify the low-income group as the reference cell for the variable `income`.

1. Select **Analyze** ⇨ **Regression** ⇨ **Logistic...**.
2. Assign `purchase` as the Dependent variable. Change the Sort order from ascending to descending.
3. Assign `age` as a Quantitative variable.
4. Assign `gender` and `income` as Classification variables. Specify reference cell coding for both classification variables.

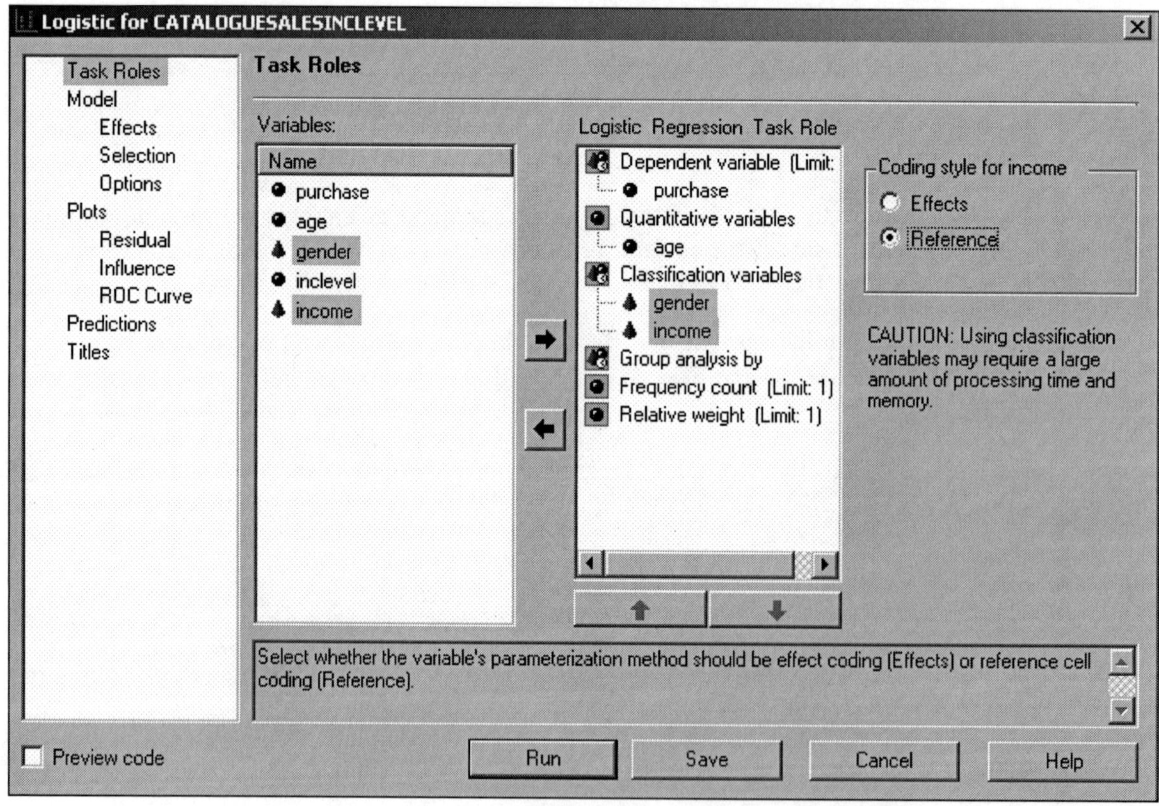

To specify reference cell coding for each class variable, you must select each class variable and select reference cell coding one at a time.

5. Select **Effects** under Model. Assign the variables `gender`, `income`, and `age` as effects by selecting all three variables and selecting **Main**.

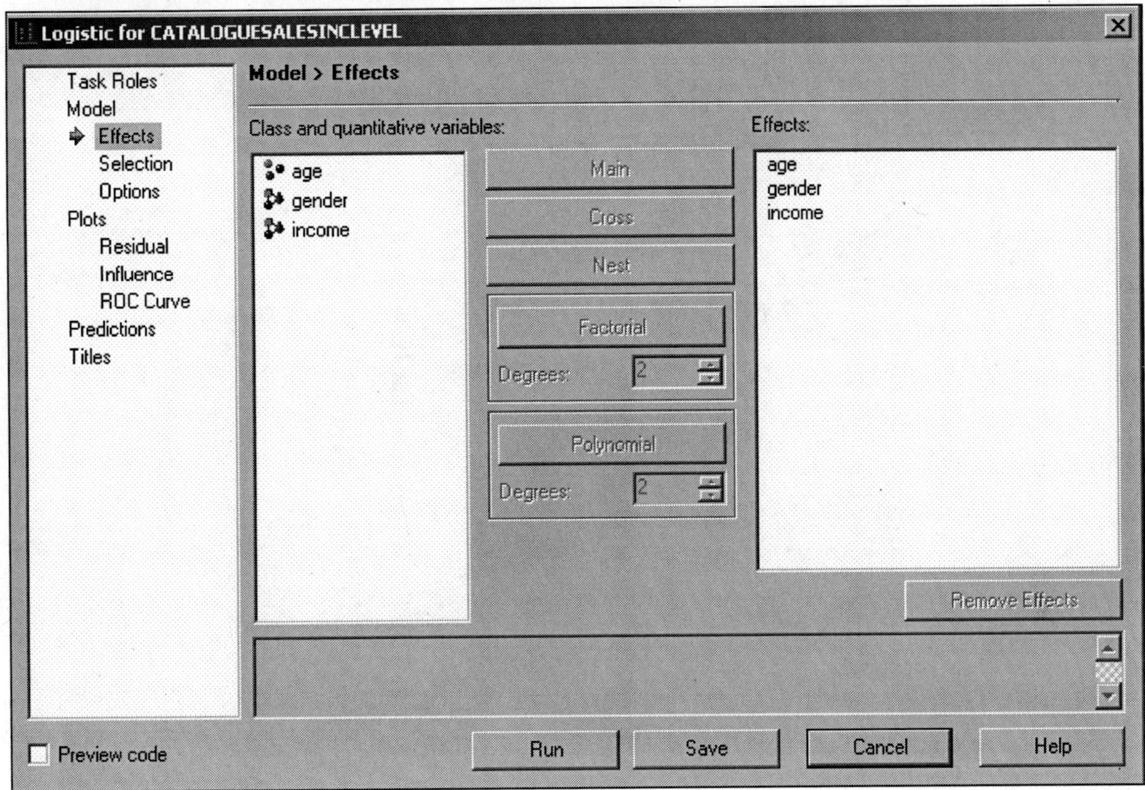

6. Select **Selection** from the pane on the left. Select **Backward elimination** from the pull-down menu.

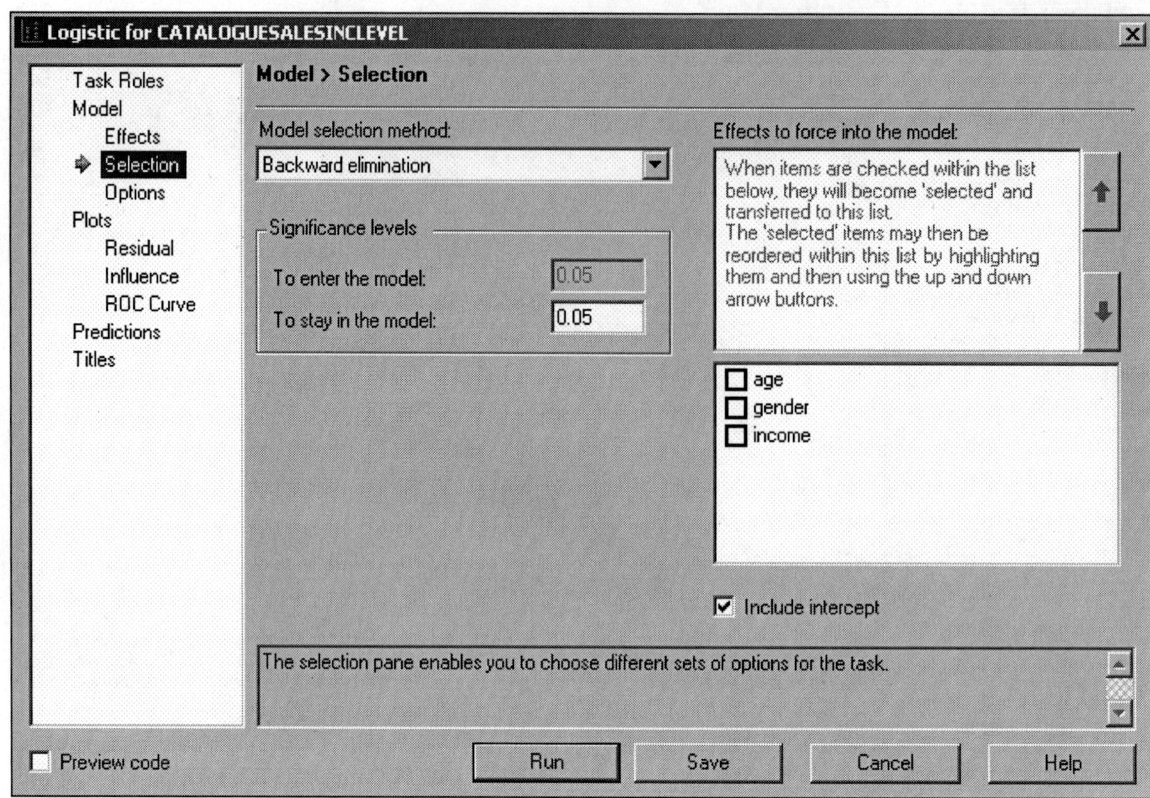

The default significance level for the backward elimination method is 0.05. If you want to change the significance level, you can specify a significance level next to **To stay in the model:**. Values must be between 0 and 1.

7. Select **Run**.

8. Scroll through the results to the Class Level Information table.

Backward Elimination Procedure

Class Level Information			
Class	Value	Design Variables	
gender	Female	1	
	Male	0	
income	High	1	0
	Low	0	1
	Medium	0	0

For **gender**, `Male` is used as the reference cell, and for **income**, `Medium` is used as the reference cell. These cells are the last groups alphanumerically. In order to use `Low` as the reference cell, edit the code that was generated by this task.

9. In the process flow, right-click on the task and select **Open Code**. If you are using the project view, then double-click the Code node under the task.

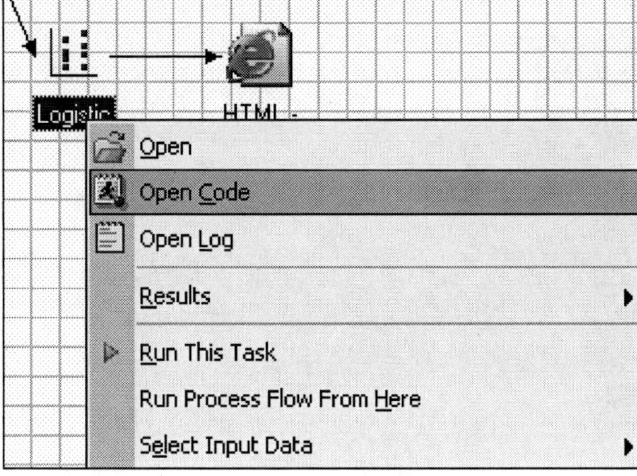

10. Scroll to the PROC LOGISTIC step in the program. Place your cursor somewhere on the CLASS statement line and press the space bar.

```
PROC LOGISTIC DATA=WORK.SORT2621
    DESCENDING
    ;
    CLASS gender     (PARAM=REF) income    (PARAM=REF);
    MODEL purchase=age gender income          /
        SELECTION=BACKWARD
        SLS=0.05
        INCLUDE=0
        LINK=LOGIT
    ;
RUN;
QUIT;

/* -----------------------------------------------------
   End of task code.
   ----------------------------------------------------- */
RUN; QUIT;
```

A window asks whether you want to add this as a modifiable code window.

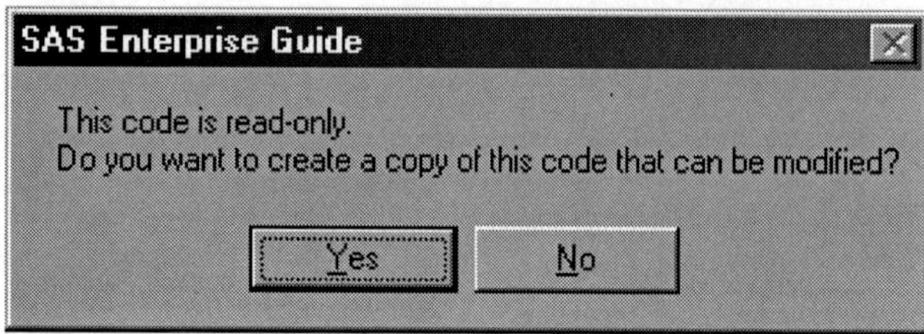

11. Select **Yes**.

A new node, **Code for Logistic Regression**, was added to the display tree.

12. Enter **REF = 'Low'** within the parentheses associated with PARAM=REF for the class variable **income**. Notice that 'Low' must be entered using upper and lower case, and enclosed in single quotes, not double quotes. Your completed code should appear as shown below:

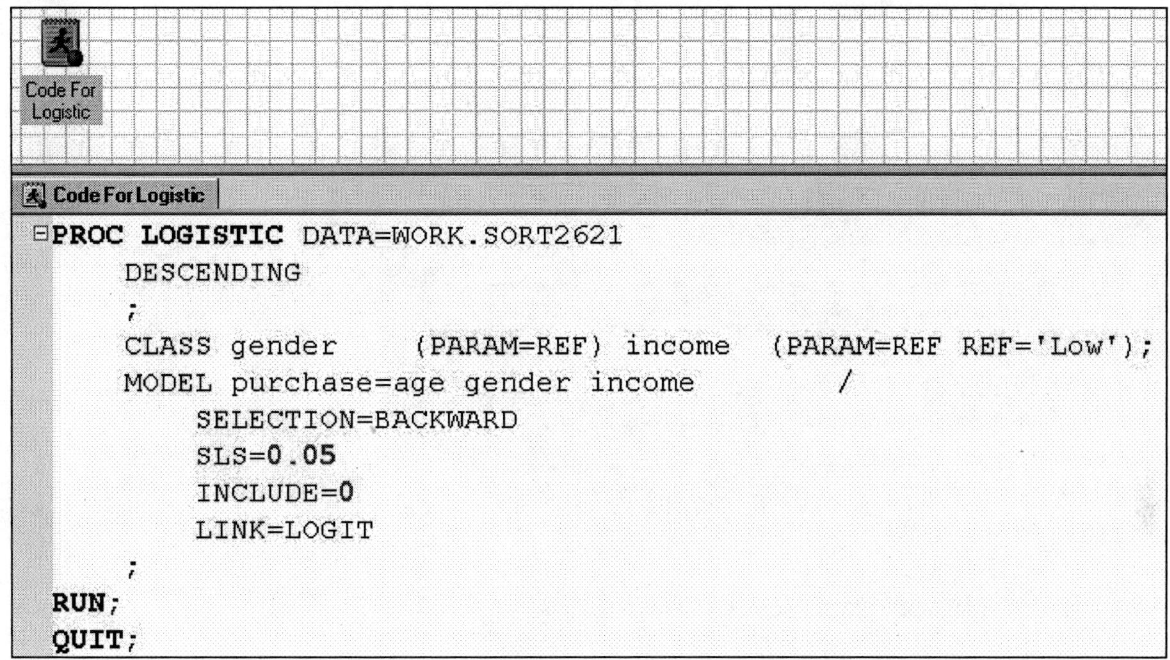
Code For Logistic
Code For Logistic
PROC LOGISTIC DATA=WORK.SORT2621
DESCENDING
;
CLASS gender (PARAM=REF) income (PARAM=REF REF='Low');
MODEL purchase=age gender income /
SELECTION=BACKWARD
SLS=0.05
INCLUDE=0
LINK=LOGIT
;
RUN;
QUIT;

> If you use `LOW` as the value for REF, you would not get the results you want. The only valid values for **income** in this data table are `Low`, `Medium`, or `High`. SAS Enterprise Guide considers that `LOW` and `Low` are two different values.

13. Right-click in the code window. Select **Run on Local**.

You modified the program to use the low-income group as the reference cell for the model.

Model Information	
Data Set	WORK.SORT73
Response Variable	purchase
Number of Response Levels	2
Model	binary logit
Optimization Technique	Fisher's scoring

Number of Observations Read	431
Number of Observations Used	431

Response Profile		
Ordered Value	purchase	Total Frequency
1	1	162
2	0	269

Probability modeled is purchase=1.

The Model Information and Response Profile of the PROC LOGISTIC output is the same as the first model.

Backward Elimination Procedure

Class Level Information			
Class	Value	Design Variables	
gender	Female	1	
	Male	0	
income	High	1	0
	Low	0	0
	Medium	0	1

The output identifies the chosen BACKWARD selection method, and then provides a Class Level Information table. The variable **income** was added to this table, and because there are three levels, two design variable columns are displayed. You chose `Low` as the reference value using the PARAM=REF and REF='Low' options in the CLASS statement. PROC LOGISTIC has generated two Design Variables for the three levels of **income**. Design Variable 1 will be 1 when **income=High**, and will be 0 when **income=Low** or **income=Medium**. Design variable 2 will be 1 when **income=Medium**, and 0 when **income=High** or **income=Low**.

The next part of the output shows the backward elimination process in PROC LOGISTIC.

Step 0. The following effects were entered:

Intercept age gender income

Model Convergence Status
Convergence criterion (GCONV=1E-8) satisfied.

Model Fit Statistics		
Criterion	Intercept Only	Intercept and Covariates
AIC	572.649	562.208
SC	576.715	582.539
-2 Log L	570.649	552.208

Testing Global Null Hypothesis: BETA=0			
Test	Chi-Square	DF	Pr > ChiSq
Likelihood Ratio	18.4410	4	0.0010
Score	18.2729	4	0.0011
Wald	17.6172	4	0.0015

At Step 0, the intercept and three predictor variables are entered into the model. The Model Fit Statistics and Testing Global Null Hypothesis tables are presented for this step.

Step 1. Effect age is removed:

Model Convergence Status
Convergence criterion (GCONV=1E-8) satisfied.

Model Fit Statistics		
Criterion	Intercept Only	Intercept and Covariates
AIC	572.649	562.190
SC	576.715	578.454
-2 Log L	570.649	554.190

Testing Global Null Hypothesis: BETA=0			
Test	Chi-Square	DF	Pr > ChiSq
Likelihood Ratio	16.4592	3	0.0009
Score	16.3718	3	0.0010
Wald	15.8824	3	0.0012

Residual Chi-Square Test		
Chi-Square	DF	Pr > ChiSq
1.9836	1	0.1590

At Step 1, the variable **age** is removed from the model and the Model Fit Statistics and Testing Global Null Hypothesis tables are updated.

The Residual Chi-Square Test table displays the joint significance of the variables not in the model (in this case, **age**). This Score Chi-Squared statistic has an asymptotic chi-squared distribution with the degrees of freedom being the difference between the full and reduced models.

Note: No (additional) effects met the 0.05 significance level for removal from the model.

When the selection process is complete, a note states that no additional variables met the specified significance level for removal from the model, and a Summary of Backward Elimination table is generated.

Summary of Backward Elimination

Step	Effect Removed	DF	Number In	Wald Chi-Square	Pr > ChiSq
1	age	1	2	1.9729	0.1601

Type 3 Analysis of Effects

Effect	DF	Wald Chi-Square	Pr > ChiSq
gender	1	5.8211	0.0158
income	2	11.6669	0.0029

In the next part of the output, the Summary of Backward Elimination table lists the step number, the name of each predictor variable (effect) that is removed from the model at each step, degrees of freedom, the number of the predictor variable in the MODEL statement, the Wald Chi-Square statistic for each variable, and the corresponding *p*-value upon which each variable's removal from the model is based.

The Type 3 Analysis of Effects table for this model indicates that the coefficients for **gender** and **income** are statistically different from 0 at the 0.05 level of significance. Please note that **income** has two degrees of freedom, because it has three levels.

Analysis of Maximum Likelihood Estimates						
Parameter		DF	Estimate	Standard Error	Wald Chi-Square	Pr > ChiSq
Intercept		1	-1.1125	0.2403	21.4255	<.0001
gender	Female	1	0.5040	0.2089	5.8211	0.0158
income	High	1	0.7605	0.2515	9.1447	0.0025
income	Medium	1	0.0963	0.2628	0.1342	0.7141

The Analysis of Maximum Likelihood Estimates table is now examined. The *p*-value for **gender=Female** (0.0158) indicates that its coefficient is statistically different from 0 at the 0.05 level of significance. In addition, you can also state that females and males are statistically different from one another in terms of purchasing 100 dollars or more.

The coefficient for **income=High** is also statistically different from 0, based on its *p*-value (0.0025). Because **income=Low** is the reference group, you can state that high- and low-income people are statistically different from one another with respect to purchasing 100 dollars or more. When you examine **income=Medium**, the *p*-value of 0.7141 indicates that this coefficient is not different from 0. Again, because Low is the reference group, you can state that medium- and low-income people are not statistically different and have a similar purchasing behavior.

What action can you take at this point? If your analysis goal is building predictive models, you can run a query or write a DATA step to, in essence, collapse the 'Low' and 'Medium' observations into a single group. The new variable (**highinc**) would be equal to High when **income=High**, or Low/Medium otherwise. You would then replace **income** in the model with **highinc**, and execute the analysis again. Remember to correctly interpret the coefficient of **highinc**.

Odds Ratio Estimates			
Effect	Point Estimate	95% Wald Confidence Limits	
gender Female vs Male	1.655	1.099	2.493
income High vs Low	2.139	1.307	3.502
income Medium vs Low	1.101	0.658	1.843

Association of Predicted Probabilities and Observed Responses			
Percent Concordant	54.0	Somers' D	0.246
Percent Discordant	29.4	Gamma	0.295
Percent Tied	16.6	Tau-a	0.116
Pairs	43578	c	0.623

The last part of the output provides the Odds Ratio Estimates table as well as the Association of Predicted Probabilities and Observed Responses table.

The effects for **`gender Female vs Male`** and **`income High vs Low`** both indicate that they are statistically significant at the 0.05 level because their 95% Wald Confidence Intervals do not include 1.000. Note that the 95% confidence interval for **`income Medium vs Low`** is not significant. The interval (0.658, 1.843) includes 1.000.

When you compare the percentages of this model with the previous model where **`gender`** was the only predictor variable, the concordant percentage increased (from 30.1 to 54.0), but the discordant percentage also increased (from 19.5 to 29.4). The tied percentage showed the most change, decreasing from 50.4 to 16.6.

The *c* statistic increased (0.553 to 0.623) from the simple **`gender`** model, which is desirable.

Comparing Models

Gender Only	
AIC	569.951
SC	578.084
-2 Log L	565.951
Conc.	30.1%
Disc.	19.5%
Ties	50.4%
c	0.553

Gender + Income	
AIC	562.190
SC	578.454
-2 Log L	554.190
Conc.	54.0%
Disc.	29.4%
Ties	16.6%
c	0.623

80

Adding income to the model decreases the AIC and SC, and it increases the number of concordant pairs. Although discordant pairs increased, tied pairs decreased. Adding `income` improved the model.

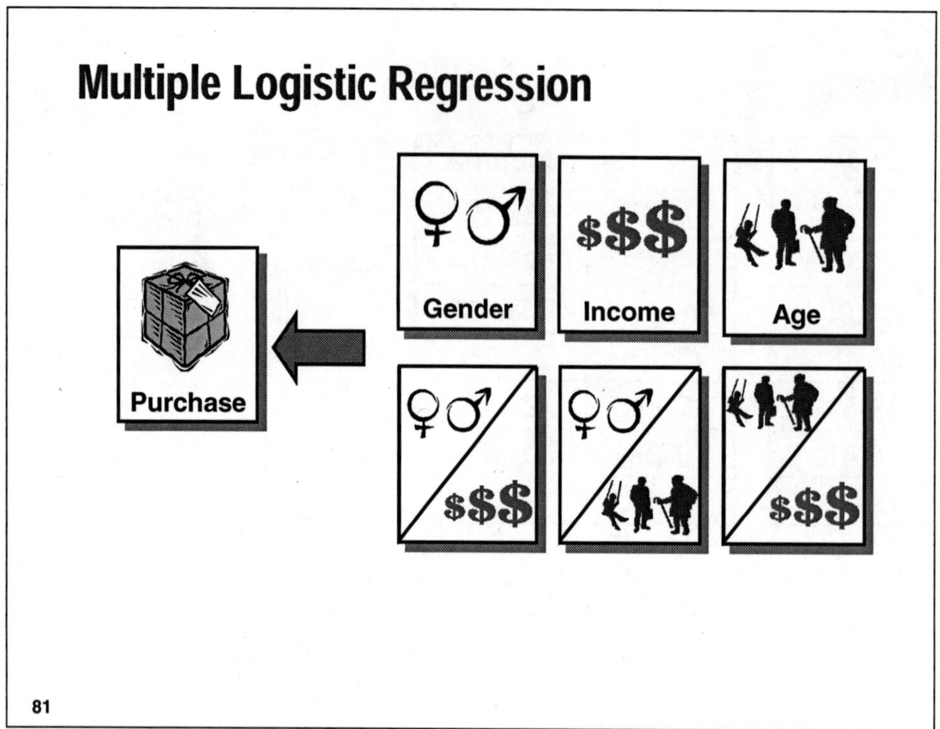

In the last example, a multiple logistic regression model was fitted with only the main effects (only predictor variables are in the model). Thus, you are assuming that the effect of each variable on the outcome is the same, regardless of the levels of the other variables. For example, you are assuming that the effect of `gender` (Female to Male) on the probability of making purchases of 100 dollars or more is the same regardless of `income` level. If this assumption is not correct, you may want to fit a more complex model that has interactions.

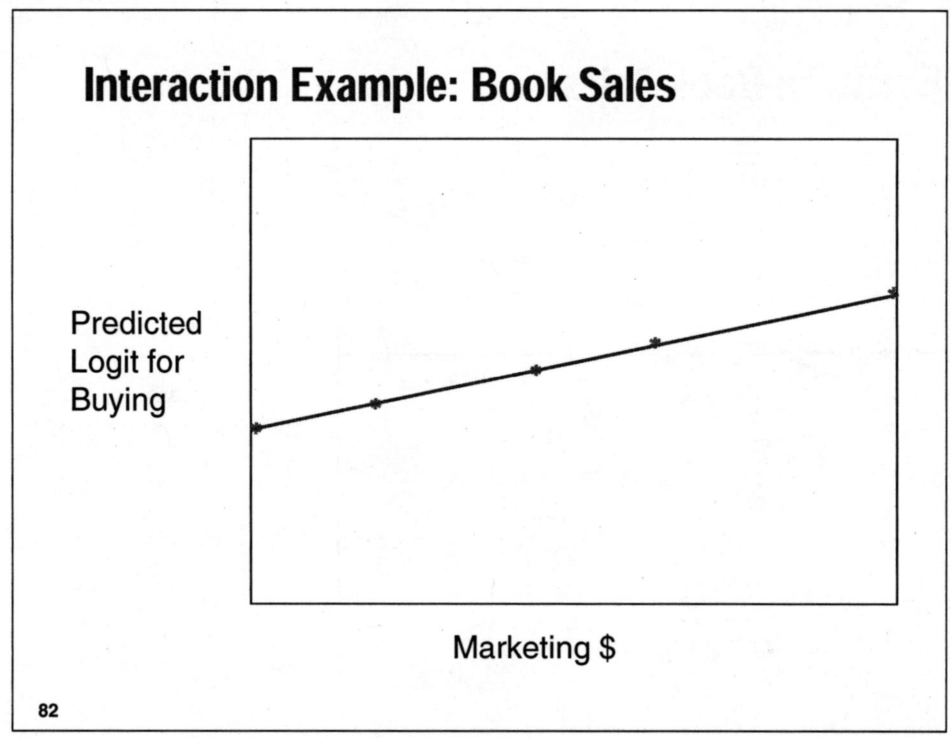

The above example assumes that one dollar of marketing money has the same effect for all books.

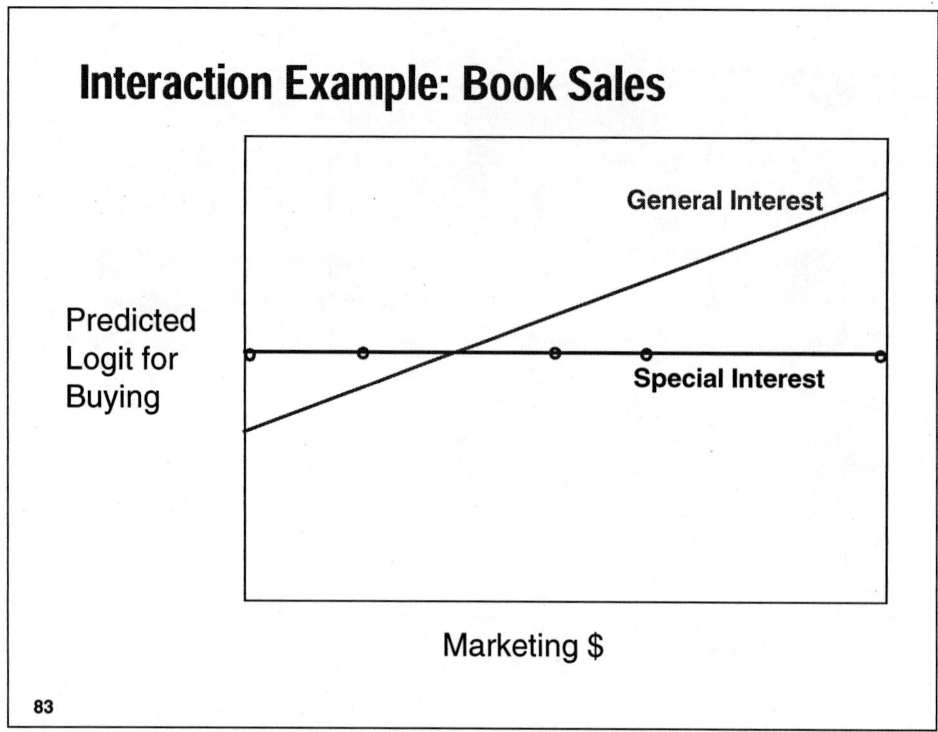

However, if you consider the type of book to be sold, there seems to be a difference in the effect of marketing dollars on general interest books versus special interest. This is called an interaction. An *interaction* between two variables A and B is said to occur when the effect of A on the outcome depends on the observed level of B, or when the effect of B on the outcome depends on the observed level of A.

In the example above, the effect of **`marketing`** depends on the level of **`booktype`**. For **`booktype`**=`General Interest`, as **`marketing`** increases, the probability of buying increases. However, for **`booktype`**=`Special Interest`, as **`marketing`** increases, the probability of buying does not change.

Therefore, there is a **`marketing`** by **`booktype`** interaction.

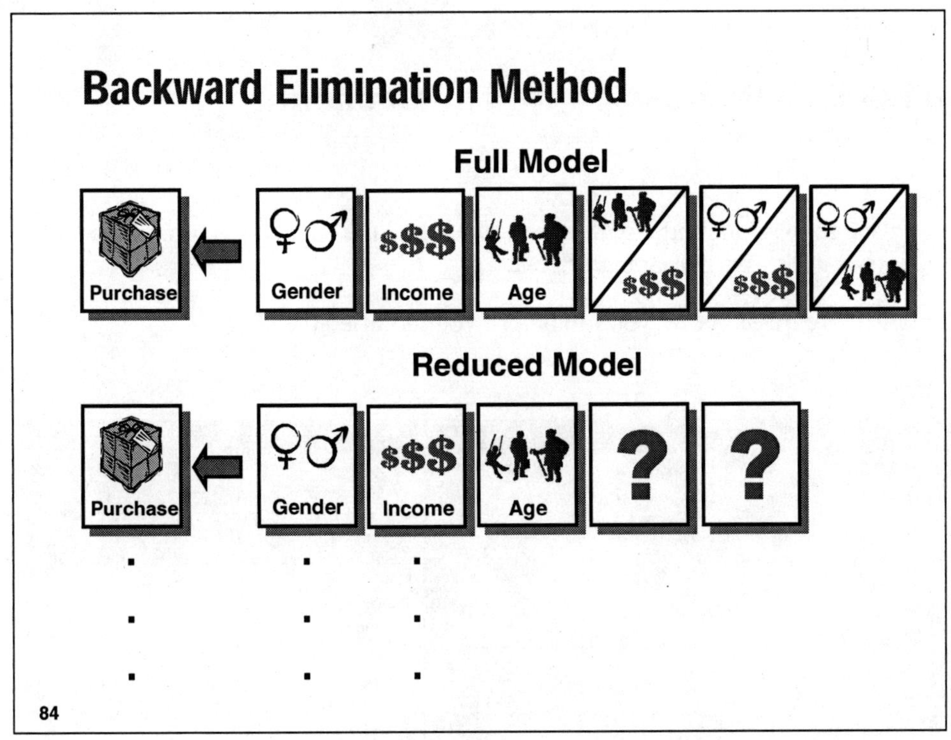

When you use the backward elimination method with interactions in the model, you begin by fitting the full model with all the main effects and interactions. You then eliminate the nonsignificant interactions one at a time, starting with the least significant interaction (the one with the largest *p*-value). Next, you eliminate the nonsignificant main effects not involved in any significant interactions. The final model should only have significant interactions, the main effects involved in the interactions, and the significant main effects.

The requirement that for any effect in the model, all effects it contains must also be in the model is called model hierarchy. For example, if the interaction `gender*income` is in the model, then the main effects `gender` and `income` must also be in the model. This ensures that you have a hierarchically well-formulated model.

For a more customized analysis, the HIERARCHY= option (a custom SAS code option) specifies whether hierarchy is maintained and whether a single effect or multiple effects are allowed to enter or leave the model in one step for forward, backward, and stepwise selection. The default is HIERARCHY=SINGLE. You could change this option by inserting the HIERARCHY= option in the task code's MODEL statement. See the *SAS/STAT User's Guide* in the SAS online documentation for more on using this option.

Multiple Logistic Regression with Interactions

Example: Fit a multiple logistic regression model with interactions. Use the backward elimination method to drop interactions that are not significant.

1. Double-click the last Logistic Regression task you ran before you modified the code.

2. Select **Effects** under Model.

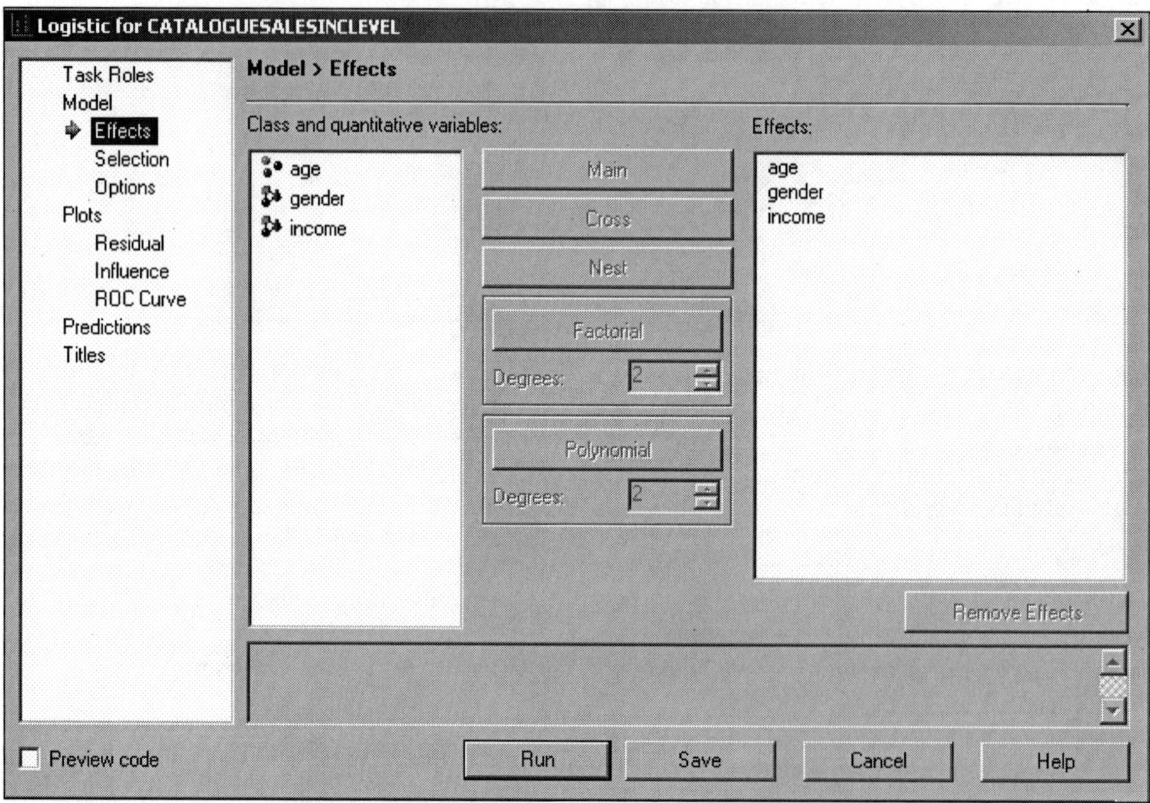

3. Control-click to select the three variables in the window on the left. Under Factorial, change Degrees from `3` to `2`. Select **Factorial** to add all two-way interactions to the model.

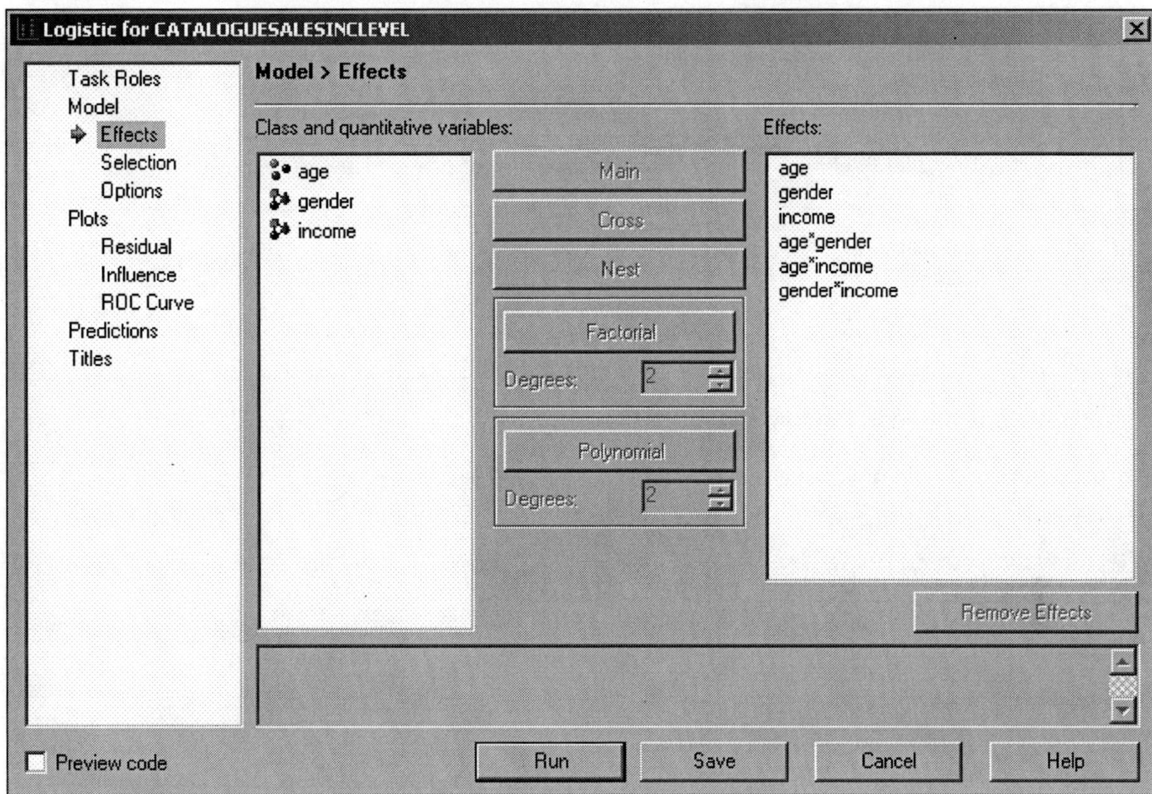

4. Select **Selection** and ensure that **Backward elimination** is selected.

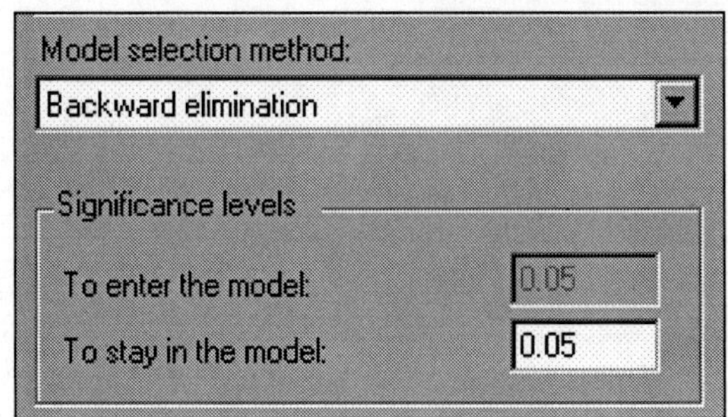

5. Select **Run**.

6. Select **NO** so that you do not replace results from the previous run.

7. After the task runs, double-click the Code node to change the reference cell for the **`income`** variable from `Medium` to `Low`.

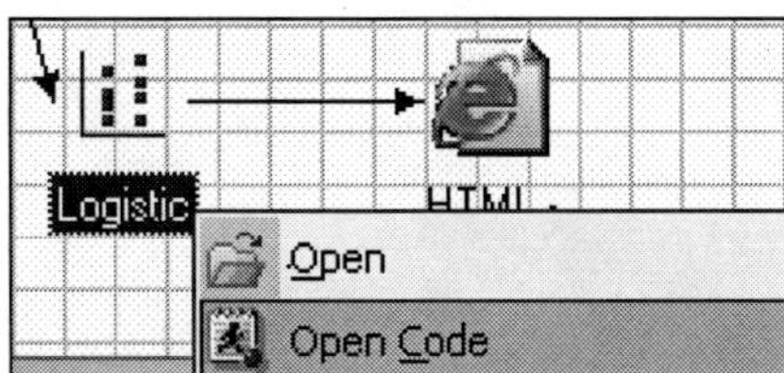

8. Enter **REF = 'Low'** within the parentheses associated with PARAM=REF in a modifiable code window as demonstrated earlier. Your code should appear as below:

Code For Logistic

```
PROC LOGISTIC DATA=WORK.SORT1567
     DESCENDING
     ;
     CLASS gender    (PARAM=REF) income   (PARAM=REF REF='Low');
     MODEL purchase=age gender income age*gender age*income gender*income        /
          SELECTION=BACKWARD
          SLS=0.05
          INCLUDE=0
          LINK=LOGIT
     ;
RUN;
QUIT;
```

9. Right-click in the code window and select **Run on Local**.

Your display tree should now have two **Code for Logistic Regression** entries.

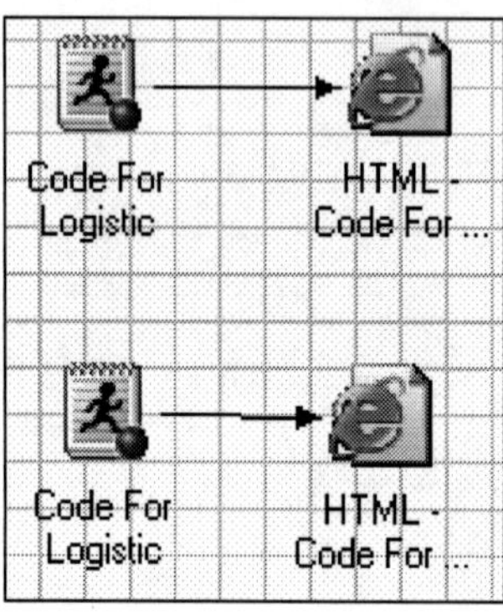

Review the results.

Model Information	
Data Set	WORK.SORT3053
Response Variable	purchase
Number of Response Levels	2
Model	binary logit
Optimization Technique	Fisher's scoring

Number of Observations Read	431
Number of Observations Used	431

Response Profile

Ordered Value	purchase	Total Frequency
1	1	162
2	0	269

Probability modeled is purchase=1.

The Model Information, Response Profile, and Class Level Information tables did not change.

Step 0. The following effects were entered:

Intercept age gender income age*gender age*income gender*income

Model Convergence Status
Convergence criterion (GCONV=1E-8) satisfied.

Model Fit Statistics

Criterion	Intercept Only	Intercept and Covariates
AIC	572.649	560.330
SC	576.715	600.991
-2 Log L	570.649	540.330

Testing Global Null Hypothesis: BETA=0

Test	Chi-Square	DF	Pr > ChiSq
Likelihood Ratio	30.3195	9	0.0004
Score	28.9614	9	0.0007
Wald	26.7755	9	0.0015

Step 0 includes all the two-way interactions.

Step 1. Effect age*income is removed:

Residual Chi-Square Test		
Chi-Square	DF	Pr > ChiSq
1.5966	2	0.4501

Selected output from Step 1 is presented above. The **age*income** interaction is eliminated because its *p*-value of 0.4501 is greater than 0.05.

Step 2. Effect age*gender is removed:

Residual Chi-Square Test		
Chi-Square	DF	Pr > ChiSq
3.2232	3	0.3585

Selected output from Step 2 is presented. The **age*gender** interaction is eliminated because its *p*-value of 0.3585 is greater than 0.05.

Step 3. Effect age is removed:

Model Convergence Status
Convergence criterion (GCONV=1E-8) satisfied.

Model Fit Statistics

Criterion	Intercept Only	Intercept and Covariates
AIC	572.649	557.194
SC	576.715	581.591
-2 Log L	570.649	545.194

Testing Global Null Hypothesis: BETA=0

Test	Chi-Square	DF	Pr > ChiSq
Likelihood Ratio	25.4552	5	0.0001
Score	24.1139	5	0.0002
Wald	22.7265	5	0.0004

Residual Chi-Square Test		
Chi-Square	DF	Pr > ChiSq
4.7980	4	0.3087

NOTE: No (additional) effects met the 0.05 significance level for removal from the model.

In Step 3, the main effect **age** is removed for the model because its *p*-value of 0.3087 is greater than 0.05.

Summary of Backward Elimination					
Step	Effect Removed	DF	Number In	Wald Chi-Square	Pr > ChiSq
1	age*income	2	5	1.5891	0.4518
2	age*gender	1	4	1.6408	0.2002
3	age	1	3	1.5965	0.2064

Type III Analysis of Effects			
Effect	DF	Wald Chi-Square	Pr > ChiSq
gender	1	4.9207	0.0265
income	2	18.8745	<.0001
gender*income	2	8.8363	0.0121

The interactions between **age*income** and **age*gender** were eliminated from the model because their *p*-values were greater than the default value of 0.05, as reported in the Summary of Backward Elimination table. However, because the interaction of **gender** and **income** was significant, the main effects **gender** and **income** must remain in the model. Because the main effect of **age** was not significant and not involved in a significant interaction, the term was dropped from the model.

Notice that by default, the Logistic Regression task maintains model hierarchy when main effects and interactions are used in backward elimination.

Analysis of Maximum Likelihood Estimates							
Parameter			DF	Estimate	Standard Error	Wald Chi-Square	Pr > ChiSq
Intercept			1	-1.4759	0.3919	14.1841	0.0002
gender	Female		1	0.9949	0.4485	4.9207	0.0265
income	High		1	1.5026	0.4549	10.9113	0.0010
income	Medium		1	0.1235	0.4873	0.0642	0.7999
income*gender	High	Female	1	-1.2223	0.5523	4.8979	0.0269
income*gender	Medium	Female	1	0.1026	0.5851	0.0307	0.8608

Association of Predicted Probabilities and Observed Responses			
Percent Concordant	54.8	Somers' D	0.261
Percent Discordant	28.6	Gamma	0.314
Percent Tied	16.6	Tau-a	0.123
Pairs	43578	c	0.631

Comparing the goodness-of-fit statistics and the statistics that assess the predictive ability of the full model and the final model shows that the full model has better predictive ability (because of the higher *c* statistic), while the final model has better goodness-of-fit statistics (because of the lower AIC and SBC statistics).

Statistic	**Full Model with all Two-Way interactions** **purchase=gender age income gender*age gender*income age*income**	**Final Model** **purchase=gender income gender*income**
AIC	560.330	557.194
SC	600.991	581.591
% Concordant	64.3	54.8
% Discordant	34.5	28.6
% Tied	1.1	16.6
c	0.649	0.631

Comparing Models

Gender, Income Main Effects	
AIC	562.190
SC	578.454
-2 Log L	554.190
Conc.	54.0%
Disc.	29.4%
Ties	16.6%
c	0.623

Main Effects + Interaction	
AIC	557.194
SC	581.591
-2 Log L	545.194
Conc.	54.8%
Disc.	28.6%
Ties	16.6%
c	0.631

86

AIC decreased (improved) for this model, but SC increased. This indicates that adding the interaction term might have improved the model's inference, but it also might have worsened its ability to predict. Overall, a model should be chosen based on the researcher's intent.

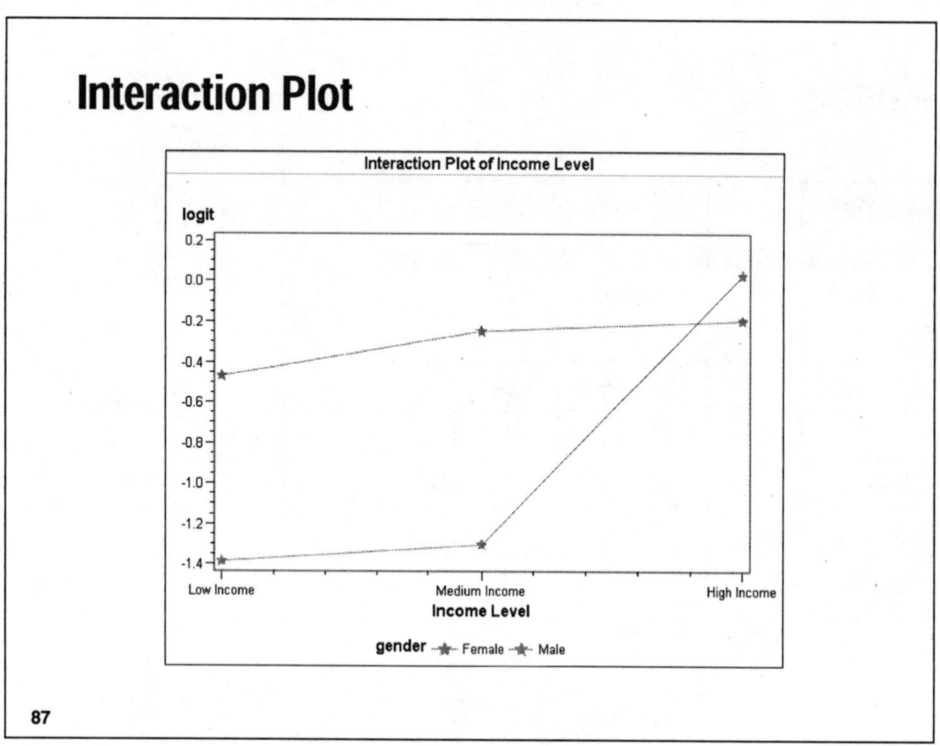

To visualize the interaction between **`gender`** and **`income`**, you could do an interaction plot. The plot would show two slopes for **`income`**, one for males and one for females. If there is no interaction between **`gender`** and **`income`**, then the slopes should be relatively parallel. However, the graph above shows that the slopes are not parallel. The reason for the interaction is that the probability of making purchases of 100 dollars or more is highly related to income for men but is weakly related to income for women.

The code for the interaction plot is shown in the Appendix entitled Advanced Programs.

5.5 Logit Plots (Self-Study)

Objectives

- Explain the concept of logit plots.
- Plot estimated logits for continuous and ordinal variables.

89

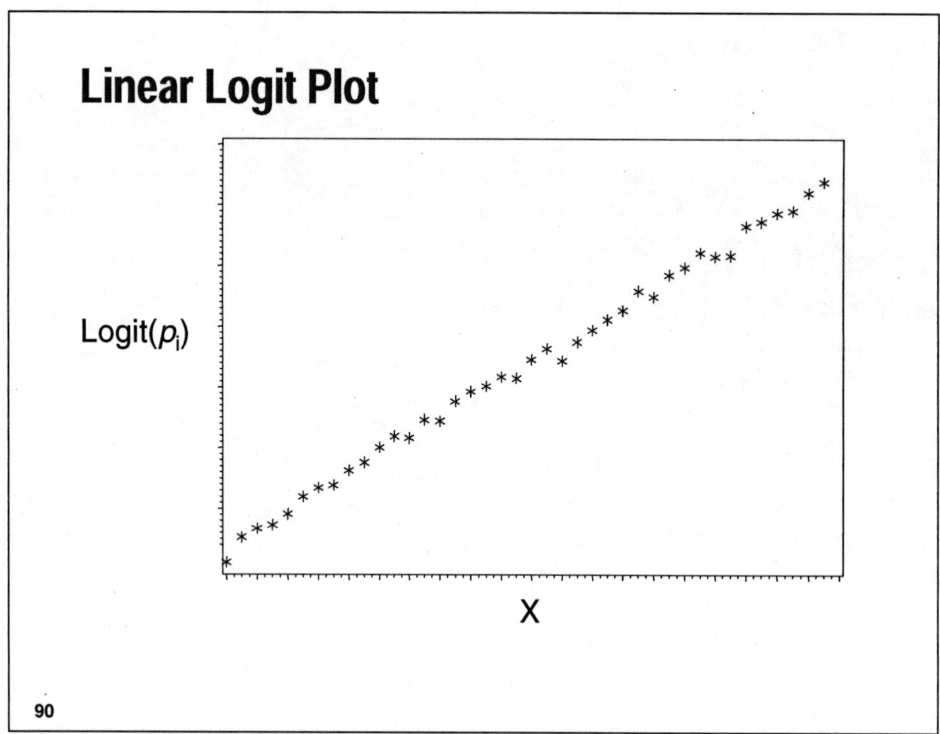

For continuous predictor variables with a large number of unique values, binning the data (collapsing data values into groups) is necessary to compute the logit. The bin size should have an adequate number of observations to reduce the sample variability of the logits. If the standard logistic regression model adequately fits the data, the logit plots should be fairly linear. The above graph shows a predictor variable that meets the assumption of linearity in the logit.

If the predictor variable is a nominal variable, then there is no need to create a logit plot.

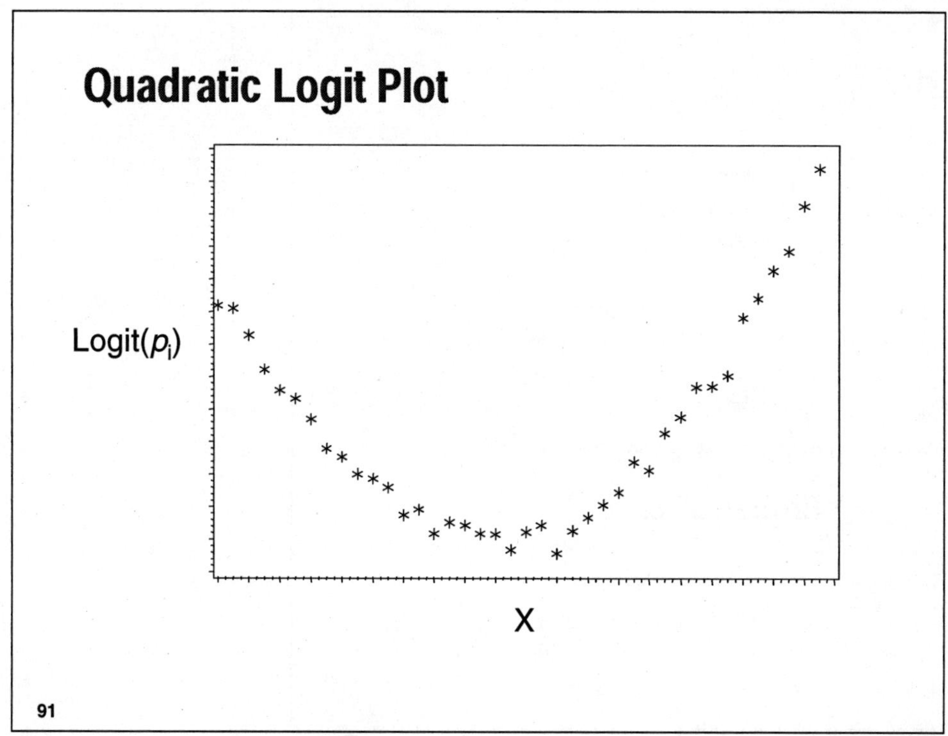

The logit plot can also show serious nonlinearities between the outcome variable and the predictor variable. The above graph reveals a quadratic relationship between the outcome and predictor variables. Adding a polynomial term or binning the predictor variable into three groups (two dummy variables would model the quadratic relationship) and treating it as a classification variable may improve the model fit.

Estimated Logits

$$\ln\left(\frac{m_i + 1}{M_i - m_i + 1}\right)$$

where

m_i= number of events

M_i = number of cases

92

A common approach in computing logits is to take the log of the odds. The logit is undefined, however, for any bin in which the outcome rate is 100% or 0%. To eliminate this problem and reduce the variability of the logits, a common recommendation is to add a small constant to the numerator and denominator of the formula that computes the logit (Duffy and Santner 1989).

Duffy, T.J. and Santner, D.E. (1989), *The Statistical Analysis of Discrete Data*, New York: Springer-Verlag.

Plotting Estimated Logits

Example: Use the Summary Statistics task, the Query Builder, and the Scatter Plot task to create a logit plot for the variable `inclevel`.

The first step in creating a logit plot for `inclevel` is to calculate the number of people in each `inclevel` group that have the outcome. Use the Summary Statistics task to do this.

1. Select the **SASUSER.CATALOGSALESINCOME** table in the process flow. Select **Describe** ⇨ **Summary Statistics**.
2. Assign `purchase` as the Analysis variable and `inclevel` as the Classification variable.

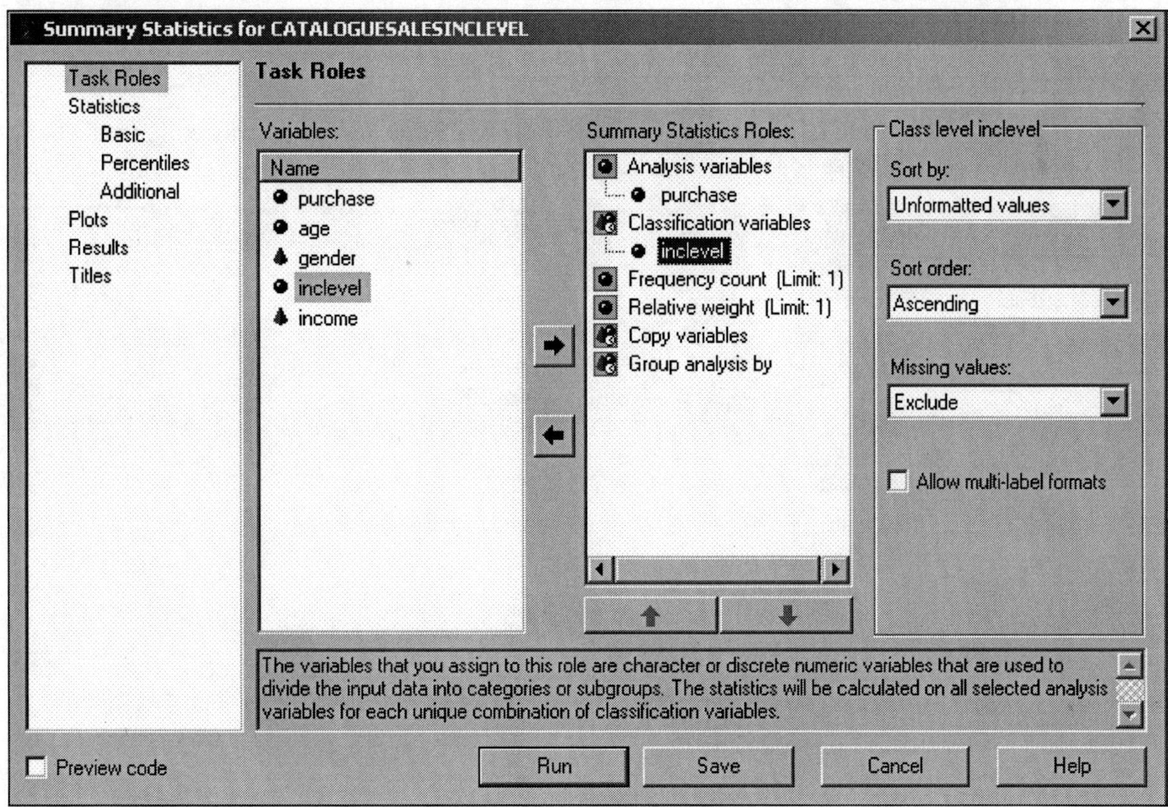

3. Select **Basic** under Statistics. De-select all of the default statistics and check the box next to **Sum**.

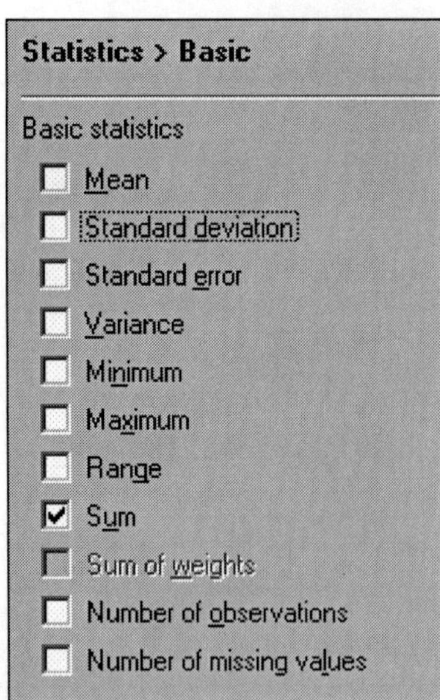

4. Select **Results** on the left. Check the box next to **Show Statistics** to deselect this option and check the box next to **Save Statistics to Data Set**. Click **Modify…**.

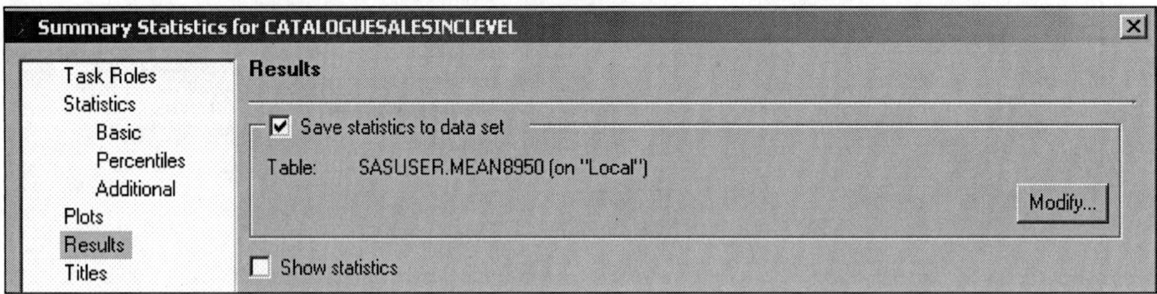

5. Change the default name of the resulting data set to **`inclevelcounts`**.

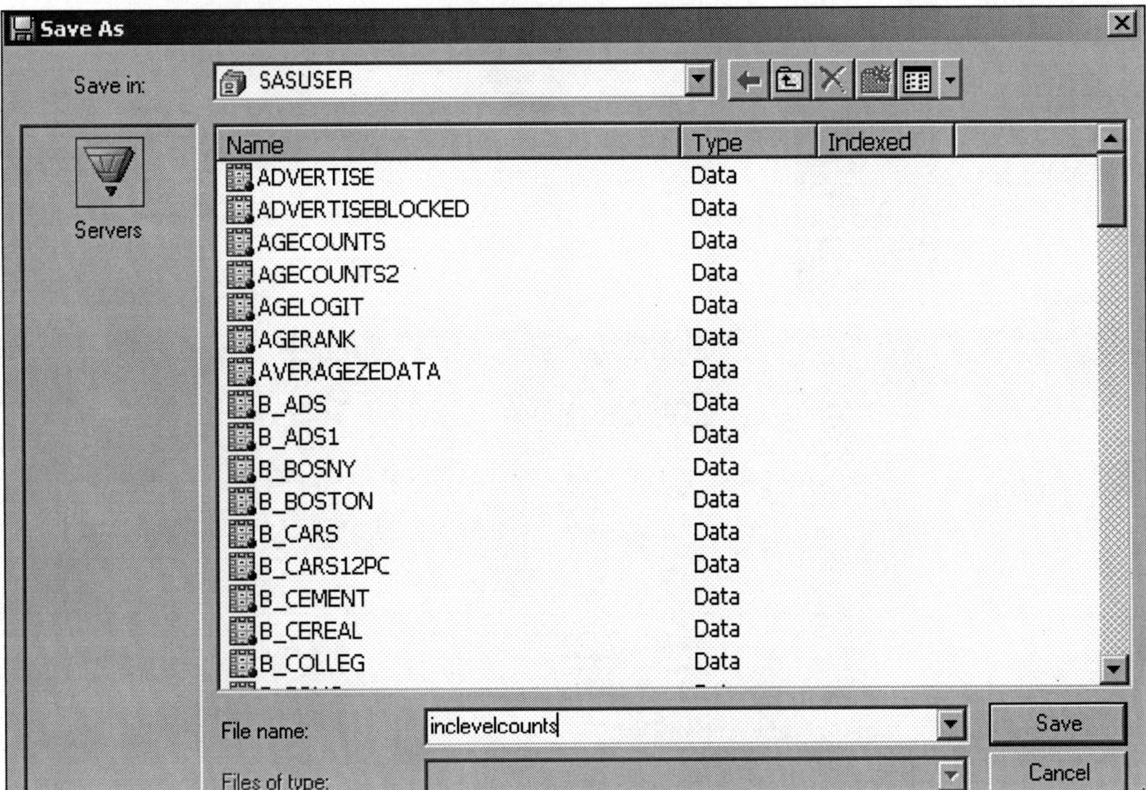

6. Select **Save**.

7. Select **Run**.

The Summary Statistics task creates an intermediate data table. The column **`purchase_Sum`** is equivalent to m_i in the logit equation. The **`_FREQ_`** variable is the equivalent of M_i. You can use a query to calculate a logit from these columns.

Summary Statistics for SASUSER.CATALOGUESALESINCLEVEL (read-only)

	inclevel	_WAY_	_TYPE_	_FREQ_	purchase_Sum
1	1	1	1	132	42
2	2	1	1	144	46
3	3	1	1	155	74

8. Select the **Summary Statistics for SASUSER.CATALOGUESALESINCLEVEL** data set in the process flow.

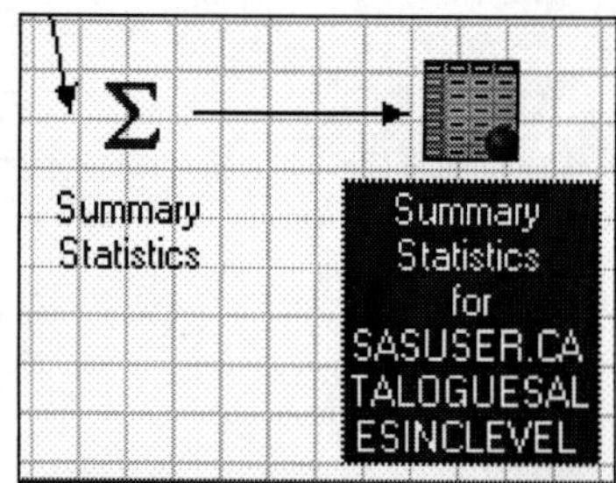

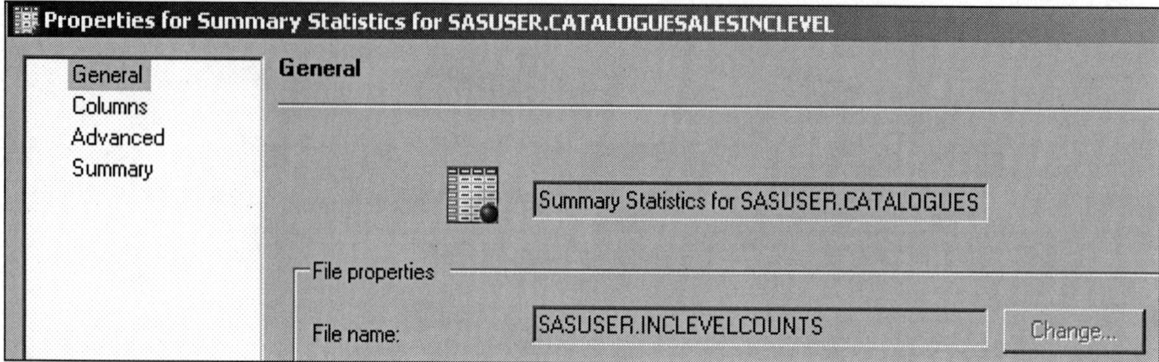

9. Select **Data** ⇨ **Filter and Query Active Data**.

10. Choose the Select and Sort tab. Click **New...** to create a new column.

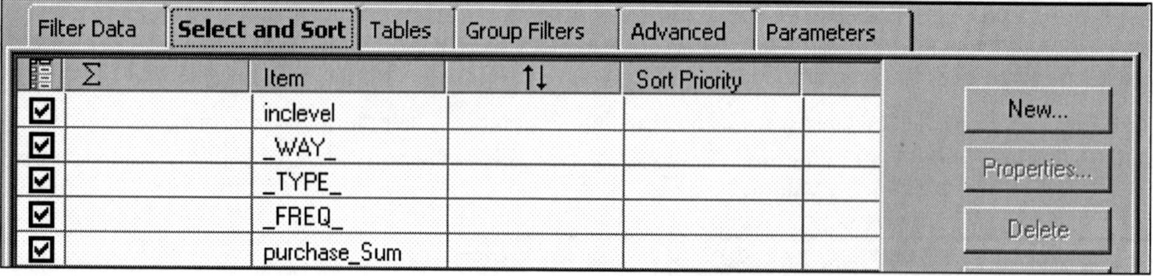

11. Specify the name `Logit_PSum` for the new column. Click **Change...** next to the **Expression** box to calculate the desired value.

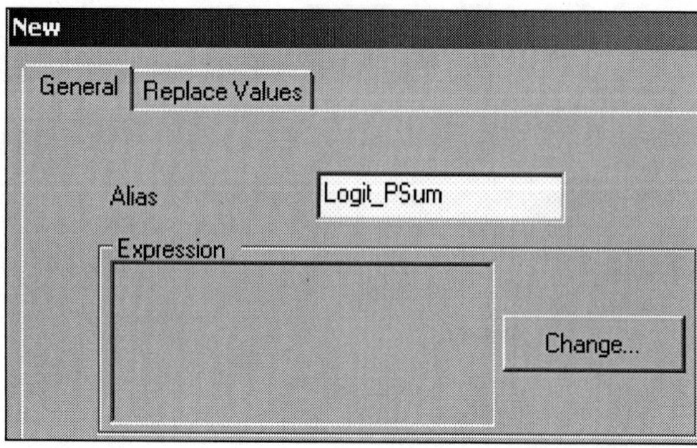

12. In the Expression Builder, select **All Functions** on the left and **LOG(argument)** on the right and click **Insert**. The outline for a log function appears in the Expression window.

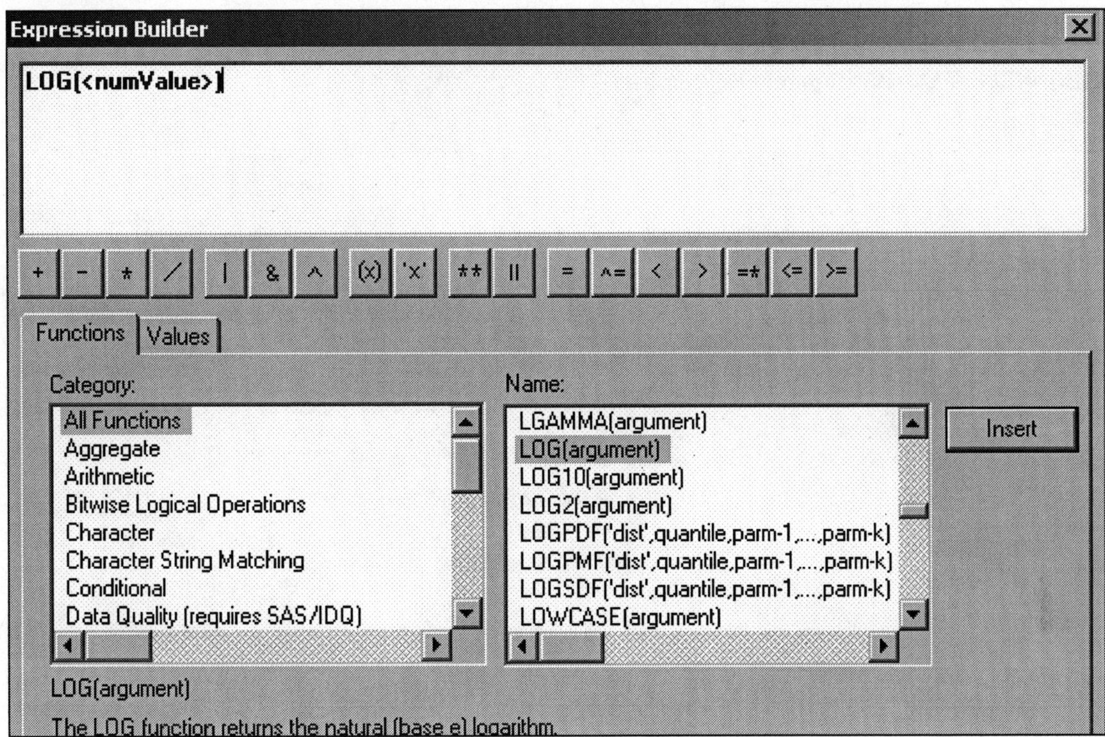

13. Select the **Values** tab.

14. Choose **<numvalue>** in the log function.

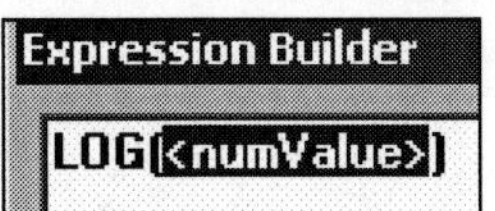

15. Select **purchase_Sum** in the **Value:** pane. Click **Insert**. For legibility, a space was inserted before and after `INCLEVELCOUNTS.purchase_Sum`.

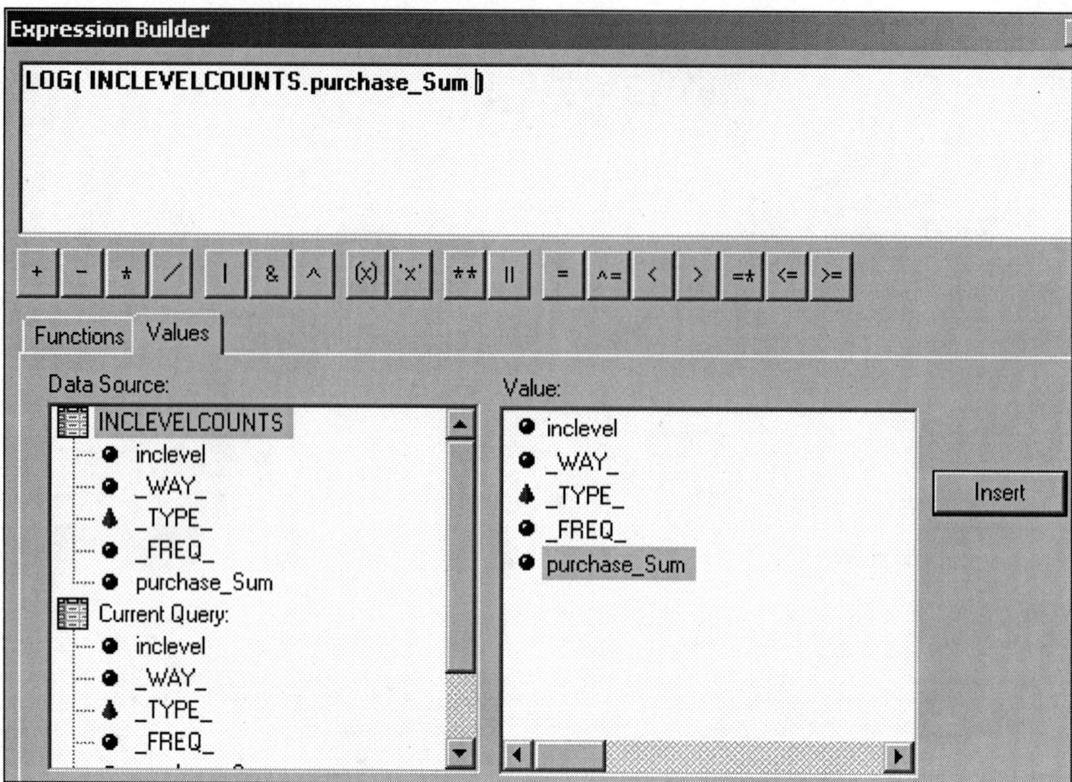

16. Choose or type the plus sign and then type `1`.

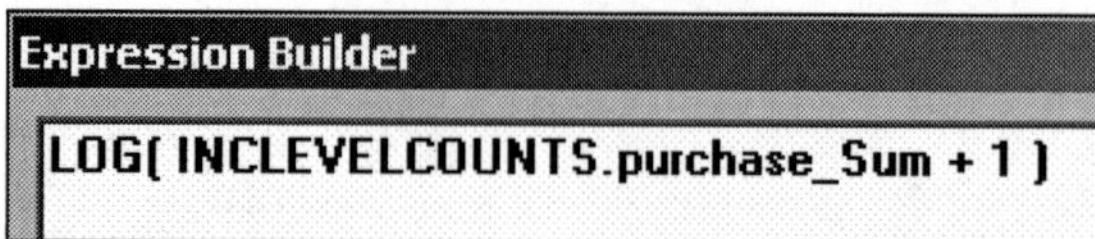

17. Select **INCLEVELCOUNTS.purchase_Sum + 1** and click (x). Your Expression Builder should now look like the following:

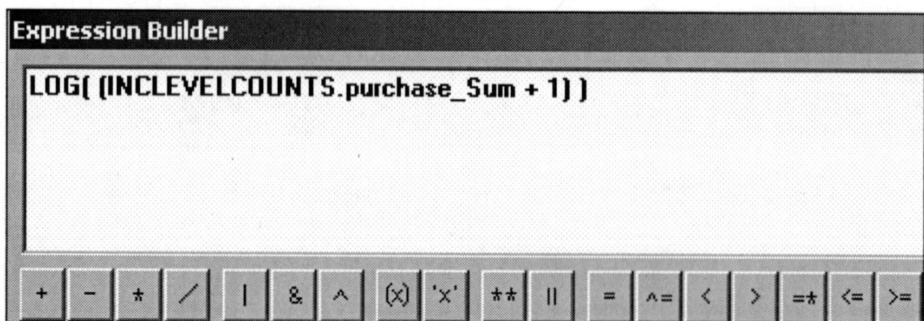

Hint: Be careful not to select the parentheses associated with the LOG function.

18. Select or type **/** after the parentheses for the expression and before the last parenthesis. For legibility, the last parenthesis was moved to the next line.

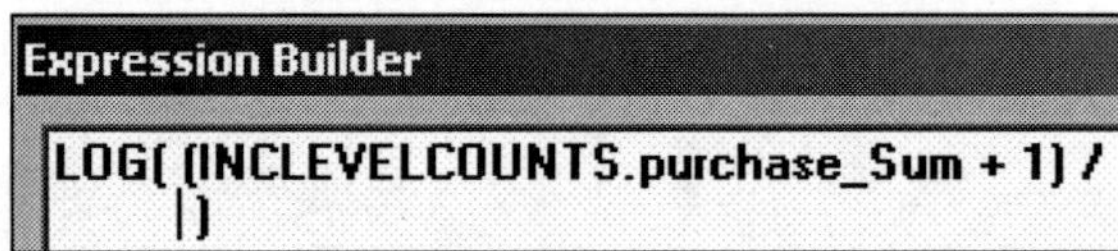

19. On the right-hand side of the Values tab, select **_FREQ_** and click **Insert**. Select or type a minus sign. Select **purchase_Sum** from the **Value:** pane and click **Insert**. Then, select or type a plus sign followed by a 1.

20. Select the **INCLEVELCOUNTS._FREQ_ - INCLEVELCOUNTS.purchase_Sum + 1** expression.

21. Click (x).

Expression Builder

LOG((INCLEVELCOUNTS.purchase_Sum + 1) /
(INCLEVELCOUNTS._FREQ_ - INCLEVELCOUNTS.purchase_Sum + 1))

22. Select **OK** twice to get back to the Query Builder.

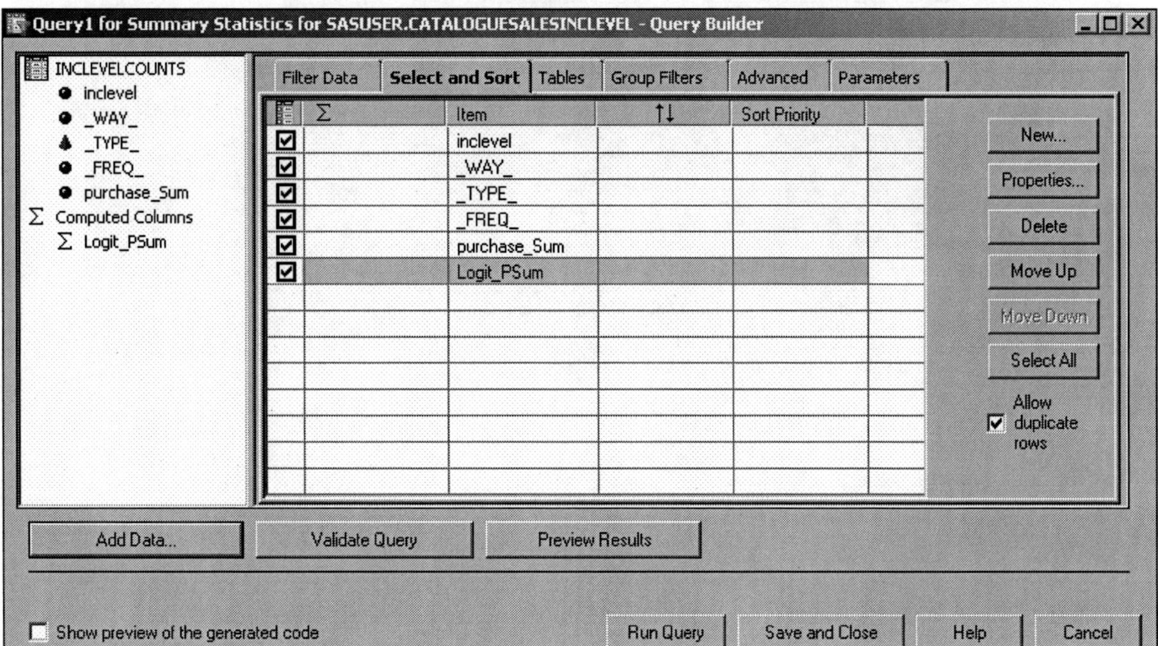

23. The Advanced tab allows you to change the name of the resulting data set. Select **Advanced** and **Change…** to provide the name of the data set, `inclevellogit`. Select **Save**.

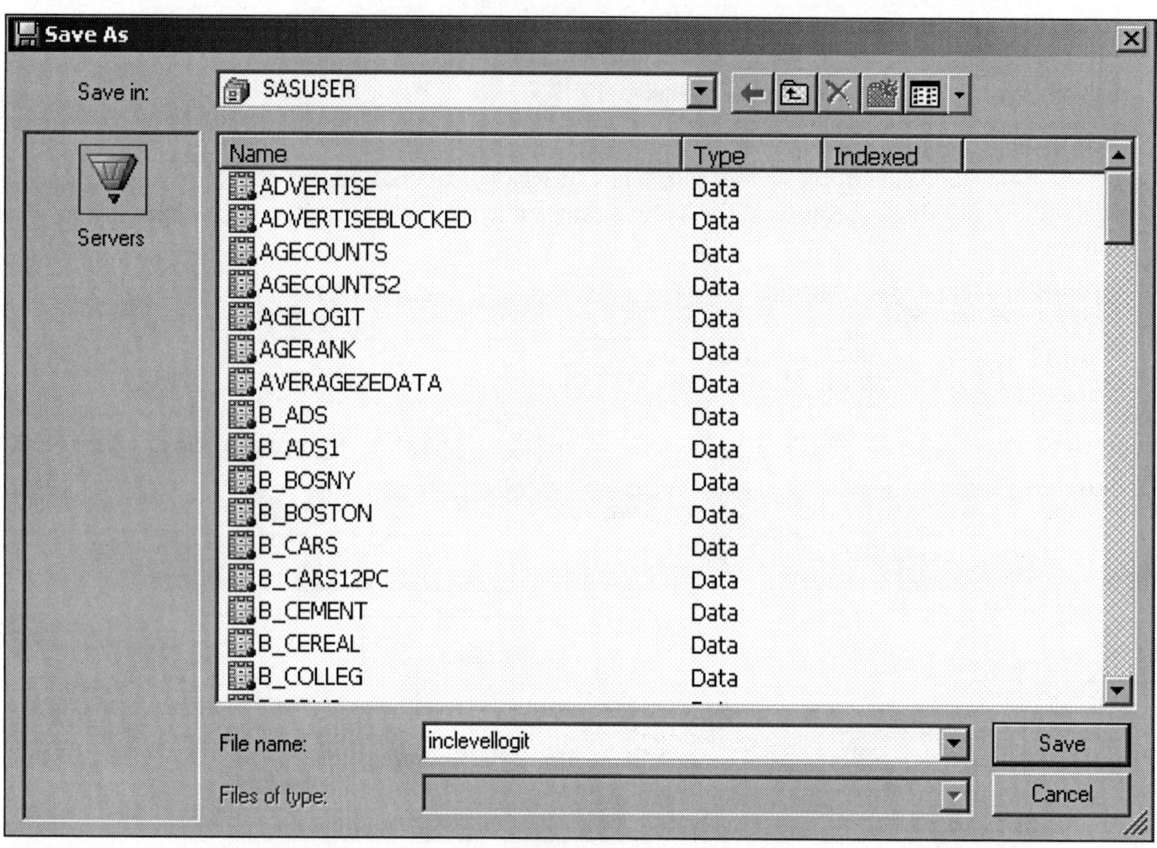

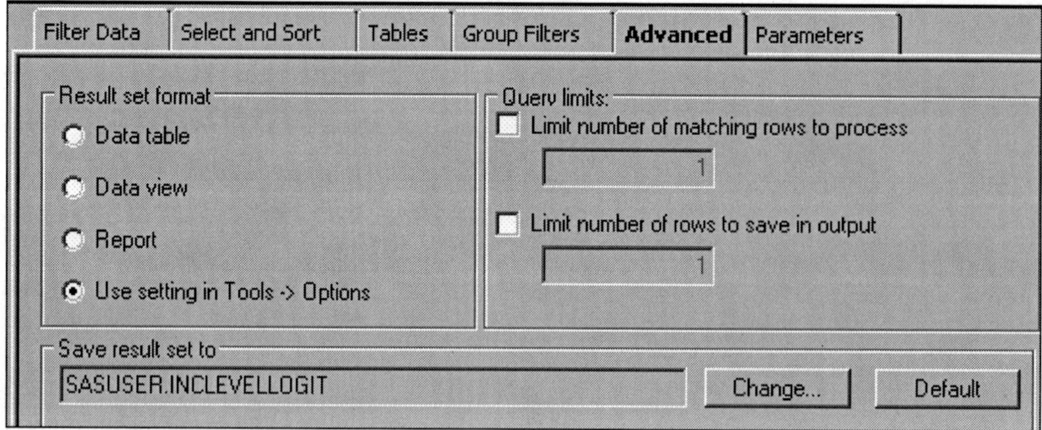

24. Select **Validate Query**. You should get a message saying the query syntax is valid.

If at this point, the query syntax is not valid, you can choose to view the SQL log created by SAS, or you can view the properties of the new `Logit_PSum` variable to double-check your expression.

25. Select **OK** to exit the validation box and select **Run Query** to run the query. The resulting data set opens in the work area.

SASUSER.INCLEVELLOGIT (read-only)

	inclevel	_WAY_	_TYPE_	_FREQ_	purchase_Sum	Logit_PSum
1	1	1	1	132	42	-0.749659391
2	2	1	1	144	46	-0.744972248
3	3	1	1	155	74	-0.089231134

Now you can create a two-dimensional scatter plot with `Logit_PSum` on the vertical axis and `inclevel` on the horizontal axis. This scatter plot can be analyzed in much the same way you analyzed the scatter plots in Chapter 3.

26. Make sure **INCLEVELLOGIT** is selected in the process flow and select **Graph** ⇨ **Scatter Plot**.

27. Select **2D Scatter Plot** on the **Scatter Plot** pane.

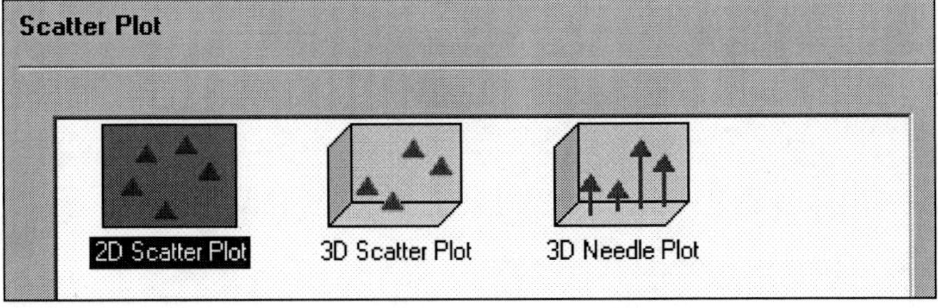

28. Select **Task Roles** on the left. Drag and drop `inclevel` to the Horizontal role and `Logit_PSum` to the Vertical role.

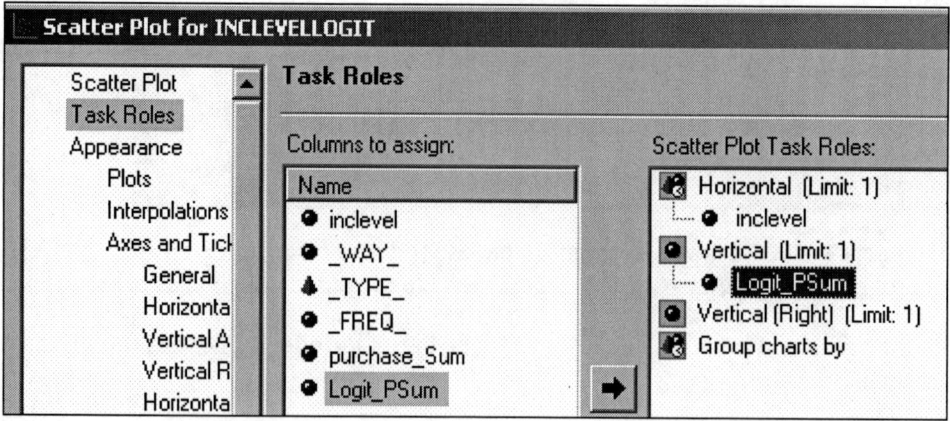

29. Select **Run** to submit the task.

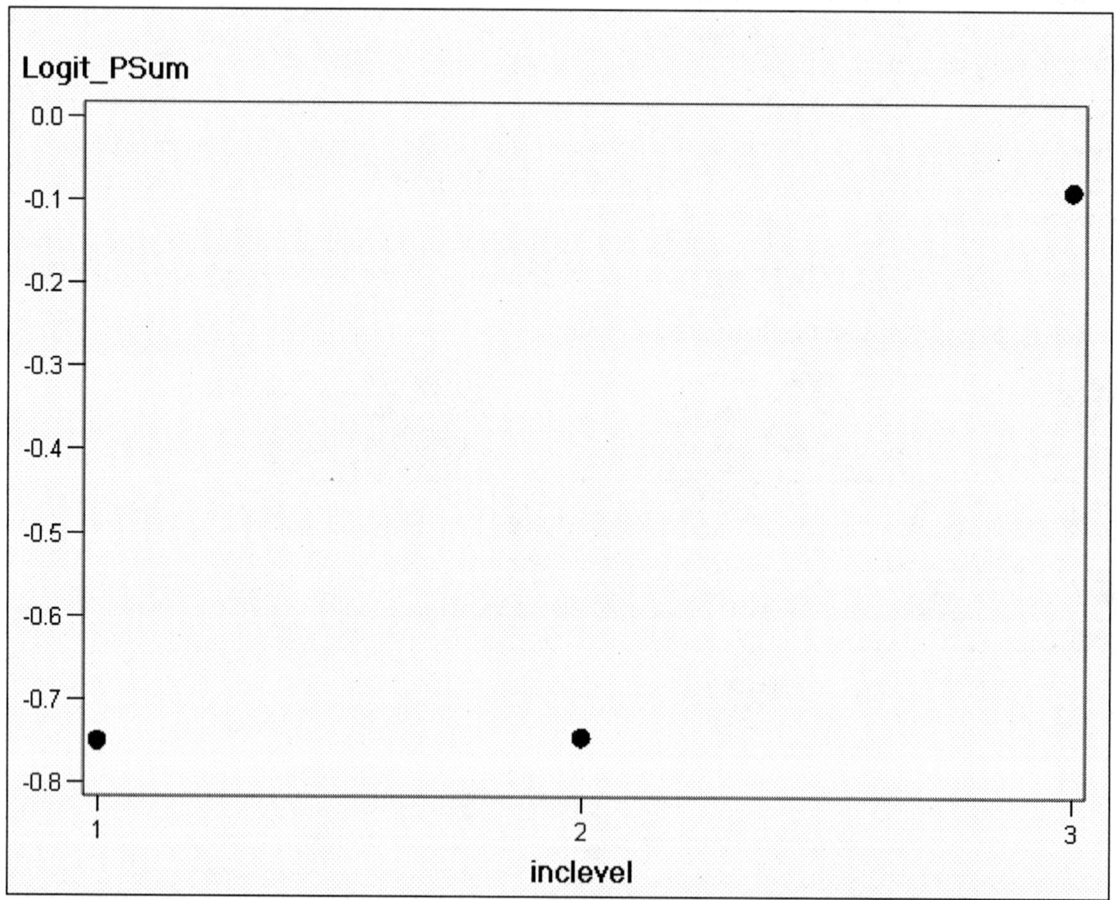

The logit plot shows that low- and medium-income customers have approximately the same probability of spending 100 dollars or more. One possible recommendation is to combine the low- and medium-income groups into one group and have income as a binary variable (high versus all other).

If the pattern were nonlinear, **income** should then be entered as a class variable. This would have created two dummy variables, which would model the nonlinear pattern.

Example: Use the Summary Statistics task, the Query Builder, and the Scatter Plot task to create a logit plot for the variable **age**.

Plot the estimated logits of the outcome variable **purchase** versus the continuous predictor **age**. When creating a logit plot for a continuous variable, you must first bin or group the continuous variable using the Rank task. This makes the logit calculations more stable. Bin the observations into ten groups to ensure an adequate number of observations is used to complete the estimated logit.

1. Make the **SASUSER.CATALOGSALESINCLEVEL** data set the active data set and select **Data** ⇨ **Rank** from the pull-down menus. The Rank task opens.

2. Under Task Roles, drag and drop **age** to the Columns to rank role.

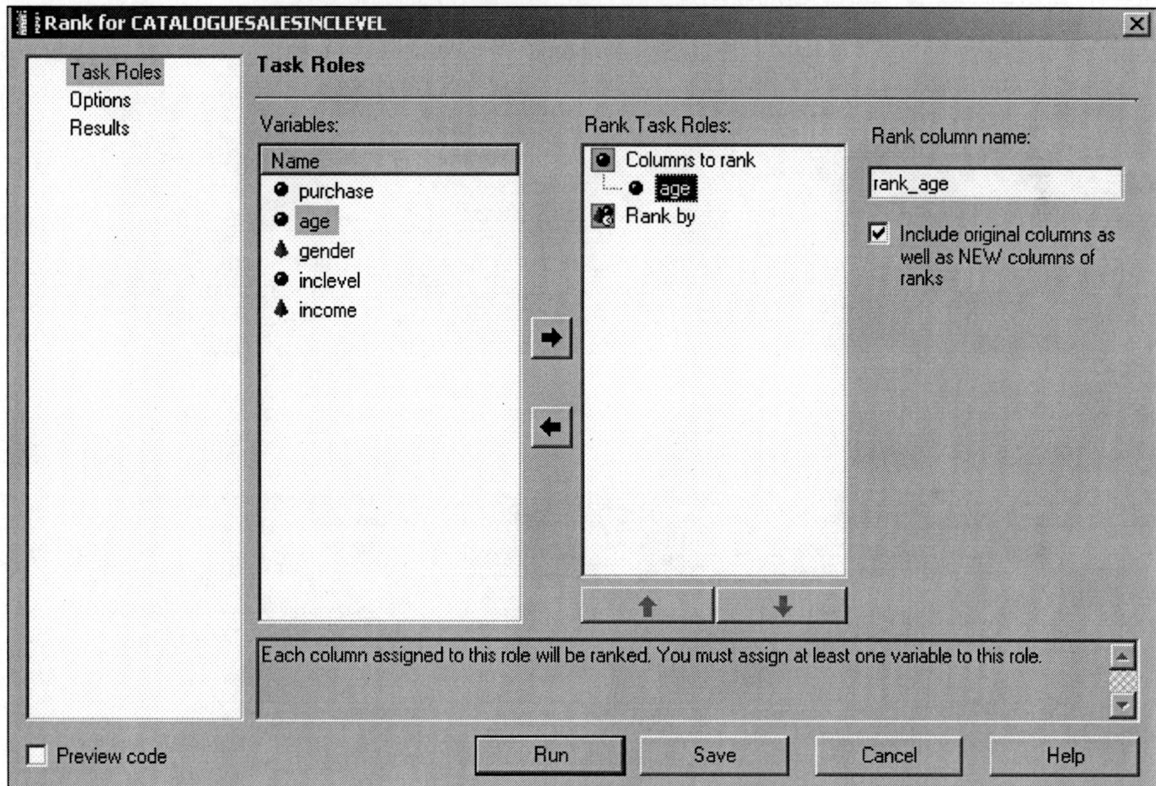

3. Select **Options** on the left and make the **Group = n** the active radio button. Change 1 to 10 in the **Number of Groups:** selection box.

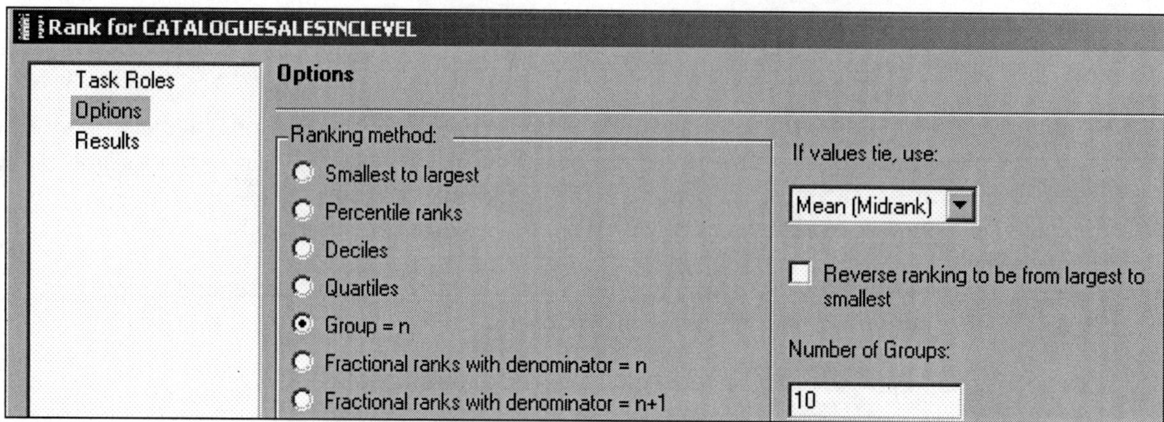

4. Select **Results** on the left. Select **Modify...** to change the name of the resulting data set to `agerank`.

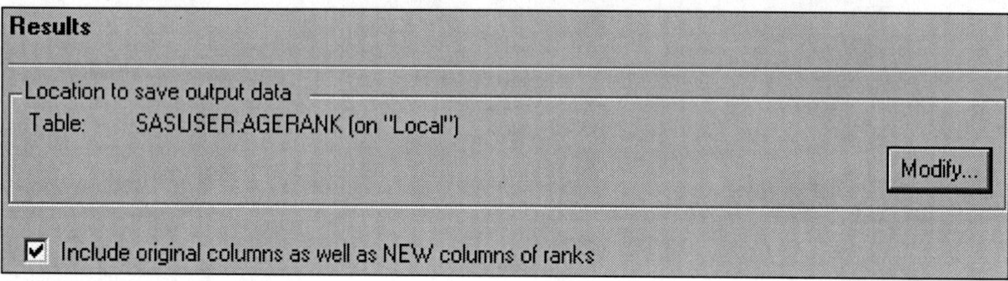

5. Select **Save**.

6. Select **Run** to submit the task.

Rank Analysis for SASUSER.CATALOGUESALESINCLEVEL (read-only)

	purchase	age	gender	inclevel	income	rank_age
1	0	41	Female	1	Low	6
2	0	47	Female	1	Low	9
3	1	41	Female	1	Low	6
4	1	39	Female	1	Low	5
5	0	32	Female	1	Low	0
6	0	32	Female	1	Low	0
7	0	33	Female	1	Low	1
8	0	45	Female	1	Low	8
9	0	43	Female	1	Low	7

The resulting data set has a new variable called `rank_age`. This variable is numbered 0 through 9 and represents ten different age bins. You can use these bins to calculate a logit.

7. Make sure the **SASUSER.AGERANK** table is the active table.

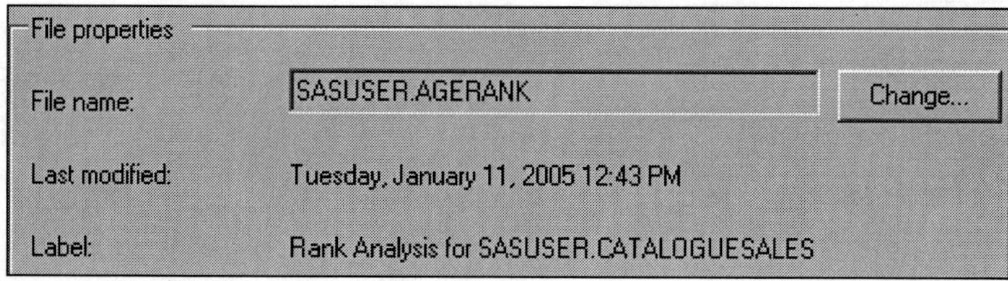

8. Select **Describe** ⇨ **Summary Statistics**.

9. Assign **purchase** as the Analysis variable and **rank_age** as the Classification variable.

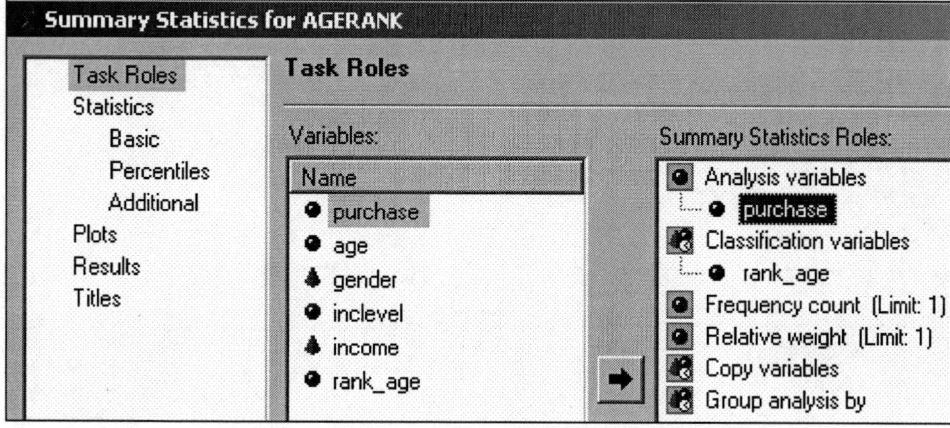

10. Select **Basic** under Statistics. De-select all of the default statistics and check the box next to **Sum**.

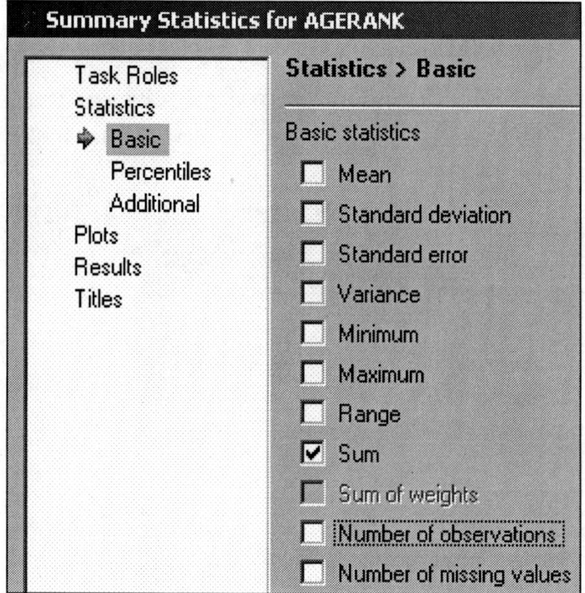

11. Select **Results** on the left. Uncheck the box next to **Show statistics** and check the box next to **Save statistics to data set**.

12. Click **Modify...** to change the default name of the resulting data set to `agecounts`.

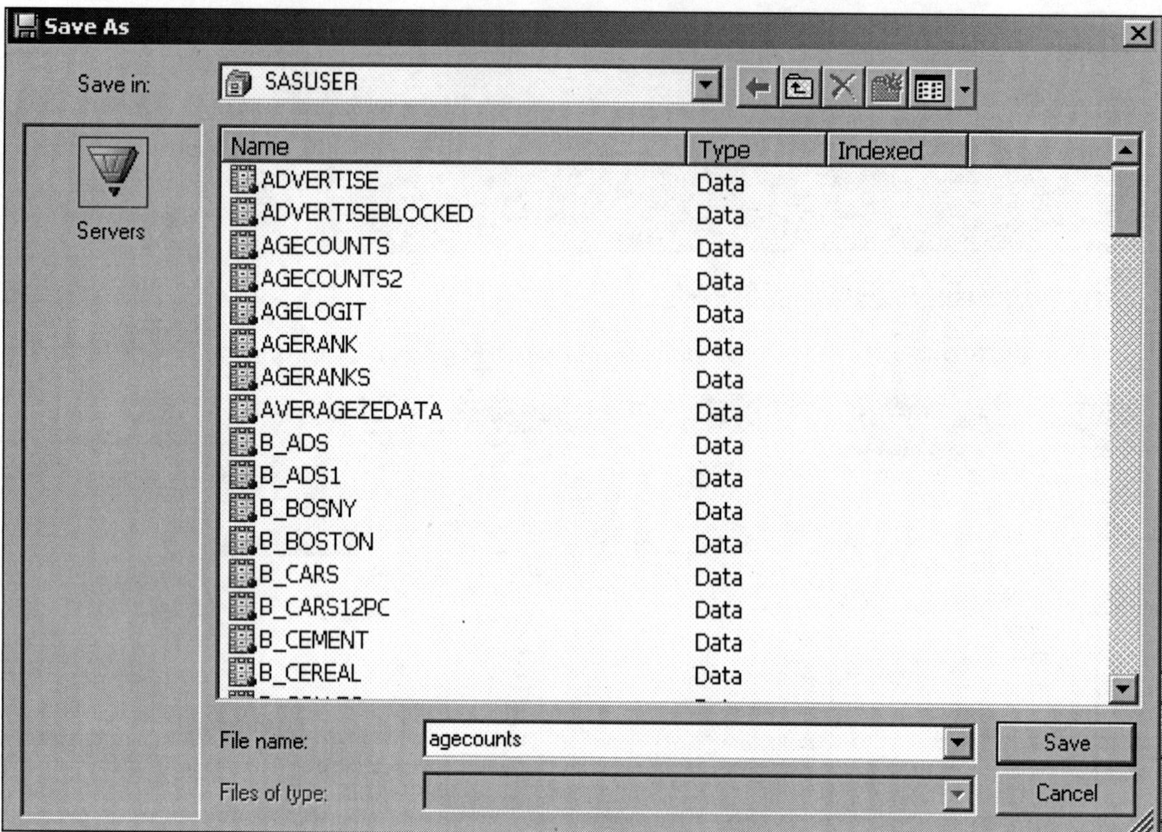

13. Select **Save**.

14. Select **Run**.

The Summary Statistics task creates an intermediate data table. The column named `purchase_Sum` is equivalent to m_i in the logit equation. The `_FREQ_` variable is the equivalent of M_i. You can use a query to calculate a logit from these columns.

Summary Statistics for SASUSER.AGERANK (read-only)

	rank_age	_WAY_	_TYPE_	_FREQ_	purchase_Sum
1	0	1	1	46	13
2	1	1	1	48	21
3	2	1	1	28	13
4	3	1	1	48	19
5	4	1	1	37	15
6	5	1	1	61	17
7	6	1	1	35	13
8	7	1	1	37	9
9	8	1	1	48	19
10	9	1	1	43	23

15. Select the **AGECOUNTS** data set in the process flow. Select **Data** ⇨ **Filter and Query Active Data**.

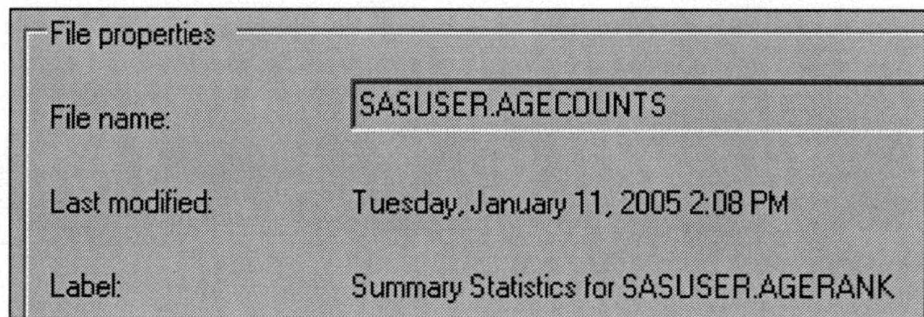

16. Choose the Select and Sort tab. Click **New...** to create a new column.

17. Specify the name **Logit_PSumR** for the new column. Click **Change...** next to the **Expression** box to create an expression to calculate the value.

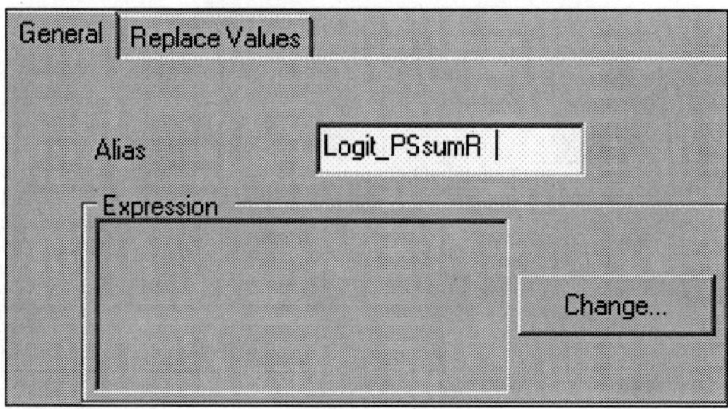

18. On the Expression Builder tab, select **LOG(argument)** on the right pane under `Name:` and click **Insert**. The outline for a log function appears in the Expression window.

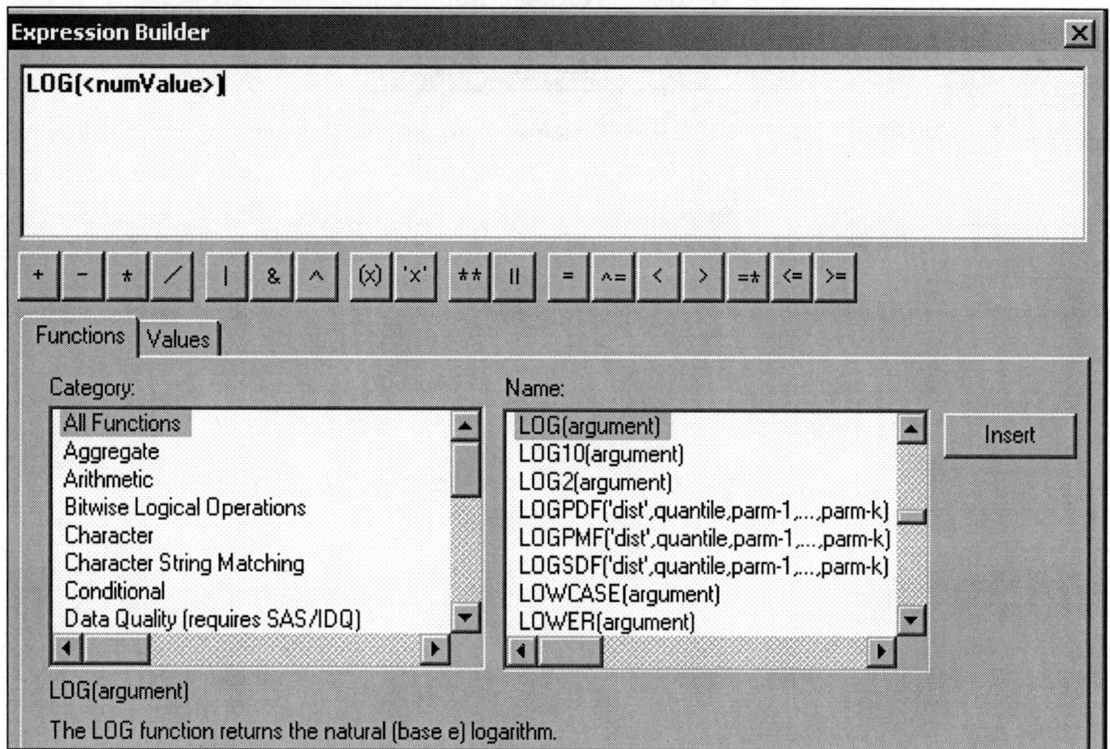

19. Select the Values tab.

20. Choose **<numvalue>** in the log function. Choose `purchase_Sum` on the right pane under **Name:**, and click **Insert**.

21. Select or type the plus sign. Then, type `1`. Select **AGECOUNTS.purchase_Sum + 1** and click .

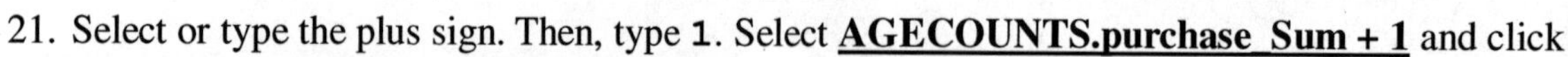

Expression Builder

LOG((AGECOUNTS.purchase_Sum+1))

22. Select or type `/` after the parentheses for the `(AGECOUNTS.purchase_Sum + 1)` expression.

23. On the right-hand side of the **Value:** pane, select **_FREQ_**. Select or type a minus sign. Select `purchase_sum` on the right-hand side of the Values tab and click **Insert**. Then, select or type a plus sign followed by a 1.

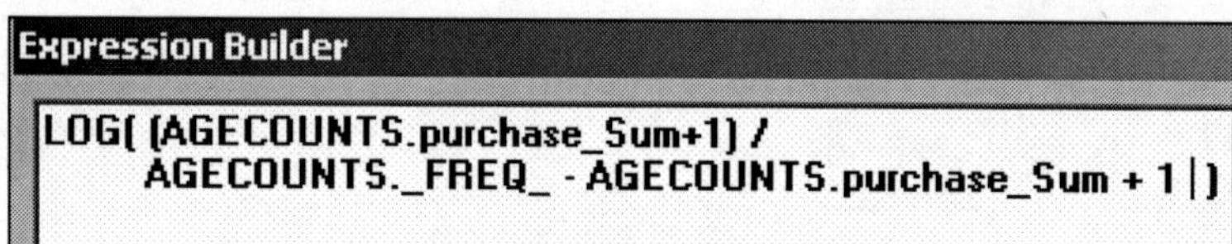

24. Select **AGECOUNTS._FREQ_ - AGECOUNTS.purchase_Sum + 1** and click .

Expression Builder

LOG((AGECOUNTS.purchase_Sum+1) /
(AGECOUNTS._FREQ_ - AGECOUNTS.purchase_Sum+1))

25. Select **OK** twice to get back to the Query Builder.

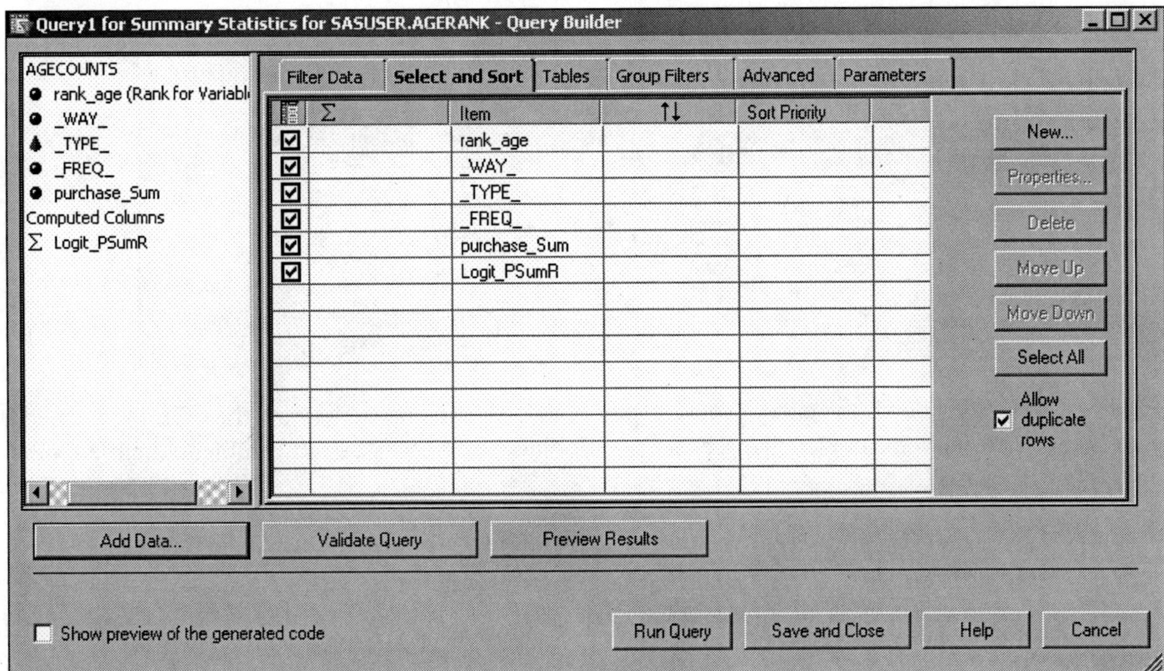

26. The Advanced tab allows you to change the name of the resulting data set. Select **Advanced** and **Change…** to change the name of the data set to `agelogit`.

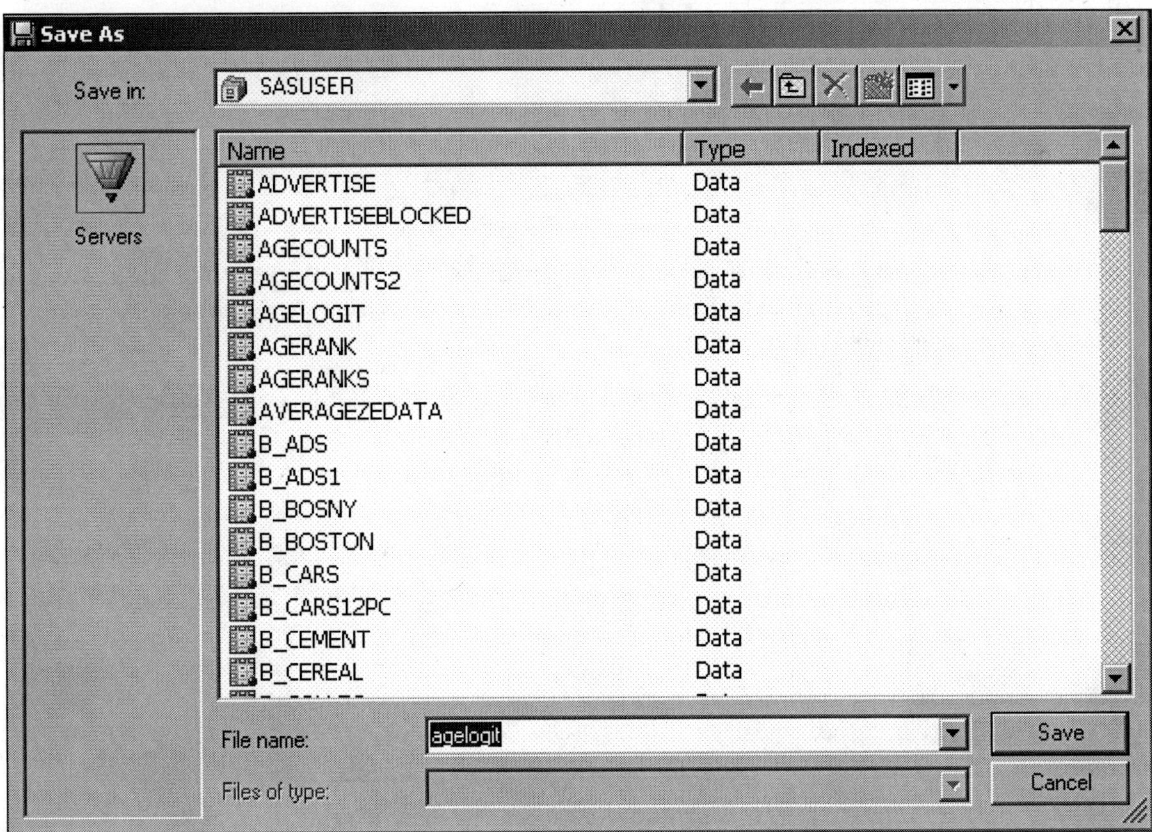

27. Select **Save**.

28. Select **Validate Query**. You should get a message saying the query syntax is valid.

29. Select **OK** to exit the validation box.

If at this point, the query syntax is not valid, you can choose to view the SQL log created by SAS, or you can view the properties of the new `Logit_PSumR` variable to double-check your expression.

30. Select **OK** to exit the validation box and select **Run Query** to run the query. The resulting data set opens in the work area.

SASUSER.AGELOGIT (read-only)

	rank_age	_WAY_	_TYPE_	_FREQ_	purchase_Sum	Logit_PSumR
1	0	1	1	46	13	-0.887303195
2	1	1	1	48	21	-0.241162057
3	2	1	1	28	13	-0.133531393
4	3	1	1	48	19	-0.405465108
5	4	1	1	37	15	-0.362905494
6	5	1	1	61	17	-0.916290732
7	6	1	1	35	13	-0.496436886
8	7	1	1	37	9	-1.064710737
9	8	1	1	48	19	-0.405465108
10	9	1	1	43	23	0.1335313926

Now you can create a two-dimensional scatter plot with the `Logit_PSumR` on the vertical axis and `rank_age` on the horizontal axis. This scatter plot can be analyzed in much the same way you analyzed the scatter plots in Chapter 3.

31. Make sure `SASUSER.AGELOGIT` is selected in the process flow and select **Graph** ⇨ **Scatter Plot**.

32. Select **2D Scatter Plot** on the **Scatter Plot** pane.

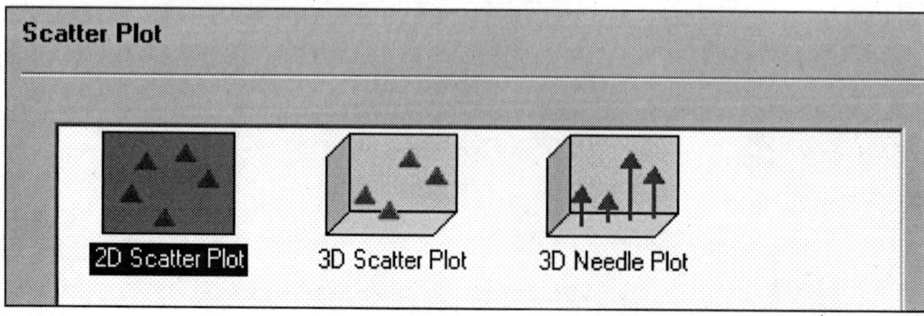

33. Select **Task Roles** on the left. Drag and drop `rank_age` to the Horizontal role and `Logit_PSumR` to the Vertical role.

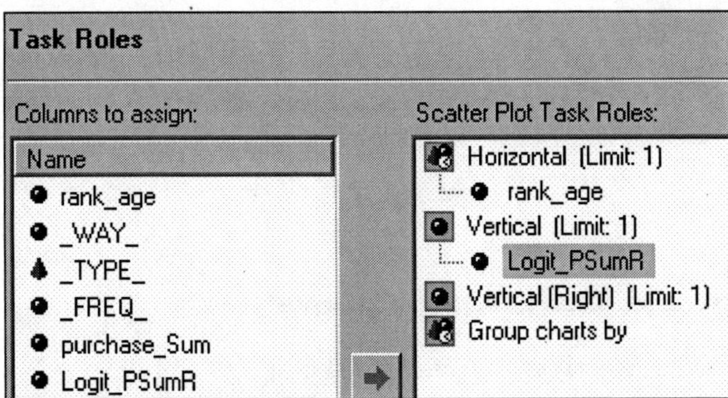

34. Select **Run** to submit the task.

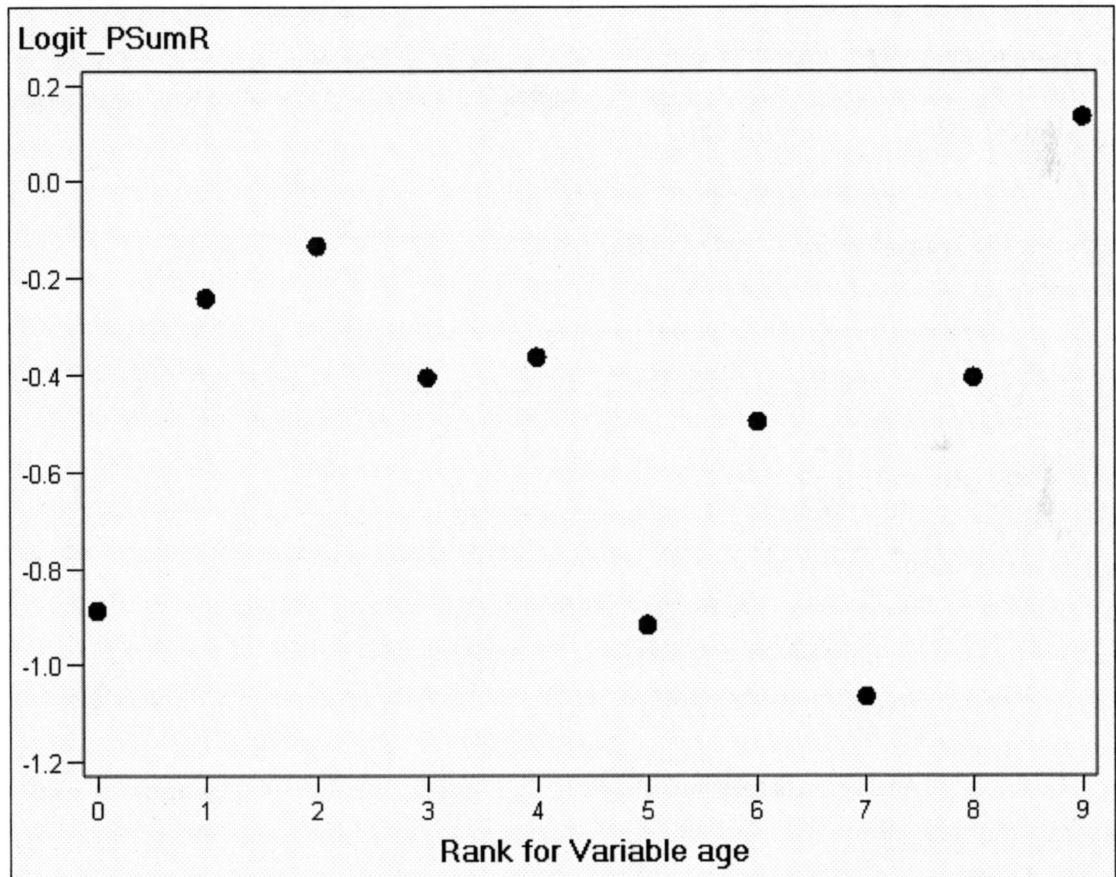

The estimated logit plot shows no apparent pattern. Therefore, `age` may be entered into the model as a continuous variable because creating several groups will probably not improve the fit of the model. Although it seems that `age` is not an important predictor for `purchase`, the estimated logit plot is a univariate plot that can be misleading in the presence of partial associations (association between the response variable and the predictor variable changes with the addition of another predictor variable in the model) and interactions. A model with two-factor interactions and main effects should be evaluated before `age` is eliminated. Estimated logit plots should never be used to eliminate variables.

5.6 Exercises

1. Performing Tests and Measures of Association

An insurance company wants to relate the safety of vehicles to several other variables. A score has been given to each vehicle model, using the frequency of insurance claims as a basis. The data is in the **VEHICLESAFETY** data set.

The variables in the data set are

safety safety score (**1=Below Average**, **0=Average or Above**)

type type of vehicle (Sports, Small, Medium, Large, and Sport/Utility)

region manufacturing region (Asia, N America)

weight weight of the vehicle in thousands of pounds.

a. Examine the **VEHICLESAFETY** data set. Use the One-Way Frequency task to create one-way frequency tables for the variables **safety**, **type**, and **region**. Generate a temporary format to clearly identify the values of **safety**.

1) What is the measurement scale of each variable?

Variable	Measurement Scale
safety	
type	
region	
weight	

2) What is the proportion of cars made in North America?

3) For the variables **safety**, **type**, and **region**, are there any unusual data values that warrant further investigation?

4) Based on the measurement scale for **weight**, suggest the appropriate SAS Enterprise Guide task to explore this column.

b. Use the Table Analysis task to examine the crosstabulation of the variables **region** by **safety**. Be sure to implement the temporary format.

1) For the cars made in Asia, what percentage had a below-average safety score? Change the output to include the row and column percentages, cell frequencies and percentages, cell contribution to the Pearson chi-square statistics, and the expected cell frequency.

2) For the cars with an average or above safety score, what percentage was made in North America?

3) Change the output to include the cell frequencies and row percentages. Do you see any association between **region** and **safety**?

4) Which cell contributed the most to any possible association?

c. Perform a chi-square test of association between **region** and **safety**.

1) Interpret the *p*-value from the test with respect to probability.

2) Do you reject or fail to reject the null hypothesis at the 0.05 level?

d. Create a new variable named **size**. Assign 1 for **type** equal to `Small` or `Sports`, 2 for **type** equal to `Medium`, and 3 for **type** equal to `Large` or `Sport/Utility`. Examine the ordinal association between **size** and **safety** using the Table Analysis task.

1) Which statistic should you use to detect an ordinal association between **safety** and **size**?

2) Do you reject or fail to reject the null hypothesis at the 0.05 level?

3) What is the strength of the ordinal association between **safety** and **size**?

4) What is the 95% confidence interval around that statistic?

2. Performing Simple Logistic Regression Analysis

a. Use the Logistic Regression task to fit a simple logistic regression model with **safety** as the outcome variable and **weight** as the predictor variable. Use the appropriate option to model the probability of below-average safety scores.

1) Do you reject or fail to reject the null hypothesis that all regression coefficients of the model are 0?

2) Write out the logistic regression equation.

3) Interpret the odds ratio for **weight**.

4) Interpret the 95% confidence interval for the odds ratio.

5) Interpret the percentage of concordant observations.

5.7 Chapter Summary

Categorical data analysis deals with the analysis of categorical response variables, regardless of whether the explanatory variables are categorical or continuous. The scale of measurement of the variables is an important consideration when you decide the appropriate statistic to use. When you have two nominal variables, the Pearson chi-square statistic is appropriate. The strength of the association can be measured by Cramer's V. Because the Pearson chi-square statistic requires a large sample size, Fisher's exact test should be used to detect an association when you have a small sample size. When you have two ordinal variables, the Mantel-Haenszel chi-square statistic should be used to detect an ordinal association. The strength of the association can be measured by the Spearman correlation statistic.

Logistic regression uses the explanatory variables, which can be discrete or continuous, to predict the probability that the outcome or response variable takes on a given value. In other words, logistic regression is designed to describe probabilities associated with the values of the outcome variable. Probabilities are bounded by 0 and 1, so a linear model cannot be used because linear functions are inherently unbounded. The solution to this problem is to transform the probabilities to logits, which are unbounded, so that a linear regression model can be used because the logits are linear in the parameters.

The output from logistic regression shows the odds ratio, which is a measure of association between the explanatory variable and the outcome variable. The odds ratio compares the odds of an event in one group to the odds of an event in another group. The odds of an event is the ratio of the expected number of times that an event will occur to the expected number of times it will not occur.

The output also shows Akaike's 'A' Information Criteria (AIC) and Schwarz's Bayesian Criterion (SC), which are goodness-of-fit measures that adjust for the number of explanatory variables in the model. Lower values indicate a more desirable model. There are also four rank correlation indices that are computed from the numbers of concordant and discordant pairs of observations. In general, a model with higher values for these indices has better predictive ability than a model with lower values for these indices.

One model building strategy is to assess all the two-factor interactions first and then assess the main effects. An interaction occurs when the effect of one variable on the outcome depends on the observed level of another variable. When a model has no interactions, you are assuming that the effect of each variable on the outcome is the same regardless of the levels of the other variables. A common variable selection technique is the backward elimination method. One strategy is to eliminate the nonsignificant interactions one at a time, starting with the least significant interaction. Then eliminate the nonsignificant main effects not involved in any significant interactions.

The following tasks are introduced in this chapter:

- One-Way Frequencies
- Table Analysis
- Logistic Regression

You are also introduced to generating formats and changing code by pressing the space bar in a code window. SAS Enterprise Guide then presents a window in which you can insert and edit your code. Numerous important options used in logistic regression were implemented with this technique.

5.8 Solutions to Exercises

1. Performing Tests and Measures of Association

a. Locate and open the **VEHICLESAFETY** data table from the EGBS node.

SASUSER.VEHICLESAFETY (read-only)

	safety	type	region	weight
1	0	Medium	N America	3.395
2	0	Sport/Utility	N America	4.18
3	0	Medium	N America	3.145
4	0	Small	N America	2.6
5	0	Medium	N America	3.085
6	0	Medium	N America	2.91
7	0	Sport/Utility	N America	4.18
8	0	Medium	Asia	3.415

1) Reviewing the columns of **VEHICLESAFETY**, you decide the following:

Variable	Measurement Scale
safety	ordinal
type	nominal
region	nominal
weight	continuous

Create a temporary format, **SAFEFMT.**, for the values of **safety** to help in understanding the values of **safety** in any reports.

a) To open the format task, select **Data** ⇨ **Create Format**.

b) Specify the new format to be named **safemt**. The type should be Numeric, and the library should be WORK (temporary).

c) Select **Define formats**. Click **New Label** and type **Average or Above** as the label. Select **New Range**. Leave the default of **Discrete** and type **0**.

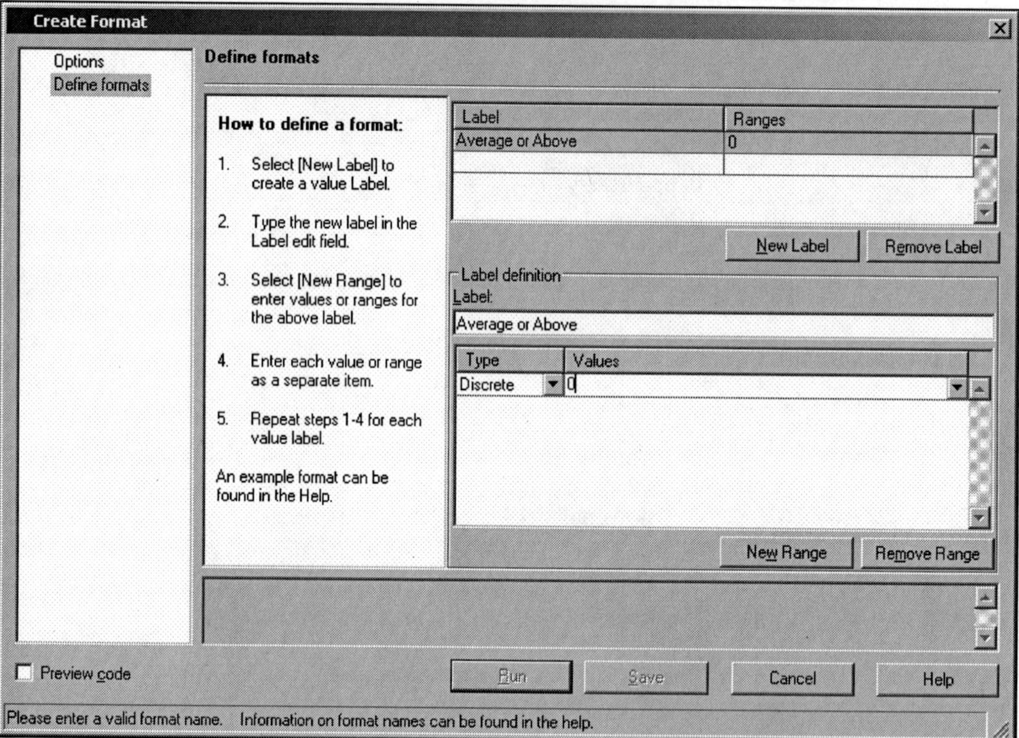

d) Using the same steps, create another label **Below Average** and set **1** as the discrete range.

e) Select **Run**.

2) Implement the One-Way Frequencies task to generate the requested frequencies.

a) With **VEHICLESAFETY** as the active data source, select **Describe** ⇨ **One-Way Frequencies**.

b) Assign **safety**, **type**, and **region** to the Analysis variables role.

c) To add the **SAFEFMT.** format, select **safety** and right-click. Select **Properties**.

d) Select **Change...** to apply the appropriate format by selecting **User Defined** on the left and **safefmt** on the right.

e) Select **OK** twice to exit the dialog.

f) Leave the default selections and select **Run**.

One-Way Frequencies
Results

The FREQ Procedure

safety	Frequency	Percent	Cumulative Frequency	Cumulative Percent
Average or Above	66	68.75	66	68.75
Below Average	30	31.25	96	100.00

type	Frequency	Percent	Cumulative Frequency	Cumulative Percent
Large	16	16.67	16	16.67
Medium	29	30.21	45	46.88
Small	20	20.83	65	67.71
Sport/Utility	16	16.67	81	84.38
Sports	15	15.63	96	100.00

region	Frequency	Percent	Cumulative Frequency	Cumulative Percent
Asia	35	36.46	35	36.46
N America	61	63.54	96	100.00

The proportion of cars built in North America is 0.6354, or 63.54%.

3) There are no unusual data values for these variables that warrant further attention.

> Notice that if there were miscoded values for these variables, the One-Way Frequencies task is an excellent tool to find this type of data error.

4) Because of its continuous measurement scale, the distribution of the variable **`weight`** should be examined using the Distribution Analysis task.

b. Use the Table Analysis task to generate the crosstabulation of `region` by `safety`. Change the output to include the requested statistics.

With `VEHICLESAFETY` active, select to **Describe** ⇨ **Table Analysis**.

Assign `safety` and `region` to the Table variables role.

Assign the `SAFEFMT.` format to `safety` using the same steps as in the exercise above.

Select the **Tables** pane on the right.

Drag and drop `safety` to Preview. It will be the column variable.

Drag and drop `region` to Preview. It will appear as the row variable.

Select the Cell Statistics tab. Make sure the boxes next to **Row percentages, Column percentages, Cell frequencies, Cell percentages, Cell contribution to the Pearson chi-square,** and **Expected cell frequency** are checked.

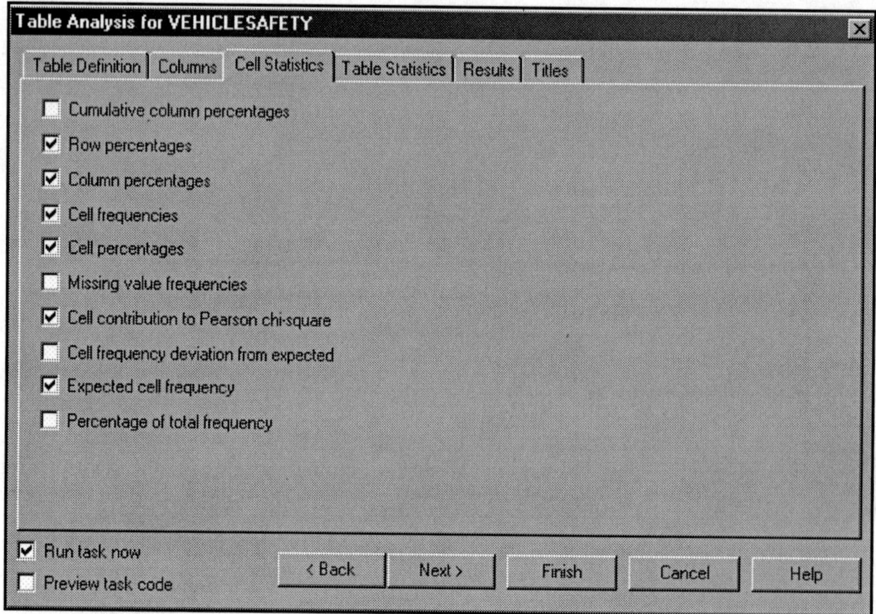

Select **Run**.

Table Analysis
Results

The FREQ Procedure

Frequency Expected Cell Chi-Square Percent Row Pct Col Pct			
Table of region by safety			
	safety		
region	**Average or Above**	**Below Average**	**Total**
Asia	20 24.063 0.6859 20.83 57.14 30.30	15 10.938 1.5089 15.63 42.86 50.00	35 36.46
N America	46 41.938 0.3935 47.92 75.41 69.70	15 19.063 0.8658 15.63 24.59 50.00	61 63.54
Total	66 68.75	30 31.25	96 100.00

1) For the cars made in Asia, 42.86% had a below-average safety score.

2) For the cars with an average or above safety score, 69.70% were made in North America.

3) Yes, there appears to be an association between **`safety`** and **`region`**. A higher proportion of cars from North America (75.41%) had an average or above safety rating than those cars from Asia (57.14%).

4) The cell where **`region`** is `Asia` and **`safety`** is `Below Average` contributed the most (1.5089) to any possible association.

c. To test for statistically significant association between `region` and `safety`, you must request and interpret the proper chi-square statistic.

Open the Table Analysis you just completed.

On the **Association** pane under Table Statistics, check the box next to **Chi-square tests**.

Select **Run** and **No** to replace previous results.

Frequency Expected Cell Chi-Square Row Pct Col Pct	Table of region by safety			
		safety		
	region	0	1	Total
	Asia	20 24.063 0.6859 57.14 30.30	15 10.938 1.5089 42.86 50.00	35
	N America	46 41.938 0.3935 75.41 69.70	15 19.063 0.8658 24.59 50.00	61
	Total	66	30	96

Statistics for Table of region by safety

Statistic	DF	Value	Prob
Chi-Square	1	3.4541	0.0631
Likelihood Ratio Chi-Square	1	3.3949	0.0654
Continuity Adj. Chi-Square	1	2.6562	0.1031
Mantel-Haenszel Chi-Square	1	3.4181	0.0645
Phi Coefficient		-0.1897	
Contingency Coefficient		0.1864	
Cramer's V		-0.1897	

1) Examine the first line of the Statistics table above. The Chi-Square statistic has a *p*-value of 0.0631, which is greater than the stated level of significance of 0.05.

2) You fail to reject the null hypothesis that there is **not** an association.

✎ SAS Enterprise Guide provides a Fischer Exact Test table for this and all 2x2 tables. Its interpretation is not covered in this text.

d. Use the Query Tool task to assign the values of `type` as requested.

Make sure the `VEHICLESAFETY` data set is active. Select **Data** ⇨ **Filter and Query Active Data**.

Go to the Select and Sort tab. Select **safety** and **Properties…**.

Select the Format tab, and then select **User Defined** ⇨ **SAFEFMT.** ⇨ **OK**.

Select **type** ⇨ **Properties**.

Type `size` in the Alias field.

Select the Replace Values tab and then click the black down-pointing arrow. SAS Enterprise Guide provides a list of the values to be replaced.

Select **…** from the menu next to the variable name. Select **Small** in the pop-up window that opens. Enter `1` in the **With** column and select **Add to List ->**.

Select **…** from the menu next to the variable name. Select **Sports** in the pop-up window that opens. Enter `1` in the **With** column and select **Add to List ->**.

✎ Notice that both `Small` and `Sports` are to be replaced by the value 1 and SAS Enterprise Guide is visually displaying this relationship:

Logically, you could verify this by selecting the Expression tab and examining the syntax of the query:

Select **...** from the menu next to the variable name. Select **Medium** in the pop-up window that opens. Enter **2** in the **With** column and select **Add to List ->**.

Select the **...** from the menu next to the variable name. Select **Large** in the pop-up window that opens. Enter **3** in the **With** column and select **Add to List ->**.

Select the **...** from the menu next to the variable name. Select **Sport/Utility** in the pop-up window that appears. Enter 3 in the **With** column and select **Add to List ->**.

When you click again, SAS Enterprise Guide indicates the duplication of the value of 3 for `Large` and `Sport/Utility`.

Change the **Replace all others with** selection to **Missing Value**.

When you are finished, the Replace Values tab should look like this:

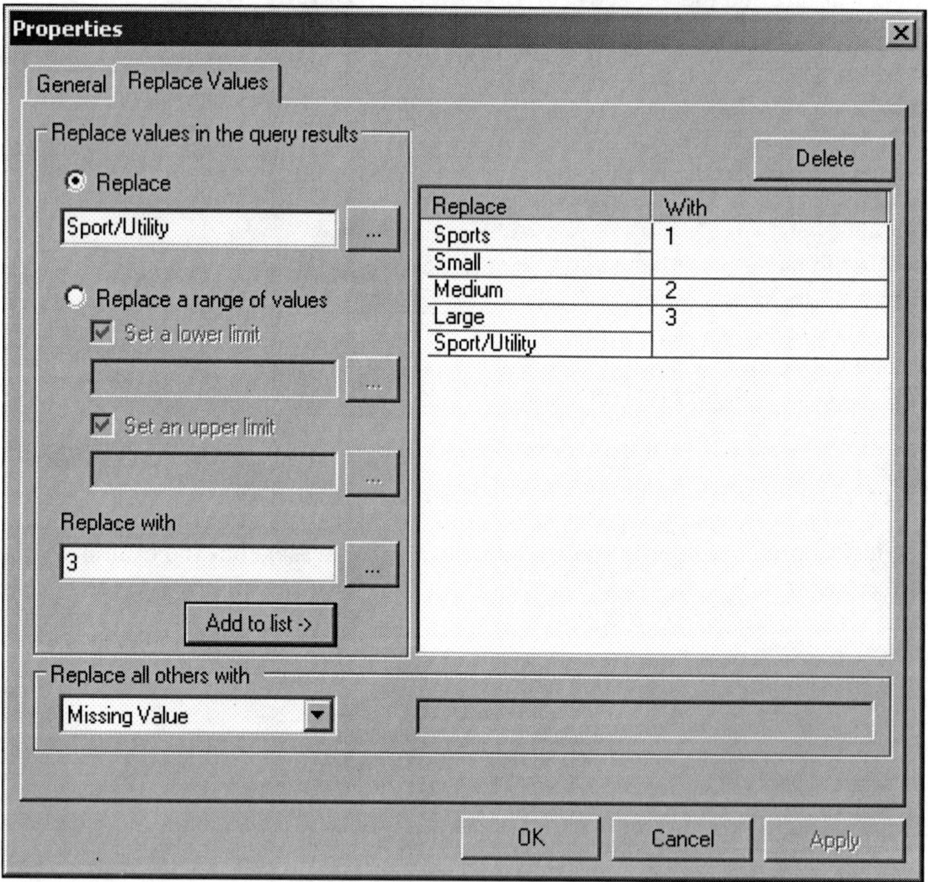

Select **OK**.

Notice that the new variable **size** has replaced the variable **type** from which it was computed.

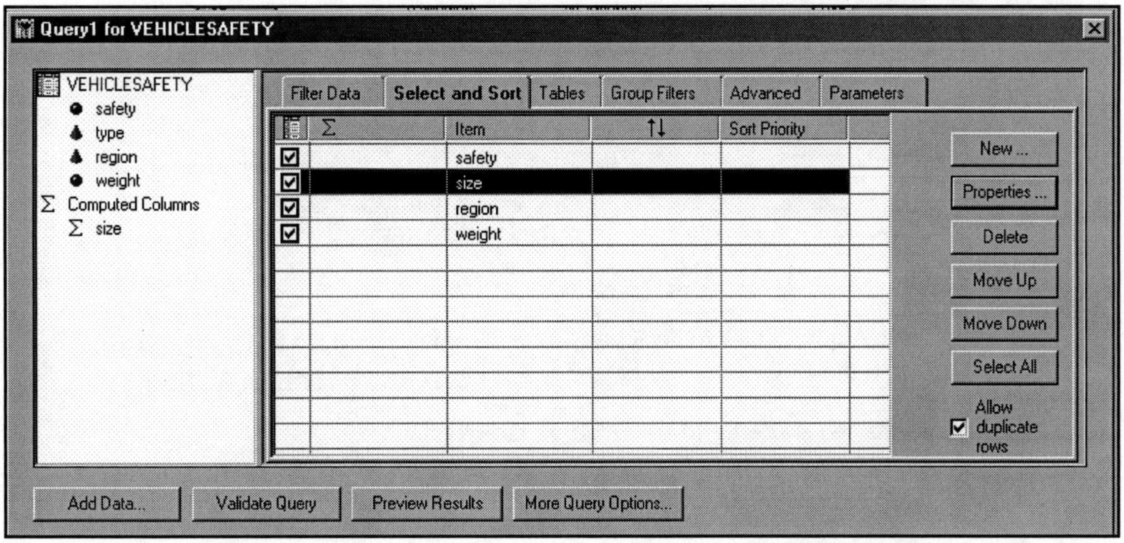

Add the original variable **type** to **VEHICLESAFETY** by dragging it from the variable list on the left to the Select and Sort tab that displays the list of columns in the table.

Select the Advanced tab. Use **Modify…** next to the table name to change the name of the table to **VEHICLESAFETYSIZE**.

Select **Validate Query**. You should get a message saying the query syntax is valid. If the query syntax is not valid, double-check your entries on the Replace Values tab for size. You can also view the log for more information.

Select **Run Query**.

Select **Results of Query1 for VEHICLESAFETY** and rename the table shortcut to **VEHICLESAFETYSIZE**.

Notice the new column, **size**, in **VEHICLESAFETYSIZE**.

	safety	size	region	weight	type
1	Average or Above	2	N America	3.395	Medium
2	Average or Above	3	N America	4.18	Sport/Utility
3	Average or Above	2	N America	3.145	Medium
4	Average or Above	1	N America	2.6	Small
5	Average or Above	2	N America	3.085	Medium

Because **size** is numeric, you should create a format to fully describe the types of vehicles in each of the three new categories.

Name the numeric format **sizefmt**, specify the library as WORK, and select **Next**.

Select **New Label** on the Define Format tab.

Type **Small or Sports** as the label's value and select **New Range**. Type **1** in Discrete Values.

Follow the same steps to create labels for values 2 and 3. The task should look like the following:

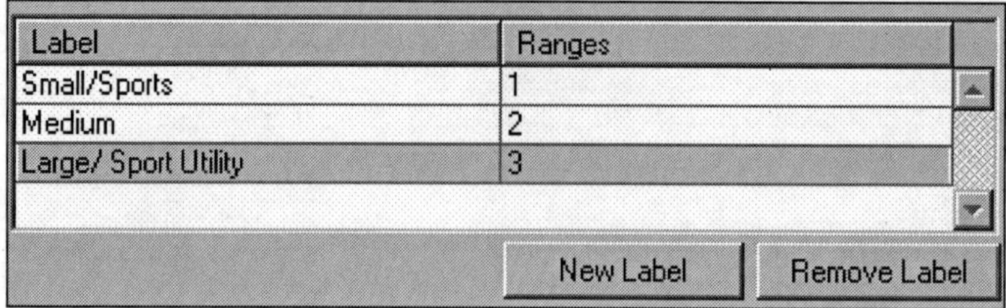

Label
Ranges
Small/Sports
1
Medium
2
Large/ Sport Utility
3
New Label
Remove Label

Select **Run**.

Use the Table Analysis task to detect any association between `safety` and `size`. Make sure the new data set is the active data source and select **Describe** ⇨ **Table Analysis**.

Assign `size` and `safety` to the Table variables role.

Add the format `SIZEFMT.` to the variable `size` following the steps outlined earlier.

Go to the **Tables** pane. Drag and drop `safety` to the **Preview** pane. It becomes the column variable. Drag and drop `size` to the **Preview** pane. It becomes the row variable.

Select **Association** on the left under Table Statistics. Check the boxes next to **Chi-square statistics** and **Measures**. Because `size` and `safety` are ordinal variables, the statistics produced by the measures selection are appropriate.

Also add the option to generate confidence intervals. Select **Preview task code**.

Select **Insert Code**. Double-click the **<double-click to insert code>** area that is part of the tables statement.

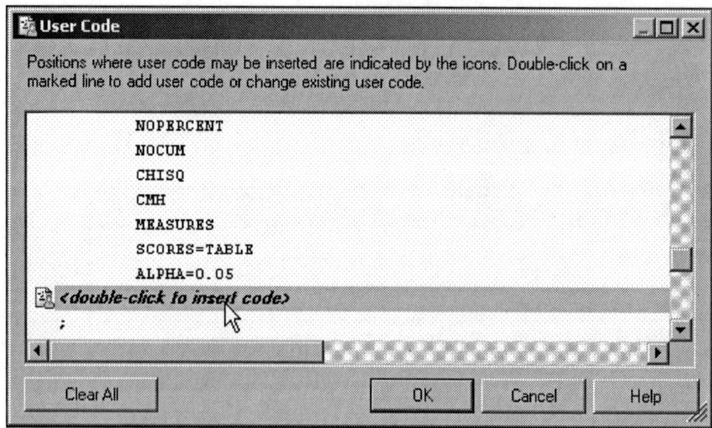

Type `cl` in the box that appears. Select **OK**.

Your typed code will be highlighted in gray in the task code.

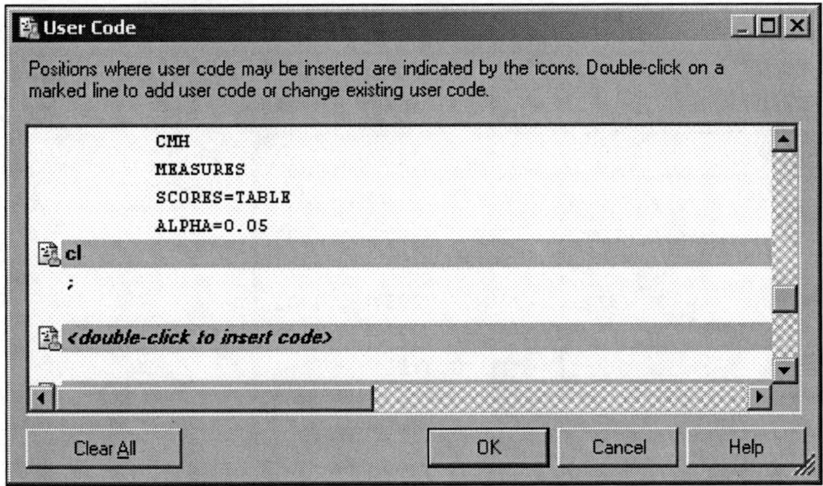

Select **OK** to close the Code Preview window.

Change the title if desired.

Select **Run**.

Test for ORDINAL Association between size and safety

The FREQ Procedure

Frequency Row Pct	Table of size by safety			
		safety		
	size	Average or Above	Below Average	Total
	Small or Sports	12 34.29	23 65.71	35
	Medium	24 82.76	5 17.24	29
	Large or Sport/Utility	30 93.75	2 6.25	32
	Total	66	30	96

Statistics for Table of size by safety

Statistics for Table of size by safety			
Statistic	**DF**	**Value**	**Prob**
Chi-Square	2	31.3081	<.0001
Likelihood Ratio Chi-Square	2	32.6199	<.0001
Mantel-Haenszel Chi-Square	1	27.7098	<.0001
Phi Coefficient		0.5711	
Contingency Coefficient		0.4959	
Cramer's V		0.5711	

1) Because both **`size`** and **`safety`** are ordinal variables, you should use the Mantel-Haenszel test to detect the ordinal association between them.

2) The *p*-value Mantel-Haenszel is <.00001, so you reject the null hypothesis that there is **not** an ordinal association.

Statistic	Value	ASE	95% Confidence Limits	
Gamma	-0.8268	0.0796	-0.9829	-0.6707
Kendall's Tau-b	-0.5116	0.0726	-0.6540	-0.3693
Stuart's Tau-c	-0.5469	0.0866	-0.7166	-0.3771
Somers' D C|R	-0.4114	0.0660	-0.5408	-0.2819
Somers' D R|C	-0.6364	0.0860	-0.8049	-0.4678
Pearson Correlation	-0.5401	0.0764	-0.6899	-0.3903
Spearman Correlation	-0.5425	0.0769	-0.6932	-0.3917
Lambda Asymmetric C|R	0.3667	0.1569	0.0591	0.6743
Lambda Asymmetric R|C	0.2951	0.0892	0.1203	0.4699
Lambda Symmetric	0.3187	0.0970	0.1286	0.5088
Uncertainty Coefficient C|R	0.2735	0.0836	0.1096	0.4374
Uncertainty Coefficient R|C	0.1551	0.0490	0.0590	0.2512
Uncertainty Coefficient Symmetric	0.1979	0.0615	0.0773	0.3186

3) To test for the statistical significance of strength of the association, find the Spearman correlation coefficient in the table above: -0.5425. The ordinal association is moderate.

4) The 95% confidence interval around the Spearman statistic is (-0.6932, -0.3917).

2. Performing Simple Logistic Regression Analysis

a. Use the Logistic Regression task to perform a simple logistic regression model with **`safety`** as the outcome variable and **`weight`** as the predictor variable. Use the appropriate options to model the probability of `Below Average` safety scores.

Make sure **`VEHICLESAFETYSIZE`** is the active data source. Select **Analyze** ⇨ **Regression** ⇨ **Logistic**.

Assign **`safety`** to the Analysis variable role. Click on **Ascending** on the right and change the sort order to **Descending**.

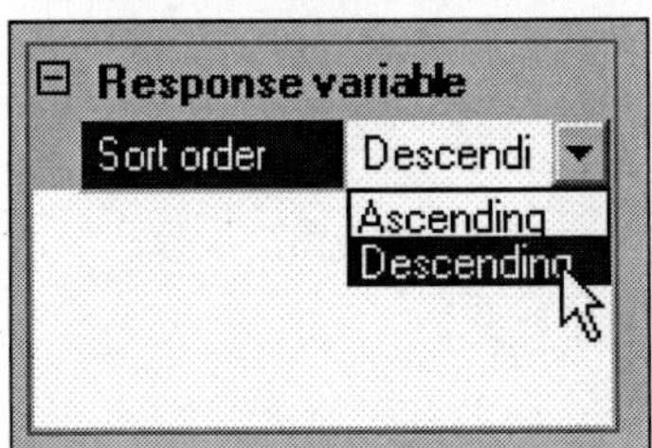

Because **`weight`** is a continuous variable, assign it to the Quantitative variable role.

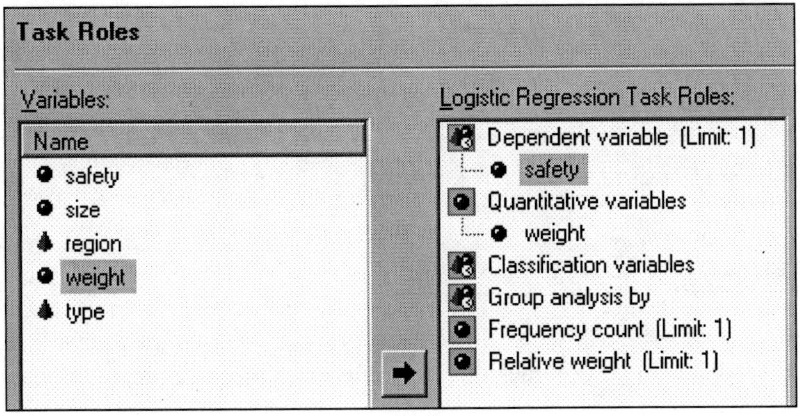

Select **Run**.

Logistic Regression Results

The LOGISTIC Procedure

Model Information	
Data Set	SASUSER.QURY4334
Response Variable	safety
Number of Response Levels	2
Number of Observations	96
Model	binary logit
Optimization Technique	Fisher's scoring

Response Profile		
Ordered Value	safety	Total Frequency
1	Below Average	30
2	Average or Above	66

Probability modeled is safety='Below Average'.

Observe that there were 30 cars with a `Below Average` safety rating. This is the attribute that you want to model, and SAS Enterprise Guide provides this very important piece of information under the Response Profile table.

Testing Global Null Hypothesis: BETA=0			
Test	Chi-Square	DF	Pr > ChiSq
Likelihood Ratio	28.6344	1	<.0001
Score	21.3147	1	<.0001
Wald	16.9690	1	<.0001

1) You reject the null hypothesis that all regression coefficients in the model are 0 because the *p*-value of the Likelihood Ratio statistic is less than 0.0001.

Analysis of Maximum Likelihood Estimates					
Parameter	DF	Estimate	Standard Error	Wald Chi-Square	Pr > ChiSq
Intercept	1	6.2896	1.6749	14.1015	0.0002
weight	1	-2.2942	0.5569	16.9690	<.0001

2) The logistic regression equation is logit($\hat{p}$) = 6.2896 – 2.2942 * **`weight`**, where $\hat{p}$ is the predicted probability of having a below-average safety score.

Odds Ratio Estimates			
Effect	Point Estimate	95% Wald Confidence Limits	
weight	0.101	0.034	0.300

3) The odds ratio for **`weight`** can be interpreted as meaning that vehicles 1,000 pounds heavier are 0.101 times more likely, with regards to odds, to have a below-average safety score compared to vehicles 1,000 pounds lighter.

4) The 95% confidence interval indicates that you are 95% confident that the odds ratio for your population is within the interval 0.034 through 0.300.

5)

Association of Predicted Probabilities and Observed Responses			
Percent Concordant	83.6	Somers' D	0.674
Percent Discordant	16.2	Gamma	0.675
Percent Tied	0.2	Tau-a	0.293
Pairs	1980	c	0.837

A concordant pair occurs when the observation with the outcome (in this case, below-average safety score) has a higher predicted outcome probability (based on the model) than the observation without the outcome (`average or above average` safety scores).

For all pairs of observations with different outcomes, 83.6% were concordant. This large percentage of concordant pairs, the small percentage of discordant pairs, and the very small percentage of tied pairs indicate that the model fits the observed data very well.

You could also create another model and compare the concordant/discordant goodness-of-fit statistics with the same statistics of any model.

Remember to use the Model Fit Statistics table to compare models. Because there was only one model, these statistics cannot be compared to any statistics from another model.

The Model Fit Statistics table for this model is shown below:

Model Fit Statistics		
Criterion	Intercept Only	Intercept and Covariates
AIC	121.249	94.614
SC	123.813	99.743
-2 Log L	119.249	90.614

The relatively large value for the *c* statistic indicates that this current model would have excellent predictive abilities.

Appendix A Random Samples

A.1 Generating Random Samples with SAS Enterprise Guide

The SURVEYSELECT procedure is used to generate random samples with SAS Enterprise Guide. Two sample methods are available: simple random sample without replacement and unrestricted random sample with replacement.

In most applications, you will generate a random sample without replacement. There are a number of options as well as advanced settings. What is presented here is a rudimentary demonstration of how to generate a random sample without replacement.

The Random Sample task also provides the ability to generate an unrestricted sample with replacement, which is not be discussed in this appendix.

A random sample will be created using two techniques, specifying a sample size and then a sampling rate.

1. To generate a random sample, select the data table from which you want to sample. In this example, select **SASUSER.CARS1993**.

2. Select **Data** ⇨ **Random Sample**.

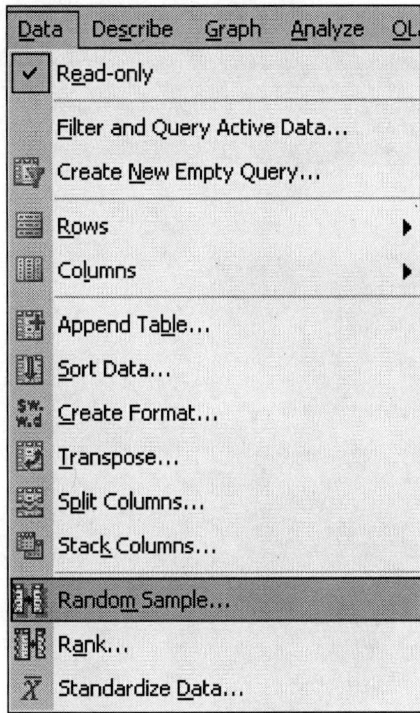

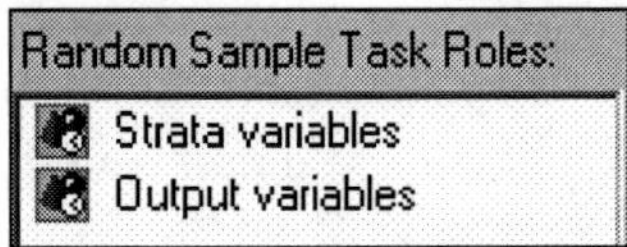

Adding Strata variables will allow you to take a stratified random sample. You can use the SAS Enterprise Guide Help facility and search on SURVEYSELECT for more information on this option. You can also use the SAS online documentation or a statistics textbook.

The Output variables role is for variables you want included in the output data set.

3. Add all of the variables for **CARS1993** to the Output variables role.

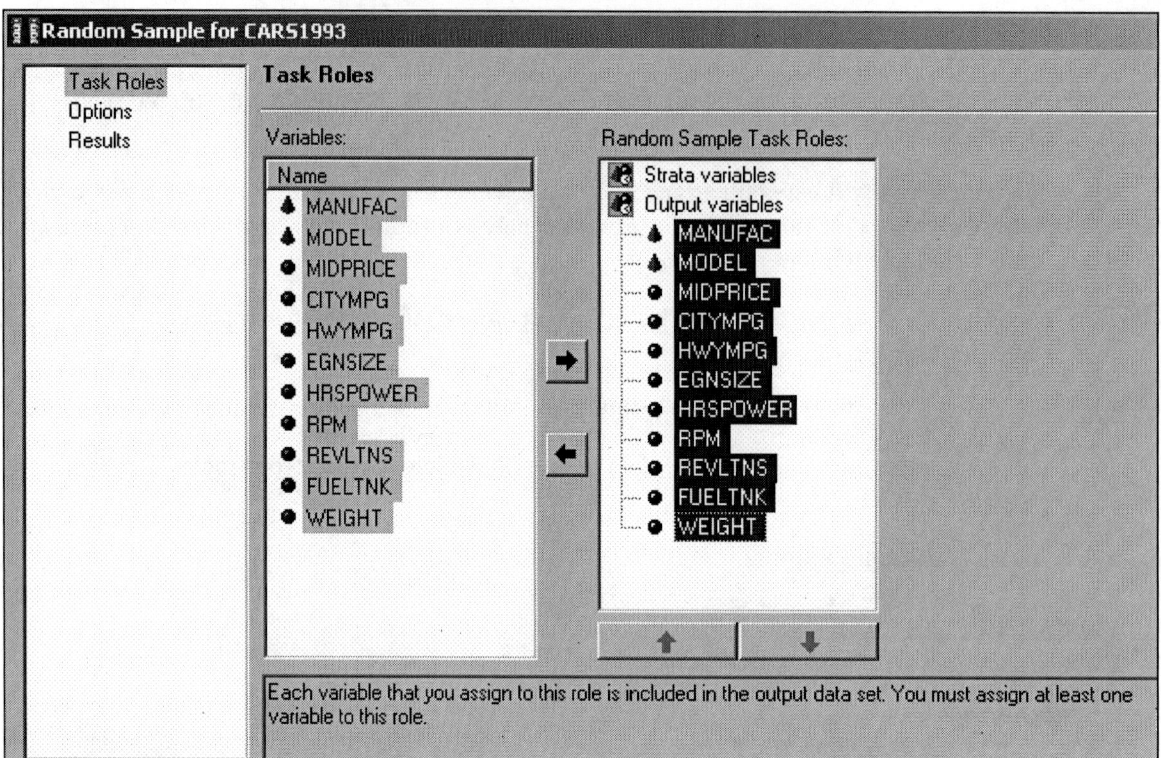

4. Select **Options** from the left pane.

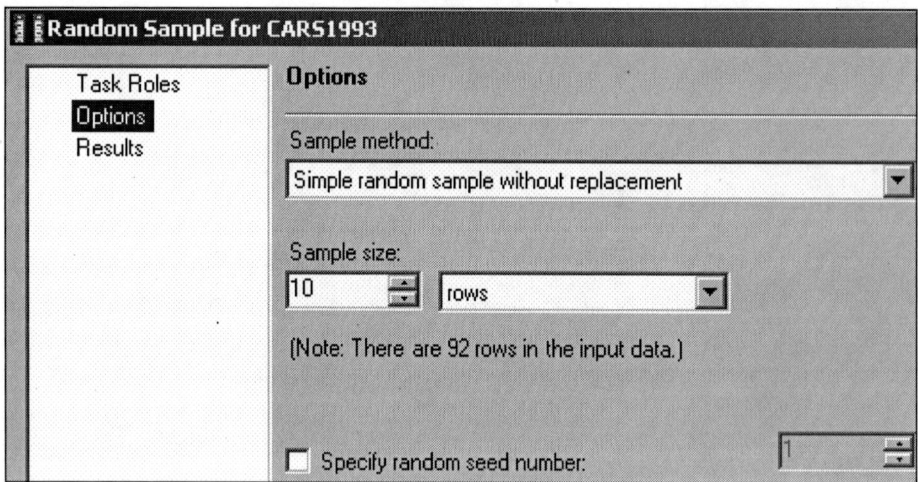

The default Sample Method is `Simple random sample without replacement`. You can also choose to sample with replacement. You can choose for your sample to be a given number of rows, or you can choose to make it a percentage of the original sample by selecting from the drop-down list. SAS Enterprise Guide displays the total number of rows in the input table and, by default, selects the sample method to be `rows` with a sample size of 10.

5. Increase the sample size from 10 to 12 by clicking on the up arrow.

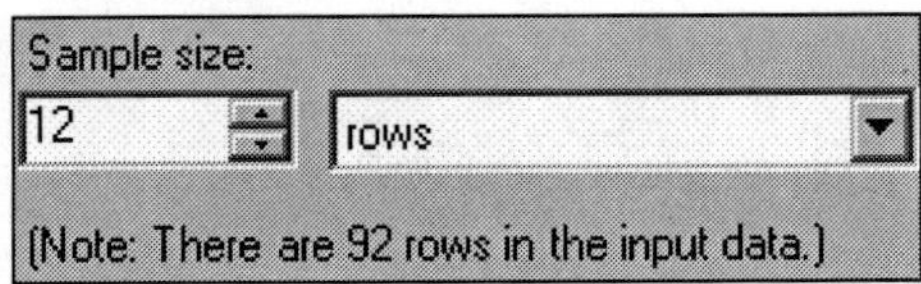

6. Select the check box next to **Specify a random seed number:**, highlight the default value of 1 and type in the value `31475`. A positive value is required and must be less than or equal to 9,999,999 because only seven decimal places are provided.

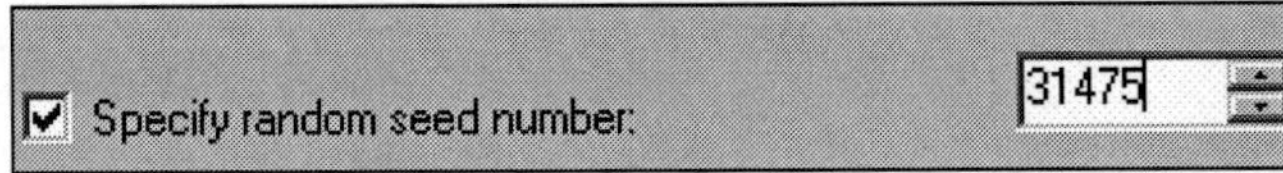

The default is to use the time on the system clock as the seed value. This will give you a different sample every time the task is run. Specifying a seed ensures that you will have the same random sample every time.

7. Select the **Results** pane on the left. You may change the name of the output data set and to select whether you want to see a report summarizing the selections.

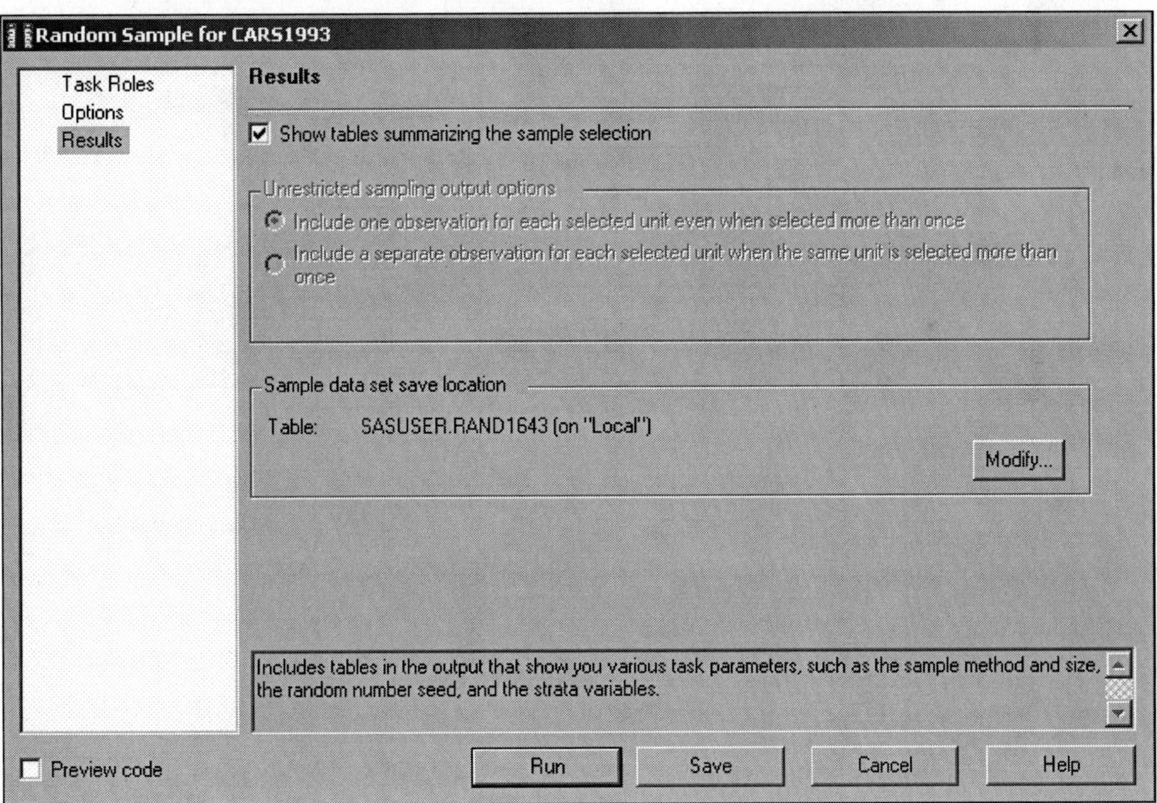

8. Select **Modify…**.

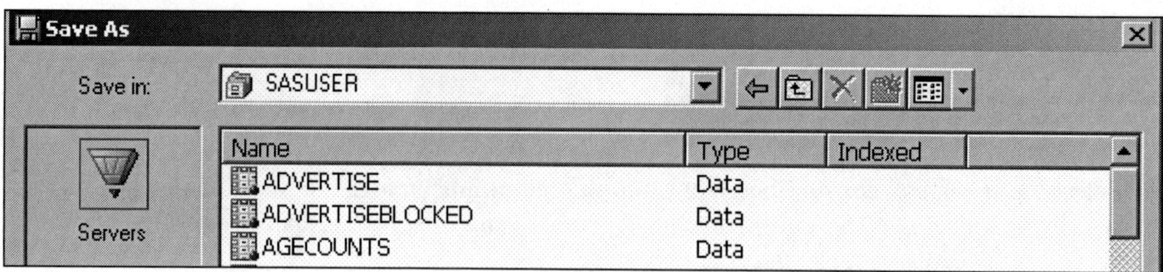

Instead of using the default SASUSER, save this sample to the WORK library.

9. Select **Up One Level**, .

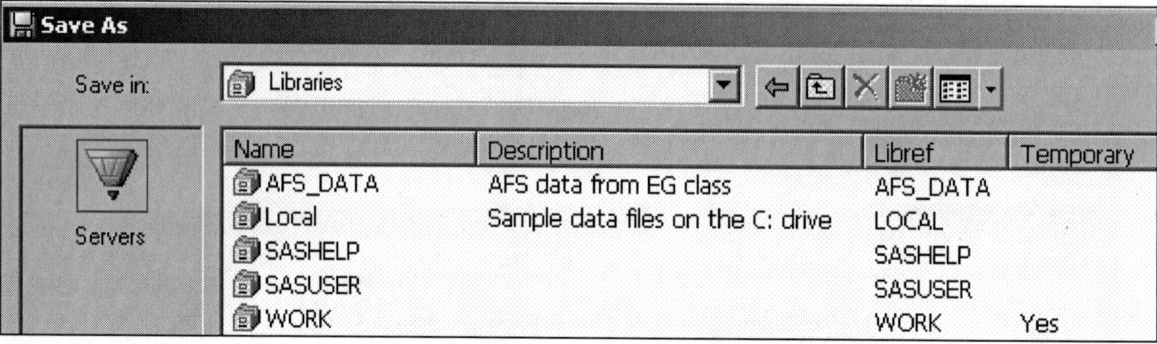

10. Double click on **WORK** and change the default name to `CarSample12`.

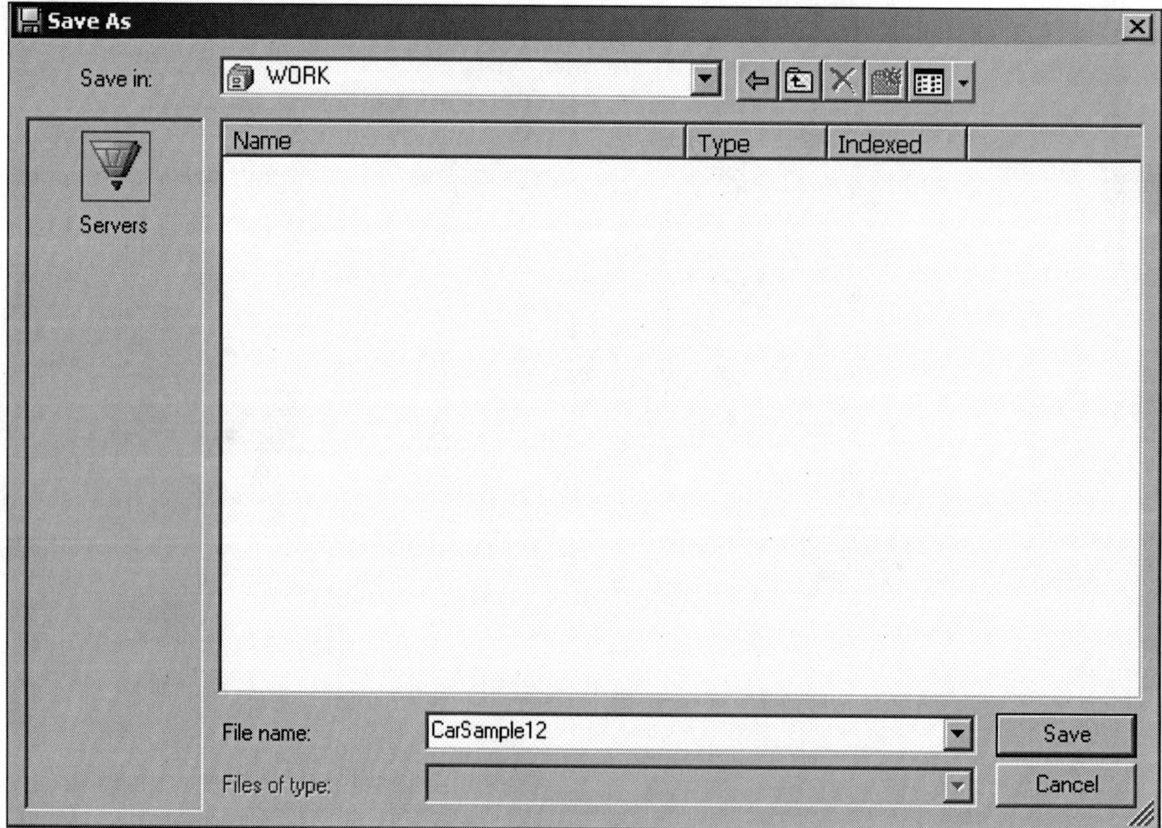

11. Select **Save**.

12. Select **Run** to submit the task.

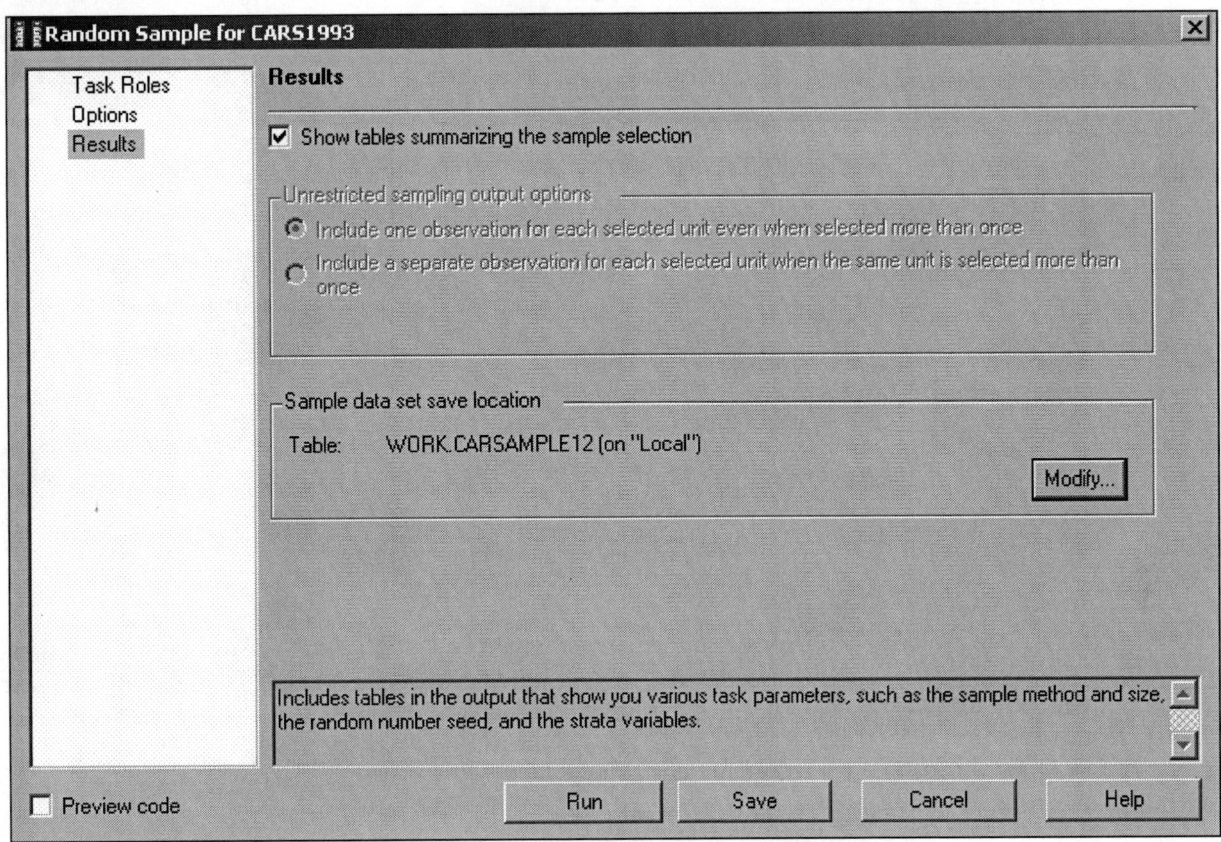

A report summarizing the sample is created.

The SURVEYSELECT Procedure

Selection Method	Simple Random Sampling

Input Data Set	SORT8539
Random Number Seed	31475
Sample Size	12
Selection Probability	0.130435
Sampling Weight	7.666667
Output Data Set	CARSAMPLE12

> The table provides two pieces of information that are beyond the scope of this book, Selection Probability and Sampling Weight. You can use the SAS Enterprise Guide Help facility and search for SURVEYSELECT for documentation of these advanced topics.

To see the new table, find the Random Sample task in the process flow.

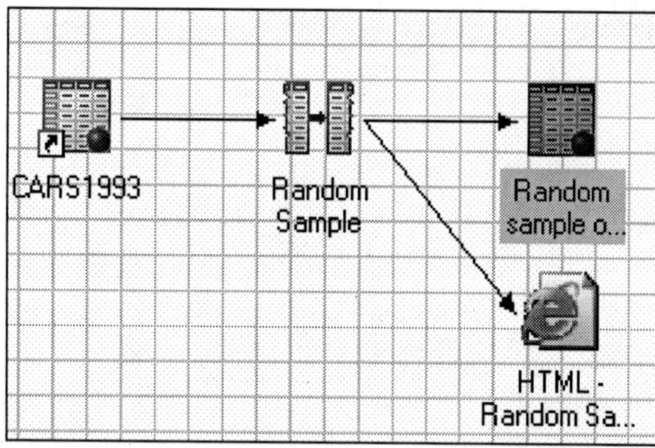

13. Open the table **`Random sample of SASUSER.CARS1993`**.

Random sample of SASUSER.CARS1993 (read-only)

	MANUFAC	MODEL	MIDPRICE	CITYMPG	HWYMPG	EGNSIZE	HRSPOWER	RPM	REVLTNS	FUELTNK	WEIGHT
1	Acura	Integra	15.9	25	31	1.8	140	6300	2890	13.2	2705
2	BMW	535i	30	22	30	3.5	208	5700	2545	21.1	3640
3	Chevrolet	Astro	16.6	15	20	4.3	165	4000	1790	27	4025
4	Dodge	Shadow	11.3	23	29	2.2	93	4800	2595	14	2670
5	Ford	Crown_Victor	20.9	18	26	4.6	190	4200	1415	20	3950
6	Geo	Storm	12.5	30	36	1.6	90	5400	3250	12.4	2475
7	Hyundai	Elantra	10	22	29	1.8	124	6000	2745	13.7	2620
8	Lexus	ES300	28	18	24	3	185	5200	2325	18.5	3510
9	Mazda	RX-7	32.5	17	25	1.3	255	6500	2325	20	2895
10	Pontiac	Bonneville	24.4	19	28	3.8	170	4800	1565	18	3495
11	Volkswagen	Eurovan	19.7	17	21	2.5	109	4500	2915	21.1	3960
12	Volkswagen	Passat	20	21	30	2	134	5800	2685	18.5	2985

14. Select **`Random sample of SASUSER.CARS1993`**, right-click and select **Properties**.

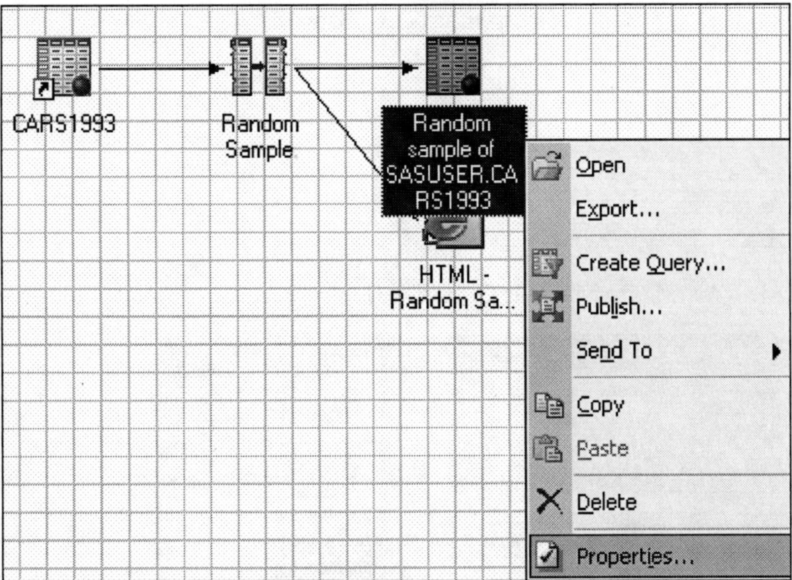

15. Notice the number of rows is equal to the desired sample size and the file containing the sample is stored in the WORK library.

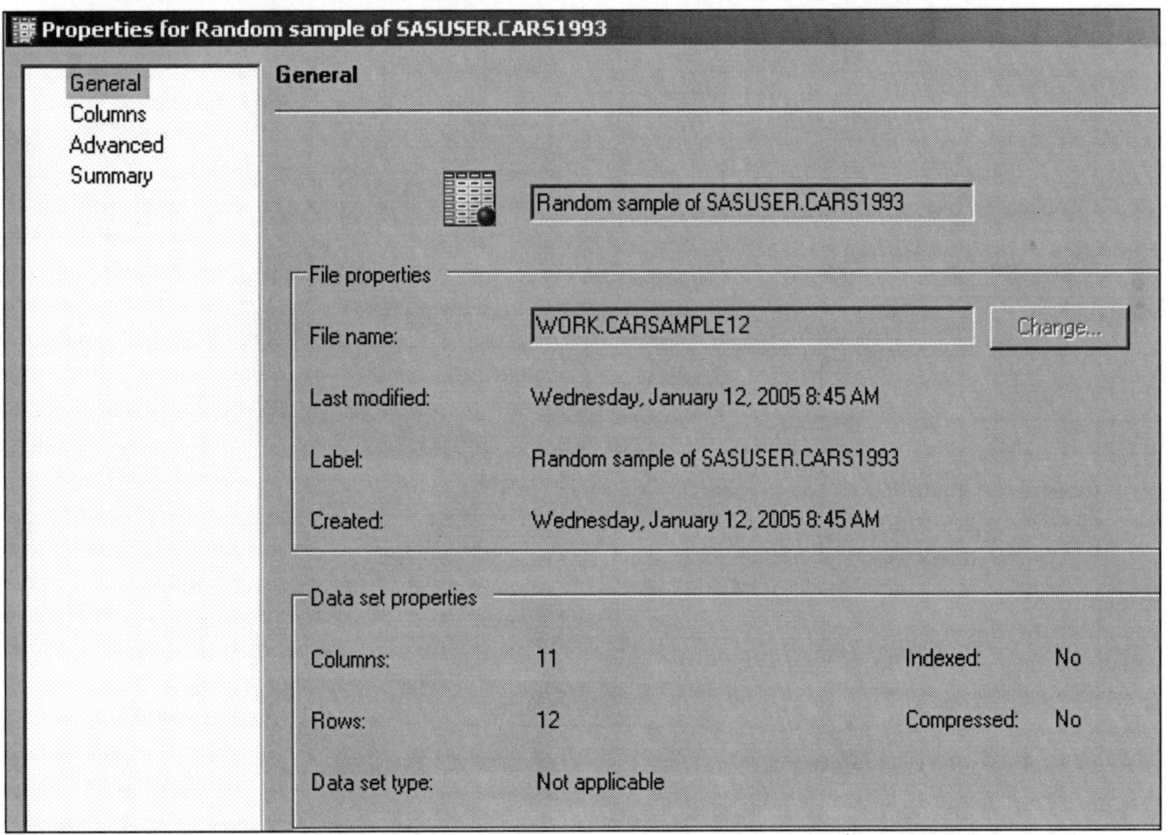

Now create another sample without replacement but choose a sampling rate of 0.05.

1. Locate and open **SASUSER.CARS1993** from the current process flow.

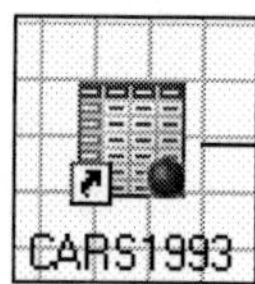

2. Select **Data** ⇨ **Random Sample**.

3. Drag and drop `Manufac`, `Model` and `Midprice` as Output variables.

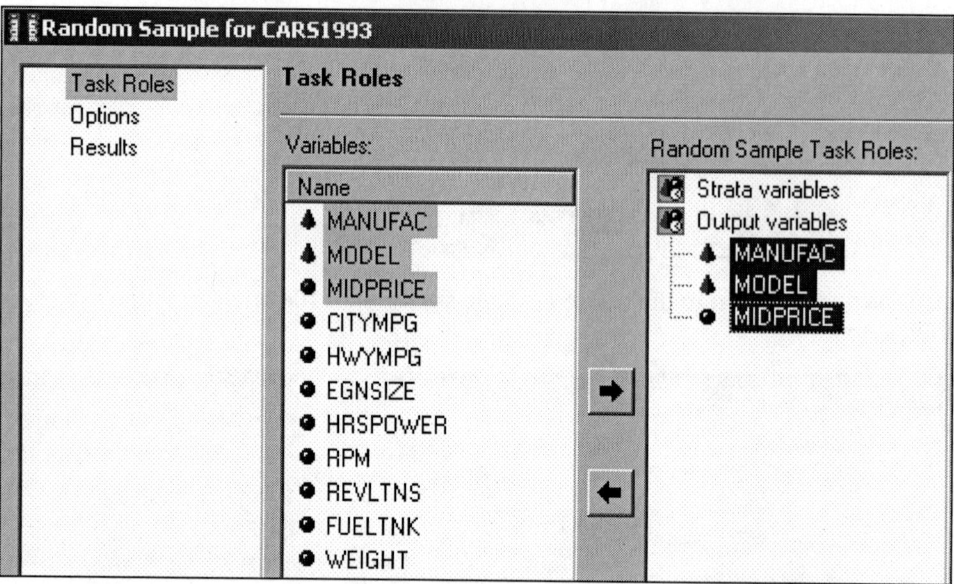

4. Select **Options** from the left pane.

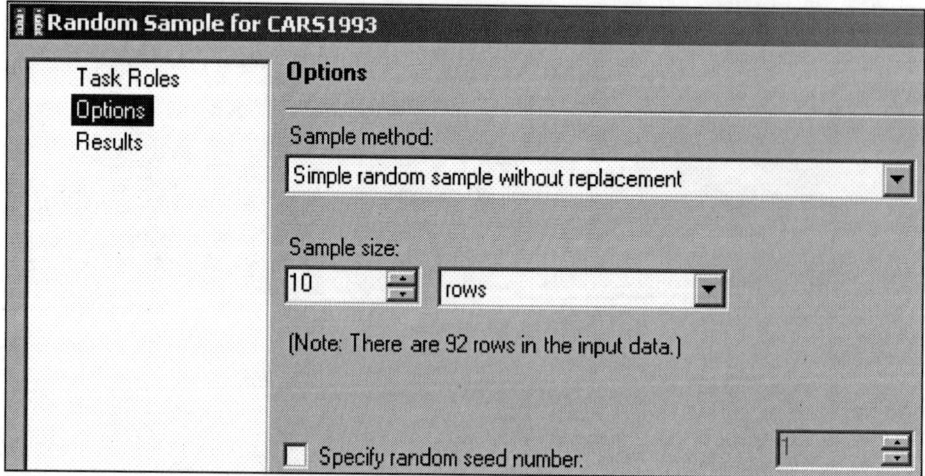

5. Click the black arrow besides **rows** and change to `percent of rows`. Change the default percentage from 25 to 5. Notice you are not selecting a random seed.

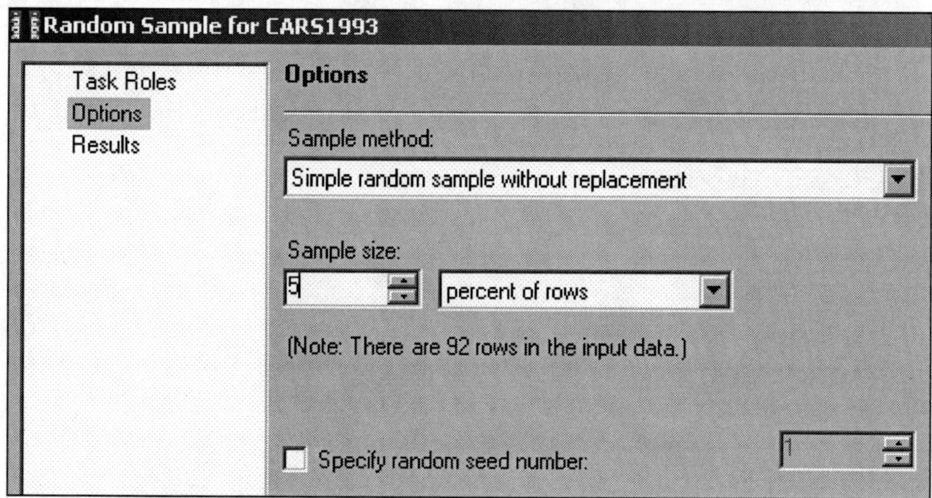

6. Select the **Results** pane on the left.

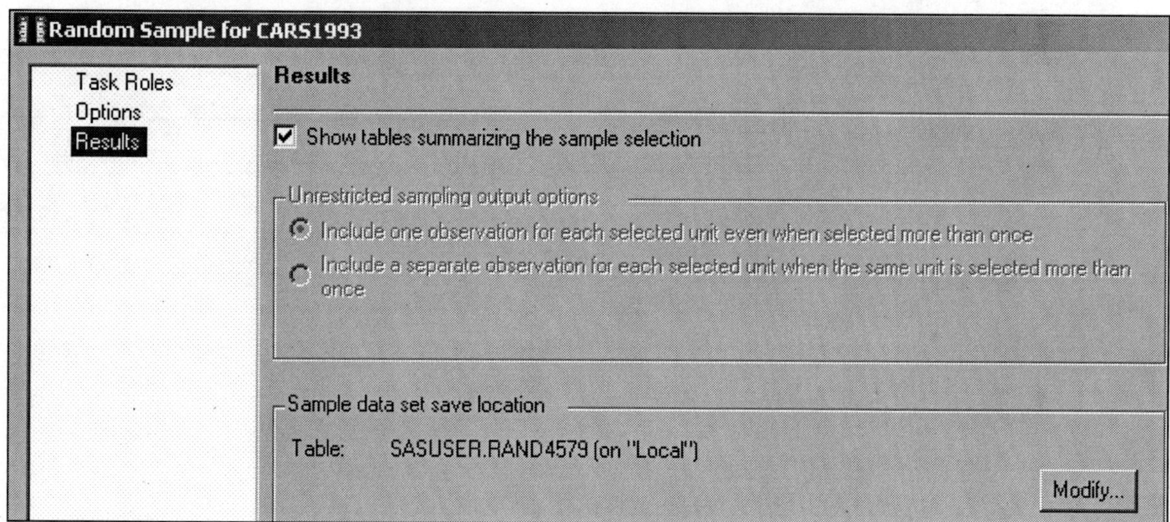

7. Select **Modify…**.

8. Change the default name to **`Cars5Percent`**.

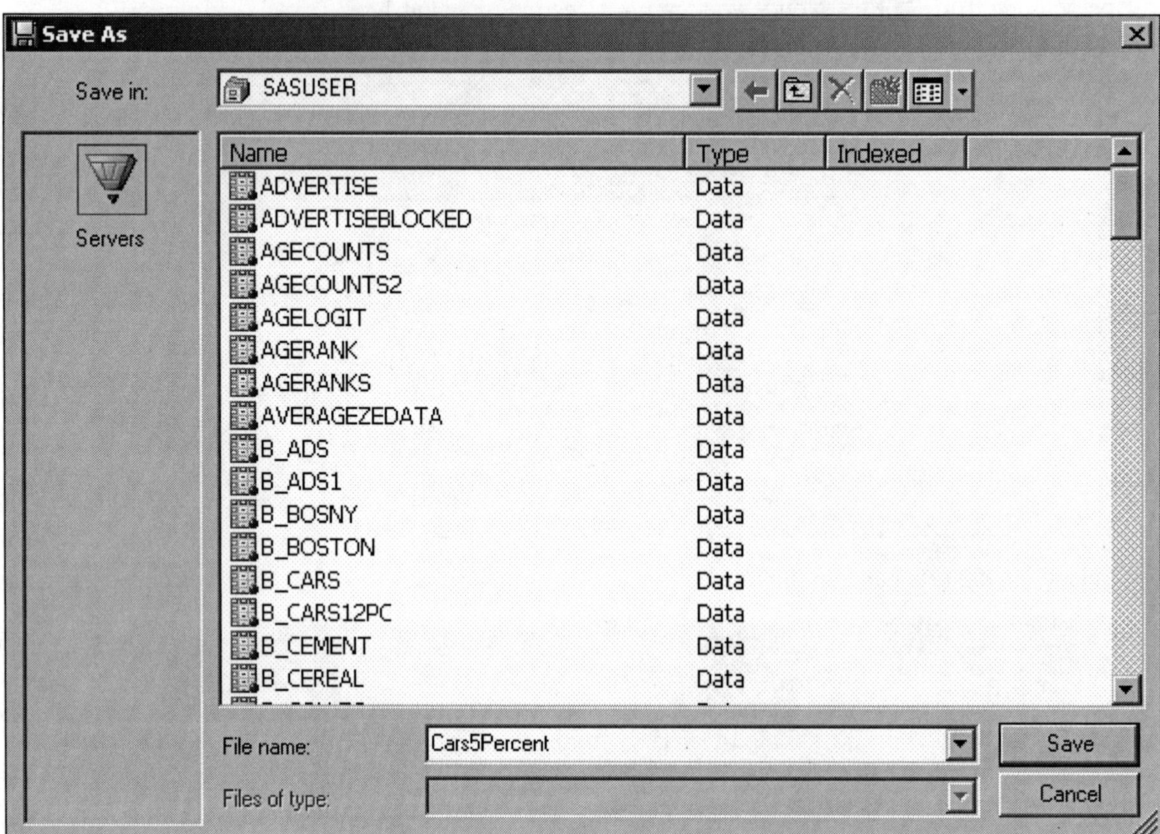

Notice the default library is SASUSER.

9. Select **Save**.

10. Select **Run**.

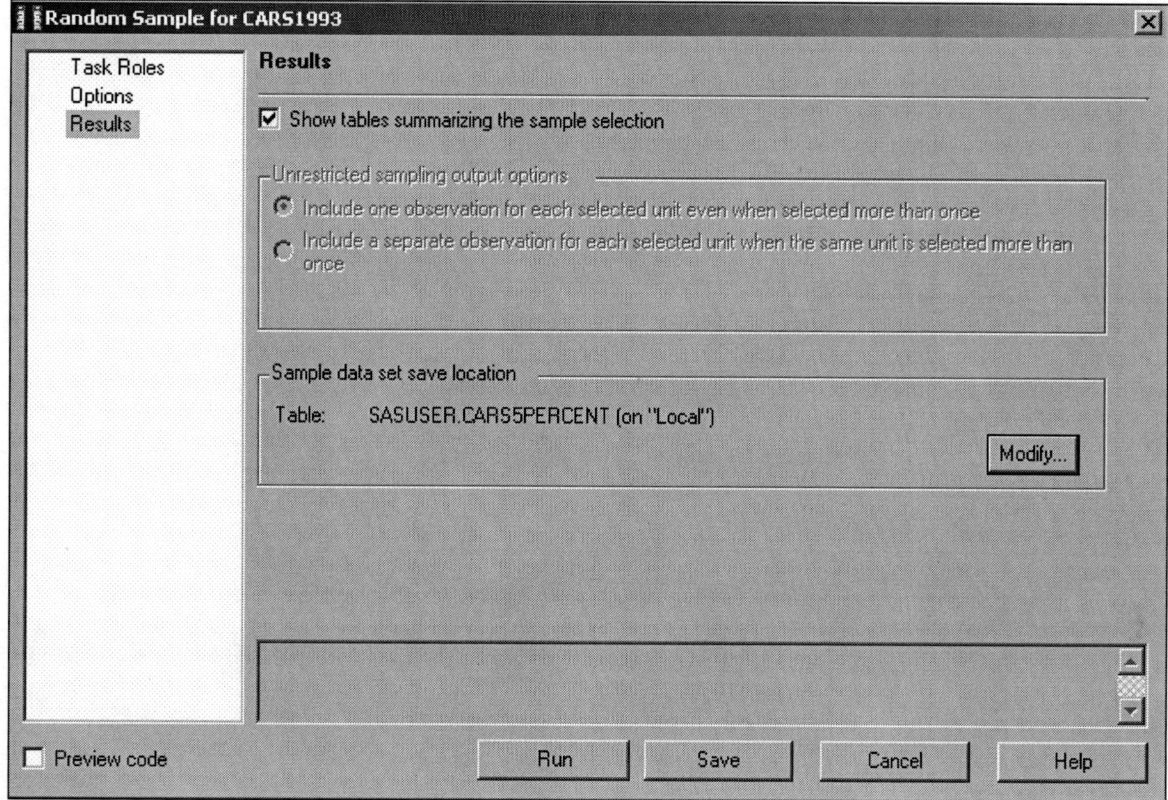

The requested summary report is generated.

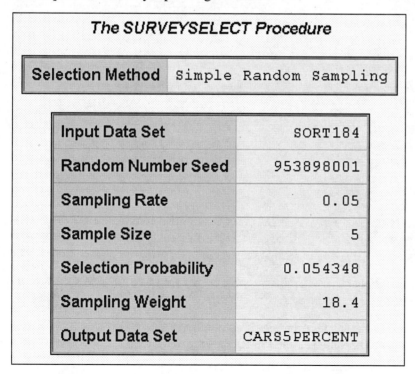

The SURVEYSELECT Procedure

Selection Method	Simple Random Sampling

Input Data Set	SORT184
Random Number Seed	953898001
Sampling Rate	0.05
Sample Size	5
Selection Probability	0.054348
Sampling Weight	18.4
Output Data Set	CARS5PERCENT

11. Locate and open the second occurrence of **Random sample of SASUSER.CARS1993** in the process flow.

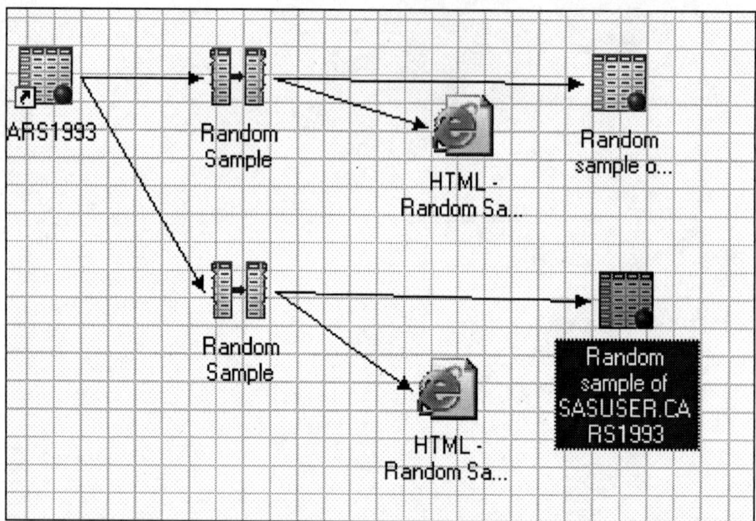

12. Select `Random sample of SASUSER.CARS1993`, right-click and select **Properties**.

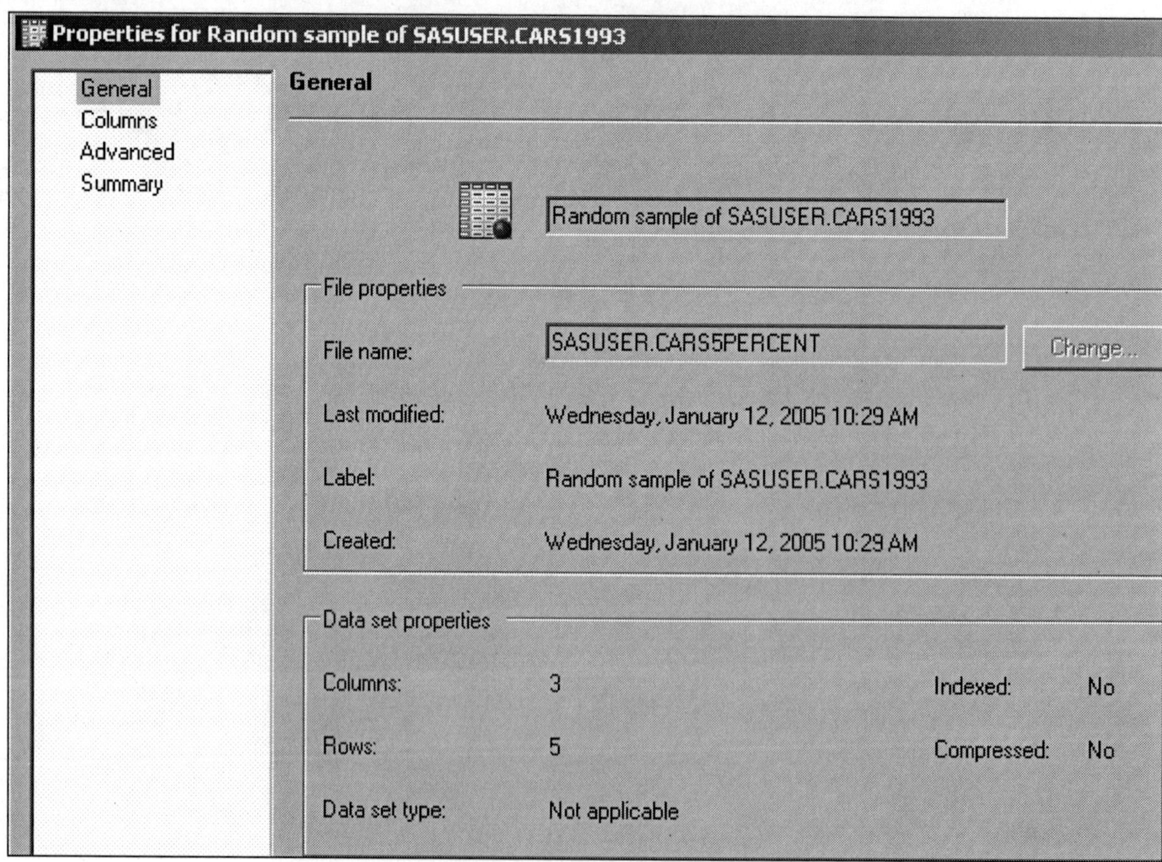

Notice the table has 5 rows and 3 columns (chosen in a previous step.) The 5 rows represent 5% of the original data table's size of 92. The table is stored in SASUSER.

13. Open **SASUSER.Cars5Percent**.

Random sample of SASUSER.CARS1993 (read-only)

	MANUFAC	MODEL	MIDPRICE
1	Dodge	Dynasty	15.6
2	Eagle	Vision	19.3
3	Mazda	Protege	11.6
4	Mercury	Capri	14.1
5	Oldsmobile	Silhouette	19.5

You can explore other options for the Random Sample task through the online SAS Enterprise Guide Help facility.

Appendix B Additional Topics

B.1 Paired *t*-Tests

This section discusses a special case scenario of a one-sample *t*-test.

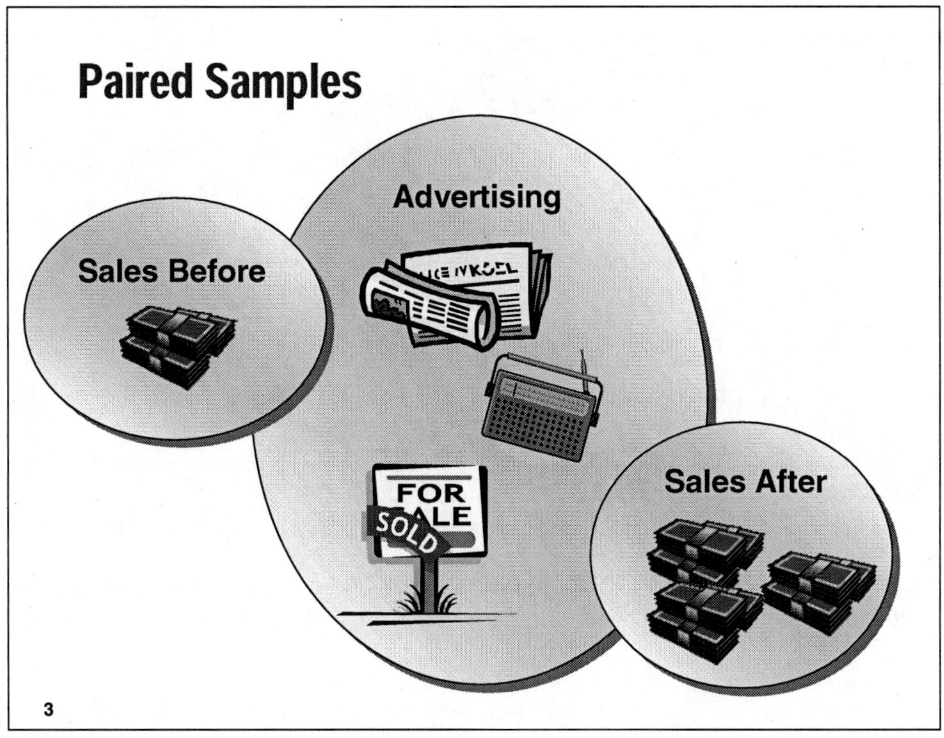

For many types of data, repeat measurements are taken on the same subject throughout a study. The simplest form of this study is often referred to as the paired *t*-test.

In this study design,

- subjects are exposed to a treatment, for example, an advertising strategy
- a measurement is taken on the subjects before and after the treatment
- the subjects, on average, respond the same way to the treatment, although there may be differences between the subjects.

The assumptions of this test are that

- the subjects are selected randomly
- the distribution of the sample mean differences is normal. This assumption can be verified by the central limit theorem.

The hypotheses of this test are

$$H_0: \mu_{POST} = \mu_{PRE}$$

$$H_1: \mu_{POST} \neq \mu_{PRE}.$$

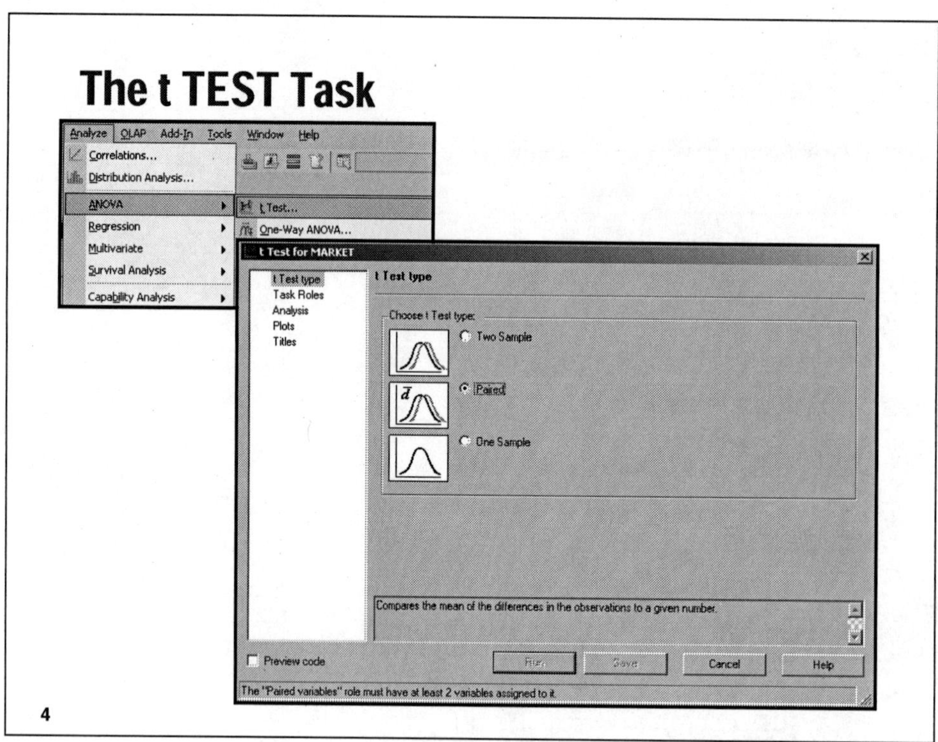

The t Test task in SAS Enterprise Guide uses the TTEST procedure in SAS/STAT software to perform one-sample, two-sample, and paired-sample *t*-tests. You will learn to use the task for paired *t*-tests in the following demonstration.

Paired *t*-Test

Example: Dollar values of sales have been collected both before and after a particular advertising campaign. You are interested in determining the effect of the campaign on sales. You have collected data from 30 different randomly selected regions. The level of sales both before (`pre`) and after (`post`) the campaign were recorded and are shown below.

1. Locate and open the data table **`MARKET`** in the project flow.

   Partial Listing

   MARKET (read-only)

	pre	post
1	9.52	10.28
2	9.63	10.45
3	7.71	8.51
4	7.83	8.62
5	8.97	10.03
6	8.62	9.45
7	10.11	9.68
8	9.96	9.62
9	8.5	11.84
10	9.62	11.95

   There are 30 observations and two variables, **`pre`** and **`post`**.

2. Select **Analyze** ⇨ **ANOVA** ⇨ **t Test…**.

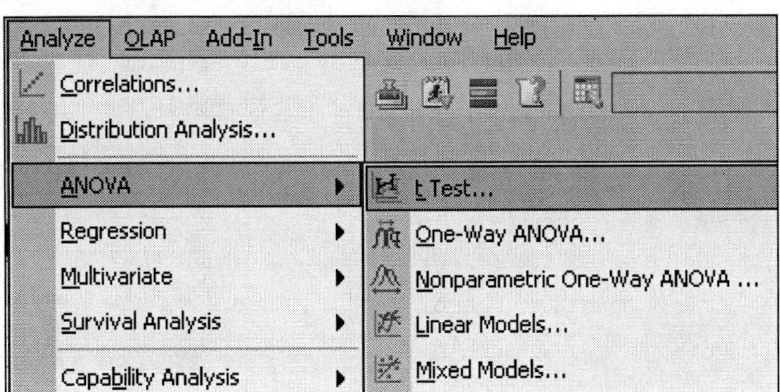

3. The **t Test type** panel enables you to specify the type of *t*-test you wish to perform. Select **Paired**.

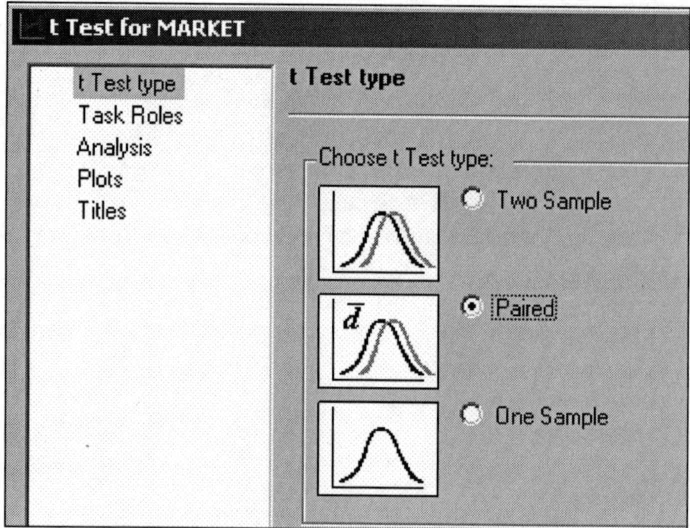

4. In the **Task Roles** panel, drag and drop `pre` and `post` to the Paired variables role.

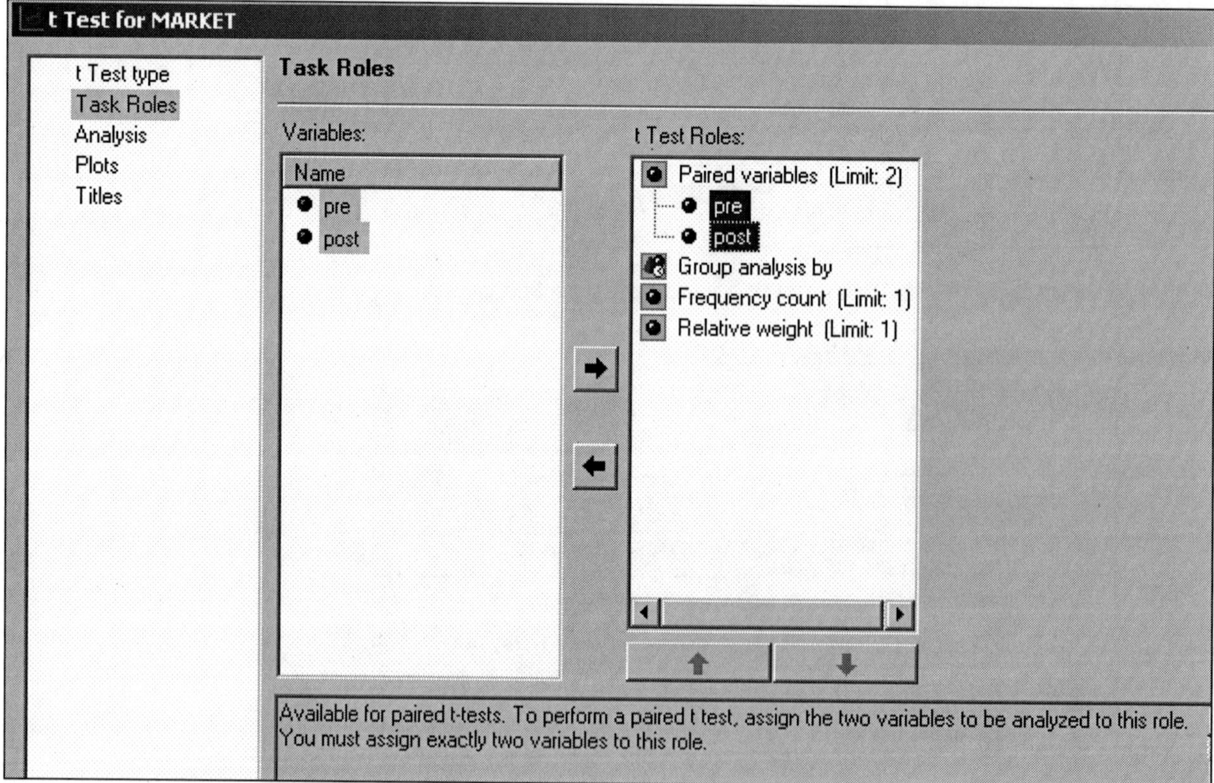

5. Select **post** from the **t Test Roles:** panel on the far right.

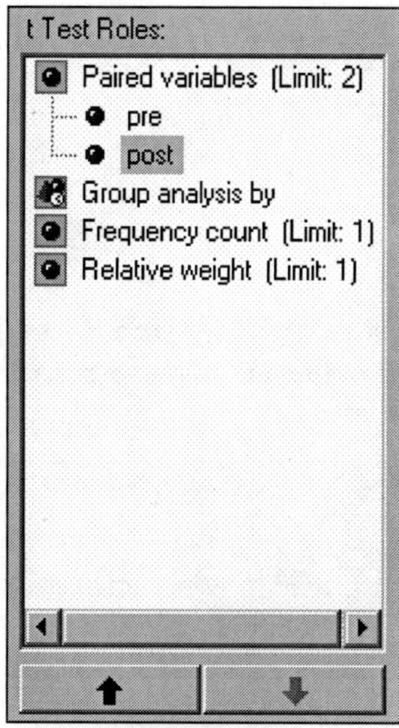

6. Select [up-arrow button].

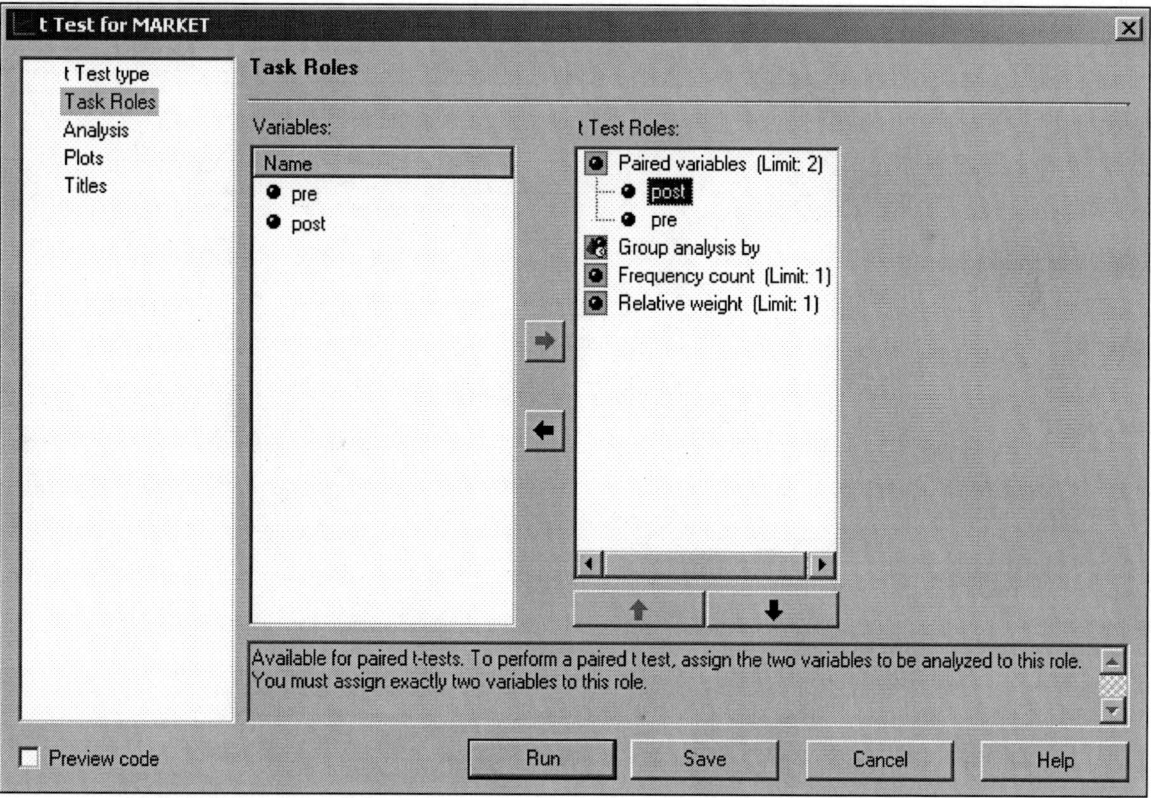

This action will generate the difference of `post` – `pre`.

7. Select **Run**.

The generated results are presented below in the logical order in which to analyze them.

T-Tests			
Difference	DF	t Value	Pr > |t|
post - pre	29	5.59	<.0001

The T-Tests table provides the requested analysis. The p-value for the difference **`post`** – **`pre`** is less than 0.0001. Assuming that you want to use a 0.01 level of significance, you reject the null hypothesis and conclude that there is a change in the average sales after the advertising campaign.

Statistics										
Difference	N	Lower CL Mean	Mean	Upper CL Mean	Lower CL Std Dev	Std Dev	Upper CL Std Dev	Std Err	Minimum	Maximum
post - pre	30	0.6001	0.9463	1.2925	0.7384	0.9271	1.2464	0.1693	-0.48	3.34

Based on the fact that the mean is positive 0.9463, there appears to be an increase in the average sales after the advertising campaign.

B.2 Two-Sample *t*-Tests

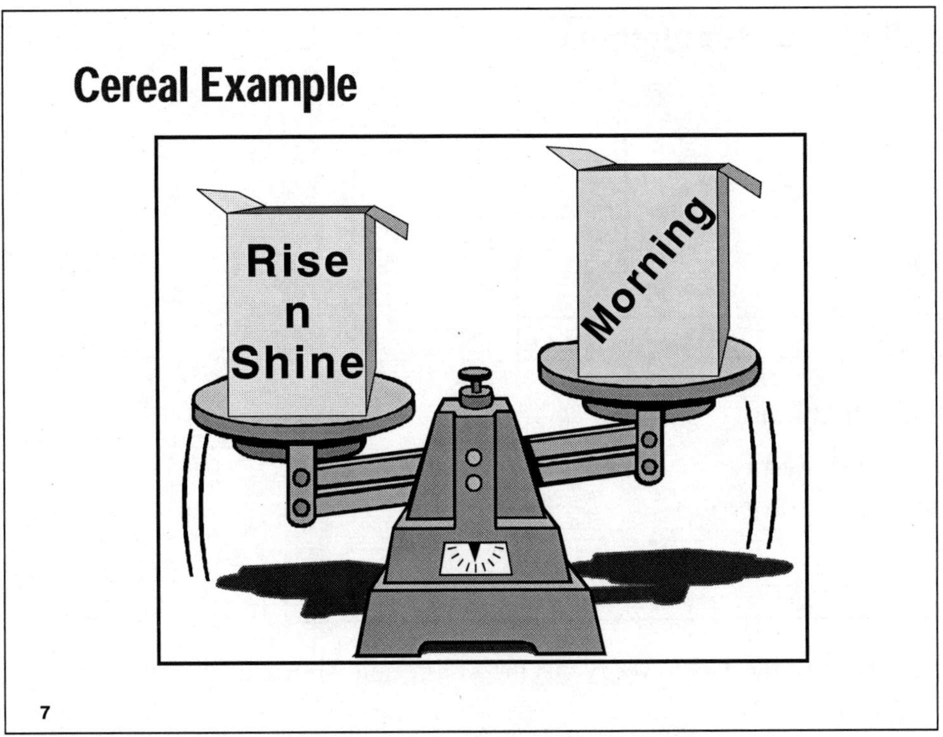

Example: A consumer advocacy group wants to determine whether two popular cereal brands, Rise n Shine and Morning, have the same amount of cereal. Both brands advertise that they have 15 ounces of cereal per box. A random sample of both brands is selected and the number of ounces of cereal is recorded. The data is stored in a data set called **`CEREALS`**.

The variables in the data set are

`brand`	two groups, `Rise n Shine` and `Morning`, corresponding to the two brands
`weight`	weight of the cereal in ounces
`idnumber`	the identification number for each cereal box.

Assumptions

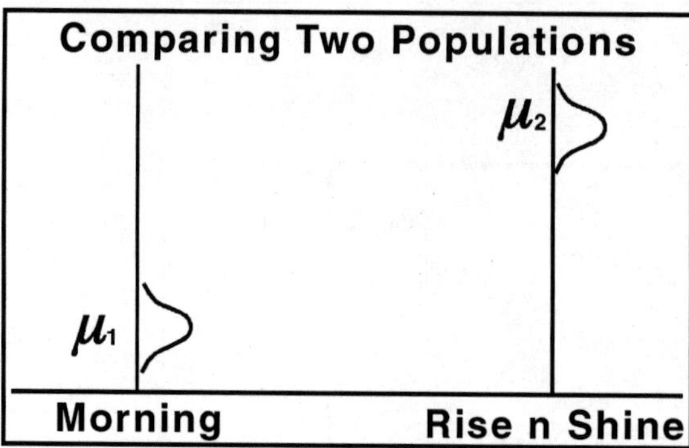

- independent observations
- normally distributed data for each group
- equal variances for each group

8

Before you start the analysis, examine the data to verify that the assumptions are valid.

The assumption of independent observations means that no observations provide any information about any other observation you collect. For example, measurements are not repeated on the same subject. This assumption can be verified during the design stage.

The assumption of normality can be relaxed if the data is approximately normally distributed or if enough data is collected. This assumption can be verified by examining plots of the data.

There are several tests for equal variances. If this assumption is not valid, an approximate *t*-test can be performed.

If these assumptions are **not** valid, the probability of drawing incorrect conclusions from the analysis could be increased.

F-Test for Equality of Variances

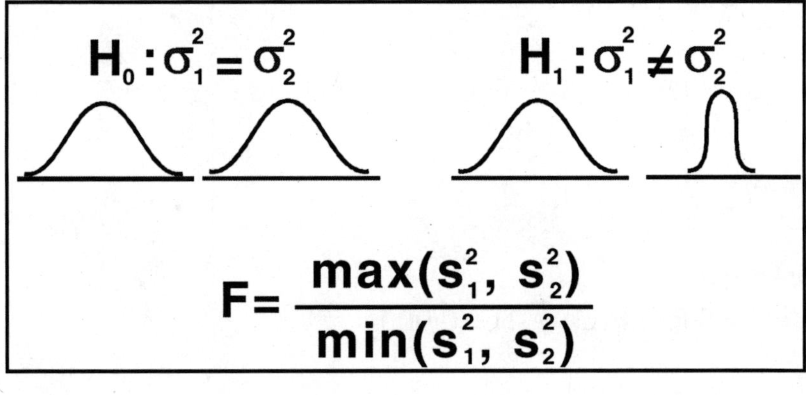

$H_0: \sigma_1^2 = \sigma_2^2$
$H_1: \sigma_1^2 \neq \sigma_2^2$
$F = \frac{\max(s_1^2, s_2^2)}{\min(s_1^2, s_2^2)}$

9

When performing this test, note that if the null hypothesis is true, *F* tends to be close to 1.

If you reject the null hypothesis, it is recommended that you use the unequal variance *t*-test in the t-Test task for testing the equality of group means.

This test is valid **only** for independent samples from normal distributions. Normality is required even for large sample sizes.

Test Statistics and *p*-Values

***F*-Test for Equal Variances:** H_0: $\sigma_{12} = \sigma_{22}$

Variance Test: F' = 1.51 DF = (3,3) Prob > F' = 0.7446

***t*-Tests for Equal Means:** H_0: $\mu_1 = \mu_2$

Unequal Variance *t*-Test:

T = 7.4017 DF = 5.8 Prob > |T| = 0.0004

Equal Variance *t*-Test:

T = 7.4017 DF = 6.0 Prob > |T| = 0.0003

10

First, check the assumption for equal variances and then use the appropriate test for equal means. Because the *p*-value of the test *F*-statistic is 0.7446, there is not enough evidence to reject the null hypothesis of equal variances. Use the Equal Variance *t*-test line in the output to test whether the means of the two populations are equal.

The null hypothesis that the group means are equal is rejected at the 0.05 level. You conclude that there is a difference between the means of the groups.

The equal variance *F*-test is found at the bottom of the t Test task results.

Test Statistics and *p*-Values

_F_-Test for Equal Variances: H_0: $\sigma_{12} = \sigma_{22}$

Variance Test:

F' = 15.28 DF = (9,4) Prob > F' = 0.0185

_t_-Tests for Equal Means: H_0: $\mu_1 = \mu_2$

Unequal Variance _t_-Test:

T = -2.4518 DF = 11.1 Prob > |T| = 0.0320

Equal Variance _t_-Test:

T = -1.7835 DF = 13.0 Prob > |T| = 0.0979

11

Again, first check the assumption for equal variances and use the appropriate test for equal means. Because the *p*-value of the test *F*-statistic is less than alpha=0.05, there is enough evidence to reject the null hypothesis of equal variances. Use the unequal variance *t*-test line in the output to test whether the means of the two populations are equal.

The null hypothesis that the group means are equal is rejected at the .05 level.

However, notice that if you choose the equal variance *t*-test, you would not reject the null hypothesis at the .05 level. This shows the importance of choosing the appropriate *t*-test.

Two-Sample *t*-Test

Example: Examine the data in **CEREALS** and do an initial check of the assumptions of the *t*-test and the *F*-test using the Distribution Analysis task. Then invoke t Test task to test the hypothesis that the means are equal for the two groups.

1. Select **CEREALS**.
2. Select **Analyze** ⇨ **Distribution Analysis…**.
3. Drag and drop **weight** in the Analysis Variables role. Drag and drop **brand** in the Classification variables role.

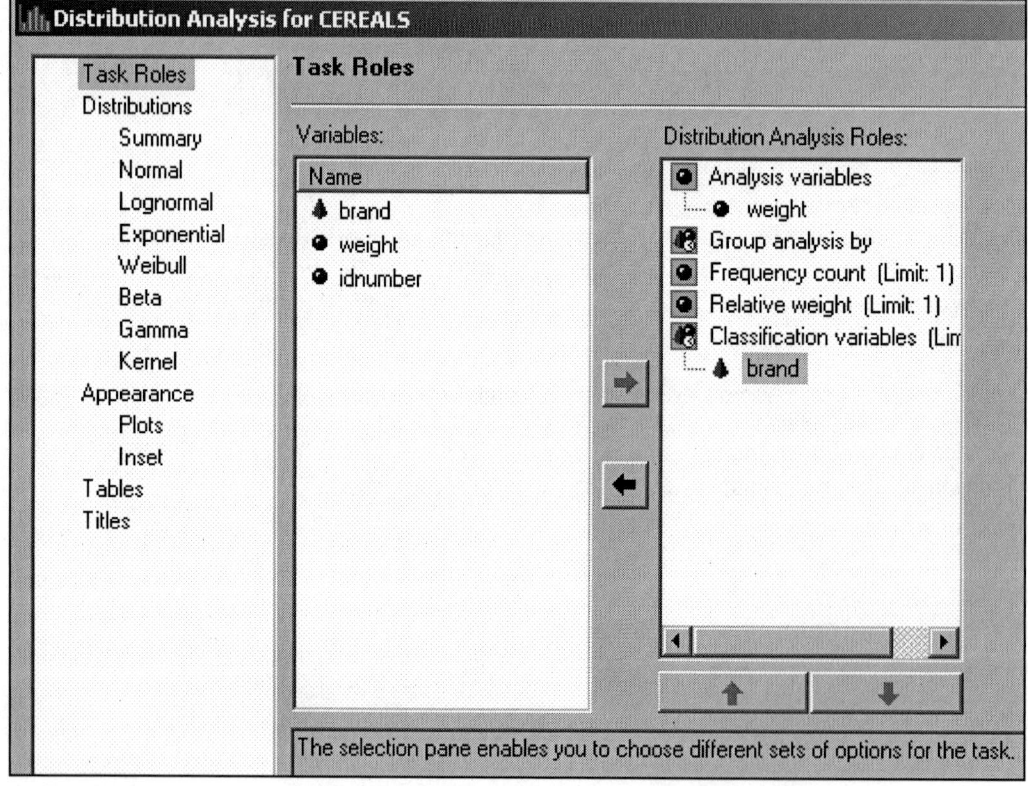

You could have also added **brand** to the Group analysis by role, which produces similar output but in a slightly different layout.

4. From the left panel, select **Normal** and request a red reference line.

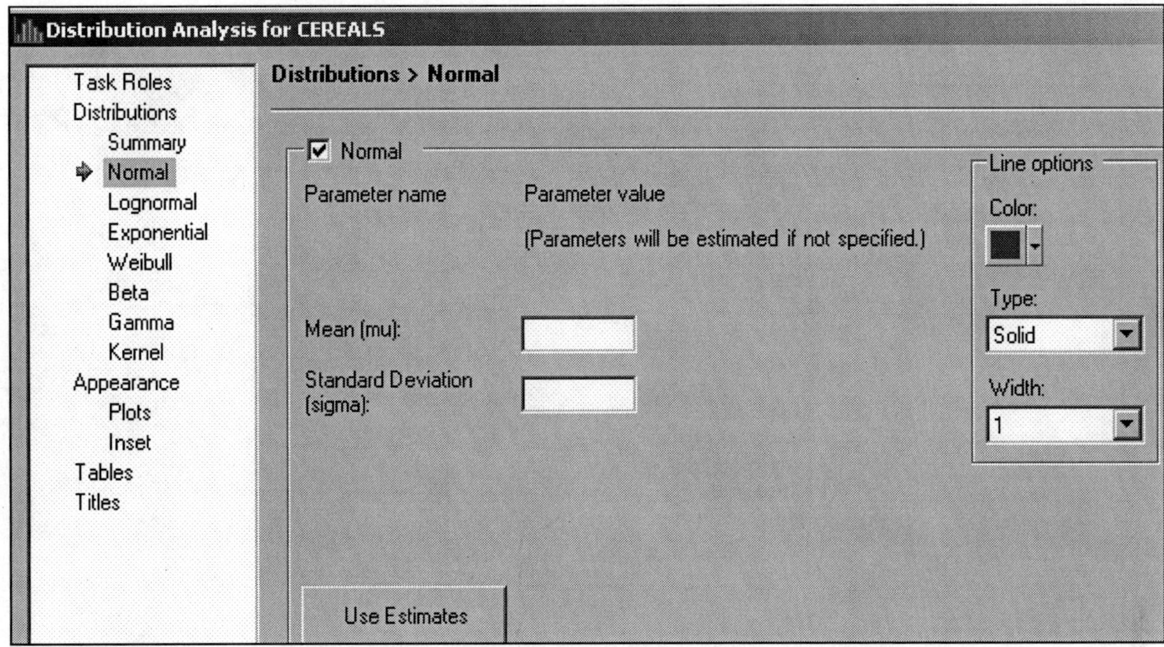

5. Select **Plots** on the left and check the boxes next to **Histogram Plot** and **Probability Plot**. Change the plot background color to white for both plots.

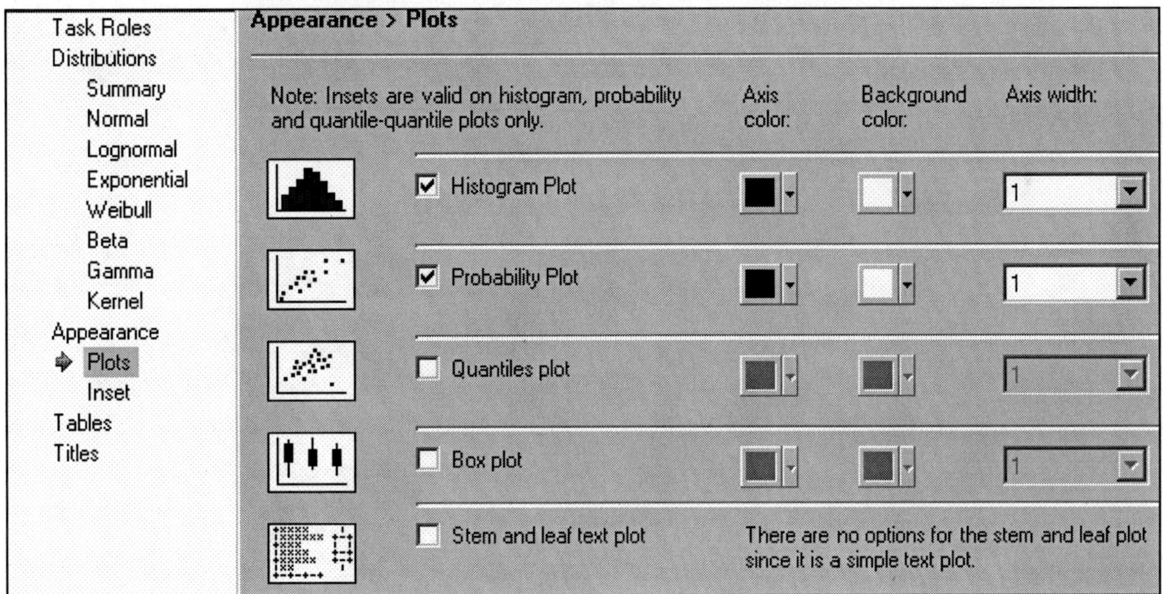

6. Select **Tables** on the left, deselect all boxes and then check the boxes next to **Basic Measures** and **Moments**.

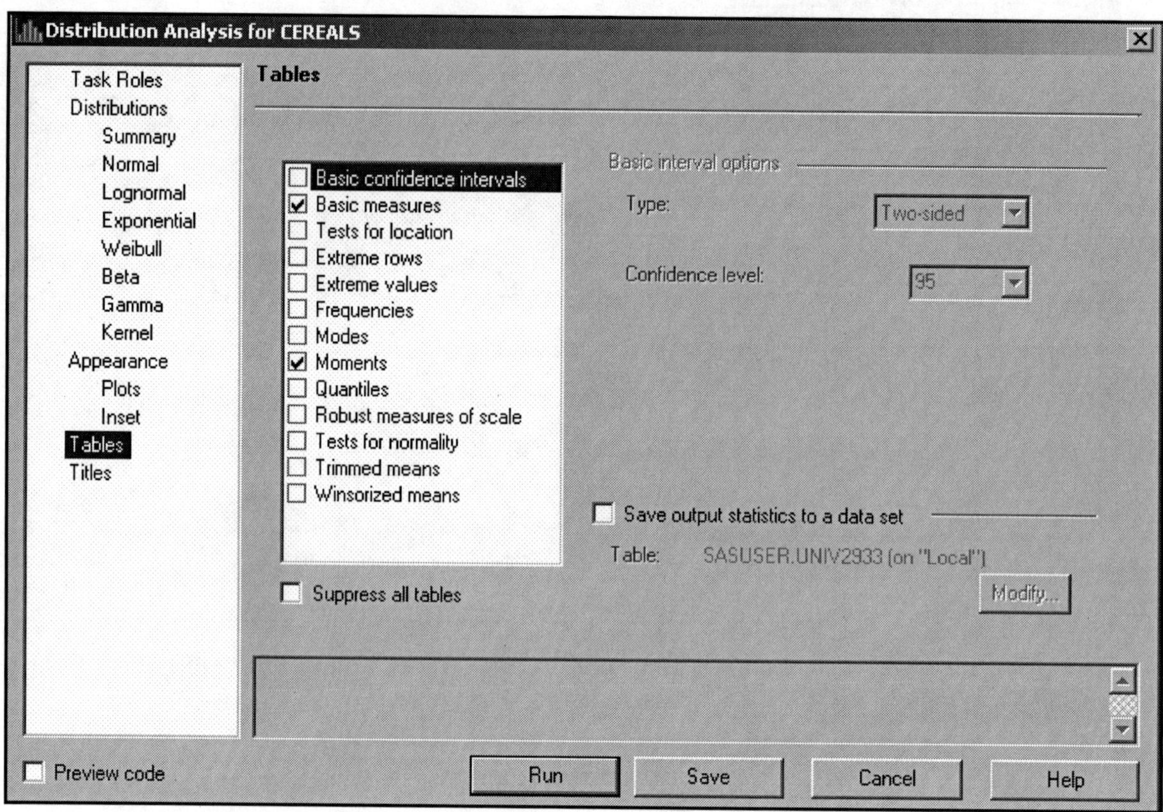

7. Select **Run**.

A summary of the output is presented below. The requested statistical tables are generated for each value of `brand` in alphabetical order.

The UNIVARIATE Procedure
Variable: weight
brand = Morning

Moments			
N	40	Sum Weights	40
Mean	14.9970125	Sum Observations	599.8805
Std Deviation	0.02201048	Variance	0.00048446
Skewness	0.87481049	Kurtosis	2.07993397
Uncorrected SS	8996.43425	Corrected SS	0.01889398
Coeff Variation	0.14676575	Std Error Mean	0.00348016

Basic Statistical Measures			
Location		Variability	
Mean	14.99701	Std Deviation	0.02201
Median	14.99490	Variance	0.0004845
Mode	14.97790	Range	0.12010
		Interquartile Range	0.03095

Note: The mode displayed is the smallest of 2 modes with a count of 2.

The UNIVARIATE Procedure
Variable: weight
brand = Rise n Shine

Moments			
N	40	Sum Weights	40
Mean	15.03596	Sum Observations	601.4384
Std Deviation	0.02654963	Variance	0.00070488
Skewness	0.39889232	Kurtosis	-0.1975717
Uncorrected SS	9043.23122	Corrected SS	0.02749044
Coeff Variation	0.17657424	Std Error Mean	0.00419787

Basic Statistical Measures			
Location		Variability	
Mean	15.03596	Std Deviation	0.02655
Median	15.03480	Variance	0.0007049
Mode	15.01220	Range	0.11490
		Interquartile Range	0.03650

Note: The mode displayed is the smallest of 2 modes with a count of 2.

The requested graphical representations are presented together for each level of **brand**.

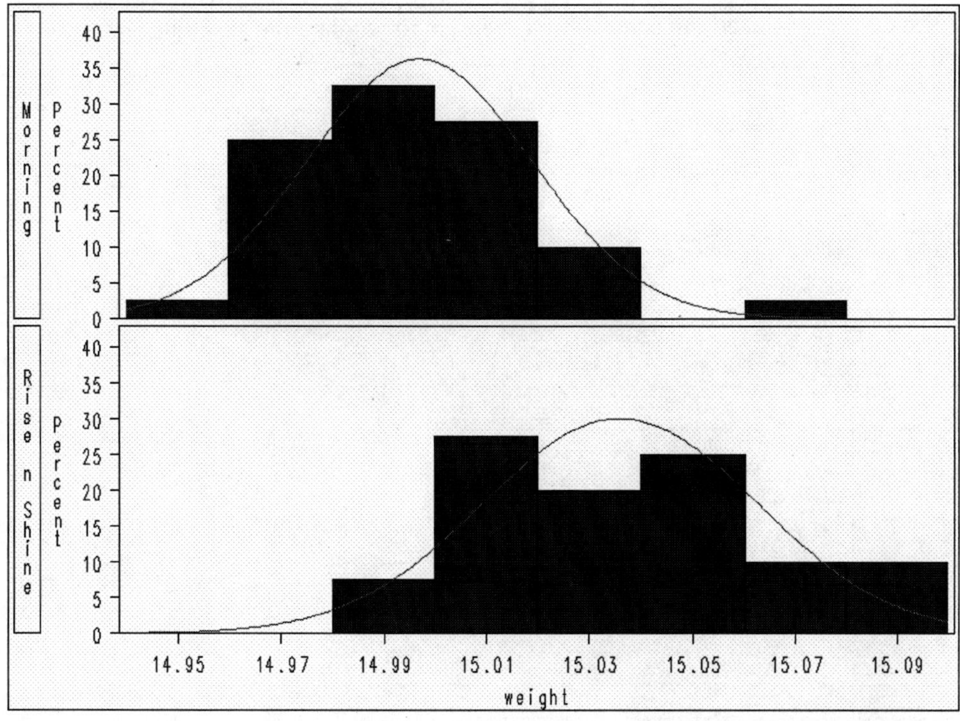

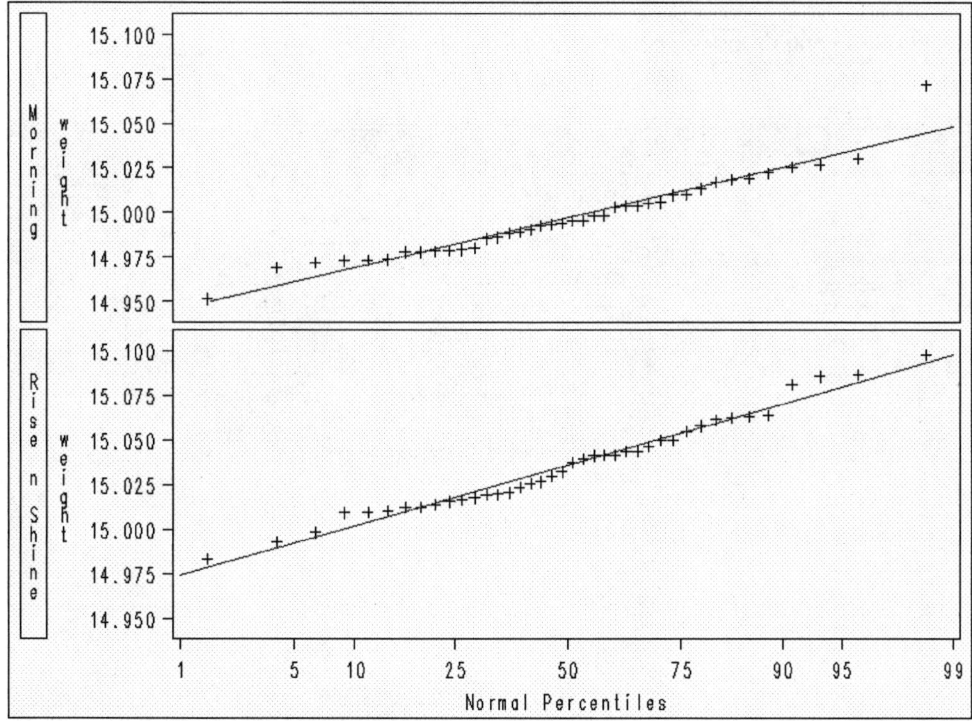

The histograms and normal probability plots show one extreme value for Morning. The normal probability plots show no serious departures from normality.

Because both brands have weights that are normally distributed, the assumptions of the *F*-test for equal variances are verified. The assumption of the *t*-test regarding the normality of the distribution of sample means is also satisfied. You could have used the central limit theorem to validate the assumption for the *t*-test because both brands have 40 observations.

8. Select **Analyze** ⇨ **ANOVA** ⇨ **t Test...**.

9. The **t Test type** panel enables you to specify the type of *t*-test you wish to perform. Select **Paired**.

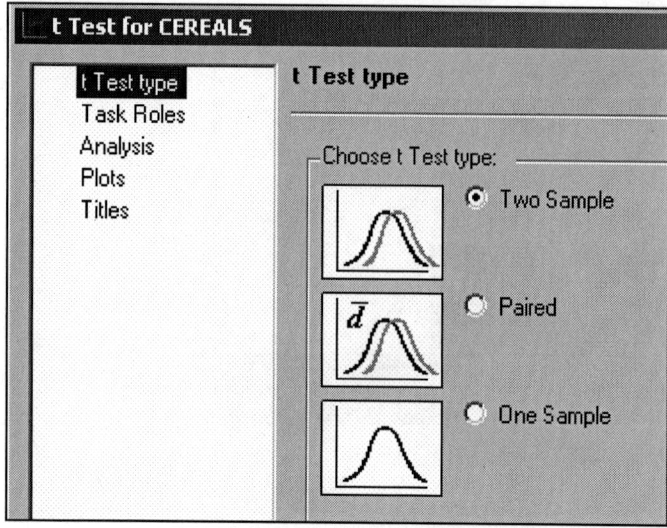

10. In the **Task Roles** panel, drag and drop `weight` to the Analysis variables role and `brand` to the Group by role.

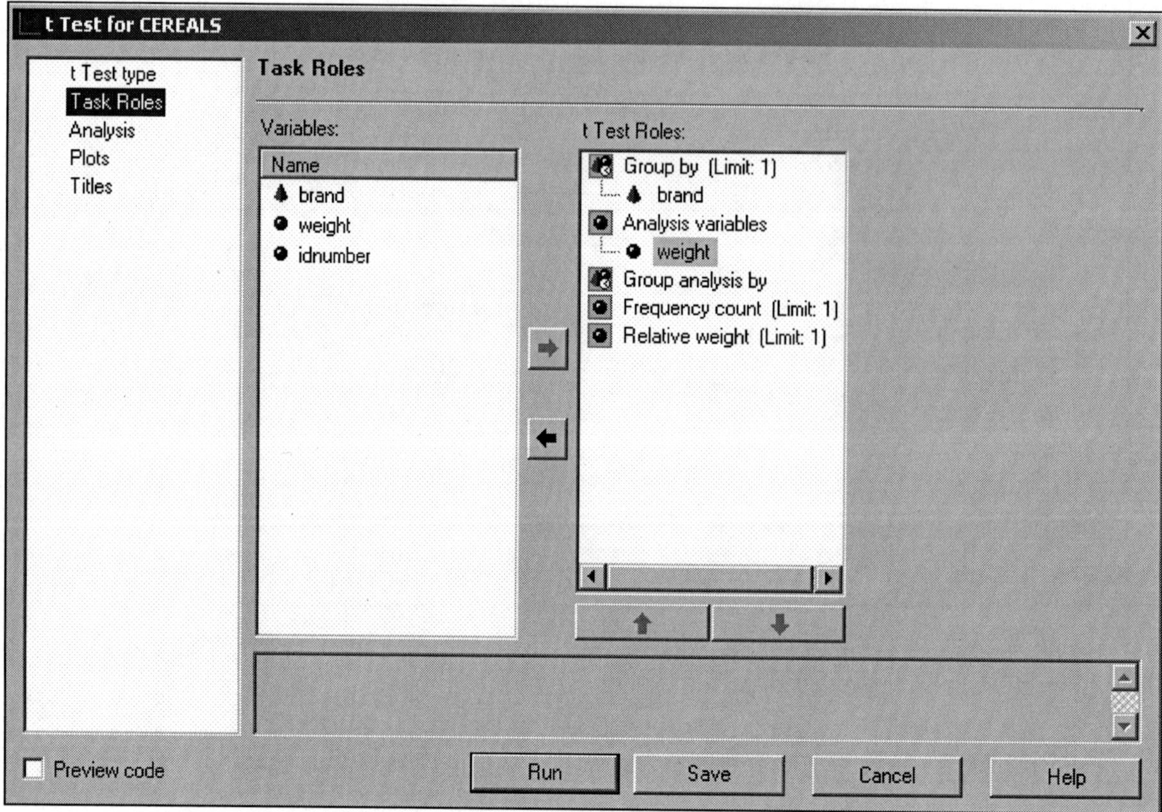

11. Select **Run**.

The generated results are presented below in the logical order in which to analyze them. Locate the Equality of Variances table that appears at the bottom of the results.

Equality of Variances					
Variable	Method	Num DF	Den DF	F Value	Pr > F
weight	Folded F	39	39	1.45	0.2460

The *F*-test for equal variances has a *p*-value of 0.2460. In this case, do not reject the null hypothesis. Conclude that there is insufficient evidence to indicate that the variances are not equal.

Find the T-Tests table immediately above the Equality of Variances table.

T-Tests					
Variable	Method	Variances	DF	t Value	Pr > |t|
weight	Pooled	Equal	78	-7.14	<.0001
weight	Satterthwaite	Unequal	75.4	-7.14	<.0001

Using the equal variance *t*-test, you reject the null hypothesis that the group means are equal. Conclude that there is a difference in the average weight of the cereal between the Rise n Shine brand and the Morning brand.

Turn your attention to the Statistics table.

Statistics											
Variable	brand	N	Lower CL Mean	Mean	Upper CL Mean	Lower CL Std Dev	Std Dev	Upper CL Std Dev	Std Err	Minimum	Maximum
weight	Morning	40	14.99	14.997	15.004	0.018	0.022	0.0283	0.0035	14.952	15.072
weight	Rise n Shine	40	15.027	15.036	15.044	0.0217	0.0265	0.0341	0.0042	14.983	15.098
weight	Diff (1-2)		-0.05	-0.039	-0.028	0.0211	0.0244	0.0289	0.0055		

Because the confidence interval for the mean (-0.05, -0.028) does not include 0, you can conclude that there is a significant difference between the two cereal means.

B.3 Output Delivery System

ODS is appropriate if you are submitting SAS code. It has been included for your perusal and possible programming benefit in the future.

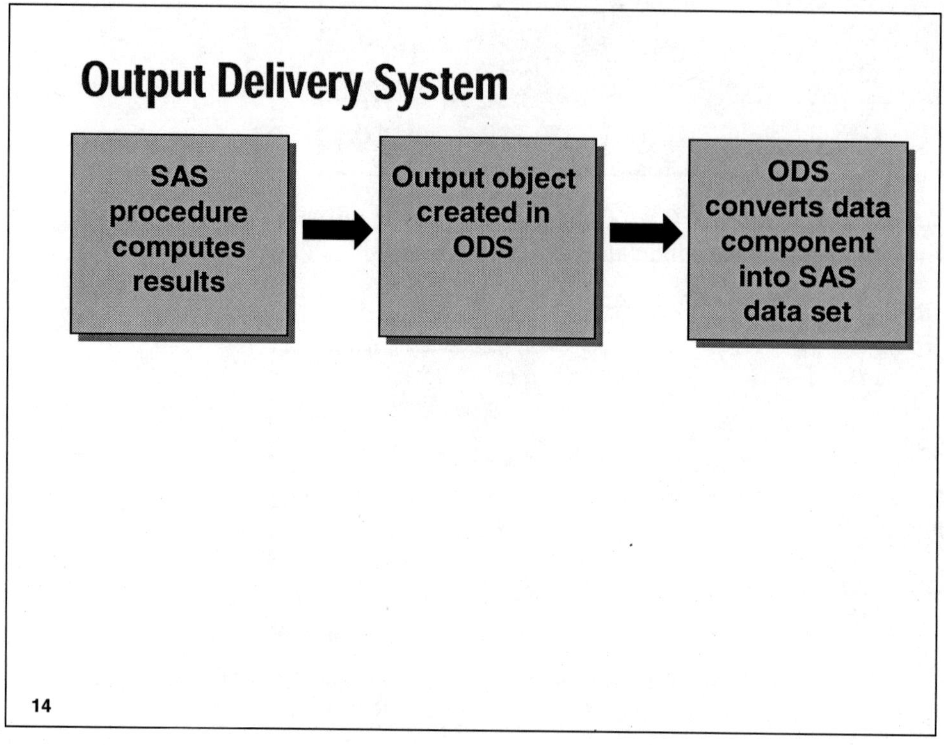

The Output Delivery System (ODS) enables you to take output from a SAS procedure and convert it to a SAS data set. Instead of writing to the listing file directly, SAS procedures can now create an output object for each piece of output that is displayed. For example, each table produced in the UNIVARIATE procedure is now a separate entity in ODS. You can then take the data component of the output object and convert it to a SAS data set. This means that every number in every table of every procedure can be accessed via a data set.

ODS Statements

TRACE
provides information about the output object such as the name and path.

LISTING
opens, manages, or closes the Listing destination.

HTML
creates an HTML file.

RTF
creates a Rich-Text file.

OUTPUT
creates a SAS data set from an output object.

15

The TRACE statement is used to obtain the name of the output object.

Output Delivery System

Example: Examine some basic functionality of the Output Delivery System using SAS code.

1. Select **File** ⇨ **New** ⇨ **Code**.

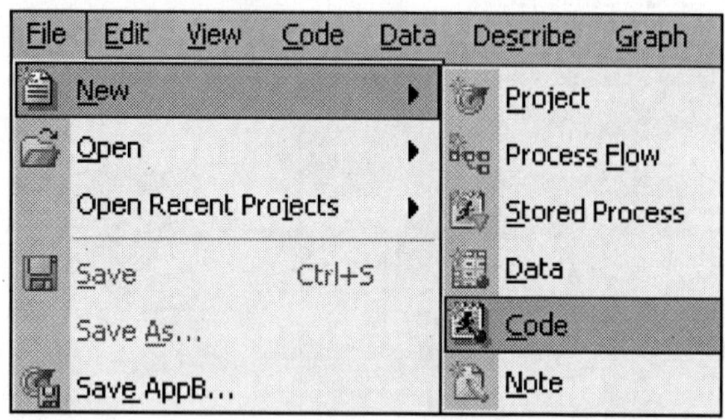

2. Type the following code into the Code1 window.

```
Code1*
ods trace on;
/*--- --- --- --- --- --- --- --- --- --- --- --- --- --- */
/* -generate and examine table definitions for UNIVARIATE */
/*--- --- --- --- --- --- --- --- --- --- --- --- --- --- */
proc univariate data=sasuser.b_rise;
   var weight;
   histogram weight / normal;
   probplot weight / normal (mu=est sigma=est
                             color=blue w=1);
   title 'Univariate Analysis of sasuser.b_rise';
run;
ods trace off;
```

The ODS TRACE ON statement produces a trace record in the SAS Log window, including the name and label of each output object. The ODS LISTING CLOSE statement instructs ODS not to produce any results in the Output window.

`Code1*` indicates that you have not yet saved this code.

3. Right-click and select **Run on Local**.

4. From the flow diagram, select **Code1** and then right-click **Open Log**.

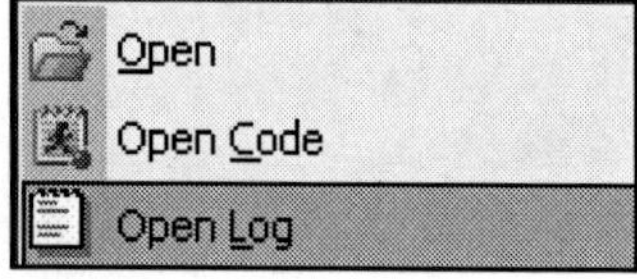

SAS Log

Code1 | Code1 (Log)

```

ods trace on;
/*--- --- --- --- --- --- --- --- --- --- --- --- --- --- */
/* -generate and examine table definitions for UNIVARIATE */
/*--- --- --- --- --- --- --- --- --- --- --- --- --- --- */
proc univariate data=sasuser.b_rise;
   var weight;
   histogram weight / normal;
   probplot weight / normal (mu=est sigma=est
                             color=blue w=1);
   title 'Univariate Analysis of sasuser.b_rise';
run;


Output Added:
-------------
Name:       Moments
Label:      Moments
Template:   base.univariate.Moments
Path:       Univariate.weight.Moments
-------------

Output Added:
-------------
Name:       BasicMeasures
Label:      Basic Measures of Location and Variability
Template:   base.univariate.Measures
Path:       Univariate.weight.BasicMeasures
-------------

Output Added:
-------------
2                          The SAS System          08:47 Tuesday, January 18, 2005

Name:       TestsForLocation
Label:      Tests For Location
Template:   base.univariate.Location
Path:       Univariate.weight.TestsForLocation
-------------
```

For each table, Name, Label, Template or Data Name, and Path are listed. Notice the name and its similarity to label, which is displayed in the results.

Moments

Basic Statistical Measures	
Location	Variability

Tests for Location: Mu0=0		
Test	Statistic	p Value

SAS Log (continued)

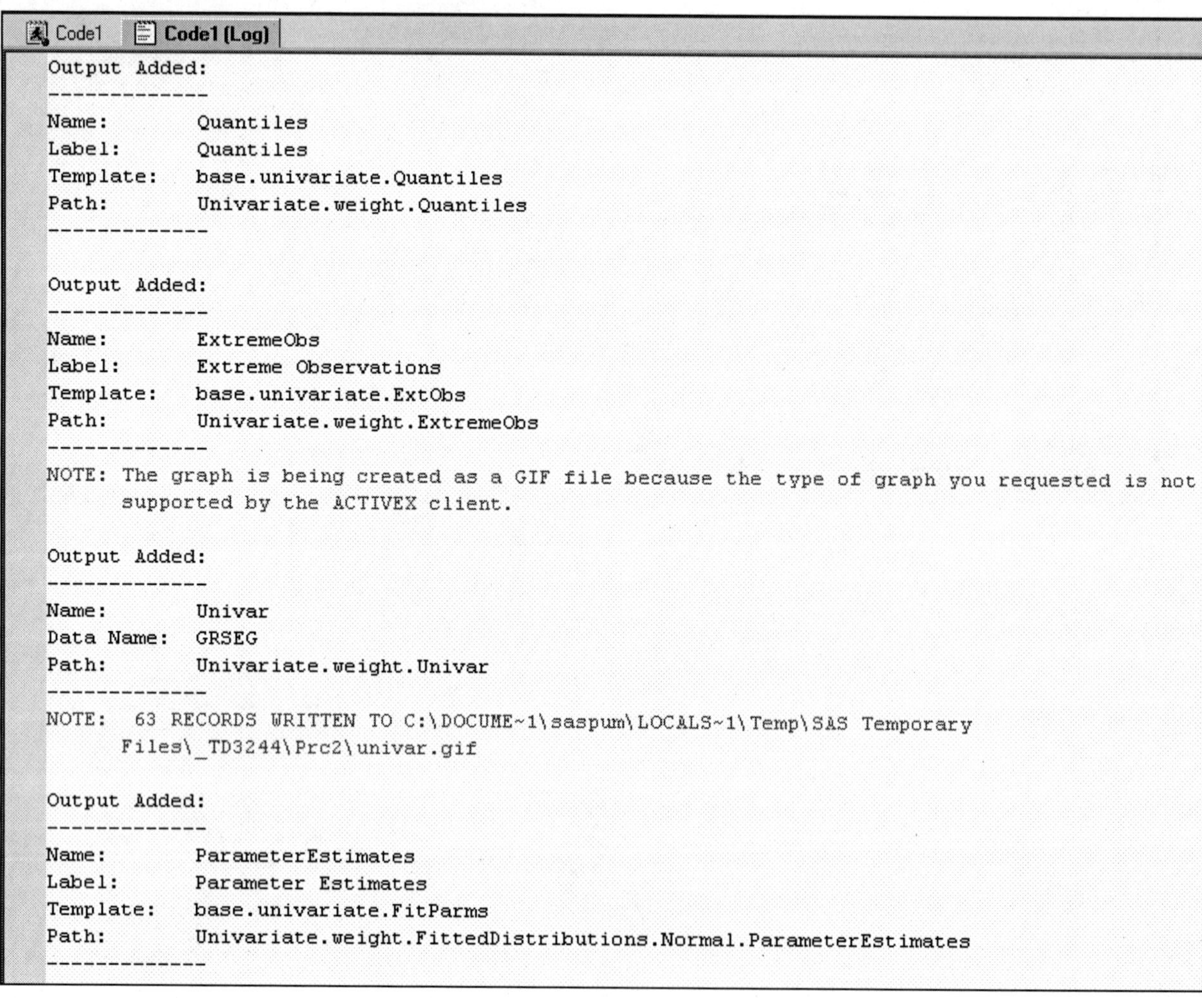

Code1 | Code1 (Log)

```
Output Added:
-------------
Name:        Quantiles
Label:       Quantiles
Template:    base.univariate.Quantiles
Path:        Univariate.weight.Quantiles
-------------

Output Added:
-------------
Name:        ExtremeObs
Label:       Extreme Observations
Template:    base.univariate.ExtObs
Path:        Univariate.weight.ExtremeObs
-------------
NOTE: The graph is being created as a GIF file because the type of graph you requested is not
      supported by the ACTIVEX client.

Output Added:
-------------
Name:        Univar
Data Name:   GRSEG
Path:        Univariate.weight.Univar
-------------
NOTE:  63 RECORDS WRITTEN TO C:\DOCUME~1\saspum\LOCALS~1\Temp\SAS Temporary
      Files\_TD3244\Prc2\univar.gif

Output Added:
-------------
Name:        ParameterEstimates
Label:       Parameter Estimates
Template:    base.univariate.FitParms
Path:        Univariate.weight.FittedDistributions.Normal.ParameterEstimates
-------------
```

Using the label, you can select a specific table in the results.

SAS Log (continued)

```
Output Added:
-------------
Name:       GoodnessOfFit
Label:      Goodness of Fit
Template:   base.univariate.FitGood
Path:       Univariate.weight.FittedDistributions.Normal.GoodnessOfFit
-------------

Output Added:
-------------
Name:       FitQuantiles
Label:      Quantiles
3                                    The SAS System          08:47 Tuesday, January 18, 2

Template:   base.univariate.FitQuant
Path:       Univariate.weight.FittedDistributions.Normal.FitQuantiles
-------------
NOTE: The graph is being created as a GIF file because the type of graph you requested is not
      supported by the ACTIVEX client.

Output Added:
-------------
Name:       Univar1
Data Name:  GRSEG
Path:       Univariate.weight.Univar1
-------------
NOTE:  47 RECORDS WRITTEN TO C:\DOCUME~1\saspum\LOCALS~1\Temp\SAS Temporary
      Files\_TD3244\Prc2\univar1.gif
NOTE: PROCEDURE UNIVARIATE used (Total process time):
      real time           1.39 seconds
      cpu time            0.39 seconds


          ods trace off;
```

Because you know a table's name, you can now select only those tables of interest.

5. Select **File** ⇨ **New** ⇨ **Code**.
6. Type the following code into the Code2 window.

```
Code2*
ods select
     Moments
     BasicMeasures
     GoodnessOfFit
     ;

proc univariate data=sasuser.b_rise;
   var weight;
   histogram weight / normal;
   probplot weight / normal (mu=est sigma=est
                           color=blue w=1);
   title 'Selected Results Using ODS';
run;
```

7. Open the results.

Selected Results Using ODS

The UNIVARIATE Procedure
Variable: weight

Moments			
N	40	Sum Weights	40
Mean	15.03596	Sum Observations	601.4384
Std Deviation	0.02654963	Variance	0.00070488
Skewness	0.39889232	Kurtosis	-0.1975717
Uncorrected SS	9043.23122	Corrected SS	0.02749044
Coeff Variation	0.17657424	Std Error Mean	0.00419787

Basic Statistical Measures			
Location		Variability	
Mean	15.03596	Std Deviation	0.02655
Median	15.03480	Variance	0.0007049
Mode	15.01220	Range	0.11490
		Interquartile Range	0.03650

Note: The mode displayed is the smallest of 2 modes with a count of 2.

Results (continued)

Selected Results Using ODS

The UNIVARIATE Procedure
Fitted Distribution for weight

Goodness-of-Fit Tests for Normal Distribution				
Test	Statistic		p Value	
Kolmogorov-Smirnov	D	0.09608648	Pr > D	>0.150
Cramer-von Mises	W-Sq	0.05930447	Pr > W-Sq	>0.250
Anderson-Darling	A-Sq	0.38776343	Pr > A-Sq	>0.250

You can also generate SAS data sets to extract specific values in later programming steps or for future analyses.

8. Select **File** ⇨ **New** ⇨ **Code**.

9. Type the following code into the Code3 window.

Code3*

```
ods output
    Moments=o_moments
    BasicMeasures=o_basic
    Quantiles=o_quant
    ;

proc univariate data=sasuser.b_rise;
   var weight;
   id idnumber;
run;
```

✎ The SAS data sets generated with the OUTPUT statement are stored in the WORK library. To store them in a permanent SAS data set, use a two-level SAS data set name. For example, `o_moments` would become `sasuser.o_moments`.

10. Examine the Flow Diagram to explore the results.

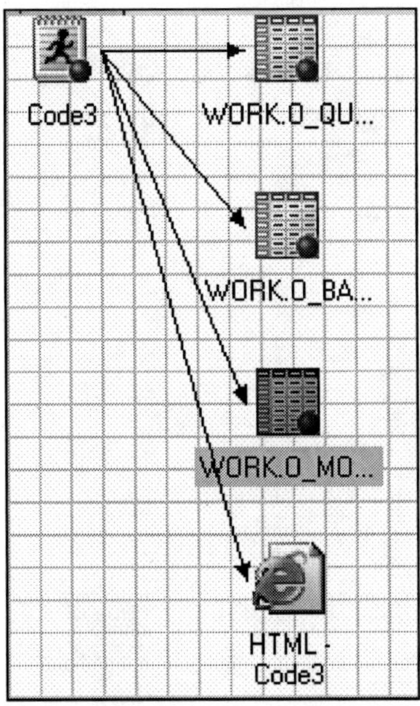

11. Open **WORK.O_MOMENTS**.

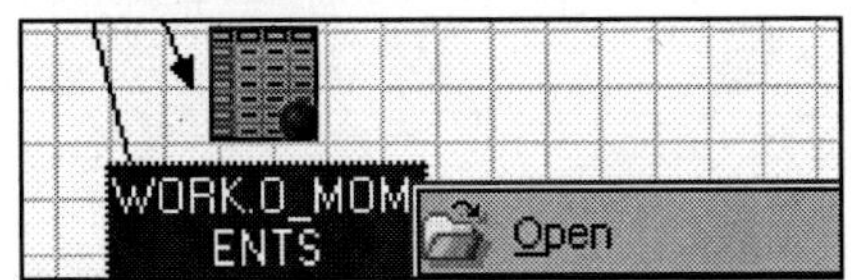

Code3 | HTML - Code3 | WORK.O_MOMENTS (read-only)

	VarName	Label1	cValue1	nValue1	Label2	cValue2	nValue2
1	weight	N	40	40.000000	Sum Weights	40	40.000000
2	weight	Mean	15.03596	15.035960	Sum Observations	601.4384	601.438400
3	weight	Std Deviation	0.02654963	0.026550	Variance	0.00070488	0.000705
4	weight	Skewness	0.39889232	0.398892	Kurtosis	-0.1975717	-0.197572
5	weight	Uncorrected SS	9043.23122	9043.231215	Corrected SS	0.02749044	0.027490
6	weight	Coeff Variation	0.17657424	0.176574	Std Error Mean	0.00419787	0.004198

`cValue1` and `cValue2` are character variables that match the displayed values in the results.

Moments			
N	40	Sum Weights	40
Mean	15.03596	Sum Observations	601.4384
Std Deviation	0.02654963	Variance	0.00070488
Skewness	0.39889232	Kurtosis	-0.1975717
Uncorrected SS	9043.23122	Corrected SS	0.02749044
Coeff Variation	0.17657424	Std Error Mean	0.00419787

B.4 Nonparametric ANOVA

This section addresses nonparametric options available with the Nonparametric One-Way ANOVA task, which invokes the NPAR1WAY procedure. Nonparametric one-sample tests are also available in the Distribution Analysis task.

Nonparametric Analysis

Nonparametric analyses are those that rely only on the assumption that the observations are independent.

18

Nonparametric tests are most often used when the normality assumption required for analysis of variance is in question. Although ANOVA is robust against minor departures from its normality assumption, extreme departures from normality can make the test less sensitive to differences between means. Therefore, when the data is very skewed or there are extreme outliers, nonparametric methods may be more appropriate. In addition, when the data follows a count measurement scale instead of interval, nonparametric methods should be used.

When the normality assumption is met, nonparametric tests are almost as good as parametric tests.

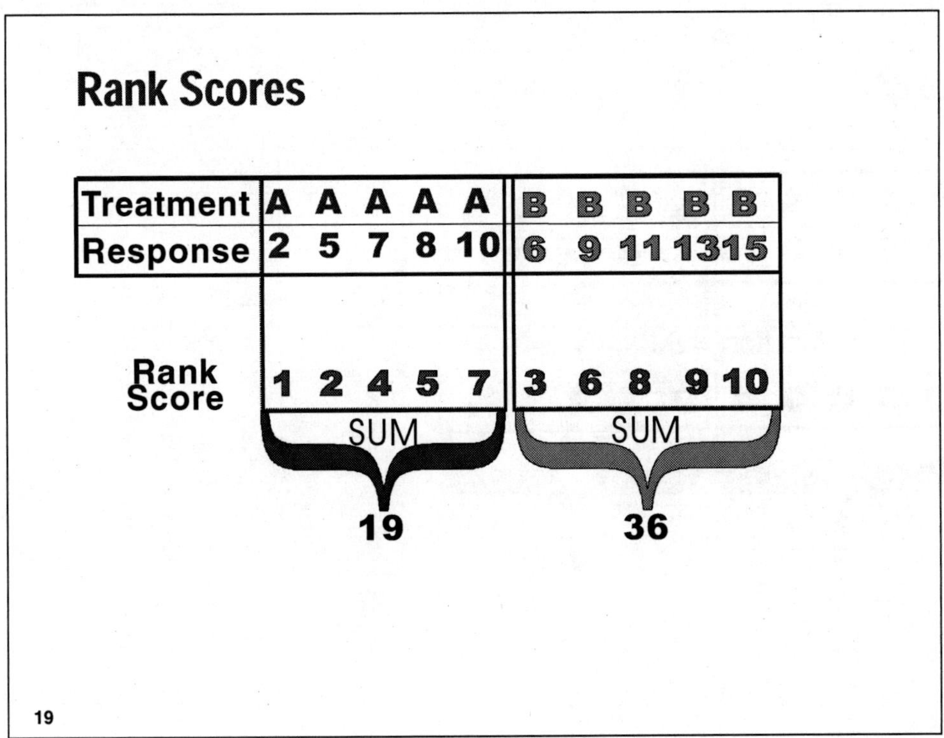

Rank Scores
Treatment A A A A A B B B B B
Response 2 5 7 8 10 6 9 11 13 15
Rank Score 1 2 4 5 7 3 6 8 9 10
SUM
SUM
19
36
19

In nonparametric analysis, the rank of each data point is used instead of the raw data.

The illustrated ranking system ranks the data from smallest to largest. In the case of ties, the ranks are averaged. The sums of the ranks for each of the treatments are used to test the hypothesis that the populations are identical. For two populations, the Wilcoxon rank-sum test is performed. For any number of populations, a Kruskal-Wallis test is used.

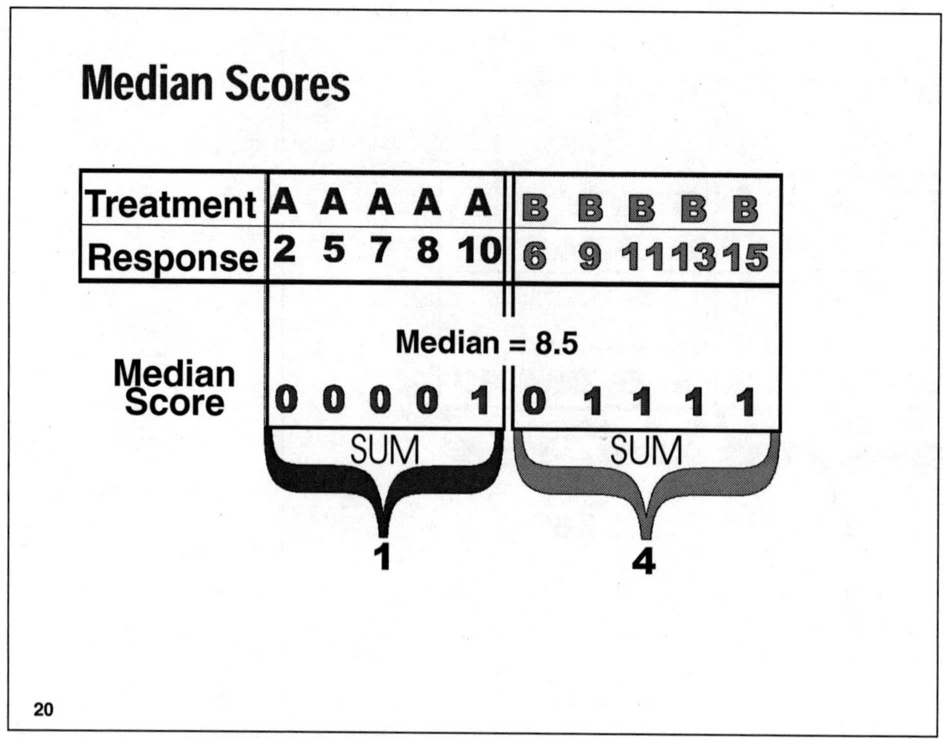

Recall that the median is the 50th percentile, which is the middle of your data values.

When calculating median scores, a score of

- zero is assigned, if the data value is less than or equal to the median
- one is assigned, if the data value is above the median.

The sums of the median scores are used to conduct the Median test for two populations or the Brown-Mood test for any number of populations.

Hypotheses of Interest

H_0: all populations are identical with respect to scale, shape, and location.

H_1: all populations are not identical with respect to scale, shape, and location.

21

Nonparametric tests compare the probability distributions of sampled populations rather than specific parameters of these populations.

In general, with no assumptions about the distributions of the data, you are testing the hypotheses

- H_0: all populations are identical with respect to shape and location
- H_1: all populations are **not** identical with respect to shape and location.

Thus, if you reject the null hypothesis, you conclude that the population distributions are different, but you have not identified the reason for the difference. The difference could be because of different variances, skewness, kurtosis, or means.

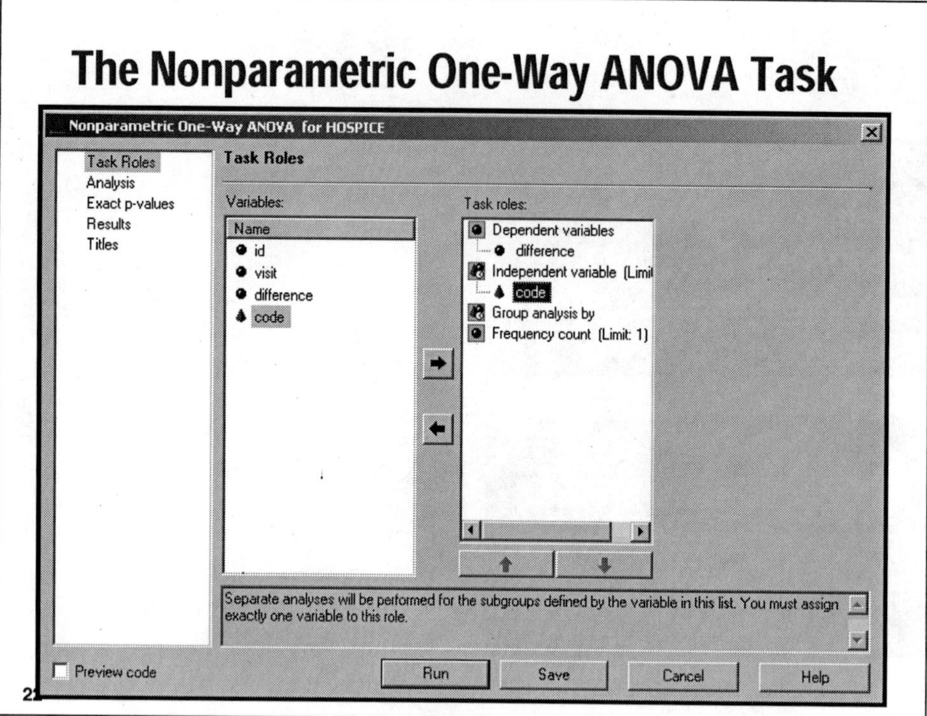

Hospice Example

Are there different effects of a marketing visit, in terms of increasing the number of referrals to the hospice, among the various specialties of physicians?

23

Consider a study done by Kathryn Skarzynski to determine whether there was a change in the number of referrals received from physicians after a visit by a hospice marketing nurse. One of her study questions was, "Are there different effects of the marketing visits, in terms of increasing the number of referrals, among the various specialties of physicians?"

Veneer Example

Are there differences between the durability of brands of wood veneer?

24

Consider another experiment where the goal of the experiment is to compare the durability of three brands of synthetic wood veneer. This type of veneer is often used in office furniture and on kitchen countertops. To determine durability, four samples of each of three brands are subjected to a friction test. The amount of veneer material that is worn away due to the friction is measured. The resulting wear measurement is recorded for each sample. Brands that have a small wear measurement are desirable.

The Nonparametric One-Way ANOVA Task

Example: A portion of Ms. Skarzynski's data about the hospice marketing visits is in the data set **HOSPICE**.

1. Select and open **HOSPICE** to view the data.

   Partial Listing

HOSPICE (read-only)

	id	visit	difference	code
1	2	1	0	Family Prac
2	4	1	1	Family Prac
3	6	1	-1	Oncologist
4	7	1	-3	Family Prac
5	8	1	1	Oncologist
6	10	1	0	Family Prac
7	13	1	-1	Oncologist
8	14	1	-1	Oncologist
9	15	1	1	Internal Med
10	16	1	1	Oncologist
11	18	1	0	Internal Med
12	22	1	0	Oncologist
13	23	1	0	Oncologist
14	24	1	1	Internal Med
15	26	1	-7	Oncologist

The variables in the data set are

id the ID number of the physician's office visited

visit the type of visit, to the physician or to the physician's staff

code the medical specialty of the physician

difference the difference between the number of referrals three months after the visit and the number of referrals three months prior to the visit.

One of the analyses to answer the research questions is to compare **difference** for the different specialties.

Initially, you want to examine the distribution of the data.

2. Investigate the distributions for each of the three specialties by using the Distribution Analysis task, Request a histogram, normal probability plot and side-by-side box plot for the specialties.

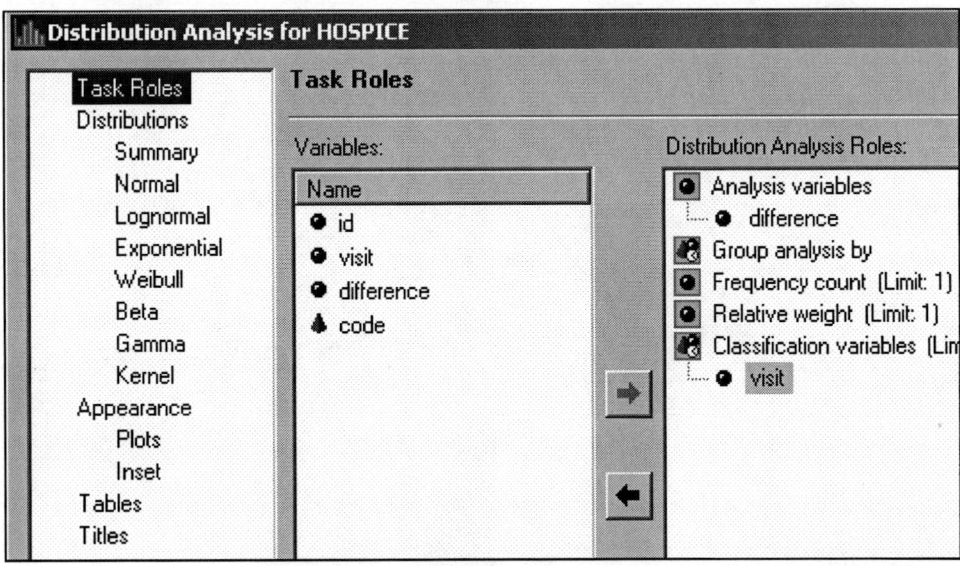

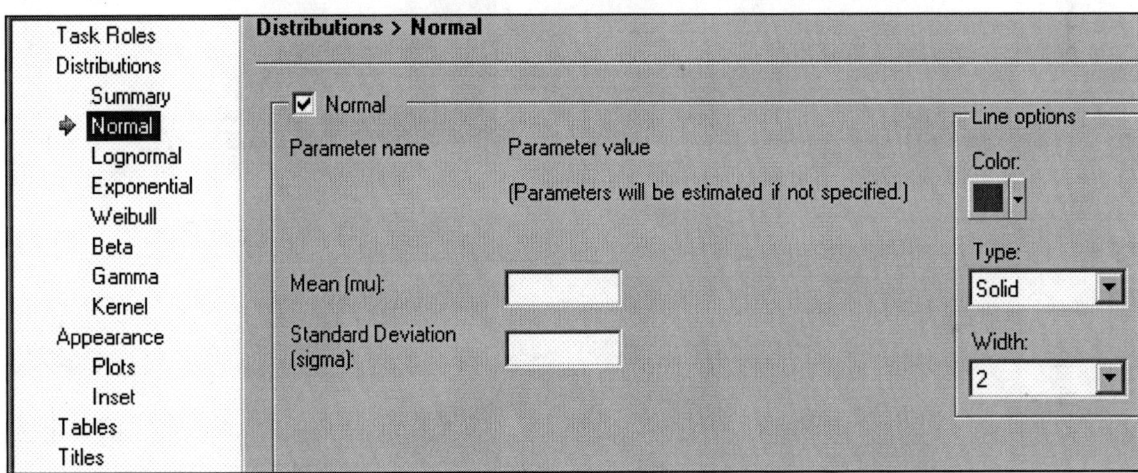

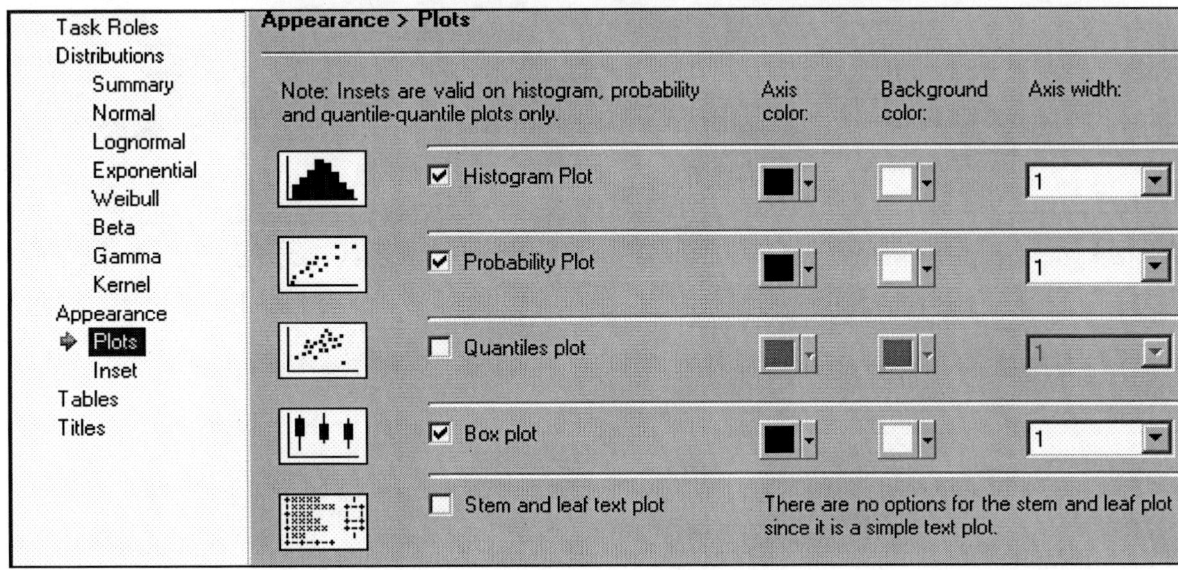

Selected Results

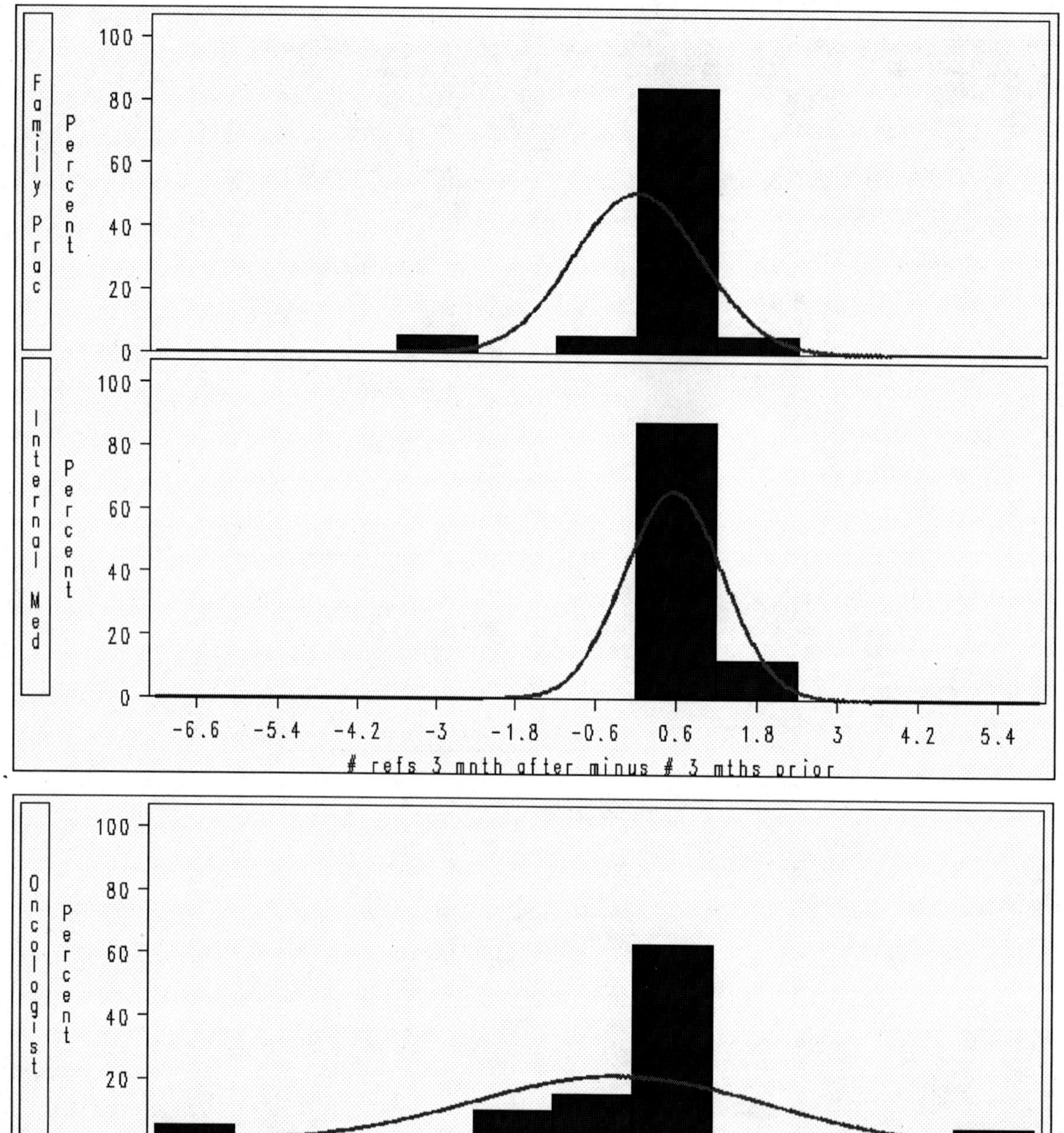

None of the groups appear normal from their histograms. There appear to be outliers for the oncologists.

Selected Results (continued)

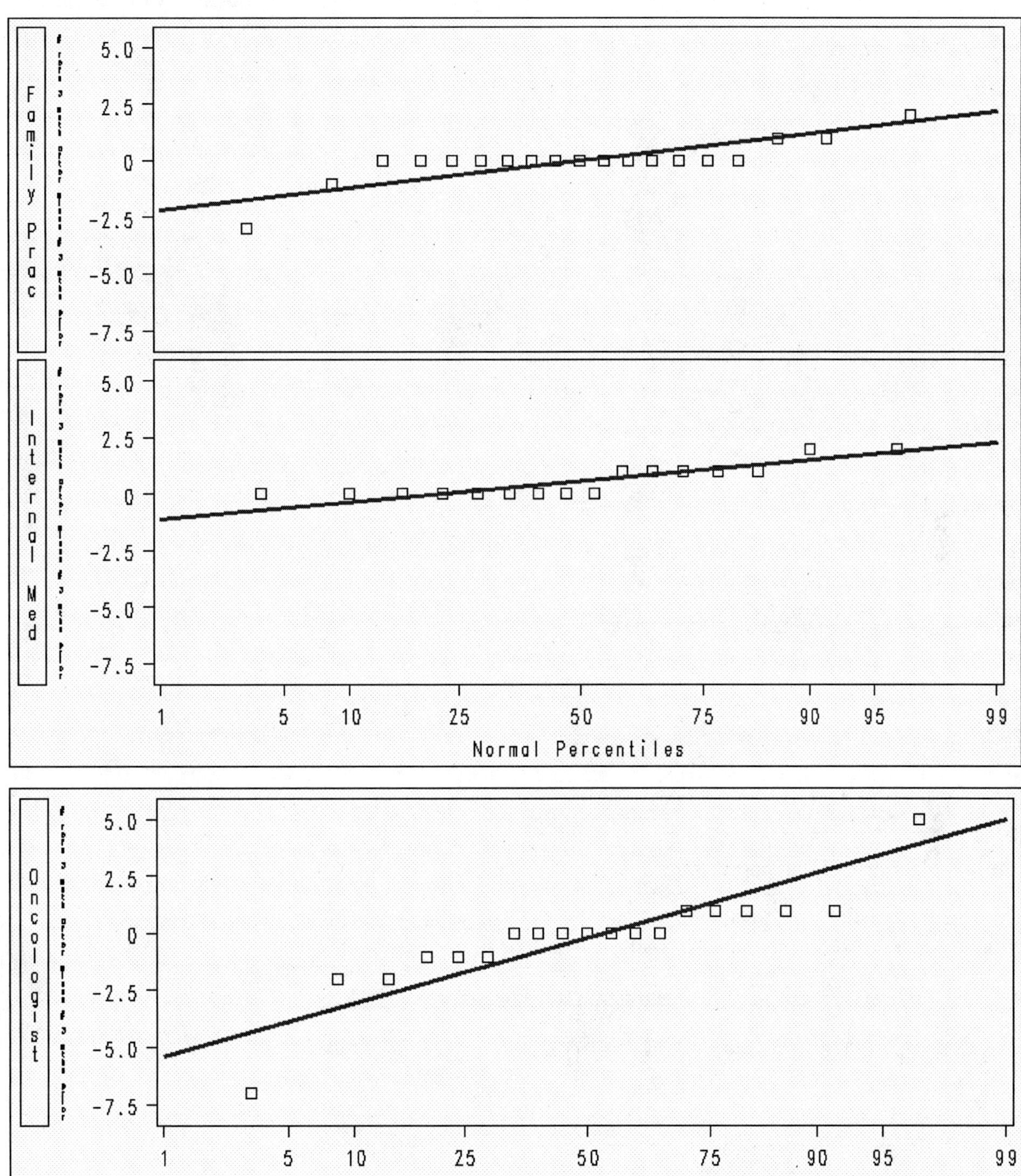

The data for internal medicine doctors and oncologists appears skewed.

Selected Results (continued)

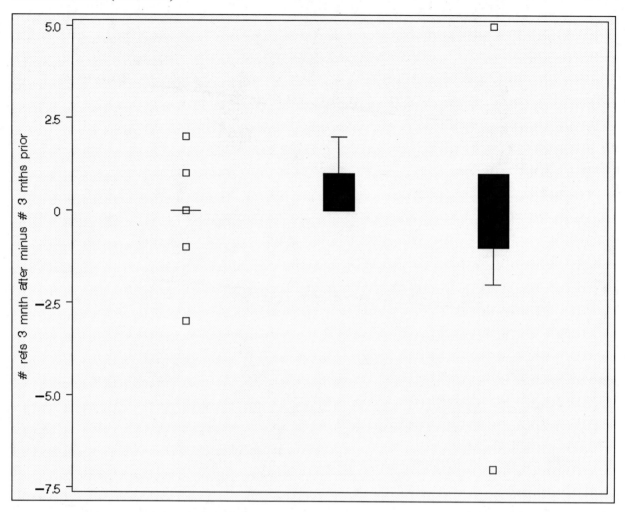

The box plots strongly support that the data is not normal.

These characteristics, combined with the fact that the data values are actually counts and therefore ordinal, suggest that a nonparametric analysis would be more appropriate.

3. Select **Analyze** ⇨ **ANOVA** ⇨ **Nonparametric One-Way ANOVA …**.

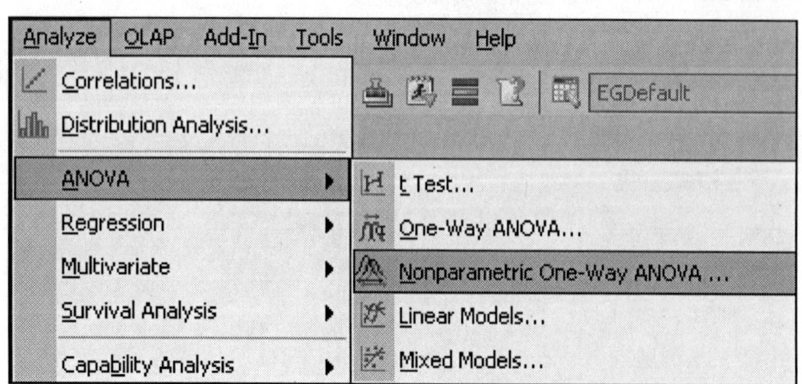

4. Drag and drop `difference` as the dependent variable and `code` as the independent variable.

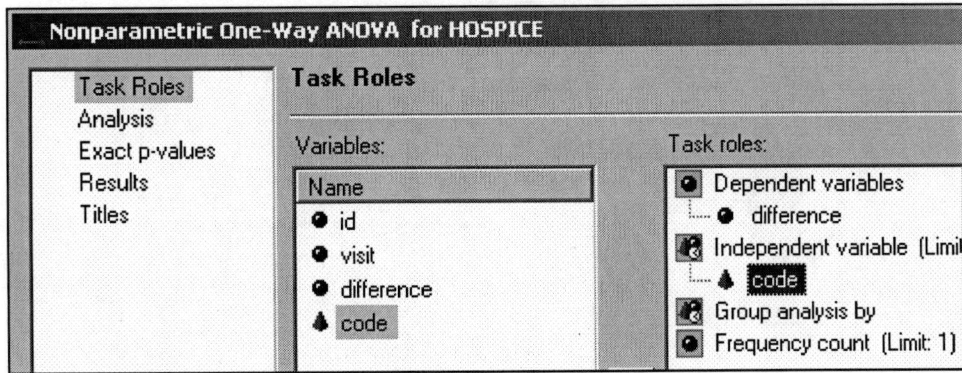

5. Select **Analysis** from the left panel.

6. Deselect **Calculate empirical distribution function statistics (EDF)**.

7. Choose the check boxes beside **Wilcoxon** and **Median**.

For illustrative purposes, use the WILCOXON option to perform a rank sum test and the MEDIAN option to perform the median test. This data was actually analyzed using the rank sum test.

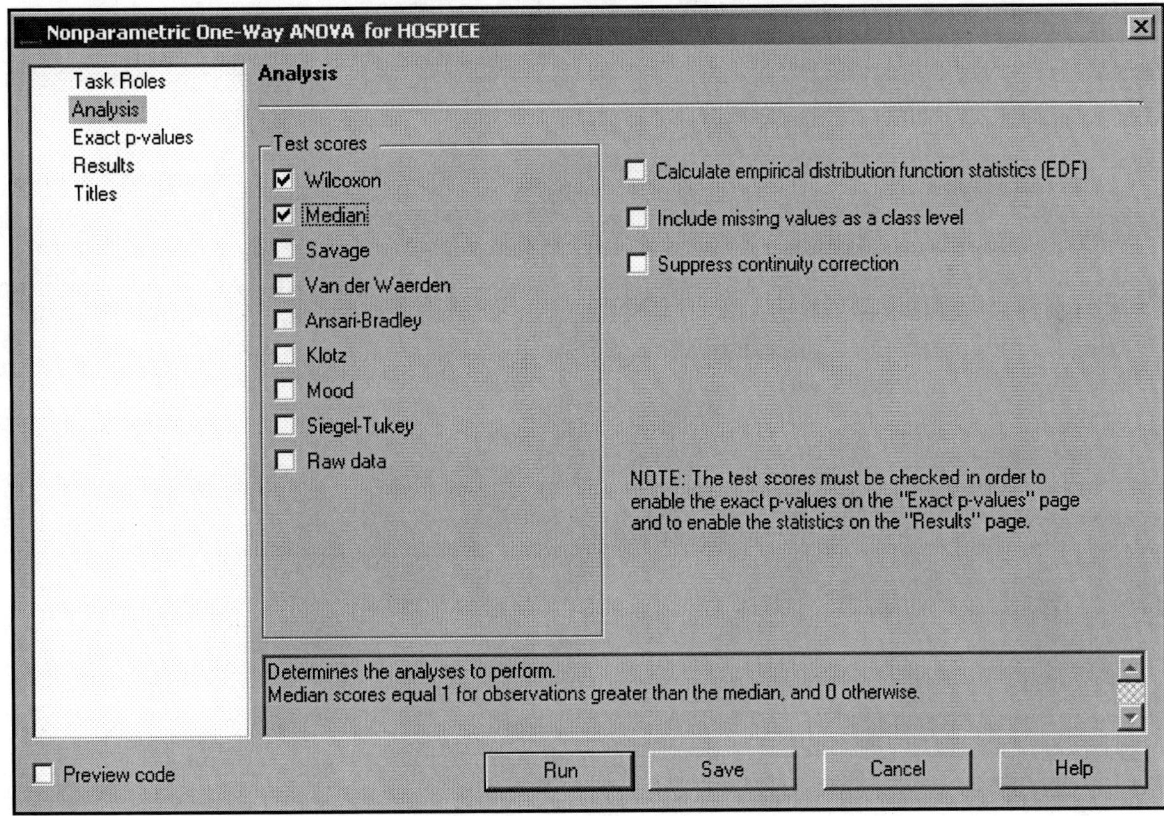

8. Select **Run**.

9. Examine the results from the Wilcoxon option.

Wilcoxon Scores (Rank Sums) for Variable difference Classified by Variable code					
code	N	Sum of Scores	Expected Under H0	Std Dev Under H0	Mean Score
Family Prac	19	478.50	522.50	49.907208	25.184211
Oncologist	19	468.50	522.50	49.907208	24.657895
Internal Med	16	538.00	440.00	47.720418	33.625000
Average scores were used for ties.					

Kruskal-Wallis Test	
Chi-Square	4.2304
DF	2
Pr > Chi-Square	0.1206

The results include the actual sums of the rank scores and the expected sums of the rank scores if the null hypothesis is true. From the Kruskal-Wallis test (chi-square approximation), the p-value is 0.1206. Therefore, at the 5% level of significance, you do not reject the null hypothesis. There is not enough evidence to conclude that the distributions of change in hospice referrals for the different groups of physicians are significantly different.

10. Examine the results from the Median option.

Median Scores (Number of Points Above Median) for Variable difference Classified by Variable code					
code	N	Sum of Scores	Expected Under H0	Std Dev Under H0	Mean Score
Family Prac	19	8.133333	9.50	1.232093	0.428070
Oncologist	19	8.566667	9.50	1.232093	0.450877
Internal Med	16	10.300000	8.00	1.178106	0.643750
Average scores were used for ties.					

Median One-Way Analysis	
Chi-Square	3.8515
DF	2
Pr > Chi-Square	0.1458

Again, based on the *p*-value of 0.1458, at the 5% level of significance, you do not reject the null hypothesis. There is not enough evidence to conclude that there are differences between specialists.

Example: Recall the experiment to compare the durability of three brands of synthetic wood veneer. The data is stored in the **VENEER** data set.

1. Select **VENEER** to review the data.

VENEER (read-only)

	brand	wear
1	Acme	2.3
2	Acme	2.1
3	Acme	2.4
4	Acme	2.5
5	Champ	2.2
6	Champ	2.3
7	Champ	2.4
8	Champ	2.6
9	Ajax	2.2
10	Ajax	2
11	Ajax	1.9
12	Ajax	2.1

Because there is only a sample size of 4 for each brand of veneer, the usual Wilcoxon test p-values are inaccurate.

2. Select **Analyze** ⇨ **ANOVA** ⇨ **Nonparametric One-Way ANOVA …**.

3. Drag and drop **wear** as the dependent variable and **brand** as the independent variable.

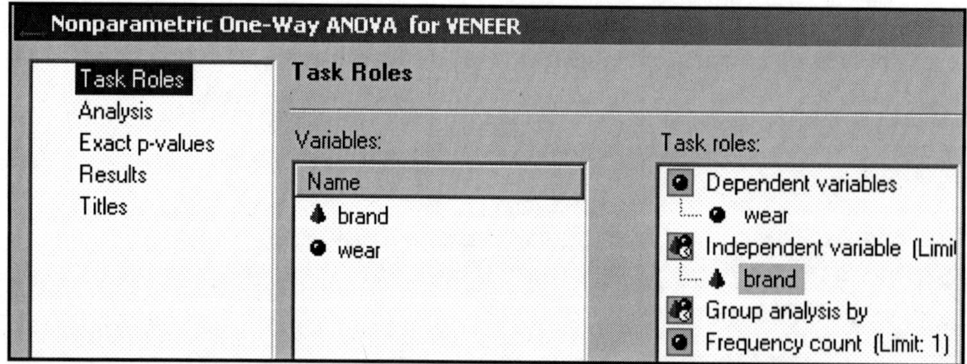

4. Select **Analysis** from the left panel.

5. Deselect **Calculate empirical distribution function statistics (EDF)**.

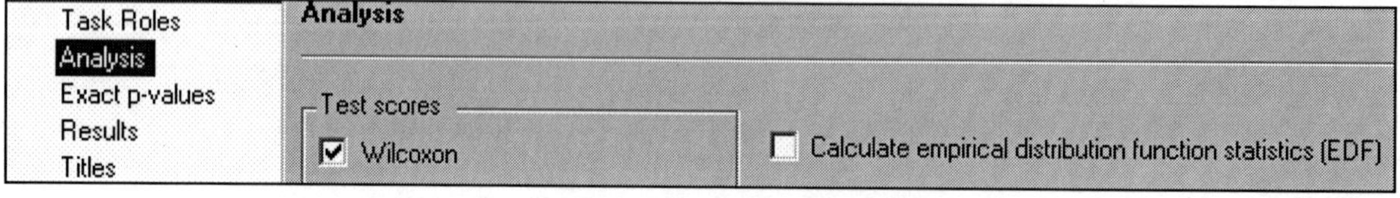

6. Select **<u>Exact p-values</u>** from the left panel.

7. Select the check box beside **Wilcoxon**.

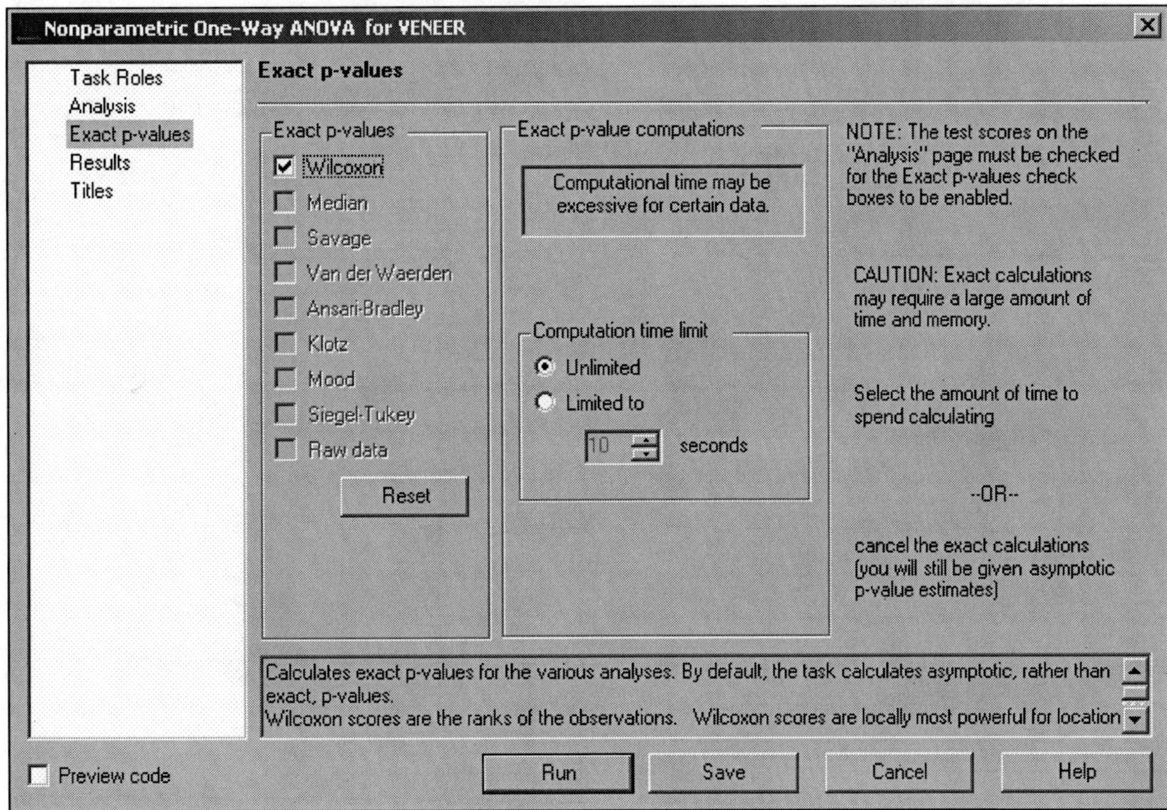

This option provides exact *p*-values for the simple linear rank statistics based on the Wilcoxon scores rather than estimated *p*-values based on continuous approximations.

Exact analysis is available for both the Wilcoxon and Median options.

8. Select **<u>Run</u>**.

Wilcoxon Scores (Rank Sums) for Variable wear Classified by Variable brand					
brand	N	Sum of Scores	Expected Under H0	Std Dev Under H0	Mean Score
Acme	4	31.50	26.0	5.846522	7.8750
Champ	4	34.50	26.0	5.846522	8.6250
Ajax	4	12.00	26.0	5.846522	3.0000
Average scores were used for ties.					

Kruskal-Wallis Test	
Chi-Square	5.8218
DF	2
Asymptotic Pr > Chi-Square	0.0544
Exact Pr >= Chi-Square	0.0480

In the results shown above, the exact *p*-value is 0.0480, which is significant at α=.05. Note the difference between the exact *p*-value and the *p*-value based on the chi-square approximation.

You should exercise care when choosing to use the **Exact p-values** panel. Computational time can be prohibitive depending on the number of groups, the number of distinct response variables, the total sample size, and the speed and memory available on your computer.

Appendix C Percentile Definitions

C.1 Calculating Percentiles

Using the UNIVARIATE Procedure

Example: Calculate the 25th percentile for the following data using the five definitions available in PROC UNIVARIATE:

1 3 7 11 14

For all of these calculations (except Definition 4), you use the value *np*=(5)(0.25)=1.25. This can be viewed as an observation number. However, there is obviously no observation 1.25.

Definition 1 returns a weighted average. The value returned is 25% (25% is the fractional part of 1.25 expressed as a percentage) of the distance between observations 1 and 2:

percentile = 1 + (0.25)(3 – 1) = 1.5

Definition 2 rounds to the nearest observation number. Thus, the value 1.25 is rounded to 1 and the first observation, 1, is taken as the 25th percentile. If *np* were 1.5, then the second observation is selected as the 25th percentile.

Definition 3 always rounds up. Thus, 1.25 rounds up to 2 and the second data value, 3, is taken as the 25th percentile.

Definition 4 is a weighted average similar to Definition 1, except instead of using *np*, Definition 4 uses (*n*+1)*p*=1.5.

percentile = 1 + (0.5)(3 – 1) = 2

Definition 5 rounds up to the next observation number unless *np* is an integer, in which case an average of the observations represented by *np* and (*np* + 1) is calculated. In this example, Definition 5 rounds up, and the 25th percentile is 3.

Appendix D Advanced Programs

D.1 Interaction Plot

To visualize the interaction, output the final parameter estimates to a data set using the OUTEST= option in the LOGISTIC procedure. It is a good idea to examine the data set **betas** to see what the variable names are.

```
proc logistic data=sasuser.b_sales_inc
     noprint
     outest=betas;
   class gender (param=ref ref='Male')
         inclevel (param=ref ref='3');
   model purchase(event='1')=gender inclevel gender*inclevel;
run;
```

A DATA step with three DO loops is used to create a data set with plotting points. The data points include all possible combinations of **gender** and **inclevel** and the interaction of **gender*inclevel**.

```
data plot;
   do GenderFemale=0,1;
      do IncLevel1=0,1;
         do IncLevel2=0,1;
            GenderFemaleIncLevel1=genderfemale*IncLevel1;
            GenderFemaleIncLevel2=genderfemale*IncLevel2;
            if IncLevel1 = 0 or IncLevel2 = 0  then
              output;
         end;
      end;
   end;
run;
```

The SCORE procedure multiplies values from two SAS data sets, one containing the coefficients and the other containing data to be scored using the coefficients from the first data set.

Selected PROC SCORE statement options:

OUT= names the SAS data set created by PROC SCORE.

SCORE= names the data set that contains the coefficients.

TYPE= specifies the observations in the SCORE= data set that contain scoring coefficients.

```
proc score data=plot out=scored score=betas type=parms;
   var GenderFemale IncLevel1 IncLevel2
       GenderFemaleIncLevel1 GenderFemaleIncLevel2;
run;

data scored;
   set scored;
   inclevel = 1*(IncLevel1=1) + 2*(IncLevel2=1)
            + 3*(IncLevel1=0 and IncLevel2=0);
run;
```

The GPLOT procedure is used to create the interaction plot. The variable **GenderFemale** (produced in the **betas** data set) is formatted and labels are written in the horizontal axis and the legend.

```
proc format;
   value genfmt 1='Female'
                0='Male';
   value incfmt 1='Low'
                2='Medium'
                3='High';
run;

options ps=50 ls=64;
goptions reset=all fontres=presentation ftext=swissb htext=1.5;

proc gplot data=scored;
   plot purchase*inclevel=GenderFemale
        / haxis=axis1
          legend=legend1;
   format GenderFemale genfmt.
          inclevel incfmt.;
   axis1 label=("Income Level");
   legend1 label=("Gender");
   symbol1 c=black w=2 h=2 i=join v=star;
   symbol2 c=black w=2 h=2 i=join v=circle;
   title "Interaction of Gender and Income";
run;
quit;
```

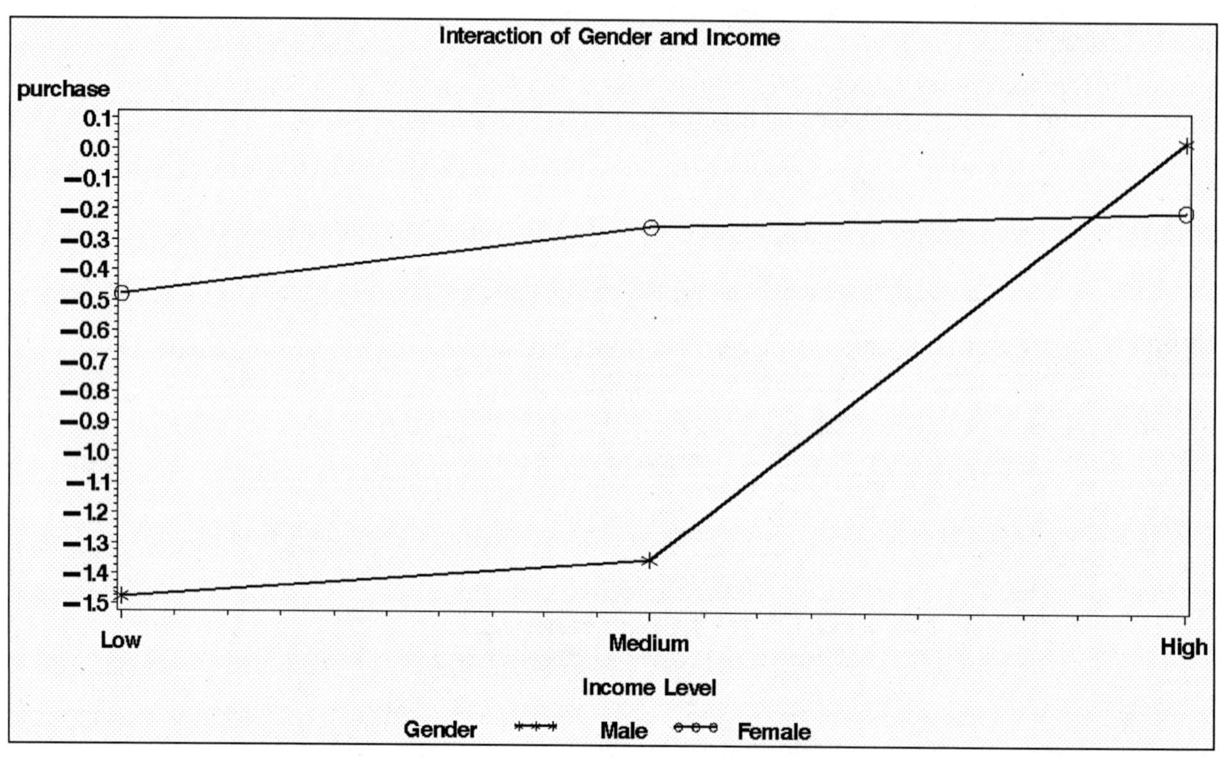

Use the following code to generate an ACTIVEX graph.

```
/* prob_logit.sas */
ods listing close;

options device=activex;

ods html
    body='elogitplot.htm';

proc means data=sasuser.b_sales_inc noprint nway;
   class inclevel gender;
   var purchase;
   output out=bins sum(purchase)=purchase;
run;

data bins;
   set bins;
   logit=log((purchase+1)/(_freq_-purchase+1));
run;

proc format;
   value incfmt 1='Low Income'
                2='Medium Income'
                3='High Income';
run;

proc gplot data=bins;
   plot logit*inclevel=gender;
   symbol v=star i=j;
   format inclevel incfmt.;
   label inclevel='Income Level';
   title 'Interaction Plot of Income Level';
run;
quit;
ods html close;
ods listing;
```

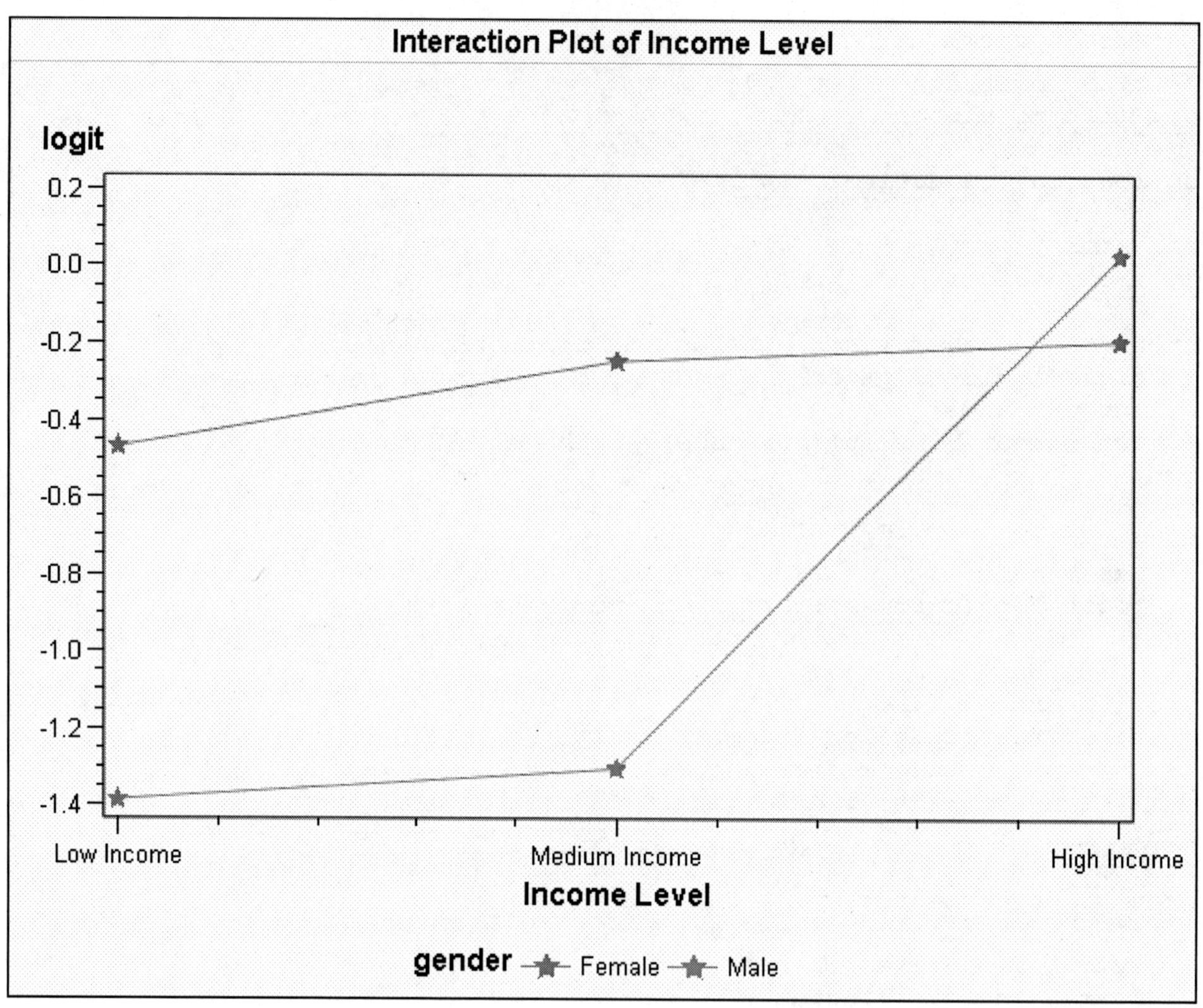
Interaction Plot of Income Level
logit
0.2
0.0
-0.2
-0.4
-0.6
-0.8
-1.0
-1.2
-1.4
Low Income
Medium Income
High Income
Income Level
gender
Female
Male

Appendix E Randomization Technique

E.1 Randomize Paints

A DATA step is used to generate the 28 observations for the completely randomized experiment. Each of the seven roads is given four stripe identification numbers. The variable **random** is generated using a seed of 47, yet any positive integer would suffice. Selected variables of the data set **stripes** are printed for verification of the data.

```
options ls=75 ps=55  nodate nonumber;

/* associate a road with a number */
proc format;
   value roadid  1='Center   '
                 2='Broadway'
                 3='Main     '
                 4='Elm      '
                 5='Station  '
                 6='Park     '
                 7='Beech    '
                 ;
run;

data stripes;

   stripe_id = 0;
   do r = 1 to 7;      /* # of roads */

      road = put(r,$roadid.);
      do s = 1 to 4; /* # of paints        */
                     /* 7 * 4 = 28 obs.   */
         stripe_id = stripe_id + 1;
         random = ranuni(47);
         output;
      end;  /* s */
   end;     /* r */

   drop
      r s;
run;

proc print data=stripes;
   id road;
   var stripe_id;
   title 'Stripe-ID for each Road';
run;

proc sort data=stripes;
   by random;
run;
```

The data set **stripes** is now sorted by the variable **random**, and the four paints, identified with values Paint-1, Paint-2, Paint-3, and Paint-4, are assigned to each of the 28 stripes.

```
/* generate values for paint based on the MOD */
/* function, described below.                 */
proc format;
   value paintid  0='Paint-4'
                  1='Paint-2'
                  2='Paint-1'
                  3='Paint-3'
                  ;
run;

/* associate the modular of 4 with a paint */
/* via the format PAINTID                  */
data paints;
   set stripes;
   by random;  /*NOTE: data is sorted by this variable*/

   break = mod(_n_,4);/*  _n_  is observation number.    */
                      /* MOD computes the remainder of */
                      /* the first argument divided by */
                      /* the second argument.          */

   select (break); /*use select instead of if-then-else*/
      when (0) assigned_paint = put(break,$paintid.);
      when (1) assigned_paint = put(break,$paintid.);
      when (2) assigned_paint = put(break,$paintid.);
      when (3) assigned_paint = put(break,$paintid.);
      otherwise;
      end;

   drop
      break random;
run;

proc datasets library=work nolist;
   delete stripes;
run;
```

The data set **paints** is now sorted in two ways: by the paint that was assigned to each stripe and by the road/stripe combination. The latter is best used in the field.

```
proc sort data=paints out=grpd_paints;
   by assigned_paint;
run;

proc print data=grpd_paints;
   by assigned_paint;
   id assigned_paint;
   var road stripe_id;
   title 'Paint #(1,2,3 or 4)  ... on Road/Stripe-ID';
run;

proc sort data=paints out=grpd_paints;
   by road stripe_id;
run;

proc print data=grpd_paints;
   by road;
   id road;
   var stripe_id assigned_paint;
   title 'On Road/Stripe-ID, Assign Paint #(1,2,3,or 4)';
run;
```

Stripe-ID for each Road

road	stripe_ id
Center	1
Center	2
Center	3
Center	4
Broadway	5
Broadway	6
Broadway	7
Broadway	8
Main	9
Main	10
Main	11
Main	12
Elm	13
Elm	14
Elm	15
Elm	16
Station	17
Station	18
Station	19
Station	20
Park	21
Park	22
Park	23
Park	24
Beech	25
Beech	26
Beech	27
Beech	28

```
Paint #(1,2,3 or 4) ... on Road/Stripe-ID

 assigned_                  stripe_
   paint       road           id

  Paint-1      Main           10
               Broadway        5
               Park           22
               Broadway        7
               Station        20
               Center          3
               Elm            16

  Paint-2      Elm            13
               Park           23
               Beech          25
               Main           11
               Main           12
               Beech          28
               Station        19

  Paint-3      Elm            14
               Main            9
               Station        18
               Broadway        6
               Center          1
               Station        17
               Elm            15

  Paint-4      Center          4
               Park           21
               Park           24
               Center          2
               Beech          26
               Beech          27
               Broadway        8
```

On Road/Stripe-ID, Assign Paint #(1,2,3, or 4)

road	stripe_ id	assigned_ paint
Beech	25	Paint-2
	26	Paint-4
	27	Paint-4
	28	Paint-2
Broadway	5	Paint-1
	6	Paint-3
	7	Paint-1
	8	Paint-4
Center	1	Paint-3
	2	Paint-4
	3	Paint-1
	4	Paint-4
Elm	13	Paint-2
	14	Paint-3
	15	Paint-3
	16	Paint-1
Main	9	Paint-3
	10	Paint-1
	11	Paint-2
	12	Paint-2
Park	21	Paint-4
	22	Paint-1
	23	Paint-2
	24	Paint-4
Station	17	Paint-3
	18	Paint-3
	19	Paint-2
	20	Paint-1

Appendix F Basic Statistics Guidelines for Analysis

F.1 Guidelines for Analysis

Basic Statistics Guidelines for Analysis

Predictor (X, Independent, Regressor, Effect, Explanatory) / Response (Y, Dependent, Target)	Categorical	Continuous	Categorical and Continuous
Continuous	Analysis of Variance (Chapter 2)	Regression (Chapters 3 and 4)	Analysis of Covariance or Regression with Dummy Variables (Statistics II)
Categorical	Crosstabulation/ Contingency Table or Logistic Regression (Chapter 5)	Logistic Regression (Chapter 5)	Logistic Regression (Chapter 5)

2

Appendix G Index

N

O

P